'THEIRS NOT TO REASON WHY'

Wolverhampton Military Studies

www.helion.co.uk/wolverhamptonmilitarystudies

Editorial board

Submissions

The publishers would be pleased to receive submissions for this series. Please contact us via email (info@helion.co.uk), or in writing to Helion & Company Limited, 26 Willow Road, Solihull, West Midlands, B91 1UE.

Titles

No 1 *Stemming the Tide. Officers and Leadership in the British Expeditionary Force 1914*
Edited by Spencer Jones (ISBN 978-1-909384-45-3)

No 2 *'Theirs Not To Reason Why'. Horsing the British Army 1875-1925* Graham Winton
(ISBN 978-1-909384-48-4)

No 3 *A Military Transformed? Adaptation and Innovation in the British Military, 1792-1945*
Edited by Michael LoCicero, Ross Mahoney and Stuart Mitchell (ISBN 978-1-909384-46-0)

'Theirs Not To Reason Why'

Horsing the British Army 1875-1925

Wolverhampton Military Studies No. 2

Graham Winton

Helion & Company Limited

Helion & Company Limited
26 Willow Road
Solihull
West Midlands
B91 1UE
England
Tel. 0121 705 3393
Fax 0121 711 4075
Email: info@helion.co.uk
Website: www.helion.co.uk
Twitter: @helionbooks
Visit our blog http://blog.helion.co.uk/

Published by Helion & Company 2013

Designed and typeset by Bookcraft Ltd, Stroud, Gloucestershire
Cover designed by Paul Hewitt, Battlefield Design (www.battlefield-design.co.uk)
Printed by Lightning Source, Milton Keynes, Buckinghamshire

Front cover: Port Elizabeth Horse Memorial, South Africa. (Author's collection).
Rear cover: Rear view of the 58th London Division Memorial at Chipilly, France.
(Author's collection)

ISBN 978 1 909384 48 4

British Library Cataloguing-in-Publication Data.
A catalogue record for this book is available from the British Library.

For details of other military history titles published by Helion & Company
Limited contact the above address, or visit our website: http://www.helion.co.uk.

We always welcome receiving book proposals from prospective authors.

"Theirs Not To Reason Why
Theirs but to do and die"
[Lord Tennyson... *The Charge of The Light Brigade*]

DEDICATION

ELINOR
EDWIN and FRITHA

My grandfathers and great uncle who fought in, and survived the 1914-1918 war

Sgt. 47983 Charles Walter Kingdon (Winton), RFA., Regular Army
1889-1963

Gunner, 172885, Frank Ambrose Brain, RFA
1889-1950

Private, S/10415, Rifleman James Bloxham
11th Battalion Rifle Brigade, POW March 1918
1892-1954

To Catherine and my personal friends whose belief in my ability gave me the confidence to undertake this book; the knowledge, advice and support of some were all too suddenly removed.

Rose E. B. Coombs, MBE, WAAF
The expert on battlefields of the 1914-18 War
Author of *Before Endeavours Fade*
1922-1991

Richard M. Y. Shackleton, Lecturer
School of History, University of Birmingham
1944-1990

Peter W. Dix
Life Guards
Sgt. Honourable Artillery Company (HAC) Light Cavalry
Gunner "B" Battery 1st Regiment HAC (RFA)
1936-1994

Contents

List of illustrations and diagrams

List of maps

Abbreviations

AAG	Assistant Adjutant General
ADAVS	Assistant Director Army Veterinary Service (also ADVS)
ADR	Assistant Director of Remounts
ADT	Assistant Director of Transport
AIR	Assistant Inspector of Remounts
AMSM	Army Medical Services Museum
ANVC	Australian and New Zealand Veterinary Corps
ANZAC	Australian and New Zealand Army Corps
AOC	Army Ordnance Corps
ASC	Army Service Corps
ASCJ	*Army Service Corps Journal*
AQMG	Assistant Quartermaster General
AVC	Army Veterinary Corps
AVC (TF)	Army Veterinary Corps Territorial Force
AVD	Army Veterinary Department
AVS	Army Veterinary Service
BAF	Board of Agriculture and Fisheries
BEF	British Expeditionary Force
C-in- C	Commander in Chief
CIGS	Chief of the Imperial General Staff
CO	Commanding Officer
CVS	Civilian Veterinary Service
DAAG	Deputy Assistant Adjutant General
DADR	Deputy Assistant Director of Remounts
DADT	Deputy Assistant Director of Transport
DAQMG	Deputy Assistant Quartermaster General
DDAVS	Deputy Director of Army Veterinary Services (also DDVS, DDAVC)
DDMO	Deputy Director of Military Operations
DDR	Deputy Director Remounts
DG	Director General
DGAVS	Director General Army Veterinary Service (also DGAVC, DGAVD, DVS)
DMO	Director of Military Operations

DQMG	Deputy Quartermaster General
DR	Director of Remounts
EAVC	East African Veterinary Corps
EF	Expeditionary Force
EEF	Egyptian Expeditionary Force
FA	Field Artillery
GHQ	General Headquarters
GOC	General Officer Commanding
GOC-in-C	General Officer Commander in Chief
GS	General Service (wagon)
Hansard (C)	Hansard's Parliamentary Debates, House of Commons
Hansard (L)	Hansard's Parliamentary Debates, House of Lords
HD	Heavy draught horse
HIS	Hunter Improvement Society
HTC	Horse Transport Company
IEF	Italian Expeditionary Force
IGC	Inspector General Communications
IGR	Inspector General Remounts
IQMG	Inspector Quartermaster General (Horse feeding)
IYC	Imperial Yeomanry Committee
JRAVC	*Journal of the Royal Army Veterinary Corps*
LD	Light draught horse (or LDH)
LHBS	Light Horse Breeding Society (also LHB for light horse breeding)
MAF	Ministry of Agriculture and Fisheries
MEF	Mediterranean Expeditionary Force
MGSC	Machine Gun Squadron (Cavalry)
MT	Motor Transport
MTC	Motor Transport Company
Mtd. Inf.	Mounted Infantry
MV	Motor vehicles
MVS	Mobile Veterinary Section
NCOs	Non-commissioned Officers
NLHBS	National Light Horse Breeding Society
PP.Cd.	*Parliamentary Papers (Cd. Blue Books)*
NA.Kew	National Archives, Kew
PVO	Principal Veterinary Officer
PVS	Principal Veterinary Surgeon
QMG	Quarter Master General
QMS	Quarter Master Sergeant
RA	Royal Artillery
RAMC	Royal Army Medical Corps
RASCQ	*Royal Army Service Corps Quarterly*
RC	Royal Commission

RCHB	Royal Commission on Horse Breeding
RCT	Royal Corps Transport
RE	Royal Engineers
RPCCA	*Report of the Purchasing Commission Canada and America*
RFA	Royal Field Artillery
RHA	Royal Horse Artillery
RSPCA	Royal Society for the Protection Cruelty Animals
SA	South Africa
SAA	Small Arms Ammunition
SAVC	South African Veterinary Corps
SVO	Senior Veterinary Officer
VBD	Veterinary Base Depot
VR	*The Veterinary Record*

Glossary

For the various Points of a Horse see the diagram in Appendix II.

Administrative Services Includes: Intercommunication, Medical, Supplies, Transport, Ordnance, Railways, Works, Remounts, Veterinary and Postal.

Administrative Troops Includes: Troops combatant or otherwise, belonging to the Administrative Services, including RE other than those of field units; ASC, RAMC, AOC, AVC.

Army Troops Troops allotted to an Army, but not to any particular division

Casting Sold alive from military service; retired through age, illness, injury or no longer required.

Catarrhal Fever Applies to any of the viral conditions causing micro purulent discharge from the eyes, nose and mouth etc.

Central Powers The major protagonists against the Allies during the First World War. The Empires of Germany, Austria-Hungary, Turkey; joined by the Kingdom of Bulgaria in 1915. So called as they were located between the Russian Empire, France and UK.

Class Military classification to indicate purpose e.g. charger, troop horse, draught.

Clipping Horses have a thicker coat in the winter. This can become a hindrance when the horse is rugged up, exercised, or standing in mud and wet conditions. Clipping, or shaving, all or part of this winter coat can prevent against loss of condition and sickness, for example through excess sweating and saving on grooming time. Minimizing sweating enables a horse to cool and dry quicker and more effectively.

Cob A horse larger than a pony standing 14.2 hands but not over 15 hands. Relatively small and compact, usually a short-legged strongly built horse. The Welsh cob is typical of the classic build of the historic cob.

Cold and hot shoeing Taking a cold shoe and shaping it to make the best fit possible, then nailing into position on the hoof. Hot shoeing is the application of hot shoes to the horses' hooves, the smith uses the anvil to make changes if necessary, cools the shoes and nails them into place.

Colic Acute equine indigestion. Sand colic is caused when a horse ingests sand, from eating off the ground, but not passing it through the system resulting in a build-up in the intestinal system, cecum, or large colon. If not alleviated, this can result in death due to intestinal rupture or large colon displacement.

Dam The female parent of a horse or mule.

Dead Loss Loss from deaths, destruction, captures, straying and casting. Does not include wastage from sickness and injury or any other animals than those paid for out of the public purse.

Dresser Assisted a Veterinary Officer in the treatment of sick animals. Checking and reporting on injuries or symptoms of illness, visiting stables, administering medicines as directed by the Veterinary Officer, responsible for the cleanliness and maintenance of the veterinary hospital as well as equipment and instruments.

Epizootics Veterinary term for an epidemic; an extensive outbreak of an infection affecting animal species and is now usually applied to things like Foot and Mouth Disease, Swine Fever, Rinderpest etc.

Establishment The strength of a unit in peacetime and wartime. The peace establishment generally lists a unit's strength by rank, numbers, employments and horses. The war establishment gave the organisation of a unit in the field, deployment of officers, soldiers, horses and transport; scale of weapons, ammunition and equipment; and arrangements for carrying equipment in the regimental transport. [Hume 2010]

Feather Hair on all four heels of a horse, of varying density and coarseness.

First Line The Regular Army with its reserves, including special reserve, liable for service anywhere.

First Line Transport That which accompanies a unit or regiment and is an integral part of its war organisation to perform its tactical function. It includes vehicles and animals: gun carriages; ammunition wagons; pack animals; limbered or GS wagons or carts carrying ammunition, tools, machine guns, technical stores, bicycles; water carts and cook's wagon or cooker.

Fistulous Withers A pocket or sinus, which discharges pus, often intermittently from the withers. It was caused by a variety of infections but classically by Brucella abortus. A condition affecting the top of the horse's head, poll evil is similar to fistulous withers.

Glanders A serious, highly infectious disease of horses and mules caused by the bacterium Pseudomonas mallei. It affects the bronchial tubes, lungs, glands and skin. Common in wartime, resulting in large number of animals having to be destroyed.

Halter A headstall of leather, rope or webbing used for tying a horse up. Sometimes made to act also as the headpiece of a bridle.

Hands A horse's height is measured in hands (4 inches) and inches. Taken from the highest part of the withers in a perpendicular line to the ground.

Haras Breeding establishment for horses.

Horse By Army Act, Section 190, the expression "Horse" includes mule, or any other beast of whatever description used for burden, or draught, or carrying persons (1912).

Horsemanship The art of riding.

Horsemastership The art of looking after horses, for example, grooming, feeding, watering and correct working use of the animal.

Hunter   A horse capable of following a pack of foxhounds hunting a fox at full speed over a countryside with numerous obstacles that the horse must jump. Distinguished as heavy, medium and lightweight hunters.

Inspector-General of Communications (IGC)   Has responsibility for the control and co-ordination of all traffic on the Lines of Communication. Commanded all lines of communication units (exclusive of lines of communication defence troops) and regulated the working of all administrative services and departments on the lines of communication.

Jobmaster   Person who hires out horses or carriages.

Lines of Communication   The logistical system of supply and communication from, base(s) of operation, to the front line(s), by for example, rail, road, navigable waterways, telegraph, telephone and visual signalling. Including the districts through which they pass, within limits determined by the C-in-C.

Lymphangitis   Inflammation of the lymphatic system, typically affecting the legs of horses, the most important form being glanders. Ulcerative lymphangitis is also caused by a bacterium Corynebasterium orvis and results in permanent discharges from limbs. Epizootic lymphangitis is caused by a yeast: Histoplasma farcimniosa. It was introduced into the UK in horses coming back from the Angl-Boer War in 1902, was eradicated, briefly reappeared during the 1914-18 War and then finally eradicated from the UK.

Mallein Testing   Skin test for glanders (bacterium Pseudomonas mallei).

Mange   Parasitic skin disease. There are three forms of mange of which the genus sarcoptic is the worst in its devastating effects and takes longer to kill. The parasite burrows under the skin and lays eggs. Cases of mange appeared particularly in the winter when coats were heavy.

Mean Loss   The addition of dead and temporary loss such as injury and sickness.

Mobilisation   Process by which an armed force passes from a peace to a war footing; the completion of units for war in men, horses and material.

Mule   The offspring of a donkey stallion and a mare or filly. Mules do not reproduce their own kind.

Periodic Ophthalmia   A condition of the horse's eye, thought to be due to Leptospira infection; although other causes may exist. The horse is usually only affected in one eye. This becomes inflamed and painful. Relapses are very common, hence 'periodic'. It was also called 'moon blindness'.

Pony   Any horse 14.2 hands or less.

Remount   MacMunn, 1930 and Tylden, 1965, state it is the technical term for a horse bought for military service before issue to a unit. Hume, 2010, states a remount was an animal that has recently been, or waiting to be, issued to a unit. A regiment would continue to class a horse as a remount until it was sufficiently fit and trained to take its place in the ranks; as with The Kings Troop, RHA today. The Remount Department provided animals for the Army and replaced unit casualties.

Reserve Parks   Carrying supplies for a division and Army Troops, maintained on the lines of communication for use in an emergency. They may be used for the transport of ammunition and stores. Organised into sections to carry two days 'iron' rations with groceries and two days oats for one division; plus 1/6th of a cavalry division and 1/6th of the total strength of the units designated lines of communication.

Second Line   The Territorial Force, to provide a force for 'home defence' with no obligation to serve abroad.

Second Line Transport   The transport trains under the ASC divided into two sections, baggage and supply.

Sickle hocked and Spavin   The hock is the joint between the tarsal bones and tibia of a horses leg and takes the greatest strain when the horse is worked. Sickle hocked is due to strained tendons and ligaments, associated with soft tissue injury in the rear, limits the straightening and backward extension of hocks, which limits push-off, propulsion, and speed. The hock is flexed so that the foot is abnormally bowed far under the belly predisposing to spavin from a trauma injury. There are two forms of spavin, bone spavin and bog spavin. Bone spavin is a degenerative bone disease type of osteoarthritis that often causes lameness. Bog spavin, a swelling condition, caused by excessive fluid in the largest hock joints, caused for example by, a stress or trauma injury, uneven loading of the hocks, poor trimming or shoeing, uneven or repeated loading of the lower hock joints.

Sire   The male parent of a horse or mule.

Special Reserve   Men who enlist into this Reserve, and any ex-soldiers who had served three years with the Regular Army, had been discharged without a pension, and not more than 38 years of age (Army Order 23 of 1912). There were Special Reserve Battalions, one to each pair of linked battalions; on mobilisation they became the depot, training recruits etc. and furnished drafts to their linked battalions on service. There were also Extra Special Reserve Battalions which did not furnish drafts, but were available for service abroad as distinct units. Special Reserve Cavalry, the two regiments of Irish Horse. Reserve Cavalry Regiments – on mobilisation surplus reserves of cavalry were formed into 14 Reserve Regiments, one to each two of the 28 Regiments of Cavalry of the Line.

Stamp   A horse's conformation, size and quality relative to intended purpose.

Strangles   Severe infection caused by streptococcos equi but precipitated by viral infection or other stress. A respiratory disease including purulent nasal discharge and abcessation of glands. Very contagious. Various complications. Choking or suffocating by compressing the windpipe.

Temporary Loss   Loss through sickness and injury.

Thoroughbred   A horse registered in the English General Stud Book. A common term for a racehorse.

Type   Horse lineage, for example Irish draught type, Hunter type.

Walers   Generic name for Australasian saddle horses, in most cases bred from a thoroughbred sire and a light type of farm or ranch mare. Originally most of these remounts were shipped from New South Wales hence the name.

Withers   The highest part of a horse's shoulder coming immediately under the pommel of a saddle. The top of the perpendicular where the height of a horse is measured in hands.

Acknowledgements

During the years of research I have enjoyed the friendship and assistance of many people. I thank all those who helped in the preparation of this publication. I owe a great debt to the late Rose Coombs, Richard Shackleton, Peter Dix, Donald Sidebotham and Elinor Winton, all of whom sadly passed away before this work was published.

I never cease to be amazed at the generosity of 'strangers' in providing information, documents and their time. So many people have given freely and with enthusiasm so that this study could be published. THANK YOU, seems a small reward. My apologies to anyone I have failed to mention by name.

Many veterans of the 1914-1918 War provided vivid descriptions of their experiences and in particular memories of horses at the battle front, including Capt. Arthur Dawkes MC., Signaller H.J. Bale and R.F. Bridger (Remount Depot, Avonmouth).

Lt-Col. (Retd) Michael H. G. Young, formerly editor of the *Royal Logistic Corps Journal* and curator of the RCT Museum, generously gave of his time in assisting my research and answering many queries. Michael was a great inspiration and provided many hours of fruitful discussion. This support has been continued by Andy Robertshaw and Gareth Mears of the RLC Museum and his team. The late Col. R. Hume was very generous in sharing his unpublished material on the Remount Department and Mrs Hume kindly gave permission to use some of his material published in 2010. My thanks to Capt.(Retd) Peter Starling, Army Medical Services Museum, for his patience and support in answering questions and providing material. John Head, grandson of Lt. Head, AVC for his enthusiasm and access to the family archive. Simon Butler has been very generous with his material and opened a new avenue of research in the West Country, in this context my thanks go to Donald Brown, Margaret Jordan, Kate Scurfield, Daphne McCutcheon, Tony Hiscock; very special thanks to Andy Chelmsford for his expertise on mules, Maggie Roberts, Petra Ingram and Lally Baker of The Brooke Hospital for Animals. Judith Lappin and Robert Alexander of the Machine Gunners Association. My thanks also to David Kenyon.

The Western Front Association is a most invaluable resource and many of its members have given generously and include: Colin Wagstaff, Chris Holland, Alan Tucker, Alan Jeffreys, Simon Davies, Brian Bird and his daughter Gillian Storey. A very special thanks to Brian Hill to whom I owe a huge debt of gratitude for sharing his knowledge, reading draft chapters and answering many questions. Also to Nigel

Neil (Lathom Park Remount Depot) for sharing his knowledge and material on Lathom.

Very special thanks to The King's Troop, Royal Horse Artillery, Woolwich, for a most amazing and informative day spent with them, Maj. MG Edwards, CO, RHA, Capt. J Gibson, Adjutant, Capt Beynon Brown and Lance Bombardier Jo Sutcliffe. Also Capt. Peter Hudson, Adjutant and Capt Derren Payne, Equine Training Squadron, Defence Animal Centre, Melton Mowbray.

Vic Simpson BVSc, DTVM, FIBiol, Hon FRCVS and Judith Morrow MVB., MRCVS., MRC.Path., provided technical veterinary advice and access to veterinary papers and archives. Clare Boulton, Librarian, Royal College of Veterinary Surgeons for her support and access to the Frederick Smith Archive. The skill of computing and word processing did not come easy, I owe a great debt to David Morris (M.A Associates) and also Ian Meadows for his patience and assistance.

In South Africa I have to give huge thanks to: Margaret Harradine and Carol Victor of the African Library, Port Elizabeth, for their invaluable help with remount material and information on the horse memorial; with thanks to Mrs Chigumbu, Director, for allowing publication of photographs. The same thanks must go to Zameka Yamile and Elizabeth Mazibuko, Zululand Historical Museum, Eshowe, for material on the Anglo-Boer War and horse memorial. Joan Marsh South African Military History Society, South African National Museum of Military History. In North America to Eric Seiferth (The Williams Research Centre, Historic New Orleans Collection), Juliana Burns (City of Lathrop) and Kristy Wallisch (Jean Lafitte National Historical Park and Preserve, New Orleans), Katherine Wilkins (Virginia Historical Society), Susan Barber (Christopher Newport University), Tim Novak (Saskatchewan Archives Board), Douglas Cass (Library and Archives, Glenbow Museum, Calagry, Canada), Karen Simonson (Provincial Archives of Alberta), Canadian War Museum, Centre for Military History (Washington, D.C),

This book began as a Ph.D thesis so my thanks remains to those who assisted in this phase of my research: Lt-Col. (Retd) P. Roffey DL, RAVC, Dr Michael Goodchild, Gen. Sir Patrick Howard Dobson, Roy Baker (RAVC), Prof. T.C. Barker, Dr Robert Bearman (Shakespeare Birthplace Trust), Maj. (Retd) W. Birkbeck, William H.I. Birkbeck, Dr John Bourne (University of Birmingham), Peter Burrell, Ann Daniels, Brig. (Retd) G.R. Durrant (Army Veterinary and Remount Services), Walter Gilbey, Helen Gibson, Kathleen Heywood, HJK Jenkins, Beryl Kerby, Marquis of Anglesey, Dr Catherine Moriarty, Mike Rumbold (Weedon Bec), Doreen and Roy Sherwood, Prof. A. Steele-Bodger, and Brig. K.A. Timbers,

My thanks are due to the staff in many libraries and the record offices in which I have worked, or who readily responded to my many enquiries: DC Thomson & Co for permission to publish from the 'Warlord', Dr Adrian Greaves, Australian War Memorial (Canberra), Bishops Stortford Local History Society (Sir Walter Gilbey Collection), Bodleian Library (Oxford), Bristol Record Office British Library, Cambridgeshire County Record Office, Cambridge University School of Clinical Veterinary Medicine Library, Essex County Record Office, Geoff Pocock – Legion of Frontiersmen, Gloucestershire Record Office, Steve Hynard Hampshire County Record Office (Winchester), Hereford and Worcester Record Office, House of Lords Record Office, Huntingdon Research Centre Library, Imperial War Museum, Leicester County Libraries and Information Service, Long Long Trail, Ministry of Defence Library (Whitehall), Museum of London, National Army Museum (Chelsea), National Horseracing Museum and National Stud (Newmarket) and Miss Terry Lane of Tattershall's Ltd, National Library of Scotland, National Light Horse Breeding Society, Northampton County Record Office, National Archive (Kew), Raymond Lowe (St. Jude's on the Hill), Richard Harman, Royal Army Veterinary Corps (Defence Animal Centre, Melton Mowbray), Royal Artillery Institution and Royal Artillery Museum (Woolwich), Royal Commission on Historical Manuscripts, Royal Engineers Museum, University of Birmingham Library, a very special thanks to staff at the University of Cambridge Library, Claire Allen Warwickshire County Record Office, Wiltshire County Record Office, Winchester Public Library, Wolds Wagoners Museum special thanks to Sandra Oakins, Col Wilson Sledmere Estate, Liz Young of Shropshire Archives, Somerset Heritage Centre (Taunton), Southwark Local History Library, Bob Stebbings family transport company Radford Bros, 1st The Queen's Dragoon Guards Regimental Museum, 15/19th The King's Royal Hussars Museum, Harry Staff of the Oxfordshire Yeomanry Association and Stanley Jenkins of *Soldiers of Oxfordshire*, Val Penketh (Bushey Museum re Lucy Kemp Walsh), Christine Woods Parish Administrator, Parish of Bushey.

A very special thank you to Duncan Rogers of Helion & Co. and his team. For his faith in agreeing to publish this book, his invaluable advice, guidance and support; a delight to work with, THANK YOU. I could not conclude without thanking Fritha, Edwin and Catherine for their support, patience and often help for a flagging spirit; many hours were spent cajoling, reading through drafts and making sense of my chaotic scribbling.

Foreword

Graham Winton's study of the British Army's horse supply between the creation of its Veterinary and Remount Services in the 1870s and its last involvements in the aftershock wars that followed the First World War in the 1920s is a welcome addition to the *Wolverhampton Military Studies Series*. It adds a further perspective to recent studies of the British Army in the late nineteenth and early twentieth centuries, filling a gap in our understanding, and providing an invaluable work of reference.

It is a truism of military history, attributed to several notable twentieth century generals (who probably all used it and agreed with it) that juniors or amateurs study and discuss tactics, while professionals and senior officers study and discuss logistics: the science and art of military supply and practical movement. More recently, it has been changed to include the point that very senior officers study and discuss not simply logistics, but force generation: the creation, training and equipping within the appropriate timescale of the armed forces needed for a war. When dealing with horses, these requirements demanded from the British Army in the period considered by Graham Winton considerable forward planning: a gun or wagon could be made in a matter of days or weeks, but a three year old horse for a cavalry troop or for heavy artillery haulage either took three years to grow, or the funds and transport had to be ready to buy them from elsewhere. This approach to military history has been routine for historians of naval or air warfare, who habitually include in their studies the civilian industrial base for building ships and aircraft, ranging from the supply of timber for masts and keels for the age of sail onwards. But until quite recently, logistics and force generation were seldom much studied by historians of land warfare, and sometimes not at all.

Partly this was due to the precedent set by the early nineteenth century founders of modern military thought, Jomini and Clausewitz, who both saw their subject as starting with generalship and with the armies in existence, trained and equipped. Clausewitz, in particular, considered peacetime supply as an entirely separate activity, irrelevant to his study of war. Partly, the neglect of logistics was due to the desire of many writers to use military history for didactic purposes, glossing over inconvenient logistical truths in their promotion of some master plan for the future, something of which both J.F.C. Fuller and Basil Liddell Hart were particularly guilty; their shared prejudice against horsed cavalry after 1919 also did much to obscure its importance and successes before that date. Partly, logistics often played at best a shadowy and secondary role to the sheer glamour – for many writing about war from a safe distance – of tactics and battles. The links between civilian supply of equipment to the armed forces, the impact of that supply on the plans and battles of generals, and the importance of the military institutions responsible for joining the two together, first became apparent in studies of the Second World War, in which old distinctions in war had visibly broken down: this included the distinction between land warfare and sea warfare, with the added dimension of air warfare and the importance of amphibious operations; the distinction that sea and air battles were fought by machines with men to work them, whereas land battles were fought by men assisted by machines, which was changed by the growing importance of the tank; and the distinction between the civilian and military war effort, eroded by total war.

Although this new thinking applied to the warfare of the industrialised age, it did not seem relevant to earlier ages in which armies were dependent on horse-power in the literal sense. There was also considerable neglect of practical military issues from historians studying the politics of the First World War, and even more so from historians of the heyday of the British Empire, including how issues of horse supply could impact directly on political calculations in the same way as battleship and submarine building programmes. This deficiency has only begun to be addressed with renewed interest in the Anglo-Boer War and in the transition of the British Army from its established role as a late Victorian Imperial gendarmerie to being a major industrialised continental army in the First World War. These new approaches have been accompanied by a re-investigation of the value of horsed cavalry, and their new tactics in a difficult period of transition between the steep rise of infantry and artillery firepower at the end of the nineteenth century, and the emergence in the aftermath of the First World War of practical cross-country military vehicles driven by internal combustion engines. But as Graham Winton shows, the issue goes beyond the administration of horse supply in peacetime, and the needs of the cavalry, whose requirements for horses have often been confused by historians with the needs of the Army as a whole. In wartime the Army needed a wide range of very different types of horses (including mules and donkeys) in the right numbers for infantry transport, cavalry, artillery, engineers, ambulances, and several smaller functions; it needed these horses trained, and it needed them fed and kept in good condition, which was a major logistical undertaking in itself. The successes and failures of the Army's horse supply for its two major wars of the period, the Anglo-Boer War and the First World War, were critical to its achievements and to their course and outcome. Without horses, the British Army could not have fought these wars; it really is that simple.

Professor Stephen Badsey
Series Editor, *The Wolverhampton Military Studies Series*
University of Wolverhampton

Introduction

For centuries, the horse had provided the principal means of mobility for the Arm, but the Great War of 1914-18 was to witness the beginning of the end of this partnership. Ironically, a unified system for providing the British Army with remounts had only been in existence for some 30 years, and an effective system for the veterinary care of animals for even less time. Maj-Gen Frederick Smith wrote "the evolution of our service began in 1876, reached its maturity in 1914, and the fruits of 38 years work were gathered during the Great War".[1]

By the Army Act, Section 190, the expression "horse" includes mule, and any other beast of whatever description used for burden, or draught or carrying persons.[2]

Most military histories and accounts of campaigns lack any reference to the vital importance of the horse. Yet for centuries, the horse provided the principal means of power and mobility for the supply of all army needs and was essential, for example, for infantry transport, the Artillery, Engineers, and prior to 1914 all ambulance units. The Army could not function without the horse. That the Army was horsed at all is taken for granted, with little or no understanding of whence they came, in what numbers, the type or quality. For many writers, the horse is seen purely in a cavalry role and even then with little to suggest any understanding of the importance of the actual animal to the trooper, or ability of the cavalry to perform traditional tasks. Yet, more importantly, the crucial motive power without which an army could not function, was provided by the horse and pack animals. Col. Dunlop, in his comprehensive work on Army reforms, 1899-1914, provides only two very brief references to horses and remounts (a remount is a horse purchased for military service before issue to a particular unit for training, or to replace a casualty).[3] 'The Army' was perceived only in terms of the fighting units; horses are included by inference and are virtually invisible. The Remount and Veterinary Departments should not, however, be seen in isolation from other army administrative services and the High Command, they were as integral to the military machine. Moore-Colyer concludes his paper on *Horse Supply and the British Cavalry* with only a very brief discussion of the major changes

1   Smith, 1927, p.241.
2   Public General Acts, Army Act 1912.
3   Dunlop, 1938, pp.106, 145.

from the 1880s, stating that "the ineptitude of both the Government and senior army personnel in ensuring appropriate cavalry provision and maintaining the capability of rapid cavalry mobilisation was, of course, to be further underlined in the Great War".[4] This statement is so vague as to be meaningless, but appears to perpetuate the myths of cavalry in 1914 and ignores the importance of reforms introduced between 1902 and 1914, including those of the Remount Department and horse mobilisation.

Some more recent works have attempted to redress the balance. Badsey in his book *Doctrine and Reform in the British Cavalry 1880-1918*, does much to dispel the conventional view of the cavalry's role during the 1914-18 war with a significant emphasis on the context and importance of the horse to the efficiency of cavalry mobility; the ability to effectively undertake the tasks required.[5] Also of importance is an article by Singleton on the military use of horses during 1914-18.[6] Although issue can be taken with a number of his findings, it is one of the very few pieces of modern research that attempts to analyse the question of horse supply and use during the First World War. Kenyon's work on British cavalry on the Western Front is an excellent reassessment dispelling many of the myths surrounding the use of cavalry, including that of the provision of fodder for cavalry and horses in general; also in highlighting the combined use of horses with motorised vehicles.[7] The one disappointing aspect of the book is that, except for the events of late 1916 and 1917, there is a lack of emphasis on the importance of horses being fit and trained to effectively undertake their allotted tasks when required to do so. Badsey covers this much more effectively. The excellent work of the late Col. R. Hume, although mostly unpublished, adds considerably to the very limited accessible material on the Remount Department prior to 1914, and is directly relevant to an understanding of the events of the 1899-1902 and 1914-18 wars.[8] Anglesey's work on British Cavalry, from 1872 to 1915,[9] and that of Tylden,[10] contain material on remounts and are useful for their bibliographies. However, the picture presented by both of these is fragmentary and often lacking in a discussion of the sources used.

Michael Morpurgo's children's novel *War Horse*, the theatre production and Steven Spielberg's film of the book, arguably poor history, have created a public awareness of the horse in the First World War.[11] Publications by Arthur and Van Emden contain

---

4   Moore-Colyer, 1992, p.260.
5   Badsey, 2008
6   Singleton,1993.
7   Kenyon, 2011.
8   Col. Hume, 1980 and private correspondence 1989. Col. Hume died in November 2010 before publishing his research on The Army Remount Service. I am grateful to Capt. (Retd) P.H Starling, Director of the Army Medical Services Museum for a copy of the compilation of his work *The Story of the Army Remount Service*.
9   Anglesey, Vol. 3, 1983, Vol. 4, 1986.
10   Tylden, 1965.
11   Morpurgo, 1982: Film *War Horse*, Steven Spielberg, released 2011.

useful and much needed reminiscences from veterans about their experiences of horses in warfare, as to a limited extent does the republication of General Jack Seely's *Warrior*.[12] Butler's, *The War Horses* is a lavishly illustrated with many photographs published for the first time, but the text, which does contain some useful information, is often disappointing and perpetuates old myths about cavalry, motor vehicles, and the welfare of horses during the War.[13]

In short, the Army could not function without mobility and motive power. Horse transport and mounted troops are only as effective as their animals. Strategic and tactical considerations are easily compromised without an adequate and reliable supply of fit, trained animals, in the right place at the right time. A simple question, placed in the context of the motor vehicle, highlights the importance of the horse. How useful is a motor vehicle without an engine, or one of the correct size and power to perform the task required of it? Saloon, estate, sports car, van, lorry or bus – all with different weights and power of engines to perform the tasks required of them. Cavalry, field artillery, ambulances, transport and supply services could not operate without the appropriate type of horse, of the right conformation and size; without appropriate draught animals the infantry could not be supplied with equipment, stores and ammunition. This, however, was not the only element in successfully horsing the Army during 1899-1902 and 1914-1918. On the outbreak of war the small peacetime cadres of the horse services and horse transport faced expansion on a massive scale to their wartime establishments in personnel, harness, fodder, equipment, buildings and vehicles. These crucial elements in mobilisation are usually ignored by historians. As late as 1918, with the massive expansion in the military use of motor vehicles, animals remained the major source of motive power and mobility. Cavalry remained the only arm capable of swift exploitation. That the authorities recognised the importance of an adequate supply of horses for military purposes can be seen in a number of significant developments from the 1880s onwards. What the authorities did not wish to recognise was the cost of maintaining that supply.

Primary source material from the 1880s to the outbreak of the Anglo-Boer War in 1899 is limited and somewhat scattered. *The Fitz-Wygram Report* of 1884 is an essential document for placing later reforms into context.[14] *The Veterinary Record* contains a wealth of information for the whole period with articles by both military and civil veterinary surgeons and extracts from other journals and newspapers. For this early period it is an invaluable source in piecing together parts of the jigsaw, as are some of the Anglo-Boer War reports. Hansard provides examples for some of the important questions of the day but often not with detailed answers.[15]

---

12   Arthur, 2003 and 2006; Van Emden, 2010; Gen. Jack Seely, 2011.
13   Butler, 2011.
14   NA, Kew, War Office Papers (WO), WO33/42.
15   Hansard, Parliamentary Papers (PP), Commons (C) and Lords (L).

The disasters of the 1899-1902 Anglo-Boer War brought forth a number of official reports and papers that relate specifically to the Remount Department. They provide a rich tapestry of material and have been quoted extensively in works on the conflict, however, they need to be used in context and their limitations as a source for the supply of remounts understood. An examination into the causes of wastage was called for and provided by the *Royal Commission* and the *Court of Enquiry*.[16] Both failed to examine the question of animal losses in the field; their investigations only related to the purchase of animals and their transport to South Africa.[17] It is to the outstanding work of Maj-Gen. Frederick Smith, AVC, that one must turn for a severe criticism of the Army system; he provides a detailed and analytical discussion of the events, sources and myriad of statistics.[18] Unlike many authors, who have accepted and quoted from the mass of information contained in the official reports and papers, and as a practitioner in the field, Smith convincingly challenges and poses vital questions for any student of the horse in war. He deserves far greater recognition and acknowledgement for his scholarly work.

There are a number of useful sources, which when combined offer an insight and understanding of the period between the Wars. The papers of the Directorate of Remounts are contained in the *Quarter Master General's (QMG) papers*.[19] These papers are somewhat limited and frustrating to use, as final decisions relating to remounts are often not recorded and official publications missing. It is to the papers of the *Board of Agriculture and Fisheries* that one must turn for clarification and copies of publications.[20] The Board's papers and those of the *Development Corporation* are a major source for the debate on light horse breeding and the supply of horses for military purposes.[21] These are fairly comprehensive but at times assume a knowledge of events for which there is no record. *Army Council Records* contain useful but limited references to horsing the Army.[22] The *Royal Corps of Transport Archive* is a most valuable source.[23] The debate over mechanisation in British and foreign armies and issues relating to horses and their future use, are well detailed; as is a new army transport system and reports on the work of the QMG's Branch. This archive with the *Cavalry Journal*

16   *Report of the Royal Commission to 'Inquire into the Military Preparations and Other Matters Connected with the War in South Africa.'* Parliamentary Papers (PP) Cd.1789 to 1792. '*Court of Enquiry on the Administration of the Army Remount Depot,'* PP. Cd.993 (Report) and Cd.994 (Evidence).
17   For example PP. Cd.963, Birkbeck (see Appendix I).
18   Smith, 1919 (Smith, see Appendix I).
19   NA, Kew, WO107. There are further papers, although few from the First World War period, in WO registered files, class WO32 Code 22, and WO33. The War Diaries of the Directorate are in class WO95, all but one relate to the Western Front.
20   NA, Kew, Ministry of Agriculture and Fisheries (MAF), Class 52. For example for WO32 cross referenced with MAF52.
21   NA, Kew, Development Commission, Classes D1/2/3/4.
22   WO163.
23   The Archive is now held in Royal Logistic Corps Museum, Deepcut, Surrey.

and the *Veterinary Record* enable one to get a feel for the period and of contemporary debates between the wars.[24] The impression is not of a conservative and totally blinkered army dominated by 'horsey types'. For the period between the wars, articles and publications in military journals and of the 'horse world' throw light on the lessons to be learnt from the 1899-1902 Anglo-Boer War and the urgency of establishing a national system for the supply of horses for military purposes.

There is precious little material from those who actually served with the Remount Department. The writings and reports of Lt-Col. Birkbeck (Assistant Inspector of Remounts in South Africa and Director of Remounts WO during 1914-1918) and Lt-Gen. MacMunn (Assistant Director of Remounts), provide an invaluable insight into the workings of the Remount Department during both Wars.[25] In contrast, the *Royal Army Veterinary Corps* is well served by histories and articles written by members of the Corps, the most distinguished being Smith, Moore, Blenkinsop and Rainey.[26] These authors cover in great detail the activities and development of the Corps during the period, however, Smith and Moore are more questioning and provide valuable insights. The comparative success of the horse services in the 1914-18 War, unlike the 1899-1902 Anglo-Boer War, did not generate the wealth of official reports, therefore material is limited. The *War Diary of the Director of Remounts (BEF)* is detailed, providing insights into routine as well as major issues facing the BEF.[27] *Remount Papers* are useful for issues relating to the expansion of the BEF in 1915, but far from detailed, whereas the *Official Statistics* for the war provide valuable basic information, although the sources are not given and it is difficult, if not impossible, to relate them to other WO papers.[28] In many cases calculations given in tables do not add up. Given the crucial importance of the horse to the military effort, it is amazing that the role of the Remount Service was ignored in the 'official history' of the war; though the Veterinary Service fared somewhat better.

The origin of the successful horsing of the British Army during the 1914-18 War can be dated to the creation of a unified Army Veterinary Department in 1881, and the Remount Department and Horse Registration Scheme in 1887, providing for a reserve of horses on mobilisation.

Part One looks at these developments, highlighting the crucial elements in effectively horsing the Army: supply, care, and organisation. These developments were severely tested during the 1899-1902 Anglo-Boer War and found wanting. The period 1902 to 1914 was therefore critical: only if the faults of the 1899-1902 War were identified, lessons learnt and reforms implemented would disaster be avoided in the next major conflict.

---

24   The 1899-1902 Anglo-Boer War and the First World War 1914-18.
25   Lt -Gen Mac Munn (See Appendix I).
26   Maj-Gen. Sir John Moore, Maj-Gen. Sir Layton Blenkinsop, and Lt- Col. J.W. Rainey (See Appendix I).
27   Brig. F.S.Garratt, Director of Remounts (BEF), WO69 and WO70 (see Appendix I).
28   WO107, and *Statistics*, 1922.

The crucial questions discussed in **Part Two** relate to solving the horse question, that of supplying the Army on mobilisation and sustaining it in the field. Significant alterations were required in the organisation of the horse services for rapid and effective expansion. For the Remount Department this meant creating a structure that permitted effective mobilisation of the horse reserve and recognising the impact of motor vehicles on the transport system. As Moore states, "in modern warfare a remount service could not maintain the supply of animals required by an army in the field without utilising those discharged as fit for duty from veterinary hospitals".[29] If this source of resupply had not existed during the 1914-18 War the horse population of the world would probably not have been adequate to meet the demands of the British forces alone. The civilian horse market was central to the supply of horses for military purposes. The big question was whether the home market would be sufficiently stimulated to provide the Army with peacetime requirements, the numbers required on mobilisation and replace wartime expansion and wastage. Were there sufficient horses in the country and how was the Army to obtain reliable information? Numbers alone were not the issue. The Army required sufficient numbers of fit and healthy animals of the right class, in the right place and at the right time. The war of 1914-18 provided the testing ground.[30]

Part Three looks at the implementation of mobilisation plans in 1914, the events of 1915-18 as they affected the horse services and demobilisation in 1918-19. As events unfolded, the situation became more complicated, the Army expanded beyond the scale envisaged in any pre-war planning; remounts were supplied to theatres other than the Western Front and to the armies of allied nations. The question of how demand for the vast number of animals, in all theatres, was met is discussed in chapters ten and eleven. As the war progressed there were serious questions about, supply from the UK and world horse markets and the transportation required for the vast number of animals from country of purchase to the battlefields, taking into account the submarine menace. There were vastly increased demands for remount depots, training of horses and staff for their specific tasks, veterinary hospitals, fodder, harness and horseshoes. A huge increase in horse services personnel was required including blacksmiths, saddlers, shoeing-smiths and ancillary tradesmen. These personnel had to be found, trained and their numbers maintained.

At the end of hostilities some 791,696 animals, in all theatres, had to be quickly disposed of, as humanely as possible.[31] The final section, **Demobilisation and Conclusion** examines the demobilisation process, the efficiency of the Remount and Veterinary Departments and whether the reforms in organisation met the demands of modern warfare. Crucial to success was an effective and efficient working partnership between these Departments and the High Command. In 1919, the horse remained

---

29   Moore, in Merillatt and Campbell, 1935, p.103.
30   Winton, 2007, *The 1914-18 War: A Horse War?*
31   *Statistics*, p.878. The figure is at 30th November 1918.

the main source of motive power, with cavalry as the main arm of exploitation, but mechanisation was firmly entrenched in the transport system. The debate between 1902 and 1914 over horse versus mechanisation for army transport had been fought and won. The Army transport system had been radically changed to accommodate mechanised vehicles, integrated with rail networks and horsed vehicles. Experiments and trials had taken place in the use of mechanical vehicles as assault weapons and although not sufficiently advanced by 1914, developments during the War were clearly acknowledged by many as signalling the end of the military reliance upon the horse. The British Army had a completely integrated horse and mechanical transport supply system with an organised reserve and mobilisation scheme on the outbreak of war in 1914.[32]

This book provides the first comprehensive study of the Army's horse services from 1878-1925, focusing on the use of horses in the 1899-1902 Anglo-Boer and 1914-18 Wars, and in particular the relationship with the domestic horse breeding industry, mechanisation and an integrated military transport system.[33]

32   Winton, 2000 (b), 'The British Army, Mechanisation and a New Transport System, 1900-14'.
33   Winton, 1997, 'Horsing the British Army 1878-1923'. Unpublished Ph.D thesis, University Birmingham.

Part One

1878-1902

Port Elizabeth Horse Memorial, South Africa

1

The Creation of Central Remount and Veterinary Services and a Horse Registration Scheme 1878-1899

The Philosophy of war knows no middle course between success and disaster; either the Army is to be properly mounted or it is not; if it is not properly mounted, it will not be efficient, and it will not win battles; and if the Army is not intended to win battles, it is surely a useless expense to the nation to keep up at all.[1]

With the massive rearmament programmes of the principal European powers in the late nineteenth century the British government was forced to review the Army's ability to mobilise in the event of an emergency, especially for the defence of the United Kingdom. With the greater destructiveness of firearms and the necessity for more rapid movement than in previous wars, the mortality rate among horses was likely to be considerably greater, therefore a larger reserve of horses would be required by the Army. As the horse was the principal means of power and mobility it is no surprise that the supply and care of suitable remounts for mobilisation was a matter of some importance. Unfortunately, this importance did not extend to accepting changes that necessitated an increase in expenditure. Maj-Gen. Frederick Smith, AVC, commenting on the lack of War Office (WO) spending, also noted that no scheme for mobilising the Army existed until 1886, it took a further four years to evolve; by the fifth year, regulations for mobilisation were issued on the basis of what was available not what was needed.[2]

In 1887 a central Army Remount Department was formed with responsibility for the purchase of all army horses. Prior to this date regiments purchased their own horses, usually through civilian agents. This regimental system of purchasing did not provide for the Army as a whole, a reserve of horses on mobilisation, or a coherent competitive method of supply during emergencies. Without a central system and trained staff, for the purchase of remounts, the Commander in Chief (C-in-C) had to

---

1   Birkbeck, 1908, p.342.
2   PP. Cd.1789, p.30; Smith, 1919, p.3.

make his own arrangements for supply. The exception, was the Royal Artillery which had maintained a centralised corporate identity that enabled many functions, common to the regiment as a whole, such as remounts, to be undertaken centrally. During the nineteenth century a Royal Artillery Riding Troop was based at Woolwich, later called the Riding Establishment Royal Horse Artillery, concerned with equestrian training for the artillery. Army Distribution Lists, introduced in 1856, show that from time to time a senior Royal Artillery officer held the appointment of 'Inspector and Purchaser of Horses,' for example, Col. F.G. Ravenhill from April 1881. In 1885 the Establishment had 138 personnel of all ranks and 100 horses. Also listed is a Remount Establishment with the Garrison Artillery, with 86 personnel of all ranks and 32 horses.[3] From April 1882 until March 1887, the Royal Artillery Distribution Lists, show a Remount Establishment, Woolwich (Royal Artillery and Royal Engineers Remount Establishment), with a Captain Royal Artillery on its strength. The Establishment is not listed after April 1887 as a Royal Artillery unit, possibly because of plans to create a central Remount Department. In 1887 the Remount Establishment, Woolwich had an establishment of three officers (including the Inspector and Veterinary Surgeon) and 87 other ranks under the command of an Inspector of Horses (Col. Ravenhill, between 1884-94). The Inspector held responsibility for training and distributing all horses required by the Artillery and Engineers (the latter holding very few horses in peacetime) stationed at home.[4]

Prior to the establishment of the Royal Veterinary College in 1792, there was no veterinary service in the Army. Regimental farriers (sometimes assisted by veterinary surgeons) held a government contract to shoe army horses, supply medicines and attend sick, or injured horses. In 1796, owing to heavy losses among army horses in various campaigns, veterinary surgeons were appointed to cavalry regiments, the Royal Artillery and Royal Waggon Train. The first graduate and therefore qualified veterinary surgeon to join the Army in 1796 was John Shipp, 11th Light Dragoons.[5] Developments in the 1790s and early 1800s provided an embryo veterinary service organised entirely on a regimental basis, veterinary surgeons were recruited directly into regiments, but with no provision for the care of sick, or lame horses when on active service. Sir Henry Evelyn Wood (Adjutant General to the Forces 1897-1901), wrote in 1914, "it is sad to reflect that from 1856 to 1900 practically nothing was done to provide for the care and feeding of our animals with an army in the field".[6] In 1859 the two separate veterinary services of Ordnance and Cavalry were amalgamated under one Principal Veterinary Surgeon (PVS) with, until 1890, a civilian surgeon at its head;

3   British Parliamentary Papers (BPP), 1884-5, Vol.XLVI, 19th Feb. 1885, pp.10-11; see Appendix I for Ravenhill.
4   I am indebted to the late Col. Hume, 1989, for information on the Remount Service; also K.A. Timbers, Secretary of the Royal Artillery Historical Trust, 1989; Hansard (C), 1887, 29th July, column (c) 494; Sessions, 1903, pp.14-15.
5   Gray, 1985, biography of Shipp.
6   Foreword to Smith, 1919, p.iv. Field Marshal Sir H. E. Wood.

also in 1859 the Army Veterinary Department (AVD) appeared in Army Lists for the first time.[7] The regimental system for the care of horses was abolished in 1878, except for the cavalry, and a more unified Army Veterinary Service (AVS) created. In 1879, a general list of non-regimental veterinary officers was available for any unit, under the newly created and centralised AVS and in 1880 an Army Veterinary School was formed in Aldershot. In April 1881, the regimental system was abolished in the cavalry, when all veterinary officers, except those of the Household Brigade, were transferred to one list, unifying for the first time all veterinary services into the AVD. The treatment of horses for practical reasons however remained on a regimental basis.

The Fitz-Wygram Committee

In 1883 the WO established a Committee under the chairmanship of Lt-Gen. Sir Frederick FitzWygram to investigate the supply of additional horses required on the mobilisation of two Army Corps.[8] According to a return presented to the Committee by the QMG's Department, an Army Corps on active service required about 12,000 horses. The peacetime establishment of I Army Corps was about 8,000 horses, of which about one-third (2,600) could be deducted for horses under, or over age, or otherwise unsuitable for active service; leaving a deficit of 6,600 horses to bring the Corps up to active service requirements, to be procured within one month of mobilisation. The Committee questioned the validity of retaining horses unfit for active service within the peacetime establishment. The peace establishment of the II Army Corps was smaller, requiring approximately an additional 9,300 horses for active service, to be purchased within two, or three months of mobilisation. The total requirement to bring the two Corps up to strength for active service was 15,900 horses. Calculations in the Return show that of the required active service strength of the two Corps (24,000 horses), an additional 40% (9,600) would be required as reinforcements, to be obtained within about six months of mobilisation. The total number required, to be purchased within a few months of the outbreak of war, for the two Corps, in addition to their peacetime establishments, was 25,500 (15,900 plus 9,600). The Committee noted that 40% might not be sufficient, as losses in the first year of the Crimean War were 80%.[9]

Horses in Great Britain and Ireland were divided into two categories, agricultural and trade/private. The total number of horses registered in the UK for the Horse Tax in 1873 (the last year the tax was collected), was 2,762,000, of which about one third were employed privately, or in trade. It was possible that about one million of these were available, without disrupting trade, of which about 20,000, would be of the right type, fit and healthy and therefore suitable for army purposes. Board of Trade Agricultural

---

7   Forgrave, 1987, p.5; Smith, 1927; *VR*, 1893, Vol.6, 30th December, p.363.
8   WO33/42, Fitz-Wygram. The four committee members included: Col. Ravenhill and Dr G. Fleming, PVO (see Appendix I).
9   WO33/42, p.1.

Statistics for 1881 record about two million horses employed in agriculture, including young horses and foals; of this number, about 50,000 were considered probably fit for active military use. Of the original nearly three million horses from trade and agriculture about 70,000 suitable horses were therefore available in the UK for military service, of which the Army would require about 36%. The majority being excluded as too heavy for army purposes, under five or over 12 years of age, or generally unfit. [10]

The question for the Army was, how many of the 70,000 suitable horses could they purchase? Probably in excess of 4,500 were in dealers' hands and thus on the open market, and of these some 500 were possibly suitable for army purposes; the remainder would have to be purchased from private owners. The Committee considered that owners kept few horses other than those required for their own use or trade, so even if they were offered a price above the normal value of a horse, they would probably part with their inferior animals, but not with their really serviceable ones. This situation would be exacerbated by a draining of the market so that replacements would be unobtainable. If horses became scarce some in the Army thought they might be replaced by mechanical draught, especially if the supply of horses permanently failed. This is an interesting early reference to the possible use of mechanical vehicles by the Army, in that senior officers of the "horsey world" were making the recommendation. The supply of traction engines could not, however, be increased in time to supply the immediate requirements of a campaign. Large employers might possibly dispense with 30% of their horses, but none would be available from the far more numerous small businesses. On the assumption therefore that a maximum of 15% of the 70,000 (10,500) could be purchased, this provided 11,000 (10,500 plus the 500 in dealers' yards). Ravenhill considered that 15% would be far beyond the number obtainable by purchase without compulsory powers, as even large owners, such as the London General Omnibus Company with 8,000 horses, could not afford to sell more than 2%, or 3% of their animals. He also believed the number of horses bred in the country had decreased, as illustrated by Board of Trade Returns between 1881 and 1882, which indicated a decrease of 18,000. Custom House Returns showed an average of 15,000 horses imported annually into the country possibly compensating for the decrease in breeding. The Committee reported that of the 25,500 required within the first year of war by the two Army Corps, a total of 11,000 could be met from the home market without recourse to compulsory purchase, at a rate of about 2,400 per month, leaving the deficit of 14,500 to be provided from other sources such as overseas purchases. These figures were based on experiences of the 1882 Egyptian War when 1,700 horses were purchased in 17 weeks, and the Russian scare of 1878 when 2,250 were purchased, by the greatest exertions, in four weeks.

The Committee concluded that:

- the total number of horses required to complete I Army Corps could be maintained in peacetime. It would not be possible, within one month, to provide the

---

10   Ibid., p.2.

4,200 (6,600 less the 2,400 purchased in the home market) required to bring the Corps up to wartime establishment as the timing was too short for foreign markets to respond, as Commissions would have to be sent out, horses collected, examined, purchased, shipped, sorted and transferred to units.

- II Army Corps required 9,300 horses to be purchased within three months. As I Corps would take all purchases from the home market during the first month; during the next two months it surmised II Corps could purchase at the rate of 1,200 per month i.e. 2,400 horses. The balance, about 6,900, would then be obtained from foreign markets.
- foreign markets would also have to supply the balance of 3,400 horses required as reinforcements within the first six months, but it was considered doubtful that any one country could supply a large number. Some countries would be closed to the UK in time of war and other countries would close markets when they chose to, for example in the Egyptian War of 1882 there was a banning of exports by Turkey. In countries such as France, Germany, Spain and Turkey all horses were registered and in time of war exportation was forbidden.[11]

The table below shows how II Corps and reinforcements could be supplied.[12] The left column gives a total of 7,100 for II Corps, which after deducting those unfit, sick and accidents, leaves hardly enough to meet the 6,900 required. The right column gives a total of 6,300 against the requirement of 3,400.

	II Corps	Reinforcements
Draught Horses:		
France	500	500
Belgium	550	500
N. Europe	700	–
United States	750	500
Canada	1,000	1,500
South America	600	
Totals	3,500	3,600
Riding Horses:		
Hungary	1,200	750
United States	700	500
Canada	1,100	1,000
Syria, Asia Minor, Morocco	350	250
Spain	250	200
Totals	3,600	2,700

11   WO33/42, pp.3, 5.
12   Ibid., based on tables p.5.

Comments were made on the various foreign breeds and prices, for example, French, Belgium and North European draught breeds were considered inferior to English ones. Few of the other countries supplied riding horses; the small Syrian, Spanish and Moroccan breeds were suitable for staff and departmental officers. Canadian horses were considered to be of good quality; a West End jobmaster (hired out horses) imported them for his London customers. The 7th Hussars in 1837 and the 13th Hussars in 1861 thought very favourably of Canadian horses as troop horses as also did all the officers of the Royal Artillery who had commanded batteries in Canada. The cost of importing would increase with shipping and the fitting out of ships specifically as horse transports. The number of horses imported from the US into Liverpool had declined but numbers were still available. Mr Erskin (US Vice-Consul), stated they exported 20,000 to 30,000 horses annually to England, dealers sending their buyers to Chicago. Small Hungarian horses were thought useful, with good reports of their work in the Egyptian War, but experience suggested large numbers were not available; the War Department sent a Commission to Hungary in about 1880 to purchase some 700 horses, but only succeeded in obtaining 350 as many were under 15 hands high. The Committee recommended that agencies be established in each of the horse-producing countries (Canada, USA, Hungary, Asia Minor, Spain, Northern Europe, France), and a limited number, about 25%, purchased from them annually; a practice that would also provide detailed knowledge on the supply, class and quality in each country. Having tried and trusted agents in each country would also speed up supply in the event of increased demand.[13]

In Great Britain the difficulty was in purchasing riding horses, numbers of which had declined, whereas draught horses existed in very much larger numbers. With improvements in roads and development of railways, fewer farmers used riding horses for work and it did not pay them to breed the light horses suitable for cavalry. However, in Ireland, which supplied horses for line cavalry regiments, the light horse was in greater demand than the draught horse.

It was not thought possible to adopt the system used by foreign countries of supplying their military horses by registration in peacetime and requisition in wartime. Instead, the system used during the Egyptian War was considered appropriate, whereby, a Central Committee was appointed by the WO, consisting of the Inspector-General of Cavalry, PVS, the Artillery Remount Agent and a selected cavalry officer. The Central Committee then selected sub-committees to be located in likely purchasing districts and communicated to them their opinions on the horses purchased; exactly the same structure applied to Ireland. Each sub-committee, on purchasing a truckload of six or seven horses, sent them to London, or Aldershot, for inspection by the Central Committee, they were then sorted and sent off to appropriate units; the assumption being that the next Army Corps to be mobilised for active service would be from Aldershot.[14]

13   WO33/42, p.8.
14   Ibid.

The Fitz-Wygram Committee reported on 29th January 1884, but little in the report appears to have been acted upon. Although from 1879 the Government purchased small numbers of remounts from overseas, it was opposed to such purchases at a time when the UK horse breeding industry was in need of stimulation. The Committee's suggestion for an increase in the permanent peacetime establishment contradicted the purpose of army reforms, that sought to produce a small standing army supported by effective resources.[15] The proposals were too expensive for consideration, as they increased the number of army animals in the UK by half; thereby increasing the cost of procuring and keeping additional horses. Stables would have to be extended, other facilities provided in cavalry barracks and the number of personnel increased to look after the additional animals.

The opportunity to establish an effective structure for mobilisation in the event of war had been lost. In just 15 years, the country would be engaged in a major colonial conflict in South Africa, the financial cost of which, in remount terms, was to be far higher than had the Committee's recommendations been implemented. Failure to obtain reliable information on potential remounts from foreign markets and in particular, the failure to establish trusted agents with local knowledge would prove costly in monetary terms and in appalling animal wastage.

A Remount Commission was sent to Canada in 1886 to purchase 300 horses and assess potential markets, but proposals to purchase a limited number of remounts each successive year as a strategy for keeping in touch with this source of supply were turned down. The Commission was subsequently criticised by the Exchequer and Audit Department of the Treasury for exceeding the authorised price for remounts by £16. The Secretary of State ordered that all future purchases should be made in the UK, however, several thousand cobs were purchased in Hungary and in South America (1896-8) for mounted infantry and shipped directly to the garrison in South Africa; horses were also purchased from Syria (1898) for the Army in Egypt.[16]

Horse Registration Scheme

The problem of providing adequate horses for the Army on mobilisation remained. A number of schemes were put forward as alternatives to those of the Fitz-Wygram Commission one of which, suggested by Ravenhill met with approval, as it avoided any significant increase in peacetime expenditure and tackled the difficulties of providing horses on mobilisation.[17] Ravenhill suggested that the War Department invite owners of large numbers of horses to place some of them, voluntarily, at the

15   WO33/42, p.4; Hume, 1989, p.4-44.
16   Hume, 1989, p.4-5; Page, 1976, p.299, from Truman's evidence to Royal Commission, Cd.1791, p35, Q12880; Cd.994, p.2; Smith, 1919, p.323; *VR*, 1897, Vol.9, 8th May, p.639 and 1898, Vol.10, 18th June, p.739 and 1894, 16th April, p.616 and 1894, Vol.7, 12th January, p.390; Hansard (C), 1887, 19th July; Amery, 1909, Vol.VI, p.415.
17   Lecture given to the Royal Service Institute, 1886; *VR*, 1888, Vol.1, 11th August, p.56.

disposal of the government in case of an emergency. This Horse Registration Scheme gained the support of Lord Harris, Parliamentary Under-Secretary, WO, who saw that it could provide the much-needed stimulus to the country's horse breeding industry. The Scheme met with approval, as it avoided any significant increase in peacetime expenditure and tackled the difficulties of providing horses on mobilisation. The Scheme was introduced in 1887, apparently with some hesitation, as an experiment, appearing in Army Estimates for 1888-9, which suggests that the WO did not believe the problem of providing horses for the Army, in an emergency, was considered solved.[18] Authorisation was given to register 7,000 horses immediately, the number progressively increased, so that by 1890 some 14,558 horses were registered.[19]

The Army (Annual) Act of 1881 allowed for the impressment of carriages and horses for the transport of baggage in an emergency, but lacked any system for implementation. The Registration Scheme provided the system and acted as the catalyst for the National Defence Act of 1888, which extended the powers of Section 115, of the 1881 Act, by adding sub-sections 7 and 8, giving the government power to requisition all horses and means of transport in the country, at a time of national danger, or when militia was being mobilised.[20]

In the event of an emergency, private owners involved in the Scheme were invited to sell their horses to the Army at a price agreed at the time of registration; in return, the Army paid an annual retaining fee of 10/- per horse. It was the owner and his stables, not individual horses, which were registered. Under the terms of agreement, an owner was required to produce on mobilisation, a specified number of horses of a particular class, 'serviceably sound and suitable', between the ages of six and ten, within 48 hours of notification. Horses had to be available for an annual inspection; a fine of £50 was payable if any were missing and the Army had the right to demand the actual horses inspected at the time of registration. The Scheme did not unduly restrict owners and the Army acquired a reserve of horses at a modest annual cost. On the outbreak of war in 1899, prices previously agreed under the Scheme were seen to be excessive; horses could be obtained more cheaply on the open market as developments in transport and changes in horse breeding had depressed purchase prices.[21] The initial response of horse owners was considered satisfactory, especially from the large railway companies, some provincial tram companies and carriers, and metropolitan firms; demonstrating that by a simple and easy process of organisation, it was possible for the War Department to obtain a sufficient number of serviceable horses to place an Army Corps in the field, within a few days of an order for mobilisation.[22]

18   Hansard (L), 1887, 8th September.
19   Page, 1976, p.298, unpublished PhD thesis; Hume, 1989, p.4-6.
20   Public General Acts, 1888.
21   Page, p.28; Hume, 1989, p.4-6; Tylden, 1965, p.25; Cd.993, p.2; WO33/271, 1903, pp.A3, A6.
22   VR, 1888, Vol.1, 11th August, p.56.

The most significant effect of the new scheme was in preparing the way for abolition of the regimental remounting system. The Fitz-Wygram Committee had recommended that on any future mobilisation, a central remount committee be formed to manage purchasing arrangements.[23] If, from the outbreak of war, the supply of remounts was to be placed under central control, a similar system operating in peacetime, would hold the same advantages, and therefore, in the interests of economy and efficiency the Registration Scheme should be administered by a central staff. Once a central administration was created it could easily assume responsibility for purchasing the 2,500 remounts required annually by the Army at home.

Army Remount Service

Army Order 172, November 1887, announced the establishment of the Army Remount Department, located in the QMG's Department, appearing in Army Estimates for the first time in 1888-89; based on the Scheme proposed by Col. Ravenhill, who was appointed the first Inspector General of Remounts (IGR) with the temporary rank of Major General.[24] For the first time in its history, the Army, based at home, had a unified structure for the provision of remounts. Maj. Tylden commented that this was the most important event in the history of remounts in the British Army, as from that time onward there was only one policy.[25] The Department was responsible for registering reserve horses for the Army and purchasing remounts for regiments stationed at home, except for Household Cavalry Regiments; units based overseas continued to purchase their own horses locally. In India remounts were provided by the Indian Government. The annual peacetime requirement for the Army at home ranged from 1,400 to 2,500 remounts, in addition, the Department was to prepare for the mobilisation requirements of up to two army corps.

The small Remount Establishment of 1887 consisted of an IGR, based at the WO, and three Assistant Inspectors of Remounts (AIR), all to be included in the General Staff of the Army. Two remount depots were created at Woolwich and Dublin, commanded by staff-captains and manned by soldiers drawn from the Artillery and Cavalry. Depots smaller than the Royal Artillery Establishment at Woolwich (which ceased to exist on creation of the Remount Department), were to receive and hold animals until fit for issue to regiments, which then trained, or schooled them for their own requirements. Each of the depots was under the control of an AIR, who undertook the purchasing of horses in England and Ireland; Woolwich remained the centre for the Artillery, which preferred English horses, with the new depot in Ireland

---

23   WO33/42, p.8; Hansard (L), 1887, 8th September, (c)1626.
24   *London Gazette*, 18th October 1887, p.3598. Col. Ravenhill, RA, was promoted from Lt-Gen, half pay, to IGR with the temporary rank of Maj-Gen whilst employed in this post, dated 1st October 1887.
25   Army General Orders, 1887; Tylden, 1965, p.25; Hume, 1989, pp.4-7, 4-8.

handling mainly cavalry remounts. Eventually, arrangements were formalised and the AIR, Woolwich, purchased all remounts for the Artillery, Engineers and transport service in Ireland and England. The third AIR was to operate the Horse Registration Scheme in its experimental form.

In July 1891 responsibility for the personnel of remount depots was transferred to the Army Service Corps (ASC), forming a remount company at each remount depot.[26] These companies, officered by an ASC quartermaster, were placed under the IGR at the WO and took the place of personnel previously seconded from the Artillery and Cavalry. They first appeared in the Army List for September 1891 as 'A' and 'B' Remount Companies, each consisting of 66 soldiers including, one company sergeant major, quartermaster and farrier sergeant; three sergeants, corporals and lance-corporals; four shoeing smiths and 50 privates.[27]

The Army purchased horses on the open market, from dealers who had been accustomed to procuring the classes required, this was considered the cheaper way of purchasing and encouraged the breeding of good equine stock within the country; unlike foreign armies who received government support.[28] The question of army purchases remained very much a concern for the horse breeding world with questions frequently raised in Parliament. For example, in 1895 Viscount Valentia asked whether any, and if so how many, horses had been purchased from breeders or farmers in country districts, during the last year (1894-5), for army purposes.[29] Mr W. St John Brodrick (Financial Secretary to the WO 1886-92, Under Secretary of State for War 1895-98, Secretary of State for War from November 1900), replied that during the year 1894-5, 503 remounts were purchased from 87 private owners and 1,116 remounts from dealers. During 1888-9 the Army purchased 1,381 horses from dealers and in 1889-90, 1,153; a total of 3,034. Of these 1,231 were purchased in London, 1,706 in Ireland (in Dublin 1,011, Navan 245, Waterford 232 and Castlenock 218), and small numbers in other places. Between 1888-90, 46 horses were purchased from breeders. In 1897, Maj. Rasch asked whether the WO would encourage horse breeding in the country districts by advertising the fact that they would be given £40 for a horse. He was informed that from April 1887 to March 1897, a total of 15,018 horses were purchased of which 61% (9,139) were from Ireland. In making these purchases many hundreds of horses, offered by agriculturists, were

---

26 *Royal Corps of Transport*, 1981; the ASC was created in 1888, technically this was a recreation. The ASC was fully combatant with its Horse Transport Depot at Woolwich and Supply and Regimental depot at Aldershot. From 1888 Supply and Transport were in one Corps; Army Orders No. 202, 1888 and No. 149, 1891; Tylden, p.2; Hume, 1989, p.4-8.
27 Beadon, 1931, pp.11-12.
28 Hansard (L), 1887, 8th September, (c)1624.
29 *VR*, 1895, Vol.7, 7th Sept., p.127; Hansard (C), 1895, Vol.XXXVI, 26th August, (c)798-9. (Valentia see Appendix I).

examined by remount officers. In addition to purchases, 7,000 horses were registered as a reserve for the Army in 1888-9, the number more than doubling during 1889-90.[30]

The annual AVD Report, 1891, records the strength of army animals as 13,327 troop horses, 1,721 chargers and 226 mules, figures that remained relatively constant throughout the 1890s. The 1896 Army General Report gives 14,603 total effective horses and mules on the British Establishment; for 1897 a further increase of 1,685 and in 1898, 690 with a total of 16,978.[31] In 1896-7 there were 14,550 registered horses of which 10,000 were draught, a large number coming from Canada. These were considered excellent for Field Artillery and horsed many Canadian batteries. Other Canadian horses were purchased for the London omnibus companies. Most of the animals purchased in Britain were now increasingly imported, other than those obtained from Ireland. Truly indigenous horses of the types required by the Army became very scarce; Anglesey states that every week about 1,200 foreign horses were landed at London, Liverpool and Glasgow docks. It was horses such as these, very few of them branded at their place of origin, which formed the majority of 'English' remounts towards the end of the nineteenth century. A view supported by Col. Hotham writing in 1906.[32]

The creation of the Remount Department and Horse Registration Scheme in 1887 did not, however, solve the problems of remount supply, or of creating a large enough reserve of horses for mobilisation. The Registration Scheme created a reserve to meet the immediate requirements of mobilisation, at a fixed price, and without risking the unpopular measure of impressment. There were, however, inherent weaknesses with the Scheme, for example, by specifying the ages of six and ten, it sought to provide the Army with horses in the prime of their working life, but it could not guarantee horses would be in hard condition (fit, not carrying fat and with muscles toned from regular working), when mobilised. If mobilisation was in the summer, hunters would probably still be at grass, mares might be in foal and even if fit, would not militarily be trained. The question of supply was not simply one of quantity, but also one of quality and suitability.[33] The situation on mobilisation was unlike that of peacetime remount supply. On mobilisation there was no certainty that the exact numbers of each type or stamp (conformation) of horse procured would reflect the different requirements of the various branches of the Army; those supplied might not be fit for service, not militarily trained, and the horse equipment available might not be adequate for military

30   Rasch see Appendix I; Hansard (C), 1897, Vol.XLVI, 4th March, (c)1597; *VR*, 1890, Vol.3, 16th August, p.91. *VR*, 1891, Vol.4, 26th September, p.174 gives the total registered horses by 1890 as 21,000 (4,212 riding and 16,788 draught); this is the only reference I have found to such a large number being registered and cannot therefore confirm its accuracy.

31   *VR*, 1891, Vol.4, 14th November, pp.269-70; Annual Report 31st March 1891; Cd.1496, Part IX, pp.65-70, for 1896, 1897, 1898.

32   Hotham, 1906, p.190; Anglesey, 1986, Vol.4, p.281.

33   Hume, 1989, p.4-6.

purposes at a time of rapid expansion and immediate action. The question was, how, on mobilisation, were the various branches of the Army to be supplied with horses of the appropriate class, and how effective would the Registration Scheme be in achieving this? This question encouraged wide ranging discussion among military personnel and the horse world generally, in particular over questions of quality and the relationship between the domestic horse breeding industry and military requirements.

Dr Fleming (1833-1901), who retired in 1890 as Colonel, Principal Veterinary Surgeon (PVS), considered that keeping the mounted men and horses, of either one or two army corps, at wartime establishment was too heavy an expense for the country, yet he saw no other way out of the difficulty. In peacetime he thought there was no difficulty in finding all the horses required, as the total for all arms of the Army barely exceeded 1,500 annually and could be picked up at leisure. This figure is usually given as 2,500 annually, only Fleming gives 1,500. The problem was how to meet requirements in the event of war and for Fleming this question had been the subject of grave discussion for several years. He saw the Government's attempt at solving the problem, by registering a few thousand horses, as being only partially successful; many were draught animals, which were most abundant in the country and could only be utilised for artillery, or transport. The greatest demand was for the light, active horse of the cavalry type that was also the scarcest. By a great effort, if the mobilisation of one or two army corps were ever necessary, sufficient draught horses might be obtained, but the required number of cavalry horses, fit to go into the field in a short time, would not be available. The issue was, therefore, how to complete, with suitable horses, the establishment of cavalry regiments. Until such provision was made, it would not have been possible to put an army of 20,000 or 30,000 men into the field with the required number of mounted troops.[34]

Considerable efforts were made during 1888 to increase the reserve of horses, but concerns remained over the shortage of trained animals to meet military requirements. For example, during 1887, 1,000 horses were added to cavalry regiments. However, the stock of trained animals (including those in training) was still insufficient to mount two thirds of troopers, about 19,100 officers and men, in the 31 cavalry regiments of the British Regular Army. When the officers (who provided their own horses) were deducted, there were 18,300 Non Commissioned Officers (NCOs) and troopers for 11,800 available horses, leaving 6,500 dismounted (equal to 13 regiments of 500 each). The nine regiments on the Indian Establishment had about 4,100 for 5,900 men and the Inniskilling Dragoons, quartered in Natal, had about 350 horses for 470 men. The three regiments of Household Cavalry (which had to provide a regiment between them for the I Army Corps) had 800 horses for more than 1,200 men. The eight regiments at home, not belonging to I or II Army Corps, or depots of regiments abroad, had amongst them 2,700 horses for 4,700 men The Cavalry Depot Staff at Canterbury

---

34 Dr G. Fleming, *VR*, 1889, Vol.1, 16th February, pp.393-4; Smith, 1927, pp.177-8 for Fleming's career.

and the Military Mounted Police (principally at Aldershot, the Curragh in Ireland and Egypt), accounted for about 130 horses to mount as many men. If these figures are accurate, 'official' calculations for the number of remounts required on mobilisation were based on 'paper' establishments, not the number physically in existence and highlight the extent of under-strength peacetime establishments. [35]

Fleming gives the number of horses required to furnish the full establishments of cavalry regiments, batteries of artillery, engineer troops, infantry and general transport of the I Army Corps as 11,483 (exclusive of 1,571 officers' chargers). The same number applied to the II Corps. A total of 22,966 horses was therefore required before the two Corps could take to the field. The total number of effective horses with the Army was only 10,371 (calculation made in 1886, but Fleming believed the situation had not changed in 1889), about 1,100 less than the number required for one army corps, and 12,600 less than for the two Corps (exclusive of officers' chargers, requiring an additional 3,142 horses). Where lines of communication would have to be maintained, an additional 2,773 horses were required for each Corps. The total deficit for the two Corps was 18,100, and even if this deficit could have been found, Fleming considered that mortality during a war would be heavy due to more rapid movements and the increased destructiveness of firearms. He suggested a large reserve of 50% to 60% should be planned for.[36] According to Tylden, in 1896-7 a cavalry division within an army corps required:[37]

3,720	for the eight regiments composing the Division
720	for the four batteries RHA
1,950	for the 15 batteries RFA
7,316	for details such as regimental transport
Total 13,706	

The breeding of saddle horses, unless they were of good quality, was not a profitable business. In England, the price allowed for cavalry remounts (about £40) was not sufficient to encourage farmers to breed and even if it were, the demand was not large enough, in peacetime, to secure a ready market for them. Simply to improve the breed

---

35   *VR*, 1889, Vol.1, 12th January, p.324; figures taken from returns made by the WO at the beginning of 1889.
36   Ibid.
37   Tylden, p.27. Cavalry brigades within the division each had their own RHA battery for support they weren't deemed divisional artillery. The Royal Field Artillery ran a confusing Brigade-Division support, where they were supporting individual infantry brigades of the same division and were considered integral to both, but also self-sufficient and therefore independent. It didn't work properly and was changed in favour of the pre-war system, so by 1914 the cavalry division did not have RFA batteries under its command, only RHA batteries. My thanks to Brian Hill and Paul Evans of the Royal Artillery Institution for this information.

of light horses for military purposes was not to increase the supply and unless breeders could find a market they would not produce them. The demand for light horse breeds, for commercial and equestrian purposes declined annually, so to provide an adequate reserve of this type would have meant an expense, which according to Fleming, would have startled the taxpayer. In addition to the original cost of the animals, there was also the cost of their keep. Cavalry horses had to be of the best quality; a good troop horse was a weight carrying hunter and could not be bred and reared at the price then being paid by the government; if inferior animals were purchased they would not meet the requirements of modern warfare. As the Army was supplied with the best possible weapons the same care was required in supplying the best horses the country could produce, with measures adopted to secure an ample supply for the demands of war. This issue Fleming considered should be settled without delay.[38]

Even for those who saw the Registration Scheme as successfully supplying the quality of horses required, the problem of supplying the numbers of light horses remained. One school of thought was that some owners would pocket their annual registration fee and not produce a serviceable animal; others questioned the fitness of the horses for military work when required. Lord Methuen's view on the Scheme (Maj-Gen. Commanding Brigade of Guards and GOC Home District, 1892-1897), was that such fears were unfounded as owners of horses had taken a pride in producing the best stamp of animals at their disposal. He appears to be commenting on a trial use of the Scheme, "the first time any attempt had been made to parade registered horses", when stating that "so good were they, that all Corps had reported favourably of them". Those sent for draught purposes were ready for wagon work almost immediately and "for gun drill at a pinch", although there were complaints that some were too heavy. In the 8th Hussars no fewer than 75% were found suitable for light cavalry duties, and the remainder suitable for transport, or mounted infantry. If such experiences were typical, Methuen thought the difficulty of providing a supply of reserve cavalry horses might not be so great. He comments that the Army Remount Staff had noted any short-comings of the trial and would take steps to prevent, as far as possible, any recurrence, "we cannot expect to run before we can walk." Remount staff who had previously been asked to work more or less in the dark, under difficult circumstances, were to be credited with their successes. Much was expected from the new Remount Department, which was therefore "evidently deserving of confidence and support."[39]

Dr Fleming wrote scathingly about the plans for horsing the Army in the event of an emergency, believing them to be woefully inadequate both in numbers and type of remount required.[40] Although details might have been prepared on paper, he considered it was questionable as to how far the actual state of readiness would allow the prompt mobilisation of even one army corps, especially the mounted sections. The

38   *VR*, 1889, Vol.1, 16th February, pp.394.
39   *VR*, 1895, Vol.8, 19th October, p.199.
40   *VR*, 1889, Vol.1, 16th February, p.393.

personnel to fill up the numbers might be forthcoming, but not the horses within the time required. It is doubtful whether the Registration Scheme and annual remount purchase of about 2,500 horses was ever capable of revitalising the domestic horse breeding industry. The annual payment of 10/- for each horse registered would not encourage farmers to breed horses for which no sale was guaranteed, even in war. Many owners registered their horses out of patriotism rather than financial gain, but for the owners of large numbers of horses or stables the Scheme had some financial merit.

Horses taken in the event of an emergency were not to be available for military training purposes in peacetime. A question was raised in the House of Commons about the number of horses registered for the retaining fee during the financial year 1897-8, the total expenditure and whether those receiving the fee were bound to let the horses for the training of militia, volunteer and yeomanry units, for a period not exceeding one week at a time, or a limited number of days per annum? The reply was that the number of horses registered annually, from 1889, was some 14,000; the proposal for making these horses available for training was considered impracticable and alien to the understanding of what constituted 'a national emergency' (the purpose of registration).[41]

The Remount Department was organised to supply the peacetime army at home; the Indian Government provided horses for the Indian Army, and other garrisons outside the UK only included two cavalry regiments and four field batteries between them. The question of what plans had been made to meet an increase in demand in the case of an emergency and what the increase might be, remained a topic of great interest and concern to military minds; as recorded in the literature of the period. Veterinary-Capt. Frederick Smith reviewed the losses of cavalry and artillery horses in battle since 1691, reasoning that to meet all casualties, the WO must be prepared to replace 17% to 20% of the total number committed.[42] He raised the question of how the WO was going to prevent the serious losses that would be suffered by artillery horses, losses which would be costly in monetary and efficiency terms, and criticised the WO for lack of foresight and failing to align with modern ideas.[43] Few of the enormous losses in previous wars had resulted from actual battle casualties, compared with those from overwork, starvation and disease. For example, in the Crimea 500 artillery horses were killed by the enemy but 2,000 died of want and disease; of 5,000 horses landed in Egypt in 1882 only 53 were killed in action but 2,500 fell sick and

41   Hansard (C), 1898, Vol.LXI, (c)1212; *VR*, 1898, Vol. 2, 30th July, p.68 and 1891, Vol.4, 26th September, p.174.

42   Later Maj-Gen. Sir F. Smith, *VR*, 1893, Vol.6, 23rd September, p.181.

43   Smith, D J., 1977, p.6; for example, unlike other nations in Europe which had recognised the dangers of the shaft system for draught, Britain had not, and was the only one still using it; this type of shaft system was not widely used in the British Army after 1900; *VR*, ibid., p.181 "Persistence in adhering to this system meant the guns would be left on the battlefield owing to the destruction of their motive power."

600 were destroyed. The figures presented by Smith highlight the dangers of an inadequate reserve, but the warning was still being ignored, as the relative position was no better than when Ravenhill formed his statistical estimate in 1888. The existing supply would only provide a fair quality and limited quantity of horses in peacetime and as Smith wrote, "we do not know how to complete our required strength for a serious conflict, much less to repair the waste of war. The subsidy paid to cab and omnibus proprietors for maintaining what is termed a reserve, are for horses that have never been difficult to obtain."[44] The question of replacing wastage remained a serious flaw in military planning.

Assessment of Planning to 1899

Prior to the outbreak of war in 1899, the General Officer Commanding in Chief (GOC- in-C) in Cape Town estimated that a 5% monthly wastage of total strength would be required. This figure appears to ignore previous experience and information contained in such reports as the 1884 Fitz-Wygram Committee, that recommended a 40% reinforcement of original strength for the two Corps. Dr Fleming (1899) had suggested 50% to 60% of original strength and in 1891 the Secretary of State for War (Rt. Hon. Edward Stanhope, January 1887 to 1892) assumed that for the mobilisation of two army corps, a cavalry division and line of communication troops, 25,000 horses would be required, including the effective animals already on strength. This figure allowed for six months wastage and replacements from weeding out animals on the peace establishment that would be unfit for active service, but did not include animals required for transport purposes.[45]

There were 11,800 horses on the peace establishment and about 14,000 on the registered reserve, therefore the difficulties of providing for an expeditionary force was considered solved.[46] Unbelievably, it is probably correct that the question of transport animals had been totally overlooked. The Royal Commission made no mention of the provision of transport animals, and the total number required for the projected fighting force was at least 34,647; in mobilisation tables they were set down as mules.[47] This would appear to be good evidence that the question of transport animals was overlooked by the Secretary of State. The QMG, in his evidence before the Commission was under the impression that Stanhope's numbers included transport; the IGR stated that transport was to be provided with horses found in England and although the evidence was not clear he did not consider they were included in the 25,000, he certainly believed they were to be horses, though the mobilisation tables stated mules. If they were to be mules, this implied purchasing abroad for which no

---

44   *VR*, 1896, Vol.9, 15th August, p.84.
45   Cd.993, p.3; WO33/271, p.A3.
46   Smith, 1919, p.20 from PP. Cd.994, Truman's evidence, p.17, Q299.
47   Cd.1789, p.97.

plans existed.[48] The Assistant Under-Secretary of State for War (Sir Guy Fleetwood Wilson), considered that with the 25,000 horses, including those already with the troops, the country would have been placed on a war footing.[49]

Appendix 33 of the Royal Commission, shows that a reserve of 10% was included in the 25,000.[50] If an anticipated campaign lasted two months this would allow a monthly wastage of 5%, probably the wastage contemplated and a figure that agrees with the assumption made by the GOC-in-C, Cape Town. According to Smith, at the opening of war in 1899 the Remount Department, which, in the whole of its existence, had in practice only supplied the peacetime needs of the Army at home, would be expected to supply a major colonial conflict. As Page wrote, since 1883 no major English mounted contingent had been required for war. The Army failed to base its plans for remounts and an expansion in personnel and equipment on realistic figures, but instead, on the cheapest options available. As the results of the War would prove, the Department's organisation remained unaltered in the belief that remount requirements, in the event of an emergency, had been met. Clearly, mobilisation plans for providing remounts were fundamentally flawed and on Smith's figures, the Army would have been 34,647 transport animals, mule or horses, short on mobilisation with no allowance for wastage.[51] The Intelligence Department (WO) did not hold information on the potential supply of horses from abroad and only limited information on the potential supply of mules, although this was not updated after 1895.[52] Despite the Fitz-Wygram Committee's recommendations and the small commissions to Canada and Argentina, little had been done to explore possible foreign sources for remounts; an exercise considered unnecessary due to the small size of the Remount Establishment and a belief that demand could be met in the UK.

The work of the Remount Department in procuring and distributing remounts, and administering the Registration Scheme was central to the provision of horses for the Army, but so also was the work of the distinctly separate and subordinate organisation, the Army Veterinary Department, responsible for the health and treatment of animals. The Veterinary Service in 1878, was a hybrid regimental system, with each commanding officer trained to retain sick animals as long as possible; each possessing a partly trained subordinate regimental staff for the care of the sick (amongst other duties) over whom AVD officers had no control. Veterinary officers had no authority over members of other regiments or units. Even with the creation of the Department in 1881, which strengthened the AVS, the treatment of horses remained basically a regimental system with subordinate personnel being drawn from within units.[53]

48   Cd.994, Q6: Lt-Gen. Sir C. Mansfield Clarke, QMG to the Forces; IGR, and, Q305 and Q309.
49   Cd.1790, p.258, Q6112.
50   Cd.1792, p.231; Smith, 1919, p.120.
51   Page, 1976, p.297; Smith, 1919, pp.5, 120.
52   Cd.993, p.7; Page, 1976, p.299.
53   VR, 1935, 5th January, p.4.

The crucial role played by the AVS is often ignored, or given scant attention when discussing army remounts, yet their work of securing and maintaining healthy, trained and effective animals was no simple task. An article of 1897, although referring to the AVD in India, highlights the importance and success of a well-run service, in comparison to lack of effectiveness of the Service in the UK it comments: "on no department probably has the pressure of military operations fallen more heavily than on the AVD. Barely sufficient, in times of peace, to perform the duties demanded of it, the strain on its resources to meet the present conditions of field service has been met in a manner, which has won universal admiration and will, it is to be hoped, be suitably recognised when the proper time comes. The importance of work done by the Department cannot be over estimated, when it is considered to what extent the condition of its transport affects the mobility and therefore military efficiency of a force; and, although much of the credit is due to the exertions of the divisional and brigade transport officers engaged, the results obtained are most credible to the staffs of the veterinary hospitals. At the same time there is room for improvement in the matter of equipment and stores carried. So much has been done, as the result of experience acquired in the past, that it is likely that on future occasions these defects will be rectified."[54]

The details below highlight the complexity of the work and structures required to achieve the tasks allotted to the AVD and assist in understanding the 'remount' debacle of the 1899-1902 War. At the close of 1893 the Department was constituted as follows:

Director General
(rank of Veterinary Colonel, administrative head of the Department and an officer of the Headquarters Staff, WO)

|

eight District (administrative) Veterinary Officers
(rank of Veterinary Lieutenant Colonel – four were stationed in London, Aldershot, Woolwich and Dublin).

|

119 Executive Veterinary Officers
(rank of Veterinary Major, Veterinary Captain, or Lieutenant)

The District Veterinary Officers had the general administrative veterinary supervision of a district, or army corps, to which they were attached, and also acted as an officer of the District Headquarters Staff. They would be available to the district GOC, for reference or advice on all points connected with the AVD. Under the instructions of the Director General and subject to the orders of the GOC, an officer personally superintended all veterinary duties of his division, or district. Duties

---

54   *VR*, 1897, Vol.10, 4th December, p.323; First Mohmand Campaign 1897 to 1898.

included frequent inspection of horses, or other animals used by the Army, stables, camps, forage, and all departmental details in his charge. The results of inspections were written in a report forwarded to the Director-General.

The Executive Veterinary Officers performed their duties under the control and direction of the Director General and District Veterinary Officers of their districts or divisions. An officer was attached to each regiment of cavalry and stations occupied by other mounted corps; also performing veterinary duties for other units at the station where he was located. They had control of infirmary stables or sick lines, pharmacies, forges, NCOs and personnel employed therein, prevention of disease and quality of forage. They were directly responsible for the quality of shoeing and the proper instruction of farriers and shoeing smiths; shoeing was carried out regimentally, as was the supply of shoes, nails, tools and management of the horses' feet. The pattern of shoes was arranged by the Director General to ensure uniformity throughout the Army.

The AVD was organised so that on active service, the Principal Veterinary Officer (PVO), was attached to the staff of the General of Communications, to direct and be responsible for all veterinary arrangements. Administrative veterinary officers were attached one to each infantry and cavalry division, one to the line of communications and base, one to each sick horse hospital and remount depot; they were to arrange and regulate the duties of executive veterinary officers under the general direction of the PVO. Executive Veterinary Officers were to be posted for duty generally, in accordance with the requirements of the Army; each officer had on charge a pair of field panniers fitted with a complete assortment of medicines, instruments and surgical stores. Base Administrative Officers were in charge of reserve stores, such as veterinary medicines and appliances, and entrusted with the duty of forwarding supplies, on requisition, to the front. Expensive stores were also to be kept at the principal depots along the lines of communication. A veterinary officer was appointed as sanitary officer and had to superintend the embarkation and disembarkation of all animals, as well as carefully inspecting them to ascertain general condition and freedom from contagious diseases. The AVD in the field would furnish reports and returns on the health, sickness, casualties and sanitary conditions of animals, supply of horseshoes and nails, as well as field forges; keeping strict watch over the quality of forage and generally everything to maintain the efficiency of animals in use.[55]

Field Army Establishments Service Abroad for December 1892, provided for a sick horse depot of 300 animals, to be treated at an advanced base, and organised into two squadrons, one for sick horses the other for remounts. In addition, there was provision for a distinct remount depot at the base for 600 horses, but with no hospital. However, the war establishment of 1898, on which the Army mobilised for South Africa, does not mention a sick horse depot, or a veterinary hospital. Provision for the care of sick and injured animals had been removed from the revised 1898 Establishment. In

55   *VR*, 1893, Vol.6, 30th December, pp.363-4.

Smith's view, "there could be little doubt that the Remount Department was responsible for the removal of hospitals from the War Establishment of 1898".[56]

The Remount and Veterinary Departments, as they existed in 1899, were totally unprepared and unsuited for the responsibilities expected of them in their first major conflict. Col. Duck (Director General of AVD, 1898-1902), giving evidence before the Royal Commission stated that as PVO in India (1894-1898), he was responsible for proposing a mobilisation scheme, preparing the AVD for war, updating all the equipment, establishing hospitals, mobile field chests etc.[57] This system was trialled and found to be successful, but on his return to the UK, as Deputy General, AVD, he found mobilisation arrangements to be woefully deficient. Smith supports such a view stating that the "outbreak of war found the veterinary service without the shadow of an organisation, nothing more, except for the post of PVO, than the British Army took with it to Flanders in 1799 and subsequently into the Peninsula and Crimea". The authorities at the base of operations in South Africa had to organise a system to meet this deficiency; their methods were not only archaic, but opposed to all common sense and experience. The AVD was to enter the war, despite early initial developments, with no organisation worthy of the name and placed under the Remount Department; a move which was to have disastrous consequences for the relationship between the two Departments, the effectiveness of the AVD and therefore of animal losses. For Smith, the 'ambitious spirits' of the AVD were suppressed by the Remount Department.[58]

The head of Remount (Maj. Birkbeck) and Veterinary services (Col. Mathews) in South Africa were placed under the Director of Transport and Supply in Cape Town. With the AVD placed under the Remount Department, the latter was therefore, charged with all the duties of providing for healthy animals and the removal and care of the sick, with the function of veterinary officers limited to treatment. On the outbreak of war in 1899 the organisation adopted was a combined system of depots for sick and healthy horses, as laid down in the 'Field Army Establishment' of 1888. Smith states, that had it been desired to ensure the general infection of the Army with contagious diseases no better arrangement could have been devised (mixing fit and sick animals together), a system resulting in Army horses being riddled by contagious disease and depriving the AVD of all means of dealing with them. Never in the history of any British Army was there such a deliberate sacrifice of animal life and of public money. AVD defects in the field, which had been apparent to veterinary officers for many years, were gradually brought to the attention of the rest of the Army and British public through the enormous losses incurred during the War.[59]

---

56   Smith, 1919, pp.113-5.
57   Duck (see Appendix I); Cd.1790, Evidence p.134, A3201; Smith, 1927, p.203.
58   Smith, ibid.
59   Smith, 1919, p.vii, and 1927, p.203.

2

The Second Anglo-Boer War: 1 October 1899 to 31 May 1902

As regards purchasing and handling horses for active service we must be guided chiefly by the experience we had in the last South African War. Most of us are probably tired of reference to this campaign, but it must be admitted that as an experience with horses and mules, its duration for three years, the various breeds of horses used, it was of enormous value, the like of which none of us are likely again to experience.[1]

The Boers declared war on 11th October 1899 and in the words of Kipling gave the British 'no end of a lesson.' According to Kitchener, the Boers were 'always running away on their little ponies'. The British public expected the war to be over by Christmas, however, it proved to be the longer (two and three-quarter years), the costliest (over £200 million), the bloodiest in human and animal lives (at least 22,000 British, 25,000 Boer, 12,000 African lives and over 377,000 horses and mules, exclusive of those 'captured' in South Africa) and the most humiliating war for Britain.[2]

The events of the War were to test the relatively inexperienced, centralised, horse services and the country's ability to supply horses for the Army in a major conflict. The appalling loss of animals, beginning with the loss of the Cavalry Division's horses in 1899, is generally blamed on an incompetent Remount Department. This is, however, only part of a much more complicated picture involving the Army Veterinary Department (AVD), decisions of the High Command and limited forward planning for a major colonial conflict.

On the outbreak of war in 1899, Gen. Redvers Buller was given command of the Natal Field Force. The War can be understood in three main phases. In the first (October 1899 – January 1900), the Boers attacked Cape Colony and Natal, besieging Mafeking, Ladysmith and Kimberley. A Kimberley relief force under Lt-Gen. Lord Methuen reached the Modder River in November but was defeated at Magersfontein in December. Buller, led a relief force towards Ladysmith, which was defeated at

---

1   Lane, 1912, p.51.
2   Pakenham, 1979, p.xv; Smith, 1919, pp.226-229.

Colenso in the same month. He was replaced by Lord Roberts (who arrived in the Cape in January 1900) with Gen. Kitchener as his Chief of Staff, undertaking an extensive reorganisation of the Army. The second phase (February to August 1900) under Lord Roberts, opened with the British adopting a more mobile strategy which proved to be more successful, despite setbacks initiated by the discredited Buller at Spion Kop (January 1900) and Vaal Kranz (February 1900). In February Ladysmith, and in May Mafeking, were finally relieved. In December, Roberts returned to England leaving Kitchener in command. The final phase (September 1900 to May 1902), a period of guerrilla warfare, saw an increase in the proportion of mounted infantry. The country was divided by nearly 4,000 miles of barbed wire and 8,000 block houses, with each section swept by mounted columns.

Mobilisation

It is beyond refute that neither the British Army, nor the public was prepared for the scale of conflict experienced in this War. If this is true for the main branches of the Army, there should be no surprise that the smaller peacetime branches, such as transport, supply, remounts and veterinary, were even less prepared to meet such demands. On mobilisation these branches had immediately to find men, horses and equipment to allow the main Army to complete its mobilisation, upon which, the initial success of the Army depended. At the outbreak of war the Remount Department had suddenly to expand from a peacetime responsibility for supplying only some 2,500 animals a year, to supplying 5,000 animals a day, for ten consecutive days, to meet the mobilisation requirements of the Regular Army; and then meet the ever-growing demands of the largest British army that had been sent overseas.[3]

The AVD found such expansion nearly impossible, as it was kept at a low establishment, which did not even meet peacetime requirements, and had virtually no emergency field force. Vet-Col. Duck, Director General of the AVD (DGAVD, 1897-1902), stated in 1904, that at no time was he instructed to make preparations for war. His information about what was occurring and his previous knowledge of Africa was drawn from newspapers, while the question of whether his Department was ready for war was never put to him by the WO.[4] The home peacetime establishment of veterinary officers was 63 (but they were five officers short of this establishment), to meet the enormous demands of war, home defence and other important commitments. On the outbreak of war, the peacetime establishment of horses increased by four fifths and it was evident that more veterinary officers would be required immediately, however, the AVD was 50 officers short of wartime requirements for the field. A total of 61 were obtained from, the veterinary establishment of India, engaging civilian practitioners

---

3   Smith, 1919, p.2.
4   PP Cd.1790, p.136, A3266-9, Evidence of Duck; Smith, 1919, pp.vii, 2, 4.

with no training in military veterinary work, or experience of military discipline, and by leaving no reserve in England except for the WO and Educational Staff.

Geography was against the British. The Orange Free State drove a huge wedge into the British territory of Cape Colony and Natal, splitting the war effort into two separate halves. In the Western Theatre (Cape Colony), all British operations had to be based on the ports of Cape Town, Port Elizabeth and East London, which were connected to each other by three single track railway lines. The Western Line from the Cape ran north through De Aar, crossing the Orange River to Kimberley, Mafeking. From Port Elizabeth the Midland Line went west to Naauwpoort then north through Bloemfontein, Johannesburg, Pretoria and Middelburg. The rail link between Cape Town and Port Elizabeth ran through Naauwpoort – De Aar and from there to Mafeking. From East London the Eastern Line ran through Queenstown to Springfontein on the Midland Line, with another connecting station at Stormberg. These stretches of line were within easy reach of the Free State border; 500 miles from Cape Town and 339 miles from Port Elizabeth. The Natal (Eastern) Theatre, was completely detached. Durban, its' administrative base was connected to Cape

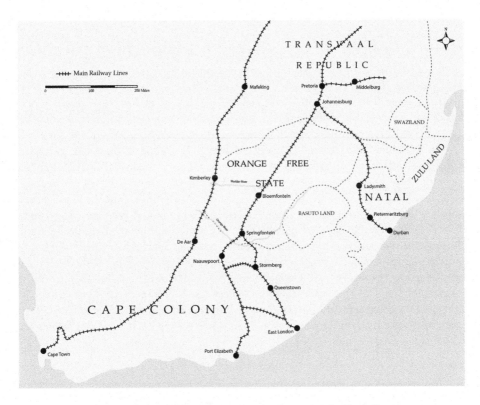

Map 1: Southern Africa 1899-1902 – main ports and railway lines.

Town only by a sea voyage of 1,000 miles. The Natal Line ran from Durban through Pietermaritzburg, and Ladysmith to Johannesburg. The British forces and remount supply were totally dependent on these four railway lines. The Remount Department established base depots at, or close to ports, with foraging points along rail lines to advanced depots. As mobility away from railway lines depended entirely upon animals, the Remount Department responsible for providing and caring for them was as important as any other army supply department.

On the 29th September, 1899, the Government decided to dispatch a field force of one army corps, a cavalry division and line of communication troops, which, according to WO *'Tables of War Establishments'* for 1899, contained:[5]

	Horses	*Mules*
Army Corps	5,210	9,111
Cavalry Division	5,006	2,332
Line of Communications	11,122	14,093
Totals:	21,338	25,536

Approximately 11,400 mules were to be purchased abroad and sent to South Africa. The UK Horse Reserve was required to supply about 9,000 horses, bringing the force up to war strength, and to provide what the authorities believed would be six months war wastage. The original plan for the despatch of two Army Corps, would have required an additional 25,000 horses, taking no account of communication, supply needs and wastage. On mobilisation, it was found that about one third of horses of all mounted units were unfit for active service.

The Remount Department in England was only responsible for the purchase, transport and shipping of horses from foreign countries to South Africa and for recommending officers for remount duty. The C-in-C in South Africa was responsible for all remount work in this country. The purchase of horses at home proceeded more or less as in peacetime. The WO had been inundated with people wishing to sell their horses to the Army, which had become the major buyer in England.[6] In order to meet increased pressures on the Remount Department, the number of purchasing staff at home was increased from four to eight. In May 1900 one officer was added to the staff at the Department's headquarters in London and two more towards the end of the year. Remount officers usually joined the Department by transfer or secondment from other mounted units such as the Cavalry and Artillery. Attempts were made to buy from small-scale horse owners, at fairs and by placing

5   For example Smith, 1919, p.122.
6   WO33/190; Cd.993, pp.3, 5, 21-22; Smith, 1919, pp.9, 120-122; Page, 1976, p.302; Amery, 1909, Vol.VI, p.415; WO33/271, pp.11-13.

advertisements, but these methods were abandoned, the results not being commensurate with the labour and costs involved. In addition to the normal army purchasing system, the Horse Registration Scheme was successfully implemented for the supply of artillery and cavalry horses from omnibus companies and large owners of van transport, such as the London Road Car Company (LRCC) and London General Omnibus Company (LGOC). As the largest holders of registered stock, they were significant providers for the Army in an emergency. From the beginning of the war to the end of 1900, 1,627 horses were requisitioned from the LRCC; the LGOC provided 1,448. Other providers included the Star Omnibus Company and Messrs Tilling of Peckham. The average prices paid by the Government ranged from £50 and £55 per horse. Over 4,000 London horses, in prime condition, fit for hard active work in the field, were taken by the Government under formal arrangements of the Registration Scheme. Despite this process of official commandeering, the London companies managed to maintain the number and excellence of their stock. Truman, Director of Remounts (WO), reported that the Scheme had only been exercised in a modified form for Artillery horses.[7]

The Scheme was less successful for the lighter class of horses required for riding. Of the approximately 14,105 horses registered on the Reserve, 3,682 were taken in 1899 and 1,679 in 1900. In addition, about 4,700 horses were purchased from other owners of registered horses not on the reserve list. In total, less than half of the planned number of registered horses were taken, as it was found to be cheaper to purchase them on the open market. By leaving a considerable number of the reserve horses untouched the Government had control of the market, which kept prices down. By this method, 73,000 horses were purchased to the end of 1901, considerably more than considered possible by the 1884 Fitz-Wygram Committee. The Scheme was considered to have been a success, except for initial misunderstandings, such as different interpretations of the term "emergency". Confusion arose around a perception that animals could only be taken for home defence, as opposed to a war in Europe, and the speed with which they would be removed.

By the first week in October 1899, it was clear an expansion of remount staff and remount depots at home would be necessary. There were no available barracks at home to accommodate the increase in horses on mobilisation. The accommodation shortage was solved, in the short term, by appropriating cavalry barracks and sending horses directly to the nearest regiments; an arrangement that interfered with the training of cavalry recruits at a time when reinforcements were urgently required. Additional remount depots were formed at Canterbury, Colchester, Norwich and Southampton, with a resting depot at Cork (for embarkation purposes only) to hold and condition remounts before shipment to the Cape.[8] All horses required by combatant units

---

7   *VR*, 1900, Vol.13, 15th December, p.326; Cd.994, Appendix B, p.312; WO33/271, p.9, ref 9th October 1899.
8   Cd.1792, p.232, Appendix 33; WO33/271, pp.11, 15; Hume, 1980, pp.26, 36-7.

leaving England during the first months of the war were found in the UK and reputedly of good quality. Up to the end of February 1900, all cavalry and artillery horses in South Africa came almost exclusively from the UK and Australia.[9] As the war progressed persistent demands for remounts (including transport mules) were only met by intensified purchasing at home and in overseas markets.

The Remount Department, with only three veterinary officers on their establishment, supplied by the AVD, but only indirectly under their control, very soon found itself short of veterinary assistance. The AVD lacking a reserve of officers and having only a small civilian profession from which to draw recruits, could not meet its own requirements and the increasing demands of the Remount Department. Before war was declared the Remount Department had taken one sixth of the officers from the AVD for purely remount requirements. The appointment of veterinary surgeons for home service was made on the recommendation of the Director General AVD, no responsibility rested with the Inspector General of Remounts (IGR). It became increasingly difficult to employ sufficient competent veterinary surgeons for examining animals in foreign countries; as early as June 1899, seven officers were required for purchasing commissions to Spain, Italy, South America and New Orleans. In August two more went to Australia. Some ships carrying horses had to leave foreign ports without onboard veterinary assistance. Very quickly it became impossible to increase the supply of veterinary officers for remount duties, so retired officers were recalled for service. This early 'grabbing' of veterinary officers by the Remount Department, according to Col. Duck, was the first cause of friction between the two services and did little to improve the unsatisfactory relations that existed throughout the war.[10]

The first phase of Buller's campaign in South Africa, from October to December 1899, saw the beginning of the appalling wastage and suffering, from which the Remount and Veterinary services never fully recovered. Buller probably attempted to accomplish too much; his Command was thoroughly defeated in the Cape and Natal and he was replaced by Lord Roberts. Following these military reverses additional forces were urgently required. It was this sudden and unexpected increase in the size of the original Field Force that placed severe pressures on the Remount service at home. The needs of the October Field Force were readily met, but the sudden and unexpected mobilisation of four additional infantry divisions and a cavalry brigade created a demand for an additional 11,900 horses and 10,000 mules. The 5th Division was mobilised on 11th November, 6th Division on 2nd December, 7th Division and 3rd Cavalry Brigade on 16th December, along with an additional twelve batteries of artillery. In January 1900, the 8th Division was mobilised and a fourth cavalry brigade. This completed the mobilisation of all regular army troops. The increasing demand for a more mobile army in South Africa had been recognised in December 1899 with the creation of a new irregular mounted infantry unit, the 'Imperial Yeomanry', to

9   Page, 1976, p.302; Cd.993, p.3.
10   Duck, Evidence, Cd.1790, A3224-5, pp.134-5; Cd.993, p.15; Smith, 1919, pp.4, 5, 10.

be recruited in the UK and colonies. By mid-April 1900 over 10,000 troops were in South Africa; further stretching the demand for horses and veterinary services.[11]

Remount Services in South Africa

The duties of the Remount Department in South Africa encompassed the purchasing of local animals, landing and issuing remounts from abroad, care of animals on debility farms and later, care of 'protection' and 'captured' stock.[12] Birkbeck states that the Department in South Africa had a curious history, placed as it was by the 'Yellow Regulations'(*Regulations for the Supply of an Army in the Field (Abroad) and for the Organisation of the Lines of Communication*, issued 1st November 1890), under Col. Bridge, the Director of Transport. Bridge was required to provide all remounts for the Army in the field and in conjunction with the Senior Veterinary Officer (SVO), arrange for the establishment of depots for all sick and debilitated animals.[13] Under the orders of Bridge, an officer was to be appointed with total responsibility for the management of all remount depots and depots for the reception of sick animals; a Remount Committee for the purchase of animals was also to be appointed working under Bridge. Animals unfit to march, and those sent back from the front as unfit, were to be placed in remount depots and all suspected cases of disease isolated. This suggests that the risk of infecting healthy animals in remount depots with sick animals was recognised. The 'Yellow Book' was not strictly followed during the campaign. Remount and Veterinary Services were administered under regulations that were obsolete and unfit for application in war, as they did not reflect changes in the Army after 1890. The enormous responsibility of providing transport for an army was sufficient to absorb the entire attention of one man, Lord Roberts. On his arrival, he separated remounts and transport, forming a separate Remount Division under an Assistant Inspector of Remounts (AIR). However, the AVD remained subordinate to Remounts with the acting Principal Veterinary Officer (PVO) being placed in a position that "bristled" with potential difficulties.[14]

The WO *Table of War Establishments*, for remount depots, was based on planning for a European war and for the care of a limited number of animals. They allowed for:

- Base depot for 1,000 horses; 7 officers and 274 NCOs and men
- Advanced depot for 300 horses; 3 officers and 56 NCOs and men

11   Cd.993, p.4; Smith, 1919, pp.54, 148, 122; WO33/271, p.14; Pakenham, p.252.
12   Protection-horses were brought in from districts in Cape Colony, under Martial Law, and held at animal centres to protect them from falling into enemy hands. They were to be available for remounts and if selected paid for. Captured-horses were brought in from districts in the Orange Free State and Transvaal with whom we were at war, from army sweeps following the order that no living animals were to be left behind for enemy use. Smith, 1919, p.200
13   Cd.993, p.21; Smith, 1919, p.114.
14   Ibid., p.22; Smith, 1919, pp.114-5, 123-4.

However, these establishments were not sent out with the First Army Corps. As a consequence of this shortage, personnel were provided as they could be found. Remount depots formed part of the line of communication troops under the Director of Transport and ASC companies formed the nucleus of all remount depots, with additional personnel obtained from transport conductors and natives. By the end of 1898 base depots had been established in the Cape at Stellenbosch and in Natal at Pietermaritzburg with Durban as the landing port. Personnel were provided from troops serving in the South African Command supported by native establishments. When war in South Africa appeared imminent, ASC companies were sent out to be employed on the lines of ccommunication; five were allotted to remount work. By the end of 1899 an additional four remount depots were formed in the Cape, established on the three main rail lines, bringing the total to five, Cape Town having Stellenbosch, with a landing depot at Greenpoint (initially Woodstock) nearer the port and an advanced depot at De Aar. The Midland Line with a landing point at Port Elizabeth and a depot at Naauwpoort; the Eastern Line used East London with a depot at Queenstown. At Port Elizabeth the Agricultural Society's showground at

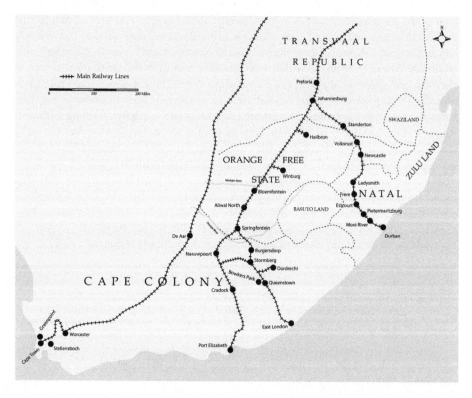

Map 2: Southern Africa 1899-1902 – Remount Depots

the northern end of the town was taken over as the remount depot; mules and cobs were taken to Kragga Kama farm outside the town.[15]

Remounts for the small permanent mounted garrison in South Africa were normally purchased in that country, except for the years 1897 (1,362 horses) and 1898 (690 horses and 701 mules), when purchases were made in Argentina. In July 1899, Lt-Gen. Butler the GOC in South Africa, was ordered to purchase a small number of animals to maintain the local Field Force, and given responsibility for the remount system. Maj-Gen.Truman, Director of Remounts at the WO, had no control of the remount function in South Africa. In addition, the garrison was supplemented by precautionary reinforcements of 2,864 horses, of which 2,253 were from India, the rest dispatched from England.[16] The WO had never contemplated forming a large reserve of horses and mules in South Africa for immediate availability in the event of hostilities, so remount purchases were kept at a very low number, mainly consisting of transport animals and cobs for mounted infantry. In comparison, Col. Mathews, the Senior Veterinary Officer (SVO), already serving in Natal (he moved to the Cape in April 1900 and by June 1901 was the PVO), made preparations for medicines, equipment and for some veterinary officers from India and England to move to South Africa.

Col. Stevenson, Assistant Inspector Remounts (AIR) at the WO, was sent to Cape Colony in July 1899, to purchase animals locally. Stevenson was to arrange for the establishment of remount depots, in addition to the two depots already in existence (Stellenbosch in the Cape and Nottingham Road in Natal), and report on the supply of cavalry and artillery horses in Cape Colony and Natal.[17] Stevenson departed for South Africa with one remount staff captain (Capt. MacKenzie, from the Woolwich Remount Depot), four veterinary surgeons, and four farrier quartermaster sergeants. He purchased cobs (small horses see glossary) for Baden-Powell's Protectorate Regiment of mounted infantry, before being ordered to leave the Cape and move to Natal (moved 30th August), where he remained. He took with him only one veterinary officer, the rest of his staff and officers were broken up and used elsewhere. One farrier quartermaster sergeant, for example, was placed with the mounted infantry to look after their horses.[18]

Stevenson stated in his evidence to the *Court of Enquiry on the Administration of the Army Remount Department* (March 1902), that he understood his position was

15 Cd.993, pp.18-19; Cd.963, p.21; Smith, 1919, pp.123, 126; Chadwick, 1992, pp.1-7; Page, 1976, p.315; I am indebted to Margaret Harradine and Carol Victor from Port Elizabeth for information on remount arrangements.
16 Truman, Appendix I; Amery, 1909, Vol.VI, pp.412, 415; Smith, 1919, p.9.
17 Page, 1976, p.301; Smith, 1919, pp.6, 84,123; Cd.994, p.3, Q.13, Evidence, Lt-Gen. Sir C. Mansfield Clarke, QMG; WO33/271, p.7. The *London Gazette* for 31st October 1899, states Stevenson was employed with the Remount Department from 9th October 1899.
18 WO33/271, p.7; Cd.994, Evidence Stevenson, p.87; Cd.1792, Appendix 33, pp.231-2; Amery, 1909, VI, pp.443-4; Cd.993, pp.18-19.

Senior Remount Officer for the whole of South Africa and that he was responsible for the purchase, and forming of the Remount Department in the whole of the country. When he reached Natal in August 1899, he stated that no remount arrangements had been made and everything connected with the Department was in absolute chaos. In Natal, the remount depot consisted of Lt. W.G. Williams, A.V.D and himself, which was not really large enough to be called a Department. He did not have any officers, clerks, or men and had to do the majority of the clerical work himself. He did, however, have the help of an inexperienced private soldier of the 5th Lancers who had been loaned to him. By the beginning of October 1899 Stevenson states he had managed to bring together two veterinary officers, two farrier-majors of his original staff and one or two regimental officers. This established a workable, although incomplete, Remount Department in Natal. Stevenson was further frustrated, when in October, Capt.R. Sparrow (with the Remount Department, 9th October 1899, from 7th Dragoon Guards) and Maj. Birkbeck (from 1st Kings Dragoon Guards), were sent out by the WO to be, he believed, under his control. However, Birkbeck was detained in Cape Town, on whose orders and why, Stevenson did not know, leaving Capt. Sparrow as the only regular officer of the Department at his disposal. This remained the situation in Natal until about the middle of March 1900 when the officers and non-commissioned officers, but not the other ranks, of the 6th and 7th Remount Depots arrived.[19]

It is clear from Stevenson's evidence that he was embittered about his treatment in South Africa. Smith, states that "every allowance must be made for this in reading his egotistical evidence of the work he accomplished in Natal". Stevenson is strongly questioned by the Court of Enquiry on his statements about horsing Indian troops and admits to only providing transport mules and not horsing the whole contingent. According to Stevenson, by ordering him from the Cape to Natal and keeping him there, he was prevented from purchasing horses, making an exhaustive report on the horse supply, and forming the Department across the whole of South Africa. By September, he had set up remount depots at Stellenbosch and Pietermaritzburg, and horsed all mounted troops then in Natal, including transport, before they left their stations for the front. He had also found transport mules for the Indian contingent and reported that it would be impossible to obtain large numbers of cobs in South Africa. This was to prove an inaccurate and costly statement.[20] The arrangements he had put in place for the care of remounts was, however, neutralised by using remount depots as places for sick animals from the front. He confirmed this error, of mixing healthy and sick animals, in his March evidence but apparently, even then, did not recognise the gravity of his action, possibly, because he had been trained in a system that regarded remount depots in war as a refuge for destitute animals. Additional

---

19   Cd.994, p.88, 2805-2809, p.94, Q2938, 2941; Cd.1792, Appendix 33 p.232.
20   Cd.994, p.88, p.95, Stevenson, 2947, 3488; Birkbeck Cd.963, 1902, July, pp.3-4; Smith, 1919, pp.6, 121-2, 124-6; Page, 1976, p.314; Amery, 1909, Vol.VI, p.415; WO33/271, p.7.

remount depots and grazing farms for resting debilitated and war worn horses were established on the Natal railway line (see Map 2) at Mooi River, Estcourt, Frere, Newcastle, Volksrust and Standerton. On landing at the Natal depot the procedure was for animals to be examined by the veterinary officer; if found free from disease and fit to travel, they were sent, as soon as possible, to the Mooi River depot, where they rested before despatch to the front. Weak, or debilitated animals were supposed to remain at Durban until fit to travel.

Dual armies sprang up in the Cape and Natal each with a 'separate' Remount Department. Nominally under one C-in-C, the Armies were in reality separate entities with little co-operation between them until July 1901. By August 1900, military operations had passed out of Natal, which then became the main supply route for remounts. Stevenson, the senior remount officer, was not given charge of the Remount Department, but returned to the increasingly important landing depot at Durban, until he left for England, 20th November.[21] Maj.William Birkbeck, the junior staff officer, was given charge of the Cape, with all the large military operations being undertaken in this area. After Stevenson's departure the Natal and Cape remount operations were united under Birkbeck as AIR. Birkbeck stated that "he was then entirely on his own. The remounts were taken away from (Stevenson?) when he came out, and he believed, that after some discussion it was decided to give him (Birkbeck) sole charge and responsibility".[22]

In January 1900, Lord Roberts undertook an extensive reorganisation of the Army and abolished the 'regimental', or 'decentralized' transport system, with the exception of technical vehicles. In its place he created a 'general' system under central control, immediately forming 28 transport companies (each with 520 mules). The Remount Department was separated from the Transport Service. Due to the increasing requirements of the Service, there was a sudden withdrawal of all ASC personnel, European and native, from remount work. This included the withdrawal of the five ASC transport companies placed, in November 1899, with the five newly established remount depots. Birkbeck considered these changes to be sensible, although they had a significant impact on his work. "With one stroke of the pen", the whole of his establishment was swept away, so after four months of careful development, the whole fabric of remount organisation went; this left him with about 58 men and 10,000 animals to look after. Birkbeck experienced difficulties in finding officers and men skilled in remount duties and accommodation for the remounts, all of which were required to

21   Cd.994, Stevenson, pp.88, Q 2809, p.94, Q2937-8, p.95, 2947; Smith, 1919, p.125 and p.87 for the difficulties and dangers of the railway journey in Natal; Amery, 1909, Vol.VI, p.435. *London Gazette*, 31st October 1899.
22   Smith, 1919, pp.125, 114, 124; Stevenson, Cd.994, p.88, A2809 and Birkbeck, p.363, Appendix F, letter dated 8th Feb., 1900 to IGR. Gen. Redvers Buller mentions Stevenson in despatches dated 30th March 1900, "...that he discharged his duties satisfactorily; of unbounded energy, he exercised great foresight in providing for possible requirements, I trust his exertions will be recognised." *London Gazette*, 18th October 1887.

Maj-Gen. William Truman (1841-1905),
Assistant Inspector of Remounts 1891 and
Inspector General of Remounts 1899-1903.
(Author's collection)

Maj-Gen William Birkbeck (1863-1929),
Assistant Inspector of Remounts South Africa
1900-1902, Director of Remounts WO, 1912-
1920. (Author's collection)

Capt. Frederick Smith, AVD (1857-1929).
Photograph taken at Bangalore on leaving
India, 1885. (Royal College of Veterinary
Surgeons, Charitable Trust Library)

Lt-Col. Eassie, AVC (1864-1943), India,
1913. (Royal Army Medical Services Museum)

enable the organisation to expand and handle the influx of animals (many of which were wild, or barely trained) and to care for the vast number of debilitated horses in need of rest. Truman states that between August 1899 and the end of February 1900, 802 personnel were send from the UK for remount depots in South Africa and up to the 27th March 2,000 natives from India.[23]

In April 1900, seven base remount depots arrived from England to take over the depots in South Africa. Two had a complement of only other ranks; the others, of which two (6th and 7th Remount Companies) were sent to Natal, had only officers, NCOs and a forage staff. Within the next three months the men of the two complete depots were withdrawn to join the Cavalry Division, or other units. One must assume from Birkbeck's comment, "no one regretted their departure", that they did not perform their remount duties to the required standard. Replacement personnel had to be improvised, with civilian and native labour supported by Indian NCOs and Syces (horse-keepers) arriving with horses from India. By July 1900 the personnel of the nine base and advanced depots, excluding Natal, under Birkbeck's command numbered 4,425 across all ranks; including 2,303 Cape Boys and Kaffirs, 1,475 Indians and 337 British NCOs and men. Additions made after July 1900 brought the number of remount depots in South Africa by 1st March 1902 to 24. Ten of these were composed entirely of civilians and natives. Poor officers were dumped on remount depots (to be 'stellenbosched') and men of remount companies were re-converted into cavalry, infantry and artillery drivers the moment they reached South Africa.[24] Birkbeck states that nearly all the cavalry officers sent out for remount duty were taken on arrival for other duties, for example to the irregular horse regiments. Smith believed it crucial for any future restructuring, that the AVD and ARD were supplied with officers and men from their own services, failure to learn this lesson risked potential disaster, as it was pointless for one branch of the service to depend upon another for their personnel in time of war. To enable a single depot to deal with the reception and issue of 200 remounts a day, including watering, feeding, and general care, required a first class organisation, which could only be effectively trained in peacetime. An organisation for which no Government would grant the necessary funds.[25]

From the beginning of the campaign, the Remount Department took responsibility for war worn horses, irresponsibly mixing them with fit horses in their depots, and when these were full, they hired debility farms, placing animals in them without inspection. There was a lack of veterinary staff, fodder, grazing, adequate space and organisation, and as the unexpected pressure of work increased the Department

23   Cd.1793, Appendix 33, p.232.
24   During the War officers who had done badly were sent to the remount farm at Stellenbosch, without losing rank, to look after horses; moved sideways.
25   Birkbeck, private letter, 8th February 1900 to IGR, WO, in Cd.994, pp.363, 366 Appendix F letter to AAG. Remounts, London, dated 12th December 1900 and p.88; Smith, 1919, pp.123-4; Cd.993, p.19; Cd.963, pp.3-4; Page, 1976, p.320; WO108/75; Amery, 1909, Vol. VI, pp.431-3.

found it impossible to closely supervise these farms. Smith believed the Department had undertaken more than it could, or had the technical ability to manage and the ignorance of the majority of remount officers on managing depots and farms was common knowledge. This included the intricacies of hiring farms, organising grazing and water-rights, providing shelter, the knowledge of the character of the varieties of herbage in each district, the acreage required per horse, and the management of large numbers of animals. Birkbeck knew he was given officers other people did not want; most were not practical men and some showed a stubbornness and disinclination to be guided, or assisted, by advice in any way.[26] By December 1900, the widely scattered farms contained thousands of diseased and debilitated animals, with personnel of poor quality. Veterinary arrangements were also poor, as the number of farms grew at a far greater rate than the number of veterinary personnel arriving in the country. Only a small proportion of these personnel were available to the Remount Department. Page writes that by the end of the war there were 17 convalescent remount, or convalescent farms, that were understaffed and suffered about 80% losses. Piquetberg Farm near Cape Town had been purchased and used for debilitated horses but did not prove to be a success. Bloemfontein's remount depot had three farms attached to it, Fischer's, Tempe and Lynch's, accommodating about 6,000 animals. A system was adopted of dividing animals into three classes according to their chances of recovery; those that could be fit within a month remained at Bloemfontein, those within two months were sent to farms in the Colesberg district, and those not fit to travel, or would not be fit within three months were sold, or destroyed.[27] In an attempt to make up for appalling and unexpected losses, the Remount Department provided fresh remounts to the forces in the field.

With the arrival in South Africa of the colonial contingents, Imperial Yeomanry and the formation of irregular corps (all mainly mounted troops) the Army had expanded to the equivalent of six army corps. With this massive increase in demand the Department operated under considerable strain. On 17th November 1899, only 125 cavalry horses and 250 mules per month had been thought necessary, but by January 1902, this had increased to about 14,000 horses and 2,000 mules being despatched monthly.[28]

In response to a cable from the Secretary of State for War (21st November, 1901), regarding the poor showing of the remount system, Lord Kitchener requested an

---

26 Smith, 1919, pp.20, 23, 137, 202; Cd.963, July 1900, pp.3-4; Cd 994, Appendix F, p.363 extract from a letter to the IGR at WO from Birkbeck, 8th February 1900 and p.25, Maj-Gen. Maurice to Truman (524); Galvayne, 1902, pp.48, 64, 76, 100.
27 Page, 1976, p.320; Smith, 1919, pp.137-9; Amery, 1909, p.433 Cd.993, pp.367-8, Appendix F.
28 Irregular forces are not part of a regular army and usually not permanent but raised for a specific purpose or campaign. WO33/271, p.14 (from GOC in C South Africa, 17th November 1899, (series No.1, 283); Hume, 1980, p.36; Cd.1792, Truman, Appendix 33, p.232.

IGR undertake a tour of inspection. Kitchener was satisfied with Birkbeck's work and so the inspection was to happen without interfering with the work of the Remount Department. Maj-Gen. Viscount Downe was appointed IGR for South Africa. He landed at Capetown on the 31st December 1901, and began inspecting remount depots, departing on 11th January on a prolonged tour of inspection arriving at East London on 29th; he then departed by sea on 3rd February for the Durban and Natal depots. The Remount Staff in South Africa at this point included Downe (IGR), accompanied by Col. Hotham (Staff Officer), and Capt. Carr, veterinary officer; Col. Long an Inspector of Remounts and Hospitals and Col. Birkbeck AIR. Kitchener, states that he later appointed an officer as a travelling inspector of all remount depots and horses in South Africa. On the 16th February in his initial report Downe found most officers employed in the various depots had no experience of remount work but where doing their best and things were improving. The class of horses imported left much to be desired, with many an entirely unsuitable and worthless animal supplied for mounted men and hard work; in a reply to a telegram on 28th April, Downe condemned Remount officers as poor purchasers. Generally the result of the inspections was satisfactory, Downe clearly understood the demands and problems facing the Department; Natal was considered to be poorly organised, but improvements were expected with a change in administration. On completion of the inspection, Downe left South Africa to report on the Remount Commissions in Australia (arrived by 29th March) and New Zealand.[29] Downe wrote (1902) that remount depots where divided into three classes (see Map 2):

- Landing depots at: Greenpoint at Cape Town, Stellenbosch, Port Elizabeth, East London, Durban
- Issuing depots, which also operated as resuscitating depots at: Bloemfontein, Bezuidenhout, Standerton, Newcastle, De Aar and Bowkers Park, Johannesburg, Queenstown
- Resuscitating depots at: Worcester, Naauwpoort, Cradock, Stormberg, Aliwal North, Burghersdorp, Dordrecht, Lynch's Farm at Bloemfontein, Heilbron, Winburg, and Springfontein. Most were associated with debility farms.

In practice some landing and issuing depots took animals requiring resuscitation.

---

29   Cd.995, pp.77-8; Kitchener, Cd.1790, p.10, 204; Cd.963, p.53; Smith, 1919, pp.189, 224-5. Hugh Richard Dawnay, 8th Viscount Downe (1844-1924). Fought in the Anglo-Zulu War 1879, mentioned in despatches; Lt-Col 10th Hussars between 1887-1892. Twice mentioned in despatches in 1899-1902 War; July 1901 promoted to the temporary rank of Brig-Gen on the Staff to command the Cavalry Brigade at the Curragh; retired from the Army in 1902, with rank of Maj-Gen.

Veterinary Services in South Africa

A Senior Veterinary Officer (SVO) of the Remount Department and his small staff were directly responsible to the Assistant Inspector Remounts (AIR) and Principal Veterinary Officer (PVO) for all veterinary duties in the Cape, with Natal remaining a separate entity. From 1900 veterinary duties relating to remount depots in the Transvaal, Orange Free State and Natal were managed by the SVO's in these commands. With the departure of Stevenson from Natal (November 1900), one SVO Remounts was appointed for the whole of South Africa. Unfortunately, this centralised management came too late to make a significant difference to the war. With the PVO not available during the first five months of the war (he was besieged in Ladysmith until February 1900), there was a lack of cohesion in the veterinary service. Sending a body of technical officers on active service, without leadership, was like sending troops into action without officers, the AVD working under these difficulties, struggled to succeed. This was also the fate of the voluntary civilian surgeons. Surgical stores were at no time during the war anywhere near sufficient to meet demand, with only the bare minimum of three months veterinary stores available, and no reserve. All efforts by the AVS to establish itself on a working basis were considered unnecessary, "as the war might end tomorrow". For the first twelve months of the war, with the exception of the Indian hospitals, veterinary officers were teaching, training and organising personnel, only to lose these trained men to other units, having to begin again with raw material. Smith comments bitterly, "Look in vain for any serious indication on the part of the authorities that they recognised the function, duties, and potential value of an efficient veterinary service; we publicly decline to be held responsible for the failure which we earnestly endeavoured to avert." [30]

There were a number of distinct, independent, veterinary organisations operating in South Africa:

- Officers of the Regular Service, including civilian surgeons, with the Field Army
- Civilian surgeons with the Sea Transport Service
- Officers of the: Imperial Yeomanry
                    Overseas Colonial Forces
                    South African and civilian surgeons

Only the British Regular AVD possessed administrative staff acting under central control, the others had no organisation or structure and were independent of everyone except the commanding officer of each regiment; such a lack of cohesion wasted a small but vital resource. In an attempt to make up for the chronic shortage of veterinary personnel, a Civilian Veterinary Service was created with surgeons employed on fixed term contracts. They received no military training, held no rank, but had to work under active service conditions. Sydney Galvayne (Hon- Lt. with Remounts in South

---

30   Smith, 1919, pp.131, 305-7, 49.

Africa), considered the civilian veterinary surgeon the most helpless creature in South Africa as he did not have a military attitude to work, lacked zeal and failed to meet the exigencies of war. He wrote that there were some glaring cases of this nature coming under the eye of the AIR, who officially had no control over the veterinary staff, but did not fail to notice them and have matters altered.[31]

An increase in the number of administrative officers was also required to cope with the training of civilian staff. There were fewer officers in South Africa at any point in the war, than were sanctioned for home service during peacetime. Eight, or nine veterinary administrative officers were required for the first phase of the war and at a later stage at least twelve such officers were required in the field. However, for the first five months of the war, there were nominally two, and one of these, the PVO was besieged in Ladysmith. In practice, there was only one officer for the whole of the Cape and Natal, to administer four bases and lines of communication and an immense number of animals for whose veterinary care he was nominally responsible. Even if both officers had been available, it would have been impossible for such a small staff to control the vast and increasing area of operations.[32]

Reference has already been made (Chapter One) to the *1898 Table of War Establishments*, which made no mention of a sick horse depot, or a veterinary hospital and none existed in the plans under which the Army mobilised in 1899. The sick horse depot, as laid down in 1892 and amalgamated with a remount depot, had disappeared. There was, therefore, an urgent need for the provision of a depot, or hospital for sick animals on mobilization. On the outbreak of war, Col. Duck, DGAVD, had suggested the borrowing of veterinary hospitals from India to meet the shortage, but they had not arrived in Cape Town when Col. Rayment, acting PVO, arrived in November, 1899. The Director of Transport and the Staff Officer for Remounts had foreseen the need for hospitals but, as they did not exist on paper in War Establishments for 1898, they did not know where they could obtained. The necessity for more field hospitals was proven with the numbers of starving horses of the Cavalry Division, Artillery, and mounted infantry after the Paardeberg campaign of February-March 1900.[33]

Throughout the war the AVD was short of senior officers and no such officer was responsible for the inspection of hospitals. This situation became more serious when, in 1901, the number of hospitals increased to cope with the expansion in mounted units, and in an effort to cope with sick and debilitated animals. Progress was made when, Lt-Col. Arthur Long, was appointed Inspector of Veterinary Hospitals, Remount Depots and Farms (1st December 1900).[34]

In December 1900, permission was given to provide one well-equipped, model, veterinary hospital at Elandsfontein, close to Johannesburg, under the command

---

31   Ibid., pp.305-9; Galvayne, 1902, pp.69-70.
32   Ibid., p.307.
33   Ibid., pp.113-4.
34   Ibid., pp.193-4.

of Maj. Pringle. The hospital, within three miles of the largest remount depot in the country, with accommodation for over 2,000 horses and stabling for 500 sick horses, was fully operational at the beginning of 1901; equipment and personnel were taken from other hospitals and existing resources. From January to December 1901 the hospital admitted a total of 24,606, with nearly 60% (14,594) of animals being cured and returned to service. A total of 6,540 were destroyed and 2,142 died; 1,330 remained under treatment. In comparison for 1901, De Aar, was returning 74% (over six months) and Stormberg 65.8% but the Orange River hospital only 26% (over six months). The WO was informed of the good results achieved by these hospitals with a request to form additional field veterinary hospitals for 2,500 animals. However, approval was only given for one hospital on this scale, a poor response to the suffering of animals when the WO knew there were generally 20,000 to 28,000 fresh cases of sickness monthly.[35]

Improvements followed Col. Long's appointment as Inspector of Remounts and Hospitals. At the beginning of 1901 there were 38 field veterinary hospitals scattered over the country, varying in strength from 300 to 3,000 animals. By the end of the year the number had risen to 50. Military considerations frequently restricted the choice of sites available for hospitals, for example, at Pretoria, Stormberg and Belfast.[36] Building operations were frequently deferred because of congested railways moving supplies, troops and blockhouse line materials. Cost, or cheapness, was the main military consideration in the provision of depots and hospitals, with local difficulties also affecting the facilities and quality of the work at each hospital. These might include lack of organisation and personnel, the inability of some of those in charge (many of whom were civilians) without experience and training, to adapt themselves to military methods. There were great difficulties in obtaining important structural details for hospitals such as shelter, or protection for the animals, water-troughs (as the supply of water was a major problem), mangers and good enclosures. 1901 saw considerable changes in horse hospital personnel. India had sent a large number of trained dressers (clinical dressing of animals in hospitals) who were distributed amongst hospitals, as were civilian shoeing smiths and Dutchmen, used, when required, as conductors. This type of personnel gradually replaced soldiers required for other duties. Some civilian veterinary surgeons returned home immediately their contract service time expired and some Kaffirs deserted after pay day, making it difficult to obtain a continuous and trained team of veterinary staff.

Mobile hospitals, which first took to the field in Natal, in May-June 1900, were the link between the sick in the field and field hospitals on the line of communications. Having proved their effectiveness a limited expansion of the system was granted for each column in November 1900. However, in December 1901 veterinary officers were withdrawn from mobile hospitals to strengthen the personnel of field hospitals. Mobile hospitals already in existence did not disappear but altered in nature, with

35   Pringle (Appendix I); Smith, 1919, pp.196-7.
36   Smith, 1919, pp.151, 197-8.

each large field hospital furnishing a mobile section. Smith wrote that the grudging methods for tackling the sick horse question even fifteen months after the war had began, was nothing less than extraordinary. Money was poured out like water by other branches, but any makeshift was considered sufficient for the needs of the veterinary service. He believed there was a genuine desire on the part of the military authorities to diminish the waste of horses and also, as far as possible, some of the cruelty. But, the efforts of the AVD to achieve this met with little substantial support; the great difficulty in all hospitals was obtaining efficient and permanent personnel.[37]

The situation regarding debility farms in 1901 was, according to Smith, so terrible that it was to be expressed with the "utmost frankness", in the hope of preventing such disasters in any future campaign. Depots, farms and hospitals were all infected with mange, glanders and other contagious diseases. He quotes Army Order 2, 30th January, 1901, "when veterinary field hospitals are located in the same place as remount depots, the field hospital will be attached to the remount depot," which meant that remount depots containing annexes full of diseased animals were placed next door to, or even in contact with, animals landed from overseas. A practice Smith made clear, the veterinary service was not responsible for. He believed veterinary opinion was not trusted, and probably only a very small proportion of the total number of war worn horses, sent to a Remount Department, were ever seen by a veterinary officer. In spite of the manner in which the remount veterinary service was handicapped, he does conclude that the service was responsible for the lack of inspections.[38]

The Remount Department thought the parasitic skin disease mange was overstated and sneered at the diagnosis of the highly infectious disease of glanders. It was a widely held and misguided view, that what was called mange, was an infection of the skin which passed away spontaneously after winter and was, therefore, a trifling question. The AIR wrote to the WO that they should not be alarmed at mange in the benighted land, as nearly every government and civilian horse got mange when left on the veldt in winter. The locals took no notice of it, as it went with the new coat; they were put through a disinfectant bath a few times, which killed it. However, there was a disease of the skin infecting the native horse, which was so like mange it could scarcely be distinguished. This was not the disease from which imported remounts suffered. Again, Smith points to the frustration and insult when the casual observation, or opinion, of a layman carried more weight than expert advice. Every mounted officer was given credit for knowing all about a horse, but trained veterinary personnel were not. The risk, therefore, of infecting farms and depots was never, in spite of warnings, taken seriously as the Department wanted useless horses removed from hospitals. All temporary unfit animals were sent south, creating an appalling waste of trained horses. In his diary Smith states that Birkbeck was anxious about mange

37   Ibid., 1919, pp. 85-6, 196, 199.
38   Ibid., 1919, pp.116, 139, 199, 202-6, for glanders pp.277-9, pp.284-6 for mange; Galvayne, 1902, pp.60-1.

and grateful that, " we had been able to help both shows along" and requested Smith joined him on an inspection trip to Bloemfontein.[39]

From January 1901, all hospitals had to complete a weekly return showing the exact position of patients, numbers admitted and discharged, types of disease, staff employed, condition of equipment and stores. Between February and August, 1,200 clinical cases of mange were destroyed in one depot and debility annex, but work to improve this situation began with the appointment in September of Maj. Layton Blenkinsop as SVO Remounts. In depots and farms in Cape Colony alone, between September and December, a total of 11,700 animals were destroyed, suffering from:

Glanders	9, 000
Mange	700
Debility and injuries	2,000

During the same period, a further 2,000 animals died and over 7,000 cases of mange were treated. This was the blackest period of the war for the AVD and demonstrated the dangers of hiding away large numbers of horses without adequate supervision and veterinary inspection. Many of the animals, clogging depots and farms, should have been sorted and returned to the front, thereby reducing the requirement for imported remounts. Towards the close of 1901, regimental rest camps for war weary horses were authorised and were a great success; columns were directed to leave men behind in charge of the horses they deposited. Lt. Head wrote, that at the time drives started each regiment received four black boys per squadron to take sick horses along the road; he mounted the boys on ponies caught in the wild and used his boys to move all his sick horses, grazing as they went. He procured ("how I do not know and dare not think of") a waggon and mules to carry forage, medicine and dressings and lines to tie the sick up at night.[40] Blenkinsop's work throughout South Africa assured an organisation and thoroughness of veterinary work that had previously been absent, with debility farms and remount depots largely being freed from disease. In the Cape, from January to May 1902, numbers were reduced to:

Glanders	1,380
Mange	120
Debility and injuries	390

In addition, a further 1,870 animals died of other causes during this period.[41]

39   Letter to the AAG at WO, dated 10th August 1901 from the AIR, in Cd.994, p.368, Appendix F; Smith, 1919, pp.139, 203 and Smith's War Diary A pp.70-71.
40   Head, letter to Gen. Frederick Smith, 29th October 1912, see Head (Appendix I).
41   Smith, 1919, pp.200, 204-5, 196, 225-6.

*Lt. Alfred S. Head, AVD
(1874–1952), Aldershot 1899.
(John Head)*

Head in South Africa. (John Head)

One of the most significant initiatives during the war was the introduction of the 'Eassie System'. Initiated and developed by Capt. Eassie AVD, at Fischer's Farm, the largest remount depot in the Free State, shortly after its occupation early in 1900. Eassie formed a model for the care of debilitated horses, on which all subsequent depots were generally based; later known as the 'Kraal System'. Smith comments that neither the institution, nor Eassie, were mentioned in the Parliamentary Paper dealing with remount work during the war, though the place commanded the admiration of hundreds of visitors, including Lords Kitchener and Milner.[42] Fischer's Farm, was no longer a place for purely sick horses but one where carefully selected, debilitated animals were sent for recovery, and to which fit remounts were sent until required by the depot in Bloemfontein. Even though Eassie had only a limited staff, the number of animals dealt with soon reached 5,000 to 6,000. His view was that with a little organisation, for example, with enclosures, shed stabling, suitable ground soil and ample mangering, horses could be made to do a great deal for themselves (see diagram below). Each enclosure, kraal, contained animals of the same class, or degree of fitness. Special features of the system included exercising horses in a large circular track with each horse enclosure connected by a gate. Horses were then moved to another, larger area, for watering (half a dozen men were employed in this process), by the use of dams an unlimited supply of water was created; then back via the track to their own paddock, or enclosure. While exercising was in progress, food was placed in mangers. The hospital was located in a separate part of the farm and arranged on the same lines as the depot, with animals grouped by diseases.

The Remount Department was better prepared for the third, or guerrilla phase of operations, from January 1901 to May 1902. It was a period of movement and attrition with large mounted columns (by May 1901 some 84,000 mounted men), covering thousands of square miles. This system of drives gave some animals steadier, slower work and increased facilities for supply when faster work was required; improvements in veterinary facilities helped to reduce wastage by a third. Operations during March to May were probably the most pressurised for the Department since those of Bloemfontein in 1900. An increase in the number of horses sent to South Africa meant an increase in the size of depots, Natal and Port Elizabeth nearly doubled. Some remount centres such as Klerksdorp and Standerton had to expand rapidly to meet demands of the Western Transvaal campaign, although it was not possible to increase water and labour supplies as easily. At Klerksdorp, in April, a 2,500 strong Australian and New Zealand contingent arrived with 90% of their horses infected with influenza; but as there were already 1,200 animals in the hospital it was impossible to find accommodation for them. A new depot was formed to take 300 sick animals. In his evidence before the Royal Commission, Maj-Gen. Kekewich, commander of one of Kitchener's four super-columns of mounted troops, provided evidence for Kitchener's

---

42   Eassie (Appendix I); Galvayne, 1902, p.118; Smith, 1919, pp.129-31 and reference to Cd.963.

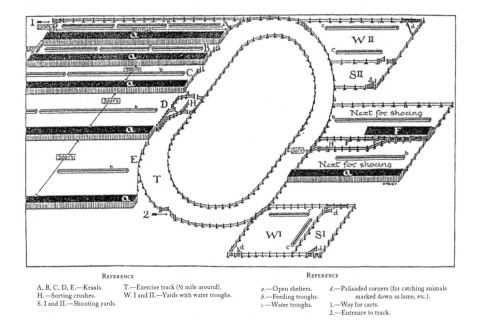

REFERENCE

A, B, C, D, E.—Kraals.   T.—Exercise track (½ mile around).
H.—Sorting crushes.   W. I and II.—Yards with water troughs.
S. I and II.—Shunting yards.

REFERENCE

a.—Open shelters.   d.—Palisaded corners (for catching animals
b.—Feeding troughs.   marked down as lame, etc.).
c.—Water troughs.   1.—Way for carts.
   2.—Entrance to track.

Fischers's Farm remount depot, Bloemfontein. The 'Esssie System', as devised by Capt. Eassie, AVD.
(Blenkinsop & Rainey, 1925)

unfortunate policy of relying on the sheer mass of available horseflesh. During the last month of the war he used up 1,500 horses, his strength at the time was 4,000, his loss being 37.5%. He blamed overwork, short rations, excessive weights and long night marches, and complained about always being short of horses, even in the later stage of the war.[43] The loss of horses and mules during the period January to May 1902, estimated in round numbers, was 73,400 and 7,800 mules respectively; not including the thousands of enemy animals, 'picked up' or captured on campaign.

During this final phase of the war most hospitals ran smoothly, with the exception of the Eastern and Western Transvaal where congestion was intense, but in general efficiency was satisfactory. Returns for the week ending 14th May, for example, show 6,000 horses discharged fit for duty, an average of 120 weekly from each of the 50 hospitals. However, such was the scale of operations that another 7,000 were admitted. Pressure on hospitals during 1902 was greater than ever, owing to specific lymphangitis (inflammation of the lymphatic system) and other epizootics (epidemics). Owing to a change in the character of work and the greater care and attention paid to animals with Col. Long's inspection of columns, the general sick rate was reduced. For the week

---

43   Cd.1791, pp.565-6, Q22004-22012; Amery, 1909, Vol.VI, pp.439-40; Smith, 1919, pp. 148, 201, 223, 225-6; Pakenham, 1979, p.556.

ending 24th October 1900, prior to his appointment (December 1901), there were 27,900 sick animals; four months later, following the great increase in the number of horses employed, the total amounted to 17,700, rising again on 14th May to 24,700.[44]

Remount Procurement

For the Remount Department at the WO, the answer to the constant demand for a regular supply of remounts was to import them from around the world; a policy not supported by the AVD. As early as June 1899, the C-in-C, Viscount Garnet Wolseley, suggested to the Marquis of Lansdowne (Secretary of State for War 1895-1900), that officers be sent to foreign markets for mules:[45]

- July 1899, small purchases were made in South Africa; three officers were sent to the United States (US) to enquire into the possibility of obtaining horses and mules should war break out.
- 15th July the QMG, supported by the Army Board, obtained authorisation to send officers and veterinary surgeons to New Orleans, Charlestown, Madrid and Naples. The first orders to purchase were sent to these Commissions on 22/23 September.
- 2nd September, approval given for the purchase of 200 cobs and 700 mules.
- 18th September approval for the purchase in Australia of 260 draught, cavalry and artillery horses (considered replacements for wastage of war during 1900).
- Approval for commissions to purchase mules in Naples (3,000), New Orleans
- (3,000 with a further 1,000 on 2nd October) and Spain (1,000).
- 13th October, a Commission departed for Argentina.
- During October, the purchase of cobs was ordered from Australia (300), Ireland (300), Argentina (200), and unsuccessfully in the West Indies.
- Further orders were given for the purchase of officers' riding mounts and mounted infantry cobs from Argentina (1600), and South Africa (700).
- In November, 3,000 additional mules were ordered from Italy (1,000) and US (2,000) to complete transport for the 5th Division. By the end of November with the mobilization of the 3rd Cavalry Brigade and 6th and 7th Divisions, purchasing orders became more numerous and larger.
- Purchasing continued in Australia.
- January 1900, the Commission in New Orleans was directed to buy cavalry horses and cobs (February), in addition to previous orders for mules; several additional officers and veterinary personnel were sent to support this work.

44   Smith, 1919, pp.141, 223, 226.
45   WO108/79; Cd.1792, Appendix 33, p.12; Cd.995, p.A2; Page, 1976, p.301-2; Smith, 1919, pp.9, 121; Amery, 1909, Vol.VI, pp.415-6. Amery and Smith both give the date of 18th September for purchase of horses in Australia, but Page states a commission was sent to Australia on 30th September.

- The Argentine Commission was directed to buy suitable cavalry horses (some were obtained from Chile).
- A second Commission proceeded to Spain to purchase mules; part of which, also attempted to purchase mules in Cyprus. A Commission departed for the US to purchase cavalry horses and cobs and ordered to begin purchasing in March.
- May 1900 a Commission was sent to Canada and another to Hungary, to purchase draught and riding horses.
- March 1901 a Commission was despatched to Canada for a second time, remaining there until the end of the war.

Purchases by Remount Commissions were generally made through middlemen rather than directly from owners, saving time in obtaining the numbers required and at acceptable prices.[46]

The Imperial Yeomanry, formed in December 1899, made their own independent arrangements for the purchase of remounts through the Imperial Yeomanry Committee (IYC). In December 1899, Mr J.J. Bell, veterinary surgeon in Carlisle, had been requested by Lord Lonsdale (associated with Lord Chesham in raising the Imperial Yeomanry), to purchase 1,000 horses for the Government. The IGR requested that the Imperial Yeomanry did not purchase in the same foreign markets as the Remount Department (WO). They began purchasing cobs in Austro-Hungary in January 1900, approximately 3,805 and 7,000 in the home market. From the 27th March 1900, the Remount Department (WO), took responsibility from the IYC for remount work and began purchasing from May, remount cavalry and artillery horses, and cobs in Hungary.[47]

Political difficulties were encountered when purchasing remounts in some countries. Enquiries were made to Holland where the price of cobs was low, but Boer sympathy, as in Germany, made purchases impossible. France, Morocco and Algeria did not allow the export of horses and in 1902 seven Russian provinces placed embargoes on exports. Purchases were made in Austro-Hungary but there was concern that the government would prohibit exports from the port of Fiume (now Rijeka, Croatia), on the Adriatic Coast; resulting in officers of the Remount Commission wearing civilian dress and purchasing as private buyers. Scandinavian prices were prohibitive and horses in Poland, Italy and Mexico were reported to be unsuitable. The West Indies proved unsuccessful for the purchase of cobs. Purchases were made in Chile (1900), but the overland journey and shipping proved this source not to be sustainable. The only totally reliable sources of supply were India, Australia, New

---

46 For Commissions generally see: WO33/271, pp.9-11, Cd.993, pp.6-11, Cd.995; Amery, 1909, Vol.VI, pp.415-7; Page, 1976, p.302; Proceedings of the Army Board, WO108/79; Smith, 1919, pp.121-2; Cd.993, pp.3-13; Cd 1789, pp.97-99; Cd.1792, Appendix 33, p.231.
47 *VR*, 1899, 30th December, p.378; WO33/271, pp.17-18 (WO letter 079/10/1,274); Smith, 1919, p.122; Cd.882, pp.4-6; Amery, Vol.VI, pp.416, 419.

Zealand, Canada, and South Africa. The US relaxed a total prohibition on export a short time before the war began. The Indian Remount Department, with a reserve of some 2,000 horses, maintained up to date information about availability in foreign markets but, this useful information was not made available to Truman, Inspector General Remounts (WO).[48]

There were problems in obtaining the considerable number of personnel required for purchasing and shipping, not least due to bureaucratic administration. Initially, the IGR was only allowed to employ purchasing and conducting officers from those on the Army Active List. On general mobilisation, for home defence, lists of purchasers were kept by the GOCs of army districts, but the necessity of buying large numbers of animals abroad was never contemplated. A list of officers, who could be used by the Department was kept by the IGR. From this list and his personal knowledge of officers from mounted units, he made selections, which could, and were, altered when submitted to higher authorities for final approval. In South Africa, the GOC-in-C, not the IGR at the WO, was responsible for the appointment of purchasing officers. Each appointment ultimately rested with the QMG, who referred to the Military Secretary for concurrence. The final order for appointment was issued by the Adjutant General's Branch. Although the number of really good horse buyers was limited, Birkbeck was satisfied he was able to obtain an adequate supply. From late December 1899 a restriction on employing officers only on full pay was removed, allowing the use of officers from the reserve, retired lists, militia and volunteers. The condition in which animals reached their destination depended very much on the efficiency of conducting and veterinary officers, who had responsibility for animals aboard ship. It was not always possible to obtain conducting officers even though it was a requirement for every shipload to have them in attendance. Hired attendants, to assist on board, in the daily labour of looking after the animals, were often recorded as undisciplined, rough and having little interest in their charges. Birkbeck's letter of 3rd January, 1900, states that attendants (on board ship) were "generally of the lowest class, and lazy to a phenomenal degree."[49]

Lt- Col. Cowans, who was to be QMG during change to First World War, was head of the shipping section. All ships carrying horses from the UK, and mules from any ports, were provided by the Admiralty, with the Remount Department responsible for all other vessels required from foreign and colonial ports. Transports carrying horses from the UK were engaged by time charters, they also carried troops and stores; some mule ships were also chartered for a specific period of time. Vessels engaged by the Remount Department carried the horses as freight, with the cost of transport varying

48   WO33/271, pp.9-10; Anglesey, 1986, Vol. 4, pp.297-8; Cd.993, pp.6-13; Cd.994,
      Appendix B/C, pp.311-36 giving tables of animals conveyed and reports from Purchasing
      Commissions, Appendix E, pp.339-57.
49   Cd.993, pp.13-15; Stevenson's evidence, Cd.994, pp.91-3, Q2894-2920, and Appendix F,
      p.363 for Birkbeck's letter of 3rd January 1900.

from about £14 per head from Buenos Aires, to £23 from Montreal. In Remount Department vessels it was usual for the owner to find all forage, fittings, water and attendants; making an additional charge for the passage of the conducting officer (if any) and veterinary surgeon. The first remount ship left the UK, with 100 artillery horses on 22nd September 1899, arriving in South Africa on 16th October. The last ship, left Fiume with 615 cobs on 3rd July 1902, arriving on 4th August. Amery gives a total of 520 outward voyages, possibly only for remount Department vessels, as he does not clarify how he arrives at his figures. Whereas Anglesey states that, from the beginning of the war, to 31st December 1902, 1,027 ships carried 459,336 animals. Truman, gives total shipments to the Cape, from 7th October 1899 to 2nd August 1902, as 387,539 (284,654 horses and 102,885 mules).[50]

Facilities in foreign countries varied considerably. In Argentina the majority of the 25,800 purchases were cobs and owing to the cattle trade there were good railways and accommodation at Buenos Aires. Over 12,000 horses were purchased by the Commission in Canada, relying on large contractors to supply mainly cavalry and artillery horses. Railways in Canada were good, but not the trucks, which caused discomfort and some loss, especially over very long distances. For example, during the 2,264 mile journey from Calgary to Montreal, the exhausted animals only found accommodation in railway stockyards. Over 25,000 horses were purchased in Australia. Dealers were informed of army requirements and it was then their responsibility to get the animals to the ports for purchasing. The market was restricted and the army faced heavy competition from other purchasers, such as the South African Constabulary and private shippers. The latter hoped to make large profits when they landed their purchases at Durban, selling to speculators, and even to the Government; purchases were also made for the Australian military contingent in South Africa. Buyers for the Army in India, purchased annually an average of 1,600 large Walers (Australian saddle horses) for cavalry and artillery. The Commission to Austro-Hungary, from late 1901 to the spring of 1902, purchased some 6,400 cobs monthly for shipment from Fiume. As the supply of cobs became scarcer, the Commission sought a supply further afield. Russia became a principal buying region, providing cobs generally more suitable for South Africa than those from Austro-Hungary. Some 28,000 were purchased between mid-September 1901 and the end of March 1902. Distances travelled by these animals were again enormous; 10 to 14 days before even reaching the railhead, then 2,000 miles to Fiume. Mules were purchased in Spain (15,299) but their poor quality ended this purchasing in July 1900. The purchase of mules from Italy (7,004) ceased due the large number of stallions; North America, Texas and Mexico remained important sources for mules throughout the war.[51]

50 Amery, 1909, Vol.VI, pp.428-9; Anglesey p.298 taken from Maurice Vol.1 pp.108-9 and Cd.1789, p.125; WO33/271, p.19, Appendix H, p.55.
51 Cd.993, pp.6-13, 24,168; Cd.882. pp.4-6; Sessions, pp.164, 166; Anglesey, 1986, Vol. 4, pp.310-11; Page, 1976, pp.304-6.

The purchasing commission to the USA became the largest horse and mule purchasing business the world had ever seen. The Commission did not experience totally smooth operations and was always undermanned. There were difficulties with local laws governing the transport of animals, ensuring they were periodically rested, fed and watered, which added to the journey time. Accommodation at the receiving stations for animals from the eastern states, New Orleans and later Kansas was poor. To overcome these difficulties (see Map 7), ranches at Chalmette (outside New Orleans) and Lathrop (near Kansas) were used. Contractors were selected, the major ones located at St Louis, in Texas, Wyoming and also further West. When Col. de Burgh (3rd Dragoon Guards), was sent out to replace Col. Scobell (5th Lancers) as head of the Remount Commissions in North America, he quickly extended operations westwards. The chief purchasing point became Ogden, north of Salt Lake City, and from there, the states of Utah, Washington, Montana, Oregon and Nevada were tapped. The distance from purchasing areas to Atlantic ports were vast; from Denver (Colorado) via Kansas City (Missouri) to Newport News (Virginia) was about 1,777 miles and from Fort Worth (Texas) to Newport News 1,465 miles. At the height of purchasing, the Commission consisted of four main departments:[52]

- The headquarters in Kansas City.
- A large number of smaller commissions scattered over various localities; each under a combatant officer supported by a veterinary surgeon doing the actual buying.
- The central depot ranch at Lathrop, Missouri, formed in the spring of 1901. Purchased animals on arrival at the depot were tested for glanders and held in readiness to be forwarded by rail to New Orleans. Approximately 3,000-7,000 animals were held at Lathrop at any one time and over 80,000 passed through during the 15 months of the depot's existence.
- New Orleans was used for shipping. Six ships, each calculated to carry nearly 1,000 horses, arrived at New Orleans approximately every four weeks.

A major concern was maintaining steady supplies of remounts from the US, especially with hostility from an anti-British faction. Sessions refers to delays in getting ships ready owing to strikes, or the work of Boer agents in torpedoing a ship, or preventing ships once loaded, from leaving harbour. He refers to the many questions, "of a nature that are not exactly public", which had to be dealt with by HQ. Samuel Pearson, a Boer commissary general, based himself in New Orleans to cause as much annoyance and injury as he could. For example, Pearson stated the Remount Commission had an armed camp at Chalmette, where horses and mules awaited shipment, and as the American Government allowed the Commission to work at

---

52   Sessions, 1903, pp.135-8. Harold Sessions, FRCVS, served on three army remount commissions, Spain, Argentine and US; Page, 1976, p.304.

Chalmette, he would collect Boer sympathisers and attack the camp. This threat was not acted out; however, the steamer *Mechanisation* had a hole blown in its side whilst awaiting loading. On 4th April 1901, de Burgh, in Kansas City, telegrammed the IGR, reporting that ships had been stopped as contraband of war, by an injunction from the Court at New Orleans until 9th April, at the insistence of South African representatives. The *Times* newspaper records that, on the 3rd April 1901 a private individual, Sessions states a Boer Agent (in fact Samuel Pearson), successfully applied to the Louisiana Court (New Orleans), with an injunction preventing the shipping of animals from the States. The New Orleans newspaper, *Daily Picayune*, records the injunction was against J. Parson, captain of the ship *Anglo-Australian*, about to be loaded with 1,200 mules and horses, and munitions of war. An amendment was requested on the 6th April to include Capt. H. Parry of the steamship *Monterey*, then loading horses and mules. The newspaper also records that on 2nd April the steamship *Rossetti* departed for Cape Town with 950 head of horses, 90 tons oats, 90 tons bran and 215 tons hay; and on 5th April the *South America* with 1,000 mules, 230 tons hay, 35 tons bran, 2,200 bushels of oats and 1,000 halters.[53]

British officers were required to show why an injunction should not be granted to prevent the export of mules, on the grounds they were contraband of war. On 4th April, the IGR telegrammed Col. Dent, remount officer in Montreal, Canada, informing him that exports from the US had been stopped and to speed up his purchases. Further assistance was to be sent and he was to report whether sufficient mules could be obtained in Canada. On the 11th April, the US Court of Law suspended judgement for two weeks so that de Burgh was at liberty to put to sea and on the 16th April, the Court, which did not have maritime jurisdiction, gave a favourable decision. Statements were made that the British were enlisting American citizens to fight in South Africa, against which, the American Government issued a press statement, that the buying of animals did not violate International Law and that there was no evidence for American citizens enlisting. By November 1901, purchases and exports from the US were greater than before although the future of this, the largest supply, was considered uncertain. The purchase of animals ceased in the US approximately a month before the end of the war; the real reason for this closure of the North American Commission might be found in Sessions suggestion, that there was, "an intimation of a diplomatic nature that it was best that our work should cease."[54]

The Remount Department was constantly under pressure to meet increased demand due to the serious losses in South Africa. This was difficult to achieve, partly because government policy was so vacillatory, for example, Commission officers sent abroad

---

53   WO108/233, Telegrams, 7th April, No.11643, 11642, 11672A, and 16th April, 11716, 11792; Page, 1976, pp.311-14; *Times* newspaper, 4th April 1901; Sessions, 1903, p.280; *The Daily Picayune*, New Orleans, 2,3,5 and 6th April 1901. I am indebted to Eric Seiferth, Historic New Orleans Collection, for much of this information.
54   Sessions, 1903, pp.138, 181, 280-81; WO33/271, pp.29-30; Page, 1976, pp.311-14; *The Daily Picayune*, New Orleans, 7th April 1901, p.3.

repeatedly received contradictory orders, and on one occasion were completely withdrawn, and then sent out again. As a result of the increased demand for mounted troops, the local Cape horse and mule resources, belatedly, began to be used; it had been known before the war that the country did not have the type of animal required at home for British cavalry, or artillery. Remount staff in the Cape should have known about the local supply, as in July 1899, the GOC, South Africa informed the WO that only 200 cavalry and Royal Artillery horses could be purchased locally and therefore arrangements for importing them should be made. Lt. Lane, AVD, for example, had toured the country to provide Lord Milner with information on local supply; information which was not subsequently used by the military authorities. Truman and the Remount Department were severely criticised for not making earlier use of this resource, the size of which was known and published by the WO Intelligence Department a couple of months before the war began, in the 'Secret Handbook,' Appendix X. This gave the numbers known to exist in parts of Cape Colony in 1896-7, as 201,535 horses and 37,442 mules. However, this was not a complete picture, as seven of the Colony's districts, including five that were supposed to contain a large horse population, did not provide returns. In December 1900 Martial Law was declared in the Colony, and by the end of May 1901 some 70,000 remounts had been obtained. The political decision not to declare martial law until late in the war, along with prejudice against the small size and appearance of the local horse, were some of the reasons given for not purchasing earlier. To have purchased on the open market in South Africa, must have been a cheaper option than importing unfit animals.[55] None of the Parliamentary reports explain why the colonial horse was rejected, or why Birkbeck could claim that the Argentine was the only animal to be obtained in sufficient numbers, and that their importation should not cease until something better was found. Smith, writes that the advice of Col. Duck and the AVD had been ignored, "with the exception of Amery and Conan Doyle, no other writers placed their fingers on the extraordinary almost wilful neglect of the local animal as a source of remount supply."[56]

Duck stated that he had suggested using local horses and warned Truman against using big English horses. Truman laid the blame on the military authorities in South Africa for not purchasing the large numbers of acclimatised local animals until 1900. If they had made use of them earlier (although in December 1899 they were reported as unobtainable), he believed the campaign would have been shorter, with a corresponding decrease in loss of life and financial expenditure. In the first nine months of the war 18,000 cobs and 11,700 mules were purchased, largely, though not entirely, for colonial troops. Towards the end of 1900 the Army was in possession of thousands of captured and 'protected' local horses. These were immune to local disease, from

55   Stevenson, Cd.994, p.88, Q2795; WO33/271, p.7, telegram from GOC to WO, 29th July; Smith, 1919, p.132-3; Amery, 1909, Vol.VI, p.438.
56   Smith, 1919, p.132; Gilbey, 1900, on the value of small horses in warfare.

which every imported horse suffered.[57] Necessity overcame prejudice as nearly double the number of local horses and mules were obtained during 1901. Truman gives the numbers purchased in South Africa as:[58]

	Horses	Mules
1899-00	54,219	18,525
1901	92,699	16,245
1902	11,898	10,520
Total	158,816	45,290

In the early stages of the war, remounts shipped from the Argentine were reported to be landed more cheaply, in excellent condition and better than the local animal as there was no change in hemisphere, which was said to have killed the English horses. Truman, who had visited the Argentine, also favoured them. However, this view was to change. In a letter from Birkbeck to Truman, he writes, that he was not buying colonials, the local horses, but leaving them for colonial regiments, who at that time only needed some 3,000. By December, however, he wrote that no one who had seen the Argentine at the front had a good word to say for them except the 10th Hussars. By September 1901, he viewed the colonial horses as best of all. This extraordinary turn around was partly explained by the view that most of the early imports of Argentines were of much better quality than later ones.[59] As larger horses were replaced by small cobs, local horses, mainly of this type, gained in popularity. This change in demand, from the larger cavalry and artillery horse, to the smaller more compact horse, is highlighted in Birkbeck's telegram of December 1901, requesting well-bred, weight carrying polo ponies as the ideal animal for all mounted troops. In December 1900, Birkbeck wrote "the light man armed with a rifle, on a hardy, wiry and enduring cob, was the cavalry soldier of the future." Gilbey also wrote in 1900 of the value of the South African small horse for scouts and mounted infantry and Galvayne in 1902, that cavalry horses for active service should never be over 15.0 to 15.1 hands.[60] In the summer of 1901 the US Remount Commission was ordered to stop buying cavalry horses and in February 1902 Kitchener reduced the standard height of cobs required from 14.3 hands to 14.1, a size becoming difficult to obtain in the US.[61]

---

57   Forgrave, 1987, p.8; Smith, 1919, pp.132, 200; Duck, Cd.1790, p.134, Q3129-33.
58   WO33/271, p.8.
59   Cd.994, Appendix F, p.363, letter 3rd January 1900, from Birkbeck to Truman, and Appendix E, p.359; Cd.993, p.28; Smith, 1919, pp.132-3; Lane, 1912, p.123.
60   Cd.963, p.54, Cable No.104, 11th December 1901, telegram from GOC Cape to QMG; also Cd.963, p.21; Gilbey, 1900, pp.3, 12; Galvayne, 1902, p.16.
61   Cd.994, Col. de Burgh evidence, Q81-83, 1901.

It is impossible to arrive at a single accurate figure for the total number of animals supplied, or used during the war. All authors vary and many do not provide the source for their figures. There are several published official tables on the supply of horses but these should be read with care.[62] Some of the most important only deal with remounts supplied by the WO and take no account of the horses in the possession of troops on mobilisation, colonial contingents, or those supplied to the Yeomanry. Only two of the official tables correspond in expressing information on the basis of January to December, and these do not agree in totals.[63] Other tables adopted the official year 1st April to 31st March, others the financial year 1st October to 30th September, so that comparison between them is impossible.[64] As Smith correctly comments, the vast wealth of available material contains no definite thread of statistical expression. Smith who does give the sources for his figures, noted that a report written by the Remount Department after the war was never published and "contained tables of income and expenditure of horses, but laboured under the disadvantage of unaccountable deficiencies, amounting to as much as 30,000 animals a year."[65] Later writers have taken from published sources without analysis, confusing an already difficult picture. Only Smith appears to make a detailed analysis of the material for supply and losses, based upon a sound knowledge and experience of remounts and veterinary matters. Even then, the figures presented by Smith, for the numbers brought into the country at each period, are not totally accurate.

The number of horses purchased abroad, during the war and the vast distances covered, over four continents, was remarkable, as shown by the figures below, based on those prepared by the QMG in 1903:[66]

62   Cd.1792, Appendices 38 and 38a, pp.258-261; WO33/271, Appendices G, H and I; Cd.994, Appendix B.
63   Cd.994, Appendix B; WO33/271, Appendix H.
64   Cd.1792, Appendix 38a, pp.259-61; WO33/271, Appendix G.
65   Smith, 1919, p.141.
66   From Cd.1792, p.258, Appendix 38, p.258; WO33/271, p.56, Appendix I, prepared by Clarke, QMG, 5th February 1903. Note there is a difference between some of these figures and those in Cd.1796, pp.260-61, Appendix 38a. The latter does not include India and has a larger total for horses by 9,010 and 1,113 for mules; Amery, 1909, Vol.VI, pp.418-9 gives the above table, prepared by the QMG in 1903, but then adds different figures in his text.

Table of Horses, Mules and Donkeys Purchased at Home and Abroad, 1899-1902:

Source	Numbers Provided		
	Horses	Mules & Donkeys	Total
Home: already with units	20,251	–	
Home: remounts	56,984	167	77,402
Home: Imperial Yeomanry with units	2,500	–	
Home: Imperial Yeomanry remounts	4,500	–	7,000
Australasia	23,028	–	23,028
Austria (Hungary)	60,352	–	
As above, by Imperial Yeomanry	3,805	–	64,157
Canada	14,621	–	14,621
Colonials: with units	27,473	–	
Colonials: remounts	1,431	19	28,923
Cyprus	–	128	128
India: with units	5,549	–	
India: remounts	3,062	1,114	9,725
Italy	7,004	–	7,004
South Africa	158,816	45,290	240,106
South America	26,544	–	26,544
Spain	15,229	–	15,229
Uganda	–	306	306
USA	109,878	81,524	191,402
Totals	518,794	150,781	669,575

The figures for the US include 3,220 horses and 1,000 mules purchased for the British South Africa Company. The QMG gives a total net expenditure of £15,339. This figure includes payments for not completing contracts in Austria (£16,862) and New Zealand (£1,052), less sales of American horses in Canada (£8,078). It does not include the cost of animals already with units on the outbreak of war.

There are no monthly returns for imports from January 1902 to the peace proclamation in May. In November 1901, there were approximately 10,000 to 12,000 remounts monthly being sent to column commanders. The WO informed Kitchener in December 1901, that they hoped to land over 40,000 horses during December – February. The total supplied from January to June 1902 was probably:[67]

67   Cd.963, p.52, Cable 98, Secretary of State for War to Kitchener, 26th November 1901;

	Horses	Mules
Overseas remounts, less loss at sea	84,688	10,447
At sea in December 1901, less loss	9,367	985
Remounts obtained in South Africa	11,898	10,520
Total	106,223	21,952

[The total figure for horses adds up to 105,953; an error in Smith's text].

Amery provides a total figure for animals supplied by the Remount Department at home and in South Africa of some, 520,000 horses and 150,000 mules; at a total cost of £15 million:

- South Africa provided some 160,00 horses and 45,000 mules and donkeys; possibly also more than 100,000 oxen (in comparison, Smith, gives a figure for the two years and three months of the war of some 146,918 horses and 16,245 mules).
- Other British colonies, or possessions, supplied some 75,000 horses.
- The US provided 110,000 horses and 80,000 mules.
- Austro-Hungary provided 90,000 remounts.
- Spain and Italy 23,000 mules.

Amery states foreign counties supplied nearly two-fifths of the horses and over two-thirds of mules. The UK provided some 80,000 horses. Less than half of the 14,000 horses registered before the war were mobilized, mainly from the London omnibus companies. Section 115 of the Army Act, which allowed for impressment of horses in the UK, was not used. The Authorities, in their post war-planning, failed to take notice of the inadequacy of the home market to meet the demands of a future large scale war.

Figures for the Boer forces cannot be ascertained. They probably took to the field with 50,000 to 60,000 horses, which were renewed several times over. Their net wastage probably exceeded 100,000.[68]

Demobilisation

The Peace Treaty was signed on 31st May 1902 and to keep down the costs of feeding idle mouths animals needed to be disposed of as quickly as possible. There is a great discrepancy in the various figures giving the number of animals in South Africa on the day peace was declared, even Smith appears to have contradictory figures.

numbers were in response to an increase asked for on the 25th November. Also, Cable No.110, p.55, Secretary of State for War to Kitchener, 24th December; Smith, 1919, p.226.
68   Amery, 1909, Vol.VI, pp.417-9; Smith 191, p.185.

His figures for 31st May are, 131,700 army horses, 76,600 mules, 12,800 donkeys and 74,200 oxen on establishment. On 1st June 1902, he states there were 161,400 horses and 93,000 mules in the country that had been paid for. The published Royal Commission tables show 151,100 horses and 94,600 mules, but do not include reinforcements from home and overseas contingents, as they were not included in WO returns. After deducting animals required for the Army of Occupation, Smith gives a figure of 140,000 horses and 74,000 mules in excess of requirements (another source gives 142,159 horses and 76,640 mules). On 31st May there were 28,700 sick horses and mules of which 19,500 were in the 50 hospitals, the remainder were on debility farms under Remount management. At the same time, members of the AVD located with Remounts, hospitals and other units consisted of:

Veterinary Officers	63
Civilian Veterinary Surgeons	113
European Dressers	79
Indian Dressers	28
Civilian Farriers, Conductors, Clerks	217
South African Natives	3,547

The end of hostilities saw an increase in the number of animals in hospitals, as those that could not previously be sent for treatment were admitted. The number of hospitals was only gradually reduced; ten months after the war finished numbers fell to nine, which was to be the future establishment for the country.[69]

The war devastated the local horse population of South Africa. Mason and Maule wrote that the war had been the death blow to the Cape Horse as Boer horses were deliberately destroyed. The Civilian Veterinary Departments were kept busy for the next few years endeavouring to stamp out mange and glanders aided by a British Government funded Repatriation Department. The Department purchased 23,700 army horses, 51,800 mules, 5,700 donkeys and 60,900 oxen, urgently needed for regeneration. Before the end of February 1903, the Cape and Natal had purchased some 86,800 horses, 9,600 mules, 3,400 donkeys and 2,000 oxen. The total sales between 1st June 1902 and 28th February 1903, were 120,500 horses, 61,400 mules and 9,100 donkeys. Over the same period approximately 19,500 horses and mules were destroyed, at least one third due to glanders. Because army horses were full of glanders and mange, the Repatriation Department insisted on mallein testing all the animals they purchased. Many thousands were inoculated, but not all, as the numbers were vast and there was an urgency to regenerate the local horse populations. By about September 1902, the Army had reduced the number of animals to a peacetime establishment.[70]

69   Smith, 1919, pp.224, 229, 297-9.
70   Mason and Maule, 1960, p.12; Smith p.229.

Causes of Wastage

The war in South Africa was essentially a 'horse war'. Pakenham states that the armies of Roberts and Kitchener "swallowed horses as a modern army swallows petrol". Lt Head, AVC, with the Inniskilling Dragoons, landed with 406 horses, but during the period November 1899 to 30th June 1902 used some 4,290 horses from various sources. The regiment furnished 4,170 hospital admissions, only 163 were due to bullets and three to shell fire; clear evidence that little of the enormous loss was directly attributable to enemy action. The expenditure of horses during the two and half years of active service approximates to the whole regiment being re-horsed ten and half times. The total lack of understanding about the use and management of horses in the field was one of the most remarkable revelations of staff ignorance, and in no small way contributed to wastage. Only horses that could not perform any kind of duty were reported as sick. Birkbeck wrote that they had done fairly well in the circumstances under which "…'s" utter disregard for horseflesh had placed them (the space is in the original text, but probably refers to Kitchener).[71] An examination into the wastage of in excess of 325,000 horses and 51,000 mules was called for, and in part, provided by the *Royal Commission to Inquire into the Military Preparations and Other Matters connected with the War in South Africa*, and the *Court of Enquiry on the Administration of the Army Remount Department*. Neither the Royal Commission, nor the Court of Enquiry, dealt with losses in the field. The Commission reported that questions connected with remounts had engaged the Court of Enquiry and two committees and it was not re-opening the issue, but accepted the Court's finding. Its investigations related only to the purchase of animals and their transportation to South Africa. Again, it is to the work of Smith that one must turn for a detailed and analytical understanding of losses in the field.[72]

There are a number of associated causes for the heavy losses. One can begin with the vast distances travelled to reach the seat of war and the limited rail transport once in South Africa; the lack of acclimatisation and the poor quality of some imported remounts. To these are added disease, starvation, overwork and lack of rest, exhaustion, neglect and poor horsemanship. In addition, inadequate pre-war planning, poor relations between the Remount and Veterinary Departments, limited numbers of trained personnel especially in the Remount Department, lack of military training, or understanding of military ways by civilian veterinary surgeons; poor organisation and limited veterinary facilities. The harsh campaigning conditions in South Africa and

71   Head, 1903, p.299 (see Appendix I); Pakenham, 1979, p.381; Forgrave, 1987, p.8; Galvayne, 1902, p.9; Cd.993, p.19; Cd.963, p.14, report from PVO at Pretoria, July 1900; Birkbeck, Cd.994, Appendix F, p.363, letter to IGR at WO, 6th April 1900 from Naauwpoort.
72   The Royal Commission, Cd.1789-92; Court of Enquiry, Cd.993-4, for the Court's findings see the Report Cd.1789, pp.97-9; Smith's *Veterinary History of the War*, was almost ready for publication when war broke out in 1914, but was delayed until 1919, although serialised in the *VR*, 1914.

the requirements of adapting to a changing military situation are also relevant. It is hard to ignore some acts of sheer military incompetence, for example, the purchasing of animals which, on arrival in South Africa, were incapable of active service. A situation that increased the work of the understaffed AVD, for example, 3,000 stallion mules sent from Italy had to be castrated on arrival, keeping transport sections, which required these animals, in their bases. The Royal Commission did not refer to such technical aspects, probably because there was no expert advice to direct their attention to these matters. Buller in his evidence to the Commission, stated that it was a grave error to purchase stallion mules for service.[73] Further incompetence is reflected in the purchasing commissions hasty acquisitions of unfit, unconditioned animals and the introduction of disease from foreign countries. Before the war had lasted eight weeks, cases of glanders were recorded at Cape Town among newly landed remounts, the first reported case of imported glanders was 5th December 1899. Diseased remounts were arriving in Natal during October 1899, for example, the 6th Inniskilling Dragoons, whose horses had suffered from mange in Ireland, but were believed to be free when embarked, brought sarcoptic mange into South Africa. Influenza and strangles (a respiratory disease) were also quickly introduced.[74]

The question of conditioning remounts for active service had probably not been considered prior to the war, as the small number of horses required for wartime establishments were to be obtained from civilian animals in hard working condition. Conditioning remounts during war, for saddle and draught work was important, but, required detailed peacetime planning, which Smith considered required centralisation, carried out in proper training establishments by the Remount Department.[75] The urgent requirement for animals, for transport and mounted troops, meant that on landing and reaching depots, they were quickly despatched on long overland rail journeys to front-line units. Here they were detrained and taken on long marches on short rations, ridden beyond the pace which best suited them, carrying weights in excess of twenty stone (280lbs), with little rest and rarely off-saddled. Transfer from one hemisphere to another, changes in altitude and being fed with grain to which they were unaccustomed, meant these animals inevitably quickly lost condition; many succumbing to injury and exhaustion. Losses in operations from Pretoria to Middelburg, in the Eastern Transvaal, July 1900, were due to using unconditioned, unfit and starving remounts. 349 cavalry horses were admitted to hospital, with a further 108 horses left dead on the veldt, or abandoned. Three days work cost the cavalry 400 horses, or 130 horses a day; losses for the mounted infantry are unknown.[76]

73   Evidence, Cd.1791, p.218, A 15,561; Smith, 1919, pp.9, 14; Lane, 1912, pp.39-42.
74   Head, 1903, pp.299-300, 307-8; Smith, 1919, pp.13-4, 24, 107.
75   Smith, 1919, p.226; Cochrane, 1913, p.167.
76   Head, 1903, pp.300-1; Smith, 1919, pp.97, 749.

Remounts for South Africa at the Grand Trunk Railway stock yards, Canada.
(Topley Studio/Library & Archives Canada PA-26058)

Offloading horses, Port Elizabeth, South Africa, 1900.
(Mrs Chigumba, Director, Africana Library, South Africa)

Remounts leaving Port Elizabeth for the front.
(Mrs Chigumba, Director, Africana Library, South Africa)

After travelling halfway round the world, already battered and bruised, animals had to travel for long periods, over vast distances in rail trucks, often without adequate food and water. Placed side by side in trucks, it was impossible to feed and water them without detraining, a lack of time and shortage of staff did not allow this to take place. The un-acclimatised English troop horses, working in tropical heat whilst wearing winter coats, carrying crushing weights, short of rations and water, suffered severely from strenuous work. They could not be clipped in the cold summer rains, nor when they stood out at night. Despite improvements following the IGR's inspection (1901), the Remount Department still failed to deal with the question of conditioning horses, even during the short time they remained in depots. Practically every depot possessed an 'Eassie' exercising track, but remounts also required conditioning by carrying a saddle and a man, but Smith believed the Department did not see its duty as riding and training horses. Unfit horses continued to be used in the front line. In 1902 efforts were made to allow time for acclimatisation, but again, due to the military pressures of campaigning, regulations were ignored.   The IGR was specifically instructed by the WO to look at the length of time given to preparing horses for work after landing, and orders issued by Kitchener were ignored, or not passed on to officers. The IGR gave strict orders to remedy this situation, calling in all horses already issued, but not acclimatised.[77] Conditioning 10,000 horses monthly was no easy task, but it was the cheaper financial option, resulting in savings and efficiency, however, such were the demands made upon the Department, it was impossible to train remounts as they passed far too rapidly through depots.[78]

Overwork and underfeeding took a heavy toll. Representations, by the acting PVO at Cape Town, early in December 1899, to increase rations were ignored; contributing to the Cavalry Division's loss of mobility. The authorised ration scale was 12lb of grain and grazing. No regular hay ration was provided and as British forces were tied down to certain localities, local grazing was rapidly exhausted. English troop horses, arriving in a strange country, used to manger feeding and comfortable stables, were helpless on the veldt; even when grass was plentiful, the pattern of the horse bit did not allow grazing. During a halt, men were not allowed to dismount without orders, or remove the bits to allow grazing, as it was considered unsafe to turn out horses with an enemy a few miles away. Feeding hay in the horse-lines was the only practicable method of maintaining the condition of horses in war. That such basic points of horse-management were ignored, or not understood, is indefensible. A week after his arrival, Buller laid down a daily ration of 12lb grain for horses and 8lb for mules. The full ration was not to be issued when sufficient grass was available; if ordered by the Commanding Officer (CO), 2lbs of hay could be substituted for each pound of grain. The ration substitute of hay was not to exceed 8lbs per day. Whenever possible horses were to be grazed, or grass cut for them, minimising the quantity of forage carried. If the CO drew all the hay permitted, the daily ration was 8lb of grain and 8lb of hay for horses, and 4lb and 8lb for mules, respectively. Maj. Haig (Assistant Adjutant General, Cavalry Division) states that cavalry and artillery were handicapped by unfit and underfed horses; cavalry horses were overloaded, exceeding 20 stone, seldom with sufficient forage. Hay was only procurable in a standing camp, or on railways; at Paardeberg the oat ration was 4lbs per day. From 10th February to 7th March 1900, horses were on reduced rations. Galvayne writes that orders were frequently issued to reduce rations, then back to full rations, and then reduced again. He did not wonder at stock dying.[79]

At the same time as the PVO was stressing the seriousness of the forage shortage, Lt-Gen. Lord Methuen (GOC 1st Division and Western District Transvaal), was

---

77   Head, 1903, pp.300-1; Hume, 1980, p.36; Page, 1976, p.321; Cd.993, pp.19-20; Amery, 1909, Vol.VI, p.421; Smith, 1919, pp. 129, 185, 225; Lane, 1912, p.39; Galvayne, 1902, pp.13-18, 150, for a detailed discussion on the poor qualities of the English horse in South Africa, except the draught type; Haig, Cd.1791, p.403, Q19299.

78   Cd.963, p.4, Birkbeck's Report, July 1900; Galvayne, 1902, p.102; Pakenham, 1979, p.381; Page, 1976, p.325; Cochrane, 1913, p.166; Vet-Capt. Blenkinsop's (SVO Cavalry Division) letter of 11th April 1900 in Cd.994, Appendix B2, p.312.

79   Smith, 1919, pp.14-15; Buller, Army Standing Orders, 6 November 1899; Haig, Cd.1791, p.403, Q19299; Galvayne, 1902, p.64. I am grateful to Capt. Gibson of The King's Troop RHA for information on the condition of the remounts in the photographs below.

13th Hussars crossing Tugela River at Trichards Drift, Spion Kop, South Africa.
(Royal College of Veterinary Surgeons Charitable Trust Library)

ordered to adhere strictly to authorised ration scales and economise by grazing mules whenever possible.[80] He informed the C-in-C that horses and mules were not efficient on a minimum oat-hay allowance of 7lb and evidence given before the Royal Commission, shows that Headquarters were informed of the poor condition of mules when grazing was exhausted. Methuen's own evidence on the grazing and ration shortage supports the Headquarters' incompetence, or wilful neglect. The authorisation of a ration suitable only for the light colonial pony, not that required by a larger English troop horse, was responsible for the starvation of horses in February 1900. This was the basis of the cavalry collapse during the Kimberley-Paardeberg operations, which, it has been suggested, prolonged the war by two years. Lt. Head, veterinary surgeon attached to the 6th Inniskilling Dragoons, wrote in 1903 that even a thoroughly acclimatised horse could not have withstood the treatment, and

80   Cd.1791, pp.119-33, Q14135-14469.

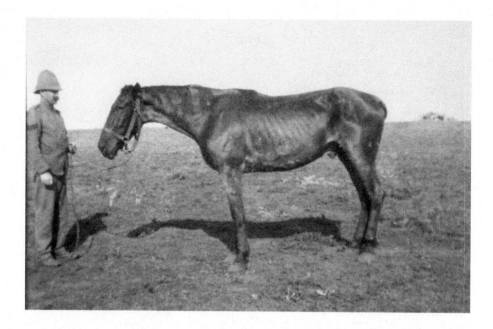

Two examples of remounts in poor condition from poor grazing and extreme work, taken by Lt. Head: (top) Remount with sickle hocked – due to strained tendons and ligaments the hock is flexed so that the foot is abnormally bowed far under the belly predisposing to spavin from a trauma injury; (bottom) in poor condition resting hind leg (Royal College of Veterinary Surgeons Charitable Trust Library)

with the number of raw, soft remounts just off ship, the mortality rate was not surprising.[81] Gen. French, giving evidence before the Royal Commission, stated that on the Kimberley march, horses had little food and could not possibly survive very hard work, unless fed, which was impossible, as fodder could not be carried with them and after Paardeberg it was not available.[82]

Orders to improve conditions for animals were continually ignored in the field, for example, a memorandum by Lord Roberts, 28th January 1900, stated that horses should be fed at short intervals and not kept too long without water. A sufficiency of grain was necessary for horses to withstand hard work, but they would never be kept in condition unless they had an ample supply of hay, or bulky equivalent.[83] Spending vast sums of money on foreign animals, yet starving and destroying trained horses at the seat of war, was an incredibly wasteful and expensive remount policy. Even allowing for difficulties of having to issue unfit horses, poor horsemastership was a major factor in wastage, a problem that both Roberts and Kitchener were clearly aware of; both issued army orders and circulars, with general and detailed instructions on horse care. Smith thought Roberts was a horsemaster but his return home in 1900 left everything in the hands of Kitchener, who he did not think knew anything about horses, his standard animal being the camel.[84]

Although there was some improvement towards the end of the war, horsemastership was poor in all branches of the Army, including the regular cavalry and mounted infantry; the exception was the Artillery, which was praised for its excellent horsemastership. Horsemastership includes four key principals, watering, feeding, the pace an animal is expected to work at and grooming. Some of the evidence given before the Royal Commission believed the Cavalry had taken good care of their horses, French for example stated that, "the horsemastership of the Cavalry is very nearly all we can desire," but also, "stable management is better understood than care and feed of horses in the field".

The introduction during 1901, of 5,800 new mounted infantry, 17,600 Yeomanry, 6,000 colonial contingents and thousands of locally raised men, with little or no experience in horsemastership, made for potential disaster. Lord Roberts stated that had the mounted infantry been better horsemasters there would have been less waste;

---

81 Cd.1790, Q3472, p.145-6, evidence of Col. Sir W.D. Richardson, Deputy Adjutant General of Supplies, South Africa, Sept, 1899. From Chief of Staff, Cape Town, to Lord Methuen, Modder River, 17th December 1899; evidence to Royal Commission Buller's Staff Officer, from his war diary, responsible for providing forage; Lord Methuen, Cd.1791, p.120, A.14162-4, Cd.1789, pp.98-99; Smith, 1919, pp.14-15, 7, 16; Head, 1903, p.30.

82 French, Cd.1791, p.304, A17183-89.

83 Cd.1790, p.533, Appendix H. Views of C in C, Lord Roberts, memorandum 28th January 1900.

84 WO105/40, Roberts Papers, Army Order 2, dated 3rd March 1900; Page, 1976, pp.328-9; Smith, 1919, p.49; Cd.1789, pp.45-47, Kitchener's and Roberts' Evidence on horsemanship and horsemastership; Smith Archive, Autobiography, pp.73-4.

only those units and men raised locally had any knowledge of horse management on campaign. Following the British disasters of 'Black Week', in December 1899, and the need for a more mobile force, the Imperial Yeomanry was created by Royal Warrant on 24th December. This new force was initially recruited on a county basis, from members of existing Yeomanry regiments, to provide service companies of approximately 115 men each. In addition, a large number of volunteers were recruited largely from the middle and upper classes. The first of three contingents to be raised, nearly 11,000 men, arrived in South Africa between February and April 1900. Not all were proficient in horsemanship, or horsemastership. The second contingent (the 'new yeomanry'), numbering approximately 16,597, was recruited early in 1901, mainly from the working classes and were very poorly trained. The third contingent, approximately 7,000, was raised in December 1901. Smith writes that both officers and men of the 1901 Yeomanry were generally, utterly ignorant of the care and management of horses; many not wishing to learn, and were, "in many cases an ordnance and remount depot for the enemy". In the Orange Free State, Lt-Gen. Rundle's mounted columns included some 3,000 untrained Yeomanry under elementary instruction at Harrismith. The majority of the officers and some 20% of the men were sent home as useless, using up horses in their training at a rate which was impossible to maintain. Lord Chesham, Inspector-General of the Imperial Yeomanry, stated in his evidence before the Royal Commission, that 75% of the 1901 contingent had not been on a horse before they passed the riding school test at home and 25% had ridden very little.[85]

In Natal, African Horse Sickness, the cause of which was unknown, was responsible for many deaths. In 1886 Dr F. Leming obtained authority from the Secretary of State for War to send out an experienced surgeon to investigate the nature, causation, and prevention of this fatal disease. The importance of the investigation can be seen as in 1887 very nearly one third, and in 1888 upwards of one tenth of horses and mules of the military force in Natal, were lost through this epizootic. Mr Nunn, the officer selected, returned to England after studying the disease for two seasons. Evidence suggested that if horses were stabled and properly looked after, the chances of contracting the disease was less than when picketed in the open. Such practices were strongly urged by veterinary officers and officers commanding mounted infantry companies, but the Authorities refused to erect even rough stables. At the highest financial estimate, by the Royal Engineers, the value of horses lost was sufficient to have built stables for three times the number of horses required. In addition there was

---

85   Cd.1789, Report, Vol. XI, Lords Roberts and Kitchener, pp.45-47; Cd.1790 Col. Lucas, DAG Imperial Yeomanry, Evidence pp.272-285, Appendix E & F pp.523-525, & G pp.526-528, and Lord Chesham, Q6731, pp.287-8; Cd.1791, p.111, Q13941, Lt-Gen. I.S.M. Hamilton, "artillery excellent horsemasters," and French, pp.301, 331, Q17883-86, and Brig-Gen. M.F. Rimington, pp.28-29, Q12663-80; Cd.994, Pringle, AVD, p.255, A7130-8; Head, 1903, p.306; Smith, 1919, pp.147, 161, 175, 23, 235 (see Amery, 1909, Vol.V, p.432).

a large cost in the wastage of lost equipment such as, blankets, reins and head ropes left out in mud and rain.[86]

It is difficult to assess the basic quality of animals supplied and the relative value of the different sources of supply, a question pursued by the WO and Royal Commission. Truman considered little reliance could be placed on much of the evidence because of its great diversity and expression of conflicting opinions.[87] The AIR in South Africa constantly received reports that he collated and forwarded, twice a month, to Truman at the WO. Many officers were asked to record their comments on each of the types of horses and mules supplied. Their views reflected both different personal criteria in judging horses and the different quality of consignments from the same source, and one cannot rule out those who may have deliberately set out to find fault, however insignificant. The real value of each class of horse could not have been fairly judged when they were not given time for acclimatisation and conditioning on arrival in South Africa; and the class required changed over the course of the war. It was often a question of survival of the fittest, irrespective of type, or country of origin. The accuracy of reports cannot always be trusted and are of little help in judging the work of the Remount Department and planning for future conflict. For example, I have not found any evidence that such reports were consulted before, or during, the First World War.

There was general agreement on the superiority of local animals as they were already acclimatised and had not suffered long sea journeys before issue. From the collapse of the Middelburg peace talks, February 1901, Kitchener had been conducting the war under protest to the WO, against the tens of thousands of sub-standard horses sent to South Africa.[88] This did not, however, stop him using them before they were ready for service. Some officers took their polo ponies out as chargers; these small compact animals were considered a great success, which accorded with the growing recognition that a good strong, well made, hardy polo pony type was required as a suitable mount for all ranks. Remounts purchased from Argentina and Hungary were often considered almost useless. Argentinean cobs, when well selected and trained, were good mounted infantry animals. Lt. Head thought Hungarian horses thoroughly useless, suggesting that Hungarian remount officers had made sure no remounts fit for their own army were offered to British buyers. North American horses generally did well and were liked, as were those from Australia, Canada and New Zealand. Not many English horses survived the first year of the war, being generally too big and heavy, however, both Truman and Birkbeck rated them highly. Russian ponies were considered better than Hungarian but only for slow harness work. The South African mule was probably the best for transport, followed by the American, Italian

---

86   *VR*, 1889, Vol.1, 16th March, pp.442-3 and 1898, Vol.11, 16 July, p.43; Cochrane, 1913, pp.164-66. Galvayne, 1902, pp.91, 122.
87   WO33/271, p.23.
88   Pakenham, 1979, p.535; Page, 1976, p.329.

and the Spanish. The great scandal was that in 1899 purchases were being made on four continents, at a time when all the local, acclimatised and cheaper animals in South Africa should have been acquired.[89]

Units created at the beginning of the war, such as transport, mounted infantry, irregular units, and Remounts, had no farrier service. Many horses and mules purchased from Australia and US arrived in South Africa unshod. Fortunately, the country was not excessively hard on the wear and tear of shoes, if it had been, there might have been an entire collapse of the military arrangements within three months of taking to the field. The chronic shortage of farriers and shoeing smiths was an important factor in animal wastage; for example, on the way to Kimberley many horses lost their shoes, which could not be replaced owing to the shortage of farriers, spare shoes and men's time. To reduce the weight placed on horses only a small percentage of spare shoes were carried resulting, for example, with remounts arriving at Paardeberg from the Modder River unshod and foot-sore. There is no evidence to suggest that the Authorities considered how the vast number of animals were to be kept shod when moving over vast areas of open country.[90] The Army had retained a regimental farrier system created in 1796, whereby a farriers' work was restricted to his own regiment, a reserve of farriers did not exist, and only with the approval of their CO could farriers assist with horses from other units.

There were not less than 200 farriers and shoeing smiths with the Cavalry Division on the Modder River, yet not one of them could be detailed to shoe animals of the mounted infantry, Transport, or Remounts. Under the veterinary officer, farriers were also responsible for the sick horses of their units; they were soldiers as well as craftsmen, and so took their place in the ranks. The regimental shoeing system had broken down in the early part of the war and was taken over by the Remount Department. Smith was appalled at the immediate breakdown in the Army's farrier system when tested under active service conditions, especially as experienced veterinary officers had seen this as inevitable. Comments on farrier organisation, from previous campaigns, appeared in nearly every veterinary report, but had been ignored.[91]

89   Head, 1903, pp.300, 302-3, 306, 308-9; Galvayne, 1902, pp.136-72; WO33/271, pp.23-4, provides a useful guide when considering comparative values of horses; Amery, 1909, Vol. VI, p.421; Cd.993, pp.27-28. Stevenson; Cd.994, p.94, A2944-7 and Appendix E, pp.358-61, gives a synopsis of opinions and reports on various classes of horses, also pp.363 in correspondence to WO from Birkbeck, and pp.6-7, Birkbeck's Report, July 1900, also, pp.19-20, 22nd December 1900; Cd.1789, p.99.

90   Smith, 1919, pp. 37, 240-1; Galvayne, 1902, pp.26-29, shoeing in relation to travel by sea, pp.34-41; WO33/271, p.22, there was a similar shortage of farriers at home where civilian labour was hired; French, Cd.1791, p.311, Q17393; Stevenson, Cd.994, pp.88, 116, A2809, 3474-9; Duck, Cd.1792, Appendix 6A, pp.101-2.

91   Haig, Cd.1791, Q19299, p.403, re unshod horses and shortage of farriers; Smith, 1919, pp.vii, 13, 49, for losses amongst farriers and shoeing smiths pp.241-3; Galvayne, 1902, p.13.

The urgent need for farriers was among the many complaints raised from January to April 1900 until finally, on 11th April 1900, the employment of civilian farriers was sanctioned. The number of civilian farriers rose with the increase in army horses and grew into a very large and expensive service. The military farrier and shoeing-smith gradually 'disappeared'. By June 1901 there were 100 civilian farriers working for Remounts alone, in addition to 35 army and 60 Indian farriers with the AVD. By the 31st May 1902, the number of civilian farriers with the Remount Department had reached 175, in addition to 60 army and 104 Indian farriers and shoeing-smiths. The numbers with hospitals and columns is unknown, but not less than another 200. Discontent arose amongst army farriers as civilian farriers were on better pay and conditions. Smith, considered an organisation on a regimental basis was bound to fail unless a very large reserve was obtainable on the outbreak of hostilities. He believed farriers should have been non-combatant, belonging to their own Farrier Corps, only posted to regiments for duties; personnel would be primarily tradesmen and provide for remount depots and hospitals. He saw the Corps as a single organisation under central control for the distribution of personnel, and during peace, or war, devoted to the care and attention of horses' feet. Emergency shoeing in the fighting line would be carried out by regimental cold-shoers (see Glossary). Truman had recommended that men complete the existing training programme, but with a special rate of pay to encourage qualification. The part previously played by regimental farriers as veterinary assistants would be taken over by personnel of the AVD.[92]

During the last 18 months of the war, every animal was shod, all round, by Remounts before issue; this covered the period of the animal's active service until returned to Remounts for rest and repair. Towards the end of the war animals were shod at the rate of 35,000 per month. However, there were many complaints about the shortage, absence, ill-sorted sizes and poor quality of shoes. Smith refers to the Cavalry Division early in 1900 as having horse shoes too heavy for the country. One particular type of nail, which represented the bulk of the stock, was so brittle that it was not uncommon for the nails in one shoe to break at the neck. Nails of all patterns and makes were purchased, even though, before the outbreak of war, Ordnance authorities at Cape Town had been advised by the AVD that the shoe most suitable for the country was the Egyptian pattern. This advice was ignored, none were stocked, or obtainable, until long after the war started. The shoes generally supplied were machine made, but the stock had run so low that the Government bought shoes from anywhere, many of them hand made and of poor quality. Gen. Brackenbury, Director General of Ordnance (WO) wrote to the C-in-C a few weeks after the war began stating that the reserve of general shoes (the authorised reserve was for 52,000 sets of horseshoes, and no mule shoes), was utterly inadequate to meet demand. He was purchasing whatever he could on the open market, for example, horseshoes from Germany and Sweden and mule shoes from the US. 35,000 sets of horseshoes and 40,000 sets of mule shoes were sent monthly to South Africa to keep animals shod.

92   WO33/271, p.22; Smith, 1919, p.243.

Even though successive governments had known that on mobilisation for foreign service, mule transport was to be used, no reserve of shoes was maintained.

Despite the collapse of the farrier system in South Africa, no further steps were taken to remedy the situation. The Royal Commission did not enquire into the breakdown of farrier organisation. Brackenbury, in his evidence before the Commission, refers to the failure of not having a 'horse' interest represented on it. Galvayne notes that even by the end of the war there was no organised system for rough-riding (breaking horses) in any depot, with exception of the stabling at Stellenbosch.[93]

Statistics: Supply and Losses

Arguably, the excessive wear and tear on animals was not due to any shortage of supply. The figures below, provided by the QMG in 1903, give the number of animals supplied by Remounts at the WO during 1901, and provides an insight into the complexity of providing an accurate and meaningful set of figures. The figures do not include those taken into the country by colonial contingents, regular reinforcements and those obtained in South Africa (see opposite page).[94]

The table shows that the total number of horses accompanying units, together with remount horses and mules from overseas during 1901, was 120,508 horses and 24,642 mules. To these totals must be added a further 92,699 horses and 16,245 mules purchased in South Africa; even though in 1899 it was reported the local supply was unobtainable. The total number obtained from all sources during 1901 was 213,207 horses and 40,845 mules. Between 1899-1902 some 146,918 horses and 16,245 mules were obtained as remounts in South Africa. To arrive at the total number of horses available to the Army, the tens of thousands of captured animals used in very large numbers, if only for a day or two, but for which there is no record, needs to be added. Gen. Mansfield Clarke, QMG, stated before the Royal Commission that in total, 518,794 horses and 150,781 mules and donkeys were supplied to South Africa; of these, the Remount Department procured 470,600 horses and 149,649 mules, including those with units at the outbreak of war, at a total cost including shipment and freight of £16,935,022 and £4,787,868. The remainder were provided by the Imperial Yeomanry, the colonies and from India.[95]

---

93   Cd.1790, Evidence, Gen Brackenbury, Director-Gen. Ordnance, pp.74, 86 (Q1782-3); Smith, 1919, p.243-4 ref. shoes and nails, and p.31 for February to March 1900, Modder River to Bloemfontein, and p.244 injuries resulting from shoeing and neglect in shoeing; Galvayne, 1902, pp.12, 132.

94   Smith, 1919, p.185 uses the table from Cd.994, Appendix B, p.311, extracting 1901 figures from: *Statement Showing Number of Horses and Mules Demanded by, and Supplied to, the Cape from the Beginning of the War to 31st January 1902.* Both Truman and Cd.994 agree in figures for 1901 although not for all other periods; WO33/271, pp.54-55, Appendix H; Amery, 1909, Vol.VI, p.417.

95   Cd.1792, Appendix 38, p.258 and 38a, pp.260-1; Cd.1789, p.97; Smith, 1919, p.185.

Number of Remount Horses and Mules supplied during 1901

Month	Monthly returns		Quarterly totals		
	Horses	Mules	Horses	Mules	All animals
January	8,439	–			
February	6,937	2,467	25,118	4,467	29,585
March	9,742	2,000			
April	8,067	3,098			
May	6,684	2,399	23,468	5,971	29,439
June	8,717	474			
July	1,442	3,650			
August	9,817	998	30,855	7,500	38,355
September	9,596	2,852			
October	12,070	2,078			
November	11,000	2,020	40,365	5,113	45,478
December	17,295	1,015			
Total			119,806	23,051	142,857
Deduct losses at sea – horses 3.63%, mules 1.56%			4,348	359	
Total			115,458	22,692	(138,150)
Add remounts on the sea in Dec 1900 (less loss), and not included in that year			5,800	2,950	
Total			121,258	25,642	(146,900)
Deduct remounts on the sea Dec 1901 not received by 31 Dec			10,000	1,000	(11,000)
Remounts from overseas received during 1901			111,258	24,642	(135,900)
Additional horses arrived into the country with reinforcements as follows:					
Six Cavalry Regiments			3,300		
Colonial Contingents			6,300		
After deducting loss at sea, total			9,250		
Grand Total (111,258 + 9,250)			120,508	24,642	(145,150)

It is equally as difficult to provide accurate and meaningful figures for losses during the war. The dead loss (not including wastage from sickness and injury, or any other animals than those paid for out of the public purse), sustained during 1901 by this immense number of animals was 142,603 horses and 14,433 mules, an average of 387 horses and about 40 mules per day. Monthly wastage varied; at the end of 1900 and again in April 1901, it was reported as 25%. The dead loss in horses in 1901 was 5.6%, per month and with a general 25% monthly wastage; 19.4% (41,400) were sick and debilitated. Approximately 20,000 went to hospital, and 21,000 to debility farms, or back to remount depots. In round figures, the mean loss in horses and mules every month during the year 1901 was:[96]

Monthly:

Deaths and destructions	Horses	11,600
	Mules	1,200
Sick, debilitated and weary		41,400
Total Wastage		54,200

Accurate information about the available motive and striking power of a force (details of losses and requirements in the field) was crucial in planning a force's potential for future action.

As with many statistics, where the basis for calculation is unknown, it is hard to obtain accurate figures for losses. Neither the Royal Commission, nor the Court of Enquiry, did more than touch upon the whole question of losses in the field. Not until early 1900, were army orders issued for the collection of casualty returns. The collection of this information did not form part of pre-war planning and was therefore introduced during the pressure of active service; when less than half the units ever saw the orders issued from Headquarters. The one exception was the Cavalry Division under Gen. French, when it existed as a separate command. The most complete and valuable information was furnished by the SVO Capt. Blenkinsop, whose figures for wear and tear from the Modder River in February, 1900, to Pretoria in December, 1900, formed the statistical basis for Smith's history of the Cavalry. The Remount Department assumed responsibility for collecting casualty returns, the AVD those for disease and injury. But, only a small proportion of veterinary staff had any knowledge of the statistical information required, or how to obtain it.[97]

Smith acknowledges that, as he calculated them, losses for a definite period probably lack a little in accuracy. However, the total loss of purchased animals for the entire period of the campaign is reasonably close. He calculates the total loss for horses in general, for the two and a half years of the war, at 66.8%, and for mules 35.3%; percentages which formed the basis for his estimate for total annual losses. His reported monthly dead loss at 5.6% for all horses, 2.9% for mules; in addition, temporary loss in the field was 19.4% for horses. The figure for mules was unknown. Total inefficiency among troops in the field amounted therefore to 25% a month.

96   Smith, 1919, pp.184-6; Cd.963, p. 47, Cable 73; Cd.994, Appendix F, p.368, Evidence of QMG, p.1, Q.18.
97   Smith, 1919, p.140; Cochrane, 1913, p.163; Head, 1903, p.299, reference records of 6th Inniskilling Dragoon Guards.

No table exists for the number of animals alive at any period, although Smith had hoped to obtain the information from a table given by Lord Kitchener to the Royal Commission. This return showed the state of monthly supplies throughout the war and number of animals for which forage was required, but without differentiating between horses and mules. The return was an estimate of probable requirements; the numbers given were only a guess of what might exist two, or three months later. Had this return been correct, it would have shown the loss for any period of the war, but after working with it for some time Smith discarded it.[98] He gives the total dead loss for the war exclusive of those "picked up" in South Africa as:

(Dead Loss)	Horses	Mules
1899-1900	110,028	29,113
1901	142,603	14,433
1902	73,442	7,853
Totals	326,073 (66.9%)	51,399 (35.4%)

In evidence before the Royal Commission, Mansfield Clarke, states 347,007 horses (67%) and 53,339 mules and donkeys were "expended during the campaign", and Col. Deane (later Director of the Army Remount Department in India), gives 120% losses during the war. Amery gives a total loss ("perished") for horses of 350,000 and 50,000 mules but does not state how these figures were arrived at. In addition, a minimum of 195,000 oxen were lost; 70,000, or 46.6% in the first 15 months of the war.[99]

Amery gave the figures for losses at sea as 13,000 horses and 2,000 mules. Losses were sustained because of accidents aboard ship, or on loading and unloading, weather, type and standard of fittings on board ship, and care on the voyage. Smith and Mansfield Clarke give the total number of 352,353 horses embarked from all ports to South Africa, of which, 13,144 died, or were destroyed on the passage, a loss of 3.7%. However, in some cases these figures and those for mules, include losses prior to embarkation. The total number of mules embarked was 105,491 of which 2,816 died, or were destroyed at sea, a loss of 2.7%. Shipping losses from each country varied considerably.[100]

98 Smith, 1919, p.142; Lord Kitchener to Royal Commission, Cd.1790, Q.190, p.9; Cd.1792, Appendix34, pp.240-41.
99 Smith, 1919, pp.226-229; Mansfield Clarke, Cd.1789, Vol. XL, p.97; Cd.1792, Appendix 38, p.258; Cd.1791, Col. Deane, member Yeomanry Committee, p.44, Q13083; Amery, 1909, Vol.VI, pp.417-8; For oxen see Col.Richardson, Deputy Adjutant General for Supplies and Transport, Cd.1790, p.139, Q339.1
100 Amery, 1909, Vol. VI, p.428; Smith, 1919, p.260-61; Mansfield Clarke, Cd.1789, Vol. XL, p.97; Cd.1792, Appendix No.38, p.258, covers the whole period of war; but does not include Yeomanry horses; Cd.994 pp.210-12, 326; Cd.963, pp.30-32, tables A, B, C; Page, 1976, p.322.

Assessment of the Remount and Veterinary Services During the War

It would appear most writers only refer to the Remount Department within in the context of the actual provision of horses and not their care once with the Army. They do not, therefore, including the crucial, but subordinate work of the AVD.

Galvayne (Hon-Lt. with Remounts) reflected that he had "no personal feelings against the Remount Department", he had "not sought to give an additional edge to an unpleasant truth," that the Department, as at first organised, was greatly to blame for the duration of the war. Page wrote that only in the Remount Department was there a demonstrable failure to adequately serve the needs of the Army. The Department suffered, like other supply depots, from a lack of preparation and an assumption that all future wars would be contained within the scope envisaged by the Stanhope Memorandum.[101] Page questions the ability and leadership of Truman, IGR at the WO, considering that unlike heads of other departments, he lacked the resource to cope with an exceptionally difficult situation, and was slow-witted even for normal activity. A view easily formulated if one considered the relatively new Remount Department of no great consequence within the peacetime army structure. Tomkinson (MP for Cheshire, Crewe), wondered how Truman "ever got into the position", being "one of the most unhorsey men in the whole service".[102] Anglesey, however, takes the opposite view, that Truman was largely responsible for a feat of organisation unparalleled in the military annals of the world. Col. Deane, informed the Royal Commission, that Truman was mainly responsible for the successful operations of the war.[103] Accusations of corruption were made against the Remount Department with attempts to lay the blame on Truman.

When Truman refused to resign on grounds of incompetence, Lord Roberts offered him a Court of Enquiry. This was held whilst military operations were still taking place and cannot have done much for the morale of an already overworked Department. None of the fraud charges were substantiated and Truman was acquitted from personal blame. The Report states that much of the popular feeling against the Department was probably due to the mistaken idea, attributed to Truman and the Department, of taking responsibility for the actions of the Yeomanry Committee. Galvayne, thought the leakage of public money, in buying remounts, was largely due to mere incompetence; he thought and heard rumours that bribery and 'bunce' (profit)

---

101 Galvayne, 1902, p.111, introduction; note page, 1976, p.343; Edward Stanhope, Secretary of State for War, December 1888, set out the overall strategic aims of the British Empire with the deployment of British forces.
102 Tomkinson, Hansard (C), 1902, Vol.CV, 17th March, (c) 287.
103 Anglesey, 1986, Vol. 4 p.289, quoting Mr. Balfour, Hansard (C), 1902, Vol.C11, 3rd February, (c) 240-44, part of a much lengthier debate on this matter; Deane, Cd.1791, p.44, Q13080.

were partial causes, but believed the purchase of remounts in South Africa, with very few exceptions, was entrusted to the wrong men.[104]

A detailed study of the campaign does suggest that the horse services in South Africa deserve greater credit than usually given. To these newly created departments, requiring initiative, drive and ability to adapt and develop in fast changing situations, fell the daunting task of wartime operations, when unprepared, in personnel, training and equipment, and an unprecedented scale of expansion. Their learning curve was steep, and upon men like Birkbeck, Cowans, Blenkinsop and Pringle, would fall responsibility for the horse services in the 1914-18 War.[105] Those in higher office and commanders in the field, were arguably to blame for a greater proportion of the suffering and losses; sending un-acclimatised and unconditioned animals into active service and failing to listen to the views of those with technical knowledge and experience.

One must question statements such as that made by Maj-Gen. French, that the Department at home had not done well and was the main cause of wastage in horse-flesh in the campaign. Col. Haig, in his evidence to the Royal Commission, thought it difficult to pass judgement on the Department; believing it had not been organised for supplying as many horses as required during the war and that the Army suffered as a consequence.[106] The supply of such a vast number of animals by the Department at the WO and its purchasing commissions, could be considered an administrative triumph. Working with a tiny staff in a cramped office, procuring in total about 620,000 horses, mules and donkeys worldwide, and some 76,830 remounts in Britain without damaging local economies.[107] It is important to note the additional responsibilities placed on the Department during the course of the war, which included, obtaining remounts for the Imperial Yeomanry (plus training cobs), Rhodesian Field Force and South African Constabulary, mules and horses for the Indian Government, and heavy demands from an increasing UK establishment.[108] During the war, 63 new batteries

---

104 Cd.993 (Report), Cd.994 (Evidence); ordered by the C in C and assembled on 1st March 1902. The Order was signed on 20th February 1902 and reported 22nd August 1902. 56 meetings were held and 59 witnesses examined. The President was Gen. Sir Robert Biddulph; also WO32/8758 and 8760, 'Court of Enquiry Remounts, Proceedings for Parliament,' correspondence within the WO as to what should be published; Cd.993, p.34; Galvayne, 1902, pp.57; Cd.882 (Welby), pp.3-8; Cd.1789, pp.97-99.

105 See Appendix I.

106 French G, 1937, p.21; Haig, Cd 1791, p.403(h) Remount Department; Cd.1791, Evidence Col. Deane, 1901, p.44

107 Cd.1789, p.97; Cd.1792, pp.258-61, Appendix 38a (38); Amery, 1909, Vol.VI, pp.417-19; Page, 1976, p.363; WO33/271, pp.10, 53-56; Cd.1791, p.44. No one set of tables given in official tables, or by later authors, agrees in detail on all figures.

108 The Rhodesian Field Force (about 5,000) was raised in 1900, commanded by Gen. Frederick Carrington, and intended to provide protection for the colony of Rhodesia. The Rhodesia Regiment, Southern Rhodesia Volunteers and the regular members of the British South Africa Company were all part of Col. Plumer's Force (serving alongside

of Artillery and five depots were formed at home and completely horsed, without interfering with the steady supply of animals to South Africa.[109] Transporting horses from foreign and colonial ports was also the Department's responsibility, including the chartering of all vessels, with their fittings and providing attendants.

Truman gives the Remount Establishment on 1st April 1899 as:

- Headquarters (WO, London) – the IGR, one AIR, one DAAG (not rated as HQ staff), one superintending clerk and four clerks.
- Woolwich: one AIR for remounting the Artillery, Engineers and Transport, assisted by one staff captain and two veterinary surgeons, and a company of the ASC commanded by a QM; one remount depot for 130 horses.
- Ireland: one AIR, one staff captain, one veterinary surgeon and a company of the ASC commanded by a Quartermaster; Dublin depot had accommodation for 78 horses and Lusk for 20.

By the first week of October 1899 it was clear to Truman that numbers of staff in the Department would be totally inadequate for the work ahead. The enormous quantities of paperwork, telegrams and post and personal contact, involving himself and his staff, was detrimental to more urgent business. The number of remount staff at the WO was subsequently increased with the employment of three lieutenant-colonels of cavalry regiments to assist purchasing under the Registration Scheme. The amendments were:

- one Lieutenant Colonel appointed from his regiment
- two other Lieutenant Colonels rejoining their Corps, replaced by qualified officers from the reserve list.
- the DAAG rejoined his regiment for active service, replaced by an officer from the Staff College (graded an AAG)
- in addition a staff captain was added from the reserve, and three clerks.

Ultimately five officers and nine clerks were necessary to deal with the official correspondence in London.[110]

If the Department's responsibilities at the WO were simply those of locating and safely shipping as many remounts as required, then it was successful. If, however, the quality of those remounts was also part of their responsibility, then serious questions must be raised. The lack of preparation and planning for a major conflict, anywhere other than in Europe, was, without doubt, a gross error for a colonial power, as was

several Australian units) in the Western Transvaal. Capt. John Moore, AVD served as veterinary officer (later Maj-Gen Sir John Moore DGAVC, BEF).
109 WO33/271, p.31.
110 Cd 1792, Appendix 33, p.12; WO33/271, pp.3, 11, 17-19, 28.

the lack of available information on the world's horse supply for military purposes. Not until July 1899, when war was a possibility, were steps taken to ascertain what animals could be purchased from abroad.[111] With hindsight, the expectations on this new Department were possibly too high. Smith argued that if the AVD been listened to, and taken into equal partnership, and had the Remount Department not taken over veterinary duties, for which they did not have the expertise, many disasters would have been avoided. Truman's success in exceeding demand has been viewed as making him responsible for some of the cruel wastage that occurred; but should he take the blame for activities in South Africa, where remount work was exclusively controlled by the GOC-in-C?[112] According to Truman, the general system on which remounting the Army was based, the staff at his disposal and preparations, were approved by the Secretary of State and considered adequate for such contingencies as might have arisen during the previous twelve years. The formation of a large reserve of animals, available immediately on the outbreak of hostilities, was never contemplated, which, with hindsight, he much regretted. It was quite evident to Truman that pre-war preparations would not have been permitted at the time, owing to political considerations, as no additional money was made available to the Department prior to the outbreak of war. The inevitable result was troops being mobilized and reaching the seat of war, before a sufficient reserve of animals and support services could be provided.

The Court of Enquiry provides valuable information about the Department but does not give a full picture of its work; for example, only three of the 59 witnesses were veterinary officers, men who had direct experience of the remount issues. Instructions to the Court contain nine terms of reference, but only dealt with the purchase and transport of animals to the point where they arrived in South Africa. The Court had no authority to go any further, having been established to look into alleged fraud and Truman's conduct; it does not therefore deal with causes of wastage at the seat of war. The Court made a number of general remarks about the Department, including the unprecedented demands made upon it, accentuated by the extraordinary wastage in horseflesh and inability of the Department, as constituted, to expand efficiently in time of war. At the outset, the Department should have been placed under the control of a general officer appointed specifically for the purpose, with sufficient authority and influence to have prevented the issue of horses not ready for active service.[113] Practical difficulties appear to have affected the entire management of the Department's work and reputation such as: a deficiency of personnel in South Africa, and an inadequacy of accommodation at the headquarters premises in London, which lacked enough desk space for the clerical staff, especially when it expanded, and no quiet room to deal with transactions and number of applicants and visitors who visited the office.

111 See for example Cd.882, p.7.
112 WO33/271, pp.7-9.
113 Cd.993, pp.19-20; Cd.994.

The distance from the QMG's buildings meant the Department was cut off from convenient communication with the WO.

The Opinion of the Court was, on the whole, favourable to the Department.[114] It found that the system of buying horses at home, whilst it did not provide a large reserve of horses, was economical, and suited conditions in the country. The Horse Registration Scheme, in providing a small reserve of horses, proved successful, although it had not met all military requirements, such as the changing requirements for riding horses. The full registered reserve had not been called out, and those that had, were replaced by fresh registrations, which were available, if need arose, to mobilise for home defence. Draught horses taken from the reserve were highly praised for their work and endurance in South Africa.

In purchasing abroad the Court thought the system adopted served the country well, but at the outset, the Department should have made greater use of local assistance and not relied exclusively on its own knowledge and methods. British Ambassadors should have been more acquainted with Remount Commissions and greater use made of military attaches. Officers employed in purchasing at home and abroad were found suitable and competent, with only three exceptions, but prompt action had been taken in withdrawing unsuitable officers. However, Galvayne considered purchasing officers were not businessmen, or horse dealers, but often infantry reserve officers who knew little about actually buying horses, and were taken advantage of by foreign and British dealers. For Col. Deane, "it was a great mistake to let officers buy horses abroad, as they were not trained or skilled in it".[115] Only the shipping of animals from Gibraltar was considered faulty and heavily criticised. Some confusion existed over the status and role of officers, ships' masters, and the lack of information supplied to conducting and veterinary officers. There were no complaints against veterinary officers of the AVD employed on board ship, but not all civilian veterinary surgeons were viewed as satisfactory. No blame was attached to the Remount Department, as so great was the shortage of officers, that practically anyone who offered his services had to be taken. Sea transport was considered good, with prompt and adequate measures taken to prevent the recurrence of any serious complaints about the condition of animals on landing. A 'voyage' report, completed by conducting and veterinary officers for the QMG, was passed to the IGR, and the AIR in South Africa forwarded letters and reports on the condition of horses disembarked. In 1901, 'offloading' reports were introduced for use by remount officers at ports of disembarkation. Serious complaints were reported by telegraph and shortcomings reported to the Admiralty and purchasing commissions.

The Court found it necessary to compare the Department in peace and war when considering whether it had shown due care and ability in dealing with the demand for

---

114 Cd.993, pp.21-34.
115 Galvayne, 1902, pp.42-57; Cd.1791, p.42, A13052, Deane; Lane, 1912, p.40, ref. Purchasing Officers; Cd.993, Appendix D, pp.336-9, for 'Instructions to Purchasing and Conducting Officers, Voyage Report'.

remounts, taking into account the great strain placed upon it. The peacetime situation has already been referred to. The Court found that speedy, or momentous decisions were never called for, as the Department was one of those whose presence was least needed at the WO; its business was not of a nature that required instant decision making. With the outbreak of war, the Department's situation suddenly changed and the IGR was suddenly required at the WO. Truman stated that the HQ office of the Department was in Victoria Street, a mile from the WO, his attendance at Pall Mall therefore caused a constant hindrance to work and many delays at critical times. The Department provided animals for the largest ever British army, with the largest proportion of mounted men; operating at an immense distance from its base and over the greatest extent of country any force had previously operated. Demands were of an unprecedented magnitude and totally unforeseen. The IGR was communicating with purchasing officers on four continents, in at least seven countries, with remount and other officers in South Africa, other branches of the WO, civilians and remount staff at home; in addition to increased remount responsibilities at the WO. The Court found that to carry out these duties required a combination of qualities rarely found in one man: great powers of organisation, extraordinary foresight, previous experience of business on a large scale and full knowledge of the resources and conditions of horse markets at home and abroad. When the Secretary of State became uneasy about the management of the Department, the QMG had replied, about the qualities of the IGR, that he did not consider him a man of exceptional ability; that he was doing work of unprecedented difficulty to the best of his ability and gave his whole time not sparing himself in anyway. The QMG believed in the IGR's absolute integrity. Truman was verbally a poor communicator and therefore did not do himself, or his Department, justice.[116]

The Court considered that the IGR and his Department, given the unprecedented demands made upon them, met with extraordinary success in achieving the task assigned to it, as many of the errors and failings were related to the magnitude of the operations. Success, meaning the number of horses actually despatched to South Africa, was in excess of demand. When horses were deficient at the front, it was not due to failure by the Department at the WO to land them on the coast, but the failure of those in command in South Africa. Here the many other demands on railway systems and exigencies of the war compelled the issue of remounts before they were acclimatised, or fit for work with the consequent excessive wastage. It was the way in which animals were treated in South Africa that wrecked the supply to the Army, for example, the combined overwork and starvation in the Paardeberg campaign (Orange Free State, February-March 1900), and with it, the sudden destruction of trained horses of the Cavalry and Artillery. From this shock and resulting strain, with no time for recuperation, the Remount Department never recovered. Under the prevailing conditions, the immediate issue of animals after long sea and rail journeys, using

116 WO32/271, p.11; Cd 993 pp.20, 33-34.

inexperienced and incompetent men in depots, and inefficient horse management by newly mounted units, all meant few animals survived for very long.

Lt- Col. Arthur Middleton arrived in Natal on 1st January, 1901 (in 1900 Middleton was a staff officer on the Midland Line at Port Elizabeth), taking charge of remounts with the departure of Col. Stevenson in November 1900. Middleton remained in post for 14 months, departing for England, February 1902. In his evidence before the Court of Enquiry Middleton stated that there was never any lack of imported remounts and considered the enormous wastage was due entirely to the readiness with which they were supplied. As there was always an influx of horses into Natal anybody who wanted a horse got one the next day, whether really entitled to one or not.[117] New horses meant getting rid of the war weary ones in order to keep down the forage bill, only leading to further wastage. The new horse appeared to be the Army panacea for meeting casualties, but so readily available was the supply, the moral obligation of looking after an animal was neglected, wastage increased and efficiency diminished.[118] In order to save forage the Department urged and carried out the destruction of trained but debilitated troop horses, not realising that when restored to health they were worth any number of soft (carrying fat, muscles not hardened for regular work), untrained, imported remounts. One of the earliest complaints made by the Department against the AVD was that they would not destroy a sufficient number of horses, considered useless for campaigning and only filled hospitals and ate valuable rations. In contrast, an article in the *St James Gazette* stated there was truth in reports that the one notion the AVD had of curing a horse was to shoot it.[119] In his article, *Veterinary Hospitals During the War*, Maj. Cochrane, AVC, considered the financial relationship between the value of a sick horse admitted to a hospital, the daily expense for keep and treatment, and length of time it was profitable to keep a horse under treatment, rather than destroy it immediately. From his experiences during the war, he considered veterinary officers did not always look at the financial aspect, which, if they had appreciated this more fully, considerably greater savings could have been made.[120] During the early period of the war, the AIR was so imbued with the wisdom, or necessity, of carrying out Buller's ration policy, enforced by the Department of Supply, that he instructed his staff officer to enforce the destruction of animals, against veterinary advice.

Unfortunately, the management of depots and Remount Department in South Africa, was generally not efficient. Neither Lord Roberts nor his Chief of Staff appeared to realise the necessity for organising a Remount Department upon which, the mobility of their troops depended. There was no directing head, system of inspection, or uniformity of management. In Amery's view, the Department presented

117 Cd.994, p.124, Q3767-3776, also p.125, Q3804-5.
118 Smith, 1919, p.134; Head, 1903, p.306; Cochrane, 1913, p.166.
119 *St James Gazette*, in Galvayne, 1902, p.70; Cd.963, p.7; Smith, 1919, pp.203, 279, 284, 134; Cd.994, p.13, Q222-223, evidence of Prince Francis of Teck, Staff Captain in Dublin until December 1899 when he moved to a remount depot in South Africa.
120 Cochrane, 1913, p.162.

an unfavourable contrast with other branches of the Army and wholly deserved the charges of lack of foresight and inefficiency subsequently brought against its administration at the WO. Smith disagrees with this view, believing Amery could not have formed any notion of what remount depots achieved under extraordinary adverse circumstances, nor seen a scratch depot at work performing in a month, as much work as fell in peacetime to remount depots in the UK in three years. Remount officers were worked hard, were bullied and badgered by everyone; not knowing from whom to take often conflicting and changing orders. Their hands were tied, yet they were frequently blamed for faults and mistakes, not of their own making and beyond their control. In the early period of the war, red tape was responsible for many of the delays and failures in responding to demands from the front. Birkbeck stated that officers sent for duty to depots were generally selected not for their knowledge of horsemastership, or experience of the duties they were to undertake, but because they had failed in the field, or there was no place for them at the front; the Department lived from hand to mouth. Galvayne believed that no one in England could realise the trials and hardships endured by remount officers in the early days of the war, and the AVD's lack of preparedness was a serious error of the Remount Department and the QMG.[121] The work was bad, it could not have been otherwise with a small staff, untrained officers unknown to each other and lacking organisation. The Department had no responsibility for the incompetent regimental officers, removed and placed in their depots, nor were the Authorities at home responsible for bad appointments in South Africa. Arguably, the central Remount Administration at the WO, defective as it was, could not have anticipated replacing the whole cavalry division in a month. Those responsible for starving horses were more to blame and not the Department, which was called upon to replace them in numbers beyond any conceivable peacetime planning. For all its faults the Department could not be blamed for difficulties it did not create and which existed outside the defects in its own organisation.

Birkbeck made some very frank comments on the little knowledge he had of remount work; the waste of public money by incompetent purchasing officers (but the only ones available) and ignorance of the peculiar conditions in South Africa. The Department would have performed much better at the beginning of the war if a force of trained remount officers had been immediately available, with experience of the country and its resources. Instead of which, there were those like himself, who arrived without the necessary technical knowledge of remount work and eager to do anything rather than remain at base, or on the lines of communication. "We have bought our knowledge at the expense of the public purse."[122] Smith comments that when this was written, Birkbeck was not aware that the skilled advice, and experience of the DGAVS had been rejected by the IGR.

---

121 Amery, 1909, Vol.VI, p.16; Smith, 1919, p.53; Birkbeck in Cd.963, p.4; Galvayne, 1902, p.115.
122 Birkbeck, Cd.963, p.22.

Birkbeck had written to the IGR, "I am all right, and do not mind the work, or the responsibility, but it is rather miserable seeing every one going up past one, half of them to command colonial corps and such like, when I know my own name has been put forward and refused because they say I cannot be spared from my present billet. However it has become too serious a business for anyone to think of their own personal considerations, and really I am quite fond of the job now, and would not care really to leave it, and I am given a staff officer now to run the office while I go away and inspect". In December 1900, he wrote to the Assistant Adjutant General Remounts (AAG), that he had just heard the King's Dragoon Guards were coming out. "Now comes the question, will I rejoin or stay at the remounts? I really do not know how anyone could take up the threads of the very complicated machine from me. I have endeavoured to decentralise it, but there is so much that I must do myself. I get on with (...?...) and I believe he has confidence in me. In fact, I really think my defection would be rather an upset all round."(the space is in the original text). Haig wrote that no one could have done the remount work as well as Birkbeck.

Smith could not help but admire the confession of ignorance and impotence, which from the beginning of the campaign had marked remount operations in South Africa. Birkbeck lacked knowledge but was not wanting in zeal and energy; he possessed a valuable capacity for organisation that supported his work throughout the war. With no experience of the work, he took on the largest remount operations known to any army since Napoleon's invasion of Russia in 1812. What he lacked was rank. As a junior officer, he had no authority over a general officer, yet was retained by the GOC-in-C at the Cape rather than being replaced with a senior officer. [123] Lord Robert's made the following recommendation in despatches concerning the "calls made upon the Remount department, under Maj.W.Birkbeck, 1st Dragoon Guards and HRH Capt. Prince Francis of Teck, have been quite abnormal ... the way in which all ranks have done their utmost to cope with difficulties, and profit by the experience gained in earlier parts of the Campaign, is certainly deserving of credit. The personnel sent by the Government of India proved of much value".[124]

The poor relationship between the Remount and AVD departments was an important factor in the failure to prevent the tragic waste of animals.[125] It was an issue that was not finally resolved until 1913, on the eve of the First World War, when the AVD was removed from its subordinate position under the Remount Department. Neither service, under the QMG, was prepared to accept subordination to the other. Though he placed on the shoulders of the AVD their full share of blame, Smith could not

123 Cd.963, p.22; Smith, 1919, p.122-5; Birkbeck to the IGR, Cd.994, Appendix F, p.363, and December 1900, Birkbeck to the AAG Remounts, WO, p.367; Haig, in Mann, 1924, p.334.
124 Lord Roberts, 2nd April 1901, *London Gazette* 16th April 1901, pp.2600-1.
125 Smith, 1919, p.114; Page, 1976, pp.318-9; Cochrane, 1913, p.169; Stevenson, Cd.994, p.89, Q.2828, 2946, does not refer to the work of his veterinary officer, Lt. W. G. Williams, AVD.

shut his eyes to the "evil genius of Remounts throughout the war". He considered the subordination of the AVD to Remounts was due to service prejudice. Whereas Birkbeck took a completely opposite view, considering the two services were so closely allied it was difficult to draw the line of demarcation between their spheres of action.[126] In the mind of the Army all questions connected with the living animal were remount questions, whether referring to questions of disease, or of health. The function of the Remount Department, in Smith's view, was merely finding the horses required and distributing them to the units; it was identical with the recruiting side of the Army. Yet, it was never considered that the recruiting department would assume the functions of the medical service, or be subordinate to it; what applied to the medical service should have equally applied to the veterinary service. There was nothing in common between the Remounts and Veterinary departments except that they both dealt with the horse. Even in army orders everything relating to veterinary matters was indexed under 'Remounts', 'horses', or 'Supply and Transport'. Birkbeck considered there should have been one head to control the general organisation of both Departments (a head of veterinary field hospitals, sick horse farms and remount depots and the disposal of animals returned from the front), a Staff and not a Departmental Officer, that is the AIR, not PVO.[127]

Col. Duck, in response to a question on the relationship between the two Departments, answered that it was very unsatisfactory and had been at variance on many points throughout most of the war; a situation, he thought that ought to be remedied.[128] Truman had placed unreasonable demands on the AVD to provide veterinary staff; the taking of one sixth of its strength for remount duty was the first cause of friction. Smith states the Director of Transport, had drawn up regulations for the treatment of animals on arrival in the country, for which there was no justification. This interference with the work of another branch of the service (the AVD), could only lead to friction and would never have been attempted with any other service. If Col. Rayment, PVO, failed to agree with the authorities in Cape Town, it was probably due to the attempted subordination of his service to another branch by placing it in a position of impotence, attempting to take his small trained hospital personnel, and the resentment created by his opinion on the ration question.[129] All added to a feeling of injustice and frustration at the attitude of the Transport Department in their unjustifiable interference with veterinary matters.

There was a clear lack of policy by the WO with regard to the AVD's lack of status, rank, authority, and subordination, which paralysed initiative and emasculated energy and zeal. Every request to create temporary administrative appointments and give

---

126 Smith, 1919, p.205; Galvayne, 1902, p.110, taken from Sir George Arthur; Birkbeck, Cd.963, p.7 in contrast to Smith, 1919, p.114.
127 Amery, 1909, Chapters V and VI, Supply and Transport and Remount Service, no mention of veterinary; Birkbeck Cd.963, p.7-8.
128 Cd.1790, pp.134-5, A3224, 3238-9.
129 Smith, 1919, p.116.

local ranks for civilian veterinary surgeons was met with refusal; neither foresight, nor judgement was lacking in the AVD at the WO. Without appropriate rank an officer had neither status, nor authority. Most of the difficulties that arose were predicted and might have been avoided had the AVD been permitted to work out its own form of organisation. In India it had been given a free hand and consequently was able, at a few days notice, to send veterinary stores and fully equipped hospitals to South Africa.[130] At the beginning of the war, the inexperienced Remount Department was given responsibility for everything connected with the provision and replacement of army animals, including collection and care of the sick. Experience taught the Department that bringing together healthy remounts and sick, debilitated animals was a recipe for disaster. It was clearly not the responsibility of the Remount Department to care for such animals.

The Remount Department had no knowledge, or experience of veterinary hospitals but, as these arrived from India, they were brought directly under their control. The representations of PVO's about the difficulties and frictions created by a system of dual control did help to reach a compromise. Hospitals, when practicable, were established in the vicinity of remount depots, removing veterinary establishments from subordination to the Remount Department. However, the AVD remained under the one administration, controlled by Remount officers endowed with authority, but with few exceptions, without training, or experience of highly specialised veterinary work. The inevitable result was the spread of disease, chaotic arrangements, confusing orders, absence of system and a veterinary service without authority, powerless to remedy the situation. The situation improved with experience, but Smith attributes this directly to the gradual extension of veterinary authority, not to the Remount Department. Yet, there were improvements in organisation and remount work generally. By 1902, more officers received training, gained experience in remount matters and entered the Department with some idea of its function. Smith praises the Mooi River remount depot (Natal, the Tugela, December 1899 to February 1900), for undertaking seasoning, conditioning and breaking of horses; the legitimate functions of a remount depot.[131]

The lack of any adequate system for horsing the South African Expeditionary Force was an important element in this discussion, as the Royal Commission reported that the IGR, with strictly limited functions and staffing, could do no more with the organisation at his disposal. The Remount Department would inevitably struggle in a major conflict when no provision had been made for expansion. Incredibly, in the planning for the mobilisation of two army corps, the IGR was to continue buying as in peacetime, through normal channels and from recognised dealers; supplying the demands of mobilisation and wastage of war. The Department was the victim of a complete failure to foresee the magnitude of the task involved in winning the war in

130 Ibid., pp.4, 48, 29, 117.
131 Galwayne, 1902, pp.113, 116; Smith, 1919, p.2; Cochrane, 1913, pp.166-7.

South Africa. Remounting, or supplying horses to an army was as important as the supply of foodstuffs and ordnance stores, or any other department of the Army.[132]

It is to these points, and failure of the High Command in South Africa, that one has to look for any failure in horse supply and care, and the military events of 1899 seen within their political context. Preparations for war were kept to a minimum so as not to alarm the Boers and precipitate aggression. Such a policy meant military preparations were restricted, including the landing of remounts in Cape Colony and Natal and the time required for their acclimatisation and forward movement. Scapegoats were found; bad horsemastership in the Cavalry, a hopeless Remount Department with Truman at its head, and a useless veterinary service. Leaving the blame here was not, however, to assist the Army in the future. Opposition by the Remount Department to veterinary autonomy died very hard and was not totally removed. Remount preparations for the War were inadequate and in the words of the Royal Commission "must not occur again".[133]

The Rt-Hon. St John Broderick, Secretary of State for War, stated in 1904 that steps for the total reorganisation of the Remount Department were being contemplated and would shortly be carried out. This was linked no doubt, to a reference to a new system, coming into operation as Truman retired on reaching his age limit; the most convenient time to make significant changes.[134]

In the words of Lt. Head, AVD, "I hope next time we may do better," but the final words should be those from the memorial at Fort Nonquai, Eshowe, to the 480,00 horses and mules killed and wounded during the Anglo-Boer South African War 1899-1902:[135]

"In a cause of which they knew nothing"

---

132 Cd.1791, p.558, Q21831.
133 Ibid.; Smith, 1919, p.74.
134 Cd.1791, ibid.
135 Head, 1903, p.310; I am grateful to Zameka Yamile and Elizabeth Mazibuko, Zululand Historical Museum, Eshowe, for the Anglo-Boer War Horse memorial details.

Part Two

Between the Wars 1902-1914

THE HORSE. "I SAY, THEY WON'T WANT ME AT ALL SOON, I'M AFRAID!"
THE CAT. "CHEER UP, OLD FELLOW! THE MOUSE-TRAP DIDN'T DO AWAY WITH ME."

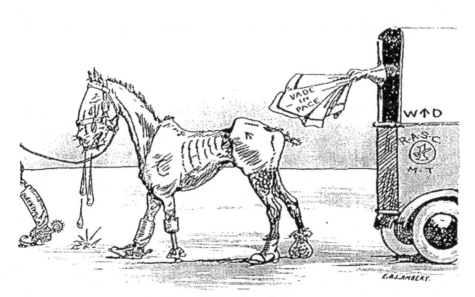

Army Service Corps Journal, *October 1913, p.286*

The Passing of the Horse Transport.

Army Service Corps Journal, *(Young, M.H.G., 'Centenary Book')*

3

Reorganisation of the Remount and Veterinary Services

The power of an army as a striking force depends on its mobility. Mobility is largely dependent on the suitability and fitness of animals for army work.[1]

The disasters that befell the Army during 1899-1902 triggered demands for military reform and the Remount Department did not escape scrutiny. It received severe criticism during and after the war as its pre-war provision and planning were considered to be inadequate. The heavy losses of 1901 were viewed as a 'Remount Scandal' with grave dissatisfaction about the methods sanctioned by the WO for the purchase of horses overseas. A number of official investigations showed that many of the persistent criticisms against the Department were unfounded. Parliamentary debates, recorded in Hansard are illuminating, but the important investigations are the:

- August 1901 *Report of the Committee on Horse Purchase in Austro-Hungary*, (Sir Charles Welby, Cd882)
- June 1901 *Report of the Remount Commission*
- 1902 *Report of the Committee Appointed by the Secretary of State for War to Consider the Supply of Remounts for the Army*, (Lord Stanley)
- 1902 *Court of Enquiry into the Administration of the Army Remount Department since January 1899*, (Biddulph; Cd.993)
- 1902 *Army (Remounts) Reports, Statistical Tables and Telegrams Received from South Africa, June 1899 to 22nd January 1902*, (Lt-Col Birkbeck, AIR; Cd 963)
- 1903 *Report of His Majesty's Commission Appointed to Inquire into the Military Preparations and Other Matters Concerned with the War in South Africa* (Elgin)
- 1903 Report on *An Account of the Work Done by the Remount Establishment of the War office During the South African Campaign 1899-1902* (Maj-Gen.W.R. Truman, IGR)

---

1 Field Marshall Douglas Haig, GHQ France, 19th September 1918, Foreword to Galtrey, 1918.

- 1902 *Reports by Officers Appointed by the Commander-in-Chief to Inquire into the Working of the Remount Department Abroad* (Cd 995).
- 1904 *Report of the War Office (Reconstitution) Committee* (Esher)[2]

The Welby Committee was requested to examine allegations made by Sir Blundell Maple (1845-1903, M.P for Dulwich), about bribes given to British officers in relation to the purchase of horses in Austro-Hungary. The Committee reported that there was no justification for any charges of bribery, or corrupt dealing and whatever errors of judgement might have been committed they were due to a desire to do the best for the public service. However, the Remount Department was criticised for its lack of peacetime planning in not studying the possibilities of different countries supplying remounts in time of an emergency. Birkbeck's Report of 1902 only added fuel to the Parliamentary debates for those supporting and criticising the Department and Truman in particular. Lord Stanley's Committee reported a need to increase expenditure for the maintenance of an expert remount staff, outlining the machinery of a system that would rely entirely upon the energy, foresight and judgement of the Department of the Inspector-General of Remounts (IGR). These Reports recommended some major alterations to the Department, which for some included the need to replace Maj-Gen. Truman, the IGR at the WO, with a competent Departmental head. However, the Court of Enquiry, instructed to consider the administration of the Department since the appointment of Truman in January 1899, judged that given the unprecedented demands made upon them and from the results of their work, Truman and the Department met with extraordinary success. The Court did criticise the errors and failings of the Department, many of which were judged to be inseparable from the magnitude of the operations with which they were engaged, but on the whole, concluded that the Department came out favourably from a long and searching enquiry. With this exoneration Truman could not be dismissed and he was allowed to continue until his retirement on grounds of his age, in July 1903.[3]

The 1903 *Report of His Majesty's Commission Appointed to Inquire into the Military Preparations and Other Matters Concerned with the War in South Africa* (Elgin), considered that after two Committees and a Court of Inquiry there was no need for further investigations into the Remount Department, or Truman himself.[4] Evidence given to all the Committees and Commissions showed that not all the problems experienced during the war, relating to the supply and care of animals, were the sole responsibility of the Department, or the AVC. The problems mentioned included: a lack of officers and men trained and skilled in remount and veterinary work, transportation,

---

2   Appendix I for Welby, Stanley and Biddulph.
3   Cd.882, pp.A1, A4; WO32/8756, Report of the Stanley Committee, 30th January 1902, p.ix; Cd.993, pp.iv, 34; Barnett, 1970, p.342; Hume, 1980; Dunlop, 1938, p.145; Page, 1976, p.355; Evidence of Brodrick, Cd.1791, p.588, Q21835.
4   Cd.1789, pp.97-98.

acclimatisation and overloading of horses, horsemastership and the treatment of animals in the field. To get the best out of animals, using them efficiently and effectively to maximise and save their strength and keep them fit requires a very considerable knowledge and experience from officers and other ranks. Although losses were high, the numbers actually killed in action were not comparatively higher than in previous wars. However, there were important lessons to be learnt such as introducing a planned system for the purchase of horses at home and abroad in times of peace and war, the provision of a better quality and quantity of fodder for working horses and the working relationship between the Department and AVC. Lord Roberts, commenting on the Commissions' Report wrote, 'we have now to see ... that the shortcomings brought to notice ... are remedied and that we are better prepared in the matter of Remounts when we next find ourselves engaged in war'.[5]

Between 1900 and 1905, two Secretaries of State for War, St John Brodrick (1900-1903) and his successor Arnold-Forster (1903-5) set in motion valuable reforms that formed the basis for the further changes made by Richard Haldane (Secretary of State for War, 1905-1912). These produced the small but professional British Army of 1914.[6] Brodrick began a process of decentralisation, the linking of auxiliary forces into the same general organisation as that of the Regular Army. In March 1901 he proposed a reorganization of the Army based on Six Army Corps, composed of Regular troops, Volunteers and the Militia, located in districts around the country. As a result of lessons learnt in South Africa, some of the reforms are attributable to less senior officers, as Dunlop suggests, the men of 1914 such as French, Plumer, Kiggell, Wilson and Haig, were already coming to the fore. He makes no mention of men like Cowans the future QMG, Smith, Moore and Pringle of the AVC and Birkbeck, Army Remount Department (ARD), even though he refers to "the many men, some in high places and some in obscurity, who laboured for fifteen years to prepare the British Army for a modern war".[7] It is into the latter category that reformers in the QMG's Branch appear to fall. It is not necessary to detail Haldane's reforms, some of which, such as the Home Command System (1905) and Territorial and Reserve Forces Act of 1907, provided the basis for reorganisation of the Remount and Veterinary Services, placed within the QMG's Branch.

Following recommendations of the 1904 *Report of the War Office (Reconstitution) Committee* (Esher),[8] for radical reforms to the British Army, including, the creation of a 'supreme' Army Council chaired by the Secretary of State for War, the abolition of the post of Commander-in-Chief replaced by a Chief of the General Staff (changed in 1907 to Chief of the Imperial General Staff),[9] a General Staff and a Committee of

5   In Hume, 2010, p.61; White, October 1921, p.562.
6   Appendix I – Broderick and Haldane.
7   Dunlop, 1938, pp.132-5, 147, 227, 305.
8   Cd.1932, 1968, 1968-1, 2002; Esher – Appendix I.
9   Originally recommended, along with the creation of a Naval and Military Council, by the 1890 Hartington Commission, Cd.5979; Dunlop, pp.198-9.

Imperial Defence to coordinate Army administration. The Six Army Corps' system was replaced with five Home Commands (1905); initially the Army Corps (Aldershot and Salisbury), Northern, Eastern, Western and Ireland. Eight Home Commands were ultimately formed: Aldershot, Southern, Eastern, Irish, Scottish, Northern, a London District and a Welsh and Midland Command (replaced in 1906 by the Western Command). [10] Each Command was headed by a GOC-in-Chief, assisted by Staff officers whose duties at Home Command headquarters were subdivided amongst administrative branches of the General Staff, the Adjutant General and the QMG. The Territorial and Reserve Forces Bill (1907) included the creation of a system of County Associations to administer the Territorial Force. The Esher Committee concluded that, the natural result of an inordinately centralised system was the destruction of initiative throughout the Army and therefore proposed a decentralised system of Directorates. The original seven directorates, under the QMG, were replaced by four, one of which was Transport and Remounts (under Maj-Gen. Heath, ASC, 1907-1911):

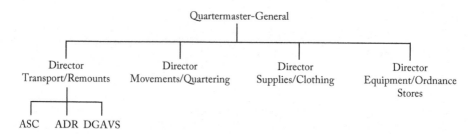

The post of IGR (founded in 1887) disappeared with remount staff being absorbed into the new directorate, with an Assistant Director of Remounts (ADR) heading the section under Col. J. Fowle (1908-1911), with a Staff Captain, Quartermaster and officer clerk. As the responsibility for Remounts would embrace the care and supervision of all animals employed in the field, whether as mounts, or for transport purposes, with units or in depots, the Committee considered that the proper position for the Director General Army Veterinary Service (DGAVS) was under the Director of Transport and Remounts. The AVD therefore remained a subordinate service to the ARD and was to remain so until 1913.[11]

These post-war reforms were part of a gradual movement away from the function of the British Army as established by the 1891 Stanhope Memorandum to Haldane's concept of an expeditionary force for use on the Continent, an overseas striking force.[12]

10   Cd.1413, 1903, The State of the Six Army Corps; Cd.1968, Part II, 26th February, pp.9-13.
11   Cd.2002, Part III, section II-3, p.9 and Appendix III; Hume, p.37, 1980; *Army Service Corps Journal*, April 1904, p.23, re Cd.1968, Sect.II, The QMG; Dunlop, 1938, pp.210-13.
12   Cd.607, *Stanhope Memorandum* written by Edward Stanhope (see Appendix I), Secretary

Stanhope's Memorandum included the provision of two army corps for home defence, with the secondary task of deploying one of these corps for service in a European war (in the belief that such a deployment was improbable). Haldane stated that, "we had therefore to provide for an Expeditionary Force, which we reckoned at six great divisions, fully equipped, and at least one cavalry division. We had also to make certain that this force could be mobilised and sent to the place where it might be required as rapidly as any German Force could be." This expeditionary force would be supported and expanded by a territorial organisation, in a decentralised scheme, administered directly by the military authorities. The Territorial forces were to be administered by County Associations as part of the National Army.[13] Haldane's very mobile expeditionary force, designed for rapid deployment in a European war, involved a significant reorganisation of the Army, which at its root required reliable and efficient mobility, principally horses. This is not to ignore the growing importance of rail and motor vehicles in a military capacity.[14] In 1911, when a German gunboat, the *Panther*, entered the Moroccan port of Agadir, alarming the British Government (the 'Agadir Crisis'), who saw it as act, or threat, by the German Government of exercising its naval power close to Gibraltar. In response, Haldane was confident enough with the progress of his reforms, to state that if the country decided to go to war, he was in a position to mobilise the Expeditionary Force and send it to the Continent. Dunlop states that in 1911, with money saved from the cancellation of the Army manoeuvres in East Anglia, final arrangements for mobilization were completed and that the Expeditionary Force as a fighting machine was ready.[15] This statement ignored totally the crucial principal factor in army mobility – the horse, the horse services and their readiness for such a war.

Army Remount Department

All the elements of this new fighting machine were not in place. Gen. Cowans, QMG, stated in 1912 that horses were the one weak spot.[16] Once again the provision of horses and transport were relegated to a position of obscurity in comparison to the actual 'fighting' elements. The Secretary of State for War was always being pressed to say that the Army was ready and the Army Council always pressing the QMG, but Cowans would not give the assurance until the horse problem was solved. In 1912 Maj. Lane,

---

of State for War, laying out the overall strategic aims of the British Empire, and the deployment of the British Army to meet them. Other priorities for the Army included: support for the UK civil power, reinforcements for India and provision of garrison units for fortresses, colonies and coaling stations.

13   Haldane, Hansard (C), Vol.153, March 1906, pp.655-686; Cd 2993, July 1906, pp.4-9; Dunlop, 1938, pp.242-3, from Haldane, 1929, p.188.
14   Hansard (C), 1906, Vol.153, 8th March, (c) p.674.
15   Dunlop, 1938, p.301; Chapman and Rutter, 1924, p.211.
16   MacMunn, 1930, p.104; Cowans (see Appendix I).

AVC, wrote that a great deal had been done during the previous decade to improve the organisation and strengthening of the Army, but the reorganisation of the horse question had not been carried out in proportion.[17] The Department had only been staffed to meet peacetime needs and lacked the ability for swift and effective expansion in time of war; this remained a major weakness in the Department's organisation. A significant development was the formation of a number of new remount depots and troops in the UK, providing the nucleus of trained manpower, as part of a mobilisation plan to facilitate rapid expansion.[18]

The 1901 Remount Committee recommended that the IGR be provided with a Remount Staff consisting of officers (other than quartermasters) specially selected from the active, or retired list of field officers, captains, or subalterns. The remainder of the Remount Establishment was to be organized as a Remount Section of the Army Service Corps. The Committee pointed out the hazards during a campaign of taking away officers and men employed on remount duties for other work, and recommended these duties be entrusted to the ASC (providing men for Remount Depots and Troops) and surplus Cavalry reservists, who had become less efficient as fighting men. Veterinary officers were to be made available to Remount Troops and placed under the control of the IGR, although in departmental veterinary matters they were subject to the DGAVD. Five remount depots were proposed, to be located within the geographical areas of the Six Army Corps at Reading, Southampton, Dublin and Lusk, Woolwich and York. Scotland and the North were to be covered by York. Dublin and Woolwich already existed.[19]

The Committee on the Supply of Remounts, reporting in 1902, was asked to consider:

- what number of horses were required, on average, during a normal year
- how many could be obtained in the UK
- what was the cost to purchase 500 or 1,000 annually from Canada, Cape Colony, or Australia
- what was the desirability of establishing remount depots in Army Corps districts
- whether the system of Registration could be extended.

The normal annual remount requirement was considered to be 2,500 although a small addition could be required in the future. The Committee placed emphasis on the fact that the small annual demand did not cause a difficulty; but the Department needed to be sufficiently elastic to obtain, at very short notice, at least ten times that number of mature horses in good condition on the outbreak of hostilities, and any number up to quarter of a million under war conditions. The annual peacetime

---

17   Lane, 1912 (a), p.47.
18   Evidence, Brodrick, Cd.1791, p.558, Q21831; Page, 1976, pp.355-6; Hume, 1980, p.37.
19   WO33/194, *Report of the Remount Committee*, June 1901, pp.3-4.

numbers could be supplied with the greatest ease in the UK, but an emphasis was required on the knowledge and organisation of existing sources of remounts and not the creation of fresh sources of supply. It was recommended that 500 horses should be purchased annually in Canada. There was a strong emphasis on the Department being constantly in practical touch and effectual command of the valuable colonial sources. The Committee were of the strong opinion that horses should be purchased at five years of age, the earliest age for being thoroughly serviceable for remount purposes; in some cases, such as an officer's charger, purchase could be made at three years, but with the animal remaining with the farmer until fit for use. The decision about where horses, once purchased, should be located was thought the responsibility of the military authorities, however, the Committee were of the opinion that the cheaper option was for them to go directly to regiments. In relation to veterinary hospitals, it was considered that maintaining the existing depots at Woolwich and Lusk (Ireland) was sufficient in peacetime. Experience from the 1899-1902 War suggested the existing registration scheme had been successful for the supply of draught, but not for riding horses. Although a system of registration was indispensable, it was not recommended to extend the maximum number allowed under the current scheme (14,500). This provided for cheapness and the first instalments in an emergency, allowing time for the purchasing machinery to be implemented. The Committee stressed the importance of a detailed knowledge of available sources of supply and the need for efficient remount purchasing officers, Assistant Inspectors of Remounts, (AIR), who had to be first class expert buyers.

In conclusion, the Committee recommended a decentralised system, with the UK being divided into five districts (two being in Ireland) according to horse populations, with a resident purchaser (AIR) attached to each, who had absolute control over purchase and registering operations. In an emergency AIRs were expected to form the nucleus of an extended purchasing system, registering reliable and fully qualified gentlemen who were prepared to assist in buying horses, for a fixed salary during their period of employment. They were not to engage serving yeomanry adjutants, but expert military, or civil, veterinary surgeons. The buyers were to be directly responsible to the IGR (WO). A resident expert purchaser was to be attached to the Staff of GOCs in Canada, South Africa and Australia. Stanley added that the Secretary of State was prepared to add an additional £100,000 for horse registration. His proposals saved the bulk of that sum with a total additional expenditure of only £9,000 annually on staff, independent of the existing Remount Establishment.[20]

The 1901 Remount Commission recommendation to increase the number of permanent depots in the UK to five, and later to six, in line with the newly created Home Commands was not accepted. In 1904, two new remount depots, Melton Mowbray and Arborfield (the latter valued at £4,500) were added to the peacetime

---

20   WO32/8756, *Report of the Committee on the Supply of Remounts* (Stanley), 1902; pp.i -ix; re expenditure, p.x Appendix, and Stanley's letter dated 6.12.01, attached to WO32/8756.

establishment. Hume writes that both were 'remount farms' for keeping horses at grass, grazing land with a few stables and agricultural buildings, staffed largely by civilians. At Dublin and Woolwich (formed under Army Order No.202, May 1888) horses were 'stable-kept in barracks'.[21] The Remount Establishment had been enlarged in 1891 with the addition of 'A' and 'B' Remount Companies (placed on the ASC Establishment); in March 1904 two additional companies, 'C' and 'D', were added, based at the Woolwich, Dublin and Lusk (a remount farm) depots. In 1911 the nomenclature of the four units was changed to 'AA,' 'BB,' 'CC' and 'DD'. Remount Companies, ASC, providing personnel for the depots, which were partly civilianised. They formed the basic remount units, which in the event of mobiliza- tion, would be expanded by soldiers recalled from the ASC reserve and cavalrymen unfit for active duty with their regiments.[22] Hume wrote that a simple and flex- ible organisation was eventually developed, with the Remount Squadron, forming the basis of all remount formations; it was an operational unit providing a mobile depot supplying remounts to units in the field. A squadron, was commanded by a major, or captain, with 200 all ranks, staffed and equipped to hold, and train if necessary, 500 horses. It could operate independently as a small remount depot, for example, an advanced or rest depot, or combine with other squadrons to form a large depot on the lines of communication.[23] A regular system of annual reports on all foreign horse markets, arranged through British Diplomatic missions abroad, was also established.[24]

War Office Lists for April 1908 (the last until July 1914) show the Remount Establishment within the QMG's Department (see opposite page).

In 1911 the Directorates in the QMG's Branch were revised. The Directorate of Transport and Remounts (Maj-Gen Heath), with the Army Transport and Remount Sections, and the Director General of Veterinary Services (DGAVS), what MacMunn called a 'Horse Directorate,' was broken up.[25] Maj. George MacMunn, DADR (WO) thought that concentrating all matters under the one director was sound. But his placing of the AVD under someone less than the QMG hurt the feelings of the profes- sion, which had made representations to Cowans, who for expediency, supported their views, and also those of the ASC that Supplies and Transport should be under one man. Heath's Directorate was split into two (QMG4 and QMG5), each under the QMG. QMG4 Remounts and Veterinary under Maj-Gen Birkbeck. Col. Fowle, the last Inspector of Remounts remained at the WO (as ADR until 1914), and QMG5

---

21 WO33/194, pp.3-4; Hume, 2010, p.66; Arborfield, BPP Army Appropriation Accounts, Vol.XVII, 1916, Paper 6-58.
22 Beadon, 1931, Vol.II, p.12; Hume, 1980, p.37; Army Order No.149, July 1891, p.16.
23 'War Establishments', 1918, Army Form G 1098-77 (Imperial War Museum); Hume, 1980, p.37; Remount Manual (War), 1923, p.9; Army Form G1098-77, Remount Squadron, September 1918.
24 Clarke, QMG to the Forces, Cd.1791, p.37, Q12919; Page, 1976, pp.355-6.
25 MacMunn, 1930, pp.91.

Transport and Supply (including horse transport). In 1911 Birkbeck made recommendations which, when adopted, diminished the ASC monopoly over the executive duties of remount companies, in that their personnel were not to be drawn solely from the Horse Transport Branch, but also from the cavalry and artillery. The companies remained part of the ASC with the men from other units transferred into them.[26]

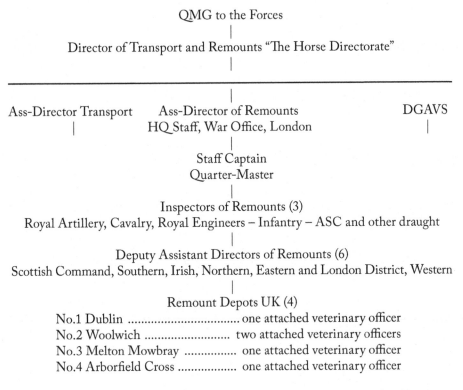

QMG to the Forces
|
Director of Transport and Remounts "The Horse Directorate"
|

Ass-Director Transport   Ass-Director of Remounts   DGAVS
| HQ Staff, War Office, London |
|
Staff Captain
Quarter-Master
|
Inspectors of Remounts (3)
Royal Artillery, Cavalry, Royal Engineers – Infantry – ASC and other draught
|
Deputy Assistant Directors of Remounts (6)
Scottish Command, Southern, Irish, Northern, Eastern and London District, Western
|
Remount Depots UK (4)
No.1 Dublin .... one attached veterinary officer
No.2 Woolwich .... two attached veterinary officers
No.3 Melton Mowbray .... one attached veterinary officer
No.4 Arborfield Cross .... one attached veterinary officer

There was also a Remount Establishment in South Africa, with an ADR and two remount depots on the Mooi River.

1911 would appear to be a watershed for the Remount Department and the horse question. In this year, with the reorganisation of the QMG's Branch, the Department became a separate directorate; with the AVC remaining subordinate to it. Three new men took office and vigorously tackled the horse problem, introducing reforms that took the Department into the 1914-18 War, Gen. John Cowans, Maj-Gen William Birkbeck, and Maj. George MacMunn, DADR (WO) who took responsibility for horse mobilisation; in association with Haldane the reforming Secretary of State

26   Beadon, 1931, p.12.

for War. MacMunn (previously serving in India), wrote that at the end of 1911, he received a letter from Cowans (then Director-General of the Territorial Force and QMG elect to the Forces. Sir Herbert Miles was QMG) informing him that arrangements for sending the Army to the Continent were nearly ready, with the exception of the horse question, which was quite untouched.[27] With no arrangement, or organisation in existence to provide for the very large number of horses required on mobilisation, a new post was being created in the Remount Directorate for horse mobilisation and Cowans wished MacMunn to fill it. Haig (due for the Aldershot Command) had already agreed to this request. MacMunn further adds that in his discussions with Haig the latter dwelt on the horse question, the requirement for nearly 160,000 horses in a very few days, which had not even been touched. So urgent was the situation MacMunn was expected to start work immediately.

Army Veterinary Service

The appalling experiences of the 1899-1902 War highlighted the urgent need for a rational and properly organised system of veterinary support in the field. The period between the wars was one of preparation and change. Maj-Gen. Sir John Moore, DGAVS with the BEF, wrote in 1930 of the imperfections under which the AVS laboured in 1914 on entering a war of such magnitude, commenting that the service desired the opportunity to prove its value and was not unprepared for war. The old system of veterinary duties largely performed by regimental veterinary officers, aided by regimental farriers, was totally inadequate for war on a large scale. It was replaced by a coherent AVS, with fully trained subordinate personnel for use in the field and hospitals, controlled by the Service. The 1899-1902 War had also highlighted the need for well-organised and adequate supplies of veterinary stores.[28]

In November 1902, on the suggestion of Maj-Gen. H. Thompson, DGAVD (replacing Col. Duck, October 1902), a committee was formed (Chairman, the Earl of Hardwicke, Parliamentary Under-Secretary of State), to enquire into conditions affecting officers of the AVD. Reporting in 1903, amongst its recommendations, sanctioned by Royal Warrant, 5th October 1903, was the creation of an AVC for NCOs, formed from men employed on veterinary duties, with voluntary transfers from the cavalry and artillery. Officers remained in the AVD. Two veterinary hospitals were sanctioned, one each at Woolwich and Aldershot. Maj-Gen. F Smith (DGAVS, 1907-1910), wrote that the Army itself was not favourable to these hospitals, as Maj. Ansell, Brigade-Major, 3rd Cavalry Brigade wrote, they aimed a direct blow at horsemastership among combatant officers and farriers. A cavalry commander protested against their presence in his barracks as it was not under his control. 1904 saw the addition of a quartermaster to the AVD to maintain veterinary stores at Woolwich.

27   MacMunn, 1930, pp.89-90.
28   Moore, 1930, Vol.1, p.10; Blenkinsop and Rainey, 1925, p.1; Forgrave, 1987, p.8.

In February 1905 the Treasury sanctioned an increase in NCOs and men (221), at the cost of losing fifteen officers, and a reorganisation into units to provide veterinary hospitals; firstly at Aldershot and Woolwich, then Bulford and the Curragh (April 1906, in County Kildare).[29]

The AVD (officers) and the AVC (NCOs and men) were amalgamated into one organisation, the AVC, by Royal Warrant, 15th February 1906. However, it would appear that the development of the AVC was not all plain sailing. Smith wrote that, "even the War Office did no more than was absolutely necessary to help the development of this young Service. Under-currents began to make themselves felt almost immediately, for example, a few months after publication of the Warrant, the Director of Transport and Remounts put forward a scheme of his own for veterinary reorganisation, for which Smith comments, "on whose prompting we do not know, but the wild scheme need not be followed any further, the intention was clear".[30]

Further important developments improved the military and technical efficiency of the Corps in preparation for war. On the question of veterinary stores, Smith stated that at a War Office conference, when all heads of departments were asked if their branch was ready for war, the DGAVS stated the Service was not, as he did not have any stores; this brought an immediate change in the situation. On mobilization, Woolwich and Aldershot were designated as training depots for drafts, with Woolwich the Corps depot and stores; a large mobilisation and reserve store was completed in 1907. Mobilization stores were also located at Aldershot, Bulford and the Curragh. Six sections of the AVC were kept in readiness for mobilization with a base veterinary store provided for in war establishments. A veterinary section was designed for 250 sick animals and located on lines of communication with a total of 104 personnel including: two veterinary officers (one on the peacetime establishment, the other on wartime establishment), one sergeant and farrier-sergeant, two shoeing-smiths, one saddler (only provided on mobilization), two corporals, 12 privates and 83 horsekeepers (specially enlisted, or Reserve, but only to be provided on mobilization).[31]

As part of Haldane's reforms a Special Reserve of Veterinary Officers was approved in 1909; and the AVC Territorial Force (TF), initially proposed by the Council of the Royal College of Veterinary Surgeons in 1908, was formed in 1910, and organised on the same basis as the Regular Army. Mobile Veterinary Sections (consisting of one officer and 24 men each) were created in 1913. These would be the most forward veterinary units for the evacuation of sick and injured animals from combat areas, linking field units and veterinary hospitals on the lines of communication. On mobilization

29   Army Order 180, November 1903; Smith, pp.208-11; Ansell, *Cavalry Journal*, 1907, Vol 2
      pp.245-6; Blenkinsop and Rainey 1925, pp.1-2; Forgrave, p.8.
30   Army Order 48 1906; Smith, 1927, p.210-11; Blenkinsop and Rainey, 1924, p.3.
31   Blenkinsop and Rainey 1925, p.3; Forgrave, 1987, p.8; Smith, 1927, p.211, 222; Ansell,
      1907, pp.245-6.

one unit was allotted for each cavalry brigade and infantry division in the BEF. In 1914 seven TF veterinary hospitals were created for mobilization.[32]

The first attempt to create a separate veterinary directorate under the QMG instead of the Director of Transport and Remounts was made in 1907. A compromise was reached, placing the DGAVS in direct communication with the QMG on all matters connected with officers. Subsequent attempts were made to obtain complete autonomy. In 1912 the Principal Veterinary and Administrative Veterinary Officers were re-designated Assistant Directors of Veterinary Services (ADVS). The impetus generated by improvements in the AVS continued after Smith's retirement under the new Director General Maj-Gen. R. Pringle (15th October 1910). In 1913 the Army Council sanctioned the DGAVS dealing directly with the QMG, not only on questions of personnel, but on all questions of administration affecting the AVS. He was to collaborate with the Director of Remounts on all general horse questions affecting the practice of the Army, as distinct from technical and professional questions. The 1914 WO Listings show the AVC, for the first time, as not subordinate to Remounts. As an administrative service of the Army, the AVC was included in two staff exercises during the summer of 1914 and in a special Veterinary Staff Exercise (three days at Aldershot) involving a series of operations set by the General Staff and in the Command Staff Exercise.[33]

To complete the war establishments of hospitals on mobilization of the BEF, the peace establishment was supplemented by 498 cavalry class "D" reservists, allotted to the AVC, as horsekeepers, or grooms (83 for each veterinary section).[34] Every effort was made to obtain commitment from approved civilian veterinary practitioners to serve with the AVC in the event of war, in a civilian capacity, for both Corps and remount duties.

After mobilisation the duties of AVC personnel in hospitals in the UK, were divided broadly into the veterinary care of horses that Regular units left behind as unfit to accompany the BEF, and care of sick of horses maintained in reserve units at home. The number of horses thought to be involved was approximately:

---

32   Army Order 181, 1909; Army Order 203, 1910, AVCTF; Army Order 66, 1914, TF hospitals; Blenkinsop and Rainey, 1925, p.5; Forgrave, 1987, p.9; Smith, p.214, 234.
33   Army Order 284, 1912; Army Order 402, 1913; WO Administrative Directory, 1913, p.68 and 1914, p.66; Forgrave, 1987, p.9; Smith, 1927, pp.216-7, 230-1, 234; Blenkinsop and Rainey, 1925, pp.4-5; Pringle – Appendix I; Moore, 1930, Vol.1, p.11.
34   Moore, 1930, Vol.1, p.10; Blenkinsop and Rainey, 1925, p.5.

Horses left behind by regular units	2,500
5% unfit of the horses obtained on mobilisation for the BEF	2,000
Total (sick horses)	4,500
14 Reserve Regiments	7,532
4 Royal Horse Artillery Brigades	780
12 Royal Field Artillery Brigades	1,728
Total (reserve of horses)	10,040

The total number of horses requiring veterinary treatment, among newly purchased remounts of Reserve units, was expected to be larger than among Regular units in peacetime. If so, existing hospitals would struggle to accommodate the 14,540 horses listed above. The establishment of veterinary personnel had been calculated on the numbers required to work the existing hospitals. At stations where more than one veterinary officer was listed, the proportion of officers to the number of horses was fixed at a maximum of one to 500, the proportion adopted in estimating the establishment of veterinary officers with the BEF. In addition, personnel had also to be found for administrative work in the Home Commands, administrative veterinary officers with territorial divisions and veterinary duties at embarkation depots.[35]

During the inter-war years the Corps had kept abreast of scientific and technical advances, and improved its organisation and administrative systems, so that on mobilisation and during the entire period of the 1914-18 War, the Corps and its equipment was generally adequate in design and detail. The Veterinary Field Manual (War) was prepared and ready for issue in August 1914, "every officer of our Service knew what his duties where in the Field", so that the outbreak of war in 1914, " found our Service prepared".[36]

35   WO33/612, p.33.
36   Smith, 1927, p.234.

4

"The Horse Question" and Mobilisation Scheme

---

*Armies exist on a different status in war and peace. In practically every nation the establish-
ment in peacetime is considerably less than it is in wartime, the difference between the two
being made up by the reserves which are either subsidised, or earmarked in time of peace. The
requirements of an army are considerably increased in wartime; the increased number of men
and animals and, increased scale of rations, expenditure of supplies e.g. ammunition. There
are therefore increased requirements in the way of transport necessitated by the outbreak of
war. Also, emphasis must be laid on the necessity of obtaining transport immediately. The
Army which can mobilize in the shortest of time gains an immense, decisive advantage.*[1]

The major question for military planners was whether there were sufficient horses in
the country, of the right class, to meet their needs on mobilisation and to incorporate
the rapidly developing motor vehicle into the transport system. In order to answer this
question, "the Horse Question", a system for a census and classification of horses was
required, set within an appropriate structure and legal framework for implementation. Once these matters were resolved a mobilisation scheme could be introduced
to provide horses for the Army in the event of war. Although the emphasis in this
chapter is primarily animals for the Cavalry and Artillery the question of horse supply
also impacted on the ASC, Royal Engineers and infantry units, both Regular and
Territorial Forces. Infantry units probably did not always get the most desirable of
animals and were possibly the least able to cope with the skills of horsemastership. The
use of mules and ponies for pack transport in military service was well established.

The Horse Question

The Stanley Committee reported that the normal annual army requirement for
remounts, under existing conditions, was 2,500, with possibly a small addition

---

1   Davidson, 1913, *ASCQ*, p.352.

required in the future. As listed in the Board of Agriculture's pamphlet (1912) they were made up of five distinct classes:[2]

- Household Cavalry and Cavalry of the Line
  (1,000 required annually in peacetime)
- Royal Artillery, Royal Engineers, Army Service Corps
  (about 1,360 annually for the three units in peacetime)
- Mounted Infantry
  (140. However, the mounted infantry were abolished in 1913)

This annual demand was a comparatively small matter and no difficulty was experienced in meeting it within the UK. Creating a sufficiently elastic remount department in the event of war was the fundamental problem. Whilst the peacetime annual demand was small, on the outbreak of hostilities the Remount Department had to obtain, at very short notice, ten times that number of mature horses in good condition. Furthermore, during a period of hostilities the Department would also be required to satisfy an indeterminate and fluctuating demand to replace wastage.

The problem was mobilising sufficient horses in the event of war, within ten days, for the Expeditionary and Territorial Forces and providing three months supply to replace wastage. The Army required a total of some 165,000 horses, fit and trained, and of the right class, type and stamp, to be in the right place at the right time; including an immediate reserve of horses for a planned wastage of 10% in the field: [3]

CLASS   Military classification to indicate purpose e.g. charger, troop horse, draught
        Riding   R1   Cavalry (Trooper and Chargers for Household and Line)
                    R2   Mounted Infantry, Yeomanry
        Light   LD1 Artillery
        Draught LD2 Transport
        Heavy Draught
        Pack   Light Draught (Ponies and Mules)
                 Heavy Draught
TYPE   Horse lineage e.g. Irish draught type; Hunter type
STAMP A horse's conformation, size and quality relative to intended purpose:
              speed, carrying capacity, height and weight

The photographs below are examples of horses of a specific classification and stamp, suitable for the task required of them. The cavalry troop (line) horse in 1912 was of a light, hunter type with substance and quality, 15.2 to 15.3 hands over four years of age. A Household Cavalry troop horse was larger and heavier, 16 hands at five years.

---

2   WO32/8756, Report, 1901, p.i; 'Types of Horses Suitable for the Army', revised edition 1912.
3   *Statistics*, 1922, p.861.

The Royal Engineers (RE) and ASC draught horses had to be able to trot with a good load but did not require much pace. A RE horse over four years would be 15.25 to 16 hands and for the ASC, 15.25 to 15.35. The Royal Field Artillery (RFA) horse had be able to fast trot over broken ground, a weight-carrying hunter type, it was heavier and did not require the quality and pace of the Royal Horse Artillery (RHA) animal. In 1912 the RHA looked for a horse of 15.2 hands to 15.3 hands at four years of age, and 15.25 to 16 hands at over four. It had to be able to gallop in a team, maintaining the pace for a considerable distance to move with cavalry. The BAF photograph of RHA 1912, shows a very plain pure bred Irish draft horse, purchased for £42. Horses of the modern King's Troop RHA, are a much finer, handsome peacetime animal when compared to their working predecessors involved in long periods of conflict and 'roughing it' on campaign. The 1912 RHA photograph is a useful example to show that even within this general classification, each horse in a sub-section gun team, although interchangeable, has a specialist role and therefore of a different stamp. Except for an officers charger, about 17 hands, all horses within a sub-section gun team are inter-changeable, including the accompanying ridden detached horses which can take their place within the traces. The six horses of the gun team perform three different functions requiring three different stamp of horse, the lead horse, centre and wheeler. The lead horse, between 15.2 and 16.3 hands or over, is lighter, more of a thoroughbred and supplies the speed for the team. The Centre horse, 15.2 to 15.3 hands is an all rounder and assists with the power. The wheeler or break horse is at the rear of the team closest to the gun, 15.1 to 15.2 hands. It is the powerhouse of the team, thick boned, stockier, heavier and slower, with a strong neck and thicker rear legs. All remounts begin their training as a centre horse, this being the least specialist role within the gun team.[4]

Lt. Lane, AVC, wrote of the absolute necessity of organising a much larger and extended system for horsing the Army, so that in the event of war a large supply of suitable horses and mules could be quickly procured.[5] He also highlighted the dangers of relying for this supply upon neutral foreign powers and sea transport. Haldane speaking in the House on mobilisation stated, "when we come to deal with horses we shall have to deal with them in a very serious fashion. It is *by far the weakest part of our whole army organisation*. We know that in the country, there is an abundance of excellent horses and that this abundance is likely to remain for many years to come." He had earlier proposed to substitute motor vehicles for horse transport on a large scale, greatly reducing the number of horses required on mobilisation.[6] The subject of horse mobilisation for a large army was, according to Maj. MacMunn, perhaps the most complicated for the administration of any modern army.[7] He saw the remount

---

4   I am grateful to Capt. Owen Beynon Brown, The King's troop, RHA and Capt Derren Payne, Defence Animal Centre.
5   Lane (see Appendix I), 1912, pp.38, 51; WO32/8756, p.vi.
6   Hansard (C), 1911, Vol.XXII, 14th March, (c) 2081-2 [author's italics] and 1st March, Vol.XXII, (c)379, for motor vehicles; Brunker, 1911.
7   MacMunn, 1914, p.433.

Cavalry Troop Horse, 1927. Required to be deep bodied, short legged and backed, well sprung ribs of the hunter type, light, active with substance and quality.
(Board of Agriculture and Fisheries, Types of Horses Suitable for Army Remounts, 1912)

Royal Engineers, 1912. This photograph shows a horse 12 years old, 15.3 hands, "a trifle plain about her quarters, but a useful sort, with plenty of strength, good shoulders and limbs".
(Board of Agriculture and Fisheries, Types of Horses Suitable for Army Remounts, 1912)

Army Service Corps, 1909. "A good stamp of slow draught horse for the ASC." Short legged, 15.2 hands, 8 years old.
(Board of Agriculture and Fisheries, Types of Horses Suitable for Army Remounts, 1909)

Royal Field Artillery, 1909 and 1912. A lead horse, 13 years old, 15.2 hands. "This horse can gallop, and looks as if he ought to have spent his life as a hunter; deep through the heart, with short legs, and the best of shoulders".
(Board of Agriculture and Fisheries, Types of Horses Suitable for Army Remounts, 1909, 1912)

Royal Horse Artillery, 1912. "A really good type of horse for the RHA." A four year old, 15.2 hands.
In fact it is a very plain pure bred Irish draft working horse of the period.
(Board of Agriculture and Fisheries, Types of Horses Suitable for Army Remounts, 1912)

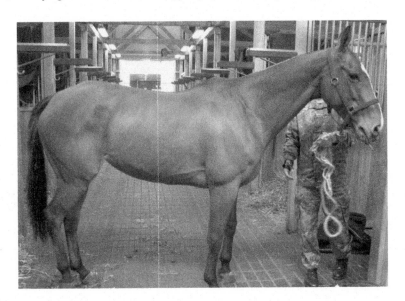

The King's Troop RHA, 2013. Lead Gun Horse. Note the difference in conformation between this
lead horse, placed at the front of the team, required for its speed and the Wheeler below.
Different animals for different purposes within the gun team.
(Author's collection with permission of The King's Troop, RHA)

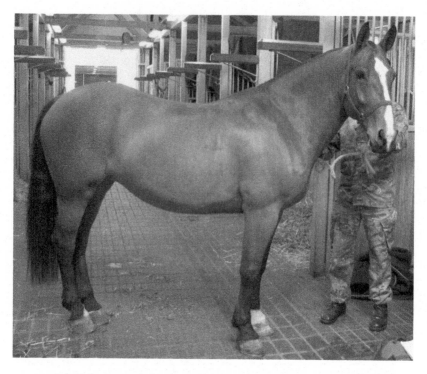

The King's Troop RHA, 2013. A wheeler or break horse, placed at the rear of the team closest to the gun, it is the powerhouse of the team.
(Author's collection with permission of The King's Troop, RHA)

The King's Troop RHA, 2013. E sub-section gun team of six horses and four 'detachment' riders at the front of the team with drawn swords.
(Author's collection with permission of The King's Troop, RHA)

problem as divided into two separate parts, the *live horse*, the actual purchase and well-being of the serving army horse, and the *paper horse*, the animal that in peacetime existed only on paper in forms and schedules.

It was with the latter that MacMunn was concerned. The peacetime establishment of horses in the UK was some 20,000; the wartime establishment, including the first reserve for the whole Expeditionary Force, was around 60,000 with a further 100,000 for the Territorial Force. This was for an army of some six infantry divisions, a cavalry division and independent brigade. To obtain the 140,000 horses required for mobilisation (in addition to the 20,000 on peacetime establishments) there were, in theory, 10,000 registered horses; the remaining 130,000 were expected to be obtained by impressment. Impressment required a complete machinery for selection and valuation, a workable law, civil structure and an accurate census of horses. MacMunn saw the first essential task as enumeration (census), followed by the organisation and machinery for impressment. The only element existing at the beginning of 1911 was a police census, which had been undertaken during 1909. Although the horse problem was far from resolved in 1911, the matter had not been ignored and a number of initiatives during 1909 had laid the foundation for further developments from 1911 onwards.[8]

Shortage of Cavalry Horses

The peacetime requirement at home for fully trained horses and men was considerably below war establishments. As a heavy burden would fall on the Cavalry Division (12 regiments) at the outset of active operations it was necessary to restrict to a minimum, the number of reservists and fresh horses taken into the ranks on mobilisation, or suffer the grave risk of initial defeat, as experienced in 1899.[9] The peacetime organisation of the cavalry at home had altered following recommendations by the Haig Committee in 1909. Reserve squadrons in regiments were abolished and six depots were formed for the training of recruits (five had been established by 1912, at Woolwich, Scarborough, Dublin, Seaforth and Bristol; Dunbar was still to be established). This change in organisation involved transferring to depots part of the personnel and horses previously included in regiments, resulting in a net decrease of 148 horses in Cavalry Establishments, but allowing for a central reserve of horses available to regiments on mobilisation. As a result of experiences gained in the 1909 army manoeuvres, the 1910-11 peacetime establishment of each cavalry regiment of the line was increased by 36 horses (and 18 men). In the financial years 1909-12, 73 'boarded out horses' were allowed per regiment and five horses in barracks (four for machine guns and one for riding). This gave each regiment a total increase of 37 riding horses in barracks, 73 riding horses boarded out and four draught horses. A 'Boarding Out system', largely

---

8   Hansard (C), 1909-1911.
9   Baden-Powell and Brunker, 1910, pp.1-2; Brunker, 1911, p.7; WO32/5073, Acland Committee Report, 1912 p.3.

based on an Austrian Army scheme, was introduced in 1909-10, with the purpose of assisting the supply of trained horses of the right class, which after training in cavalry ranks were boarded out (allotted) to farmers and others who undertook to produce them in good condition, or pay a fine if not, when required, for manoeuvres, or war. [10]

The 'Acland' Committee (Chairman F.D. Acland, MP, also Finance member of the Army Council) was appointed in March 1911 to consider and report on the extent and best means of remedying the shortage of trained horses for the Cavalry Division on mobilisation. It also included in its brief, the remaining two line cavalry regiments based at home, belonging to Army Troops, bringing the total number of cavalry regiments to 14, but not including the RHA, or RE units of the Cavalry Division. The eight Committee members included Maj-Gen. E. Allenby, Col. J. Fowle and Maj-Gen. Pringle. The eight witnesses included Maj-Gen. Heath, Director of Transport and Remounts, Brig-Gen. De la P. Gough, CO 3rd Cavalry Brigade, Col. F.S. Garratt, lately commanding 4th Cavalry Brigade, Lord Willoughby De Brooke, Master of Foxhounds, Warwick and Mr R. Tilling, of Thomas Tilling Ltd., Jobmasters, London. The Veterinary and Remounts Departments, GOC's Home Commands and Cavalry Brigades, and COs of cavalry regiments were also consulted.[11] After consultation and comparisons with foreign armies, the Committee made a number of far reaching recommendations, including the supply and training of remounts, increases in establishments and the supply of officers chargers. The effect of these recommendations was to provide the Cavalry Division with immediate access to properly trained and seasoned horses, so that the peacetime organisation would be able to meet mobilisation requirements and undertake an immediate and effective part in a war on the Continent. A regiment was expected to maintain 480 horses (469 with the regiment and 11 with the depot) plus 73 'boarded out' horses, a total of 553, with on average 50 being cast annually (see Glossary). On average about 700 remount riding horses were required annually by the cavalry at home.

The Committee issued an Interim Report for introducing a system in which riding horses were purchased for, and posted to, the cavalry at home, a matter the Committee considered should be dealt with immediately.[12] The system in use did not allow for uniformity as horses were purchased throughout the year, at between three and eight years of age, then posted immediately in small batches to regiments. This was not considered to be an efficient system as it shortened the service life of horses to less than nine years and made systematic and progressive training almost impossible. A new system was proposed whereby remounts were purchased annually, held at grass farms and then sent to regiments in one batch, about October each year. This 'Annual Batch System' was meant to remove the bad effects of the existing system and extend the service life of horses from less than eight, to eleven years. Remounts, on reaching their regiments, at between four and a half and six years of age, would

---

10   Haig Committee, 'Cavalry Organisation', Report, January 1909; WO33/5073, pp.1, 3, 10.
11   WO32/5073, Report 1912.
12   WO32/5073, Interim Report, 28th July 1911, pp.3-4, and Report 1912, paras.9-13.

receive 18 months systematic training. Some 62% of cavalry horses were purchased between the ages four and five years. The Committee recommended, that as far as possible, horses be purchased at four years of age, on 1st May (the official birthday of army horses), in the year issued to regiments, with the bulk of buying taking place before September of that year.[13] On purchase they were to be placed on grass farms. The Remount Department considered it necessary and cheaper to purchase all year round and although the Committee accepted this view, it recommended that as far as possible, purchasing should fit into the new system and be restricted to winter and spring. The QMG was convinced restrictions should not be placed on the purchase of horses all year round as prices would increase inconsequence.[14]

Regiments usually replaced veterinary castings and wastage from accidents throughout the year, the majority being cast after annual manoeuvres; under the 'Batch System' remounts would be supplied in October. Horses unfit for further service, being expensive to keep, were to be cast, or disposed of at once and any not fit for the cavalry, but fit for other units of the Service, such as transport, or the military police, were to be quickly transferred. Animals unfit to perform their duties were cast from the service, sold off alive, under three main groupings – Veterinary cases such as chronic disability; Remount cases, unsuitability from various causes such as unfit and prematurely worn out (under 15 years of age), crib-biting, failing to develop suitably, dangerous or unsafe to ride; finally, 'worn out', animals over 15 years of age that failed to meet the standards of fitness to perform one month's service in the field under continental conditions within its own branch of the service; there was no age limit if an animal met fitness requirements.[15]

The majority of cavalry remounts were purchased in Ireland, straight off grass, with many reaching their regiments badly shaken, in very poor condition and quite unfit for training, especially in winter and spring.[16] The Committee recognised the important fact that fit cavalry horses were not immediately available in civilian life and therefore recommended all purchases should be placed on grass farms for rest and conditioning, as with the existing farm at Lusk in Ireland. A strong recommendation was made for the acquisition of additional farms as they were seen as an economic way of holding new remounts, and for holding horses already with regiments who required care and rest. In 1911, a Mr Pinckard of Combe Court, Chiddingfield, Surrey, offered his farm ((Pinckard's Farm, Witley), as a gift, to the Government for 21 years, for use as a remount farm; later forming part of the Arborfield Remount Depot.[17]

The additional draught horses required on mobilisation did not require special military training, therefore, civilian horses registered, or requisitioned for the purpose

---

13   King's Regulations, para. 1216, 1912; Army Order 519, 1888, p.18.
14   WO32/5073, 116/GN/5238, QMG4, Minute (8a), 24th April 1908.
15   *Remount Regulations*, 1913, pp.2-3.
16   *VR*, 1913, Vol.XXVI, 13th December, p.375.
17   Brian Hill personnel correspondence; Hume, 1980, p.38.

could be taken immediately. An estimated three months training during peacetime was necessary for the seven pack animals required for the war establishment of each regiment.[18] As pack saddlery formed part of the machine gun equipment of cavalry no difficulty was anticipated in obtaining sufficient numbers of trained and experienced draught horses for regiments in peacetime; being replaced on mobilisation by registered, or requisitioned draught horses.

The 'Boarding Out System', which existed to secure fit horses on mobilisation by providing regiments with an additional number of horses over their peacetime establishment, without additional stabling or men, was acknowledged as being in an experimental stage. Improvements were to be made as needed, for example, a restriction of the boarding out area, to within a day's march (20 miles) from regimental headquarters was to be abolished.[19] Any necessary rail expenses in sending horses to allottees and bringing them in when required for manoeuvres and mobilisation, would be paid from Army funds. An amendment to the Army Act was approved by the Army Council in June 1913, so that private owners would have to dispatch impressed horses and vehicles to any point within ten miles of their residence. Motor vehicles were to be included, if delivery could be secured within 200 miles, if not, the QMG preferred to omit motor vehicles. The Council finally agreed to ten miles and 100 miles, not 200.[20] The cost of returning by train any horse found on inspection not to have been adequately cared for, was to be met by the allottee. Horses boarded out within a radius of about 30 miles of a headquarters were to be inspected by a regimental officer and any at a greater distance by a remount officer belonging to the Home Command. Horses were to be inspected half-yearly, with the exception of those seen by COs in the hunting field, and could not be used by allottees for racing and working trade vehicles. Preference was to be given to allottees who used horses for riding purposes, thereby encouraging allotment to Regular, and other officers. Horses were not to be boarded-out before the autumn of the year in which they became eight years old and not to be called in for training more frequently than once every two years, and then only for regimental and brigade training, not for manoeuvres. Allottees who kept a horse for about seven years, with favourable reports throughout, were allowed to keep it on reaching fifteen and a half years of age, on payment of £10 (the army received an average of £12 for cast cavalry horses). This was seen as an additional inducement to encourage more allottees to join the Scheme.

By implementing all these improvements the Committee hoped a proportion of boarded out horses would be fit for the ranks directly on mobilisation; whereas under the existing conditions, of the 73 horses per regiment boarded out, only the 48 required

---

18   Possibly including one for veterinary equipment and two per squadron for scouts or machine gun pack animals.
19   WO32/5073, paras. 28-38, pp.10-12.
20   WO32/5073, para.30, p.10; WO163/20, Army Council Précis No.789-79/4102, *Impressment of Horses on Mobilisation* and Army Council, 22nd June 1913 and Council meeting number 12, 14th March.

for first reinforcement, would be fit and available. This was a matter of some debate. The Inspector General Home Forces, Gen. C.W. Douglas, considered 50% of boarded out horses would be immediately fit for the ranks. The Army Council considered this probably an exaggerated estimate, even though reports from inspecting officers showed that boarded out horses were much better treated than previously. However, the Remount Statement allowed for only 26 of the 73 horses being available per regiment on mobilisation. In 1914, 32 boarders out of 83 would be considered fit to go into the ranks. Douglas reported in October, 1913, that in general, cavalry horses were of satisfactory quality, stable management was generally good, but too many remounts were still cut, bruised and permanently blemished during the first few weeks after being in regimental stables. The allotment of boarded out horses was considered to have progressed satisfactorily with an improvement in the class of allottees.[21] A request from the Territorial ASC, for a small proportion of civilian horses to be available for training, and a suggestion that TF Associations devise a system of modified registration to provide a supply of serviceable horses for drill purposes and for annual training camp, was not considered to be feasible to administrate and did not provide any financial benefits over the Boarding Out System.[22]

Remount depots maintained 150 horses of all arms of the service, available throughout the year to replace wastage. In addition to this number, the total annual wastage in horses (an average of 50 per regiment) was to be met from those held at farms during the summer months, for issue to regiments. In the event of this supply not meeting demand the Acland Committee suggested the creation of a 'pool' of horses, about 378, to meet the short fall. All remounts were required to undertake eighteen months training and no horses under six years of age were to take their final place in the ranks, or, to be sent on manoeuvres; nor, as laid down in the Remount Manual, were they to be regarded as fit to take their place in the ranks on the out-break of war. To meet the requirements for a spring or summer mobilization, without calling on boarded out horses, the Committee recommended that the peacetime establishment of horses in stables be increased immediately by 40 per regiment (20 were finally sanctioned, over two years, in the Estimates for 1912-13), with a gradual increase of boarded out horses, if feasible, to 120 (10 per regiment was sanctioned). If not feasible, or if the system proved unsatisfactory, the number of horses in stables was to be increased by 32 per regiment in addition to the 40. The age groups of horses placed in regiments under the existing system were to be balanced by transfers between regiments.[23]

---

21 WO163/20, Army Council (34/2204), p.447, Report of Inspector General Home Forces, Ref. 'Mobilisation of Cavalry'; WO163/20, 34/2228, 'Annual Report of the Inspector General Home Forces, October 1913, p.340.

22 WO32/5073, paras. 39-43, pp.12-13; also *ASCQ*, 1914, Vol.7, April, pp.184-5, ref. Territorial ASC.

23 WO32/5073, pp.4-5, 15-16, 19.

The regimental peacetime establishment of officers' horses, in 1912, was 45. Following the recommendation of a War Office Committee in 1903 (approved 1904), the establishment of officers' horses, provided with free forage, was reduced from three to two per officer. The Army Council in February 1909, suggested that every officer entitled to be mounted, should be supplied with a free charger, or chargers, the use of which would be restricted to the officer's military duties. He should be allowed to use his chargers for general purposes (the Director of Remounts observed the desirability of hunting) on payment of an annual £10 charge for each horse. To assist with the issue of making cavalry commissions more attractive, the Acland Committee considered the offering of financial inducements, whereby free forage was allowed to each officer for a third horse that could be requisitioned on mobilization. Failing this, spare horses owned by cavalry officers were to be classified under the Army Act and as many as required taken on mobilization, on payment from the public purse. No government charger allotted to an officer was to be used for general purposes until it had been passed by the CO as fully trained for military work; it could then be issued on hire, but not hunted before October of the year in which it was five years old. The practice of officers not taking their chargers to manoeuvres, but using troop horses, was to be stopped and if any officer persisted, he was to be made responsible for finding a suitable replacement. In 1913, the Inspector General Home Forces reported that officers of RHA and RFA were generally dissatisfied with the class of chargers supplied to them, being below the standard issued to officers of the Cavalry, and their duties, as artillery officers, demanded they should be well mounted. The Army Council commented that the average price paid for chargers had been raised, the class and quality of horses was maintained, and batteries of the RHA and RFA were well horsed. [24]

During a period of reduction in military spending any new system that might increase peacetime spending was rigorously scrutinised. For the QMG Finance (QMGF), the main financial feature of the Acland Report was the immediate addition of 40 horses to each of the 14 cavalry line regiments, based at home, to provide the numbers required on mobilisation; with a further increase at a later date, of either 43 per regiment boarded out (bringing the total to 120), or 32 per regiment in barracks. [25] No decision on these two alternatives was to be taken pending further experience of the Boarding Out System. The QMG Finance (QMGF) noted that with the increase of 40 horses in stables, with boarded out horses remaining at 73, the Army was placed in a better position on mobilisation than the German higher establishment of 600.

---

24   WO163/20, Army Council Précis No.782, 53/Southern/1027; ref. 'Forage Allowance for Officers' Chargers Taken Away From Their Station During Leave'. Question of officers' chargers, Army Council, 4th February 1909 (précis 409); WO163/20, Army Council (34/2228), p.355, ref. 'Horses for RHA and RFA officers' chargers', also Précis 782 ref. Battery Horses.

25   WO32/5073, J.A. Corcoran (QMGF), circa, 4th January 1912, 'Financial Remarks on the Report of the Committee on the Horsing of the Cavalry Division'.

(Germany did not have boarded out horses). The proposal that older horses, sent from regiments to the new grass farms for rest in winter, was to be left for departmental consideration. The several changes proposed by the Acland Committee approximately balanced one another out financially, leaving only the net cost of the increase in horses to be found. In relation to the 'pool' of 150 horses to replace incapacitated horses, the QMGF wrote that if the Acland Committee's Scheme had been in existence this 'pool' would probably not have been agreed to for the Cavalry (it was sanctioned January 1909).[26] On the principle of leaving cavalry units short of remounts until October each year, the proportion of the existing 'pool' maintained for the Cavalry, about 50 horses, could be dropped. A table of castings in the Acland Report, shows 11.4% average wastage for 1907-11, and statistics presented to the Committee showed the number of aged army horses had increased, possibly a result of increased purchases during the 1899-1902 War. The QMGF considered a proposed saving of £6,700, with an increased service life of horses, was too high an estimate, and the earmarking of officers' private chargers was possibly an extra expense on mobilisation, as these horses would be more expensive (this was also true for Hunt horses). Birkbeck was of the opinion that boarders and horses in stables (judged by any continental standard), were alternatives and the Committee's Report did not justify the suggested increase of boarders to 100, or 120 per regiment, in addition to the increased number in stables. He therefore thought the Council should not approve, in principle, any increase beyond the 40 in stables, providing the establishment of the new system of supply, training and improvement of the Boarding Out System was successful. He supported the proposed sale of boarders at fifteen and a half years for £10. [27]

In March 1912 the QMG wrote to the Parliamentary Under Secretary stating that the Acland Committee had dealt exhaustively with a remedy for the shortage of trained horses in the Cavalry on mobilisation. He entirely agreed with the recommendations on supply and training, which in his opinion and those of the Remount Department, should result in economy and increased efficiency. [28] He had, therefore, already made preparations to carry out the recommendations so that they could be put into effect as soon as the report received the Army Council's approval. It was not, he understood, the intention to buy all remounts in the spring and summer, as such a system would make the price of horses prohibitive, a point emphasised by Birkbeck. Purchases had to be made as opportunities occurred. Summer months were good, as also was October, when purchases would be made for issue in that year. The age grouping of horses in a regiment was important, so as not to have an undue proportion of old, or young horses with the consequence of placing an abnormal annual demand for remounts. The recommendations for boarded out horses were being implemented,

26   Ibid., document (2a); the 'pool' sanctioned, January 1909 on 116/GN/5238.
27   Birkbeck, WO32/5073 (6a) and (6e), 116/GN/5470; also 116/GN/5238.
28   WO32/5073, Minute Sheet, 116/GN/5470 from QMG, 20th March 1912; WO32/5073, paras. 9-13, pp.4-5.

and the QMG agreed with the Committee's conclusions about the registering and training of horses for use on mobilisation, but doubted that 40 horses (in stables) could be added to the establishment without an increase in personnel. The Commander in Chief General Staff (CIGS) had concurred with the Committee's recommendations except for the forage allowance to officers for a third horse, which he doubted would have any effect on the supply of candidates for cavalry commissions, stating that "in 1902 or 1903 we took steps to reduce obligatory expenses in the cavalry by providing each officer with two chargers at the public expense, and I think saddlery at cost price. Did this reduce the average cost of living in cavalry regiments?" He thought not. [29] The QMG agreed with the CIGS, but thought the question of allowing forage to the third horse would have advantages for increasing the establishment. He concluded that the result of the Committee's recommendations would be an improved economy and increase in efficiency.

At a conference in June 1912 the Parliamentary Under Secretary stated that the recommendations would not require further ratification by the Army Council, which had generally approved the Report.[30] A second conference, under the QMG's instructions, considered how Vote 6N (purchase of horses and mules), or 7B (forage), could be used to meet an expenditure of £2,800, the estimated net cost of 280 cavalry remounts bought at five years old (at £50 each), instead of at four years old (at £40 each).[31] To offset this cost, savings were considered in the general provision for the purchase of horses at home (on Vote 6N1), and the ADR promised a saving of £1,200 on the provision of forage (Vote 7B), for these horses. The ADR undertook to purchase these horses at a time that allowed for the saving of one month's forage, out of the eight months provided in estimates. He proposed to buy 140 horses between 1st July and 31st August and 140 horses between 1st September and 31st October; the cost of forage rations taken into estimates therefore, amounted to £600. Owing to a reduced forage ration for horses at Pinckard's Farm, an estimated average saving of a quarter of the annual ration could be made for 80 horses, which at prices in the estimates came to £500. This gave a total saving of £2,300. The cost took no account of the increase in forage prices, to be met from sources other than Vote 7B.

The Army Council informed the Secretary to the Treasury in July 1912 of the background to the Acland Committee, it's Report and the Council's general acceptance of the recommendations.[32] With the Treasury's approval, they intended to take immediate

29   WO32/5073 (6e), 6th February 1912, signed by CIGS: extract re para. 59 and 89 of the Acland report. The CIGS Precis 557 p.1.
30   WO32/5073 (10a), 25th June 1912; Birkbeck, WO32/5073 (6e). The Report was approved at the 139th meeting of the Army Council.
31   Army Finance Vote 6 was for Quartering, Transport and Remounts, Vote 7 for Supplies and Clothing; Conference on 25th June 1912, WO32/5073, 26th June 1912, following on from 12A and options A/B.
32   WO32/5073, 116/GN/5470, letter 26th July 1912, Secretary of Army Council E.W.D. Ward to Secretary of Treasury.

action on certain recommendations, the most important being the increase in peace-time establishments of 40 horses stabled with their regiments. The Council proposed purchasing 20 additional horses per cavalry line regiment at home (total 280 horses) out of money provided in the 1912 estimates, leaving the further 280 horses recommended by the Commission, for subsequent provision. It was calculated that 40 was the largest number of horses that could be added to each regiment without requiring an increase in personnel and additional stabling costs. No immediate increase in the authorised number of boarded out horses was proposed as it had not been possible to find allottees for the existing number of 73 per regiment. Failing an improvement in the number of applicants for boarded out horses, it was considered necessary to increase the number of horses and men with the regiments, but this was the more expensive plan. The Council proposed to adopt the recommendations relating to boarded out horses, including the inducement of allowing allottees to purchase horses (over 15 years old), which they had boarded out for about seven years, on payment of £10.[33] The question of forage for an officer's third charger was reserved for further consideration. Great importance was attached to the introduction of newly purchased remounts being sent to grass farms and then issued in October, as a batch, to regiments; the Batch-System was viewed as essential to the introduction of a progressive 18 months training period with a regiment.[34] The existing remount depots, together with the recently acquired Pinckard's Farm, were considered adequate for requirements if supplemented by grazing facilities in Ireland, where the majority of horses would be purchased. The financial estimates were generally accepted by the Council except for the saving of £2,600 on forage, which the Veterinary and Remount Departments considered overstated by some £600-700. In a draft letter to the Treasury referencing the 'pool' system, a note in the margin reads 'omit as it will only raise questions'; probably because the Treasury had been requested to sanction the expenditure during the current financial year, at the earliest possible date.[35] The Treasury replied that as they were not being asked to agree to more than the actual purchase of 20 horses per regiment, it was not necessary to go more fully into the details.[36]

The Acland Committee Report was favourably received and generally adopted. MacMunn stressed the importance of the Report, as it became the "Law and the Prophets" in solving the problems of the Cavalry Division and mounted brigades, laying "down certain principles and proclaiming certain bedrock facts", essential to drum into the ears of the non-expert and the Finance Department". [37] These principles were: that horses put into the ranks before six years old did not last their full economic life and were not to be put into military training before five years old; that

---

33 WO32/5073, paras. 28-38, pp.10-12.
34 This had no connection with the Scheme for horse breeding farms which was rejected by Lord Stanley's Committee, WO32/8756, p.iii, in 1902.
35 WO32/5073, 116/GN/5470, letter, 26th July 1912.
36 WO32/5073, letter 30th July 1912, signed E.N. Behrens, ref. 116/GN/5470, QMGFa of 26th July.
37 MacMunn, 1930, pp.97-8.

the civilian horse world did not provide fit and trained cavalry horses for the Army, without which, impressment would not be effective. The principle was accepted that every cavalry regiment must have sufficient horses of six years of age and over to ensure it could provide wartime establishments, plus 10% for reinforcements, and all horses under six were regarded as in training and not in the ranks.

The Horse Mobilisation Scheme

The Stanley Committee (1901-2), did not consider the main requirement for a scheme was creating fresh sources of supply, but the practical acquaintance with, and organisation of, existing sources. The purchase of 500 remounts annually from Canada was recommended, with a strongly expressed view that the Remount Department should, at all times, be in practical touch with, and effectual command of, the sources of supply in the Colonies. [38] There had been conflicting evidence as to the practical gains of the existing registration system, which had worked well for the supply of the draught class of horse, but not for the riding class. The Committee therefore considered the system was generally unsatisfactory and did not desire its continuation for the riding class. The system had enabled the Department to obtain quickly, a large number of seasoned horses to meet the first strain of the 1899-1902 War, thereby allowing time to organise the purchasing machinery for further requirements. Within these limits the Committee considered a system of registration extremely valuable, if not indispensable. They did not recommend any extension to the existing system of an authorised maximum of 14,500 registered horses. Little of the Stanley Committee's Report appears to have been acted upon.

Much attention was devoted during 1908-9 to the difficult question of horse supply in wartime.[39] It was evident that the essential basis for any scheme was the possession of accurate information on the number horses, of the several classes required for military use, in each military district. The census and classification of the country's horses was an essential first step in developing a horse mobilisation scheme. It was therefore proposed to take a countrywide census of horses, with the co-operation of County Associations and Police Authorities; noting that arrangements had already been made for a trial census.

Census and Classification

The *Times* reported that a Home Office circular issued to the police, requested them to collect statistics on the number of horses and horse drawn and mechanically propelled vehicles, which might be available for army purposes in the event of an emergency.

---

38   WO32/8756, pp.ii, iii, v, vi, *Committee on the Supply of Remounts*; *VR*, 1914, Vol.26, 2nd May, p.712; Williams, 1909, pp.290-2.
39   Baden-Powell, 1909, p.6.

The Census was to include horses used by private individuals for their own conveni-
ence, or for pleasure, as well as those used for purposes of trade; the information was
confidential to the War Department and would not be used in connection with tax
collection.[40] Haldane considered the results of this census absolutely useless, except for
giving him the approximate number of horses in the country. MacMunn thought it
almost valueless for the classification of horses for a mobilisation scheme, but important as a basis for future work as it showed, to some extent, where the different types
of horses were located and that there was a far larger number in the country than had
been imagined. This exposed the view of many people that the country had insufficient horses for the army. [41]

   Lt. Lane, thought the Census was of little practical value, but pointed out the
extremely large number of very heavy horses shown in it and that those in some parts
of Scotland were almost entirely of this class.[42] In 1910, Baden-Powell and Brunker
wrote that the important task of organising the horse supply of the country to meet
the needs of both Regular and Territorial Forces (TF) in war, had been taken in
hand.[43] MacMunn stated that the General Staff and even the QMG urged him not to
bother so much about the TF, as to be successful, all overlapping between these Forces
was to be avoided. However, he felt with the plentiful number of horses the TF should
be on the same footing, not differentiated, except for giving the BEF the better horses,
if necessary, and with no mistake about their dates for readiness.[44] Complete decentralisation and an intimate knowledge of local resources and conditions was required.
To achieve this, a combination of Police Authorities and County Associations was
to be used, each working within its own well-defined sphere; with the work of the
Regular Army limited to taking over, at given places, the horses required in the event
of mobilization.[45] Using the results of the Census, the WO would assign to County
Associations the quotas required on mobilisation and then as drafts. The Associations
were to inspect and classify a sufficient number of the horses to provide the quotas,
with an adequate margin, and at the same time to organise the necessary machinery for
immediate collection when ordered to mobilise. This task was to be accomplished so
as to be 'the least onerous to the civil population'. The whole scheme relied upon using
people who knew local conditions as the task would involve them in a considerable
amount of work and organisation, but kept government expenditure to a minimum.
This Classification Scheme proved too simple an idea and the workload far greater

40   *Times*, 'Census of Horses and Vehicles', 1909, in *ASCQ*, Vol.3, January 1910, p.515.
41   Hansard (C), 1911, Vol.XXII, 14th March, (c)2081; Brunker, 1911, p.339; MacMunn,
     1930, pp.92-3.
42   Lane, 1912, p.39.
43   Baden-Powell and Brunker, 1910, pp.5-6.
44   MacMunn, 1930, pp.98-9.
45   County Associations were created by the Territorial and Reserve Forces Bill (1907) to
     administer the Territorial Force.

than the Associations could cope with; the scheme implemented after 1911 involved a greater use of army personnel.

In the summer of 1911, before MacMunn's arrival at the WO, Cowans initiated a census using adjutants of territorial units and although many of them were not, in MacMunn's view, competent to carry this out, the results generally confirmed figures in the police census.[46] During 1909 some counties, for example Devonshire, undertook experimental classifications of horses, raising some important questions on the organisation and process.[47] A circular sent to Associations in January 1910 explained the general policy and invited their observations, but until the quotas to be found by each Association were fixed, it was not possible to assess the extent of the task being asked of them; but the proportion of horses to be found by any given district upon mobilisation was not expected to be excessively high. In 1911 Brunker wrote that using the results of the police census, quotas to be found by counties had been worked out and allotted, though further progress, in some parts of the country had been uneven. Some Associations had the work of classification and organisation for collecting the horses well in hand, others found various difficulties interfered with progress. He thought a variety of methods might be required to suit the conditions existing in the different districts, however, many of the problems that at first confronted the WO and Associations were becoming routine. [48]

Haldane reported to the House of Commons, that there were very large numbers of horses in the country, the problem was how to organise them to obtain those required on mobilisation. The Police Census had served its purpose, but a reorganisation was necessary, so that on mobilisation the Cavalry, Artillery and other arms of the service would be guaranteed their required supply of horses. To do that, horses had to be thoroughly sifted and classified, but classification alone was not the answer to the problem. With barely enough quality horses of cavalry and artillery type in the country, for mobilisation of these units to be accomplished, those that were suitable had also to be properly trained. The Acland Committee had considered the question of ensuring that cavalry horses required for war purposes were fit for the work. Twelve County Associations were involved in the work of classification and some had made remarkable progress, but through the Army Annual Bill, Haldane stated he was seeking further legislation in a new clause to assist with the problem. The difficulty remained in knowing the class and location of horses. He proposed putting a large staff of expert officers, under the aegis of, and at the disposal of, the Associations, to work out the classification; at the same time the Remount Department was to be strengthened. Territorial horses would be earmarked for the TF; horses for the Regular Army would be chosen and looked after by the Remount Department to avoid any duplication,

---

46   MacMunn, 1930, p.93. Cowans presumably undertook this in his capacity as Director General of the Territorial Force, but I have been unable to link this directly with the classification undertaken by the County Associations referred to by Brunker, 1910, p.9. It could be the initiative of Circular Memorandum 231, 10th January 1910.
47   Hansard (C), 1911, Vol.XXI, 20th February, (c)1688; Brunker, 1911, p.329.
48   Brunker, 1911, p.7.

with officers given powers to inspect and report on horses. Substantial additions were to be made to the number of boarded out horses as they were considered a first reserve for Regulars. Haldane proposed to introduce an entirely new machinery for dealing with the horse question during 1912. [49]

County Associations had encountered difficulties in achieving their task of organising the supply of horses for the Regular and TF, so after a full investigation, responsibility for completing the work was transferred to GOCs Home Commands. A small staff of remount officers was to be provided for the purpose with assistance from adjutants of the TF. Their task was to inspect and classify a sufficient proportion of horses in each county to provide the required quotas on mobilisation, after allowing for casualties and rejections. April 1912 was the date assigned for the completion of the first classified lists, thereafter the lists were to be continually revised to show changes in the country's horse population. [50]

The Assistant Director Remounts (ADR) recommended to the QMG that he should immediately see the reports from Commands on the classification of horses, which fully bore out the information already given, as to the scarcity of generally suitable horses for army purposes and more particularly, those of the light draught types suitable for the gun teams of the RHA and RFA. [51] Only the Northern Command had forwarded a detailed report and the ADR thought very little care had been taken in completing reports with the necessary details to make a judgement on how the military horse supply stood for mobilisation.

The ADR highlighted some of the special points noted by the Commands. In Northern Command all the adjutants except one had been used for classification, but many had no knowledge and had not been able to complete the work and on completion the deficiencies could not be corrected. Horses that had been classified had not been inspected. There was an excess of riding horses for the Regulars and a deficiency of light draught especially for RHA and RFA. Between 2,000 and 3,000 riding horses, of the valuable hunter class, were available for reinforcements, but they would not be in hard condition between May and October (the traditional campaigning season). Eastern Command's report was considered unsatisfactory, as it gave no details; the Command proposed to report with 'greater confidence' by 31st March. Western Command had difficulty in finding light draught horses suitable for RHA and RFA, estimating that roughly 16,000 horses were available for reinforcements. Aldershot Command regretted their report was incomplete, but would be forwarded within a few days (received 20th February 1911), a situation noted by the ADR as 'serious'. Information had been obtained through gentlemen who were to act as horse purchasers. There was a difficulty in finding RHA horses; RFA were easier, but few were in hard condition. Cavalry and riding horses were easy to get except during the

---

49   Hansard (C), 1911, Vol.XXI, 14th March, (c) 2081; Brunker, 1911, p.338.
50   Brunker, 1911, p.7.
51   WO32/9131, 17th February 1911.

summer months. Southern Command had no difficulty in finding cavalry horses in small numbers, but RHA and RFA horses were difficult to find. Only requirements plus 25% had been classified and reinforcements had not been considered. Scottish Command reported that no Cavalry, RHA or RFA units of the BEF were mobilising in the Command. They could find the horses required for Aldershot and Woolwich from registered horses, but possibly only 300-400 cavalry horses were available as reinforcements, to be purchased from various hunting centres; also about 1,000 for the RFA. If the TF mobilised at the same time as the BEF the former would take all the best horses. Some adjutants were not capable of classifying and another DADR was requested. This was not an auspicious start!

Amendment to the Army (Annual) Act 1911

In 1911 Parliament passed an Amendment to Section 114 of the Army (Annual) Act.[52] This permitted any officer, duly specified by the Army Council, to enter any premises at any reasonable time, for the purposes of inspecting horses and vehicles with a view to their classification and selection, if found to be suitable for military service in an emergency. It was to be understood that the classification of horses and vehicles made by officers authorised to enter premises, was for the sole purpose of meeting military requirements in time of a national emergency. The Act, as amended, further provided that if any authorised officer was obstructed in the exercise of his powers of entry, a search warrant could be issued by a Justice of the Peace if he was satisfied by information given on oath, that the officer had been obstructed. This authorised a Constable accompanied by the officer to enter the premises. As the law for impressment already existed, this Amendment made it lawful to enumerate, and gave officers involved the necessary support to carry out their task. The powers of impressment also extended to motor vehicles.

When MacMunn inaugurated his new Horse Mobilisation Section, he found this Act and the Territorial adjutants' census, valuable data on which to commence work.[53] He was content that there were enough horses, of sorts, in the country to be organised for mobilisation. If there was a summer mobilisation, hunters would all be at grass and not in hard condition for active service; with the increased civilian use of motor vehicles it was the class of working horse known as the light 'vanner', bus and trotting delivery-van, that was fast disappearing. Representations had been made to the Army Council that these Acts and Amendments were often not well circulated in boroughs and rural districts, in response the WO issued a letter referring to the implementation of the Amended Section 114.[54] It was considered of great importance that before officers began the classification of horses and carriages for mobilisation, every effort was to be made to avoid friction with owners by acquainting them with the

---

52   Public General Acts, 1911; WO32/9129, 116/GN/5432.
53   MacMunn, 1930, p.93.
54   WO32/9129, 116/GN/5422 (QMG4), June 1911.

Amendment. To assist classifying officers in the various commands, the Department, with permission from the Home Secretary, would circulate pamphlets to all those known to the police as being in possession of horses, or vehicles.

The WO wrote to all GOCs Home Commands introducing and enclosing a copy of the new Horse Mobilisation Scheme, advising them of changes to Section 114 of the Army Act, and the new arrangements for the classification of horses in peacetime, together with their supply on mobilisation for both the Regular and TF. [55] This replaced proposals in Circular Memorandum No.231 (14th January 1910) and any experimental classification being undertaken by County Associations was to cease. The letter briefly outlined changes to Section 114 and the steps being taken to inform owners of horses and vehicles. It was stressed that officers engaged in visiting premises for the purpose of classification should exercise the greatest tact and care in dealing with the owners. In selecting horses and transport they were to bear in mind the importance of interfering, as little as possible, with the business, or trade in which the owners were engaged, and that all information obtained during inspections was to be considered confidential. The importance of working closely with the County Associations was not to be overestimated, their assistance and goodwill were essential features of the Scheme. Two Deputy Assistant Directors of Remounts (DADRs) were to be added to Commands to assist implementation; these officers would receive their orders direct from the GOCs, or their Staff and would be responsible for supervising the classification and working out details of the Scheme. It was anticipated that the services of adjutants of the TF would be utilised, observing that the months of October to January were probably the most convenient for them. If these arrangements could be made an average of only some 400 horses would have to be selected and classified by each adjutant. It was pointed out that a further 25%, over and above the actual number of horses required on mobilisation, would have to be classified to allow for casualties. In addition to the number of horses required for Regular and TF units mobilising in Commands, the following numbers were to be supplied by them to the Aldershot Command:

	Riding	Light Draught	Pack	Total
Western	1,000	2,000	200	3,200
Southern	500	1,000	200	1,700
Northern	1,500	4,000	100	5,600
Eastern	500	1,000	-	1,500
London District	500	3,000	-	3,500
Total	4,000	11,000	500	15,500

55   WO32/9129, 116/GN/5432, 1st August 1911, from R.H. Brade; and 116/GN/5422, (QMG4) reference Circular Memorandum No. 325, 28th March 1911.

These horses were to be collected at railway centres that had good communications with Aldershot and where sufficient trucks could easily be obtained for their entrainment. The GOC Aldershot Command was instructed to arrange with the Commands, those stations in the neighbourhood where the horses were to be consigned. Under Section 115 of the Army Act,[56] owners were required to provide ordinary articles of harness, saddlery and stall gear with their horses; it was not necessary therefore for unit horse-collecting parties to take any equipment to collecting centres. The GOCs were asked to submit, as early as possible, their general remarks on the Scheme and in relation to Paragraph 4 the exact arrangements they proposed to make.[57]

New Scheme for Classification and Mobilisation

The new scheme for classification and supply of horses on mobilisation was as follows:[58]

- Amendment of Section 114 of the Army Annual Act, 1911, Section 4, which gave Police Authorities, or County Associations power to authorise officers, specified by the Army Council, to enter any premises for the purpose of enumerating and classifying horses required on mobilisation for the Expeditionary and Territorial Forces.
- The GOC of each Command was responsible under the Scheme, for the selection and classification, during peacetime, of the horses required to complete units to wartime strength (plus 25% provision for casualties). He was also responsible for the collection and distribution on mobilisation of the horses required for the Expeditionary and Territorial Forces.
- GOCs were to take steps to secure the assistance and co-operation of County Associations, remembering that the Police had undertaken a census of horses and the Returns were in possession of County Associations. These Returns, although possibly not altogether accurate and requiring further careful examination, could be utilised in the selection of horses for both forces. Classified lists taken from the police census had already been made in certain counties and could be useful.
- The selection and classification of horses required on mobilisation for the Regular and TF was to be carried out by Remount Staff Officers, assisted by adjutants of TF units. It was therefore essential for the efficient working of the Scheme that these officers worked in close co-operation under the direction of the GOC.
- Adjutants were to be employed for classification only, at times that would not interfere with their primary unit duties. In many instances officers of the TF could probably, without expense to the public, obtain useful information that

---

56 Paragraph 15 of the Scheme.
57 WO32/9129.
58 Ibid. This copy of the Scheme was not dated but almost certainly that sent out with the WO letter of 1st August 1911.

would assist in the selection and classification of horse. Adjutants carrying out the duty were to be instructed to bear this in mind.

- GOCs were to impress on County Associations the importance of decentralisation for the provision of TF unit horses on mobilisation and their collection at that time. Arrangements were to be made with Associations for COs to collect the pre-selected horses at fixed centres, approved by the GOC, or at unit headquarters, whichever was more suitable.
- In order to facilitate classification, it was suggested Commands were divided into areas corresponding with petty sessional areas, or with territorial recruiting areas, whichever was more suitable.
- In selecting horses for the TF, those more suitable for the Regular Army Expeditionary Force (EF) were not to be included, for example those that from their age, condition, quality, and general fitness were capable of immediate and prolonged work. Horses in possession of Associations or TF units, and horses noted at the headquarters of the unit, as being earmarked for the use of officers, or men, for annual training would be allotted accordingly on mobilisation. The wording of this last sentence was changed on 7th November 1911, in a letter to all Commands to read: 'Horses which are the property of a County Association, or are owned and ridden on parade by members of the TF units who are entitled to be mounted, will be classified but reserved for their owners on mobilisation'.[59]
- In the areas where two units overlapped, Remount Staff Officers would issue special instructions to the adjutants concerned. The procedure for selection and collection of vehicles and harness, as well as complete "turnouts," was to be carried out on the same basis.
- Adjutants would be granted any necessary travelling expenses and usual allowances for journeys on this duty. Whenever practicable the work was to be carried out during normal visits to out-stations.
- The selection of horses for the EF was to be very closely and continuously supervised by Remount Officers.
- It was desirable to draw horses from areas as near as possible to the troops to which they would be issued. In the case of Aldershot this was not practicable and horses were to be selected and classified in other Commands during peacetime, and on mobilisation collected and despatched to Aldershot Command.
- During peacetime, GOCs were to arrange, in preparation for mobilisation, the services of purchasing officers and civilian veterinary surgeons to carry out the work of inspection and purchase in such a way as to ensure fast delivery to units. In peacetime each purchasing officer was to be provided with lists of horses he had to purchase on mobilisation and their destinations. On mobilisation the pay for purchasing officers was to be three guineas a day and for veterinary surgeons two guineas. One clerk per purchasing officer was permitted at 7/6d a day. Men

59 WO32/9130, R.H. Brade.

required for delivery of horses at collecting stations would receive 5/- a day.

- Under Section 115 of the Act the seller would be required to deliver the following articles with each horse: one watering bridle, head rope, horse blanket or rug, body roller and pad. The following articles were to be provided with each turnout: harness as used by each horse; for each horse one nosebag, horse brush, rug or blanket, body roller and pad; one pail per vehicle, 3lbs. of lubricating grease per cart and 6lbs. per wagon. Where necessary, arrangements for storing picketing gear, if required at the depot nearest to the fixed centres, was to be made in peacetime and a scheme prepared for horse collecting parties.
- A list of horses registered at Army Headquarters was to be furnished to each Command, so that they could be distinguished by having the letter 'R' placed against them in the column of remarks on the classification form.
- To supply the necessary drafts for replacing casualties after mobilisation, the Remount Staff Officer, purchasing officer and veterinary surgeon, pending further instructions, would remain in the districts after troops had moved away.
- Certain horse vehicles were to be exempted from classification: royal stables, foreign embassies, those employed in government service, police and fire brigades and chargers of officers on the active list.

On 12th August the WO issued Circular Memorandum No.352 (cancelling No.231) informing County Associations of the new scheme in accordance with the amendment to Section 114.[60] The Army Council expressed its high appreciation of the work already accomplished, especially of those Associations that undertook preliminary classification trials, ensuring them that the work already done would not be wasted. The Circular concluded by pointing out that the success of the new scheme largely depended on the close co-operation between Associations and GOCs and that the Council was confident in relying on the loyal assistance of the Associations. In September, a letter was sent to Chief Constables and Boroughs advising them of changes to Section 114 of the Act.[61]

It appears that the WO issued details of the new scheme with an accompanying letter of 1st August 1911, as a process of consultation to refine the Scheme, with subsequent correspondence between the Home Commands and the WO from August to October. Some of their queries were related to the transfer of horses between units and other Commands, with the WO tending to reply that fuller details would follow. This phase of implementation raised many questions about administration and staffing, which appear to have caused delay and frustration to the WO and Commands:

Western Command requested a map, or maps, giving petty sessional and police divisions within its area; Northern Command required 76 maps.[62] A request was made

---

60   WO32/9129, 16/GN/5432. There is a draft of this letter in the files dated July 1911.
61   Ibid.
62   Ibid., letters dated 12th August and 27th September 1911.

for Remount officers and adjutants acting as Assistant Remount Officers (ARO), to be given some idea of the average prices allowed for different classes of impressed horses, and whether horse purchasers would have the authority for valuing impressed horses on mobilisation. Comment was also made about the unsatisfactory state of stationery boxes containing the forms for impressment.[63] Owing to the volume of correspondence with adjutants of Territorial units, their secretaries and horse purchasers, and keeping registers of horse amendments up to date, it was necessary to increase the number of clerks to the offices of DADRs from one to four, one for each DADR.[64] In addition, one clerk was required for the DADR who performed the duties of Staff Officer for Remounts in the Command.[65] The WO allowed two additional clerks for DADRs in Northern Command and one in the London District.

Scottish Command noted that eight of their counties did not have TF adjutants (the WO replied that adjutants from Special Reserve battalions could be employed for the purposes of classification), that transport was a problem in very rural areas and, owing to poor railway communications, motor transport would have to be used.[66]

Eastern Command were concerned about the unreliability of the police census and the possibility of a considerable overlap in supplying horses for the Regular and TF, as by far the greater number used by the Yeomanry during training, might not be available on mobilisation. Many came from London and other Commands and were used by several other regiments during the training period. Under such circumstances, it appeared unavoidable that the Yeomanry, with few exceptions, would be unable to mobilise for some considerable time, and other units of the TF would be delayed in taking to the field fully equipped. The TF in the Command required approximately 18,000 horses.[67]

Maj. H. Williams Wynn, DADR London District, forwarded a detailed letter to the WO concerning the process of earmarking firms from which TF units would obtain their horses on mobilisation.[68] It highlights some very interesting and no doubt unthought-of details about the horse supply. The first difficulty was the impossibility, on impressment, of treating all owners equally. The enforcement of Section 115 of the Army Act would arouse discontent amongst horse owners, unless it was clearly shown that all were treated equally, according to their ability to supply the class of horse required. According to the Police Census, 272 owners of 50 plus horses in London owned 27,738 horses and 375 owners possessed fewer than 50 but more than 25, totalling 12,737 horses. A number of owners with fewer than 25 horses had not been involved as the loss of time in examining and purchasing such horses would, it was felt, have seriously delayed mobilisation. Therefore, upwards of 40,000 were (in 1910)

63   Ibid., letter, 4th September 1911.
64   Ibid., volume of correspondence, 180 for example in the Northern Command area.
65   Ibid., letter 5th August 1911.
66   Ibid., letters 14th August, 22nd September, 30th September 1911.
67   Ibid., letter 18th September 1911.
68   Ibid., 29th September 1911.

in the ownership of large firms. TF units in the Command required 10,544 horses on mobilisation; they could call on the owners for roughly 25% of their horses. In practice however, it was not found possible to adopt such a policy when earmarking firms to supply certain TF units. There was little call for using heavy draught horses, or ponies in some units, and if these were deducted from the 40,000, only 24,400 light draught and saddle horses were available for impressment. This inevitably meant that owners of light horses would feel a greater hardship compared with those whose studs comprised a larger proportion of carthorses. Many owners of large studs carried out duties which, if on mobilisation were to be discontinued or interrupted, would seriously affect the public service and even safety, for example, the fire brigade, contractors for the Royal Mail, various Borough Councils and other Municipal Authorities. This amounted to between 10% and 25% of horses. Williams Wynn had not planned to include these horses, as with the exception of contractors for the mails, they had a number of horses registered that would all be purchased in the first few days of mobilisation.

In another class were the railway companies with termini in London and the large carrying companies, for example Carter, Paterson and Co., Pickfords, and Thompson McKay and Co. All together the railway companies had 885 light horses registered and if all these were withdrawn during the first two days of mobilisation, some delay in the transportation of goods would be unavoidable, reacting unfavourably upon the mobilisation of certain units. He assumed that as companies registered their horses, they took steps to replace them, if sufficient warning was given. He had therefore arranged not to call up their registered horses until the third day of mobilisation. Carrying companies were in a similar position to the railways, but he was compelled to call up a large number of their registered light horses on the first day of mobilisation. The companies had met him in a very obliging spirit, expressing their readiness to provide a large number of horses within 12 hours notice. However, if further calls were made upon them, for the second and third days of mobilisation, public and probably the military authorities would suffer considerable inconvenience and delay. He was not planning, therefore, to make further calls upon their registered horses until after the fourth day of mobilisation; this would allow 72 hours to replace them. He did not propose calling upon the railway, or carrying companies, for any horses beyond the number registered. It was, he thought, a matter of discussion whether any consideration should be given to the nature, or trade of a business, when impressing horses.

There was no doubt that the general public would at once feel inconvenience and perhaps scarcity from the impressment of horses belonging to dairy companies, provision dealers, wholesale bakers and other similar trades; whereas the withdrawal of horses from drapers, jobmasters, or cab proprietors would cause little inconvenience or distress. He was not therefore proposing to discriminate against trade in earmarking firms supplying horses, as it would be difficult to draw any hard line, owing to the large number of stores and universal providers. He requested advice on whether any account should be taken of the value of an owner's horses before earmarking them for purchase by impressment. The purchase price was not to exceed £60, but one or two firms known to him had horses with a higher average value, whilst their best horses were probably worth £120 to £150. If such horses were purchased, under compulsion for £60 each, there would be much grumbling that valuable carriage horses in private ownership were not also impressed. He did not see his way to earmarking horses of private owners and doubted that the number in London was sufficient to justify the trouble and delay involved in purchasing them. Someone at the WO had noted comments along the left hand margin of this letter, for example, 'all riding horses with contractors could of course be taken', 'it was presumed that companies realised their liability and only registered a small proportion of their horses, 'that great inconvenience would undoubtedly be caused when mobilisation came and that can't be helped', and 'dairy companies and bakers should be kindly dealt with'.

That the plans were at this stage still fluid can be seen from Northern Command's correspondence with the Director of Transport and Remounts, as to whether it was intended to concentrate the whole of the remount staff at York.[69] The Command's reply was that it would be divided into three districts allotted to the three DADRs:

- No.1 District: Northumberland, Durham, Yorkshire N. Riding, (Maj. C.W. Gartside-Spaight)
- No.2 District: Yorkshire W. Riding, Derbyshire, Staffordshire, (Capt. E.F. Hood)
- No.3 District: Yorkshire E. Riding, Lincolnshire, Leicestershire, and Rutland, Nottinghamshire, (Col. L.A. Hope)

York was considered the most suitable centre for the officers as all three districts met at York and with good railway facilities for reaching all parts of the Command. On the 18th November the Command had been divided into two districts:

- No.1: Northumbria, Durham, Yorkshire N. and E. Riding, and northern half of W. Riding. (under Col. Hope)
- No.2: Southern half of W. Riding, Lincolnshire, Leicestershire and Rutland, Nottinghamshire, Staffordshire and Derbyshire (under Capt. Hood)

Gartside-Spaight was to be the DADR for the whole Command. However, the Command's return to the WO of 14th February 1912, showed a structure based on the original three districts, sub-divided into adjutant areas on which the 1910 police census returns were compiled. [70]

The chairman of Southampton's Territorial County Association wrote that horses on the Army Reserve List mostly belonged to the owners of firms who had often supplied them for the Association, and if 450 horses were withdrawn from this supply for army

---

69   Ibid., 14th August 1911, Command's replies 15th and 18th August 1911.
70   Ibid., letter 19th December 1911; Col. Hope departed as DADR.

purposes, the efficiency of the TF, especially artillery, would be seriously affected.[71] The Association was loyal, but the chairman pointed out that this would be the result of actions by the Military Authorities in appropriating their supply of trained horses, without consultation or co-operation. A letter from the Major in charge of Administration for Southern Command, to the TF, provides an extract from an Army Horse Reserve list for the County of Hampshire (see table below), showing registered horses for the financial year administered by the Association, and requesting them to furnish him with a statement of companies whose horses were registered in the event of mobilisation.[72]

Name & occupation of owner/film	Address	Address of Stables	No of horses kept	No class of horses registered R LD HD P				Total	Purchase price per horse
J. Bradford, Jobmaster	Rose & Crown Hotel Brockenhurst	Same	28	20				20	£50
R.J. Bradford, Jobmaster	Ave. House Brockenhurst S	Same	80	50				50	£50
G.R. Metton Ltd, Jobmaster	Landsdown Stables Bournemouth	Same	60	20				20	£40
W. Graham Fisher, Riding Muster	St Pauls Rd Bournemouth	Same	15	10				10	£40
C.H. Home, Contractor & Farmer	Privett, Gosport	Varied Gosport & Salisbury	200 - 500	100	50	50		200	£45
Curtiss & Sons Ltd, Carriers	Gunwharf Rd Portsmouth	The Hard Portsmouth	58		40			40	£45
H.G. Bradford, Jobmaster	Royal Hotel Mews Southampton	Same	60 - 70	40				40	£50
G. Parker, Jobmaster	Southgate Winchester	Same	80 - 150	60				60	£55
George & Railway Mews Ltd, Jobmaster	Winchester	1) G & R Mews Winchester L & SW Rly State Yd Winchester	28	10				10	£40
TOTALS				310	90	50		450	

WO32/9129 (Code 22A)

List of Horses in the County of Hampshire, Registered Army Horse Reserve, 1911-1912. (WO32/9129)

Commands were notified by the WO that under Section 114 it was necessary for GOCs to obtain consent from County Associations, or the Police Authority, before any registration and classification could begin in a county or police district.[73] In Great Britain the consent of the County Association was to be sought in the first instance, with application to the Police Authority only being made if the former refused consent. In Ireland, consent of the police authority had to be obtained.[74] That all officers were not showing the requested tact and care towards owners was highlighted in a letter to Commands (except Ireland) from the Army Council, having heard that officers

71   Ibid., letter 17th July 1911.
72   WO32/9129.
73   From R.H. Brade, QMG4, 12th September 1911, ref. Memo 351, para. 3.
74   A copy of this letter had been sent to the chairman of the TF in Southampton, see his letter above.

engaged in the classification of horses had visited without first obtaining the consent of the owner.[75] Instructions were to be issued stopping such practices.

A captain and adjutant from Northern Command were refused permission to inspect by a cab proprietor in Sheffield.[76] Advice was requested as to whether he should apply for a warrant under Section 114 (1A), but no result is recorded. The WO received a letter from a J.F. Mason of Eynsham Hall, Witney, Oxfordshire stating that on 10th December his wife met a gentleman, accompanied by a police constable, coming out of his hunter stable and informed her that he had been looking at the horses for army purposes (Mrs Mason thought the officer's name was Capt. Hamilton, from Salisbury Plain); the stud groom was absent and neither he, nor his secretary, had received any intimation of the visit. The GOC Southern Command was asked to investigate and report; Capt. Hamilton replied, apologising. [77] The HQ of Lowland Division, Scottish Command, also had problems with an owner when classifying. An incident was recorded in November 1913, when a request was made for a search warrant in respect of horses belonging to W.D.C. Knox of Upper Bagnton, Westbury. Capt. F.S. Kennedy Shaw (DADR No.2) wrote to Knox about objecting to one of his officers, Capt. Martin, involved in the census, not being allowed to see his horses. Shaw wrote asking to see Knox about the registration of his horses, but Knox refused to give information he considered useless and was informed of Section 114 of the Army Act, relating to refusing information for the census. The GOC Southern Command wrote to the WO requesting a search warrant under Sect 114, which was granted; however, the GOC informed the WO that Knox had permitted Capt. Martin to visit and classify horses without a search warrant. [78]

Commands were notified by the Army Council that the classification of horses and vehicles, in accordance with the Scheme, was to be completed by 1st February 1912.[79] They were to report to the Council, giving any difficulties in finding the types of horses required on mobilisation, especially for the Cavalry, RHA, RFA, and also the probable number of horses left in the Command and available for reinforcements. The Council pointed out the desirability of the new scheme being in working order by 1st April 1912, so that on, and after that date, the existing scheme for mobilisation could

75   WO32/9130, from R.H. Brade, 14th November 1911.
76   Ibid., 20th November 1911.
77   Letter to Col. J.E.B. Seeley (Appendix I) at WO, 7th December 1911; letter to Southern Command 22nd December 1911; Letter to WO, 22nd December 1911 and reply 21st December 1911.
78   WO32/9134, 116/GN/5725, letter Capt. Martin to Shaw, 5th November 1913, and Shaw to Knox, 6th and 17th November 1913; from Knox 21st November 1913 and Shaw to Knox 22nd November 1913. Letter to WO, 9th December 1913, reply from Brade 24th December 1913.
79   WO32/9129, Brade, 16th December 1911; WO32/9130, Army Council Conference, 9th November 1911, for the Major Generals in charge of Administration, or a representative, and all DADRs. Second conference 27th February 1912, to include the Major Generals in charge of Administration, or representative, and one or more of the DADRs of each Command.

be cancelled. Commands were required to request their remount officers to register as many horses as possible of the riding and light draught type for the year commencing 1st April 1912, at 10/- annually per horse. They were also required to make it clearly understood that these horses would only be taken on mobilisation, in accordance with special instructions from the Council's office. The Commands were asked to consider the question of collecting horses on mobilisation and report to the Council. Replies from Commands suggest how far the scheme for horse mobilisation had progressed since 1st August 1911 and the problems still to be overcome.

Eastern Command had begun work on classification during the autumn of 1911, but had not covered the whole Command, nor complied with recent instructions.[80] Horses returned by adjutants as fit for the regular cavalry and artillery were subsequently found by DADRs, in many cases, to have been quite unsuitable. Having received more definite instructions as to the mode of classification, adjutants were able to proceed with their work more thoroughly. Until the reorganisation for impressment of horses was in thorough working order, arrangements had been made with large dealers to supply horses on mobilisation, but it was impossible to say definitely whether they could produce them in the time requested.

In London Command, horses for EF units mobilising in the district, those for contingents detailed to supply Aldershot Command and for advanced and base remount depots, would be supplied almost entirely from registered horses.[81] For yeomanry and artillery of the TF the number required was covered by those classified, with over 25% as a reserve. Those classified as riding horses were scarcely of the type for the Regular Cavalry and in most cases had received little training in saddle work. Those classified as RHA and RFA draught horses for the TF were on the whole satisfactory. The Command's instructions were that only 25% over the actual requirements were to be classified for reinforcement; however, a much larger proportion had actually been classified with a very large number in the district available for further classification, but only an estimate could be made based on the 1910 census. It was thought that the removal from London's commercial life of only the numbers classified would dislocate many businesses; in the event of a national emergency an estimated further 5,000 heavy draught and 8,000 light draught horses, could be obtained by impressment, probably the property of small owners entailing considerable time and trouble to collect.

Western Command found that farmers were giving up breeding the light draught type required by the RHA and RFA, in favour of heavy draught classes, with a similar difficulty with the cavalry type in North Cheshire. There was difficulty in estimating with any accuracy the number of horses left in the Command for reinforcement,

---

80   WO32/9131, 116/GN/5456, Eastern Command, 8th December 1912.
81   London Command, 13th February 1912, this ends with a very similar message to the letter of 29th September 1911.

possibly 11,000 in Cheshire and the counties north of it, 5,000 in Wales and counties in England south of Cheshire. [82]

In Scottish Command horses suitable for the RHA were very scarce. About 1,000 were available from various cities for the RFA, but only if TF units were not ordered to mobilise at the same time. Returns showed certain counties with a surplus of riding horses available for TF units, which could be increased by using lighter draught horses. Where there was a surplus, for example in Roxburgh and Dumfries, they were mostly hunters, many being suitable for the EF and included in the estimate of 300-400 available for cavalry reinforcements. In counties such as Ayr and Berwick, where many riding horses had been expected, there was a scarcity and horses were of an inferior quality. If heavy draught horses were considered suitable for dismounted TF units, a large number of high-class ones could be obtained. For classification generally throughout Scotland, 22,072 horses of various types, in excess of the original allotment to each Adjutant, had been inspected and classified, but of those, 15,707 were heavy draught. In the returns, individual horses had not been earmarked for specific units. [83]

Northern Command reported that many of the officers who carried out the classification had very little knowledge of the essential qualifications required in horses for military purposes. They assumed that many of the horses in cab proprietors' stables and similar establishments, listed as suitable for light draught for the Regular and TF would, on inspection, be found too light for the work of RFA, RE or ASC draught horses. Of those listed as suitable for the Regular Army, a large proportion of the riding horses were valuable high class hunters, the price for which would prohibit their purchase, or impressment, except in the event of the gravest national danger. They would not be available for immediate use from April to September as they were mostly out to grass. Of riding and light draught horses many were in small studs scattered in outlying country districts and could not therefore be rapidly purchased, collected and despatched to the Aldershot Command for mobilisation of the EF. There was a very serious deficiency in riding horses for the TF and light draught for the Regulars, but only a small deficiency in light draught for the TF. It was possible that on inspection a number of horses classified as light draught could be reclassified as riding horses thereby, reducing the deficiency in riding horses for the TF. However, for both Forces deficiency in light draught would be increased. By using heavy draught (an unlimited supply) for units of the TF and the majority of all vehicles from civilian sources, the number of light draught required would be reduced to a minimum. If light draught for the RHA and RFA were to be found on mobilisation, none would be left in the Command for reinforcements. [84]

82   Western Command, 13th February 1912.
83   Scottish Command, 13th February 1912.
84   Northern Command, 14th February 1912.

Southern Command made an initial response to the WO stating that completion of the Scheme was doubtful by the date suggested and there was an initial shortage of artillery type horses. Farmers did not breed, to the same extent as previously, the class of horse required for the RA. Further correspondence stated that it was doubtful the new scheme would be in working order by 1st April. The WO reply to this statement was to the point, 'hard luck.'[85]

Aldershot Command's only available resources for RHA horses were a comparatively small number of brougham (four wheeled horse carriage) and livery stable horses, the majority of which were aged and worn out for military purposes. RFA horses were not so limited, but among a number of light farm horses, corn fed and in hard condition, there were few that could be put straight to trotting work without a risk of at least temporary breakdown. The situation was more favourable for cavalry riding horses, particularly if the age issue was stretched. Command resources for first supply in May (with the above qualifications) were estimated as a maximum of 251 draught, 478 riding and 130 pack; it was probable that the number remaining in the Command for reinforcements approached 1,000 heavy draught, 550 light draught, 400 riding and 200 pack and ponies.[86]

The WO forwarded another general circular to Commands on 8th March 1912 requesting further updates on the situation:[87]

Scottish Command thought counties such as Roxburghshire would produce more horses of the hunter class. There was a surplus of 1,615 pack animals. As none of the cobs on the islands such as Mull, Skye and Hebrides had been classified, a considerable surplus of this class would be available for reinforcements. The most serious shortage was likely to be in riding horses, which could be supplemented by transferring light draught horses. The prospective total of horses available and suitable for military requirements on mobilisation did not actually exhaust the resources of Scotland. But it was considered very few would be left and probably only sufficient to adjust any inaccuracies in classification, without causing a considerable amount of hardship to owners and businessmen. The counties of Caithness, Clackmannan, Kinross and Selkirk had not been included in the returns as no units were mobilising in those areas.

In Southern Command requirements for units of the Regular and TF units, plus 25% had been the primary consideration. When all arrangements to transport and purchase horses were complete, no difficulty would be found in classifying a considerable number, in excess of those shown in returns for reinforcements.[88]

85   Southern Command, 31st December 1911, 15th February 1912, 8th March 1912, WO reply 21th March 1912.
86   Aldershot Command, 17th January 1912.
87   WO32/9130, 116/GN/5486, circular 8th March 1912; WO32/9131, 13th March 1912.
88   Southern Command, 14th March 1912.

Eastern Command stated they were in a period of considerable stress because of strike operations at the time of the survey and directly afterwards foreign complications (but no details of these problems are given). Some 23,000 horses had been classified out of a total of about 25,600 required on mobilisation by the Regular and TF. In Surrey, horses had not been properly classified. The Command submitted a further report to the WO stating that the total number of horses classified was nearly 50% above the actual requirement as it then existed, but with a considerable deficiency in riding and light draught horses. It was possible that selecting and transferring the more suitable of the heavy draught could make up this deficiency. According to their returns, only about half of the riding horses required (including 25% for casualties) were available, possibly because they were poor hunting counties. The number of suitable riding horses in the Command was comparatively few. According to the police census, the total number of riding horses was 15,108, but judging from their own inspection, a larger number of the horses were unfit for army purposes. Yet, in accordance with instructions, very few owners of one or two horses had been visited and only half of the horses in one stable (as a maximum) had been included in the returns. A certain number of officers employed in classifying did not have sufficient knowledge of horses to make the lists entirely reliable.[89]

London Command showed a marked deficiency in riding horses for the TF, but anticipated that this deficiency would be made up by the small owners. If the District had to provide the same number of horses to the advanced and base remount depots at Woolwich, as listed for the previous year, this would add a further 275 riding and 1,050 light draught horses.[90]

Northern Command had a shortage of riding horses for the TF, but after further inspection it was possible that a proportion of light draught could be classified as riding, however, the shortage would probably continue to exist. There was a surplus of riding horses for Regulars of the EF, which could, on mobilisation, be allotted to the TF, but if further riding horses were required for the EF, after mobilisation, they would be taken from riding horses allotted in the first place to the TF. Although possibly depleting the TF, it would enable a reserve of horses to be obtained and trained for the EF, allowing time to obtain those riding horses for the TF, which would, at first, not exist on mobilisation.[91]

Eastern Command issued a document for distribution to horse and vehicle owners within the Command, informing them of the proposed scheme for purchase and collection of horses and vehicles on mobilisation. It included, a copy of the Scheme, List A (horse depots arranged for in the Command), List B (articles of camp equipment required for a collecting station raised for the reception of horses on mobilisation) and List C, a circular stating that "in accordance with Section 114 of the Army

89   Eastern Command, 15th March 1912, 22nd April 1912.
90   London Command, 16th March 1912.
91   Northern Command, 21st March 1912.

Act, in the event of mobilisation they would be required to send their horses and vehicles, as shown on the lists to the collecting station". Those horses and vehicles finally approved at the collecting station would be paid for on delivery by draft, including a sum to cover the cost of bringing the horses and vehicles from their stables. If not purchased they would be returned, a sum being paid to cover the cost of taking them to the collecting station and return. They would be required to furnish 'leading gear' to convey the horses from their stable to the collecting station.' [92]

MacMunn wrote to all Commands to clarify arrangements for classification in peacetime and purchase on mobilisation, of the various types of transport required. New instructions were to replace all those previously issued. "Turnouts" (an animal complete with harness, saddlery and spare equipment such as shoes, as required in the field to perform its tasks) required for the EF would be classified by officers of the ASC and Remount Branch working together, as directed by the GOC and impressed on mobilisation by the ASC. Transport (other than mechanised) including "turnouts", for TF and those units not allocated (unalloted), would be classified and purchased under the same arrangements as horses for TF units. Instructions regarding the impressment of motor transport were to be issued separately. He wrote again informing Commands that they must collect through civilian agencies. Aldershot was to send parties to Southern Command to fetch horses being 'marched' in, but not to any other Commands. Horses sent by Commands under railway supervision would be without collecting parties. Railway Council Authorities would be responsible for making sure there were no delays. [93]

Problems remained to be resolved before the new scheme could be considered complete, but a Minute was forwarded to the CIGS in March 1912, informing him that progress was sufficiently advanced with the new scheme to rely upon it in the event of mobilisation. "The existence of any other scheme tends to duplicate the work in Commands, I therefore intend, unless you have any objections, to cancel previous schemes formally. The old scheme was not that introduced by Circular Memorandum 231 of 14th January 1910. The history of the old scheme is buried in the archives of the "old" WO." The CIGS replied, concurring. Commands (except Ireland) were notified by the WO of the Army Council's decision that on, and after 1st April 1912, horses and vehicles required on mobilisation would be supplied in accordance with the Scheme issued on 1st August 1911, and that the scheme known as the "old scheme" ceased to exist after the 31st March 1912. [94]

Further insight into the arrangements to make operational the machinery for impressment can be seen in a letter to the WO from Eastern Command. This advised

---

92   Eastern Command, WO32/9131, 116/GN/5495, 8th April 1912; submitted with EC49558R.
93   WO32/9129, 16/GN/5432, MacMunn, 7th May, on behalf of the ADR, 21st May 1912.
94   Minute sheet No.33, dated 6th March 1912; reply from CIGS, 14th March 1912; WO32/9130; WO letter to Commands from Brade, WO32/9130, 20th March 1912.

that an application had been made to all Territorial County Associations in the Command, to register the names of officers, NCOs and men of the National Reserve who might be willing to assist purchasing officers in the collection of horses and vehicles on mobilisation.[95] Satisfactory replies had been received from all the Associations, except the counties of Bedford and Northampton. Steps were therefore being taken to organise staff for collecting stations. The Command proposed, if possible, to obtain substitute civilian grooms in place of the National Reserve for the counties of Bedford and Northampton. The GOC also requested payment for certain TF officers who had offered to classify horses. The Army Council did not accept this, but was considering providing travelling expenses to gentlemen not in receipt of pay from Army funds, but who offered to classify horses, therefore saving an army officer, or DADR from doing the work. It was also pointed out that responsibility for detailing officers from units to carry out classification, in cases where the ordinary classifying officers could not do it, lay with the GOC.

Commands were informed, that where conditions permitted they were to make every effort to implement provisions of the provisional Chapter V of the new Remount Regulations, so that mobilisation of the EF and TFs could, if necessary, proceed simultaneously.[96] Classification for the coming season had been laid down and was to be strictly adhered to:

- The census should include single horses
- All pleasure horses were to be allotted if necessary.
- Horses were to be classified into the subdivisions of: Riding (R1 and R2) and
- Light Draught (LD1 and LD2)
- Only those horses working under pack, in certain counties, were to be classified as pack; horses suitable but untrained were better classified under R2, or LD, as appropriate.
- There were no clear restrictions for classification, but grey and white horses were only to be allotted to medical units, trains and administrative services on lines of communication (except remounts for the 2nd Dragoons (Scots Greys) which might be grey). All grey and white horses should be marked with an X in classification lists.

In August, Commands were issued with a reminder of the provisions of the 'Horse Mobilisation Scheme' for raising wartime establishments by the following methods:[97]

- The transfer of fit horses from units and establishments not belonging to the

95   WO32/9130, 116/GN/5432,(QMG4); WO32/9132 (CR, EC, C/2205/R).
96   Remount Regulations, provisional Chapter V, Mobilisation Section 3 (6) and amplification of the Regulations, Section 2 (3) C.
97   WO32/9132; WO32/9127, 19th August 1912, ref. Army Council.

Field Army as ordered in the annual Remount Statement. The calling out of the Reserve Horses (registered, or subsidised) by impressment, of the civilian horse population.

• Impressment was provided for by:
a) the annual preparation of lists for military purposes, compiled as a result of an annual inspection of private stables by duly authorised military officers. Owing to the scarcity of horses fit for military purposes and the need for gauging the resources of the Kingdom, this classification had to extend to every stable.
b) the organisation of the country into purchasing areas, in which appointed persons would purchase horses from stables indicated in lists, supplied by Command Headquarters.
c) arranging lists and purchasers, so that purchases for the EF and reserve units would, when possible, proceed simultaneously and separately without over-lapping. TF units would purchase the horses allotted to them using their own officers, or specially attached purchasers.
d) organising local arrangements for the collection of horses and their despatch to destinations, using the rates payable for civilian labour laid down in the Regulations.

In order to provide for these various services, the following documents had, or were about to be, issued after consultation with GOCs:

a) *'Remount Statement'* (to be issued annually), containing details of all EF, TF and Reserve Units, to receive horses; with instructions for the transfer of horses from units etc not mobilising, and the disposal of horses left behind temporarily unfit.
b) *Chapter V of 'Remount Regulations'*, printed in advance of the regulations them-selves; containing the regulations for mobilisation and conduct of classification and impressment.
c) Copy of *'Instructions to Purchasers.'*[98]
d) Revised and simplified forms for impressment, classification, payment on purchase and despatch by rail. In this connection Law Officers of the Crown and Treasury Solicitors had been consulted and the impressment form arranged, so that the fullest interpretation could be put on Section 114 and 115 of the Army Act.

To assist the Army Council in judging to what extent the organisation was fit for purpose, Commands were requested to answer questions that had been drawn up on an attached form and also make any other remarks. It was not necessary for them to refer to the question of extra DADRs for the present organisation, clerks for remount duties, or despatch boxes for purchasers, as these points had been fully reported on.

---

98   WO32/9127 (22A), *Instructions to Purchasers*, 1912.

GOCs were further requested to reply to questions that would be used to improve the system; but any minor points, recently forwarded in special letters, were not to be repeated.

MacMunn wrote to all commands with reference to the Remount Regulations, forwarding a memorandum on 'Prices to be Paid in Wartime', issued by the Director of Remounts as a guide to purchasers of impressed horses on behalf of the WO. [99] The prices were only a guide, as the purchaser was expected when necessary to complete his tally of horses by buying more valuable animals; he was considered the sole judge of what was a fair and reasonable price. The owner, if objecting to the price offered, had to accept it, but with the right to appeal to the County Court Judge to arbitrate as to price; nothing was to hinder the impressment of the horse:

Class	Size	Price
A horse fit for – an officer's charger	any size	£70
a cavalry trooper	not under 15 hands	£50
A cob fit for – Yeomanry or Mtd. Inf	14.2 to 15 hands	£50
for transport	not under 15 hands	£45
A heavy draught horse	15.2 hands and over	£60

These prices were for horses between five and eight years of age, with one tenth being deducted for every year after eight; no horses older than 14 were to be purchased.[100] Northern Command responded pointing out that if the order not to purchase over 14 was followed, many horses suitable for TF would be excluded. It requested consideration be given to extending the age of purchase for the EF to 14, and 16 years for the TF. MacMunn notified all headquarters that the phrase had been changed to read 'that no horse was to be bought that was not fit for a year of military service'. [101]

Artillery Horse Subsidy Scheme

A Committee looking at the 'Scheme for the Registration of Horses' under the chairmanship of Birkbeck reported on 11th October 1912.[102] Its terms of reference were to

99   19th September 1912; ref. Remount Regulations, Chapter V, Section 3-7.
100 WO32/9132, 116/GN/5526, (QMG4); Types of Horses for the Army, 1912, Board of Agriculture and Fisheries, circulated illustrating for breeders the types of horses to be purchased.
101 WO32/9132, CR.NC.22888/84/4/R, Northern Command, 5th October 1912; MacMunn's letter 18th October 1912.
102 WO32/8767. The Committee included: Lt-Col. Acland, Maj. MacMunn, DADR. Five meetings were held and seven representatives from the business world and military personnel were examined.

consider the proposed Scheme for the Registration of Horses for Army Purposes, with special reference to the principle and amount of subsidy involved. The Committee saw the military problem as the mobilisation of RHA and RFA for the Regular Army alone, as the peace establishment of batteries and ammunition columns was small in comparison with their wartime establishments. Reliance was placed on a supply of civilian horses being immediately available. To mobilise RHA and RFA brigades of the EF, approximately 16,000 light draught horses were required for the ranks within three to ten days, of which 9,000 had to be gun team and first line wagon horses. The essential qualification for civilian horses was to be of a suitable stamp and in hard condition, as it was considered worse than useless to send horses in soft condition into the field, as they would be incapable of work and their presence in a team accelerated the breakdown of other horses. The only class of horse that would fulfil the requisite conditions was the light draught horse in daily work in the large cities and towns, precisely the class of horse being superseded by the introduction of motor traction. There was then the issue of the specific training of horses to fit into RHA and RFA gun teams.

In order to prevent, or at least retard, the disappearance of this class from the streets, the United Horse Owners and Allied Trades Protection Association had forwarded a project to the Military Authorities for an annual subsidy, to be paid to horse owners who undertook to maintain horses of a suitable stamp and condition to meet the wartime requirements of the Artillery for three years. It was thought, the suggested £4 subsidy would have no influence on companies for whom the employment of horses continued to be an advantage, other than in maintaining standards. For companies like Messrs Tilling and Co, that contracted out horses to a wide range of trades, and supplied Territorial mounted troops for annual training and mounted drills throughout the year, the subsidy would, in the opinion of the Committee, produce good results in keeping up business and act as an inducement to keep the class of horse required by the Army. Tilling and Co., were the largest firm of jobmasters in London, supplying horses on contract; in 1912 they owned some 5,000 horses of which 1,200 were for horsed omnibuses. Mr Paterson (Messrs Carter, Paterson and Co), whose Company had recently combined with three other delivery firms, owning about 6,000 horses, stated the subsidy would be insufficient to really influence him in maintaining his total stud when the time came to change to motor traction. They were considering introducing more motors for long distance work, although the horsed van was most economical for door to door work. The Committee thought that about 1,000 of these horses would be suitable for the RA.

The Report states that the advantage to the Government, in assisting these and similar firms with a subsidy, was in having the knowledge of where to obtain instantly, a large number of horses that were in good condition and well cared for. This also induced companies to keep more horses of the artillery type, rather than lighter or heavier animals. Mr Hawkins (Secretary of the National Union of Horse and Vehicle Owners), representing the owners of some 35,000 horses, suggested the provincial towns, rather than London, were more likely to welcome the subsidy. Although there were fewer large studs, the subsidy was likely to influence provincial owners in keeping their studs, rather than move into motor traction. Williams Wynn (DADR, London District), estimated the number of firms in London, owning more than 150 horses each, suitable for the RA, was about 6,000.

The Committee concluded that in trades where motors would replace horses, no subsidy would influence firms. Those companies for which horses were still economical, came within the provision for impressment under Section 115 of the Army Act and so could be called upon, without the payment of any subsidy. The £4 subsidy would influence and assist owners to retain their studs longer than otherwise possible, especially those in the provinces, who for reasons such as sentiment, or lack of capital, would retain the horse. This included companies who obtained income from their horses for Territorial and army manoeuvres, it was therefore important to keep them in existence. The Committee were of the opinion that very few horses currently used in agriculture in England were suitable for artillery, being too heavy; there were lighter horses in Ireland working on the farms, but their condition and feeding made them unfit for the ranks on mobilisation.

As horses were being substituted by motor vehicles a subsidy of less than £4 would be of no value in halting the trend. The subsidy was to be allotted throughout the country in consultation with officials of local horse owners' associations. The Committee therefore recommended that a £4 subsidy, per horse, should be trialled as a cheaper alternative than any other scheme. The WO would apply the subsidy to encourage firms likely to be assisted in maintaining their horse businesses, recognising that it would not be possible to discriminate precisely between firms; this was to be left to the DADRs to make contracts appropriately. As an experiment 10,000 horses were to be subsidised, as originally proposed by the Army Council, for a period of three years; the WO would review the situation annually. They emphasised that the Subsidy Scheme was not the final settlement to the problem of supplying the RA with horses, noting that the Scheme only provided for 62% of artillery horses required for the EF. The organisation of the Army rested on adapting the country's resources to the requirements of a war, as the time was not far distant when the Army would have to further adapt motor traction to military needs, or it would be compelled to greatly increase its peacetime establishments.

After much consultation with horse owners the Government was persuaded to adopt the Artillery Horse Subsidy Scheme. The condition of subsidy was to be the same as that for the old registered scheme, in that horses were to be available whenever any portion of the Army Reserve was called up. This gave the Army the advantage of being able to take horses for small wars, for which the impressment laws could not be used.[103]

103 MacMunn, 1930, pp.93-4.

Remount Statement

The first Remount Statement was issued in August 1912, the culmination of 30 years work to obtain both a structure and system for preparing the Army for war, to provide a reserve of horses of both class and quality for mobilisation. The Statement contained the detailed requirements and instructions for horses, for the Army, on mobilisation. The amended edition of the Statement, was the one on which the Army mobilised in August 1914.[104]

The principle amendments from the 1913-14 edition related to the Expeditionary Force tables with changes to the peacetime establishment of the Cavalry; pairs of heavy draught horses were to replace light draught for trains and ambulances and Station Horse Establishments of home garrisons. [105] For the TF, table alterations included changes to the turnouts of heavy draught horses; for Reserve and unalloted units, the numbers of Reserve Artillery brigades were changed and certain unalloted units were added to Eastern Command and London District. As a general principle, Commands other than Aldershot, were to complete with horses those units mobilising within them, or remaining after mobilisation, from their own horse resources. Special Reserve Units that did not have peacetime establishments, were to be issued with their wartime establishments at their war station by the Command in which the station was located; this included the war establishments for Coastal Defence Stations. Priority was for the prompt mobilisation of the Aldershot Command. Commands were instructed to use their reserve horses to complete quotas for Aldershot, unless impressment provided the same quality of horses in equal time. The contract to deliver reserve horses at a specified place within 48 hours, was to ensure they were available faster than impressed horses. Reserve horses, surplus to Aldershot requirements, could be used for a Command's requirements as they should have registered in peacetime the requirements of the EF.

Calculations for wartime establishments were based on the principle that 10% of the peacetime establishment (20% for cavalry), as laid down in Remount Regulations, were likely to be unfit and had therefore been deducted, except in the TF in which all peacetime establishments were assumed to be effective. Six of the draught horses of each peacetime establishment were trained as pack and shown as such. The peacetime horses of all units and establishments in the ranks were assumed to be fit for service, except those included in the 10%, or 20%. All artillery horses, except chargers and heavy battery horses had been classed as Light Draught 1. Extra horses for wagons carrying blankets were to be provided, if required, at the port of embarkation by the Director of Remounts. Some Light Draught II horses would be surplus to requirements in ASC companies owing to heavy draught horses forming the wartime establishment of trains.

---

104 WO33/628, for 1913-14; WO33/669 (Amended) for 1914-15.
105 The following details are taken from WO33/669, pp.4-5.

The number of boarded out cavalry horses had increased from 73 in 1911 to 83, all of which were to be called in prior to mobilisation. It was anticipated that not all would be immediately available as some would be unfit, and distant boarders might not arrive in time. The figures for availability had been adjusted accordingly, showing that only 58 out of 83 were expected immediately for mobilisation and to join the first reinforcements:

Boarders that would join in time:-	fit for the ranks	30
	for first reinforcement	28
Boarders that would only be fit for, or join in time for the		
	Reserve Regiment	25
Total		83

The calculations below show the peacetime establishment of a cavalry regiment, fit for the field, for the purpose of estimating the number of horses required (total 69) from outside a regiment, bringing it up to a wartime establishment of 528 horses on mobilisation (including chargers and interpreters horses):

Troop horses in ranks[106]	509
Troop horses at depot (to join unit on mobilisation), average	7
Total	516
Less 20% possibly unfit and untrained	103
Balance	413
Add fit boarders	30
Add fit chargers (45 less 20%)	36
Fit on Peace Establishment: Total	479
War Establishment in riding horses	528
Less horses fit on peacetime establishments	479
Less deficiency per regiment	49
Less deficiency (48 less 20%) for 1st reinforcements	20
Total	548
Deficiency, per regiment: (548-479)	69

There was no age limit for horses going into the field, the decision was left to the CO; the only laid down condition was that a horse should be fit for one month's work

---

106 This figure did not include the additional seven boarders added to the 1914-15 Establishment.

under Continental conditions in the 'service arm' to which it belonged, as laid down in the Casting Regulations. The CO of a regiment could select the 528 horses required (including 14 horses for interpreters) for war establishments from:

Troopers in ranks	509
Troopers from depots	7
Officers chargers[107]	45
Boarders (if all arrived on time)	83
Remounts (reserve or impressed)	69
Total	713

From these 713 horses a regiment required:

Riders for the Regiment	528
Riders for 1st Reinforcement	48
Total	576

For Reserve Regiment	137
Total	713

Reserve units were to receive the surplus, or unfit horses on mobilisation and horses of unalloted units and establishments were to be used for completing the EF. For the TF, those Commands in which Divisional Transport and Supply Columns were using mechanical transport, the necessary amendments to horse requirements were expected to be made by them to supply TF units. Horses required with "turnouts" were included in the calculations. TF units permanently allotted to Coastal Defence did not require 2nd line transport, so Commands were to make necessary adjustments The whole of the 2nd line draught, "D" horses, were shown as heavy draught, except in the divisional transport train, where the supply wagons and spare "D" horses were shown as heavy draught.

After providing an explanation and general instructions, the Remount Statement was structured so that the whole provision and disposal of horses was placed into a series of tables, including: listed by Commands and units, the detailed requirements for each Command and units mobilising under its orders, and how the horses of the unallotted Regular Army units and establishments which did not form part of the BEF, or Home Defence Troops, were to be disposed of. A summary of the Statement showed mobilisation Field Army requirements, listed by classes of horses to be provided by each Command and by other arms and services of the BEF, and a list of unalloted and reserve units and establishments, and Station Horse Establishments of ports and garrisons, requiring horses.

---

107 Or officers' private chargers liable for mobilisation if drawing a forage ration.

In wartime some new reserve units would be formed, whilst certain training and miscellaneous peacetime establishments would be maintained and others would cease to exist. All fit horses of unallotted units and establishments were to be transferred to EF army units on mobilisation, the unalloted artillery units becoming reserve units. The reserve units consisted of 15 reserve cavalry regiments, three reserve horse artillery brigades and 12 reserve field artillery brigades. All drafts of horses to reinforce the EF, for Cavalry and Artillery, were furnished from reserve units, and for other arms and services from special depots. These reserve units, depots and the miscellaneous establishments were filled by the Commands to which they were allotted, immediately the mobilisation of EF army units was completed. Commands were warned of the possibility that the EF might not vacate its barracks immediately and should therefore be prepared to billet, or otherwise accommodate horses impressed for reserve units.

Once the wartime establishments of EF units had been completed, Commands and TF units would cease to purchase and refilling would be carried out by the Remount Service. If a Command reported it was unable to provide horses of the required class, from its own resources, the WO was to make other arrangements to provide them. Reserve units would have a nucleus of unfit, or untrained, horses left behind by units mobilising; this would be 10% of the peacetime strength of Army Corps except the Cavalry. Remount Depots, No.4 Arborfield Cross and No.3 Melton Mowbray, were to act as reserve units (Arborfield held horses for the ASC and Engineer units; Melton horses for mounted infantry). Remount Farm No.1 Lusk and No.2 Woolwich Depot, when filled, were to form a reserve at the disposal of the Remount Department. Horses left behind, by units mobilising, or giving up their horses, were to be transferred to reserve units under Command arrangements. The Remount Statement listed the horses available for reserve units and establishments, detailing the approximate number of army horses left behind by serving units on mobilisation from various sources, under Cavalry, Artillery, ASC, and miscellaneous establishments.

The WO informed Aldershot Command it was considering the question of Aldershot receiving the large number of horses required on mobilisation.[108] Staff officers concerned with horse mobilisation were asked to attend an informal conference with the Director of Remounts to discuss the existing general horse mobilisation scheme, in relation to their Commands and Aldershot's requirements.[109] Commands were notified that not all TF Associations had been informed of the mobilisation system for TF units; this was to be corrected and they were to receive, *Chapter V of 'Remount Regulations'*, the pamphlet on *'Impressment of Horses in Time of National Emergency'*[110] and *'Instructions for Purchasers'*.[111]

---

108 WO32/9132, 23rd October 1912, E.W.D. Ward, Secretary to the Army Council; WO33/669, in Part III, A of Remount Statement.
109 WO over the 29-30th of October with the Southern, Western, London District and Northern Commands, each in turn discussing with Aldershot mobilisation details.
110 Wo32/9132, 116/Home Stations/332.
111 WO32/9132, 26th October 1912, Ward, Army Council.

On 11th November the WO informed all Commands of their understanding that all horse mobilisation preparations were complete, as detailed in Chapter V of Remount Regulations and the Remount Statement, which had been with the Commands for several months along with the necessary forms. The only exception was the modifications to the Remount Statement affecting the Irish and Western Commands and horses for two Territorial Divisions.[112] The preparations included the appointment of purchasers (with substitutes in case of an emergency) and the completion of purchasers' lists from the previous year's classification. It understood that forms and stationery were complete in the existing purchasers boxes, or otherwise temporarily packed, pending the arrival of despatch boxes that had been ordered, and that 'requisitions of emergency' with their schedules were ready. The increase in DADRs had been sanctioned but provision of an extra clerk was still under consideration, and although classifications completed under the existing allotment were not that good, the whole Scheme was otherwise ready to be put into operation at any moment. It was made very clear to Commands that the WO publications in circulation, subject to any specified amendments, were those then in force. Suggestions and improvements discussed at the informal conference in October, would not have effect until embodied in the next revision of mobilisation schemes, resulting from the classification then in progress and issue of the annually revised Remount Statement and War Establishments. The annual amendment to the Horse Mobilisation Scheme was to be completed as soon as possible after the conclusion of the annual census, in accordance with the Remount Statement, to be issued about 1st January and come into effect for the 1st February.

Mobilisation Scheme

In October 1913, MacMunn described the full extent of the new mobilisation scheme of which there were two elements, Partial (highlighted in chart No.1 below) and Full Mobilisation (highlighted in the chart below). MacMunn stated that Partial Mobilisation was calling on military units and the Army Horse Reserve, in a situation where the Government would not want to obtain, or would not rely on, the general support of Parliament and the country, for putting the Impressment Laws into effect, for example, the sending of reinforcements to South Africa.[113] The Army Horse Reserve was essentially the old Horse Registration Scheme introduced in 1887, but now formed of two sections: the Artillery Horse Subsidy Scheme introduced in 1912, and a Miscellaneous Section (the "old registered horse scheme"):

112 WO32/9132, 11th November 1912, R.H. Brade, Army Council, and Ward 29th November, 1912.
113 MacMunn, 1914, pp.435-443, lecture given October 1913; Brunker, 1913, pp.7-8; MacMunn, 1930, pp.100-101.

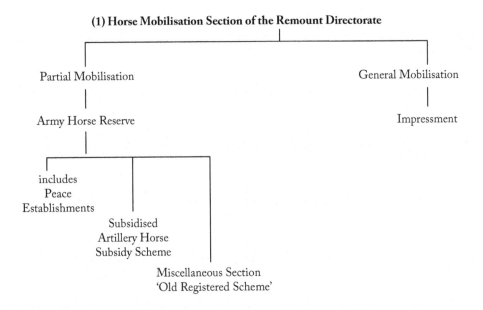

(1) Horse Mobilisation Section of the Remount Directorate

Partial Mobilisation

General Mobilisation

Army Horse Reserve

Impressment

includes
Peace
Establishments

Subsidised
Artillery Horse
Subsidy Scheme

Miscellaneous Section
'Old Registered Scheme'

The development of motor traction had resulted in a large reduction in the number of light draught horses of the artillery stamp working in the large towns. Representations were made to the WO, largely by deputations from some of the country's largest horse owners, especially business horse owners, requesting assistance to continue breeding this type of horse for the Army. Such pressures forced the WO to acknowledge that the payment of a higher subsidy would help many of the firms to make up their minds to maintain their studs and not change to motor transport. An annual subsidy of £4 per horse, paid six monthly in arrears, was agreed. The contract was for three years with a £50 penalty if the owners defaulted, but they were allowed to withdraw from the agreement at any time under certain penalties. On acceptance, horses were inspected by artillery officers and then every six months before payment. By October 1913 some 7,800 had been registered under the Artillery Horse Subsidy Scheme. MacMunn did not anticipate any difficulty in registering the full establishment of 10,000 horses. The Miscellaneous Section had an establishment of 15,000 horses and an actual strength in October 1913 of approximately 14,000, including saddle and transport horses of various classes, some of artillery type and some heavier. The Army Horse Reserve amounted to some 21,800 horses in October 1913, available to the QMG, within 48 hours, for any lawful emergency, from within a ten mile radius of their stables; in addition to the Army peace establishments.

Including all the horses from the peacetime establishment and Army Horse Reserve, impressment was then the main source of supply for a general mobilisation. The starting point for implementing the impressment process was the Amendment to Section 114 of the Army Act of 1911, followed by the Horse Census of 1912 and Remount Statement of 1913:

(2) Horse Mobilisation Section of the Remount Directorate

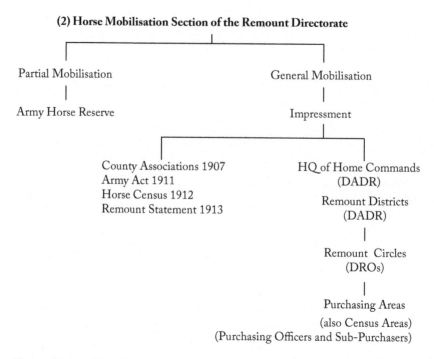

Partial Mobilisation

Army Horse Reserve

General Mobilisation

Impressment

County Associations 1907
Army Act 1911
Horse Census 1912
Remount Statement 1913

HQ of Home Commands
(DADR)

Remount Districts
(DADR)

Remount Circles
(DROs)

Purchasing Areas

(also Census Areas)
(Purchasing Officers and Sub-Purchasers)

To implement the administrative machinery and support the work of the County Associations, a small Remount Staff was organised, providing a reserve of officers for purchasing and administrative appointments. At least one Deputy Assistant Director of Remounts (DADR – there were 24 in July 1914) was appointed to the Headquarters of each Home Command. The Commands were divided into Remount Districts each with a DADR to manage the Registration Scheme.[114] Their appointment to the Command's Headquarters was to allow a more rigorous approach to the task of collecting information on the country's horse population. Districts were further divided into Remount Circles under District Remount Officers (see Appendix III Remount Service - Southern Command, October 1919); enumerators concerned with the administration, allotment of horses to units, and the finding and handling of horses on mobilisation.[115] These officers (total of 85), first appear in the April 1914 Army Lists.[116]

---

114 In his 1913 lecture, MacMunn, 1914, pp.438, 439-40, does not refer to 'remount districts', or 'district remount officers'. The division of Commands he calls 'remount circles' each with a DADR. His next division was into 'purchasing areas.' In the absence of other evidence one must conclude that the nomenclature of the system changed very soon after. The structure given here is from MacMunn, 1930, p.99; also WO107/26 and Hume, 1980, p.42.

115 Ibid., p.438, states there were 19 in Great Britain, apart from Ireland which was different; Brunker, 1913, p.9, gives 23 in Great Britain and Ireland. Figures in the text are from the Army List for July 1914.

116 MacMunn, 1930, p.99; Hume, 1980, p.37; *VR*, 1914, Vol.XXVI, 7th February, p.523.

Remount Circles were further divided into Purchasing Areas (also the census areas) under Purchasing Officers, appointed to the Remount Department and were generally, for example, retired officers, country gentlemen, Masters of Hounds. They were informed of the number of horses to be requisitioned within their areas, their locations and unit destinations; they were issued with a purchasing, or despatch box containing all the administrative material required to implement horse mobilisation (including Army Form A.F.A2029). They were appointed on the basis of having a sound knowledge of the type of horse required, the skills to judge a horse quickly and accurately, and the ability to drive a bargain with horse dealers. Three Purchasing Officers (Inspectors of Remounts) were included in the organisation; one responsible for cavalry remounts, one for artillery and one for draught horses. Their duties included purchasing, distribution of animals to regiments and corps and a measure of supervision over the activities of the remount depots. [117]

The legal machinery gave the GOC of a district, or any authorised officer of field rank, the power to impress horses for units under his command.[118] The machinery for impressment was initiated with an order for the Army to mobilise. To impress a horse four documents were required, bound in sets contained in Army Form A2029 and each of a different colour:

- Form A   The Requisition
- Form B   The Demand
- Form C   The Justices Warrant
- Order D   The Warrant ... served on the owner(s)

The purchaser, who had the complete set in Army Form A2029, pre-signed and complete except for the name of the Secretary of State, awaited a telegram stating that the Secretary of State had issued the necessary 'Proclamation' in *Form A 'the Requisition'*. [119] The Purchaser then proceeded to the magistrate presenting him with the above and filled in *Form B, 'the Demand'*. This called on the magistrate to issue a warrant for the provision of horses and vehicles as shown in his attached schedule. It was then attached to the 'schedule of horses for impressment.' The magistrate issued *Form C 'the Justice's Warrant,'* an order for the police to provide the horses shown in the attached list. The Purchaser was then ready to pick-up his allotted Constable and begin collection, with a veterinary officer accompanying the purchaser. The Constable had to complete *Order D, 'The Warrant'*, according to the scheduled list of the names of owners who were to supply the required horses; this demand, or Warrant, was served on the owner to hand-over the horses.

---

117 MacMunn, 1914, p.99; Hume, 1980, pp.7, 37; Todhunter (IWM, reference 87/53/1).
118 Army (Annual) Act, 1911; MacMunn, 1930, pp.100-101, and 1914, pp.442-3.
119 Todhunter (IWM, ref. 87/53/1).

The Constable left copies of the Order D, so serving the Warrant to owners of the horses (see Impressment Order below to Stratford-upon-Avon Corporation). Horses were then taken, if ready, or at a prearranged collection time. When taken, horses were paid for by cheque, at a previously agreed price and branded by the assistant, or clerk, with a broad arrow on the near forefoot (the same mark was used for vehicles). The owner could not, at the time, refuse the price but could appeal to the County Court for enhancement after delivery of the horse. MacMunn states they would have liked an addition to the law, making it incumbent upon the owner to deliver an impressed horse immediately, within a ten mile radius of his house, under threat of a penalty; the WO would then pay the man who brought the horse.[120]

It was the duty of the Purchasing Officer to employ any grooms, or other help, to take the horses into various villages and collecting centres, where they were inspected by a veterinary officer, then entrained, or handed over to a military collecting party. These arrangements were within the discretion of the Purchaser and the two sub-purchasers who were to assist him. This collection, in most Commands, was to be done by employing civilian labour, for which the Purchaser had full authority. On the order for mobilisation he was given a cash imprest of £100 to meet expenses. The same machinery applied to the TF, except that a Purchaser was generally not appointed for an area, but to a Territorial unit or group of units.

This was the main system of impressment. Commands had limited authority for modifications to meet any very peculiar conditions that might apply in some parts of the country. They each had a 'railway truck programme' agreed by the railway for impressment. It was the responsibility of the Purchaser to get horses, held at collecting centres, often yards close to the railways, or cattle markets, into the trucks, corresponding to the requirements of his schedule. Generally, each Command mounted the units contained within it, and sent a quota to Aldershot. The Aldershot quota and the Remount Reserve were the 'pools' by which they equalised the burden according to the resources of each command. It was not proposed to resort to impressment in Ireland, except for gun horses in the large cities, as it was felt purchasers "need only chink a bag of sovereigns to get all they wanted".[121]

By April 1914, MacMunn states the QMG was informed "that we were ready" and reported accordingly to the Army Council and Secretary of State, who informed Parliament that the horse problem was, in principle solved.[122] Brunker wrote that in the light of experience, with some possible slight further improvement in the machinery of collection, "the arrangements for this important branch of mobilisation may now be regarded as complete".[123]

120 MacMunn, 1914, p.443.
121 MacMunn, 1930, p.101.
122 Ibid.; Col. J.E.B. Seeley, Secretary of State for War, Hansard (C), 1914, Vol.L1X, 10th March, (c)1095-6.
123 Brunker, 1913, pp.7-8.

**Impressment Order to Stratford on Avon Corporation
(received 11 August 1914)**

In the Stratford on Avon Corporation Horse Book, held at The Shakespeare Birthplace Trust, reference BRR 60/9

G. R.

National Emergency.   Impressment Order under Section 115 of the Army Act.

To *Stratford on avon corporation*

    His Majesty, having declared that a national emergency has arisen, the horses and vehicles enumerated below are to be impressed for the public service, if found fit (in accordance with Section 115 of the Army Act), and will be paid for on the spot at the market value to be settled by the purchasing officer.   Should you not accept the price paid as fair value, you have the right to appeal to the County Court (in Scotland the Sheriff's Court), but you must not hinder the delivery of the horses and vehicles, etc. The purchasing officer may claim to purchase such harness and stable gear as he may require with the horse or vehicle.   *Thomas H Bazeley PB110*

Horses and Vehicles required—

4 horses

At the unicorn Hotel at once

Place_____

Date *9 august 1914*

*Impressment Order to Stratford Upon Avon Corporation, Warwickshire. Dated 9th August 1914.
(Shakespeare Birthplace Trust BRR60/9)*

During 1913 MacMunn made several trial samplings of the impressment lists of remount circles in Great Britain and felt sure that it would work. As the Army itself was most sceptical, the QMG sent him lecturing to various Commands and to communicate articles to the leading papers. Whereupon, Lord Esher wrote "that cheery optimist Col. MacMunn suffered from two delusions; first, that there were enough horses in England and secondly, that even if there were, that it was possible to impress them". When 160,000 horses were mobilised and correctly placed, in 14 days in August 1914, MacMunn wrote to Esher telling him so, signing himself "the cheery optimist".[124]

Located in the QMG's Department, the organisation of the Remount Department in the UK, in July 1914 immediately prior to the opening of hostilities was:

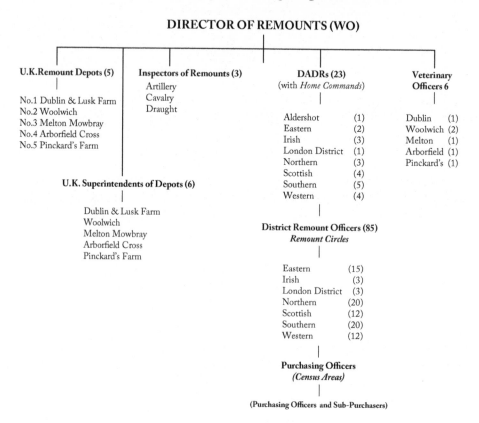

DIRECTOR OF REMOUNTS (WO)

U.K.Remount Depots (5)	Inspectors of Remounts (3)	DADRs (23) (with *Home Commands*)	Veterinary Officers 6
No.1 Dublin & Lusk Farm	Artillery		
No.2 Woolwich	Cavalry	Aldershot (1)	Dublin (1)
No.3 Melton Mowbray	Draught	Eastern (2)	Woolwich (2)
No.4 Arborfield Cross		Irish (3)	Melton (1)
No.5 Pinckard's Farm		London District (1)	Arborfield (1)
		Northern (3)	Pinckard's (1)
		Scottish (4)	
U.K. Superintendents of Depots (6)		Southern (5)	
		Western (4)	
Dublin & Lusk Farm			
Woolwich		**District Remount Officers (85)**	
Melton Mowbray		*Remount Circles*	
Arborfield Cross			
Pinckard's Farm		Eastern (15)	
		Irish (3)	
		London District (3)	
		Northern (20)	
		Scottish (12)	
		Southern (20)	
		Western (12)	

Purchasing Officers
(Census Areas)

(Purchasing Officers and Sub-Purchasers)

During 1913 the Veterinary Directorate became independent of the Remount Department and placed directly under the QMG, the veterinary officers listed in

124 MacMunn, 1930, p.101.

the chart above are therefore attached to the Remount Depots from the Veterinary Directorate. In addition to the above, the Remount Department in South Africa retained: a remount depot at Robert's Heights, Pretoria, with a Superintendent of Depots, a DADR and an attached veterinary officer at the Depot.

The effectiveness of this decentralised Hose Mobilisation Scheme was demonstrated on the outbreak of war, when 115,000 animals were impressed for military service within 12 days.[125]

125 Hume, 1980, p.42.

5

Mechanisation and a New Transport System

There is nothing which a horse can do which cannot be better done by motor traction.[1]

The horse is noble animal, but there are lots of things a motor vehicle can do which he is unfortunately unable to carry out.[2]

Mechanical traction had been used to a limited extent during the 1899-1902 War. The successful results of this experiment, along with the activities of other major European armies and the steady spread of motor vehicles in civilian use, meant the Army could not ignore its potential in any future conflict. The increased use of motor vehicles in military service after 1902, led to the introduction of a new transport system that integrated motorised transport with the use of rail and animals.[3] Forward thinking officers like Col. Paul, Assistant Director of Transport, could write in 1911 that "road transport will be considered as the organisation by means of which supplies of all descriptions in war are conveyed from the railways, or other sources, to the field units, and which also undertake the evacuation of sick and wounded, and the conveyance to the rear of impedimenta no longer required at the front." [4]

Mechanisation

The threat to the monopoly of the horse as the motive power of the British Army was first seriously challenged by developments in mechanically propelled vehicles during the first two decades of the twentieth century. Railways would also play a major role in diminishing the monopoly of military horsed transport, although the cavalry horse was not under such threat until well after the First World War. In transport terms

---

1   Wells, H.G., "The use of cavalry" in *VR*, 1917, Vol. XXIX, 14th April, p.432.
2   White, O.W, 1921, *RASCQ*, October, Vol.9, p.576.
3   Winton, 2000.
4   Paul, 1911, *ASCQ*, Vol.4, p.535.

the world was in revolution: steam, petrol, rail, electric tramways, air, shipping, motor transport and road improvements. In 1911, Lt-Col. St John Parker, ASC, wrote that it did not require a prophet to see by what means supplies would be transported during the next European war.[5] Capt. Cumberlegge, ASC, who had been sceptical about the, "oft repeated claim that the horse would always remain a necessary component of the army machine," now considered that with aeroplanes, submarines and the large variety of motor vehicles, it was "well to beware of judging the future by the present and of condemning rashly". He saw that mechanical transport must, before long engage, the serious attention of the Army generally, and of all ASC officers in particular.[6]

It was a transport revolution the military could not, and did not, ignore. The introduction and development of mechanically propelled vehicles went hand in hand with developments in organisation and structure. In 1912, Lt-Col. Carter, ASC, wrote "recent inventions had an enormous effect on the conduct of war, the repeated improvements in modern weapons and machines of every kind had, and would continue to, produce changes in the tactical handling of troops".[7] The mobility of the large contemporary armies, with their enormous unwieldy mass of horses and vehicles, were dependent on the availability of effective railways. St. John Parker, reviewing wartime establishments, estimated some 20,000 additional horses would be required for ammunition and supply columns and about 173,000 for mobilization generally. It was therefore imperative to adopt suitable means to reduce horse transport and he saw the only practicable alternative was mechanical road transport.[8] The introduction of motor propelled vehicles, of a reliable type, compelled the military to take note of this new factor in warfare, as it had a distinct and direct bearing on the solution of strategic problems, in the same way as the improvement of firearms had a bearing on of tactical problems.[9] Capt. Davidson, RE, thought it accepted by all the leading Powers that an army that had no mechanical transport would be most seriously handicapped on mobilisation.[10]

As muzzle-loaders gave way to breech-loaders and these to magazine rifles, machine guns and quick firing cannon, Capt. Green, RA, believed the demand for greater quantities of ammunition to feed the new generation of guns and rifles, introduced a new complication for transport and would be a major incentive for change.[11] Significant increases in the consumption of ammunition would place serious strains on transport services, as the waggon train of an army increased to transport the enormous increase in the bulk and weight to feed the higher rates of expenditure.[12] Transport would be

5   Parker St John, 1911, p.374.
6   Cumberlegge, 1910, pp.28-29.
7   Carter, 1912, p.673.
8   Parker, St John, p.365.
9   Paul, 1911, p.538; Carter, 1912, p.673; Beadon, 1931 pp.48-49.
10   Davidson, 1913, pp.352-3.
11   Green, 1905, pp 609-10.
12   Fortescue, p.xix, introduction to Beadon, 1931.

difficult to mobilise in highly concentrated areas and when mobilised, more difficult to manoeuvre. There would be numerous disadvantages to the large horse transport columns working in advance of the railways. These disadvantages included:

- relatively greater costs
- volume of fodder required was greater than fuel for motor transport
- difficulties with organisation and control
- the horses and number of personnel required, per ton of useful load, consumed a relatively larger percentage of the total they carried
- a days march was limited to an average of 15 to 20 miles
- the pace was slow with lengthy columns, making them vulnerable to enemy action with the roads immediately in the rear of fighting troops congested with traffic of all kinds, possibly hindering movements to the rear, or flank
- the supply of draught horses was becoming more difficult
- humane reasons, dead and dying horses were distressing to men who cared for them

The pace at which animals undertake their work is important for health and longevity. The regulation trot was 8 mph. White writes that divisional horse transport could do no more than 3½ mph by themselves, including halts, or 3 mph with infantry, or 2½ mph when large bodies of troops are moving. Motor transport could move at 8 to 10 mph in convoy formation.[13]

The advantages of motor, over horse transport, were reinforced as motor vehicles improved in design and performance, and as Green points out, their capacity to reduce the bulk created by an increase in road transport.[14] This could be seen by simply observing the spaces occupied by motor and horsed vehicles respectively, then applying this to an army on the move. By using motor vehicles there would be an enormous reduction in length of columns, "reductions in checks, blocks and all the weariness of the flesh attendant upon such movements". The number of animals to be fed and equipped would decrease, as would the quantities of forage and equipment, as the greater number of animals disappeared replaced by the motor car and lorry for transporting men and supplies. Fortescue saw that the introduction of motor transport would relieve the misgivings of many that animal transport, on the scale and under the system which prevailed at the opening of the 1899-1902 War, would hopelessly encumber roads in the rear of a large force operating in any European country.[15]

Mechanically propelled vehicles were introduced into the British Army in 1858. The earliest recorded British use of motor transport on active service was the Ashanti War of 1873-74. The Germans employed two British made tractors in the Franco-Prussian

13   Pratt, A., 1918, p.333; White, *RASCQ*, 1921, pp.556-557.
14   Paul, 1911, p.538; Carey, 1906, pp.213-221; Green, pp.610-11.
15   Fortescue, ibid.

War, 1870-71, and the Russians used 12 British tractors in the Russo-Turkish War, 1878. Britain was the first nation to employ mechanical power in any numbers in warfare, when using traction engines and several steam lorries, operated by the Royal Engineers, during the 1899-1902 War (see photograph below). Given the technical limitations of motor traction, these experiments had proved its usefulness and stimulated further experiment and development. Maj. Scholfield, RE, Director of Steam Transport in South Africa, highlighted the considerable success, and also the lack of understanding, of the abilities and use of this new technology in warfare.[16] Maj- Gen. Wood, remarking on Scholfield's Report, wrote of the excellent results of this new type of transport, but also the lack of fully trained personnel and the need for the use of vehicles to be governed by expert advice in these earlier stages of its development. In contrast, Maj-Gen. Smith, AVC, wrote that motor transport (MT) was disappointing in South Africa.[17] It is difficult to judge the extent of the success of motor transport during this War, however, it had its successes and caught the attention of some forward-thinking officers intent on expanding the use of mechanical vehicles in the army.

Before the 1899-1902 War was over, developments initiated by the WO were sanctioned for the future use of MT in the army. A Mechanical Transport Committee (MTC) was formed in 1900 and given considerable powers for experimentation and reporting, with four sub-committees: Experiment and Motor, Royal Artillery, Royal Engineers, and ASC. The principal feature of these early deliberations was to establish that MT came within the brief of the ASC. During 1901 the WO organised its first trials for 'self-propelled' lorries, with a view to purchasing the best types for the Army, although petrol vehicles were not to be included.[18] 1902 saw the formation of 'motor volunteers' utilised during the 1903 Army manoeuvres and an Inspectorate of MT was formed, within the ASC, in 1903. From 1903 MT became the responsibility of the ASC under Maj. McNalty, ASC. All army vehicles, including those of the Royal Engineers, were transferred to Aldershot. Army Estimates (Vote VI) for motor transport vehicles rose from £22,000 in 1909-10, to £46,000 in 1911-12. Between 1904 and 1912 the transport and supply services of the British Army were gradually transformed, so that when the BEF took the field in 1914, a large proportion of its horse transport had been replaced with motor transport units. This was the result of implementing a new transport system and a mobilisation plan for motor vehicles similar to that for horses.[19]

All these changes, as with the far reaching developments relating to army remounts, took place in the peacetime army. Forward thinking officers recognised the problems of transport and supply, saw the potential of motor vehicles being developed in the

16 Ventham and Fletcher, pp.1-3; *The Automotive Monthly*, June 1964 in RCT B2 -8962; Scholfield, 1903.
17 Elliott Wood, Commander R.E., First Army Corps in 1903, South Africa, in Scholfield, 1903, p.3; Smith, 1919, p.269.
18 *Motor Traction*, 1909, 6th March, pp.208-9; Cd.991, 1901.
19 Brunker, 1911, pp.11, 16.

Royal Engineers Fowler traction engine and train fording a drift in the Transvaal 1899-1902, with a Burrell 224 engine in the foreground. (Royal Logistic Corps Museum)

Steam tractor trials, Aldershot 1904, Wallis and Steven (Basingstoke) Tractor 004.
(Royal Logistic Corps Museum)

commercial world, and had the vision to translate into practice the advantages of MT over the horse, as the future source of motive power for the military. The foundations for mechanisation had been firmly laid within the twelve years from the close of the 1899-1902 War. The shortage of certain types of horses was a central factor, in the process of mechanisation by 1914. It should therefore be of no surprise that the British Army in 1914 was using a large number of mechanically propelled vehicles. As with all continental armies, the British retained a dependence on animal transport. The Army had not been slow to learn its lessons and mechanisation was not the slow and painful progress suggested by some writers.[20]

The earliest forms of mechanically propelled vehicles, although possessing some superiority over horse drawn wagons, had inherent disadvantages for military use. Early steam vehicles were heavy, consumed a large proportion of the load they carried in fuel, had a high initial cost of introduction, complex machinery and breakdowns, and a shortage of trained personnel. Lt. Lyon and Lt. Unwin, ASC, in their 1908 article on the future development of mechanical transport gave a detailed breakdown of the advantages of mechanised vehicles over horse transport, in tonnage carried and costs. A horse transport company on the higher establishment could carry an average of 12 tons over 15 miles in one day, with a maximum of 12 drivers, giving a figure of 15 net tons miles per man per day. In comparison, a traction engine hauling a load of 18 tons in three 6-ton trucks with three men, travelling 25 miles a day gave 150 net tons miles per man per day, or ten times as much as horse transport. In economic terms the traction engine cost about £1,000 and each truck £80, so the total cost of the train was about £1,240. For horse transport there would be at least nine General Service (GS) wagons at about £90 each, 36 horses at about £30 each, adding the value of the harness, the total cost would be £2,000. Lyon and Unwin concluded that MT would do nearly twice the mileage per day compared with horse transport for a little less than 30% of the cost.[21]

The major limitation to extending the use of MT and replacing animals in first and second line divisional transport, was the inability to go across country, but Maj. Hazelton, ASC, thought this was not a serious limitation considering military planning was focused on its use in Europe.[22] By 1911, some of the main advantages of the latest type of motor vehicles included: increased mobility and greater speed, with the latest motor at least four to six times faster than any horse transport. MT was cheaper, took up less road space and required fewer personnel. The smaller area in which it could be concentrated and the increased radius of action were also important aspects, as was the freedom from the panic of animals and sanitary advantages. Mobilisation would be quicker and less costly; with fewer vehicles, and without animals, it was easier to move troops and goods by rail or sea. Capt. Hayter, ASC and others, believed that increasing

20   For example Crouch, 1984, p.6.
21   Lt. Lyon and Lt. Unwin, ASC, 1908, p.416.
22   Hazelton, 1911, p.486.

No.2 Horse Transport Company, RASC, Bulford, 1929. (Royal Logistic Corps Museum)

commercial use was proving motor transport to be the cheaper option.[23] Such views were not confined to British officers. Although Britain took the lead in the development of motor vehicles for military purposes, Germany, France, Italy and Austria were all experimenting with motor vehicles. Their views and findings on the military value and future development were exactly the same as the British. Animal transport was by no means obsolete, but it now had both a rival and a partner.[24]

The Army closely monitored the continual and rapid improvements in design and performance of motor vehicles in the commercial world. The early arguments against the introduction of motor vehicles were quickly negated by the speed of development and increased reliability. Following the WO trials of 1901, the Motor Transport Committee (MTC) continued to purchase and experiment with various types of motor vehicles, concentrating on lorries and tractors, using both steam and internal combustion engines as sources of power. Some 26 traction engines and 10 lorries were used in the manoeuvres of 1903. [25]

It is commonly assumed that the major debate taking place within the Army between the wars, on the future of 'motive power', was the horse versus the motor vehicle. This was an important issue, but so also was that surrounding the advantages and superiority of the internal combustion engine over steam propelled vehicles. The Army required vehicles that consumed less fuel, had an independence of operation and carried a useful load. The debate over steam versus the internal combustion engine

23   Hayter, 1910, p.720; Hazelton, 1911, pp.482-3; McNalty, 1904, February, pp.58-70.
24   Article in the French Journal, *Revue du Service de l'Intendance Militaire*, (ASCQ, 1906, Vol.1, October, p.587) refers to the lead taken by England; Sutton and Walker, 1990, p.69.
25   McNalty, 1904, p.69.

faced the same issues as between the horse versus motor vehicles: mobility, speed, radius of action, reliability, initial cost and maintenance. The Army could not move forward with mechanisation without considering adequate supplies of fuel for the vehicles it adopted, especially in time of war.[26] In 1902, the WO carried out consumption trials with steam engines to demonstrate the practicality of supplying an ammunition park, for an army corps, with mechanical instead of animal transport.[27] Results from the trials of 1908-10, together with reports from trials in various manoeuvres, in both the British and Continental armies, led to the conclusion that steam vehicles could be abandoned, except for those functions for which it was specifically suited, and substituted by internal combustion engines. This decision was made in 1910, largely influenced by the work of Col. Paul, Assistant Director of Transport (WO), notably following a visit made to the 1910 French manoeuvres. On his return Paul wrote to the QMG describing the British system of employing mainly steam vehicles, as being 'archaic' and 'a relic of the Stone Age'. The internal combustion engine had asserted its superiority over steam as the next best method of transport after the horse, although, the Army would use both types of vehicles in the 1914-18 War.[28]

During the opening decade of the twentieth century the MTC spent £30,000 on experimental work, a considerable sum at that time, yet small when one considers its expensive nature. This Committee maintained close links with the Inspection Branch and the civilian motor industry. These links were central to the successful mechanisation of military transport and supply services, and their successful employment during 1914-18. In 1902 a newly formed Motor Transport Section (MTS) was given five years to develop, but it did not appear formally in wartime establishments until 1907-8. The first Motor Transport Unit, 77 Company, ASC, was formed at Chatham, 1903, under Brevet-Maj. C.E.I. McNalty. The use of cars for staff purposes was especially encouraged in the 1903 and 1904 manoeuvres; both service cars and private cars were used, and from 1904 onwards, motor transport companies formed the nuclei for formations in the field. The first static workshop was constructed at Aldershot in 1905, followed by mobile workshop trailers and then mobile workshops constructed on lorries.[29] By the end of 1906, a scheme had evolved whereby a certain proportion of motor transport was included in the mobilisation establishments of the Field Army. This coincided in date with the London General Omnibus Companies' decision to convert from horses to motor vehicles. MT was to provide for the supplies and ammunition of one cavalry division and six infantry divisions, on the assumption that twice the distance could be covered compared with horse transport. In the provisional Wartime Establishments for 1907-8, two sections of the transport and supply park, originally consisting of 80 horsed GS wagons, occupying a road space of roughly 800

26   Hayter, 1910, pp.722-3; Sutton and Walker, p.71; Beadon, p.32.
27   McNalty, 1905, pp.73-78.
28   Paul, 1911; Parker, St John, 1911, p.366; Hazelton, 1911, p.485; Beadon, 1931, pp.34-35.
29   McNalty, *ASCJ*, 1904, p.59; Beadon, pp.27-30, 35-6, 56.

yards, where made into motor transport sections. Motor cycles and lorries were used in army manoeuvres of 1909. Col. Edye, ASC, noted that the advantages of MT were again highlighted during the Irish Manoeuvres of 1910, which he believed were the first manoeuvres in which all the transport used behind the horsed regimental transport was mechanical.[30]

The continued need for horse transport was still recognised especially for first line divisional transport. Although MT was about to revolutionise supply in the field, motor lorries could not always guarantee going right up to the troops in camp or bivouacs, as they needed some form of road. Animal transport was therefore the link between a motor transport supply train and front line troops. It was becoming clear, that only fast moving motor transport had the required radius of action capable of linking up regimental wagons and field bakeries. For Capt. Cumberlegge, and others like him, it was inevitable that ASC supply trains of the future would be composed entirely of motorised vehicles.[31]

One of the objectives of the 1910 Army manoeuvres was to consider the maintenance of an army in the field by extensively trialling motor vehicles for the transport of supplies and ammunition. Maj-Gen. Robb, commented that many of the vehicles called out on the Motor Vehicle Registration Scheme were in poor condition, and commented on the lack of trained horses and personnel. Light tractors were used for the ammunition supply of a divisional ammunition park, which Lt-Col. Brunker stated, would have required 1,048 horses for each divisional ammunition column.[32] GS wagons were fitted out for horse and motor transport, one engine drawing three wagons. The divisional ammunition column returned to the park with empty wagons; the mechanical draw bar was unshipped and horse teams hooked into the full loads, whilst the engines drew the empty wagons back to the rail for refilling and exchange. The experiment was generally considered a success, for example, one tractor and two men took the place of 18 horses and six men. Following the 1910 Cavalry manoeuvres Haig recommended organizing a 'Signal Squadron' that would include cars and motor cycles.[33]

By 1911 there was a variety of motor vehicle types in use by the Army. Lt. Verney, ASC, commented enthusiastically on the great change in motor omnibuses. Having reached a sufficiently high standard of efficiency, he considered they were the finest method of moving dismounted troops for distances up to 200 miles in 30 hours. Three buses per company of infantry (average seating capacity of 34 per bus) provided transport for about 5,000 men. Verney stated he had driven one of the finest of the new motor buses, built in 1908, accomplishing 90 miles in 4.5 hours but he acknowledged that would not be the case when carrying heavy loads and road traffic.[34]

---

30   Brunker, and Baden-Powell, 1910; Sutton, 1998, p.53; Edye, 1911, p.384.
31   Cumberlegge, 1911 (a), p.245.
32   Brunker (editor of the *Army Annual Year Book*), 1911, pp.247-50.
33   Ibid., pp.258-50, 259; Robb, in Carter, 1912.
34   Verney, 1912, pp.2-7.

In the 1911 War Establishments, the supply park consisted of three sections, one and two being MT. Horses were to be substituted for light tractors drawing the Regular Army wagon equipment, the considerable stock of which, Hayter, considered would probably affect future policy for some time.[35] A light tractor was able to pull three GS wagons, replacing twelve horses, conveying a load further in one day, at a faster pace, thus shortening the length of a column and requiring fewer personnel.

Attention was also given to the use of motor vehicles for hauling guns. Cumberlegge thought that in the future, guns and teams might be conveyed rapidly from point to point with horses only being used to drag the guns into position at the end of a march.[36] Capt. Walker, RE, held the same view, reinforcing the point that in addition to economising on horses, the adoption of motor vehicles by the RHA would reduce the length of a column. There were normally 18 guns, 54 wagons, 7 small arms ammunition (SAA) carts and 74 GS wagons, all horsed, as well as 70 spare horses, giving the column on route a total length of approximately 2,500 yards (2,286 metres). By using lorries this could be reduced to 18 guns, 18 wagons all horse drawn with 100 spare horses, 25 lorries towing 18 wagons and 7 SAA carts. In addition to carrying the loads of 18 wagons and 34 GS wagons the column length would be reduced to 1,250 yards (1,143 metres). [37] During 1911, trials took place in the Long Valley, Aldershot, with a Caterpillar tractor drawing a 64 pounder gun against a team of eight horses drawing a similar gun. The object of the trials, with each team undertaking three identical tests, was to ascertain if the tractor showed any advantages over horsed teams. The conclusion drawn from the trials was that MT was best deployed over long distances, carrying big loads; the work of the tractor only began where the work of the horses left off. Horses could not compete, for example, on excessively severe and long gradients and in speed over long distances.[38]

In March 1913 the Aldershot Command carried out a 'billeting' exercise involving two divisions, necessitating the feeding of some 10,000 men and 2,000 horses; the supply sections of trains were not used, thereby greatly reducing the need for horse transport. Supply for the exercise was carried out by MT; the column, consisted of only five, 1.5 ton lorries, with one in reserve, containing sufficient food for men and forage for horses.[39] Such were the developments by 1914 that Henderson could write, in relation to the Territorial ASC, in Scotland, that no better object lesson for the value of the motor lorry, for transport purposes, could be furnished than the experience of supply officers in the training camp at Boards. The contractor's bakery was in Glasgow, a distance of 25 miles by road from the camp. A very efficient service of motor lorries took the bread into camp each afternoon punctually at 3pm. Had the

---

35   Hayter, 1910, p.725; also Paul, 1911, p.147.
36   Cumberlegge, 1911 (b), pp.566-71; Ventham and Fletcher, 1989, pp.8-14.
37   Walker, 1909, p.279.
38   Brunker, 1913, p.135-144.
39   Ibid.

service been by rail, or horse transport, there would have been considerable trouble in transportation and probably frequent delays in delivery. It seemed reasonable to Henderson that on mobilisation much of the transport work of the Territorial ASC would be done by MT.[40]

A memorandum from the Secretary of State for War, referring to the Army Estimates for 1913-14, states that the chief change in establishments was a reorganisation of the Horse and Field Artillery, in part due to the development of MT.[41] Experimental work continued right up to the outbreak of war, for example, in July 1914, a demonstration of gun towing, using 30 HP (horsepower) Sheffield Simplex Cars and 15 pounder guns of the Territorial West Riding RHA, was carried out for the first time by Northern Command.[42] The object was to repulse an imaginary enemy landing at Grimsby eight miles away. The advancing ammunition party had a journey of 118 miles to complete before they picked up their loads and joined the guns, which were manoeuvred by the Simplex cars into battery position off the road. The experiment proved satisfactory, given the limitations of a standard touring car not being designed for artillery work, travelling over bad roads, or in shell torn country. The average running time was 21 mph, the whole journey occupying between five to six hours, compared to 14 hours by rail, or between four to five days using horse transport.

Two troop movement trials using motor vehicles were carried out during 1908, in conjunction with civilian organisations, independently of the work of the MTC. On the 6th December, the first mobilisation exercise in transporting British troops with double-decker buses was carried out with some success. 81 men of the 5th Bn. Essex Territorials (Eastern Command) were carried in two buses, 14 miles in 67 minutes, in poor weather conditions, from Chelmsford to Latchingdon, Essex. Ammunition and commissariat supplies were carried in a motor van. The three motors completed the course simultaneously. On the return journey, 50 men were carried from Latchingdon to Maldon in one bus without difficulty.[43] Another exercise, on the 18th December, carried out under service conditions, over heavy roads and in bad weather, was also considered successful. With 25 ordinary London General Omnibus Company petrol driven vehicles, conveying 500 men, an average of 20 men per car, of the 1st Bn. Norfolk and 3rd Bn. Essex Regiments, from Warley barracks, Brentwood, to Leigh, Essex. Clarkson commented that this experiment was useful in showing the unsuitability of the undisciplined London bus driver to operate upon country roads, as about 25% of the cars were soon ditched, and only an average speed 7 mph was achieved.[44]

40   Henderson, 1914, p.187.
41   Brunker, 1913, p.1.
42   Beadon, 1931, pp.34-35.
43   Clarkson, T, 1910, p.452; Sutton and Walker, 1990, p.74, states a company of 120 men.
44   Beadon, 1931, p.33, state 94 vehicles to assist in the concentration of troops at Shoeburyness; Sutton and Walker, 1990, p.74, state 24 vehicles London to Shoeburyness; *Motor Transport Corps Report 1908-9*, in RCT Archive, A6/8920, 1908, pp.43-46. Clarkson, p.452.

Clarkson estimated there was work in London for at least 2,000 of the improved type of double-decker bus, capable of carrying 60,000 men, which if used for military purposes would free railways to deal with heavy traffic such as guns and horses. During the May 1909 Yeomanry manoeuvres, four double-decker motors were used to move men into action quickly; the same vehicles moved about ten tons of regimental baggage 35 miles, from Wickham Market to Sudbury, in three hours. In June an experiment took place to determine how far men could be conveyed in one day in a double-decker steam bus, between Chelmsford, via Woolwich Ferry to Folkestone return; the total distance of 186 miles was achieved in 13 hours 38 minutes, at an average speed of 13.6 mph In July, 160 men of the 5th Bn. Essex Territorials were transported 22 miles, in five cars from Chelmsford to Colchester, in 125 minutes.[45] The most publicised trials took place on the 17th March 1909, involving a composite Guards battalion (Grenadier, Coldstream and Scots Guards), with all arms, personal kit and battalion equipment, moving from London to Hastings, using 316 privately owned and driven cars, of various makes, with about 30 civilian drivers and commercial lorries to carry the Battalion's equipment. It was organised by the Automobile Association with the agreement and attendance of Haldane, Secretary of State for War. In Clarkson's view, it showed very conclusively the unsuitability of private cars for such a duty; he had no hesitation in stating that the chief value of the experiment was in showing how the transport of troops should not be done, with vehicles occupying an excessive amount of road space. Sutton and Walker however considered it a highly successful event, although not of a tactical nature.[46]

The use of motor vehicles as field ambulances was not ignored. Lt-Col. Cree, RAMC, stated that in reducing the number of wagons required for a division the present 30 horsed ambulance wagons could be cut to 16 motor wagons, reducing space and time. The motor cycle was also considered as being important for military use; Maj-Gen. Fraser saw it as an alternative for mounting yeomanry and some of the Regular Army, as there would not be enough suitable horses. The Army purchased ten motor cycles, which could achieve speeds of 40 mph again with the intention of replacing riding horses for communication purposes.[47]

To obtain the number of motor vehicles required for military purposes the Army would have to rely on the forms of transport in civil use during peacetime. Standardisation, not only in vehicle design, but also, as far as possible, in component parts was important. Of all continental countries, Britain laid down the greatest degree of standardisation, and insisted on the closest compatibility between the different makes.[48]

---

45   Clarkson, 1910, p.453-4; see Maj. P.O.Hazelton, editor of *ASCQ*, in Verney, 1912, p.7 and Lt-Gen Paget, G.O.C Eastern Command, on the advantages of the motor bus as a means of rapid troop transport.

46   Beadon, 1931, p.33; Clarkson, 1910, p.451 he states 400 vehicles were used; Sutton and Walker, 1990, p.77.

47   Cree, 1914, Vol.7, July, pp.252-73 (lecture, Aldershot, 24th December 1914); Fraser, in Clarkson, 1910, p.464; Sutton, 1998, pp.54-55.

48   Col. HCL. Holden, RA, 1913, pp.345-352; Davidson, 1913, pp.356-7.

Motor Vehicle Subsidy Scheme

In a memorandum to the General Staff, December 1910, Col. Paul, put forward a scheme for the reorganisation of the supply and transport system, including a recommendation that the 900 motor vehicles required to complete the numbers for mobilisation, over and above those held with units, should be obtained by means of a subsidy scheme. The first motor vehicle Registered Subsidy Scheme was introduced in 1908, with a subsidy of £2 per annum, largely aimed at obtaining the light steam tractor. As Maj-Gen. Robb stated in relation to the 1910 manoeuvres, the registration, or subsidy fee, was not sufficient to ensure a supply of vehicles, or that vehicles were maintained in an efficient condition for military purposes. When those on the Scheme were called out many were in poor condition. In 1911 two schemes existed for the supply of vehicles for mobilisation and for a standardisation of vehicles and parts; a "Provisional" and the "Main Subsidy Scheme".

The specification for a lorry for military purposes had been agreed with manufacturers; the Army would purchase a number of these and obtain the rest, on mobilisation, from civilian owners, who were encouraged to buy the type, with an annual subsidy, registered under the "Provisional" Scheme, This Scheme was designed as an initial stage until sufficient "subsidy" type vehicles could be produced. It was expanded and a larger subsidy offered of between £38-£52, but only for the petrol lorry, the vehicle then required under the new system of Supply and Transport. The Scheme could not provide for the entire mobilisation requirements of the BEF so an Impressment Scheme, which along with the "Provisional" Scheme formed the "Main" Scheme, was introduced to obtain other types of civilian-owned vehicles. Although complicating the provision of spares and repair system, the Impressment Scheme, was well planned and supervised, so that the BEF was not short of transport, nor the ability to maintain it, on mobilisation.[49]

'Subsidy' vehicles were divided into two classes: 'A', a heavy lorry carrying a 3-ton (3.05 metric ton) load, with a maximum speed of 16 mph and 'B', a light lorry carrying 30-cwt (1,524 kg) load with a 20 mph maximum speed; all powered by petrol engines. In 1912, the owners of subsidised vehicles received a purchase premium and an annual subsidy, together working out at £110, or £120, spread over three years, provided inspection requirements were met. Vehicles could be compulsorily purchased whenever the Army Reserve was called out on permanent service, but the WO could not require them to be used for manoeuvres.[50] Capt. H.N. Foster, ASC, was appointed Inspector of Subsidised Transport (WO), under the Director of Transport, with responsibility for the Subsidy Schemes and for arrangements in the event of mobilisation.[51]

49   Sutton and Walker, p.78; Beadon, 1931, pp.37-40.
50   *Army and Navy Gazette*, 24th August 1912, in Brunker, 1913, p.160
51   Paul, 1911, pp.543-550; Beadon, 1931, pp.37-40, 52-55; Young, 2000, p.32.

3-ton Dennis 'subsidy' type lorry waiting for recovery, France. Dennis Bros of Guildford, built 7,000 lorries of this type. (Royal Logistic Corps Museum)

30-cwt 'subsidy' type lorry. (Royal Logistic Corps Museum)

It is important to acknowledge that the mobilisation of motor vehicles in August 1914 was no last minute panic, picking up any available type of civilian vehicle, but a well thought out strategy to be implemented, as with remounts, using a pre-planned registered Subsidy and Impressment Scheme.

A New Transport System

The Army required a completely new transport and supply system linking MT and other existing methods of transport to their best advantage, including horse drawn vehicles and railways, making full use of existing stocks of mobilisation equipment.[52] The new system appeared in the 1911 Wartime Establishments, with provision for some 1,400 lorries for the BEF, of which about 900 were to be provided from the Subsidy Scheme. By the outbreak of war in 1914, 600 vehicles had been registered for subsidy. Maj. Reckitt, RASC, stated that these vehicles were far superior in quality and condition to those impressed and obtained at random from a very indifferent civilian market. The commercial lorry eligible for enrolment under the Scheme had been modified to suit army requirements and by 1914 was known in the automobile trade as the 'Subsidy Type', and was considered by some as a hallmark of efficiency. A Motor Volunteer Corps was formed in 1903. Drivers had to complete a certain number of hours and received a payment and the cost of their fuel; it was disbanded in 1906. With the formation of Haldane's Territorial Force in 1908, an Army Motor Reserve was established to provide for commissioned officers, and in 1912 a 'Special Reserve' of the ASC to supply drivers (initially 1,000) for the subsidised vehicles; these Category "C" reserve men, were paid an annual retaining fee of £4 for a commitment to appear on mobilisation and were then paid six shillings per day.[53]

The greater part of the administrative transport of the BEF, for supplies and ammunition, was converted into MT, effecting at the same time, a radical simplification in the organisation of supply services in the field. Brunker wrote in 1911, that the large scale substitution of MT for horsed transport would involve considerable changes in army establishments, but would reduce the pressure on the supply of horses and the number of transport drivers required on mobilisation.[54] When introduced in 1910-11, the new transport system:[55]

- left untouched First Line, or regimental transport, which accompanied troops into action, and Second Line, or the 'Divisional Train' and the Divisional Ammunition Column (which remained an artillery, not, an ASC unit). These

---

52   Carter, 1912, p.673.
53   Reckitt, 1925, October, p.544; Brunker, 1912, p.264-5, 'Special Reserve'; Beadon, 1931, p.38; Young, 2000, pp.21, 32.
54   Brunker, 1911, pp.7-8; Hobbs, 1913, p.415; RCT, 1981, p.19.
55   Paul, 1911, pp.539-40; Carter, 1912, p.674; Beadon, pp.56-7.

lines of transport would probably all work off roads and therefore remained horse drawn, as did field ambulances.

- swept away rear echelons replacing them with two MTCs for each division; one to carry supplies and stores to the divisional train, the other ammunition to the divisional ammunition column.
- as motor transport had not fully proved itself, it was considered appropriate to have a mobile, two day reserve, in Reserve Parks, of preserved food and grain, carried in horse transport.

In September 1914, the separate Directorates of Supply and Transport, within the QMG's Department, were amalgamated into a single Directorate of Supply and Transport, under Brig-Gen. S.S. Long:[56]

QMG's Department

|

Director Supply and Transport

|

Lines of Communication

|

In front of Lines of Communication
First and Second Line – Regimental and Divisional Transport

With the above changes in place the Structure of the new Transport System (see diagram of New Transport System below) for supplying Divisions and individual units in 1914 was:

- **Main Supply Depots** forming part of the **Advanced Base**: established at some point on the railway system, well in the rear of the Army.
- **Regulating Stations**: provisions sent by rail from an advanced base (ammunition and supplies).
- **Railheads**: receiving trains from regulating stations. The furthest point on the railway line to which provisions would be transported. At this point supplies would be transferred to the MT of divisional supply columns, for distribution to brigades and divisional troops.
- **Rendezvous Point**: situated not more than 40 miles from railheads (limit of the authority of the Lines of Communication). The Inspector-General Communications (IGC) was solely responsible for supply up to, and including, the railhead and rendezvous points. But the location of the rendezvous point, day by day, together with the time that columns were required to arrive, rested with General, or Army HQ. Supply columns were to be met by a representative of the Division receiving supplies and taken by the shortest route to the:-

---

56 Paul, 1911, pp.546-8; Carter, 1912, pp.677-84; Beadon, p.81; Hobbs, p.693.

THE NEW TRANSPORT SYSTEM

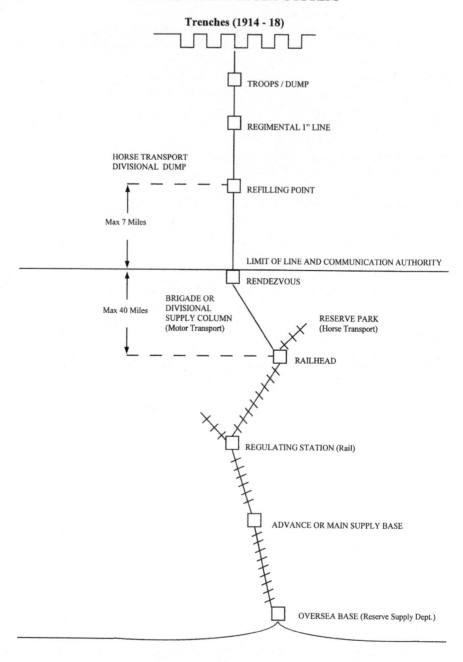

The New Transport System. (Author)

- **Refilling Point**: loads were transferred here from lorries to horse drawn wagons of the supply section of the Divisional Train or Second Line Transport. Supply sections of the train were loaded on a unit basis by Brigade Transport Officers. This point marked the furthest point reached by MT and its selection was partially dependent on the lorries radius of action. It was laid down that this distance should not be greater than about 47 miles from the railhead, except for cavalry. The horse drawn divisional trains then went forward to the troops. If MT was to be used for the removal of sick and wounded it was to be at this point.

This covers the echelons of transport under the immediate control of the ASC ...

- The **Final Stage**: set at a maximum of 15 miles from the refilling point, was the First Line or Regimental horsed transport, carrying the next day's rations for men and animals in the front lines.

The Cavalry Division was supplied by fast moving lorries of cavalry supply columns and ammunition parks. A cavalry supply column consisted of five motor cars, nine motor cycles, six 3-ton and 136 3-cwt lorries (including 40 for hay), four workshop and four store lorries with a total of 305 drivers. During a period of battle, ammunition was supplied by fast moving motor vehicles from divisional ammunition parks[57].

The most important changes to the 1911-12 War Establishments were those affecting general transport, ammunition and supply columns. What had previously been a unit's 'second line transport' (baggage and supply) was taken over by the ASC, one train, or unit to each division. By relegating the old second and third echelons of supply to the control of the Inspector General of Communications (IGC), the impedimenta of a division was reduced, relieving the Divisional General of responsibility. For ammunition and supply columns, the "old columns" were broken up into two sections; the first consisted of retained horsed vehicles forming part of the Division and regimental transport; the other section, consisting of MT, was relegated to the lines of communication behind the Division. MT was not included in the divisional organisation, they were only to be used on the lines of communication. Reserve Parks, on the lines of communication, held supplies and ammunition for a Division and Army Troops, for use in an emergency, carrying two days 'iron' rations with groceries and two days oats for one division; plus 1/6th of a cavalry division and 1/6th of the total strength of the units designated lines of communication.

The function of the lines of communication were modified; communications were no longer lines terminating at a well defined point, or points, on a railway system, but were extended on a more elastic basis to road points, varying day by day between the 'rendezvous' and 'railhead'. MT formed the link. The administrative functions of the several Staffs of the Army in the field had become more complicated and required

---

57   RLC Archive, Box 9, B1-8250.

co-ordinating; the GHQ's, Army and Divisional staffs, and Lines of Communication, all had to deal with the problem of food and ammunition supply, linking into the executive work of the ASC.[58] In 1913, Brunker compared the old and new transport and supply systems, writing that in place of the long tail of transport vehicles, moving no faster than 3 mph, dragging five days food for man and beast, which an army had to protect, a supply column of motor transport had been substituted. Moving at 15 mph to link an army with its source of supply and with the shorter columns they would be more difficult to locate by enemy cavalry, and if located the drivers had to be disabled, as opposed to just shooting the horses.[59]

Wartime Establishments for 1907-8, contained the words 'Expeditionary Force' for the first time, printed on the cover, giving the first definite idea that the Force was to be used in a civilised country with a temperate climate. The new transport system was therefore based on the assumption that the Army would be organised for operations in a highly civilised and thickly populated country, for example Western Europe, which had a network of railway lines so close together that the full distance between them would be well within the radius of action of MT. It envisaged using lateral roads for MT connecting with railways and the main roads used by troops; selecting 'railheads' as points on the line that were sufficiently in the rear of troops to be secure from attack, but would permit the MT supply columns to use these lateral roads to reach divisions.[60]

Once the new system had been accepted, the necessary steps were taken to form the cadres of motor transport units required by the BEF on mobilisation:

> 6 units for supply columns of divisions
> 1 unit for supply columns of cavalry divisions
> 1 unit for supply columns of Army troops
> 8 units for supply columns of ammunition parks
> 2 units for supply columns overseas depots, base and advanced base
> (or more if the bases, or advanced bases, were duplicated)
> 1 depot to remain at home.

It was proposed to maintain small peacetime cadres that could be quickly expanded on mobilization to 19 cadres (as above), equipping the first 18 companies with sufficient vehicles for training the personnel and performing work which had previously been undertaken by horse transport companies (HTC), which they were replacing. During 1911-12, steady progress was made in converting the third and fourth lines of transport from horse to MT. One depot company and 14 service companies of MT, had been formed with a nucleus of vehicles, leaving the other four companies required

---

58   Carter, 1912, pp.674, 686.
59   Brunker, 1913, p.211; Hobbs, 1913, pp.415-6.
60   Cumberlegge, 1912, pp.362-71; Carter, 1912, p.676.

for the BEF to be completed during 1912-13. Corresponding with this formation of MTCs was the reduction in HTCs, so that by the autumn of 1912 the remaining horse transport establishment was only the number of companies required for three home depots, seven units abroad and the 40 units still required for the BEF. The peacetime establishment of MTCs was fixed, tentatively, at eight vehicles (six lorries and two tractors), anticipating that this establishment, in addition to its employment for the purposes of training and manoeuvres, would make a considerable annual saving in expenditure on hired transport.[61]

The 3-ton motor lorry could carry 224 rounds of 18 pounder ammunition, whereas the artillery battery, with its six-gun limbers and 12 ammunition wagons only carried 1,056 rounds; so, five lorries carried more than the lengthy column of a battery at full war strength. The effect of these changes to the total strength of a division, before and after, was a saving of 1,164 horses:

old war establishments	7,316	horses to the division
new war establishments	6,152	horses to the division

This gave a net saving on the six divisions of 6,984 horses, after taking into account an increase of 1,350 horses from an additional six howitzer batteries shown in the 1911-12 War Establishments and a corresponding expansion of ammunition columns. A divisional ammunition column previously used over 1,000 horses. Each of the old supply columns required about 300 draught horses, a total of 1,800 for the six divisional supply columns. If, with the new system, the Remount Department did not have to find these horses on mobilisation, more would be available for the RFA.[62]

Army manoeuvres of September 1912 provided the first opportunity for testing the new Transport System (introduced in 1910, but manoeuvres did not take place during 1911, and only one element operated the new system during the 1912 manoeuvres). This was also the opportunity for the Army to handle petrol for the first time on a large scale. For Col. Hobbs, ASC, the outstanding feature of the manoeuvres was the triumph of the motor lorry (both civilian and military).[63] The roads were exceptionally good, the distances travelled, although considerable were well within the maximum; the weather was fine and the manoeuvres did not last long enough to cause any serious strain in the way of repairs on the MT workshops. The supply columns did especially well, justifying for Hobbs, the prominent position given to the motor lorry for the transport of supplies. No difficulty was experienced in transferring supplies from trains to supply column lorries at the selected railheads, and at refilling points MT met brigade-horsed vehicles. Each brigade, composed of an eight or nine wagon convoy, was not required to move back to refill, but waited for the lorries, loaded up,

61   Paul, 1911, pp.540-2; Beadon, p.58; Brunker, 1911, p.311 and 1912, p.8.
62   Carter, 1912, p.695; Hobbs, 1913, p.416; Brunker, 1912, pp.405-6.
63   Hobbs, 1913, p p.415-30; also Carter, 1912, pp.694-5.

and moved to join the troops. This constituted a considerable saving in the number of horses required on mobilisation, clearly one of the most important features of the new organisation.

Hobbs did not consider the new transport system perfect in every detail, but the main principle was not, he considered, open to challenge at any point. The system would more than keep pace with the most mobile infantry, any difficulties would be with the fast moving cavalry. As the experiment took place under favourable circumstances, it remained to be seen whether prolonged hostilities, a long line of communication between railhead and the Army, and bad roads, would discover flaws in the system.[64]

In the context of wartime establishments for 1914, the Editor of the *Army Service Corps Quarterly* wrote, that it was public knowledge that the question of reducing the number of horses in the trains and reserve parks was under consideration.[65] Rumours had been rife for some months that a scheme was being devised to equip cavalry formations with a fast moving section of transport. With the disappearance of mounted infantry units and mounted brigades, provision had been made for an additional cavalry brigade, making it necessary to lay down separate establishments for a cavalry brigade with a cavalry division. The same reorganisation applied to other field units, services and lines of communication units involved in the supply of cavalry formations.

Following the 1913 army manoeuvres, considerable alterations were made to the entire system of supply and transport from railheads to cavalry formations. The Cavalry Divisional Train, consisting of a headquarters and five HTCs of the ASC, each divided into a headquarters, supply section, and baggage section was abolished, and replaced by a Headquarters Cavalry Divisional ASC (consisting of 11 horses and one motor car); with a cavalry supply column consisting of two MTCs, ASC for supply and requisitioning. The supply lorries, although they could not operate off road, would be right up with the troops instead of only advancing as far as refilling points.[66] These changes were embodied in the 1914 War Establishments, the immediate result of which was felt in every cavalry formation and cavalry unit, and those units of the RA, REs and Royal Army Medical Corps (RAMC) that were allotted to a cavalry division, or isolated cavalry brigade. The establishment of first line transport was considerably increased with the train transport simultaneously disappearing.[67]

Alterations were also made to the organisation of an infantry divisional train. With a reduction in the number of lighter draught horses being used in the commercial world the Army replaced four lighter draught horses with two heavy draught horses in

---

64   Brunker, 1913, pp.211-13.
65   Editor, *ASCQ*, 1914, April, p.95-108.
66   Wilson, 1914, p.247 (Lt-Col. F.M., ASC).
67   Editorial, *ASCQ*, 1914, Vol.7, pp.96-99; Wilson, 1914, pp.247, reference War Establishments, Part 1, EF, Army Orders, 1st January 1914.

all GS wagons, although lighter draught horses were retained for all carts. The effect was to reduce the total number of draught horses as follows:

- Headquarters and Headquarters Company:
  - on mobilisation from   51   to   29   (7 draught and 22 heavy draught)
  - after concentration from   280   to   144   (16 draught and 128 heavy draught)
- For each of Numbers 2, 3, and 4 Companies:
  - on mobilisation from   30   to   17   (5 draught and 12 heavy draught)
  - after concentration from   104   to   55   (7 draught and 48 heavy draught).

There was also a reduction in personnel, including saddlers, farriers and field ambulances (from 57 to 39 ambulances, further reducing horse numbers). These reductions amounted to a total saving in horses of a Divisional Train between the Wartime Establishments of 1913 (652) and 1914 (369), of 283. With this reduction in horses and personnel, the weight of one days supplies for the divisional train was lightened by approximately 5,000 lbs.[68] By April 1914, the only horse transport formation of any significance remaining with the BEF was the Divisional Train composed of four HTCs. One HQ and HQ company, for the transport and supply services of the HQ and Divisional Troops; and three other HTCs, one to each infantry brigade. [69]

Although the new system was tested to a limited extent during the manoeuvres of 1912, the manoeuvres of 1913, for the first time in the history of the Army, made it possible to fully test the Transport and Supply System.[70] The scheme was designed to trial the working of GHQ at its wartime establishment, an approach march of one cavalry division and two armies, each of two divisions, marching on one road with its supplies; with the supply services confined to the same roads as the troops. Valuable lessons were learnt, especially for example, in the practice of moving large numbers of transport vehicles in congested areas. The Cavalry Division numbered about 4,000 men and 3,600 horses; the lorries of each supply company, to convey their supplies, would have consisted of seven for bread, meat and groceries and thirteen for oats.[71] This was the first and last opportunity for the Regular Army to familiarise itself with the reorganised transport system before the outbreak of war in 1914. A reorganisation which included modifications to the organisation of cavalry supply, to Army Corps and GHQ troops, which in war establishments were provided by MT units of corps troops and GHQ troops supply columns; no horsed units were involved.

The new transport system maximised the use, in turn, of railways, mechanical transport and horse drawn vehicles. This greatly increased the speed and reliability

68   *ASCQ*, 1914, Vol.7, pp.105-7; also *Motor Transport Corps Reports (MTC) Reports*, 1910-11, pp.15-16, in RCT Archive, A6/8921-24.
69   *ASCQ*, 1914, Vol.7, pp.105-6; Courtney, E.A.W., 1914, p.152.
70   *MTC Corps Reports 1912-13*, p.7, in RCT Archive, A6/8921-24; Beadon, pp.59-61.
71   Wilson, 1914, p.251; *ASCQ*, 1914, April, pp.101-5.

of mobilisation, mobility, radius of action, and movement of the BEF; enabling large reductions in the number of horses required on mobilisation and for transport in the field. In 1914, British and foreign armies, including Germany, were still dependent on animal transport; however, as Beadon wrote of the British Army, "no army in Europe had better equipped maintenance services".[72] Pre-war planning allowed for the co-ordinated and effective working of mechanical and animal transport, capable of adapting, changing and expanding as the war developed. One would take issue, for example with Singleton, when he states "the internal combustion engine had a poor record of reliability, and in 1914 the British Army could muster a mere 507 assorted motor vehicles".[73] The use of motor vehicles by the British army in 1914, was not, as often perceived, a panic decision, brought about by a shortage of horses during the period of mobilisation, the 'Great Retreat' of September, or the 'Race to the Sea' of October 1914.

The New Transport System was only just completed and tested in time for the outbreak of war in August 1914. Motor vehicles were not sufficiently advanced to be effective other than on hard road surfaces. Their introduction into the military system was therefore concentrated on the lines of communication and not with forward units (division, or regimental first line transport), or for hauling RHA, or RFA guns. In 1914 there was not a single vehicle that could be called an artillery tractor.[74] Up to the outbreak of war, MT was controlled by the WO Mechanical Transport Committee, through the Transport Branch of the QMG's Department, which also dealt with questions of animal transport. The actual executive work was performed by various ASC, MTCs, based with Home Commands, under the instructions of the Assistant Director of Supplies and Transport at the HQ of the individual Commands.[75]

The BEF went to France in August 1914 with motor transport in quantities that hardly seemed possible in the time taken since the MTC made its recommendations in 1911. It was supported by a properly trained and organised ASC, a Special Reserve of officers and drivers, a degree of standardisation and a motor vehicle subsidy and impressment system linked to mobilisation plans, on the same basis as the provision of horses for military purposes.[76]

---

72   Beadon, Vol.II, p.46.
73   Singleton, 1993, p.194; WO161/18, 'History of Department of the Senior Inspector of Motor Transport 1918.'
74   Ventham and Fletcher, 1990, p.14.
75   Beadon, Vol.II, p.41.
76   Sutton and Walker, 1990, p.78.

6

The Domestic Market and the Supply of Horses for Military Purposes

---

The general national interest in having a sufficient number of capable horses to run the economy and fight in the country's wars was confidently entrusted to the 'unseen hand' of competition, private enterprise, and market forces. Provision for the specifically military dimension of national security was seen narrowly in terms of the existence of a sufficient pool of strong, healthy, and properly graded horses, kept in being by ordinary commercial and individual requirements, upon which the army could draw as need arose.[1]

Army horses were not a special breed, they came from the regular civilian supply of the country and so the military relied on the national herd for its supply of horses, in both peacetime and on mobilisation. Competition from foreign buyers, cost of production and increasing mechanisation meant the maintenance of this supply, in both quality and quantity, was of major concern to horse breeders and the military.

The horse supply of the country was a complex matter involving the different requirements of agriculture, urban centres, transport, the military, and recreation such as racing and hunting. Agriculture was the nursery of the entire horse economy and most horses, and virtually all heavy horses, were bred on farms.[2] Buyers and dealers from urban studs and yards purchased a wide variety of horses from farms, fairs and provincial stables in order to feed the insatiable demand of urban centres, principally London. The quality of horses varied considerably and was generally never of a very high standard. Heavy horses were mainly employed for goods transport, the largest and best by the railway companies, breweries and the better class of coal merchants and hauliers. Light horses were mainly used for bus and cab work, and passenger transport. Work in the towns made far heavier demands on horses than agricultural work, wearing them out far more quickly. Large haulage and passenger companies sold on their cast horses into a vibrant second hand market with many that had survived their urban work lives ending up back in the countryside.

1   Thomson, FML, 1983 (a), p.54.
2   Collins, 1983, p.77.

Horse breeding in the 19th Century

Horse breeding during the nineteenth century was affected by a number of factors at home and abroad. Britain's estimated horse population grew from 1.3 million in 1811 to a peak of nearly 3.3 million in 1901.[3] The peak year for horse drawn traffic was 1902; half a million private carriages were on the roads, 133,000 public passenger vehicles and cabs, and a fleet of about half a million commercial vans, wagons, carts and drays.[4] Most of the increase occurred during the second half of the nineteenth century, with the growing urban centres requiring horses for goods and passenger transport, hunting and riding.

Horse breeding was adversely affected by, for example, economic changes in agriculture, industry and transport, changes to fashions in the horse market, depressions, war and fear of war.[5] With an increase in the price of beef and mutton around 1860, farmers were provided with a financially more rewarding market than horse breeding. Maj.Gartside-Spaight, ASC, wrote, that in Ireland prior to 1879, there was a large number of brood mares of the best quality, but in 1879 and succeeding years, acute agricultural depression swept the country and farmers sold their good mares, retaining for breeding only those which were not saleable.[6] The system of using travelling thoroughbred stallions to improve the countries breeding stock had proved unsuccessful as many of those used were of poor quality.

Thompson considered the railway age was the greatest age of the horse.[7] The decline in long distance coaching traffic brought with it the development of railways, generating an increase in local horse transport. The Franco-Prussian war of 1870-71 sent the price of horses soaring, as both France and Germany looked to the British and Irish markets for remounts. The export of horses from the UK in these years, mainly to France and Germany, was 80% higher than it had been in the 1860s, with the reported prices for medium and heavy draught horses, for use by bus and railways, rising by 20% to 40% within a couple of years. By 1872, bus companies and breweries were being pushed out of an overpriced and dwindling British horse market. Horses were imported in large numbers from the Netherlands and North Germany; these rose in 1872 to 12,618; nearly eight times higher than normal levels seen in the 1860s.[8] All these examples contributed to market fluctuations and added to a perception that the UK supply of horses was drying up and demand was falling. It should be stressed that horse breeding is a slow process. Fluctuations in the breeding pattern cannot be made up in the short term, except by an increase in imports, which in itself affects the

3   Barker, 1983, p.102, in Thompson, F.M.L, 1983 (a).
4   Thompson, 1968, p.12.
5   MacGregor-Morris, 1986, pp.16-17.
6   Gartside-Spaight, 1906(b), *ASCQ*, April, p.312.
7   Thompson, 1968, p.13.
8   Thompson, 1983 (b), p.52.

horse breeding market. The number of births at any one time bears a direct relationship to the number of births in the preceding 20 years.[9]

The closing years of the nineteenth century saw some improvement for the horse breeding industry, at least for the superior breed of horse, to meet both a home and a well established, growing export market. There was, for example, an increasing number of horsed implements used in agriculture and agricultural shows awarded prizes for improvements in breeding. An improvement in farming fortunes and the country's trade saw a rise in the value of good quality, well-bred hunters, high-class carriage horses and officers' chargers.[10] Hunters worth over £50 gradually became more difficult to find and costly to purchase; in the autumn of 1889, for example, the trade of some dealers was restricted owing to the scarcity of this type of horse. By 1905 the situation in Ireland, as presented by Gartside-Spaight around 1879, had not improved; many of the best fillies were sold abroad; sires to produce the right class of weight-carrying hunters were scarce and generally deficient.[11]

The 'Horse World' of London

The quality of the working life of a horse in London depended on many factors, including its stabling, feed and general care; the quality of which could possibly be ascertained by its average working life. Much of the horse world was dominated by jobmasters, keepers of livery-stables who hired out horses and carriages. In 1893 the largest master in London was Thomas Tilling of Peckham. By 1897 the company possessed a stable of around 4,000 horses for renting out, as well as horse-drawn vehicles; rented, for example, to private individuals, the Post Office, the War Department and the Fire Brigade, in addition to operating over 200 horse buses.

Gordon gives a most vivid and instructive picture of the 'horse world' of London in 1893, an interwoven network of a wide variety of some 300,000 working horses. The horse economies of the farm and town were largely complementary in that, the former bred and schooled horses, the latter took new young horses, ready for work, from the countryside and second hand sale yards. It was from this 'horse world' that the military sought its supply of horses.

There were some thoroughbred horses, the royal horses of the State and the 700 or so black Flemish funeral horses, but thoroughbreds were rare in London, the majority being of the indifferent and worst types, "the fag end of greengrocers' drudges and cab yard screws. [12]

It has been estimated there were about 22,000 omnibus horses in London in 1893; two out of every three died in service. The largest user, The London General Omnibus

9   Collins, 1983, p.77.
10   MacGregor-Morris, p.17.
11   Gartside-Spaight, 1906(b), April, p.313.
12   Gordon, 1893, p.130; Collins, 1983, p.87.

Crown Mews, Middlesbrough c1900. Robert Walker (on left) was the stable owner and horse dealer.
These would be the types of horses available to the Army for impressment. (Dr Alan Dowson)

Company, owned about 10,000 mares, mainly English with a few foreign horses, working a 1,000 omnibuses. Mares were purchased at five years of age, averaging £35, and cast after five years. Around 10,000 tram horses were owned by thirteen London companies, accounting for half of all tram horses in England. These were generally Irish mares, many shipped from Waterford. The average working life of a tram horse was four years. In 1892 there were some 22,594 cab horses in London, mainly British with some foreign imports. Unlike the omnibus and tram horse, which was increasing in numbers, cab horses were decreasing.[13]

There were about 19,000 carrier's horses, mostly British, of all grades, but generally of poor quality. Pickfords owned about 4,000 horses. Carter Paterson owned 2,000 of a lighter type than the railway horse, in twenty depots around London. Shipping carriers generally used poorer quality horses around the docks and wharves. Smaller carriers probably only kept about 250 horses in total, averaging £25 each. It was the railway companies that dominated the carrying trade, keeping about 6,000 horses of different types for the range of work undertaken, for example, walking in heavy traffic, or trotting horses for lighter loads, averaging £60 each. The vast majority, and

13   Ibid., p.10; see Gilbey, 1913 p.10 for the change to using mainly foreign animals.

typical railway horse, was the 'van' horse. These light carthorses, or 'vanners', were of no particular type, or pedigree. The Great Western Railway Company employed about 1,100 horses with an average working life of five years, and the Midland Railway Company over 1,350 horses. Whereas, in the Great Northern stable, with 1,350 horses it was four years. The North Western only kept about 650 horses as the bulk of its work was contracted out. Including the railways, the London carrying trade employed some 25,000 horses; added to those of the omnibus, tram and cab trade, this gave a total of 72,000. In addition, there were ponies, donkeys and hackneys.[14]

The Post Office did all its work by contract, generally using English horses but not from any particular county, averaging £36 each. The jobmaster McNamara for example, supplied 600 horses with an average working life of six years. About 1,500 heavy vestry, or carthorses, all English, collected London's refuse, with an average working life of eight years and cost of £75. There were 3,000 heavy brewers' horses, with an average working life of six years, usually some of the Shire and Clydesdale types. Courage's brewery generally sold their cast horses for an average of £32. There were probably over 5,000 coal horses, of which about 1,500 were of fairly good quality, some Clydesdales and Shires, valued at between £50-£70, belonging to the leading coal merchants. These were the better class of heavy dray horse going down to the worst type of horse owned by the smaller and poorer dealers.

22,204 carriage licenses were issued within the Administrative County of London in 1891, the vehicles they pertained to were pulled by about 40,000 carriage horses such as the home bred Cleveland Bay, Clydesdale, Yorkshire coaching horse and some foreign types. They ranged in value from £20 for a pony to £400 for a state coach horse. A Cleveland Bay might fetch £30 to £160 depending on age. Other trades groups employing horses were distillers, millers, soap merchants, timber merchants and contractors.[15]

Also in London were some 375 mounted police and two regiments of Household troops with 275 horses each. Gordon states that originally the Household Cavalry was almost entirely mounted from Yorkshire and North Lincolnshire. Horses were later purchased from Ireland by the Army Remount Department, mainly from dealers, such as Daly, in Dublin. They were at least 30% cheaper than the old Yorkshire horses; a troop horse costing £40 instead of £60, bought as rising four years of age. Including the police and military, only 1% of London horses were used for riding. For reasons of traffic congestion, price and scarcity, many gentlemen had ceased to run their own horses and carriages and instead hired them from one of the great jobbing masters such as Tattershall's.[16]

It was from within this complex horse world that the military sought the types of animals it required. It is a misconception to believe that army horses were a special

14 Gordon, pp.9-67.
15 Ibid., pp.69-83, 101 -112, 129-134.
16 Ibid., pp.149-50; Thompson, 1983, p.18.

breed existing outside the civilian framework. The country's domestic horse population and the military supply were all part of the same intricate economy and network
However, the Army was never a major factor in the horse breeding industry; its
demands were always a mere drop in the ocean.

The question of the supply of horses for military purposes

In 1873 the House of Lords established a Select Committee to 'inquire into the
condition of this country with regard to horses, and its capabilities of supplying any
present, or future demand for them'.[17] The Committee did not consider the case
proven that horses in the UK had deteriorated in quality and took a strong view that
the government should not interfere with private enterprise. It did not propose any
special scheme for providing army remounts which it viewed as remaining part of
the general question of horse supply. In 1873, the Government was not prepared to
finance an improvement in the quantity, or quality of the nation's horse stock, or to
provide the Army with its horses. The supply of army remounts was to be safely left
to market forces, with the military as ordinary customers in the open market. Such
a view was acceptable before the advent of electrification and the development of the
motor vehicle brought the demise of the light horse. However, the policy of 1873 was
not considered acceptable in the years between the 1902 and 1914.

Concessions were made in the 1880s. For example, in 1887 a scheme was established
to provide a reserve of military horses, and the Royal Commission on Horse Breeding
was created, which was to indirectly support military needs. The Government was still
not taking responsibility for horse breeding. Finance was made available to the Royal
Commission; this marked a small and inexpensive move away from total reliance on
unaided private enterprise, towards an official policy of providing some state aid. The
Government was not prepared to grant funds directly, or to manage the industry, but
considered if it did not provide some support, the industry would continue to decline.
In these circumstances Col. Bridge, Inspector of Remount Depots from 1906, saw an
'impasse'.[18] Previously, it was the large landowners who had chiefly interested themselves in the improvement of horses, but this situation was threatened, with the prob-
ability that their desire and power to spend money on maintaining the excellence
of the breeds was likely to diminish. The declining values of large landed estates,
caused to some extent by the imposition of death duties, and the looming introduction of taxation on land values, was perceived as paving the way for the parcelling
out of land and the creation of smaller holdings. In such circumstances, the state
of horse breeding in the country looked likely to grow worse, unless, some system
for its improvement was found, free from great expense, but with the merit of being
practicable and financially rewarding to the breeder. Expensive schemes involving

---

17   BPP, 1873, Vol.XIV, Report, pp.xiv-xv; Thompson, 1983, pp.54-55.
18   Bridge, 1909, p.298.

the creation of large government breeding establishments and increased expenditure might have been practical in improving the number and quality of horses required by the military, but they were outside the range of possible options in relation to government policies. The military were not prepared to support any scheme that involved them in greater expense; simplicity and cheapness were their requirements.

The *Veterinary Record* of 1891 records that "the question of the supply of horses for military purposes was having one of its periodical revivals". For Birkbeck, the military efficiency of the nation largely depended on the successful solution to this question. He wrote, "the British nation appears to be awakening to the fact, which has for long been weighing on the minds of soldiers, that all is not well with our supply of horses for war". [19] Sir Walter Gilbey, writing in 1902, stated that experience gained from the 1899-1902 War made it evident that the system then in operation for obtaining remounts for the Army could not be depended on by the nation for future emergencies. Maj. Armstrong, ASC, agreed with Gilbey, in considering that during the previous eleven years the situation had undergone a change for the worse, due mainly to the increase in motor traction, with tens of thousands of horses being discarded. Gilbey added that horses used by the great bus companies were not bred in Britain but were almost all produced on the grazing grounds of Canada and America, and brought over to England in large numbers. The impact of the increased use of motor traction on the number of imported horses is reflected in import figures:

> 1895-98 inclusive 167,209   (average 41,802 over the four years)   (pre-motor era)
> 1908-11 inclusive 56,192   (average 14,048 over the four years)   (post motor
> established)

This decrease of over 27,000 horses annually, of which the 'bus type' formed a very considerable proportion, was mainly of those riding and draught classes, essential for military purposes.[20] Thompson wrote that in 1906 there were barely 10,000 motor vehicles in the entire country, but by 1909 Bridge gives a figure of 89,365. Without a profitable economic market farmers reduced the breeding of horses, except for the heavy horse of the shire stamp. Gilbey was convinced, along with many others prominent in the horse world, that horses which would have best served as army remounts, were eagerly purchased by foreign buyers and taken abroad. He stressed that the time had come to ensure, within Great Britain, a supply of horses, upon which, both in numbers and quality, the Army could depend.[21]

19   *VR*, 1891, Vol.4, 25th July, p.52; Birkbeck, 1908, July, p.327.
20   Gilbey, (1902) 1913, Introduction, p.10. Originally published in 1902, but I have been unable to obtain a copy of this edition so have used the revised reprint of 1913; Armstrong, WHM, 1908, p.496.
21   Thompson, 1968, p.12; Bridge, 1909, p.286; Gilbey, (1902) 1913, Introduction; Hotham, 1906, p.189.

The supply of horses from the colonies for military purposes was also changing. Australia was feeling the impact of the loss of many of its young horses shipped to South Africa during the 1899-1902 War, and for remounts and breeding to the Indian Government. The German Government purchased in the country for the 1900-1901 Boxer Rebellion, or China campaign and Japan was buying some 15-20,000 horses. Sales which added to the constant drain on Australia's best young mares and with the quality of its horses falling. In South Africa horse breeding was developing slowly from the impact of the War, even with the Government auctioning off nearly 6,000 horses to dealers, 80% of which were sold on to German agents. Col. Hotham, RA, believed some 25, 000 transport animals (horses, mules, donkeys and bullocks) had left the colonies during 1904-5 including nearly all of the Governments surplus transport mules. When the need arose they would have to be replaced from North America and the Argentine. The average selling price for mules and horses was £20, for purchasing including shipping costs about £45-£50. [22]

The state of horse breeding in Great Britain and Ireland, and the supply of horses for military purposes in time of war, was one that afforded inexhaustible debate for the military and those involved in the 'horse world'. "A repetitive debate was eagerly taken up by the daily and weekly press, whatever their specialism." It was a subject upon which most Englishmen thought they were qualified to speak, as shown by the many letters to the press. Bridge thought it difficult to name any other subject that arose so frequently in one form or another, though it did not usually get much further than the question stage in both Houses of Parliament (a view supported by a glance in the index volumes of Hansard (C) under 'horses').[23] Literature from the period illustrates that the prevailing view of the military and 'horse world' was one of despondency. The assertion being that, horse breeding was dying out; foreign buyers were ruining the industry and depriving the UK of all its best brood mares; the WO did not buy army horses in the proper way, or give a fair price, and the Government needed to put a prohibitive duty on the export of horses and turn to the breeding of horses. Bridge believed, the country had come to accept this as true, but arrived at no definite course of action.

Lt-Gen. MacMunn, rounded on the "nice, kind folk" who wrote on the subject to the press and WO about its whole attitude towards war-horses, but who did not understand the points though offering every sort of panacea. He believed the facts of the case were different and was glad the Army resisted all the charlatans, doggedly resisting all options that were contrary to their policy of cheapness, non-interference with individual enterprise and simplicity of operation. Armstrong believed change was required and the reason for it could be summed up in five words, "The Age of Mechanical Appliances".[24]

22   Hotham, pp.191-2.
23   Bridge, 1909, pp.282-3.
24   MacMunn, 1930, p.95-6; Armstrong, 1908, p.496.

The main point under discussion was the perceived danger to the country of the imminent failure of the nation's horse supply and consequent inability to supply horses for military purposes in time of war. The two basic questions, the condition of the national horse breeding industry and the supply of horses to the Army in war, had become inextricably intertwined. Horse breeding in the UK was unsatisfactory simply because it could not supply the military in wartime. During the 1899-1902 War foreign markets were frantically sought to make up for the lack of available horses from the home market.[25] This was, however, an overreaction to the remount policy adopted during that War, and a fear the same mistakes would be repeated. The relevant questions in relation to the national herd and the supply of horses for the military included:

- Were there sufficient horses in the country to supply the requirements of the civilian population and the military in peacetime?
- What evidence was there to conclude that, in the foreseeable future, the ability to supply the required number, and type of horses, would fall so far short as to cause a danger to national security?
- What exactly were the needs of the military in both numbers, type, stamp and class of horse and at a price they were prepared to pay?

The question of horse supply in peacetime

Much of the debate on horse supply was based on value judgements and personal experiences, with few reliable figures. The lack of detailed, or accurate statistics on the national herd, was a problem for military planners. Official statistics, for example, do not give details of the number of horses exported in each class, only value and sex, not even whether they were serviceable animals. In 1909, Bridge wrote that no one knew how many horses there were in Great Britain; it was not therefore possible for the Remount Department to draw up accurate horse mobilisation plans when they did not have the basic information on the total number of horses available, by age or class; for example, saddle, carriage, heavy and light draught and cobs. Articles from the period contain varying crude figures and interpretations, some with minor variations and some with significant differences of up to a million horses. Statements such as that by Gartside-Spaight, that the "difficulty of providing remount horses of a suitable stamp for the Army, at reasonable prices, has always been great", are difficult to support without clarification. He provides no figures, nor time frame.[26]

Statistics compiled by the Board of Agriculture and Fisheries (BAF), were limited to returns giving the number of agricultural horses (including brood mares) and young stock actually on farms in Great Britain. They did not include the necessary

25   Bridge, 1909, p.283; Birkbeck, 1908, p.335.
26   Bridge, 1909, p.283; Baden-Powell, 1909, p.6; Gartside-Spaight, 1906(b), April, p.312.

information required by the military on class and age. Thompson wrote that figures for horses kept on farms were a treacherous guide to the state of the total population as returns from farmers, if completed, were not filled in properly and did not, for example, include horse drawn vehicles.[27] There was no national horse tax, or census. Police and military authorities had endeavoured to collect statistics in a piecemeal way, but little reliance was placed on the results. Bridge and others saw clearly the need for an exhaustive census, of all horses in the country and their locations, by county and borough. Until such information was available, thereby providing a complete picture, it was not possible to state with any accuracy, whether the country's horse supply was sufficient to meet the demands that would be placed upon it at a time of national emergency, to put the Regular and Territorial Forces on a war footing. There were many difficulties in obtaining accurate information. The horse population was migratory, being bought and sold many times over; horses were moved about Great Britain, for example, from England to Ireland, from market to market and between dealer and farmer. In addition, horses were sold from Britain and Ireland to foreign countries as demand and trade dictated.

Ireland was of great importance in supplying army remounts, providing more than 90% of cavalry and 80% of draught horses; negative trends in this market were therefore of concern. Mr Winter of Limerick stated that he had seen truck loads, thousands of horses, predominantly mares, purchased for the foreign market. In an attempt to arrive at the numbers of good quality mares leaving the country, he consulted Board of Trade returns, but found only 107 horses had been sent abroad in 1904.[28] This was accounted for by the fact that all horses for the Continent went to England first, practically all horses sent abroad were entered in the Board's returns as only going to England. The Irish Department of Agriculture and Technical Instruction collected statistics giving the number of agricultural horses, brood mares, young stock, commercial, pleasure and recreational horses, but none by class. Returns for 1907 gave a total of 596,144 horses on farms and elsewhere, in Ireland.[29] Over 400,000 were used for agricultural trade and transport purposes, in addition to those kept for recreation, and young animals under two years old. There were also nearly 30,000 mules and jennets (small Spanish horse), and over 240,000 donkeys.[30] In Ireland, as in Great Britain, it was not possible from available information, to establish whether the decrease of 8,269 horses from 1906 to 1907 was in young stock, harness, or saddle animals. In 1907, 3,982 horses were imported into Ireland from Great Britain and 33,253 exported to Great Britain.[31]

27   Thompson, 1968, p.20; Bridge, 1909, pp.283-4; Le Mesurier, 1904, *ASCJ*, April, p.21.
28   Gartside-Spaight, 1906 (b), *ASCQ*, April, p.330.
29   Bridge, 1909, p.283.
30   Gartside-Spaight, 1906 (a), January, p.181.
31   Bridge, 1909, pp.287-8.

Figures supplied by BAF for Great Britain, gave exports and imports for the UK, but only the number of agricultural horses and young stock. Returns for 1906-7 show a decrease of 20,581 horses in the UK:[32]

Great Britain	12,312
Ireland	8,269
Total	20,581

Unfortunately, the class of horse was not recorded, although the bulk were young stock (under one). The 12th Report of the Royal Commission on Horse Breeding, October 1909, produced figures showing the fall in the population of horses under one year old:[33]

For the UK (including Ireland)	208,269	1904-5
	184,602	1907-8
	(drop of 23,667)	

For Ireland alone	68,978	1904-5
(with few, or no carthorses)	57,446	1907-8
	(drop of 11,532)	

Although these figures do not correlate with Bridge, they are consistent with the general trend in a decline in the horse population after 1905. Figures given by Collins show a fall in the number of unbroken horses, under one, in England and Wales, from over 125,000 in 1905 to 107,420 in 1907. He states that the decline in horse breeding was first noted in 1907 and that horse births and imports began to decline about 1904. The decline in births was possibly, entirely among light horses that comprised only 30% of the agricultural herd. This reduction was probably offset by an increase in the numbers of heavy horses. In 1911, slightly fewer than 50% of horses lived on farms and out of a total working population of 2.6 million, only 35% were occupied in farming.[34]

It is possible, that this decline in foals was exclusively confined to the light harness class. BAF put it down to an unfavourable foaling season and reduction in breeding owing to a feared reduction in demand, brought about by the rapidly increasing use of motor vehicles. Writers, associations and societies rigorously propounded this latter reason. The decrease would, however, appear to have been temporary, as figures for 1908 and 1909 do not follow the same pattern. A fall in the horse population from 1895 was recorded as:

---

32   Ibid., pp285-6.
33   MacGregor-Morris, 1986, p.45.
34   Collins, 1983, p.19, note 10 from Agricultural Statistics, 1911, Pt.1, pp.17-19, 756.

45,588   horses and young stock in the UK   from 1896 to 1897
29,522   from 1897 to 1898

Numbers steadily decreased from 1896 to 1900 and then rose steadily until 1905. BAF returns for 1907 show 2,088,932 horses on farms in the UK with little change in 1908. The decrease in 1907, of young unbroken horses, had practically all been made up, suggesting that the threatened fall off in breeding had not occurred. Between 1900-1921, there is little evidence for a significant change, up or down, in the size of the agricultural herd.[35]

Gordon wrote that in 1876, 40,700 horses were imported, mostly for the cheaper kinds of work. Exported horses were those required for heavy work, breeding and for food. Sometimes exports exceeded imports, but more often the balance was the other way; however, it was always on the right side as far as cash flow was concerned. Imported horses averaged £17, exported horses were, for example, worth £54. During 1889 there were 3,800 imports and 14,200 exports; in 1890, 19,400 imports and 12,900 exports. London always took the largest share of all classes. The bulk of imports were not of high quality and came from nearer home: draught horses from Denmark, Holland, Belgium, France; ponies from Norway, Sweden, E. Russia, Poland, Finland; riding and driving horses from Hanover, Hungary; also horses from the United States and Canada and South American mustangs.[36] The demand for remounts during the 1899-1902 War was of course an exception with nearly 50,000 imported in 1900. The importing of 38,000 horses in 1897 when compared to the 1907 BAF Returns showing approximately 15,000 foreign horses were imported highlighting this continual decline.

It should be emphasised that the army horse in the UK was at the bottom end of the market, it was the 'misfit', the half-bred hunter for example, which failed to grow big enough to command high prices in the fashionable market. Hunting men wanted big, striding blood horses, whereas the cavalry preferred the smaller horse. Lt-Col. Blenkinsop, PVO, Irish Command and Lt-Col. Herbert, CO of the 6th Inniskilling Dragoons, were of the opinion that although officers required the same type of horse in peace as on active service, the weight-carrying hunter made an admirable charger in peacetime, but was not the ideal horse for active service. Gartside-Spaight complained about the scarcity of good quality weight carrying hunters, commenting that the class that could be purchased at the authorised army price, left much to be desired. In his report to the Hunter Improvement Society (HIS) of 1891, Mr. G.S. Lowe wrote that if a hunter failed to reach the highest echelons he may still be worth £100 as an ordinary hunter, from £50-£60 as a harness horse, or £45 as a cavalry horse. In Bridge's opinion, the hunter was too highly priced, yet this was the class of horse required for sport, officers' chargers and the cavalry in peace and war. The demand for hunters had

35   Bridge, 1909, pp.285-6; Collins, 1983, p.76.
36   Gordon, 1893, pp.106-7.

not declined, owing to the significant increase in numbers engaged in hunting, a sport which had increased three to four fold during the Victorian period. By 1900, there were probably some 200,000 horses kept exclusively for hunting.

English and Welsh farmers bred fewer hunters. Breeding did not repay the special care and attention required and was something of a lottery. Too many failures might occur before producing one good foal; for example mishaps (disease and injury) between birth and the saleable age of four to five years, lowering prices in a limited market. Opinion varied, but generally the problem was thought to lie in the choice of dams not the sires in the selection and mating process. From 1887, good sires were made available by using 'King's Premium' stallions, but little care was taken over the selection of mares. To reward the breeder, hunters had to sell at a good price, but this might be before the age at which they commanded the higher prices. It was the finished, well-bridled and well-mannered hunter that realised the large prices; with the dealers, not farmers, realising the real profits. A breeder aiming for the high-priced markets, might only achieve this with possibly three out of four horses. Selling the misfit was the breeder's difficulty. With the demise of the hansom cab, British and Continental armies were the only markets for hunter misfits, with smaller mares being sold to the British cavalry. British army buyers almost always had the pick of misfits before continental remount agents, "partly from goodwill and because our price was a pound or so more".[37] Ireland continued to produce the hunter in both numbers and quality as there was a ready demand from the home and foreign markets.

Those, whose experience went far enough back, stated that the cavalry horse of 1908 was not what it had been many years before. Capt. Ryan, Adjutant, American 15th Cavalry, who visited England and Ireland, 1904-5, during his tour to observe European cavalry wrote most enthusiastically of horses in England, and praised the qualities of the Irish hunter, 'finding saddle horses in large numbers, more than could be found in most other countries and the cavalry securing horses better suited to their requirements.'[38]

The Department of Agriculture and Technical Instruction devoted special care to the improvement of horse breeding, introducing a system of advancing money to localities for the purchase of suitable stallions. The Department registered stallions and mares, after inspection and approval, with premiums and prizes awarded to the owners. Breeders in Great Britain could have produced more for the home market at that time, if they had thought the returns were worth the time and expense.[39] Ireland practically monopolised the supply of horses for hunting in England, but did not, and could not, meet all the demand at this time.

37   Gartside-Spaight,1906(b), April, pp.331, 334, 292-6, 313; Lowe in Macgregor-Morris, p.20; Bridge, 1909, pp.292; MacMunn, 1930, pp.95-6 and Army Council Statement in MAF/53/2/A43091/1915; Thompson, 968, p.15.
38   Ryan, 1905, pp.205-6, 225.
39   Birkbeck, 1908, pp.338-41; Bridge, 1909, p.292-6.

Farmers for whom the breeding of the hunter type was not an economic option, turned their attention to breeding the heavier horse, mainly Shire and Shire crosses, supplemented by local breeds such as Clydesdale, Cleveland and Suffolk. There was a ready market for these heavier breeds in the urban centres where they remained in demand for the transport of goods and provided the majority of horses used for heavy agricultural work. The heavy horse was easier to produce, the price was not subject to great fluctuations and their temperament meant they were not as susceptible to injury through high spirits. No special feeding was required, they were easier to break and could be put to work by farmers and breeders long before the age at which a hunter could profitably be sold. The Hackney was in great demand from the colonies, continental and American buyers, but in the home market, a decline in this breed had effected trade, influenced to some extent by the growing use of motor vehicles. Every encouragement was given to breeding Shires and Hackneys by providing for example, a plentiful supply of good sires at agricultural shows and prizes; these realised high prices, especially when shipped abroad. Cattle breeding at this time offered farmers a more profitable, steadier market and price, than the fluctuating horse breeding industry. Maj. Lane, AVC, writing in 1912, believed, the decline in breeding heavy horses was not so marked as that of the light horse, but the former was useless for army purposes except for heavy transport, which would in the future, he believed, be carried out by motor traction. He shared this view with Maj. Armstrong, ASC, who at the earlier date of 1908, had considered that within 25 years, motors would be requisitioned as a reserve for war, on similar lines to horses.[40] This threat to the horse breeding industry from motor traction is a constant theme in all the contemporary literature.

The impact of motorised vehicles and scarcity of light horses

The electrification of tramways saw the beginnings of mechanised road transport, and the replacing of tramway horses (some 10,000 in London in 1893), but did not halt the growth of horse populations in urban centres, as an increasing number were still required for other passenger and freight transport. Until 1914, the urban horse was only seriously challenged in those areas of passenger transport that used light horses; over 300,000 such horses were displaced for resale in the horse market. The demand for heavy horses in the transport of goods remained exceptionally buoyant.[41] The mechanisation of horse drawn buses in London progressed rapidly, with the number of horses falling from 2,500 in 1907 to 376 in 1912, disappearing completely soon afterwards. A London traffic census for 1911, showed that only 13% of all passenger vehicles were still horse drawn, falling to 6% cent by 1913, while 88% of goods traffic

---

40   Lane, 1912, pp.38-9; Armstrong, 1908, p.496.
41   Collins, 1983, p.85.

remained horse drawn. The effect of mechanisation on agriculture was slight with little decline in non-agricultural horses until after 1919.[42]

For the Army, the decrease in numbers of available light draught horses, especially the carriage horse, light draught 'busser', 'gunner' and 'parcel-vanner', was critical. These were the types from which the Army obtained its gun-teams and transport horses. However, the scarcity, which Bridge thought was due more to the reduction in imports than in breeding, was felt more in the quality available than the quantity. The number of horses displaced by motor vehicles and electric tramcars far exceeded the falling off from greatly reduced importation and from restricted breeding. There was still a demand for horses and a market for the breeders, the horse had not been ousted at the same rate and in the same proportion as mechanical transport had increased. Returns for the number of mechanically propelled vehicles in the UK for 1909, showed a steady rise to 89,365 motor vehicles:[43]

71,131   private, or pleasure motor cars
17,981   industrial vehicles, or public service conveyances.
  253   motor cycles?

Col. Hobbs, (Assistant Director of Supplies and Transport, Eastern Command), writing on the new system of army transport, considered that the rapid disappearance of the 'busser', or trotting draught horse, made it increasingly difficult to obtain annually, the numbers of light draught horses suitable for army vehicles. During the army manoeuvres of 1912, 1,490 hired horses were used, mostly of the "country" type. Some were used by heavy batteries of the Royal Garrison Artillery, but the greatest number was used for transport purposes. Even in 1911, there were not enough 'bussers' and the numbers had to be made up with London 'vanners', these and even heavier types were the ones that Hobbs considered would probably have to be used on future manoeuvres. The number of commercial companies tendering to supply horses in large quantities was few in number; it was also a recognised practice for companies to tender for the total number of horses required by one Army Command, or for none at all. In 1861 the London General Omnibus Company owned 6,391 horses increasing to 17,183 in 1904. However, not a single horse had been procurable by the military from this company in 1912, as they had given up all horses (in 1906 they had decided to spend £1 million on motor omnibuses). The Associated Omnibus Company supplied over 100 horses for the 1912 manoeuvres, but these were then sold and replaced by motor buses.[44]

The available evidence does not suggest there was a numerical deficiency in the national herd to meet the normal requirements of the civil population and military in peacetime.

42   Barker, in H.M.L. Thompson, 1983 (a), p.108; Baden Powell, 1909, p.388.
43   Bridge, 1909, p.286-7.
44   Hobbs, 1913, p.427; RCT Archive, A6/3521; Paterson, 1927, pp.68-75.

An immense number of badly bred, nondescript horses flooded the market, purchased by people who needed horses but could not pay high prices for them. Scarcity generally raised prices and provided a market benefiting the breeder and dealer. In 1913 MacMunn wrote that sufficient horses existed in the country to enable the military to take what they required in a national emergency, without crippling the horse life of the country.[45]

The question of the future supply of horses for military purposes?

In 1909, Maj. Fife, council member of the HIS had no doubt that horse-breeding in England was declining. The reasons he gave for this perceived decline of horses in home markets, was the demand for electrification, motor vehicles and the particular evil of importing foreign horses. He did not agree with the widely held opinion that the purchase of mares by foreign buyers was detrimental to breeding.[46] Fife was one of many involved, or interested in, the nation's horse breeding industry, who held the view that if nothing was done the extent of the decline would result in the country being unable to meet military requirements.

The question of whether or not, and to what extent, foreign buyers were taking the best quality animals and breeding stock out of the country, therefore diminishing the supply for military requirements, remained a central element of debate. Once again, it appears difficult to obtain consistent, detailed, or accurate figures to support the passionate debates for, or against, the export of horses. In 1891, Mr Lowe of the HIS reported that the practice of selling young mares at three, or four years, to foreign buyers had for years been draining the country of its best blood.[47]

For Gordon, in 1893, the 'van', or railway horse, was a 'Britisher' to the backbone, but was not as easy to acquire owing to foreigners collecting so many of them. So large was the continental trade that at Harwich, the Great Eastern Railway Company provided stabling for 80 horses, which was frequently full. Gordon states as many as 120 had been exported in one boat, most being Irish, and that the whole Belgian army had at one time been horsed from Ireland.[48] Col. St Quinton, in his 1897 report to the Commission on Horse Breeding, commented on the erroneous idea that the English Army experienced difficulty in obtaining its annual number of remounts, or of any problem with horse supply in Ireland, giving the example that between February and March, he had placed 738 horses into service with their different regiments.[49] He considered himself in the unique position of regarding foreign buyers as friends, witnessing daily how their demand improved and guaranteed supply; free trade being the safeguard against the

---

45   MacMunn, 1914, pp.435, 443.
46   MacGregor-Morris, pp.39-40.
47   Ibid., p.20.
48   Gordon, 1893, pp.50 and 106.
49   *VR*, 1897, Vol.10, 3rd July, pp.7-8.

Queen's Own Oxfordshire Hussars, possibly in summer camp 1914. Two contrasting examples of the domestic working horse available on impressment and for hire by Yeomanry regiments.
(Author's collection)

inevitable development of electrical and motor cars, and for any large supply of horses required in an emergency. The patriotic view clearly comes through in the writings of gentlemen breeders and dealers, but there is little evidence as to what extent this permeated to the smaller and poorer ones; however, one would suggest it was a sentiment they could ill afford with the need to make a good return on their investment.

Armstrong, believed the root of the problem in providing remounts lay in establishing a scheme for retaining the best mares in the country. If foreigners were allowed to purchase them wholesale, then the UK breed of horses would deteriorate and eventually become a thing of the past.[50] Such arguments were countered by those who believed that if more horses were purchased in the UK, and especially Ireland, more would be bred and therefore, the horse population at any given moment would be larger. This debate should be considered in the context of the class of horse being exported, bearing in mind that the Army was particularly concerned with the supply of riding and light draught horses. For example, during the 19th century a large export market developed for heavy horses which, until the end of the 1880s were mostly of breeding stock. This export trade increased throughout the century, partly because some British breeds (not only thoroughbreds), were valued by the many developing new countries, especially the Americas, which were still comparatively short of heavy horses and required draft stallions. The United States also bought from France and Belgium.[51]

It was frequently stated that foreign purchasers generally paid better prices than home buyers for the class of horses they required, but similarly the home buyer could often purchase the type required more cheaply from abroad. Col. Granet, Assistant Director Remounts (WO), understood that foreigners were competitors in the purchase of young horses required for army purposes and paid a better price; but he had not heard of any very good evidence that they paid very much higher prices.[52] In 1907 a total of 58,028 horses were exported from Great Britain and Ireland (other than to British possessions) with a declared value of £947,000: [53]

> 46,089   under the value of £10 per head (for slaughter)
> 1,155   with a value £10 to £20,
> 10,784   with a value of £20 plus, not all equally valuable as £20 was a low sum, or only a fair value.

Bridge suggests that from these figures, the extraordinary low value per head of the horses exported, for example £16, was largely due to the fact that four fifths were for the meat trade. Of the 10,784, some would have been very highly priced thoroughbreds, but he was certain the general average (per head of the majority) must have been

---

50   Armstrong, 1908, p.512.
51   Chivers, 1983, p.42.
52   D4/100, 1910, p.1: Granet, Evidence before the Development Commission.
53   Bridge, 1909, pp.288-90.

priced at the lower average figure of £50 to £55 each, the remainder probably at £40 each. Of 4,918 mares exported for slaughter, or breeding, 50% went to Belgium, or the Netherlands, with an average value of importation from the UK of only £10–£13 each. Not, Bridge suggested, good stock. The average price for exported serviceable animals was:

Stallions	£273	per head
Mares	£60	per head
Geldings	£9.10s	per head (probably all went for slaughter)

Bridge thought the widely held and freely expressed opinion, rarely contradicted, that foreign purchasers took all our best brood mares, which was prejudicial to the national breeding industry, was an absolute fallacy. Under normal circumstances, he thought it was difficult to accept that farmers and breeders would have sold their breeding stock and therefore their livelihoods. Birkbeck thought it difficult to state with any accuracy that the best brood mares were leaving the country to the detriment of the country's breeding stock, but argued that good mares were at all costs to be kept in the country by premiums, or an export tax.[54]

Gilbey argued strongly against exports and used figures to reach the opposite conclusion to Bridge, that good horses were still being purchased by foreign buyers. He argued that the potential of the Light Horse Breeding Society, introduced in 1911, as a nucleus for a dependable supply of horses for the Army, was being lost, at least for those branches requiring the hunter type. From statistics provided by Customs and Excise, he calculated that far more horses of the hunter type were sent abroad than were, or could be, produced under the Light Horse Breeding Scheme. He assumed young horses, when four or five years old, were worth £50 to £100 each. Figures from previous years were, he stated, not available to him but for 1912, 6,942 horses of this price had been exported; it was, he believed, the old story; "the best of our good horses had gone to foreign buyers". The French and German purchasers willingly took three or four year olds at a price that was profitable to the breeder. The French, for example, purchased three year olds for their army, but from dealers in France; from abroad, they purchased four to six year olds, even some at eight, except for a few hundred thoroughbred mares annually at three years old. However, British Remount buyers, restrained by regulations, were unable to pay higher prices, with the result that a large proportion of the best horses were exported. The 6,942 horses formed only a small proportion of the total number sent abroad; in 1912, no fewer than 10,592 horses were sold of a value between £20 and £50. Where Bridge considered horses of this price were mainly for the meat trade, Gilbey concluded that many, very many, were of the stamp sorely needed for remounts. Gilbey, Bridge and Birkbeck all agreed, however, that the

54   Bridge, 1909, p.290; Gartside-Spaight, 1906(b), April, p.312; Birkbeck, 1908, p.340.

method of classifying exported animals did not provide the information required to give an accurate estimate of losses, of this class, to the nation.[55]

For Maj. Lane, AVC, the comparatively small demand in horses for commercial purposes during the previous few years, had already greatly affected the supply of breeding horses, especially light horses.[56] The best of those being bred found their way into foreign armies, whose agents were always prepared to pay 20% to 40% more than the British Remount Department. The purchase of three year old horses by foreign buyers was strenuously denounced, although there were no statistics giving the ages of those exported to back up the claims. Lane also commented on other factors affecting breeding and the keeping of horses, such as increased expenses, notably the increased cost of land, forage and labour.

Overall the available evidence does not suggest that purchasing by foreign buyers was prejudicial to breeding in the UK. In 1914 Maj-Gen. Cowans, QMG, wrote that people frequently asked him why he let foreigners come and buy our horses, why they were let go out of the country? He believed that stopping them would stop horse breeding altogether; it was in fact "a great assistance to us". In 1912, 66,000 horses were exported, out of which, only 20,000 cost more than £20, so the real exportation of suitable horses was very small.[57] To prohibit, or place a duty on the export of horses, would not have assisted the breeder and almost certainly have dealt a heavy, if not fatal blow, to the industry by reducing the stimulus for breeding. Foreign buyers did purchase a number of expensive high-class horses and paid well for them, but they also purchased a larger number of the poorer type, for which there was practically no market in the UK. Bridge concluded that the export trade would stimulate breeding and reduce imports, increasing reserves required by the military. In the event of war, the foreign supply would be available to the British Army, which could no doubt order a ban of all exports.[58]

There is no clear evidence of a significant decrease in the national herd which was sufficient to supply both the needs of the civilian horse world and the military in peacetime. There was however, a growing deficiency in the supply of good quality riding horses and light draught horses for the Artillery, due to reduced breeding in this class. The deficit was in the maintained reserve necessary for a national emergency and for the far greater numbers required for immediate mobilisation and subsequent replacement of the wastage of war. Amongst the suggested solutions was the establishment of government breeding farms, haras, or stallion depots on the French model. Supplying at government expense approved brood mares, paying greatly enhanced prices for remounts, purchasing horses two, or three years before the age at which they were fit to take their place in the ranks, and running these younger horses on specially purchased government farms, or boarding large numbers out with farmers.

---

55   Gilbey, 1913, pp.4-6; Bridge, 1909, p.29-10.
56   Lane, 1912 (a), pp.38-39.
57   Cowans, in MacMunn, 1914, p.450.
58   Bridge, 1909, p.290.

The use of influential societies was another solution, which would be empowered to advise and supply approved stallions at lower fees, to duly approved and registered mares. Such societies were already in existence, notably the Brood Mare Society; but they had not received public recognition, or encouragement and failed to use their influential networks and potential in supporting the nation's horse breeding industry.[59] Any such schemes would ultimately have involved the Government in providing far greater financial assistance.

The Government had not traditionally seen itself in the role of supporting private industry. Such a policy made it highly unlikely that it would agree to increasing public expenditure on horse breeding. In most proposals to improve horse breeding and supply, there was the perceived problem, fear, or threat, by some of those actively involved, or interested in the industry, of government interference with private enterprise. Col. Douglas William, Assistant Inspector Remounts, Irish Command, thought it "a rather ticklish thing to interfere with private enterprise in the way of horse breeding".[60] For the government to intervene in horse breeding, on continental lines, by establishing state depots would, Gilbey believed, court failure.[61] Parliament would have to grant the WO compulsory powers to purchase large tracts of pasture-land, whilst the initial expense of buildings and stock would be enormous. The cost of maintaining large numbers of mares and young animals in the country would be out of all proportion to the results one might expect in the way of troop horses. Moreover, a state establishment would, beyond question, militate seriously against horse breeding by private individuals and damage the commercial industry.

Schemes to improve horse breeding and supply to the military

The vital importance of properly horsing the Army was never questioned but, the measures taken to encourage the breeding of suitable horses had never been commensurate with their needs.[62] The existing means of supplying the military was seen by most interested parties as inadequate. The future of the light horse was clearly seriously threatened and major initiatives were required to provide the financial incentives to encourage farmers to breed this particular class. In 1909, the Board of Agriculture published a booklet (revised, 1912), containing information, supplied by the Assistant Director Remounts, on the type of horses required for remount purposes.[63] The purpose was to bring to the attention of horse breeders in Great Britain the knowledge of which types were required for remount purposes. It specified general conditions relating to age, colour and soundness, dividing them into five fairly distinct

59   Ibid., pp.298-99.
60   Gartside-Spaight, 1906(b), April, p.329.
61   Gilbey, 1913, pp.15-17.
62   Ibid., Introduction.
63   Board of Agriculture and Fisheries, 1909; 1912 (revised).

types: for Household Cavalry, Cavalry of the Line (about 1,000 cavalry horses were required annually in peacetime), Royal Artillery, Royal Engineers and Army Service Corps (about 1,360 horses purchased annually in peacetime for the three units), and Mounted Infantry (about 140 purchased annually in peacetime).

Where did the responsibility lie for supplying the Army with the number of horses required? As there did not appear to be a problem with supply in peacetime, the question only really related to mobilisation in the event of war. Birkbeck was firmly of the opinion that it was the Department of Agriculture's responsibility to find the staggering difference between peacetime and wartime demand. The type suitable for military requirements could only be found by ensuring that horses in general working use were hard and fit, were used to eating concentrated foods and able to work hard under adverse conditions often with scanty food intake. Lane also emphasised the necessity of procuring only seasoned animals; soft and immature ones being a very serious hindrance on active service. Bridge and many others believed the lesson had been learnt from the 1899-1902 War, of the absolute unsuitability of using inexperienced young horses, not in hard working condition, for campaigning. He thought it would be possible to leave young horses out of the first mobilisation and retain those in the country due for export on the outbreak of a future emergency. [64]

If the Department of Agriculture was to find the means of supplying the military's requirements, it had to do so without interfering with private enterprise. This could be achieved by placing the necessary resources for producing the class of horses required at the breeder's disposal, encouraging him to make use of the resources and not exporting the end product. Birkbeck argued that no government, or country, could possibly meet, out of public funds, the expenditure necessary to maintain all the horses required, even for the Army's first mobilisation and could not see how any such scheme could have been practicable. Even though all the armed nations of Europe spent large sums of money on horse breeding, with a view to meeting their military requirements, in not one, did the money come from army funds. Nor was the WO held responsible for this purely agricultural matter. The War Department was concerned with the end product, the Department of Agriculture with finding the means of supply. It was not practical for a government in peacetime to manage, or to be responsible for, any scheme to supply the numbers required by the Army in time of war.

Bridge wrote in 1909, that the Army purchased annually, 2,500 horses of which some 1,500 were for riding and the rest for draught. 160,000 horses, plus those already with units, were required on first mobilisation for war, some 60,000 were for riding. It is difficult to find one agreed figure for the annual peacetime requirements for army remounts:

---

64   Birkbeck, 1908, pp.328, 335-6, 338; Lane, 1912, p.39; Bridge, 1909, p.291.

Stanley Report (1901)   2,500
Birkbeck   (1908) about   2,700
Birkbeck   (1914) some   3,000 Development Commission evidence
Granet   (1910) average   3,000
Gilbey   (1913) between   2,500-3,000

Gilbey is the only one to state that there was difficulty replacing the annual peace-time wastage. There were changes to establishments affecting the number of remounts required, for example, ceasing to provide for overseas garrisons, increasing the number of cavalry horses maintained with regiments during peacetime and the introduction of motor vehicles.[65]

Bridge did not think it possible to predict the actual wastage of war, but thought it was not an over-statement to suggest at least an annual remounting of 2,500, although he does not give the period of wastage to be covered by this figure. Birkbeck states that roundly 174,000 would be required for mobilisation alone, approximately 60,000 being riding horses, estimating 332,000 for the first year of war, including probable wastage, of which 180,000 would be riding horses. In his evidence before the Development Commission in May 1914, he gives a figure of 85,000 riding and light draught horses would be required within ten days of mobilisation.[66] As he does not enlarge on, 'including probable wastage', it is possible wastage for one year of war, would be around 158,000. This is a considerably larger figure than Bridge provided, assuming 2,500 as 'an annual remounting'. Col. Granet giving evidence before the Development Commission gives figures of:[67]

57,000 riding horses required for mobilisation
54,000 of all kinds for the Regular Army, in addition to those already in service
80-90,000 for the Territorial Force

He gives a total for the above of 144,00 (90,000 + 54,000), which appears to ignore the riding horses.

The Army Council's Statement of April 1914, gives the general mobilisation figures as:[68]

36,374 riding horses
49,076 light draught
13,054 heavy draught
4,057 pack
Total 102,561

65 Bridge 1909 p.296; Stanley Report, WO32/8756; Birkbeck, Evidence before the Development Commission 1908, p.335, WO32/9128, 1914, 22nd May, pp.2-5; D4/100, 1910, Granet; Gilbey, 1913, p.15.
66 Birkbeck, 1908, p.335; WO32/9128, 1914, 22nd May, p.3, Q36.
67 D4/100, 1910, 21st Sept., p.14, Q1047; also p.15, Q1078-83.
68 MAF53/2/A43091/1915.

The Council's Statement does not clarify any of these figures. They do, however, represent the alterations, especially for heavy draught, relating to changes in the Army's transport establishments, notably the increased use of motor vehicles. Again, the figures given in much of the contemporary material vary, some quite considerably, although many are fairly compatible. The major problem is in understanding what the figures do, or do not, include, for example, just the Regular, or the Territorial and Reserve Forces? Do they include those horses already in service? Do they mean a full mobilisation of all forces, including first and second lines, or a partial mobilisation? The rounding up of figures is also very common and confusing.

Birkbeck considered that beyond laying down the type of animal it required, the WO could do little to help. It could possibly reduce its demand for draught horses by increasing the use of mechanical traction for second line transport and ammunition columns (which it had done by 1914). It could keep the number of riding horses in cavalry regiments at war strength with mature horses, exclusive of untrained animals. It could also possibly help to create supply by purchasing remounts at 3.5 years of age, and follow France's example, in utilising its young and old mares for breeding, in a liberal spirit, without any frustrating restrictions. The problem lay in realising the number required. For Armstrong the answer was simple, "we must breed them". Maj. Eassie considered it essential in horse breeding to have a fixed policy and to give it a long trial. [69] Unfortunately, such advice was not to be heeded.

The Hunter Improvement and Light Horse Breeding Societies were founded in 1885 to improve and encourage the breeding of horses for hunting, riding, driving and for military purposes. In 1887, Lord Salisbury's Administration diverted £3,000, which had been given annually since the reign of Queen Anne (1702-1714) as Royal Plates, to be won at race meetings in different parts of the country; with an additional £2,000, to be administered by the newly appointed Royal Commission on Horse breeding. [70] The Commission was to award premiums to thoroughbred stallions, distributed throughout the country for stud purposes, serving mares at a two-guinea fee. The statement appointing the Commission, declared that the Queen's Plates had been failing in their original purpose of encouraging the breeding of sound horses and that in recent years there was an increasing necessity for encouraging the breeding of horses, apart from the influence of private enterprise; largely due to the UK being swept by foreign government agents purchasing stallions and mares, leaving the country with the rejected inferior and often unsound animals, and in the gradual, marked deterioration of the general breed.

Between 1888 and 1910, the Commission awarded annually some 28 premiums. The Commission was the only official directing body charged with the supervision

---

69   Birkbeck, 1908, p.335; Armstrong, 1908, p.498; Eassie in Gartside-Spaight, 1906(b), April, p.337.
70   Thompson, 1983, pp.54-55; Gilbey, 1913, Introduction; Birkbeck, 1908, p.378; *Selborne Committee Report*, 1915, in MAF.52/3TL21438.

of the home breeding policy in England. It was to consider how public money would be best spent for the purpose of encouraging the breed and maintenance of a race of sound horses; certain numbers of which would be purchased by the Army. Successive governments from 1887 saw the Premium Stallion Scheme as being sufficient, in the long term, at minimal cost to the taxpayer, to meet the national requirement for a pool of good quality horses and provide a reserve of horses for the military. In comparison with foreign governments, Birkbeck considered this was "absolute child's play". The meagre assistance given by the State was supplemented by agricultural societies and many associations for the improvement of particular breeds of horses, giving premiums for stallions and prizes at their shows. He noted that much that was done in this country by private enterprise was done abroad by funds provided by governments.[71]

The Hunter Improvement Society (HIS), having started the movement to promote horse breeding and having handed some of its powers over to the Royal Commission, had by 1891 turned its attention to mares and young stock. This decision was no doubt influenced by the export of good, young breeding stock and a recognition that ready markets existed for the hunter class. In 1909, the Society's Council decided to take over the work and duties of the original Brood Mare Society and a special committee was appointed to promote the interests of horse breeding. This included the duty of keeping before Parliament and the country, the importance of making proper provision for the distribution of brood mares and supplying information and statistics to members of Parliament. Maj. Fife believed that due to the advance of mechanisation and the importation of foreign horses, there was never a time when horse breeding was more in need of the Society's assistance. In the event of war, the larger the country's export of horses, the better prepared it would be, as these animals could then be withheld in this country. Conversely, the larger the imports, the weaker would be the country. In 1906 and subsequent years representations were made to the Government from various quarters concerning the urgent need for further financial assistance.[72]

The military authorities were only concerned with the supply of horses appropriate to its needs. Birkbeck's view was that however excellent the work of all the societies and associations, they did not aim to produce a war horse, level up the general utility horse, or ensure the horse in general use was of a class fit for war. The only solution was state aid, legislation and scientific direction on a scale never before contemplated in Great Britain. A first step towards the scientific direction of a breeding policy was establishing a stud school, where officials, who were to guide the work, could themselves be taught. A scheme had already been proposed for the formation of a national stud for 12,000 brood mares, let out to farmers at £2 per year, under the conditions of the Brood Mare Society.[73] According to Birkbeck, the mare reproduced

71 Birkbeck, 1908, p.339.
72 Macgregor-Morris, pp.20, 39.
73 Birkbeck, 1908, pp.339-41; also Birkbeck, 1907, for a comparison with the French remount system.

herself possibly once a year, while the sire multiplied many times; therefore, it was to the provision of stallions rather than mares, that state funds should be devoted. He recommended:

- The establishment of stallion depots in districts where horses were bred, to serve mares at a nominal fee. These depots were to contain several hundred stallions.
- Premiums for approved, privately owned stallions, provided they served mares at a reasonable sum.
- Compulsory registration of all stallions and elimination of those whose services were likely to be injurious to the breed.

In England, the upkeep of a brood mare stud for the production of sires to fill stallion depots, was considered unnecessary, as there was no difficulty in buying all those required.

Birkbeck's view is an interesting contrast to others who considered that emphasis should have been placed on the selection of better quality mares. If encouragement was required to use government stallions, this could be achieved by giving prizes for young stock at county shows which would also provide opportunities for judging the results of the Stud Department's policy. Good mares were to be kept in the country, at all costs, by means of premiums, or an export tax, because if farmers could not find a profitable market for their horses they would not breed them. The Remount Department's annual requirement was too insignificant to provide the required market, though the purchase of three-year-olds would have been an incentive to breeders. Breeders needed to focus on the fashionable and general markets, which Birkbeck considered depended largely on the encouragement of equestrian sport and discouragement of the use of motor vehicles. As the excellence of the country's saddle horses was due to hunting and polo, a heavy tax on motor cars, cabs and buses, would aid the sale of hacks and harness horses. Racing, which had formerly been subsidised by the State, had ceased to fulfil the purpose of encouraging a stout breed of horse.

For Gilbey, the alternative to state breeding was changing the system of purchasing, recognising that farmers could not breed a horse, keep it until five years old and then accept the regulation £40 army remount price.[74] The Government had to buy horses aged rising three, or raise the price limit, so that three-year-olds had to be kept at the public expense until they were fit to join a unit; a policy Gilbey had recommended in 1886. Lord Ribblesdale (Liberal peer and captain in the Rifle Brigade) had stated that if horses could be purchased a little younger and at a better price, he was certain more would be bred.[75] Five years of age was the minimum at which a horse could safely undertake the heavy work demanded by military service, the Horse Registration and Subsidy Schemes stipulated horses not less than six years old. A scheme was needed that profit-

74   Gilbey, 1913, pp.17-22; also Stanley Report, WO32/8756, pp.iv-v.
75   Lord Ribblesdale, Hansard (L), 1906, Vol.CIV, 13th March, (c) 1236.

ably employed horses between the date of purchase and reaching five years old. The Duke of Devonshire (Secretary of State for War 1882-85), in his reply to Lord Ribblesdale, stated that the most effective means of improving the supply of horses would be for the WO to increase the price they paid; the Government could not expect to buy an animal for £40, for which a private purchaser would bid £50 or more. The Government should take horses from the breeder when they were over three years old, breeders could then readily sell at a price from £30 to £40. Horses, if taken at this age, could be purchased in larger numbers and of a better stamp; a proportion of four year olds should also be purchased. The expense would be considerable, but any scheme which aimed at the efficient mounting of the Army, would have to be conceived on a more liberal scale. Gilbey suggested that money could be raised by introducing the Totaliser (a lottery) on racecourses, a scheme also recommended by Birkbeck; the French had used a lottery, the Paris-mutuel, to create income for the national treasury. It had been used in 1913 at a point-to-point meeting and had proved exceedingly popular.[76]

The ultimate option for obtaining horses in an emergency was impressment. The powers to implement this had already been extended with the Army Act of 1881. 'Emergency' was defined as calling out the reserves, although, it is not clear whether this meant the full reserve, or part of it. Bridge had called for clarification of this question believing a special Act was required, placing it beyond all doubt, that the Government had the power, in the event of a national emergency, to take on due payment, those horses which were the property of public companies, traders, private individuals or others, as required for the service of the Army. [77]

The October 1909 Council meeting of the HIS instructed the Brood Mare Committee: to consider and submit a report, as to the best means of meeting the requirements of the nation in improving the condition of light horse breeding in the UK.[78] The Committee was of the opinion that not less than an annual £50,000 should be allocated to support light horse breeding; France spent £185,000, Germany £370,000 and Austria £210,000 annually. The 28 King's Premium stallions were considered totally insufficient for the needs of the country, noting that in some districts, great use was made of unsound, weedy thoroughbreds and unauthenticated half-bred stallions. The continuous export of many of the best stallions was regretted and measures were required to counteract this bad practice, as referred to by the Royal Commission of 1887. To assure a real and permanent improvement, the considerable number of stallions exported should be retained in the UK, but this was only achievable with support and resources from the Government, organised by the Board of Agriculture. With good organisation and liaison between the WO, Royal Commission and HIS, the standard of excellence could be greatly improved, the cost of production reduced and the industry made more profitable. The Council appointed the Brood

76   Gilbey, 1913, p.21; Birkbeck, 1908, p.341.
77   Bridge, 1909, p.297.
78   MacGregor-Morris, pp.45-53.

Mare Committee to draft a detailed scheme for consideration of the Commissioners under the Development Act. The Development Commission had been instituted by Parliament in 1909 at the instance of Mr Lloyd George when Chancellor of the Exchequer. The sum of £2.9 million was assigned for certain purposes, previously unaided by the state, or in receipt of scanty and fitful assistance.[79] The Committee met on 17th February 1910, and resolved to constitute the Horse Supply Committee, with cooperation from the Polo and Riding Pony Societies, to investigate the whole question of horse breeding and report to the Council.

The Horse Supply Committee, having met on six occasions between 15th and 23rd May 1910, submitted its report to the HIS Council on the 6th June. In the context of horses for the Army the report states:

- There was a need for an accurate census of horses in the UK which, to be of value needed to provide an accurate classification, repeated at least every five years. Owners were to be under statutory obligation to return forms.
- The decline in light horses was partly due to the increase in mechanical traction and the consequent decline in a market for misfits; in part owing to the majority of farmers no longer being able to afford to hunt and therefore had lost interest in light horse breeding
- There should be no restrictions on exports, thereby encouraging breeding, as foreigners were to a great extent the best customers for breeders of light horses in the UK. Had this not been so, light horse breeding would have suffered even more seriously.
- An adequate supply was to be maintained. Demand for high-class hunters and polo ponies had to be the main stimulus for breeders. It was from these breeds that the Army obtained its supply of the larger hunter and polo pony of approximately 15.1 to 15.2 hands. These 'misfits' offered the smallest commercial return and so breeding was likely to decline in the future unless, the WO assisted in encouraging breeders. The heavy horse was generally sufficiently profitable to ensure a plentiful supply and did not therefore require support.
- The Army only purchased about 3,000 horses annually in peacetime. This annual purchase should be used to encourage, rather than discourage, the breeder. Army horses were bought at four years and upwards, at a price that gave the breeder no profit, probably a loss. If purchased at three years plus, at the same average price given for older horses, this would just pay the breeder.
- Although it might be inconvenient for the Army to purchase all horses at three years old, they should buy as many as possible at that age and give a higher price for older horses. This would increase army expenditure, but give the advantage of being first in the market and using their annual purchase to encourage the breeder, help maintain and foster a valuable asset in time of war.

79 Development Commission, D3/10.

- The Army should purchase many more horses directly from the breeder. It was, however, more convenient for Army buyers to purchase from experienced dealers, who collected considerable numbers of horses for inspection at local centres, saving army purchasers time, gaining better prices and a better selection.
- Army policy should be to purchase annually a certain number of mares of a better stamp than the ordinary troop horse, at two or three years old. A thoroughbred, or registered sire, left with the breeder until the foal was weaned and then passed into the Army in the ordinary way could then serve these mares. This process would offset the breeder's costs of keeping mares and assist with retaining a certain number in the country. The Army could further assist breeding by casting a few of their best mares at about 12 years old, or preferably sooner, before they became altogether worn out.

The above measures were considered important for the Army to adopt, so supporting horse breeding, but they only touched the fringe of the problem. However, the military did not wish to adopt many of these options as they would increase costs in actual money and time. Other measures recommended by the Committee included:

	cost per annum
Stocking districts where there was a shortage of mares, operating along the lines of a scheme in Ireland.	£7,000
Giving free nominations (no fee) for approved stallions to service approved mares in each district	£14,000
Purchasing an adequate number of sound stallions with money set aside for a government agent, appointed to buy selected thoroughbred race horses that would otherwise go abroad.	£5,000
Making loans available, as in Ireland, to individuals or associations to purchase stallions, registered for free nomination to mares	£6,000
The Royal Commission's scheme for registering stallions and free nominations for mares would not interfere with giving premiums for stallions	£5,000

After experience of the proposed scheme, the Royal Commission could modify their system to bring both forms of encouragement into greater harmony.

Castrating fewer colts which the Government could then purchase as a reserve of stallions, to be reared on government farms and disposed of at four years of age to breeders, or placed with private breeders. The annual cost would be equivalent to the annual expenses of a government farm and 30 colts.	£2,700

Passing legislation which did not allow stallions to travel the public highway for hire, without a veterinary certificate of freedom from hereditary disease.

An organisation was necessary to carry out the above proposals. It was recommended that the £50,000 allotted under the Development Act, for the encouragement of horse breeding, should not be distributed to the various societies, but administered by the Board of Agriculture, the President of which would be the Minister responsible to Parliament. He was to be assisted by an Advisory Council with representatives from the Board of Agriculture, Royal Commission, Councils of the HIS, Polo and Riding Pony societies and officers recommended by the Army Council. Part of the function of this Council would be to arrange for the appointment of small local district committees. Funds for Ireland (£10,000 in addition to existing grants) were to remain separate from those of Great Britain. These recommendations, it was stated, were popular with breeders.

In July 1910, the Board of Agriculture applied to the Development Commission for an Advance of £50,000 to aid light horse breeding.[80] The proposed expenditure was for the:

- payment of premiums to stallion owners
- encouragement to keep suitable brood mares
- free nomination for the services of mares by Premium Stallions
- purchase (for re-sale) of stallions
- voluntary registration of stallions
- administration.

In September, Col. Granet was called to give evidence before the Development Commission.[81] His evidence provides an insight into the current military thinking and practice in relation to remounts. He stated that the Army, had not, to any appreciable extent over the previous three years, experienced increased difficulty in procuring the small number of horses required annually in peacetime; an average of 3,000, of all sorts, riding and heavy. The average was not likely to increase under conditions existing at the time and could decrease as the Remount Department was to cease sending horses to South Africa and Egypt. Territorial Forces mostly hired their horses for training, owning, he thought, very few. The Yeomanry owned about 40% of their horses; a breakdown for 1910 shows: [82]

Owned	Relations and Friends	Hired	Total
5,791	1,091	1,517	8,399

---

80   D4/100; 1910, 19th July, No.A7580/1910, under the Development and Road
       Improvement Funds Act of 1909.
81   Ibid., 21st September, pp.14-16, Q1042-1106.
82   Cd.468, pp.484-5.

The decline in the number of horses would continue if nothing was done, but Granet agreed that the Board of Agriculture's application to the Commission would intend to increase the supply of horses suitable for army purposes. All army purchasers reported that the quality of horses had deteriorated, although the price remained the same. The stamp of horse required by the Army was a second grade hunter (the misfit) and the Army was only allowed to buy a few horses under four years old, about 100 being purchased towards the end of the year. Granet was questioned about the suggestion that the Army should purchase horses at three years old, giving the owners a part payment to keep the horse for the Army for a year, or until wanted, paying a fair price for their keep and the balance of the price when taken. He thought this could act as a financial incentive to the poorer farmer. Asked about proposals being made to the WO that they should have horse depots and retain animals in time of peace, he replied that he did not think it had ever been definitely suggested because the Army would require an enormous number of such depots. Such an answer seems a little strange in the light of Birkbeck's writings on the need for depots, but, perhaps the emphasis is on 'definite suggestion'. Others such as Armstrong in 1908, wrote about the need to establish government stud farms, referring to one at Lusk near Dublin, as did Gartside-Spaight in 1906, with one at Moore Park, Ireland, a farm already to hand.[83]

The question of remounts in peacetime was a very small, almost insignificant matter. However, Granet stressed the difference between peace and wartime requirements and the very great importance of having an efficient supply of suitable horses for wartime conditions. Questioned about the decline in horse supply, Granet thought it would be very much worse in wartime, even compared to the previous ten years. There were no reliable figures for the country's horse population; the Police Census of 1909, for horses in the UK, was unreliable as it was voluntary and owners were not compelled to give information; it gave a total of 184,664 riding horses: [84]

146,792   riding horses in Great Britain
37,872   riding horses   in Ireland

The supply of Irish horses was of vital importance to the WO as England alone could not supply the need in time of war. On mobilisation, taking riding horses alone, including artillery riding horses, 57,000 would be required for the Territorial and Regular Army. This was more than 30% of the 184,000 of this stamp recorded in the Police Census, which did not take account of such factors as age, or soundness. For Granet, the question of the supply of riding horses was very serious as it was not possible for Great Britain and Ireland together, to supply the numbers required. Therefore, the WO considered the industry in both islands required fostering (the Irish Department had also placed a bid for funding with the Commission).   Army   demands   for

83   D4/100, Q1052-3; Armstrong, 1908, p.495; Gartside-Spaight, 1906(b), April, p.321.
84   D4/100, Q1031-33.

draught horses would not be as serious a drain on national resources, though the quality was not as the Army would have liked. The Army had been hiring 6,000 horses for manoeuvres, the quality of which in many cases was wretched (see the Queen's Own Oxfordshire Hussars); if they were a fair sample of what the Army would get, they would not be satisfied. The Army would like any scheme to include light heavy horses as well as riding horses. Nearly all artillery draught horses were purchased in Ireland and the quality, in relation to numbers, was excellent. He proposed that Irish draught horses should be strengthened to get a higher class of animal with more substance, to supply army purposes.

Two systems of registration were in operation for maintaining a small reserve, by payment of a retaining fee and 'boarding out'. The Army had some useful brood mares that could be utilised as part of a breeding scheme, provided the Treasury sanctioned the cost of removing them from establishment. Some army horses proved more valuable than others, although the same price was given for all horses; Granet agreed that it was very important the country should have access to them for breeding, if they could be spared, at the cost of replacing them by an average horse. A mare lent out on such a scheme could not be counted as on the reserve, as she might be in foal (only about 50% to 60% of mares went into foal). He stated that the Army Council would consider sympathetically any proposal for such a scheme. An arrangement had been reached between the Board and the WO in 1912, to experiment with the sale to the Board, of 20 selected artillery mares of an exceptionally good and suitable type; placed out, with certain County Committees, as brood mares, six to Wiltshire, four each to East and West Sussex and three each to Northamptonshire and Warwickshire.[85]

From information obtained, for example from Granet's evidence before the Development Commission and the Report of the Horse Supply Committee, it would appear the Government faced continual lobbying by influential members of the horse world. This resulted in government recognition that support was required for the horse breeding industry, probably best seen in the Development Commission's decision of 27th September 1910, to award a grant of £40,000, in addition to the £5,000 from the Royal Commission and £5,000 from the Livestock Breeding Scheme; a total of £50,000. The grant of £40,000 from the Commission, authorised by the Treasury in January 1911, was to be used to establish the Light Horse Breeding Scheme (LHBS) to upgrade the country's horse stock, especially riding horses.[86] At the same time, the functions of the Royal Commission on Horse Breeding were transferred to the Board of Agriculture. The Board issued a statement that the Lords Commissioners of the Treasury had, on the recommendation of the Development Commission, made an

85   MacGregor-Morris, pp.63, 74-75 ref. Brood Mare Scheme, 1911-12.
86   D3/2; *Second Report of the Development Commission* to 31st March 1912, which states for 1910-11, grants to the Board of £41,050 and the Department of ATI of £10,000; also D4/100 and D3/2; *Norton Committee Report* in WO163/29, p.133; *Selborne Committee Report*, 1915, p.5; MacGregor-Morris, 1986, pp.54-55.

annual grant to the Board of Agriculture and Fisheries (transferred to the Board of Agriculture's Vote in 1916), from the Development Fund of £40,000 for the ensuing year. This was for the encouragement of light horse breeding in Great Britain by means of: the award of premiums to stallions; grants for the purchase of half-bred working brood mares (to be located in selected districts), free nominations of suitable mares for services by Premium, or approved stallions and the purchase, for resale, of stallions and voluntary registration of stallions.

The President of the Board proposed to appoint immediately an Advisory Council, composed of persons from various parts of the country, intimately acquainted with the industry. The Council was to advise and assist the Board generally in all matters connected with the horse breeding industry. The Advisory Council met in February 1911; Lord Middleton was appointed Chairman with a standing committee of 20 members (including five members of the RCHB, and representatives from the HIS, NLHBS and several pony societies); one of its first tasks was to advise on how to use, to best advantage, a gift of £10,000 from Capt. Dealtry C. Part of the, 21st Lancers, for furthering the Board's LHBS. In 1912, a Committee for improving the native breeds of ponies and horses was formed under Lord Arthur Cecil.[87] Further progress was made when the Secretary of State for War agreed that the WO would be prepared to purchase annually a certain number of the remounts, at three years plus, it also promised co-operation and assistance from the Army Council on the Advisory Council. The recommendation to award grants to the Board of Agriculture (also Ireland) for 1910-11, was accompanied by a promise to consider favourably applications for a renewal, provided the Commissioners were satisfied with the working of the Scheme.[88]

The aim of the LHBS was to award premiums to selected stallions (for example thoroughbreds, cobs and ponies) which were required, in return for a small fee, to serve mares that received nominations from local committees. The most valuable premiums were those known as 'Super Premiums' and 'King's Premiums'. Thoroughbred stallions were to compete for the premiums at the Annual Spring Show, with successful stallions being required to travel prescribed districts, along routes laid down by the Ministry, after having consulted the wishes of the owners. Until 1920, six to eight premiums were provided for Scotland. Before the outbreak of war in 1914, in addition to subsidising selected stallions, the Board purchased nearly 1,000 brood mares through the County Committees and leased them to allottees under specified conditions. For various reasons this part of the scheme was not a success and most of the mares were sold.[89]

The Army Council wrote to the Board expressing their approval of the LHBS, making it quite clear that they did not see the primary function of the Scheme as

87   MacGregor-Morris, pp.63-4.
88   D3/2, *2nd Report of the Development Commission* to 31st March 1912.
89   WO163/29, *Norton Committee Report*, p.133.

producing horses for the military.[90] The Scheme, they wrote, was devised primarily in the interest of breeders, for the purpose of stimulating a languishing industry and for encouraging the breeding of a better class of horse; the military requirements of the country were taken into consideration only incidentally. The Development Fund, out of which the Scheme was financed, could be utilised for aiding and developing the breeding of horses, only to the extent of assisting agriculturists in placing the industry on a paying footing, and not for securing the provision of remounts for the Army. The Board requested from the Development Commission a continuation of the grant for 1912-13 and an additional grant of £10,000, enabling them to allocate further grants to County Committees during the forthcoming autumn for the purchase of mares for service during the breeding season of 1912. This additional sum was agreed. Advisory Council reports clearly state that a minimum of five years, more realistically ten, must elapse before meaningful judgements could be expressed on the value on the LHBS.[91]

Despite the initial enthusiasm greeting the increased state assistance, it was soon recognised that such support was still very short of what was required. At the Board's Advisory Council meeting in July 1913, Maj-Gen. Brocklehurst indicated that he, at least, did not consider sufficient was being done, to reduce the risks and increase rewards, for keeping good stallions in the country. He considered that with the continued improvement in motor traction the day would not be far distant when almost the only support for light horse breeding would be the remount buyer and dealers in horses for riding and driving for pleasure. The government grant was, he believed, to prevent the remount horse from becoming an extinct animal. Mr Lort Phillips spoke against the Brood Mare Scheme as it encouraged the breeding of half-bred horses and did not improve breeds; he felt the only way to put the horse breeding industry on a sound footing was for the Government to pay a price for its remounts that induced farmers to breed them. It was absolutely essential that money was spent on the badly needed artillery stamp of horse; the artillery depended on misfits, but the time would come when it would not be possible to purchase them and they must be prepared to meet the deficiency with an alternative. At the same meeting, Mr Cheney, Assistant Secretary to BAF, commented on the idea that the object of the Board was to induce farmers to breed light horses for remount purposes; that this was not the primary object of the Scheme, as the Board was endeavouring, by the provision of high-class sires, to secure the breeding of horses of a better stamp than that required by the WO for remounts. The Scheme would no doubt, incidentally, produce many horses suitable for remounts, as there were bound to be many misfits produced in the attempts being made to breed horses of superior quality of the hunter weight type. Cheney emphasised this point, so as to correct the idea that the Scheme was one for

---

90   Army Council 116/Gen.No./5385, 1910, 24th December, in MAF.52/2/A43091/1915.
91   D3/2, *2nd Report of Development Commission*, to 31st March 1912; MacGregor-Morris, p.71.

breeding remounts, a business that could not be advocated by the Board, as it was not sufficiently remunerative to the breeder.[92]

Gilbey (who had been a member of the RCHB until its replacement in 1911), considered the Government had been pressurised into taking action because of the impact of motor traction on horse breeding. These government actions, it was hoped, would promote the breeding of a good stamp of horse and secure for the Army an adequate supply of horses in time of an emergency, for example, an invasion of the east coast. However, he believed there was a fatal flaw in the new scheme, as with the old one it encouraged farmers to breed horses without providing a market for the produce (a point raised by Birkbeck in 1908). Gilbey criticised the whole scheme, including the system of making a substantial proportion of the stallion's earnings dependent on the number of foals that were alive, some months after birth, helping farmers meet the cost of loss through accidents and disease. He commended the fact that, unlike the old scheme of King's Premiums, 'Board stallions' were not to be chosen from one particular breed, an example copied from the Continent, and that Board stallions had to be over three years old and entered into the studbook of their breed. This system meant a greater variety of stock was possible other than just using thoroughbred sires. The new scheme was meant to produce greater results, assuming that each of the 50 King's Premium horses sired 65 foals in a season, and 40 of those survived, giving 2,000 young horses of good class annually. Gilbey, however, feared that though the Board's scheme was helping the British farmer to breed horses for sale, these might end up abroad. Probably more worrying was a letter, in July 1913 from the Development Commissioners to the Advisory Council, enquiring into a reduction in the grant for LHB, owing to increased expenditure incurred in the heavy horse industry.[93]

The Advisory Council were all agreed that light horse breeding was in far greater need of assistance and any reduction would militate against the success of the Scheme, which required at least five years in operation before any useful conclusions as to its value could be reached.[94] The Development Commission had agreed a continuation of the Board's grant of £40,000 for 1913-14, but £36,500 in England and £3,500 released to the Scottish Board (received until 1915) was for light horse breeding. The Board wrote to the Commission in October 1913, asking for assurances that the advance of £36,500 would be renewed for 1914-15, but was informed the grant would be reduced and by a similar sum in 1915.[95] However, in September 1913, the Commission decided not to grant the Board's application for 1914-15 with a request to revise its estimate, reducing it by £5,000 for 1914-15 and 1915-16. On financial grounds alone, the Commission considered such a reduction necessary. When they had agreed to the annual grant of £40,000 for light horse breeding in Great Britain,

92   MacGregor-Morris, pp.79-80, 82.
93   Gilbey, 1913, pp.1-4.
94   MacGregor-Morris, pp.78-9.
95   D1/1, 1st October 1913.

they had done so based on information that the requirements for other livestock would
be an annual £5,000. This amount had risen considerably and large, unanticipated
demands were being made on the Development Fund for another proposal connected
with the livestock industry. They also thought it possible that by means of certain
economies in other directions, a grant of £31,500 would be sufficient to carry on the
Scheme during 1914-15, without any loss of effectiveness in its most useful parts. The
Scheme had been modified, deleting provision for the purchase of stallions and brood
mares by the Board and by reductions such as the purchase of brood mares by County
Commissions, a provision the Board had not made use of during the previous year.
The most important parts of the Scheme, the award of stallion premiums and the issue
of free nominations to mares, was not reduced, but extended.[96]

The supply of light horses and military requirements for mobilisation, including impressment, on the eve of war

The proposed reduction in the grant for light horse breeding by some £5,000 was
taken seriously by the WO. In December 1913, Col. J.B. Seely, Under Secretary of
State for War, wrote to Lord Cavendish, Chairman of the Development Commission,
expressing concern, that the question of the adequacy of horse supply for purposes
of army mobilisation, had been pressed upon them from many quarters and he was
constantly urged to embark upon ambitious and expensive schemes of stud farms, or
the purchase of three-year-olds. He considered that, at that moment, there was no
actual shortage, however, the position with regard to light horses, due to the growth
of motor traction, was one that gave rise to particular consideration. Cavendish replied
that the Commission had already decided to reduce the grant by £5,000 for 1914 and a
further £5,000 for 1915-16, and he could not give a great deal of weight to the Army's
point of view, as the object of the Fund was the development of agriculture and rural
industries. The reduction for 1914-15 was not, in his opinion serious, as it would be
obtained, in part, by reducing administrative costs. The two most important headings of the Scheme, premium stallions and nominations for mares, were expected to
increase, not diminish. He concluded that if the WO would like to be heard, before
the further reduction for 1915-16 took effect, the Committee would be willing to give
the opportunity in the autumn of 1914, but doubted whether they would succeed in
altering their views.

Seely wrote to Lord Haldane, Secretary of State for War, informing him of the
Commission's reductions in grant.[97] The decision, he wrote, was peculiarly unfortunate for the WO, which had constantly been pressed to spend large sums of money on
various schemes to ensure the continuing supply of light horses suitable for military

96   D3/4, 4th Report to 31st March 1914, and D1/1, 35th meeting.
97   WO32/9128, File No.116/GN/5719; Seely's letter to Cavendish, 2nd December 1913,
     Seeley to Lord Haldane, 18th December 1913.

purposes. Seely, along with Maj-Gen. Cowans (QMG) and Gen. Birkbeck (Director of Remounts), shared the view that the proper course was to reject all expensive schemes, relying instead upon measures that would improve the breed of horses, ensuring that a large and growing proportion would be fit for military purposes. As the total number of light horses decreased and mechanical transport increased, the shortage would be made good by an ever increasing proportion of suitable animals out of a diminishing total. He requested help from Sir W.M. Haldane, Lord Haldane's brother, who had taken much interest and helped greatly in military affairs. At a meeting of 4th December 1913, the Development Commission accepted the Board's revised estimate of £31,500 for light horse breeding during 1914-15, stating a further reduction of £5,000 was to be made in 1915-16. In December, an advance of £10,000 was granted to Ireland for 1914-15, to aid heavy horse breeding; a similar grant, of £4,600 was made in October to the Scottish Board, provided that the temporary nature of the assistance was accepted.[98]

R.H. Brade, Secretary to the Army Council, wrote to the Board in April 1914, informing them that, in accordance with the express wish of the Commission, as intimated personally by Sir W. Haldane to Col. Seely in January 1914, they had prepared a statement of their views on the imperative necessity for taking early steps to improve the quality of horses in daily work throughout the kingdom, upon which, the Army relied for its supply on mobilisation. Haldane intended that representatives of the Board and WO would appear before the Development Commission's May meeting and that the Director of Remounts was to represent the Army Council at this meeting.[99]

The Army Council's Statement to the Board contained its views on the importance of increasing the scope of the Board's Scheme for the improvement of light horses.[100] This was a very carefully crafted letter, clearly highlighting the Army's concern at the possibility of paying higher prices for remounts. It placed responsibility for the supply of military horses on the State, through the Board of Agriculture, with an increased expenditure to ensure that in defence of the State, the Army could mobilise effectively. The Statement also provides a view of military thinking, on the eve of war, about the condition of horses in the country and requirements for mobilisation. It begins by stating that the horse mobilisation of the British Army was a more formidable task than for the Continental nations. The Army had to extend its horse strength in proportion from 1 to 5.5, compared for example with France at 1 to 2.75 and following the custom of all European nations, the British Government relied for this increase on mobilisation upon the civilian resources of the country.[101]

98   D1/1, 12th March 1913.
99   MAF/52/2/A43091/1915; the War Office Statement attached as Letter 1A.
100 WO Statement, as Letter 1A, accompanied WO letter, 16th April 1914, to the Board, in
     MAF53/2/A43091/1915 and WO32/9128.
101 MAF52/2/A43091/1915; WO32/9128, Letter 1A, Army Council Statement, 1914, "WO
     views on the necessities of increasing the scope of the Board of Agriculture's Scheme for

To avoid enormous peacetime expenditure on horses, the WO considered that on mobilisation the numbers and quality required could only be obtained by impressment. To achieve this an adequate supply of suitable horses in civilian life was required, upon which they could draw, otherwise it would be impossible to mobilise the Army. If the supply was not available the Army would be compelled, at vast expense (which it could not afford), to maintain establishments constantly at war strength, along with adequate reserves. The situation in England and Wales, in the event of a general mobilisation meant the Army would require (April 1914):

Riding Horses:

4,116	for	the Expeditionary Force
26,457	for	the Territorial Force
5,761	for	Reserve units and Remount Depots
36,334		Total

Light Draught:

13,992	EF
30,536	TF
4,548	RUs and RDs
49,076	Total

Heavy Draught:

5,530	EF
6,711	TF
813	RUs and RDs
13,054	Total

Pack:

663	EF
3,340	TF
54	RUs and RDs
4,057	Total

Total 102,521

As far as was possible, the Army perceived it had moved with the times with a large and increasing number of motor vehicles on Establishment, but the demand for large numbers of riding and light draught horses would always remain. Ireland had practically the monopoly of the hunter and cavalry remount trade, in peacetime the Army purchased 80% of its requirements there. The cavalry horse, the 'misfit' hunter,

the improvement of Light Horses."

was a smaller horse of a quality that could withstand the hardships of campaigning, exposure and scanty rations, could be purchased in Ireland at remount prices, yet the WO saw no reason why English farmers should not breed hunters. An equally large percentage of army light draught horses came from Ireland, a type that could also have been be bred in England, usefully replacing the very indifferent light 'vanners' found on the streets.

In the event of a general mobilisation, it was stressed that time and condition were essential factors. Animals were required quickly and had to be fit for hard work. The Census and Classification of horses undertaken during the winter of 1912-13 showed the following numbers suitable for military purposes:

Riding	LD	HD	Pack	Total
87,340	132,498	148,163	7,621	375,622

From these figures the Army considered their requirements on mobilisation could be met, but the State had to take adequate steps and in good time, to make sure this situation continued. Once again, the WO highlighted the detrimental effect of motor vehicles on the supply of light horses. The motor vehicle, for passenger traffic, especially in the big towns, had already virtually ousted horses; in the provinces they were creeping in. Horses had held their own in the carrying trade, on short routes, but for long and continuous journeys the motor was more economical. In agriculture and for the delivery of heavy goods, heavy draught horses were still in demand and with every prospect that the supply of this type would improve in quality and quantity.

England was not the only country whose horse production was being affected by motor vehicles. An increasing number of continental nations were buying their horses in the UK, suggesting that the market for all classes of good horses was likely to be maintained. The WO perspective was that the general condition of horses in the countryside, or urban districts, was appalling; numbers of which, by faulty conformation, or obvious unsoundness, were quite unsuited for hard work. For the foreseeable future, the WO considered there would be plenty of light horses at work throughout the country to meet the requirements of mobilisation, but only if the majority were useful, sound animals. Various traders were content with the very sorry animals that the WO wanted to eliminate, including, some 2,000 misshapen Russian ponies imported annually. It was the quality of the equine population that required levelling up, improvements for which, the WO considered the Board of Agriculture was responsible, with consequent increased expenditure. The WO did not consider it was only in the interests of the Army that the light horse breeding industry required reorganisation; the Army horse was required to be stout, active, with courage, docility and constitution, the same animal as was required in daily civilian use, so any improvements were mutually compatible. It was in the interests of the breeder, horse users and the State that an adequate supply of good quality horses was available.

In May 1914, Birkbeck was called to give evidence before the Development Commission.[102] Strangely, when asked, if a few years earlier he remembered a representative of the Remount Department (Col. Granet, 1910) giving evidence before the Commission, when they were contemplating a scheme for encouraging light horse breeding in England, he replied that he had not been aware of that. Birkbeck was informed the Commission had to decide whether to continue the grant for the encouragement of light horse breeding and it had certain misgivings as to whether the grant was being well applied and doing really useful work. Most of Birkbeck's answers correspond with the WO's statement in April, but he adds further detail on the military perspective of the horse supply problem immediately prior to the outbreak of war in August 1914.

Birkbeck believed a healthy and growing export market was a valuable stimulus to breeding and about 12,000 horses and ponies were imported annually. The only cavalry horses purchased in England were from dealers in York and Carlisle, although the best of these originated from Ireland where quality had been maintained. A significant number of ASC and Royal Engineer horses were still bought in Wales and West of England, but even for this class Ireland was found to be better. Nearly all horses were purchased through large dealers, not directly from the breeder; in Ireland it would have been practically impossible, as army purchasers did not attend fairs to buy horses. The Army had increased its prices for chargers to £65; they had wanted to increase from £60 to £70 but the financial authorities would not allow it. On average during 1914, the Army paid £45 for cavalry and artillery horses, instead of £42 at four years old. For general mobilisation there would be sufficient horses of the right type in England and Wales; a total of 135,000 horses were required, of all types, 85,000 riding and light draught horses immediately, within ten days. 11, 000 horses were included in these figures for Reserve Units and Remount Depots on mobilisation, as an allowance for war losses, 75% of cavalry and 25% of artillery horses. A cavalry regiment only required about 60 horses on first mobilisation, as the peace strength was above its war strength, but cavalry horses required more technical training before going into the ranks than draught horses, which could be trained in a couple of days for a gun wagon.[103]

The Horse Census of 1912-13 classified a total of 589,401 UK horses as fit for military service with the Regular and Territorial Forces, of these 231,868 were heavy draught horses, of which only 16,630 were required for various forces (an excess of 215,000), leaving 374,000 light horses classified as fit for military service. Birkbeck thought the census, although not accurate, acted as a guide, but hoped they would have a better census list in 1915. The census did not show a very large margin against

102 MAF52/3/TL21438 and WO32/9128; 22nd May1914, Birkbeck's evidence, pp.1-5, Questions 1-112.
103 WO32/9128; Question 3, p.1, re Granet; Birkbeck, p.4, Answer 75, p.1, Q8, p.5, Q12 and, Q101-3.

the numbers required, which was of concern for the future. He wished to ensure that in ten years time they would be in an equally favourable position.[104] The Army did not have a claim on the census horse, except by law of impressment under Section 115 of the Army Act, and no extension of this system had been contemplated by the WO. The Horse Reserve cost an annual £45,000, whereas impressment cost nothing, therefore being a cheaper way of obtaining horses. Asked whether there was a reserve in Ireland to draw upon in case of mobilisation, Birkbeck thought they were not kept fit and in working condition, a large number of farm horses, except in towns and hunt horses, were poorly maintained, mostly out to grass and unfit for mobilisation. WO statistics for Ireland showed 160,000 horses fit for military purposes, of which 17,000 were to be taken for the mobilization of the two divisions based there. As soon as the Army had mobilised and reserve regiments had been completed, the WO proposed replacing wastage by voluntary purchase in Ireland and Canada. These horses would go in as a 'second line', as they were not fit for immediate mobilisation. [105]

Birkbeck did not think the WO had ever contemplated starting its own stud farms as there was no parallel for it in any country, except the Indian Government. In France, Germany, Russia and Austria, it was always the civil agricultural departments that bred horses, none actually bred horses for its army. Birkbeck considered it a great mistake to withdraw, or curtail, the Board's LHB Scheme, as it had, in his experience, met its objective. The Army felt the scope of the present Scheme was totally inadequate to meet the circumstances and wanted something on a much bigger scale, as there were a fearful number of misfits and miserably bred little horses around the country. Draught horses purchased in Ireland were of very good blood, the type required for artillery and rarely seen in England, a very stout horse with a great deal of quality. The aim of the Board's Scheme from his point of view was to introduce this strain into England. [106]

In 1914 there was a good market for foreign buyers from Russia, as well as the regular traders who had purchased for years, Italians, Dutch, Belgians, Swiss and Swedes. In 1913 the French and Germans entered the market, although not buying directly in the UK; the Germans had made a clean sweep of Breton horses, attending all big sales, purchasing, or causing to be purchased, about 180,000. They had also purchased during the last few years 100,000 horses annually in Russia. The French bought in Paris from import dealers, purchasing between 2,500-3,000 horses in 1913; statistics showed farmers imported 12,000 horses into the country annually, mostly Russian ponies. Birkbeck thought the market for misfits was reduced locally, but was sure the foreign army market would remain. Asked whether foreign countries would be short of horses under their mobilisation schemes, he replied he had spoken to some French officers recently, some of whom thought they would be; they paraded their

104 Ibid., Q12, p.1; also WO33/669, p.101, *Remount Statement* for 1914-15.
105 Ibid., pp.1-2, Q12, 14, 18, Q29-30.
106 Ibid., p.3, Q33-35; p.2, Q19, 23-24.

horses past the mayor of each district annually for a military inspection. Asked when Austria mobilised, was there any shortage of horses; Birkbeck replied Austria was full of light horses, little bits of horses, many of which were sold to France. [107]

Following Birkbeck's evidence to the Commission, Cubitt (WO) wrote in July to the Secretary of the Board, stating that the Army Council was not aware what line the Commission might decide to take in regard to the amount of grants.[108] He called to the Board's immediate attention the Council's grave concern about an ample supply of light horses of suitable stamp for military purposes, vital to the successful mobilisation of HM Forces, and was compelled to ask for a definite assurance that the Board contemplated taking adequate steps, at an early date, to allay anxiety on this point. The Board replied they fully recognised that the decrease in light horse breeding called for action to improve the quality of those being bred, they had prepared, in 1910, their LHBS, of which the Army Council had expressed approval. A Scheme primarily devised, in the interests of breeders, for a languishing industry and to encourage breeding of a better class of horse, only indirectly for the military needs of the country. The Board was glad to extend the Scheme if funds were provided, and asked whether the WO was prepared to make the necessary provision in their Estimates.

The Commission wrote to the WO in July, requesting statistics on how many horses, the Army purchased in Great Britain that had been bred in England, Wales or Scotland, during each of the previous three years; also, how many Irish bred horses had been purchased in Great Britain. The WO was requested to note how many of the horses they purchased were as a result of the LHBS supported by the Commission. Birkbeck forwarding the following statistics:[109]

	Horses Purchased at Home		
	GB	*Ireland*	*Total*
1911-12	697	2,467	3,164
1912-13	769	2,874	3,643
1913-14	492	3,723	4,215
Total	1,958	9,064	11,022

107 Ibid, pp.2-3, Q31; *VR*, 1913, Vol.XXVI, 6th September, p.154, 4th April, p.652; WO32/9128, p.3, Q48-9; WO Statement which states some 2,000 ponies; WO32/9128, p.5, Q111-12.
108 WO32/9128 and MAF52/2/A43091/1915, Cubitt to Board, 1914, 20th July, referring to letter of 16th April (ref.116/5719), and the Board's reply, 1st August from E.J. Cheney, Assistant Secretary to the Board, referring to WO letter 24th December 1910 (116/GN/5385), the WO expressed approval of the Scheme.
109 WO32/9128, to QMG4, 3rd June 1914 (ref.3489/14). Birkbeck replied 8th June 1914 with the figures. Also WO letter to the Board, 15th June 1914 ref. purchase of three-year-olds during 1914-15, part of a letter from Cubitt, 9th July 1915.

The Commission decided to postpone further consideration of the evidence pending reports from representatives of the HIS and NLHB Society, which followed on 23rd July 1914, along with receipt of a formal application for further assistance. Evidence taken before the Commission from representatives of the HIS, Lt-Col. Sir Merrick R. Burrell, member of the HIS Horse Supply Committee and Norton Committee 1923, provides much the same information as Birkbeck. Foreign markets were to be encouraged, as the best horses were consumed at home; foreigners were the great outlet for horses that the country did not want. There were many countries, Italy and others, who took a small horse in large numbers, for which there was no market in this country. The Scheme was beneficial but could be improved to meet its object to breed the highest class of horses. Burrell favoured a government stud farm for stallions only, but wanted to give the present scheme, in a slightly altered form, a few more years to run. Heavy horse breeding was very prosperous and did not need support, it was the light horse that was nearly extinct and in one or two aspects, the light horse-breeding grant was not fulfilling promoters' expectations. [110]

The Army believed the measures it had taken to establish a reserve of horses for a national emergency, encouraged horse breeding by motivating owners to keep horses in this country. The remodelled Horse Registration Scheme involved the creation of a special section for artillery horses, with a significantly larger sum paid per horse, than for other classes, highlighting the serious problem of the supply of light horses. The Scheme offered those who registered their horses with the Army an annual payment of 10/- for each 'Registered' horse and £4 for each 'Artillery' (bus-type) horse. Gilbey thought it exceedingly doubtful that home resources could have furnished the Artillery with 10,000 horses, of the 'bus' stamp, to fulfil the WO's Subsidy Scheme, a view probably supported by Hobbs' experiences with the lack of 'bussers' for the 1913 manoeuvres. [111] The weak point of the Registration Scheme was, he believed, that it provided for immediate needs and nothing further. It did not offer any inducement for farmers to breed horses; a farmer would not start horse breeding for 10/- annually, or £4 (only obtainable for four years); if he bred at all, it would be the type he already bred, the Shire type, for which there was a certain market.

There were still a considerable number of heavy horses in the country in 1913. Official Returns for Agricultural Horses showed 23,500 less than in 1898, from which Gilbey doubted any sound inference could be drawn. [112] The numbers fluctuated from year to year, in a manner that made it difficult to draw any definite conclusions, though figures for the two series of five years, 1898-1902 and 1908-12 did show changes in the agricultural horse population. He considered that from the breeder's point of view,

110 D1/1, 49th meeting of Commission; D2/15, Burrell, Q3, Q29-30; *VR*, 1914, Vol.XXVI, 18th April, p.687, re LHB and the declining market for misfit hunters and reduction in LHB grant.
111 Gilbey, 1913, pp.11-14; Hobbs, 1913, p.427.
112 Ibid, p.14.

the Government was doing something to encourage breeding by providing good and cheap stallions under the Premium Scheme and breeders were taking advantage of it to produce a better class of horse. To the breeder it was purely a matter of business as he would sell to the best market. The Board's Scheme, whilst helping the British farmer to breed horses for sale to foreigners, was not good for the supply of horses to the Army. He concluded that horses suitable for military purposes were not bred to anything like the same extent they were as in the 1890s and that nothing was being done to specifically encourage the breeding of army horses. The purpose, to which the Board quite properly applied its grant, was the improvement of horse breeding and not an increase in numbers, for national purposes, quantity as well as quality was needed. Definite encouragement was required for farmers to breed horses that would form some reserve in a prolonged conflict and to replace the inevitable loss and wastage in war. There was a significant difference between improving horse breeding and breeding for the Army and the only way of doing that was to create a market, which did not, at that time, exist.

The picture offered by Gilbey and others on the eve of the 1914-18 War would not have encouraged military planners, or those interested in supplying horses to the Army. Those speaking for the military, may of course, have painted a slightly blacker picture in an attempt to improve funding for the number and quality of animals they required. However, the results of the long, and frustrating struggle, to upgrade the quality and numbers of horses required by the Army was soon to be tested. The Army's involvement in assisting horse breeding in these pre-war years, is probably be best summed up by the Norton Committee's Report on Light Horse Breeding, that prior to the 1914-18 War:[113]

> *the Army, in time of peace, did little, or nothing to help the horse market in Great Britain.*

In contrast MacMunn confidently wrote:[114]

> *We went on our way, fairly satisfied that we were on the right road.*

113 WO163/29, Army Council Records, 1923, Précis No.1145, Appendix A, *Norton Report.*
114 MacMunn, 1930, p.97.

Part Three

The 1914-18 War

58th London Division Memorial, Chipilly, Northern France

58th London Division Memorial, Chipilly, Northern France

7

Mobilisation 1914

It is known that far from railways and motors causing the disappearance of horses, they have opened up new fields of work for them, and there are as many as ever there were, though perhaps not in the same places and not of precisely the same types. Thus it is to be anticipated that the horse will always have its place in the Army as long as armies exist, though it may not occupy the same place as it occupies today.[1]

The outbreak of war in August 1914 provided the second test for the horse services and the ability of the national herd to supply the military with the required number and quality of horses. Once again, the scale of the conflict was one that surpassed all expectations and pre-war planning.

There can be no doubt that animals (including the horse, mule, donkey, camel, bullock, dog and reindeer), were the principal sources of motive power and that the horse was used in the greatest numbers in all theatres of war, France, Egypt, Gallipoli, Salonika, Mesopotamia, East Africa, Italy and the United Kingdom. The table below illustrates the enormous number of animals involved in all these theatres on 11th November 1918:[2]

UK	94,644
France	404,000
Egypt	167,000
Salonika	120,000
Mesopotamia	88,145
East Africa	1,499
Italy	20,482
Total	895,770

1 Maj. Cumberlegge, ASC, *ASCQ*, 1911, pp.566-7.
2 *Statistics*, 1922, Appendix I, p.877.

This is not to ignore the crucial role played by mechanical transport in many of these theatres of war. Statistics do not show the complexity of organisation and provision required to horse the British Armies. Capt. Sidney Galtrey wrote, "it is certain that people know little or nothing of the horse and mule that help to move the guns, the transport wagon loaded with food, ammunition and stores, and in hundreds of ways keep armies moving and make them formidable in offence and sure in defence".[3] Horses are often perceived mainly in terms of cavalry, but this arm made only a small demand on remounts and supplies. A cavalry division in 1914 required approximately 9,815 horses; the XII Royal Lancers for example, left England and landed at Le Havre on 17th August 1914, with 548 men and 608 horses. An infantry division at full strength required approximately 5,592 animals, which could rise to 5,800 with animals required for such units as divisional artillery, ammunition columns, supply train transport, field ambulances and signal companies. Horses, or mules, were required for the Royal Engineers (bridging teams, water carts, mobile pigeon lofts and travelling cookers), Machine Gun Corps (cavalry), Labour Corps, Road Construction and Railway Companies, Ordnance Corps, riding horses for the Chaplain's Department, Tank Corps (89 horses on 7th December 1918), agricultural units, timber companies (Canadian), riding horses for HQ and other Staff, for training camps (e.g. artillery, cavalry, ASC drivers), units on Lines of Communication and medical services. Even the RFC has some horse drawn transport. This provision was for both the Regular and Territorial forces.[4]

"What," wrote Galtrey, "is the artillery that predominates in modern warfare? The field gun, which is the weapon of the RFA and RHA. Each must have its own team of conditioned horses, and so when you count up the guns in a battery, the batteries in a brigade, the brigades in a division, the divisions in a corps, and the corps in our Armies on all fronts, you arrive at a first calculation of the vital necessity of horses and mules in many tens of thousands ... then, with the artillery of every division, there must be a divisional artillery column, which means several hundred more animals, and again there is the divisional train transport, chiefly horsed by weighty draught horses."[5] In November 1912, the total peacetime establishment for Royal Artillery units was 6,106 horses; the wartime establishment was 24,868 horses, representing on mobilisation a colossal increase in men, equipment and horses.[6] These totals are made up of:

- RHA units of a cavalry division:
      peace establishment   558
      war establishment   1,526

3   Galtrey, 1918, p.13 (June 1918, a Staff Captain Remounts).
4   Money-Barnes, 1968, p.76; Stewart, 1950; Marcosson, 1918, p.69.
5   Galtrey, 1918, pp.14-15.
6   WO32/8767, November 1912.

- Two mounted brigade batteries:
  - peace establishment   270
  - war establishment   758
- For divisional artillery of six divisions including heavy batteries:
  - peace establishment   5,278
  - war establishment   22,584

One of the first major problems on mobilisation was the improvisation of remount depots for horses, and training centres for the men handling horses for the first time; with the single most important demand for horse power coming from the transport and supply units supporting infantry, artillery and cavalry units. More than 200,000 horses were killed in France, most of them employed in transport work. An outstanding achievement of the administrative services was the expansion of the ASC, which was divided into three main sections, horse, motor and supply transport. This expansion not only included the provision of trained personnel, remounts and equipment to complete and reinforce them in the field, but also the provision of large horse transport depots that had to be staffed and equipped. There was an enormous expansion in the ASC Horse Transport Section. With mobilisation plans, based on an establishment for the Expeditionary Force of six divisions, of the more important units only, this meant an initial provision of six divisional trains and six reserve parks. Subsequently, 72 divisional trains, 36 auxiliary transport companies, 28 local service companies and 23 reserve parks were formed. On the outbreak of the war the ASC provided fodder for approximately 28,742 animals, by 11th November 1918 this had risen to approximately 895,000.[7]

Animal drawn transport of the original BEF consisted of first line transport and the technical vehicles of field units, with a divisional train and reserve park for each division. A divisional horse transport train consisted of 375 animals and 198 wagons. Most ammunition columns were only formed on mobilisation, some only ten days before embarkation. Few of the men had any previous training and many were unfamiliar with horses.[8] The 'Wolds Wagoners' Special Reserve (Category "C"), were an interesting exception (see photographs below). In 1905 Col. Sir Mark Sykes, conceived the idea that more could be made of drivers of horse drawn vehicles in solving army transport problems. Richard Sykes wrote that his father's idea fell on deaf ears, with few highly placed officials being able to see the use, or practical wisdom in taking such a course, and although he persisted, over the years he received only discouraging reactions. In about 1909 Sykes decided to organise driving demonstrations from amongst professional wagoners on the Sledmere Estate and district, Yorkshire; proving to be very successful and popular meetings. A WO committee headed by Gen. Cowans was

---

7   *Statistics*, pp.181, 859; Fox, 1920, p.6; Marcosson, 1918, p.69; Henniker, p.147.
8   See Glossary for definitions of First Line Transport, Divisional Train and Reserve Parks; Farndale, 1986, p.4; Chapman, p.43-44.

invited in 1911 to see for themselves that civilian drivers could qualify as army transport drivers; the WO was impressed and recommended the creation of a new auxiliary force. Sykes formed the Wagoners in 1913, initially numbering 400. They expanded to approximately 1,000 on mobilisation in August 1914 and were mainly allocated to ASC reserve park, horse transport companies; 200 were posted to Royal Engineer bridging trains in Ireland. Embarking for France on 20th August the Wagoners served through 1914 and with changes to Reserve Parks in 1915 the majority of Wagoners remained as drivers with their original units throughout the War.[9]

Each divisional ammunition column consisted of 723 horses and 113 vehicles. The light General Service (GS) wagon was for two men and four horses and the heavier GS wagon for three drivers and six horses, but in April 1914, following an Army Council decision of October 1913, transport trains changed and GS wagons in trains and all ambulances, except for cavalry, were issued with two heavy, instead of four light draught horses.[10]

The figures below illustrate the Remount Departments response to the increasing wartime demand for men and horses:[11]

Strength in August	Animals	Officers	NCOs/Other ranks
1914	25,000	121	230
1915	534,951	366	16,294
1916	789,135	406	18,373
1917	869,931	423	20,560
1918	828,360	450	19,488
1919	210,090	258	6,731

It was a notable achievement, from a peacetime establishment in 1914 of 25,000 animals (UK), to mobilisation in August 1914 of 165,000, and its greatest provision in August 1917, on the Western Front, of nearly 870,000 animals. So too was the provision of trained personnel to manage the expansion. The procurement of animals was, however, only one aspect in providing for the Army. The figures below illustrate increases in some units, Regular and Territorial Forces combined, involved in

---

9   Sykes, 6th Baronet, 1879-1919, Sledmere Estate. Commissioned 1897 into 3rd (Militia) Battalion, Green Howards, served in the 1899-1902 War for two years, Lt-Col, C.O. 5th Bn.(Res) Green Howards, 1914-18 at WO, placed by Kitchener on the de Bunsen Committee advising the Cabinet on Middle Eastern affairs. Died of Spanish Flu 1919. Boddy and Wilson; RLC Archive Box 2, 3970 (RCT, B2/1550), letter Richard Sykes 1974; Young, 2000, pp.39, 50. My thanks to Sandra Oakins of the Wolds Wagoners Museum.

10   Farndale, 1986, p.4; *ASCQ*, 1914, Vol.7, p.105; MacMunn, 1930.

11   *Statistics*, pp.396, 862.

Wolds Wagoners – three horses and pole draught, probably 1913, taken at a Driving Competition at Fimber Nab, near Sledmere. (Wolds Wagoners Museum)

Wagoner Dolby, No.CHT1101, with ASC, riding postillion, light draught horses somewhere in France. (Wolds Wagoners Museum)

the care of remounts and those receiving a major proportion of them. Along with those of the Remount Department, all these figures include the increase in drivers, riders, saddlers, veterinary staff for remount depots convalescent hospitals, and base supply depots. This staggering increase in personnel involved a comparable increase in training needs, with the Remount Department providing the ever-expanding Army with animals for training personnel.[12]

12   *Statistics*, pp.221, 224, 396; *VR*, 1935, Vol.XV, 4th May, p.521, lists 362 officers with the

		Officers	Other Ranks	Total
Army Veterinary	August 1914	300	208	508
Corps	April 1918	1,333	28,119	29,452
Cavalry	August 1914	2,104	44,392	46,496
	July 1916	5,792	134,666	140,458
RHA	August 1914	270	7,268	7,538
	May 1917	465	17,544	18,009
RFA	August 1914	1,887	49,341	51,228
	April 1917	10,095	339,951	350,046
ASC	August 1914	819	13,672	14,491
	September 1918	11,480	316,123	327,603

The AVC provides a useful example of rapid expansion with its need for skilled and qualified personnel, although the many figures given are confusing and inconsistent. The Establishment pre-war was too small to provide trained personnel for cadres of all veterinary units required on mobilisation, but registers existed of those veterinary practitioners prepared to serve in a civilian capacity with the Corps. Army Order 181, 1909 created a Special Reserve of Officers and Order 203, 1910, created an AVC Territorial Force (TF). In August 1914 the total number of officers holding commissions with the AVC was 364, including two Quartermasters. The total is made up of: 169 Regular Officers, of these, 64 were serving in India and 32 in overseas Colonies and Egypt, so not available to the BEF in August 1914; 19 Reserve of Officers, 28 Special Reserve and 148 Territorial Force not available for duty with the Regular Army, BEF. The number of AVC officers required for the BEF on mobilisation was 192, but only 109 were available, the deficiency was made up by granting temporary commissions to civilian veterinary surgeons, so that on 11th November 1918, 1,100 civilian veterinary practitioners were holding commissions.[13] Home requirements were met to some extent by employing surgeons locally at civilian rates of pay. By constant advertising in the UK, assistance from the Colonies in sending home suitable graduates and by means of the Military Service Acts, it was ultimately found possible, on a minimum basis, to meet all demands for veterinary officers required to complete Establishments of the BEF, Indian and Home Commands. On 1st November 1918 the total number of officers was 1,356 of whom 182 were from the Colonies. On 4th August 1914, there were 322 Warrant and Non-Commissioned Officers, and other

---

AVC, 1914 and Blenkinsopp and Rainey, 1925, pp.5, 23 also give different figures.
13   VR, 1914, Vol.XXVII, 24th October, p.243: 20th March 1915 p.495; 3rd April 1915, p.517. During 1914 and 1915 there were disputes over the rank and promotion of these civilians – a situation similar to the 1899-1902 War see VR, 1915, XXVI, 8th May, p.579; Vol.XXVII, 3rd April, pp.517.

ranks (ORs) and on 11th November 1918, 26,146. Maj-Gen Sir John Moore, Director Veterinary Services (DVS -BEF), stated that at the end of the war, in all theatres, 1,668 Officers including Special Reserve, TF and Temporary Commissioned Officers and Quartermasters, had served with the Corps, and 41,755 NCOs and ORs, the maximum number at any given time was 27,950. In France the total effective strength of the Corps including Canadian, Australian and Indian personnel rose to 765 Officers, 16,446 Warrant officers, NCOs and ORs.

Obtaining and training personnel was one problem, keeping them was another. Both the AVC and Remount Service suffered from the continual loss of trained Category "A" personnel to active units, replaced by lower category, untrained, army personnel. During the course of the war, the establishment of other ranks in the AVC was completely changed three times. Such transfers threw a considerable strain on reserve hospitals at home; involving nearly 50% of their establishment in training replacements, these duties were in addition to the normal work of hospitals and with no extra establishment.[14]

Mobilisation

Mobilisation took place in two phases. The first was the automatic assembly and despatch overseas of the BEF, as laid down in war establishments and mobilisation plans, requiring approximately 49,000 riding, 80,300 draught and 5,500 pack horses, a total of 134,800 animals. These were to be purchased within a few weeks, along with an assumed wastage of between 22,000 and 27,000 animals, to be provided till the close of 1914, when shipments from North America became available.[15] The second phase was the formation and despatch of the New Armies and their line of communication units. The provision of animals was only one aspect of the supply problem, which included fodder, veterinary care in the field, shoeing, provision of remount depots, transport in the UK and to theatres of war, personnel and equipment such as harness and saddlery. The main ASC depots for horse transport were Aldershot and Woolwich; for motor transport Bulford; for Supply Deptford, Avonmouth, Liverpool, Northampton, Manchester, Newhaven, Leeds, Glasgow, and Southampton.[16] On mobilisation every one of the eleven branches of the QMG's Department formed two separate mirror organisations; one based at the WO in England and the other an exact replica at GHQs in France with its own QMG and heads of directorates:

---

14   *Statistics*, pp.187, 863.
15   *Statistics*, p.861; MAF52/2/TL3770, letter from President of BAF to Secretary of Treasury, 1919.
16   Blenkinsop and Rainey, 1925, p.6; *Statistics*, p.861; Chapman, 1924, p.43.

- Gen. J. Cowans QMG (WO)   Lt-Gen. Sir R. Maxwell QMG (BEF)
- Maj-Gen.W. Birkbeck,   Brig. F. Garratt
  Director of Remounts (WO)   Director of Remounts (BEF)
- Maj-Gen. R. Pringle Director of Maj-Gen. J.M. MooreDirector of
  AVC (WO)   AVC (BEF)

(See Appendix IV Remount Directorate, BEF, 1918, and Appendix V Directorate Veterinary Services, BEF, 1918).

Mobilisation orders, for the BEF, Special Reserve and TF, were issued on 4th August, the annual training season and the worst time for a crisis, especially in the week when Territorial units were in camp. On the 6th August, marked " Secret", the CIGS informed the QMG that, "it has been decided that (1) the BEF will commence to embark on 9th (2) Third Army will not embark with remainder of BEF," and "the War Council will warn South Africa (GOC-in-C) to bring all troops home, with stores, horses, equipment." [17] Asquith was requested to order troops to their peace stations; horses were mostly close to their peace stations, except for Territorial units in training with many artillery and riding horses away from their census and therefore impressment areas. Eventually, on the 1st August, the Remount and Mobilisation Directorates were issued orders "to go home", thereby giving them valuable time to prepare for the first day of mobilisation, and on the 31st July the Remount Service was given permission to appoint purchasers. This, states MacMunn, "gave us a chance".

A WO telegram issued at 7.50 p.m., 2nd August, to all Commands, ordered all troops, Regular, Special Reserve, Officer Training Corps, or TF, in training places other than at their peace stations, to return to these stations immediately.[18] Commands sent their DADRs to purchasers, issuing them with their purchasing boxes, explaining their contents, giving them the programmes and times of horse trains and schedule of horse boxes, especially those required for Aldershot. Civilians on WO lists, usually retired officers, who were to assist the mobilisation programme, received urgent telegrams on 3rd August. Lt-Col. McFall, District Purchasing Officer for Waterford, received a telegram from the Remount Officer at Limerick, dated 31st July, telling him to "be prepared for emergencies", followed on 3rd August by one telling him to "be at your post, pay begins from noon today, purchasing does not begin till further notice". Lt-Col. Todhunter received a telegraph 31st July from the Adjutant Essex Yeomanry, Colchester, "are you at home ready to begin buying horses if required" and on the 5th August, "Mobilise." On the 13th August he was informed the purchasing of horses and vehicles for these Yeomanry regiments and TF units was completed and he was not to continue purchasing, being paid £72.4s for time and expenses. MacMunn

17   WO107/19, 2nd August 1914; WO107/19, War Council, 6th August, Secret, to QMG from CIGS, and WO, ref. 4th and 6th Divisions, letter 2nd day 6th August, War Council re South Africa.
18   MacMunn, 1930, pp.107-8.

stated, "The fun with impressment was soon to begin". Capt. Fyrth, AVC, attached to 8th Brigade RFA, 5th Division from August 1914, went over to the Curragh on 14th August for remounts. He records that on the 19th August horses were slung aboard at Dublin for transfer to Le Havre where horses and guns landed down ramps without a casualty; he proceeded "with a couple of sick gees to the sick horse depot, Quai de Pondicherry."[19]

Overzealous soldiers did impress some favourite pet animals and of those too old, or unfit, a number were returned, but the myth that the country was stripped of horses dies hard.[20] The family bakery and confectionary business of E. J. Bird and Son, of Sutton Coldfield, Birmingham is typical of the many family stories handed down from the 1914-1918 war (see photographs below). The family owned six horses, used for delivering bread, supposedly all were commandeered to serve in France; in fact only two horses were taken and replacements were quickly obtained. The son, Walter Bird, enlisted in the 1/5th (Territorial Bn.) Royal Warwickshire Regiment in September 1914 and was allocated, no doubt because of his experience with horses, to the Transport Section, in which he served throughout the war, in France and Italy. On demobilisation he returned to the family business and his working horses. A story related by his sister in 1964 refers to a horse called "Bob" that Walter had looked after and worked with at the front; on returning from leave, walking past a field in France, he was surprised to hear the whinny from "Bob" who had recognised him.[21] Typical reports, such as that in a Western Super Mare newspaper, refer to ASC teams in 1914 seizing horses from the shafts of carts and carriages in the streets; an action which would, I believe, be very rare, or highly unlikely.[22]

An article in the *West Somerset Freepress*, 8th August 1914, would have been the more normal experience. Under the heading *Purchasing Horses for the Army, First Drafts from West Somerset*: "Immediately the Army mobilization orders were posted, steps were taken … to supply a number of horses for army draught purposes. On being warned by the police, horse-owners brought horses already registered to several depots where they were examined to see if they were fit for army purposes". The purchasing officer accompanied by a civilian veterinary surgeon commenced their duties by purchasing 25 horses with about another 25 the following day, they were of the light draught type, "of excellent quality". They were entrained at Williton and Bishop's Lydeard, West Somerset, by a RFA collecting party, consisting of one corporal and six privates from

19   National Army Museum, 8407-20 (2 to 47), telegrams 31st July, and 3rd August 1914, Personal Service Record of Col. A.W. McFall, OBE, 1881-1920; Todhunter, IWM reference 87/53/1; MacMunn, 1930, pp.110-112; Capt.W. Fyrth, AVC (IWM reference 97/4/1).

20   Anthea Cox relates the story of her grandfather's carriage horse, impressed but returned later as too old; Cooper, 1983, p.40; Chapman, 1924, pp.89-102.

21   I am grateful to Brian Bird and his daughter Jillian Storey for this information and photographs.

22   Correspondence with Margaret Jordon and Don Brown.

Private Walter James Bird, in Italy with the transport section, 1/5th Royal Warwickshire Regiment. (Brian Bird & Jillian Storey)

Bulford Camp. A further 40 horses for the RFA were to be sent off from Taunton. The article concludes, "It is probable that there will be further calls on horse owners in the district yet." A Bideford paper gave notification that a Maj. Eyre had been authorised by the Army Council "to impress by purchase in North Devon, such animals as may be required for the use of His Majesty's Forces".[23]

Debates in the House of Commons on impressment illustrate a few over enthusiastic remount officers (notably in East Anglia), but generally mobilisation was completed with little disruption to agricultural and commercial life.[24] There were examples of people cheating the system for profit, "unfortunately individuals in England, and to a far greater extent in Ireland, used the national peril for their own gain;" this was the exception and the WO brought some offenders to justice.[25] There were claims against the WO for the price given for animals, an article in the *Horse*

23   I am grateful to Maggie Robertson for Somerset material and Simon Butler for the Devon material.
24   Hansard (C), 1914, Vol.LXV.
25   Chapman, pp.89-102, ref. an article in the *Times*, 1915, 5th January, '*How the Remount Scheme Had Worked*'; Singleton, 1993, p.184; BPP, 1916, Vol.XVII, pp.91-2, Army Appropriation Accounts, 1914-19; *VR*, 1914, Vol.XXVII, 24th October, pp.245-6, 'Alleged Fraud in Requisitioning Horses'.

The E.J. Bird shop and horse drawn vans. This photograph and the subsequent one illustrate well the type of horses taken on impressments. (Brian Bird & Jillian Storey)

Tom Smalley, delivery driver, E.J. Bird Bakery, c1905. (Brian Bird & Jillian Storey)

Horses mustered in the Square, Beaminster, Dorset, for impressment 1914. (Simon Butler)

Buying horses for the War at the village of Stourton, Warwickshire.
(Warwickshire County Council, PH924-5)

and Hound, for example, states "there is evidence that there has been no inconsiderable amount of incompetence in the purchase of army remounts. I would rather not suggest that there has been, in certain instances, an attempt to make money on the part of the buyers". Remount regulations prescribed that horses from public bodies and of the food distributing trade were, if possible, to be spared.[26] The Railway Executive Committee made representations to the WO about the dangers to mobilisation plans if their horses were impressed. Instructions were issued prohibiting the impressment, or the compulsory acquisition, of horses owned by the railway companies, other than those already registered in the Reserve Scheme.[27] The number of heavy draught horses required on mobilisation was an insignificant proportion of those available in the country and it was not anticipated that the withdrawal of those required for military purposes would have any serious effect. The 1912-13 Horse Census classified a total of 589,401 UK horses fit for military service, of these 231,683 were heavy draught, of which only 16,670 were required.[28]

It was soon evident to MacMunn that the actual impressment was going with a precision "that surpassed their wildest dreams". Maj-Gen. Allenby, commanding the Cavalry Division, complimented the Remount Service on the working of the Boarding Out System, as 'boarders' were rejoining in very good condition.[29] From 10th to 17th August inclusive, the railways moved into Southampton 21,523 horses and by the 31st, a further 37,649. The heaviest day of arrivals was between 10 p.m. on 21st and 6 p.m. on 22nd August, when 4,583 horses reached the docks.[30] On the 18th August the QMG reported that the BEF was complete with horses and the Territorial Force almost complete. 165,000 horses had been raised in 12 days, an incredible achievement, increasing the horse establishment by 700%.[31] Equally remarkable was the mobilisation of motor transport as shown below:[32]

26   *Horse and Hound* in *VR*, Vol.XXVI, 19th September, p.186, 'Remounts', the author refers to the number of horses purchased and afterwards cast for a few sovereigns; *VR*, 1914, Vol. XXVII, 31st October, pp.255-6; 12th December, pp.326-8; Hansard (C), 1914, Vol.LXV, 9th August, (c)2064.

27   Pratt, E. 1921, Vol.I, p.47.

28   WO33/669, note in Remount Statement 1914-15.

29   MacMunn, 1930, p.111.

30   Pratt, E., Vol.I, pp.113-4.

31   WO107/19, QMG Reports to Secretary of State, 1914, 16th August, Parliamentary Secretary to Secretary of State from QMG; Chapman, p.41.

32   *Statistics*, p.852.

	Motor lorries, Tractors etc.	Motor cars and vans	Motor cycles	Total
Available on Peace establishment 1914	807	20	15	842
Balance provided on mobilisation	334	193	116	643
Total	1,141	213	131	1,485

Singleton wrote that any charges that the British army was technologically back-ward in the period between 1900 and 1920 would be difficult to sustain. The British Army was in the forefront of mechanisation and even Bond's statement that the British army compared favourably with Europe is to misrepresent the extent of exper-imentation, and adoption of motor vehicles into a new military transport system.[33] Motor transport for the original six divisions consisted of motor cars, motor bicycles and some 500 lorries in the supporting columns of the various formations, with 650 in cavalry and divisional ammunition parks. Only about 80 motor vehicles were actually owned by the WO at the outbreak of war, but on mobilisation the Army had planned to rely on the Motor Vehicle Subsidy Scheme and impressment, which was completely successful, so that on the 17th August, the QMG was able to report that all estab-lishments for lorries abroad were complete, with an additional 25% for breakdowns, gradually being increased to 75%.[34]

Royal Artillery batteries had completed their annual training camps when ordered to mobilise on 4th August. Regular horse and field batteries were ready and up to strength, no hasty reorganisation, or improvisation was required. Quick exercises and route marches had been undertaken to toughen and harden men and horses. Heavy artillery, however, had not fared so well, as owing to a shortage of funds prior to 1914 heavy batteries had been reduced to only 12 horses, extra horses for annual manoeu-vres had to be hired. Siege artillery batteries fared even worse, having last manoeuvred in 1912 and then only with a number of hired horses.

Capt. Brownlow joined his artillery brigade ammunition column at Bulford on the third day of mobilisation. Many such columns were newly formed in their entirety on mobilisation. These horsed columns consisting of 200 horses and approximately 36 wagons would be obsolete by 1918. Brownlow states that horses arrived in batches and at odd moments, often in the middle of the night, with impressed horses coming from a variety of sources, straight from grass, butchers and bakers carts, livery stables and private stables. They were carefully sorted into teams and allotted to various subsec-tions. The hard yellow military harness was stamped, punched, fitted, dubbined and

---

33   Singleton, pp.193-4; Bond, 1980; Winton, 2000, *JSAHR*.
34   WO107/19, 17th August 1914, Parliamentary Secretary to Sec. of State from QMG; also QMG Reports to Sec. of State; Chapman, pp.44-6; Henniker, pp.147-48.

soaped; hundreds of articles were checked and issued, such as buckets, nosebags, picketing ropes, head ropes, harness, blankets and tools. Horses tied to picketing ropes, gave vent to not being in their accustomed stables, by kicking and squealing, when fed in strange nosebags, threw their heads indignantly in the air, the corn being spilled and wasted. Bakers' horses pulled themselves to pieces; grass-fed horses sweated, sat back in the breechings and refused to move and the aristocrats from private stables kicked with indignation as they trained in marching order. About the 14th August, he states they had accomplished the impossible and were ready for the field. Lt- Col. Arbuthnot, RFA, wrote, that the artillery claim to have come well through the war as regards horsemastership, was largely due to their old peacetime training and regime. Many a battery commander of 1914, he states, will remember with horror, when, on about the third, or fourth day of mobilisation, he realised two thirds of his horses were untrained, unkept, grass fed and totally unfit for active service. Recollecting his own battery in Ireland he had several young mares that had never even been saddled, or harnessed, but had just been torn from their foals and required milking every morning. Detailed lists of equipment for each horse with a unit and the fodder ration was all prescribed and authorised against nominal returns. Any additional equipment or rations would have to be authorised by the QMG's Department.[35]

The AVS was ordered to mobilise at 5 p.m. on the 4th August. They had been anticipating mobilisation for some days and in accordance with Command Mobilisation Schemes, had carried out veterinary inspections of animals for fitness, checked veterinary equipment and valued the private chargers to be taken into service. The personnel of the AVS, allotted on mobilisation to the BEF and despatched to France, to look after 54,000 animals (this figure varies from 53,000 to 55,000), was 122 Officers, administrative and executive, and 797 ORs. The increase from peacetime establishments was made by special enlistments, or transfer of lower category men from combatant units, and Class "D" cavalry reservists, used as horse attendants for hospitals. The accompanying units of the Corps in the first phase of mobilisation comprised of six veterinary hospitals and sections, each for 250 animals; eleven mobile veterinary sections for the evacuation of ineffective animals; two base depots of veterinary stores and one record section at the Base (3rd Echelon).[36] The Veterinary Manual (War) proved to be a weak spot in the organisation and was not complete by 7th August 1914. Standing Orders for the BEF, 9th August, with reference to the AVS states that, a Veterinary Manual (War) had been approved and copies would be issued to all concerned as soon as possible. Maj-Gen. Moore (BEF) states he was sent 150 copies for issue. The system inaugurated proved unequal to the strain of the early stages of war and was replaced

35   Farndale, p.6; Brownlow, 1918, pp.7, 9-11; Arbuthnot, 1919, pp.337-8.
36   Moore, 1930, pp.10-12 and 1934, p.19; Blenkinsop and Rainey, 1925, p.9; *Statistics*, p.864, differs from the previous authors, giving eight veterinary sections for 250 patients each, 14 Mobile Veterinary Sections and one Veterinary Base Depot stores; RCT Archives B1 0754, p.43.

Members of the 5th Howitzer Battery, 4th South Midland (Howitzer) Brigade, RFA, loading one of the Battery's horses onto a wagon at Rugby Station, Warwickshire, before departure for Swindon, 11th August 1914. (Warwickshire County Council, PH815/21/5)

200 horses of a RFA ammunition column, along Greatheed Road, Leamington Spa, Warwickshire, 1915, or earlier. (Author's collection)

by a workable method, incorporated into Veterinary Manual (War) 1915, which stood the test of the remaining period of war. Standing Orders for the AVS included establishing hospitals at selected points, on lines of communication, for the transfer of sick and inefficient animals to mobile veterinary and collecting stations. Responsibility for fixing collecting stations and notifying the Inspector General Remounts (IGR), rested normally with armies and cavalry formations.[37]

The initial phase of mobilisation was achieved without any serious problems. However, no sooner had the BEF been despatched, than it was obvious increasingly large demands would be made for remounts, personnel, equipment and motor vehicles, of all kinds, to meet the initial high losses in the field, and for the New Armies being raised in the UK. The Army's vast expansion resulted in increased demands for horses that had not been envisaged, or planned for.

Following the horsing of the BEF, the procurement of remounts by means of impressment virtually ceased. In order to supplement the reserves of horses, make good wastage and provide for the New Armies being created, it was essential to use every possible source of supply. Buying continued on the UK open market and purchasing

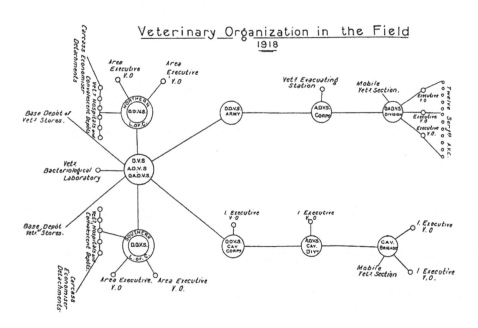

Veterinary Organisation in the Field, 1918. (Blenkinsop & Rainey 1925)

37   Moore, 1930, pp.12-13.

commissions were sent to Canada and the United States; it was soon found necessary to increase the personnel of these commissions, at a time when every available officer was required, civilians were therefore retained after the initial period of mobilisation. During this early period no limit was set on the price paid for horses although it was rare to pay more than £100; later purchasers were limited to about £90 for chargers, riding horses and gunners, but no limit was set for heavy draught horses, which sometimes cost over £100 each. Horses were taken to pre-arranged collecting stations in each district before moving to remount depots in specially arranged trains.[38] A special report to the Secretary of State on horse supply, listed additional reserves to those already planned for on mobilisation:[39]

Mobilisation completed according to programme as follows:

BEF	55,000
TF	83,000
Coast Defence Garrisons	3,000
Res. Cav. Regts etc (by 24th August 1914)	19,000
Total	160,000

Pre-Arranged Reserves

Overseas	3,200	600 in the Advanced Remount Depots, 2,600 in Base Remount Depot (10% of War Establishment)
At Home (reserve units)	12,400	14 Res. Cav. Regts., 9,000; 6 Res. Artillery Bdes. 3,400.
Remount Depots	2,000	(12,400 plus 2,000 being 45% of War Establishment)
Total	17,600	(55% of War Establishment)

Additional Requirements

Mobilisation of:

• Unallotted batteries and brigades	5,000 (nearly completed)
• 7th Division and cavalry from abroad	6,000 (being bought in UK)
• Two Territorial Force divisions and Dominion troops (Reserve Parks etc.), approximately	2,000
• New Army	30,000 (of these 20,000 Canadian horses to arrive by Christmas)

---

38 Chapman, 1924, pp.41-3; also Army Appropriation Accounts, BPP, 1916, Vol. XVII, pp.91-2.
39 WO107/19, 21st August 1914, part of a rough draft for special report to Sec. of State, Memo as to Horse Supply.

A similar report gave the position of the Transport Services as:

A) Expeditionary Force:
- Horses Transport: mobilisation effected as for the rest of the EF
- Mechanical Transport:
  - Personnel: cadres raised to wartime establishments by special enlistment
  - Vehicles: numbers raised to wartime establishments by calling up subsidised lorries and impressing the remainder.
  - Reserves: with each unit 25%; being despatched to overseas base 25%; being maintained at home 50%; total of 75%.
  - Spare Parts: provided for every vehicle sent overseas.
B) Central Force TF:
- the organisation of the transport system on lines of BEF being completed
C) 7th Division requirements:
- 5 HTCs ASC, formed from companies from foreign stations and reservists
- 2 MTCs: officers from the Special Reserve, who have little experience of personnel, only to be found from MT Depots and special enlistment.
- Dominion Contingents: Supply Columns and Ammunition Parks (MT), no regular MT officers or NCOs were available to form a nucleus.

The serious problem of accommodation for the massive increase in remounts was resolved with the formation, in September and October, of three new remount depots, each for 3,500 animals. These depots, taking horses and mules arriving from America and Canada, were formed at Lathom Park, Ormskirk, for horses and mules landed at Liverpool; Shirehampton for horses disembarked at Avonmouth, Bristol. Swaythling near Southampton received remounts before issue to Expeditionary Forces and veterinary evacuations. These developments necessitated acquiring the land, providing temporary stables and other buildings, and practice camps; employing mainly civilian personnel, where possible, from surplus employees of large horse farms.[40]

In August 1914 AVC accommodation was also stretched. The Corps depot was at Woolwich, with small veterinary hospitals at Aldershot (No.1), Woolwich (No.2), Bulford (No.3) and Curragh (No.4). Veterinary sections were located at Colchester, Woolwich and Shorncliffe. Army Order 66, March 1914, established seven TF, AVC divisional hospitals, to work alongside divisional bases and regimental sick lines at mounted stations, to provide, on mobilization, an organized system for dealing with the large numbers of sick animals and to prevent the inevitable wastage resulting from hastily improvised arrangements. Small detachments were to be sent out to collect sick animals from mobilising units and taken to the hospitals. The establishment of each

---

40   I am heavily reliant on Rainey and Blenkinsop, pp.6-8 for information in this and next two paragraphs; WO107/19, 18th August 1914, Parliamentary Sec. to Sec. of State from QMG, extract Note 5 re embarkation: Moore, 1930, p.18; WO107/26 and WO107/27.

hospital, for 500 animals, was one veterinary section (wartime establishment: 104 men and officers) and an additional 200 horsekeepers registered with a division to join each hospital on mobilization. The available veterinary facilities could not deal with a tenth of the requirements. Existing provision was quickly expanded taking full advantage of stabling and sites allotted for veterinary purposes under billeting schemes in home commands. The first large new hospitals, each for 1,000 patients, were formed close to the remount reception depots at Ormskirk, Swaythling and Shirehampton. Demands at these centres remained fairly constant throughout the war, whereas at other centres it fluctuated in accordance with the distribution of troops during mobilisation and training. Moore wrote that the WO had suggested forming a hospital near Southampton to receive ineffective animals from France, however, this did not happen and hospitals with the BEF in France were informed, 22nd August, to prepare for twice the number of sick, with an increase in ASC personnel; six officers and 118 NCOs and men were sent to France on 25th August. The facilities at the bases of Le Havre, Rouen and the advance base at Amiens, were for handling 3,000 sick animals.

From mobilisation the heaviest workload fell on Southern Command, for training the majority of the New Armies, a portion of the Canadian Expeditionary Force and many TF formations. Veterinary accommodation at Bulford, Tidworth and Larkhill was expanded to its limit with small centres established wherever possible. However, all these measures were insufficient at a time of exceptionally high pressure, when the admission rate of sick animals from remount depots and horse ships was at its highest, and with divisions evacuating their casualties before proceeding overseas. Sick animals were boarded-out with selected civilian veterinarians at a fixed daily rate, initially of 5/-, but abuses of this experiment led to difficulties and it was abandoned.

Reports to the QMG (WO) during August show that mobilisation supply arrangements were working smoothly. Three weeks supply of forage for the whole of the BEF was available, increasing daily until there were 49 days reserve supplies overseas; a further 14 days' supply was then being collected at Newhaven. At the eight home defence supply depots there was just over seven days reserve supplies for 80,000 horses, rapidly building to 40 days forage.[41] Fit animals in the base remount depot, Le Havre, France, numbered 736 cavalry, 180 artillery, 113 transport and 308 heavy draught; these numbers would fluctuate with new arrivals and demands from units. On 1st September, two ships sailed for France with about 800 artillery and draught horses (including 200 heavy draught). Owing to events in France and changes of base, Garratt (Director Remounts-BEF), requested the despatch of cavalry horses be delayed (900 were ready to go). The QMG reported that, since mobilisation, the work of his Department included the provision of:[42]

41   WO107/19, 1914, 20th August, from S. Long, D12 to QMG, reply to request 11th July 1914, supply situation.
42   WO107/19, 1914, letter to QMG from Birkbeck, 2nd September 1914; Base Depot Report (Le Havre?) on 30th August 1914; 31st September 1914, notes on work of the

Horses:

Sailed with EF	55,000
Reinforcements despatched since	5,000
Issued to regular units at home	21,000
Total	81,000
TF etc.	83,830
Fit for issue at home	6,900
Total	171,730

Of the above total, only 135,000 were in war establishments, so from a peacetime establishment of about 20,000, a further 151,730 horses had been provided from impressment and the Subsidy Scheme.

The QMG stated that for the first time mechanical transport had been used extensively for carrying supplies and ammunition in the field, with its use being extended more than anticipated, including for the supply of forage: up to the 10th August, Mechanical Transport sent abroad was:[43]

Motor Lorries	1,468
Motor Cars	326
Motor Ambulances	58
Total	1,852

This supply of horses and vehicles had been obtained with a minimum of interference to the general supplies of the country and more economically than in any previous war. Movements by rail and sea from 9th August to 12th September included embarkation to France of 57,600 horses, 7,700 vehicles and 2,400 mechanical transport vehicles; in 250 ships. On 31st September there were 70,000 animals and 160,000 men on their way to England in 260 ships, from India and the Colonies.

Having horsed and despatched the I and II Army Corps, BEF (first four divisions, the Cavalry Division and a Cavalry Brigade) attention was turned to completing other divisions. The III Army Corps was formed in France 31st August with the 4th Division reaching Le Cateau on 24th August and 6th Division the Aisne on 16th September. In relation to horses for transport, Birkbeck reported the 7th Divisional Artillery was fully horsed, except for ammunition columns, for which horses existed and could be issued when required; requirements for horse transport could also be met. For the 8th Division, all batteries in England were horsed, with horses available for ammunition columns when equipped. For the 2nd Cavalry Division; 5th Cavalry Brigade was horsed and 6th Brigade was bringing 800 horses with them from abroad, but would need three weeks rest. 1,873 horses were required, the balance of 1,073 were

QMG Dept. since mobilisation, for Sec. of State.
43   Detailed breakdown in WO107/18, 'MT with EF', dated 2nd October 1914.

taken from the Yeomanry; the 7th Cavalry Brigade (Household) were to be completed by about 10th September. The Yeomanry, Territorial Divisions and Reserve Battalions were all horsed, but without farriers; but it was then impossible to horse the duplicate Yeomanry regiments, 50% of whose horses, would probably have to be replaced before they took the field. Reserves of horses were held in Reserve Cavalry Regiments and Reserve Artillery brigades, which were filled up with drafts of horses, then sent to complete BEF units. 10,000 horses were due monthly from Canada, the first landing on 5th October. Heavy draught horses, or complete pair-horsed heavy wagons, were available in large numbers from depots at Deptford and Islington markets. [44]

On the supposition that the 7th (landed Zeebrugge 6th October) and 8th Divisions (landed France 6th November), three cavalry divisions (3rd Cavalry Division landed Zeebrugge 7th October) and two Indian divisions joined the BEF, on the 14th September, there would have been in France, including one TF division in Egypt, a total of 82,132 animals made up of:[45]

Class	Riding	Draught	HD	Pack	Total
1	32,406	37,789	10,284	1,653	82,132

The complete picture included the following:

Training at Home and en route:

	Riding	Draught	HD	Pack	Total
2	68,690	55,906	17,908	2,554	145,058

For units in course of formation:

	Riding	Draught	HD	Pack	Total
3	54,763	51,360	25,945	3,911	135,979

Total					363,169

(Allowing for the duplication of 54 Yeomanry regiments, but not for duplication of any TF divisions)

It was assumed casualties in each class would amount to:

Class 1	10%	per month	of	82,132	or	8,213
Class 2	1%	per month	of	145,058	or	1,450
Class 3	1%	per month	of	135,979	or	1,360

---

44   WO107/17; from Birkbeck, 5th September 1914, 'Horses' (reference transport).
45   WO107/17; WO107/19, 14th September 1914 draft document; and telegram. 'Fessitude,' London, September 1914, Q800, 3rd/R855, re. horsing two new batteries, one Field, one Horse Artillery and replacing wastage the field; and 8th September, 'Horse State of the EF' and Statement of Remounts Overseas.

It is interesting that the casualty figures had been altered; in a draft WO document the higher percentage had been crossed out in Classes 1 from 30%, Class 2 from 10% and Class 3 from 10%. To complete the 48 infantry and five cavalry divisions planned for abroad, with provision for a monthly replacement of 11,022 horses, the Remount Department had to meet the first provision to units of 141,900, broken down as:[46]

FIRST PROVISION:

Class		Riding	Draught	HD	Pack	Total
2 (Res.Parks)		323	85	5678		6086
3		54763	51360	*35945**	3911	135979
Provisional Totals:		55086	51445	31623	3911	*142065**
Replacements	1	3240	3779	1028	165	8212
	2	687	559	179	25	1450
and later	3	547	514	260	39	1360
Replacement Totals:		4474	4852	1467	229	*11022**

The WO document gives first provision as 141,900 horses, but the table calculation above makes this 142,065*, a difference of 165. There is also an error under HD, *35,945** (WO107/19) which should be 25,945 (WO107/17) and a replacement of 11,022 not 11,023*; this had been changed from 52,700 to 11,023 as stated in the percentage changes above.

This requirement was to be met from horses still available in the UK, from Australia and the 10,000 expected monthly from Canada. The supply of remounts was considered so serious that it was suggested the Indian Government should be asked how many Australian and Indian horses they could to obtain and send home by 1st April 1915, to avoid them over wintering in England.

British Expeditionary Force[47]

The BEF landed at Le Havre, Rouen and Boulogne between 12th-17th August, moving to their concentration areas around Le Cateau by the 20th, also the location of GHQ (see Map 3 below). The HQ for Inspector General Communications (IGC) was at the advanced base, Amiens. Units then moved to Maubeuge and positions on the left of the French line. The Battle of Mons opened on the 22nd, with II Corps falling back on the 23rd. On the 24th, I Corps covered the retirement of II Corps on the line

---

46   WO107/19; WO107/17.
47   I have used extensively in the following sections, WO95/69, War Diary of Director of Remounts (Garratt), BEF and Moore, 1930, pp.14-24, 111-117.

Le Cateau – Cambrai. Retirement continued on the 25th covered by the Cavalry, with successful rearguard actions by I Corps at Landrecies, and II Corps at Le Cateau on 26th. The BEF retirement continued on the line Compiegne-Soissons then Marne-Seine. This was a period of extremely intense, fluid and confusing actions, with heavy casualties in men, equipment and animals.

The first priority for Garrett, Director of Remounts (BEF), who landed at Le Havre 9thAugust and Moore, Director AVC (BEF), who landed at Le Havre 10th August, was establishing base and advanced depots and hospitals. They began inspecting ground allotted by the French for, No.1 base remount depot, hospital and horse transport depot, but chose a different site on 13th August, a disused silk factory, excellent in very wet weather, at L'Usine Bundy, Le Havre; with land stretching nearly to Harfleur. Nos.1 and 2 veterinary sections and base depot veterinary supplies also moved to this site. Remounts took land nearer the docks with sheds for 2,000 animals, also occupying a disused brick factory; water troughs and fencing were ordered from the Director of Works, which surprisingly, had to be made, or obtained from England, as they appear not to have been part of equipment shipped on mobilisation. No.2 base was at Rouen, with Nos.5 and 6 veterinary sections located on a small racecourse at Petit Quevilly. Garratt and Moore moved to Amiens on 15th August, the location of the advanced base and HQs of the IGC and Administrative Services, to inspect suitable ground for two advanced remount depots, a hospital, and a horse transport depot. Remount depots were sited at Berancourt (1st and 2nd Advanced depots arrived from England on the 21st and 23rd respectively). The hospital at L'Usine Cauvin (Cauvin Yvose) was located in a tarpaulin factory with warehousing and accommodation for 1,000 animals (No.7 veterinary section arrived 24th).

Sick animals were being treated before any battle casualties were moved back from the front, for example, sickness was reported amongst chargers of the Administrative Staff in the confined and hot stables at Amiens, and the Cavalry evacuated 47 horses from Maubeuge before moving forward from their concentration area. Moore was called to Boulogne, a port not intended as a base for veterinary purposes, but units passing through the docks had left sick horses behind; these were placed in temporary accommodation until they could be moved to Amiens, as Boulogne was closed as a base on 25th August 1914. Battle casualties began to arrive at Amiens on the 23rd; 193 by the 26th. Mobile veterinary sections (MVS) were mobilised with their allotted units (Nos.1-11), but with the fluid nature of the campaign it became difficult to keep track of the sections, and impossible to arrange their supplies when the BEF was retiring. Some veterinary sections (Nos.1,2,4,5) had disembarked at Le Havre, but their arrival was not reported to the IGC, or HQs of the Veterinary Directorate, so it was surmised that they had proceeded to the front with their allotted formations. With railheads changing daily, sometimes twice a day, some sections were separated from their original allotments. No.1 MVS moved towards Valenciennes to evacuate horses, unaware it had been captured by the Germans, but luckily the GOC 5th

Map 3: Remount depots (BEF), August–September 1914

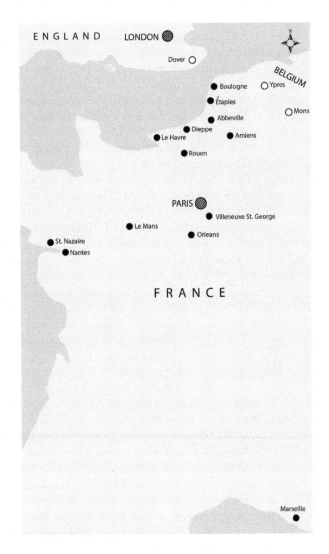

Cavalry Brigade ordered them to march with his unit. No.5 MVS, evacuating sick horses was severely shelled before getting away from the station. [48]

With the BEF in retreat, the advanced remount base and hospital were moved from No.1 Base Amiens to No.2 Base Rouen on 26th August; the advanced depots and 193 sick horses went by road as there was insufficient rail transport. Nos.1 and 2 Advanced Remount Depots were ordered into Rouen to entrain for Le Mans. On the 29th Le Havre and Rouen were ordered to be abandoned and units to move into the Loire

---

48   Moore, 1930, pp.20-21, for the full location of AVC units at this time.

basin with St. Nazaire and Nantes as bases, and Le Mans an advanced base. Garratt was informed the base remount depot was being shipped from Le Havre, which was contrary to the arrangements made by the AQMG, Lines of Communication, as Garratt had stressed the importance of it being railed direct, to save the sea voyage and any delay in fitting out first line cavalry reinforcements. On the 31st, No.1 Veterinary Section at Neufchatel and No.2 at Forges, the Base Veterinary Stores and 653 sick horses were moved by sea to St Nazaire. Nos.5 and 6 Sections at Rouen and Nos.7 and 8 at Amiens, with 350 sick animals went by train to Le Mans. No.6 Mobile Section went by road (see Map 4 below).

Despite this upheaval the requirement to provide remounts and veterinary hospitals did not cease. For example, the 1st Division requested removal of 80 sick animals, and 5th Division 360; the DDVS wired that 1,000 cavalry horses required evacuation. Dispatch of these animals to Le Mans was delayed until it opened on 4th September; the base was located at Chateau Le Que with unloading facilities at Quai de Debarquement near Yvre l'Eveque. During the months of September and October it accommodated a large number of animals with a limited personnel. By 29th September the situation had stabilised and Havre was re-opened, on high ground to the north of the town, as No.2 Base Remount Depot, accommodating 2,600 animals and a veterinary hospital for 1,000. Stabling huts were sanctioned for 5,000 horses for the winter. The same establishments were opened at Rouen, on their old site at Petit Quevilly. The decision not to concentrate all establishments together at Havre showed that lessons about controlling sickness had been learnt from the 1899-1902 War. Moore states that on his August journey by road to Rouen whilst moving through Gaillefontaine and Forges les Eaux he was attracted to the rich pasture lands, which were eventually used as the location for convalescent horse depots. He put forward a scheme to the WO (from his experience with remounts at Lathrop in USA during the 1899-1902 War), for establishing a convalescent horse depot in the Gournay en Bray area, for 1,000 animals only requiring rest, feeding and a minimum of attention; but this was turned down at the time owing to the military situation in the area.

A new base remount depot was opened at Nantes, and a receiving station at St Nazaire, using a remount section from Nantes; but it was not a healthy site being marshy and exposed to Atlantic winds. 1,600 horses were landed at St Nazaire, after a sea voyage, which had left them in poor condition, 280 were reported sick. As St Nazaire was ill provided for veterinary purposes, Nantes became the base hospital. However, with the longer sea journey for remounts from England, and the prevalence of the respiratory diseases strangles and catarrhal fever, the number of sick horses at St Nazaire gradually rose until, on 8th September they totalled 1,058, making it necessary to move a number to the hospital at Nantes. The Ecole de Dressage et d'Equitation (accommodating 500 animals), was taken over and staffed by Nos.5 and 6 Veterinary Sections. An extension was also arranged at La Chapelle. The base depot for veterinary stores was also located at Nantes until moving to Le Havre.

With allied success at the battles of the Marne (6th-9th September) the Germans retreated to the Aisne, with battles there opening on 13th September. Sick horses

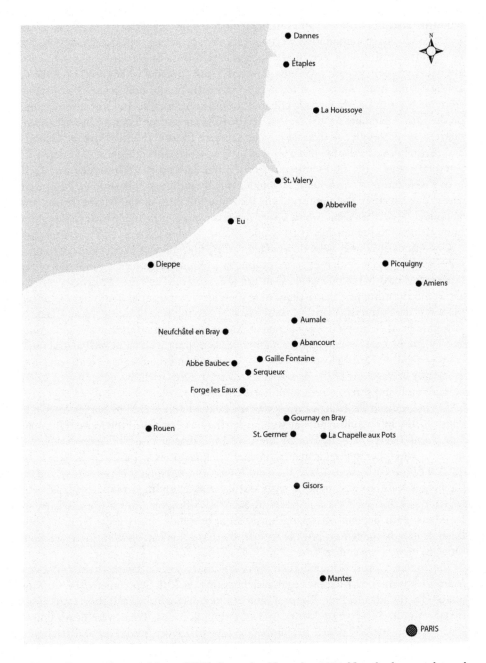

Map 4: Remount bases and farms (BEF), September–November, 1914. Note the change and spread in locations compared to Map 3

from the front poured into the advance base hospital at Le Mans, the majority only requiring rest. Between 6th and 9th September the numbers rose from 722 to 1,959. Extra paddock accommodation was requisitioned; picketing ropes and halters had to be obtained locally. No.1 Veterinary Section moved from St Nazaire to assist and 500 animals were despatched to Nantes. It was difficult to know which unit, or division, animals came from, some were loose in trucks without any equipment. The distance from the front to Le Mans made efficient administration difficult. Orders were issued on the 12th September for the removal of the IGC and Administrative Services head-quarters to Abbeville. A disused copper sulphate factory at Villeneuve St Georges and surrounding fields, SE of Paris, was used as an advanced hospital and depot for veterinary stores, for 1,000 animals. For the ten days up to 28th September, 1,714 horses were received, with about 80 remounts daily adding to this number. Most were cases of exhaustion and debility from the close billeting in the Marne region and subsequently on the Aisne, where a two-day fever was contracted, which ceased when units changed to the northern line of operations.

Conditions at Nantes were unsatisfactory. The hospital was overcrowded owing to very heavy remount casualties from respiratory sickness and injuries; about 866 of the latter were admitted in one week. Concern was expressed amongst veterinary officers about the alarming rate that halters were used up at the front and number of trifling cases sent to hospitals; many of these were minor injuries resulting from a lack of picketing gear. A hospital was opened at Abbeville, near Serqueux railway junction, and by late October was receiving many injuries from gunshots as well as the usual cases of debility. No.10 Hospital went to Neufchatel and the Dannes-Neufchatel area eventually became one of the principal veterinary centres with four hospitals of 2,000 animals each and three convalescent horse depots of 1,200 each.

The hospitals at Le Mans and Nantes were closed and moved to Forges-les-Eaux, but difficulty in obtaining railway wagons for the horses delayed the move. Hospitals Nos. 7 and 8 were also to be located there. No.1 Hospital at Ville St George was closed on 12th November and relocated in tile and brick factories at La Chapelle-aux Pots; quickly filling with about 1,800 animals. An advanced remount depot was placed on the Forges-les-Eaux site, making the Gournay district an important centre, particu-larly for sick and ineffective animals. A small convalescent farm was established at Le Mans, 24th September, taking horses from hospitals, and a grass farm at Abbe Baubec, near Serqueux on 3rd November, the latter took its first animals, 40 from Orleans, on 8th November.[49]

The Indian Corps, bringing their own veterinary sections with them and using Marseilles as their base depot, began disembarking on 30th September 1914; Orleans was used as the advance base. The provision of remounts for Indian transport units (divi-sional trains and reserve parks) was beset by complications. These were heavy horses sent out from the UK which succumbed to catarrhal fever (pink eye) and strangles;

49   *VR*, 1917, Vol.XXX, 10th November, pp.192-3.

225 cases were recorded by 11th October. With the urgent need for speed, animals were rapidly gathered together. Journeys by sea and rail were long and exhausting, with was no proper covered accommodation, or shelters for healthy, or sick animals; the weather was bad, camps were foul and infectious and respiratory diseases spread. Of a shipment of 319 animals sent directly from Deptford to Orleans for the Indian Cavalry Division, all except 82 fell sick, 21 dying, of which, five mares had 'picked foal' (aborted) and others were presumed to be in foal. In a second shipment of 250 horses from Havre, 165 fell sick within a week, six mares in foal were separated. A third attempt, from the Remount Depot at Le Mans, also failed. On 23rd November, influenza was reported amongst 50% of heavy draught horses at Orleans, with a large number of catarrhal cases. Many horses that came out direct from England had no rugs and those obtained locally were too small. Transport for the Indian cavalry was eventually completed with horses that had been in the country some time, mostly drawn from the convalescent horse depots. Looking back to 1899-1902 war experiences when animals were issued before they were fit and acclimatised, the question was again raised of retaining horses in depots for three weeks before issue to units.

In the early days of operations around Ypres, Armentières and Bethune the journey for casualties to Havre was long and exhausting. In a consignment of 71 horses from Hazebrouck to Havre, three were dead on arrival and three more destroyed. Of 197 horses sent by 3rd Cavalry Division from Boulogne, eleven were dead on arrival at Le Havre. Discussions between the IGC, Moore and Garratt, on 22nd October, about the evacuation of sick horses to the rear and the formation of remount depots near hospitals, resulted in the decision to establish hospitals at Boulogne (No.3), Abbeville (No.5) and Forge-les-Eaux (Nos.7 and 8). The remount depot at Boulogne was kept (No.3 Advanced Remount Depot, sent from Ostend 13th October), and a remount rest camp established between Forge-les-Eaux and Rouen. By October, a section of the remount depot at Rouen had been taken as a cavalry depot for mounting and equipping reinforcements and details. On the 18th October there were about 600 cavalry horses at Rouen and about 500 more expected, but there were only about 500 saddles at Rouen, or on rail to Rouen from Le Havre. Regiments sent men down to the depot to be mounted and along with reinforcements, they were sent back fully mounted, equipped and trained. By this system men took to the front horses they had personally ridden and helped to train. The Orleans Indian Depot was considered unsanitary and by 1st December, closed and moved to Gournay, along with a new rest farm. As soon as 2nd Indian Cavalry Division had entrained for the front, the IGC approved the removal of No.1 Advanced Remount Depot from Orleans to Dieppe, by rail on 12th November; with No. 6 Depot moving to a new base at La Houssoye Farm, 23rd December, opening with 89 horses. A base remount depot for 2,600 was established at Dieppe (agreed 30th November), along with No.5 Canadian Remount Depot moving to St Germere from Havre; No.9 hospital was transferred to Dieppe from Abbeville.

The railways experienced increasing pressure to move troops and supplies to their concentration areas. This caused problems for the Remount Department, which by late August was beginning to experience what was to become a continual problem of meeting requests for remounts, but not being able to move them to the front by rail in case this caused disruption to railway arrangements. Garratt raised questions on several occasions about the extreme difficulties experienced when moving animals forward from the base depot, and suggested sending forward a small advanced remount depot to the railhead, before the movement of troops, or to increase the percentage of spare horses with regiments. The solution, though not ideal, was to attach trucks to supply trains going to railheads at night. Requests from the front, for the replacement of equipment shortages, were telegraphed to supply bases.

The Cavalry Division requested all remounts be sent forward saddled, but in so doing their first batch of remounts were delayed. The Director of Ordnance ordered 400 saddles from the base depot to be moved to Amiens and on 24th August 2,000 were ordered from England. On the 26th August, eight trucks, with 200 saddles on board went missing and remounts for the 3rd Cavalry Brigade were delayed owing to a shortage of saddles. Very few saddles were coming back from the front, Ordnance had run out and there was also a scarcity of picketing ropes. Orders were issued for Ordnance to send saddles for cavalry horses to Le Havre for fitting out, thereby saving the horses a railway journey round by Le Mans. The horse transport section of the ASC had to provide complete 'turnouts' (horse, driver, harness and vehicle, not all of which came from the same depots), with all components to be available at one assembly place, the advanced horsed transport depot. During a war of movement this was a difficult task. During September and October, bases were constantly moved and with rail transport unreliable, or unavailable, it was impossible to move by rail with any rapidity.[50]

It was not long before the old problem of insufficient farriers and shoeing-smiths became a difficulty; some units arrived from England with them. The DDR at GHQ complained that horses sent from the base remount depot were not properly shod. The reply was that only one shipload of personnel, consisting of two officers and 58 men were at the base when horses arrived from England and they had to deal with 960 horses in three days. It was an impossibility, owing to the lack of men and materials to get horses shod in time. This problem was not helped by a change in the location of the base depot from Havre. [51] DDVS reports stated remounts were arriving at the front without hind shoes; Garratt replied that he was not in a position to shoe them. The 1st Cavalry Brigade complained that the shoeing of some remounts was not good and on the 14th October, Garratt noted the very great shortage of shoeing-smiths. Agreement was reached on 10th November that Remounts (not the AVC, which was short of personnel), would undertake shoeing at veterinary farms, and the IGC cabled the WO for 250 farriers to be sent out. The establishment of shoeing-smiths in all depots was supposed to have been completed in November, with extra smiths being included for farrier sergeants. However, by late November, remount depots were still

---

50   WO95/69; Henniker, p.14.
51   WO95/69, 11th September, telegram from DDR, GHQ to base remount depot.

not able to get horses shoes tapped with screw holes, in accordance with orders to have all horses shod by 1st December, although they had been requisitioned earlier.

With increasing numbers of casualties, sick animals and expansion of the BEF, the shortage of personnel gave cause for serious concern, especially for veterinary establishments. On 26th August all cavalry reservists with remount depots were ordered home and Garratt requested 200 ASC personnel to replace them. In September, the Nantes depot reported a shortage of men; the IGC requested 400 men from England who were used to horses. Orders were received on 1st November to send artillery officers and some cavalry officers from remount depots to England and in September RFA drivers were removed from hospitals. In October the Adjutant General issued instructions that no reinforcements were to be employed in hospitals as they were required for other units; 905 reinforcements and 146 Class 'B' men were employed at that time. This was a severe setback as was the loss of RFA drivers who had been with depots and hospitals since September. A statement prepared on 26th November showed they were 35 officers and 931 other ranks short of sanctioned hospital establishments with a deficiency of 61 veterinary officers and 1,539 other ranks; a situation that threatened similar disasters to those of the 1899-1902 War. In desperation the AVC recruited their own specially enlisted personnel by their own branch of the WO and rushed them over to France, "saving an ugly situation". They were permitted to retain Class 'D' cavalry reservists who went out with the original sections as horse keepers.

This lack of establishment meant some work suffered and was not carried out to the desired standard. The original plan laid down in the 1914 Veterinary Manual (War), of engaging local labour for conducting sick horses by train proved impossible, with wagon loads often dispatched without attendants. On arrival at stations, hospitals were notified by railway staff that animals were ready for collection, but this had to be done by hospital personnel. In a batch of 412 horses received at Villeneuve St Georges on 21st September, four were found dead in the train and five had to be destroyed at the station. This problem of conducting sick horses was pursued until a Routine Order of 2nd October, ordered one man per truck, with an NCO for every 100 horses; conducting parties being furnished from personnel at railheads under the orders of Railhead Commandants. When transfer was between hospitals, conducting parties were to be found from hospital personnel. Moore, however, considered conducting sick horses was the responsibility of mobile veterinary sections with additional veterinary personnel; a view supported by the WO, resulting in additional men being sent out.

The sheer volume of work at depots and hospitals also caused severe difficulties. The congestion of sick animals at Villeneuve St Georges became so great, and the number of veterinary personnel so inadequate, that 200 Royal Artillery reinforcements were taken from the base to help; 100 reinforcements were also obtained for the same purpose at Le Mans, and Nantes. Many of these reinforcements would be untrained in remount and veterinary skills and routines, only adding to the workload in training and monitoring them. In anticipation of a WO meeting, a request was made for 300 veterinary personnel and six officers. The congestion was only relieved by transferring 400 horses to Le Mans and turning them out to grass, securing additional paddocks for 250 animals. This organisation was followed until the adoption of Veterinary Evacuating Stations in 1918. The conducting parties of mobile veterinary sections, except Cavalry, were reduced to partly provide for personnel of the evacuating stations. One should recognise the untiring energy of Moore and Garrett and their HQ staff as the administrative work also greatly increased, in response to which, an additional DADVS was added to the Veterinary Directorate.

Supply of Remounts

On the 24th August the IGC was informed that the Cavalry had sustained heavy casualties, although it was not until 29th that the first rough estimate of casualties was received from the front. A request had already been sent to England for 300 cavalry, 200 artillery, 100 transport and 100 heavy draught remounts, to be further supplemented with a request for 1,000 riding horses. Garratt also impressed on the Director of Ordnance the need for more saddles, blankets and extra rugs for winter.

The fluid nature of the war meant the Remount Service had to be alert and adaptable to quickly changing demands and circumstances. The inability to meet some demands did not always rest with the Service. During September, for example, the IGC requested the formation of a new field battery and 1st Line reinforcements, but was informed horses could only be supplied if other demands were not met, and cabled the WO for more horses. An additional burden came with instructions to replace the wastage of the Indian contingent; England was cabled for 1,000 more cavalry horses, and owing to heavy work an increased supply of light and heavy draught horses. The landing of horses in port was delayed to allow for the disembarkation of the 6th Division; once landed the remounts could not be received at railhead and four trains of animals were kept waiting.

By 19th September a weekly shipment of 1,200 horses was leaving the UK for the BEF. An additional 1,000 light and 500 heavy draught were requested, along with pack animals to complete 28 machine gun packs. On the 20th, the weekly shipment was raised from 2,900 to 3,000, consisting of 1,600 artillery and light draught, 400 heavy draught, 200 pack and 800 cavalry horses. In addition, on the 21st, owing to heavy casualties, a further 2,300 horses were requested from the WO. By the 26th October, the total number of cavalry reinforcements mounted and despatched to regiments since war began was 125 officers and 1,760 other ranks. By late November, the general situation of the BEF's remount reserve was such that, no horses were to be sent to France as all depots were practically full. The WO was cabled to stop sending cavalry horses until further notice as the Rouen depot would be full and cavalry divisions did not require any more horses, for example, 1st Cavalry Corps reinforcements were going to the front without horses as they had sufficient. On 19th December, for the first time since war began, all demands from the front were completed, or en-route by rail; weekly shipments decreased from 3,000 to 1,000, as only draught horses were required. For example, on the 7th December, 400 heavy draught horses were urgently demanded for reserve parks. The WO wrote to Garratt, 8th December, proposing not to ship mules to France for some weeks as they would be fully trained at home. Also, no ordinance mules were currently available and horses, or ponies, suitable for pack were to be issued instead. On the 23rd December orders were issued to provide pack transport for extra machine guns; 100 pack mules were ordered from Marseilles and 80 pack horses from Rouen.

There was concern that the UK supply could be temporarily halted, in which case, the size of the reserve of remounts kept with the BEF required consideration. In October Garratt considered that by the end of November there would be in France, in three base remount depots each holding 1,700 animals, and four advanced remount depots with 900, a total of 6,000 animals. He thought it also necessary to keep a large reserve in the Indian base remount depot as these horses would require at least a fortnight's rest before being fit for issue. A conference with the IGC, on 9th November, discussed the serious supply shortage of light draught horses, especially for the artillery. The QMG sanctioned a suggestion to reduce numbers by issuing heavy draught in place of light, to the 7th Divisional Ammunition Column, in the same Corps as 8th Division, which already used heavy draught for its Columns (two heavy and two light draught horses were used instead of six light horses in divisional ammunition columns). The QMG (BEF) thought mules unsuitable to replace light draught in British divisions, but by the end of 1914, imported mules were being trialled, with positive results, as substitutes for horses in the Army. The much maligned mule was never popular in England, even after the war when available to farmers at much lower prices than horses. They were increasingly used during the war for transport and pack work when their qualities for hard work, hardiness, reliability and more resistance to disease than a horse, were quickly recognised. Cubitt at the WO pointed out in 1915, that mules were equivalent in weight to the ordinary light 'vanner' horse … "were exceptionally quiet and hardy, lived longer and did more work on less food than a horse … if once the value of the mule was realised in England and bred in any large numbers they would be a valuable asset to the mobilisation of the Army".[52] By 31st December the situation had improved to the extent that, for the first time since the beginning of the war, it was unnecessary to ask for any horses from England for the following week. All depots by the end of that week were expected to be practically full and horses of all classes were ready to be brought in from remount farms.

52   WO95/69. November 1914; MAF 52/2/A4 3091/1915, 27.4.15, WO to BAF; Fox, 1920, "the Gunner", *The Mule's Virtues* pp.6, 8; Nicholls, p.102; my thanks to Andy Chelmsford.

Hutments and Stabling

Remount depots and hospitals were routinely inspected for stable management, condition of the animals and building works, highlighting both short-term problems and some of a more serious nature. The QMG, for example, reported that not all remount depots were satisfactory and at an IGC conference, on 26th September, stated that action had already been taken and a base remount depot commander changed. Garratt had spoken to Moore about the number of sick animals in depots, which he considered too high. In the early days a considerable number of mares, purchased as remounts, were in foal; fifty were collected at Nantes and sent to Le Havre for shipment to England, and Abbeville had 80 mares in foal ready to be sent home. Garratt visited 1,000 horses sent to Abbeville from the front, noting that the draught horses looked very bad.

The provision of hutments and stabling was essential for the well being of animals, but they were difficult to provide in the early days of the war. The construction of stabling at Le Havre Base Depot was begun early November, but by mid December was only about half completed. Most of the work was put out to local contract as the Director of Works, although responsible for the service, had few men of his own so progress was slow. Later, when the AVC was provided with a reasonable establishment, its own men assisted with building under the direction of Works Services. Buildings were laid down to approved plans and layouts on an understanding with the Director of Works that they were not occupied before completion. Difficulties were increased by bad weather. December saw a deterioration with reports from most depots about the poor state of the ground. At Havre, for example, the mud was very bad, at Rouen the ground was deep in mud from heavy rain, at Forges, horses in paddocks did considerable damage to fencing and at Boulogne a cement works was rented to place 180 horses under cover.

The experiences of the winter mud of 1914-15 were not to be forgotten. The hilltop at Havre was dreadful with one horse drowning in liquid mud and dung. Sometimes it was even difficult to reach the animals to feed them. At Gournay, where animals were not confined, two drowned in mud. At Abbeville, where 450 were accommodated at a briqueterie (brick factory), in farm buildings and 160 in a circus tent, straw was put down in the open lines. As mud presented the greatest difficulty in all places, a priority in the building of a hospital, or depot, was a substantial corduroy road made from railway sleepers so that neither transport nor animals became bogged down. The disposal of manure in wet weather became a serious problem and a report was requested from all remount depots, with special attention drawn to the importance of not allowing it to accumulate in remount lines.

The provision of accommodation for hospitals and convalescent horse depots presented many difficulties especially early in the war; the distance of reception hospitals from the front line being an important factor. Long railway journeys for debilitated animals from the Marne and Aisne fronts resulted in many deaths en route, though hospitals at base ports were conveniently situated for receiving newly landed

3rd Reserve Veterinary Hospital, Aldershot, 28 May 1916: mares with foals born in camp.
(Army Medical Services Museum)

respiratory sick animals. Large brick factories provided excellent, readily available accommodation for men and animals, which with reconstruction and additions eventually provided some of the best hospitals. Circus tents purchased from Paris were used for holding 24, or 48 horses in hospitals at Abbeville, Rouen and Neufchatel, until more permanent stabling was available. Some hospitals were constructed of

No.9 Veterinary Hospital, Dieppe, France: utilization of brick sheds for stabling.
(Army Medical Services Museum)

iron fittings sent from the UK and erected by veterinary personnel; others were of wood with galvanised iron mangers erected by local contractors and POW labour. All construction work was under the direction and supervision of the Directorate of Works. One important feature of stable construction was the provision of solid, hygienic flooring and approaches to hard standings, with various materials being tried: concrete, stone slabs, bricks on edge, beech planking, beech blocks set in tessellated form in chalk and cinders or sand.

With large influxes of sick horses into hospitals and an increase in the size of the BEF, a re-organisation of hospital establishments became necessary. The small veterinary section for 250 animals became unsuitable and on the 11th November the WO designated that all hutments and stabling in France should be rearranged on a new establishment of 1,000 animals; the original for 250 sick animals was retained as a guide for working sub-divisions, or as a basis for increases to either 1,250, 1,500, or 2,000 establishments, as adopted later in the war. As the war progressed, admissions into hospitals ranged from 2,500 and 3,500 weekly; the highest number in any week was 4,512. Experience showed that it was easier to work a hospital for 2,000 horses, and also cheaper to make additions to existing hospitals, than create new ones.

Injury, Sickness and Disease

Sickness, disease and inefficiency took their toll on animals from an early date with cases of poverty, debility and exhaustion soon being treated. There were complaints about the issue of unfit remounts, for example, 90 'absolutely useless' remounts were issued to 5th Cavalry Brigade; horses were known to have been three and four days in a train before reaching brigades, and similar complaints were received later in September relating to 1st Cavalry Brigade. Gunshot, shell and bomb casualties were infrequent at first, mainly coming from the first battle of Ypres (18th October – 18th November) onwards. A large number of fistulous withers (see Glossary) were encountered where animals had been under harness and saddles for days and foot cases, cracked heels, injuries and lameness were common. The parasitic skin disease, mange did not appear until the end of November, when it was detected in evacuations to Abbeville from the 1st Division and also reported in the 4th Division. Steps were initiated to watch for the highly infectious disease of glanders, the first case was reported in a captured German pony on 23rd October, with the weekly supply of mallein (for skin testing) from Woolwich increased to 2,000 doses. It was not until the autumn of 1915 that the frequency of reactions to testing, amongst animals evacuated from the front, indicated the strong menace from glanders, resulting in testing of the whole force during the winter of 1915. The most serious sickness in the early days of the war was the group of infectious respiratory diseases, strangles and catarrhal fever of the influenza and pneumonia type, which predominated amongst remounts from overseas. It continued at the new base in Le Havre and was particularly prevalent amongst heavy draught horses which suffered greatly from catarrh; this was thought to have originated from animals kept in stables in England. The AVC was ill equipped to deal with it, due to a lack of accommodation and periods of bad weather. From 10% to 40% were admitted to hospital almost immediately after landing, with a heavy mortality rate. About 25% of sickness cases with colds were contracted when on board ship. The 8th Division, on arrival at Havre, placed in hospital 426 sick animals, mainly heavy and draught horses of the infantry transport. At one point, only 132 from 400 animals were fit for issue.

From the beginning of the war to 16th October, 104,000 remounts were admitted to hospital, an average of 500 per week, of which 8% to 12% were admitted direct from ships. Strangles and respiratory disease were very prevalent at St Nazaire, Nantes and the advanced remount depot at Le Mans. Anglo-Canadian horses recorded with 'pink eye' (catarrhal fever) were segregated and held at base. The Indian Corps', to supply their urgent demands, were authorised to purchase locally, as were DDRs at GHQ for the supply of reserve parks. Eventually, it was decided that all remounts were to be retained at base remount depots for 14 days before issue. Despite the large number of animals in hospitals, by late November some 1,500 animals per week were probably being returned to remount depots, but as they were not all fit for immediate issue the demand to create more convalescent farms increased.

With the onset of bad weather and increased possibility of mange there was much discussion about the policy of clipping horses coats (allowing thick winter coats to dry more quickly after exercise and make grooming easier), a subject that remained a contentious issue throughout the war. Moore was in favour of general all round clipping, but Garratt did not think it advisable except in special cases and telegraphed Cavalry Corps commanders and DDRs at GHQ for their opinions. The DDR, 1st Cavalry Corps replied, that clipping was not advised. However, orders were issued, 18th November, for draught horses on lines of communication to be clipped trace high, with legs left unclipped. For the control of contagious diseases in hospitals, clipping was to be carried out as circumstances necessitated. The QMG (BEF) suggested clipping might be allowed as the majority of horses were stabled at the front,

Wastage

In contemporary accounts, there are often only fleeting glimpses of the condition of horses during the war of manoeuvre in 1914. The RFA and RHA were heavily involved in the events of August, for example at Nery, 1st September, L Battery RHA, lost 150 of its 228 horses. Lucy wrote that many artillery horses fell out fatigued and lame with the men out marching them; some horses were shot, others stripped of harness and left alive standing, or limping, along the line of retreat. With the pace of the retreat from Mons and problems with locating units and supply dumps, there were increasingly fewer opportunities to feed and water animals[53] Brownlow writes that as the horses became exhausted their best pace was no quicker than a walk, occasionally a sweating and panting team would stop dead and could only be made to move again

53   Lucy, p.151; Farndale, p.57.

by using outriders and men heaving at the wheels. On the retreat from Le Cateau he recalls an abandoned horse with galls (sores) like scarlet saucers on its back and sides, standing still as a statue, gazing as his masters passed by. During the October move to Flanders, he records horses being so exhausted that even on a small incline they were unable to move and one, or two, dropped and died from sheer fatigue. In the Kemmel sector (near Ypres) during November, horses without stables, or cover, had to stand week after week in a sea of churned mud, often up to their hocks; the consequence of which was mud sores, in some of which it was possible to place a fist down to the bone. [54] Arbuthnot wrote that on reaching France, for the first critical month or two when the Artillery fought and marched, seldom an officer, or No.1, could be spared to look after horses.[55] Uncertain forage, days and nights under harness and an outbreak of strangles added to the trials. Yet Mitchell, AVC with the Guards Brigade, in December wrote "horses working wonderfully well, in spite of the weather" and "the 'Black Watch' just looking as if they were ready for an agricultural show".[56] Although horses suffered, especially the unfit mobilised remounts, many recovered. By the spring of 1915, in spite of an appalling winter, Artbuthnot states they marched with sleek coats to the second battle of Ypres (22nd April-25th May, 1915).[57] The importance attached to horsemastership by the Artillery in peacetime was fully justified during the first six months of the war.

In December, Birkbeck wrote that the wastage question was serious and indeterminate.[58] The BEF took the field with some 54,000 horses, with 20% wastage during the months of August to October. Wastage from 15th September to 14th November was 12,000 monthly. By 25th November there were approximately 100,000 horses with the BEF and Remounts (WO) was sending 5,000 monthly to meet wastage. It was thought the wastage of 20% was due to the abnormal conditions of the first month of the war and was unlikely to be repeated. With the number of animals being returned from hospitals, an average allowance of 15% was considered adequate to meet future demands. There were about 11,000 animals in hospitals and convalescent farms, with over 500 per week going back to the ranks. Moore records that the first useful statement of casualties they received, not including the Cavalry Division, was on 21st September, showing 777 having died at the front, 1,213 destroyed, 1,504 missing,

54   Brownlow, pp.64, 93, 175, ammunition column, 25th August 1914.
55   Arbuthnot, p.338.
56   William McGregor Mitchell, letter written 8th December 1914 from HQ 1st Guards Brigade, 1st Division (unpublished letters, kindly loaned by Helen Gibson). Mitchell served in France throughout the war reaching rank of Captain; becoming a Professor at the Royal (Dick) Veterinary College.
57   Arbuthnot, p.338.
58   WO107/19, 'Estimate of Horse Supply Demand,' 25th November 1914 and part of a draft document from Birkbeck, 20th December 1914, to Maj-Gen. Lawson; also a document headed 'Remounts' in WO107/19; WO107/17, 20th December 1914.

3,692 transferred sick, 3,672 cured and 1,388 under treatment.[59] There were a further 4,546 in hospitals on the lines of communication, which by 26th September had risen to 5,432.[60]

Casting and the Disposal of Dead Animals

This presented an initial difficulty. A policy was adopted of not charging contractors for carcasses; although in certain places it was possible to obtain 15 francs per carcass from contractors. The most satisfactory method of disposal was burial in a designated place by AVC personnel; this was the only possible method in the area of fighting troops. In the latter stages of the war special structures for dealing with dead animals were obtained, and considerable profits resulted. The French Army had mobilised so many civilian horses that the British authorities were asked if they could be replaced by those British Army horses considered of no further use for military service. French Authorities were given permission to purchase horses unfit for further service; they were sold at public auction by the British Army once approved by the Directors of Remounts or Veterinary Services. Under casting regulations formulated under Routine Order No.280, 3rd November; cast horses were branded with an inverted broad arrow. Auctions were held under the orders of base commandants with a deputed officer in attendance. At his first casting parade at Abbeville hospital, 18th November, Moore records that of 21 horses were cast and sold; one was aged 30 years another 28 years, two at 22 years, six at 20 years, four at 18 years and two at three years. This range in ages is not surprising for a period of rapid mobilisation and the collection of large numbers of horses to supply wastage. The great majority of older horses did remarkably good service during the war and the old peace time rule of excluding horses aged under six and over 12 years for active service was relaxed in favour of an open policy.[61]

59   At Villeneuve St Georges 623; St Nazaire, 611; Nantes, 1087; La Chapelle, 336; Le Mans, 1899; Total: 4,546. By 26th September at: Villeneuve. St Georges 1370; St Nazaire 525, Nantes 1029, La Chapelle 545; Le Mans 1963; Total 5432. Table of casualties was supplied to the QMG and taken from Moore's war diary, WO107/19, 25th November 1914; Moore, 1930, p.25.

60   Chivers, 1976, gives a 12% loss in animals by end of December 1914, equivalent to an annual loss of 36%.

61   Moore, 1930, pp.118-119.

8

Expansion and Horsing the New Armies 1914-15

German horse dealers travelled to Sweden, on being officially informed that the Government had raised the embargo upon the shipment of horses, and some 12,000 animals were said to be available for foreign purchasers. One of the Germans stated: "we want these horses very badly, and we are quite ready to buy 100,000 animals on the basis of money no object. Since the commencement of the war the Army has squandered its stock of horses, and the military authorities apparently never for a moment considered the difficulties ahead. These troubles they are now experiencing. During August and September 6,000 horses a day were worn out or killed, so it will be readily understood that 12,000 horses will not go very far towards filling the gaps.[1]

After successfully supplying the mobilisation requirements of the BEF, the already stretched Remount Department and AVC had to turn their attention to supplying and caring for the requirements of a massively expanded BEF and Territorial Force (TF), which by December 1918 included some 90 infantry and eight cavalry divisions, in five armies, in all theatres. This was no easy matter and went far beyond the planning of the inter-war years.

Horsing the New Armies and Divisions returning from overseas

The Remount Department had hardly completed establishments for the BEF when a policy was implemented to bring back Imperial troops from Egypt, Africa, the Mediterranean and India and raise new armies, initially the first six Kitchener (K1) Divisions, all of which required horses and equipment. The magnitude of the task was daunting, requiring a massive increase in horse purchasing arrangements both in the UK and overseas. The Remount Department increased purchasing on the UK open market, where the supply was to prove greater than anticipated, as MacMunn stated,

---

1   *VR*, 1915, Vol. XXVII, 1st May, p.572.

"the BEF could have taken more horses from the UK if more accommodation and equipment had been available". [2]

Troops returning from foreign stations formed the 27th, 28th and 29th Divisions (27th and 28th were at Ypres by April 1915; the 29th to the Dardanelles, March 1915). Over the winter of 1914, against advice from the Adjutant General and QMG, Kitchener insisted on putting the 27th and 28th Divisions into camp on the Downs at Winchester, when they could easily have been billeted.[3] Horses and men suffered severely, animals were taken sick from exposure in large numbers, retarding their efficiency. The *Veterinary Record* for March 1916 states that since the outbreak of war, approximately 8,000 animals from training camps had been admitted to hospitals with disease, with the annual mortality running at 2% higher than in peacetime.[4] WO papers relating to the mobilisation of the 27th and 28th Divisions provide an insight into these problems. For example, a report on mobilisation, comments on the extreme haste with which it was being attempted, combined with appalling conditions in the camp, bad weather, and the general lack of understanding in the use of English harness and equipment, all militated against efficiency.[5] To assist with these problems, the QMG notified Gen. Bulfin, CO of 28th Division, that 15 lorries were working between their camp and Portsmouth providing ordnance stores and that remounts were ready when they could take them.[6]

During December there was a serious outbreak of mange amongst horses in training for the 28th Division; all 180 horses were swiftly isolated to a tannery near Cosham, and replacements issued. However, in early January the Division still lacked some harness and pack saddles and required re-equipping throughout.[7] The winter proved very difficult. In January 1915 Bulfin informed the WO that conditions in the camps, owing to continuous rain, were deplorable, it was like one huge quagmire with men and horses wading about and therefore it was quite impossible to allow troops to remain. Wagons were constantly mired and horses worn out, militating against the speed and efficiency of mobilisation. Maj-Gen. Thomas D 'Oyly Snow (injured in command of 4th Division at the Battle of the Marne and given command of 27th Division), wrote to the WO suggesting improvements, based on the Division's experiences, to facilitate any future mobilisation should Morn Hill Camp, Winchester, be used again.[8] The most important concern within the camp area was providing good

2   MacMunn, 1930, pp.118-9; WO95/69.
3   Ibid., p.124.
4   *VR*, 1915, Vol.XXVIII, 9th October, pp.164-5: The health of animals kept in camps over winter and possible extension of the system of issuing horses on 'meat for work' at 25/- weekly; 1916, 25th March, p.429 ref. 'Mortality Amongst Army Horses'; Hansard (C), 1915, Vol.LXIX, February 2-18, (c) 242, 1135, 1305.
5   WO107/19; 27th Division to QMG, 20th December 1914.
6   WO107/19, 28th December; and Bulfin's reply to QMG.
7   WO107/19, telegram from Bulfin to WO, 28th December, (2265Q), ref. mange, and further communications; and 10th January 1915, Bulfin to WO.
8   WO107/19, 1st January 1915, 'Notes on Suggested Improvements to Facilitate Mobilisation'.

metalled roads of sufficient breadth to allow wagons to pass each other; when roads were provided, it was recommended units should be forced to use them and horses moved to water, or exercise, only by road. Watering places should be enclosed and the times of watering agreed for the various units and horse lines drained, as it was impossible to keep horses fit when up to their hocks in mud. Stores should be collected in advance of a Division's mobilisation, as some equipment was only dribbled to them over a number of weeks. Snow further suggested that in the case of a camp with no hut accommodation, staff should be provided solely for assembling harness as it was impossible to do this satisfactorily in a muddy camp and pouring rain; harness, horses and vehicles should be issued first, equipment later.

A lack of horse equipment in the early stages of the war rendered training and exercising very difficult. The necessity of issuing harness and saddlery to the Regular and Territorial units that followed the BEF, put great strain on the QMG's department. At Tidworth in Hampshire, for example, where the reserve cavalry regiments were formed, there were very few bridles and saddles, and on one occasion amongst 1,000 horses there were only 57 bridles and no saddles. The *Upton News* for 26th September, 1914, carries a fascinating "Appeal to Sportsmen," as the supply of saddles was deficient and impeding the training of Reserve Cavalry regiments, the WO appealed for owners of gentleman's hunting or colonial saddles, in good repair with fair sized seats, if possible with girth and stirrups also bridles and bits; polo or pony saddles were not suitable. Owners were to send their saddles to the Chief Ordnance Officer, Woolwich Dockyard.[9]

There were two major problems in providing the enormous quantity of harness and saddlery. Firstly, the shortage of leather, particularly that required to stand the hard wear of active service, and secondly, the very limited number of UK businesses capable of making military pattern harness and saddlery. Harness had to be imported from India, America and Canada; from San Antonio in South America to St Paul in the North, and from Omaha in the West. At one stage harness and saddlery was being manufactured in 24 different American cities. Not until the end of February 1915 did any large supplies arrive from America, but even then the rapid mobilisation of successive divisions prevented the accumulation of a reserve. Congestion at ports and on railways further delayed the distribution of supplies arriving into the UK. From August 1914 to December 1915, the sets of harness in use had increased from 40,000 to 518,000, however, by the latter date difficulties of supply had been overcome and as output at home improved, purchases in America were reduced and then stopped. Great Britain ultimately supplied harness to the BEF in France, Egypt, Mesopotamia and East Africa and in 1916 to forces in Salonika. The Russian Army was provided with 36,000 sets of machine gun saddlery and 30,000 sets of saddlery, as well as many

9   I am grateful to Brian Hill for the *Upton News* article.

thousands of sets of artillery harness; Serbians were also supplied with thousands of sets of pack saddlery.[10]

Calculations in WO documents for the number of horses required, those available, and the percentage allowed for wastage, present a confusing picture. Some documents are undated making it difficult to understand the figures chronologically, with tables and totals frequently not agreeing; the percentage calculations for wastage vary from 10% to 20%.[11]

In September, GOCs Home Commands were instructed that no horses in excess of those detailed in the Remount Statement were to be issued to Regular units without Birkbeck's specific instruction.[12] Birkbeck provided figures for horse requirements, up to 15th May 1915, totalling 244, 948, which included a presumption that the monthly wastage rate for units already overseas remained at 10%, and that the additional units took the field on the planned dates of:

2nd Indian Division	15 October
1st Indian Cavalry Brigade	15 October
3rd Indian Cavalry Brigade	30 October
1st Indian Division	30 October
7th British Division	15 October
8th British Division	30 October
2nd British Cavalry Division	30 October
7 TF Divisions	15 February

The planned wastage figure for the above including the BEF was 82,630, in addition the assumed wastage for new provision was for 69,480 mules and 92,838 horses, required for 14 TF divisions, 14 mounted brigades and four New Armies. The total of 244,948 horses and mules can be summarised as:[13]

								Totals	
R1	RII	LD1	Mules	LDII	HD	Pack	Mules	Horses	Mules
64,409	1,294	63,358	66,432	6,616	27,805	1,986	3,048	175,468	69,480
								(244,948)	

---

10   Chapman, pp.95-6.
11   See earlier, ref. WO107/19, variations from 10% to 30%.
12   WO107/17, 'Horsing the First Four New Armies and Territorial Army, Horse Transport';
     Letter from MacMunn to Director of Remounts, 9th September 1914 from WO, (R922;
     QMG4) to 'the General Officer, Commander in Chief, Commands'.
13   WO107/17, probably 18th September 1914, 'Horse Requirements', to QMG from
     Birkbeck.

Heavy draught horses (HD) were obtainable in England, in addition to another 40,000 good horses from the UK. Birkbeck considered this then exhausted UK horse resources if the country's distribution trade was not to be seriously affected.

177,000 animals would then have to be imported, requiring a significant increase in the horse purchasing commissions in Canada and the USA. It was estimated that 50,000 horses might be purchased in Canada and the northern states of America, although Canada's horse supply was not very large and was equipping its own forces.[14] Maj-Gen. Benson, commanding the remount commission in Canada, reported that he did not envisage any difficulty in keeping up a monthly supply of 20,000 horses of good type and 10,000 excellent mules, but it was difficult to see beyond June 1915. Benson was not anxious about the provision of riding horses, but had some uncertainty about the ability to maintain the standard of supply in artillery horses, so mules were being considered as a backup position. It was soon realised that demand for artillery horses for the New Armies' would be more than the light 'vanner' horse population of the world could supply, therefore, the decision was made to use a combination of horses and mules.[15] The main focus was centred on the US where it was thought 75,000 animals could be purchased, but the British were not the only ones purchasing in these countries, France was buying large numbers in the US, which was willing to supply any, and all, belligerents. Supply from the Argentine was handed over to France, being in the wrong hemisphere for British remounts. Birkbeck saw the continued supply of horses from America as problematical. The estimated US horse population was over 30 million, of which 8 million were thought to be broken horses; barring political complications, as experienced in the 1899-1902 War, this provided an inexhaustible source of supply. In addition, a communication had been sent to Uruguay to assess its value for supply, with the assumption that 72,000 animals could possibly be purchased.[16]

Arrangements were made to purchase mules in Spain and US. The Indian Government was asked to purchase 50,000 horses in Australia and import them to India during the winter, where they would be partially acclimatised, conditioned and trained at less expense than in England; they would then be shipped to England in the spring when they would be of more use. This left a balance of 52,000 animals, for which Birkbeck's solution was to substitute mules (70,000) for horses in the Artillery and the four New Armies, except for the gun teams themselves and for spare horses. This resulted in:

---

14   WO107/17, draft to Maj-Gen. Lawson, assistant to CIGS from Birkbeck, 20th December 1914.
15   WO107/17, 26th November 1914, memo New Army's document (1A), Lawson to Director Remounts; MacMunn, 1930, pp.117-8.
16   WO107/17, document 16th November 1914, re. 'Estimate of Horse Supply and Demand re Uruguay' from 15th March 1915.

Number required: 245,000

To be supplied from the:

UK	68,000
USA	75,000
Australia	50,000
(Mules from America)	70,000
Total	263,000

Birkbeck provided a financial breakdown for supplying the above, taking the average initial cost as:[17]

28,000 English Heavy Horses	at £60	£1,680,000
40,000 English Light Horses	at £50	£2,000,000
75,000 American Light Horses	at £40	£3,000,000
50,000 Australian Light Horses	at £40	£2,000,000
70,000 American Mules	at £40	£2,800,000
Total		£11,480,000

Freight of 145,000 American horses and mules	at £10	£1,450,000
Freight of 50,000 Australian horses to India, then onwards to England or Marseille	at £25	£1,250,000
Total cost of purchase and freight		£14,500,000

The calculations for remount requirements took no account of the formation of a new Territorial Army at home and Birkbeck earnestly urged that the new Reserve Yeomanry regiments should not be given more than 50 horses per regiment for training recruits. There was a serious problem in supplying chargers for officers of the New Armies. The method in use for providing chargers was to use riding schools in the big towns to train and handle them, creating a very large business in London. This changed when Tattersalls was adopted as the issuing depot for chargers for the senior staff. Tattersalls is the oldest bloodstock auctioneers in the world, founded in 1766 by Richard Tattersall at premises near Hyde Park Corner, in what was then the outskirts of London. A later Richard Tattersall (1812–1870) moved the business to Knightsbridge in 1865.[18]

New formations on being raised and trained were sent a batch of animals discarded from other units going overseas, which was a more efficient system of utilising poorer quality animals. As skills improved they were given better quality animals and on

17   WO107/17, Birkbeck to QMG, dated 18th September 1914.
18   Ibid., pp.119-20; Orchard, 1953. I am grateful to Miss Terry Lane of Tattershalls for information on the Company.

being ordered abroad were supplied with good animals, their unfit and unsound animals sent to another new formation.[19]

A further forecast for completing supply to the New Armies shows that the TF of six divisions, earmarked for the Continent, was mostly complete.[20] If the TF was required for service abroad on, or after the New Year, it could be made ready by slightly holding back the New Armies. Birkbeck on being asked to comment on the remount aspects of this forecast, commented that the Territorial divisions were not as complete in horses as they appeared on paper; to fit each one for service overseas 350 horses were required for the ammunition park and about 1,000 for replacement of losses suffered from indifferent horsemastership.[21] However, he thought they could meet the completion dates. At the beginning of December 1914 dates for completion of the New Armies (each one of six divisions requiring 33,000 horses) was given as:[22]

No.1   New Army: by middle of   March 1915   (governing factors were guns, horses and mechanical transport (MT).

No.2   1 May
No.3   15 May
No.4   15 June   (difficulty with MT)
No.5   possibly 15 July   (with the possible exception of MT).

The Territorial Force (six divisions for the Continent), which were competing for mechanical transport, would be ready by about December 1914. Revised estimates in December, for completion dates for horses was proposed as:[23]

1st   New Army   28 July
2nd   30 April
3rd   30 June
4th   30 June
5th   problematical
6th   problematical
Territorial Army   anytime with two weeks' notice

---

19   MacMunn, 1930, pp.119-20.
20   Draft document to the Secretary of State, November-December 1914, WO107/17, (1A).
21   WO107/17, Memo, New Armies, Document (1A); Lawson, 26th November 1914, to Director Remounts.
22   WO107/19, 3rd December 1914, to QMG, memorandum and table dealing with probable dates of completion of New Army Horses, actually issued 30th November to Director of Remounts; 107/17 document 1a, 26th November; WO107/26.
23   16th December; WO107/17, extract letter from Lawson to Director of Remounts.

Birkbeck preferred not to give dates for the Fifth and Sixth New Armies until he knew what Uruguay and Australia were likely to produce; a similar position existed for saddlery, harness, carts and wagons, and figures for wastage in the field.[24] He considered the horse question would be a problem of great magnitude and difficulty. There would be 400,000 animals when all formations were in the field, providing for four New Armies, six TF divisions and two mounted divisions, overseas contingents and the 27th, 28th and 29th Divisions. To maintain this number, with an average monthly wastage rate of 15%, 60,000 remounts would be required. It was hoped that with increased experience it would be possible to discover ways of reducing requirements and prevention of wastage, thereby achieving the original estimate of 10% in the Remount Statement of 1913-14. Even if it were possible to achieve this, 40,000 animals would still be required. The situation was not encouraging as the estimated rate of supply during June 1915, when the six TF divisions and four New Armies were to be horsed, and after, was calculated at 46,000 a month; leaving only a small margin for further new armies.[25] A remount statement for December 1914 shows a total availability of 159,576 animals as:[26]

Overseas:

Demands	937	
Assets	3,902	(Fit for issue)
Available in a short time:	4,530	(Temporarily unfit, recently landed and from hospitals)
	500	(On the sea)
Total	5,030	

i) Available in UK (fit for issue):

In depots	9,939	
In Reserve Cavalry Regiments	2,136	
In Reserve Artillery Brigades	541	
In Household Cavalry	620	
Total	13,236	(Total fit for issue)

---

24 WO107/17. Birkbeck's draft to Lawson, 16th and 20th December.
25 WO107/19; document not dated, headed 'remounts'. WO107/17, extract draft document (1A) to Secretary of State.
26 WO107/17, 18th December 1914, 'Supply of Remounts 1914-15, for New Armies, TF, EF Wastage'. Other WO tables in WO107/17, undated but similar to one of 6th October 1914, present a confusing picture of the actual numbers received from overseas to 15th July 1915, giving a possible total of 434,100 from Canada, Australia and UK (212,700 riding, 192,000 light draught and mules, 29,400 heavy draught), but totals vary considerably.

ii) Available in UK (not fit for issue):

In depots including Canadians on call	21,006	
In Reserve Cavalry Regiments	7,049	
In Reserve Artillery Brigades	2,729	
In Household Cavalry	302	
Total	31,086	(Could be fit for issue in a short time)

With Territorial Units	69,095

In Veterinary Hospitals (week ending 5 December 1914):

Overseas	11,275
In UK	9,432
Total	20,707

Already issued to New Armies	10,554

Expected during December but not yet landed:

From N. America	5,716
From Spain	250
Total	5,966

Birkbeck noted that the world's horse supply had changed since the 1899-1902 War and with other countries also purchasing, the supply would be exhausted if the war went on for long. He stressed the importance of replacing horses as much as possible by mechanical traction, "we have not yet touched the light-motor resources of the country. Col. W.M. Cave tells me that the Belgians were entirely supplied by the ordinary motor car, without even changing the bodies and cycles. Cyclists could be relied upon for home defence and usefully replace horses in many capacities with the divisions of the New Army and the TF, as mounts for orderlies and even for administrative officers." To accommodate the increased numbers of animals, the IGC (France) decided to ask for one and a quarter additional base remount depots, three advanced remount depots for each army, and one rest farm with an advanced depot for each base or line of communications.[27]

---

27   WO107/17, 18th September 1914; WO107/18, papers 3rd September to 28th November 1914, ref. 'MT for the New Armies'; WO95/69, IGC conference, France, 7th December.

Demand for Additional Remount Depots and Veterinary Facilities in the UK

Accommodation for remounts presented the QMG with a problem only a little less serious than obtaining the remounts themselves. There are a variety of figures giving the number of animals held in remount depots, before and during the war, some of which are clearly rounded up. Before the war UK remount accommodation was for 1,200 horses, in August 1914 for 1,695 animals (rounded to 1,700), on 21st October 1917 for 47,371 (to 50,000) and on 30th November 1918 for 31,667. During active operations remount depots in France kept establishments for up to 16 -17,000 animals. In contrast, in 1932 accommodation had reduced to under 6,000.[28]

In addition to those depots that existed before the war such as Arborfield Cross (Berkshire) Melton Mowbray (Leicestershire), Woolwich, Lusk and Dublin (Ireland), a massive expansion of depot accommodation was necessary, for the reception and conditioning of the huge number of animals imported into, and purchased in, the UK, including accommodation for the expansion in related personnel. The main remount depots, formed in August and September 1914, were situated at Shirehampton near Bristol, Ormskirk near Liverpool, and in Swaythling near Southampton. Romsey depot was opened in March 1915. All depots had veterinary hospitals attached to them. The primary function of a remount depot was to deal with the reserve of horses, issues to units and provision of personnel for forming any field depots required. Animals were kept under veterinary observation for three weeks before distribution to units, or in smaller remount depots for conditioning and training, prior to their transfer to base remount depots abroad.[29]

Shirehampton and Ormskirk were reception depots for animals from North America. In the absence of any suitable site nearer to Liverpool, the park at Lathom House, near Ormskirk, was placed at the War Department's disposal by the Earl of Lathom, at an agreed rental. The original establishment was on a civilian basis, but changed in January 1915 to military personnel (as did Shirehampton), partly for financial reasons, with many of the civilians enlisting. The depot included a regimental headquarters and ten remount squadrons, laid out in squadrons of 500 horses, each with one superintendent, two assistants, six foreman, 150 grooms and riders and a number of smiths. Each squadron was sub-divided into troops of 100 horses with separate stables and hut for a foreman and 25 men. The squadron HQ consisted of shoeing-smiths, a foreman and 25 special riders to handle horses requiring exceptional treatment. Horses were landed under veterinary supervision at the Canada Dock, or the Riverside landing stage. Those unfit to move, owing to injury or sickness, were taken to a veterinary hospital in Liverpool, the remainder travelled the short distance by rail to Lathom Park. Daily veterinary inspections were made at

---

28   *Statistics*, pp.862, 396; Chapman, pp.92-4.
29   WO33/673, Second Report of the Commission on War Establishments 1914; Chapman, ibid.

the depot and all sick or ailing horses removed to a neighbouring hospital. In three weeks animals were usually ready for transfer to either a reserve unit of cavalry, or artillery, or to a remount training depot. Within about three months they were fit for transfer overseas. Between its establishment and 18th November 1917, the Ormskirk depot received 215,313 animals and issued 210,850; with 4,463 in depot on 18th November. Personnel were constantly changing owing to the despatch of squadrons, the reinforcing of drafts overseas and drafting of category "A" men to combatant units. Over 7,000 men passed through the depot, which had a strength of 1,782 in November, 1917.[30]

The port of Avonmouth was used for landing horses and mules from North and South America. The Great Western Railway Company carried over 14,000 tons of building materials and fodder to the Remount depot at Shirehampton, two miles from the docks, on land of a Mr Napier Miles. In total over 339,000 animals were landed and moved inland from Avonmouth Dock Joint Station. The straggling remount depot was built on low lying ground, but in an excellent situation for receiving horses from the docks; laid out and organised on a plan similar to Ormskirk and changed from civilian to military personnel almost simultaneously. The squadrons were originally commanded almost entirely by local officers employing civilian grooms and stable lads known to them, but owing to the number of squadrons posted overseas and the drafting away of Category "A" men to combatant units, this experienced personnel soon disappeared. The less skilled men replacing them, for example townsmen, "some short sighted, or even lame", were not as efficient, but with their goodwill and willing-ness soon handled horses and mules fearlessly. Over 7,000 men passed through the depot with 5,359 transferred to other units and overseas. Between October 1914 and 1st November 1917, the depot received 183,956 horses and issued 177,214, with 3,149 deaths; 176,200 mules were received, issuing 174,849 with 470 deaths. [31]

During the civilian phase of the depot a unique organisation, the Legion of Frontiersmen, provided much needed skills and experience in working with horses and mules. The Legion of Frontiersmen was a civilian group, formed in Britain, 1905 by Roger Pocock, with its headquarters in London. Pocock had served with the North West Mounted Police and in the 1899-1902 War. On the outbreak of war the Legion's riding and horse breaking skills were offered to the WO, with many men returning to England from Canada. Reluctantly it would appear, the WO used them in remount depots notably at Shirehampton, Swaythling, and probably Romsey, near Southampton. In 1915 the WO finally authorized the formation of their own unit within the British Army, the 25th (Service) Bn. Royal Fusiliers (Frontiersmen), which served in the East Africa campaign, 1915-17.[32]

30   WO107/26; see also *Horses for the War*, 2012. My thanks to Nigel Neil.
31   WO107/26; Pratt, Vol.II p.939.
32   My thanks to Geoffrey Pocock for information; Legion of Frontiersmen website.

In March 1915 the increased import of horses necessitated establishing a third port of landing. The Admiralty selected Southampton, with a new remount depot at Romsey (Hampshire). However, submarine activity prevented the use of Southampton and many of the horses for Romsey were landed at Avonmouth and railed to the depot. To save the expense of an additional large depot with the arrival of very large numbers of mules, it was decided to run them on farms in the warm and well-watered West Country. The Somerset, or 'Taunton Mule Depots', under Lt.Col.Badcock, were organised to accommodate 6,000 mules in scattered, hired quarters on farms. An advertisement for tenders to supply hay to these depots, from 1st May to 31st July 1915, also provides a list of their locations. Twelve in number around Bridgwater, Taunton, Highbridge, Wiveliscombe, Minehead and Wellington; also two convalescent horse depots at Lowton and Trull, Taunton. The depot at Lowton, was on the land of Ernest Mattock of Lowton House; he appears to have been running War Department horses from December 1914. He was paid 2/6p per horse weekly; 30/- weekly for hire of sheds for mixing grain, storing hay and grain, for shoeing purposes and sick accommodation; 10/- for hire of carts, or wagons, including harness. Labour for tending the horses was found by the War Department. In February 1915 there is reference to a Superintendant at Lowton Convalescent Horse Depot. In January, an additional 400 convalescent horses were expected at the depot, which had a complement of 500. However, there were clearly issues with the lack of water and good pasture at the depot and brood mares not being properly fed. In April Mattock was relieved of 100 horses running on his land and his contract was not renewed at the end of October. 101,043 mules, all landed at Avonmouth, passed through these Somerset depots. [33]

Swaythling Depot was formed immediately on mobilisation. Its function differed from Ormskirk and Shirehampton in that it was used as a collecting depot, for the reception of remounts from reserve units and training depots prior to despatch to France; supplying animals to replace casualties from mounted units, sustained on rail journeys to port of embarkation. It was originally laid out on the same basis as Ormskirk, but only for three squadrons (1,500 horses) and subsequently increased to ten squadrons (5,000), with the depot extension laid out in a more compact form. The work of the depot fluctuated more than at other depots as it was dependent on demands from France. Sometimes the movement of animals was small, less than a few hundred weekly; in contrast, during May 1917, 1,500 horses were embarked on 15 consecutive days. The WO records, 274,376 animals received by the depot between

33 WO107/26; *West Somerset Freepress*, 3rd April 1915 with thanks to Maggie Robertson; Somerset Historic Environment Record No.12772; Somerset Heritage Archives DD/CPHS/35-8. In 1875 the Mattocks were contracting with the 1st Somerset Militia for a camping ground on Leigh Hill, food, fuel wood and straw. In 1877 reference to a lease for Leigh Hill camping grounds and practice range; again in 1873, 1876, 1877 and 1883. In 1887 the Leigh Hill Camp and Rifle Range was being used by the Somerset Light Infantry.

Mules in Minehead railway station yard, Somerset; shipped from the United States.
(Daphne McCutcheon)

Mules at Wiveliscombe railway station, Somerset. (Tony Hiscock)

September 1914 and December 1917. However, *The Times* records that up to 1st April 1919, 342,020 horses and mules were received; 317,165 from US, 6712 from Ireland, 9,357 purchased at home and 8,856 returned from France. On 1st April 3,530 animals were stabled and cared for by 757 men.[34]

These three large depots were all laid out on a scattered plan, taking every precaution against epidemics. However, it was soon recognised this plan caused difficulties with supervision. Construction of the fourth major depot at Romsey began in November, 1914 with the first two horses arriving on 9th March 1915. It was constructed on a gravel site, on a more compact plan, covering a smaller area; divided into two wings, with the officers, stores and institutions at the centre; huts and stables were closer together making it an efficient, economic and administratively easier depot to run. It was the only one with entirely military personnel. Unless other landing depots, such as Shirehampton, were pressed for space, or ships landed animals at unusual ports such as Devonport and later Southampton, Romsey was used largely as a training and conditioning depot, receiving horses from other depots and hospitals, many of which were embarked direct to France without transferring to Swaythling. The WO records show that from 1915 to October 1918, Romsey received 69,846 animals and issued 65,060, sending out 2,369 men; but does not give dates for these figures. However, Col. Jessel, CO of the Depot, records, 118,755 animals were received and 114,636 issued. Jessel's history of this Depot provides information not always obtainable for others. The rent payable per month for the Depot was £61.13s.10d and £5.15s. 3.5d for veterinary establishments, a total of £67.9s. 1.5d. In addition there was compensation for tenant rights, restoration and severance. Compensation was settled at £222. 15. 6d to be paid off during 1917-1918. The average daily strength was 4,162 animals, between May 1917 and October 1918, 5,458 (average 303 per month) were sent to hospital, 7,795 (av. 433 pm) treated in squadron sick lines and 35 (av. 1.9 pm) were destroyed, or died. During the same period 69,396 were dipped at the Wessex Divisional Veterinary Hospital, Romsey, with one death due to dipping and nine due to accidents at the dip. The average daily cost of an animal varied between 3s.10d (av. 3,750 animals daily July-September, 1915) and 6s (av. 3,632 April-June 1918). The rise in costs relates to a significant rise in prices, for example, oats by 93%, hay 57%, bran 110%, linseed 77%, wheat straw 80%, rock salt 41% and molassine 220% (a molasses-based feed).[35]

Towards the end of 1915, the Admiralty decided that ships should go straight to their final port of destination without calling elsewhere. This resulted in horses being landed at ports other than the recognised remount depots. Remounts were regularly landed at the ports of Glasgow, London and occasionally Hull, Devonport and Southampton. Those landed at Glasgow were railed to Ormskirk and Ayr in Scottish Command. The depot in Ayr, with a capacity for 500 horses, occupied a show-yard

---

34 WO107/26; *The Times*, April 1919.
35 WO107/26; Jessel, 1920, pp.82-84, 87, 92.

and other hired stabling in the town, receiving animals from Glasgow too ill to travel any further, Clydesdales and other horses purchased in Scotland. Established on the 1st November 1914 Ayr received 13,603 animals an issued 13,248. Landings from the Thames went to Woolwich depot, expanded for their reception, to Romsey and to a newly formed depot at Luton, on a military basis in empty government stables. Established on 22nd October 1917, with a capacity for 1,500 animals, Luton received 455 and issued 84. Animals landed at Hull went to York or Kettering; landings at Devonport and Southampton went to Romsey.

In addition to the four large depots, there were many civilian, semi-civilian, or military depots, located within the Home Commands. These served different purposes, for example, the collection and conditioning of horses purchased in England; the exchange of animals with neighbouring units; the issue and withdrawal of animals placed in civilian hands for conditioning and care; the purchase and reception of horses issued from hospitals and the issue of animals to the local War Agricultural Committees for the Food Production Department. Many of the smaller centres established throughout the country were for sick horses, managed by women, with women grooms looking after two or three horses each, such as the depot at Russley Park, Southern Command, No.2 Circle, Wiltshire. Managed by Lady Birkbeck, it had a capacity for 100 horses and was immortalised in two paintings, *The Straw Ride* and *The Ladies of Russley Park*, by the renowned female artist of the period, Lucy Kemp Walsh. From the 6th Janaury 1916 the depot received 365 horses and issued 308. In Western Command, No.3 Circle, a depot was accommodated in the Midland Railway sheds, Shrewsbury, close to a German POW camp. It had a capacity for 500 animals, managed by Mr Knill a local manufacturer and run on civilian lines taking horses that have been placed out to grass. There were two interesting annexes to this depot. Mrs Corbett's Charger Training Stables, taking horses on a weekly basis at 25/- each, using other ladies and some lads as labour, "turning out fit and well mannered animals". The second, Mr Rimmington's Reformatory Stables, taking "all the wicked horses and mules" that other depots, or units in the Command could not deal with. The personnel consisted of Rimmington, his wife and six ladies. The Shrewsbury depot, established 28th August 1914 received 6,027 animals, issuing 5,493.[36]

In Northern Command, for example, in Remount Circle No.3, Leicester had a number of centres: a training squadron for 500 animals initially civilian, then militarised, based in the boxes at Oadby (Leicester) racecourse and Trentham Hall stables accommodating between 500-1500 animals. At Market Rasen a Mr Cartwright had a similar but smaller facility taking the poorest convalescent horses. In Southern Command, No.3 Circle, Mr G Miller organised facilities for 300-600 animals. On mobilisation a polo stables at Springhill was utilised becoming a centre for conditioning horses from hospitals, or those recently landed. Miller placed animals at various farms for grazing, when ready to be prepared for issue, they where moved to his own and neighbouring stables, employing a considerable number of lady grooms.

36   WO107/26; WO107/27; Chapman, 1924, p.92-3; Wortley, pp.117-32.

Since its establishment on 22nd October 1914 it received 2,719 animals and issued 2,434. Mr. A Jones the principal purchaser in the West Midlands bought mainly cavalry horses for his Worcester depot before issue. This was a scattered organisation with stables hired in the cattle market and other parts of the city for some 200 horses; within a few miles radius neighbours gave free use of their stabling, for example, Lord Dudley of Witley Court and Lord Sandys at Ombersley. The personnel were civilian, with two yards in Worcester staffed by ladies. From its establishment on 12th August 1914, 6,396 animals were received and 6,060 issued. In Eastern Command, No.1 Circle, Kettering stables built by the Scottish Horse in 1913 were subsequently occupied by 57th and 58th Remount Squadrons in June 1915. This formed a depot close to Grantham for the supply of trained mules for machine gun companies mobilising there. The depot was then used for conditioning horses landed at Hull, the squadron commanders being the Masters of the local packs of hounds. From its establishment on the 30th June 1915, 18,833 animals were received and 17,036 issued. In Irish Command at Ballsbridge, Dublin, a depot for 800 animals was located in the Royal Dublin Society show-yard; a civilian depot receiving chargers and other horses purchased in Ireland for issue to units, or sent to English depots. From 4th August 1914, 38,912 animals were received and 37,038 issued.

The personnel of depots frequently changed, owing to the necessity of releasing fit men from remount squadrons. Military depots were augmented by local civilian organisations employing labour unfit for military service. The attraction of better paid civilian work, increased by the shortage of men and consequent rise of wages, made it very difficult to maintain the personnel of non-military depots. The 40% annual turnover of men from remount squadrons during 1916-1918 was continuous. They were replaced by men with fewer skills, inferior physique, and generally without previous knowledge of horses; making the work of training and conditioning animals and maintaining the rate of output increasingly difficult. Remount depot personnel increased from a peacetime establishment of 352 officers and other ranks, to 21,00 in 1917, and to 18,766 by 30th November 1918. During the six months from 1st January to 30th June 1918, 2,534 men of all ranks were transferred to other units; 816 were released, for example, for coal mining and shipbuilding.[37]

To meet fluctuations in demand, sick animals, capable of travelling, were moved around hospitals within the various Commands, as were AVC subdivisions, each with personnel for looking after 250 sick animals. Adequate veterinary accommodation in Southern Command was not met until halfway through the war, when the AVC took over Pitt Corner Camp, Winchester, forming No.6 Reserve Hospital accommodating more than 3,000 horses, initially used mainly for the sick and injured. Capt. Head, who had served as the AVC officer with the 6th Inniskilling Dragoons during the 1899-1902 War was recalled for service in 1914 and embarked for France, returning to England as

37   Chapman, 1924, p.92; WO107/26; Hume, 1980, p.42; MacMunn, 1930, p.116; *Statistics*, p.862.

a major in command of Pitt Corner; retiring again in 1919 as a Lt.-Col. He would serve again in the 1939-1945 War, organising the local Home Guard in Helston, Cornwall until 1943. Woolwich hospital expanded to take 1,000 evacuees from mobilisation and training units and the large remount depot. In Aldershot Command existing veterinary accommodation was expanded with two reserve hospitals each for 1,000 sick animals taken from mobilising divisions, remount depots and for the mobilisation and training of most veterinary units being formed for service overseas. Towards the end of the war substantial reductions were made in the Commands' facilities.[38]

The winter of 1915 saw a temporary easing of the pressure on veterinary work in Southern Command when New Army divisions moved to Northern and Eastern Commands for training. However, considerable veterinary accommodation was then required in Northern Command, notably at York, Doncaster, Catterick Bridge and Newcastle upon Tyne. For a short period, heavy demands from mobilising units were placed on facilities in Irish Command; additional facilities were opened at the No.5 Reserve Hospital, Curragh, for 500 sick animals, with other centres in Dublin and elsewhere. Western Command felt the pressures for veterinary facilities from mobilising Welsh Division units and also from purchasing by the Remount Department. Thereafter, the demand came from sick animals evacuated from Ormskirk remount depot and smaller depots in North West England. No.7 Reserve Hospital at Ormskirk, for 1,000 animals was considerably expanded. Scottish Command facilities were met by the Lowland Divisional hospital at Stirling and other temporary centres as required.[39]

Major Head, AVC, OC No6 (Res.) Section AVC, Pitt Corner Camp, Winchester, seated in the middle, with the Sergeants' Mess, August, 1917. (John Head)

38   Blenkinsop and Rainey, pp.7-8; Head collection, with thanks also to Brian Hill.
39   Ibid., pp.6-9; *VR*, 1916, 30th September, p.140, description of a southern veterinary hospital.

9

The Western Front 1915-18

Concerning the war I say nothing ... the only thing that wrings my heart and soul is the thought of the horses ... oh! my beloved animals ... the men ... and armies can go to hell but my horses: I walk round and round this room cursing God for allowing dumb brutes to be tortured ... let him kill his human beings but ... how can he? Oh my horses.[1]

Christmas 1914 did not see the end of hostilities; it was not to be a short war. With the prospect of a lengthy conflict, detailed planning was required to meet an increasing demand for animals, particularly for transport purposes; with additional burdens being placed on the horse services in supplying and caring for remounts to the American Expeditionary Force and other allies. The major offensives took their toll of animals, as did the constant routine transport work, in all weathers and conditions, and with accommodation and fodder not always of the required quality, or quantity, to keep hard working animals in good condition.

Winter of 1915-16

With insufficient hard standings and shelter the winter of 1914-15 had been hard for many animals. Planning to avoid similar experiences during the winter of 1915-16 was done early, including discussions for the withdrawal of horses from their billets and the front lines. Gen. Cowans (QMG, WO) informed Lt-Gen. Maxwell (QMG, BEF) he was to consult with Garratt (Director of Remounts, BEF) and Moore (Director AVC, BEF), and arrange for all existing billets and shelters to be used, with two alternatives possible to provide for the remaining animals. Firstly, horses were to be stood in the open on permanent standings to prevent wastage from gangrene and other sceptic infections of the lower parts of the limbs; the inevitable result of standing continuously in the deep mud of highly fertilised soil. Standings could be made from bricks or railway sleepers, the sides sheltered from prevailing winds by

---

1   Letter from Elgar to his friend Schuster, 25th August 1914.

Tented veterinary hospital, France. (Army Medical Services Museum)

forests, plantations or temporary screens. Secondly, to provide temporary overhead shelters using, for example, the sealed pattern corrugated iron sections cost of about £3 per horse), or tents, as used by the French, (which had the advantage of being movable when the original site became foul and the ground needed cleaning). For economy, overhead shelters without standings were the cheapest option and therefore considered preferable; or sometimes a combination of the two were used. Cowans recognised that with each horse, costing an average of £50, and the world's supply rapidly diminishing, it was economic sense to make horses as comfortable as possible during the winter.[2]

Experience had shown the four essentials for keeping horses in the best condition during the winters of Northern France was, shelter from rain, dry hard standings, dry hard approaches to the shelter and watering places, and hard, dry standings around water troughs. Some troughs were placed by roads with firm surfaces. Watering by bucket was forbidden except, on the road, owing to the uncertainty of knowing how much a horse had drunk, as a shortage of water was very damaging to a horse. In hot weather and hard work a horse required 20-25 gallons of water a day.

Preparations for the winter did not stop the suffering for those animals continually involved in transport and supply work. Animals had to be nursed through a second severe winter of appalling ground conditions, with heavy losses. Many spent the winter in the open, cold and wet, with mud attacking their hoofs. Labour and materials were lacking for the building of new stable accommodation, less than 1% of animals could

2   WO107/15, 14th July 1915; Fox, 1920, p.7.

be housed in existing stables. Standings were normally made of bricks, as the Army requisitioned all available brickyards in occupied areas, with shell ruined buildings providing another source, but rubble brick was of no use for standings as the bricks had to be properly set. It did not help that many of the men in mounted units were inexperienced in horse-management. There were some positive comments about how the horses looked in the early Spring of 1916 although this cannot have been true for many animals. Stewart, for example, wrote that during this period the 12th Lancers took the opportunity to fatten up their horses after the bad conditions of the winter.[3]

Cavalry and their horses

When financial savings were required, cutbacks in expenditure on horses was a frequent target especially in relation to the cost of cavalry horses. In November 1915, the Army Council considered the horse had played an unexpectedly small part in the war and questioned whether all possible savings had been made, as did Henry Asquith (Prime Minister, 1908-1916) commenting on the need for stringent controls over expenditure. If Asquith and the Council were in any way conversant with the use of horses during the war then this comment can only have been aimed at cavalry and not transport horses.[4] Cowans thought nothing was to be gained by keeping horses at home rather than abroad, nor could rations be reduced without grave risks as cavalry horses had to be kept absolutely fit in case an opportunity presented itself for a substantial advance, for example, after the fighting at Loos (October, 1915). He proposed, ironically, when motor transport was being more heavily used and had replaced horses for a number of tasks, that horses kept in the reserve parks could be put to daily use to save petrol and wear and tear on mechanical transport. Change was taking place. At Neuve Chapelle (10th-12th March) a battery of 9.2inch, howitzers drawn by Holt caterpillar tractors, marked the first all mechanised battery of guns.[5]

It is not appropriate in this work to dwell on the role of the Cavalry but that of its horses to perform the tasks required of them. The Cavalry's inaction, or inability to fulfil expectations in their offensive role should not remain a matter of ill-informed and heated debate given the more recent works of Badsey and Kenyon. These provide a radical re-evaluation of the role of the cavalry during the war, convincingly demolishing the myths around cavalry being unable to operate on a modern battlefield due to machine guns, and their horses incapable of negotiating trench systems, shell holes and barbed wire; and the disappointing offensive capability of tanks which left cavalry as the decisive offensive arm of exploitation in the victory of 1918. Badsey, more than Kenyon, links the importance of the actual horse to the Cavalry's ability to perform

3   Fox, 1920, pp.6-7; Stewart, 1950, p.276; Kirk, January 1916 (IWM).
4   WO163/21, Army Council, Minutes of Proceedings, 27th November 1915, 'Reduction in Military Expenditure', (79/8388), p.2, 'Horses'.
5   Farndale, 1986, pp.87, 135; WO163/21, 27th November 1915.

successfully the tasks required of it and of their horses central role in doing so. We now have a much clearer, and more accurate picture of the fundamental misunderstanding of the roles of cavalry and their horses in the war.[6]

Cavalry were most uneconomical troops in trench warfare since at least a quarter of the men were occupied caring for the horses and therefore not available for the firing line. Horses caused congestion on the roads to a level not often appreciated or even considered; these drawbacks were not, initially, experienced with motor transport. Whilst employed in the line troopers were not available for mounted training. Their horses generally lost condition through a lack of attention and exercise as there were insufficient men to look after them. They were then inefficient if called upon to immediately perform their traditional tasks. Gen. Allenby, for example, was always reluctant to keep his mounted troops (dismounted) in the trenches. Indifferent forage and constant exposure to cold was nearly as serious when units were at rest as when they were in the front line. Frequent cavalry movements from one part of the line to another were hard on the horses, before enemy action took its toll. Some of the marches in winter, on roads covered with mud and ice, or blocked with other troops, told severely on their condition.[7]

Three riders in the rain, France. Notice the mud and rain but spare a thought for how these conditions affected the horses. (Army Medical Services Museum)

6   Badsey, 1996, and 2008, Chapter 6; Kenyon, 2011; Crutwell, 1934, p.268; Home, 1985, p.157.
7   Stewart, 1950 p.287; Tylden, 1965, p.38; Preston, 1921, pp.155-6.

The British cavalry did its work well during the retreat from Mons, was disappointing in the advance to the Aisne and invaluable (dismounted) at First Ypres. It did not then spend the rest of the war inactive only to be used in dismounted operations, but developed both technically and operationally. Examples include, the introduction of "cavalry tracks" and mobile trench bridging teams and equipment so that mounted troops could operate in the front line areas; the introduction of the Machine Gun Corps (Cavalry) provided additional firepower; combined operations with infantry, tanks and armoured cars; and also changes in Command and control structures enabling greater flexibility and impact of operations. Any poor showing of the Cavalry can be related to the ineffective use by the staff in charge, as at Loos 1915 where they were held too far back. Crucially, cavalry was also dependent on the condition and ability of the horses to perform when required. Crutchley, with the 3rd Machine Gun Squadron (Cavalry), wrote, "we often knew that a stunt was coming by the massing of lines of tethered horses in the back area".[8] The ominous phenomena occurred every year, when a cavalry division was being assembled to exploit a hoped for breakthrough. Few such opportunities for exploitation were offered during 1916 and failure of those that were can be seen as a failure by higher command and ineffective control of available units.[9] The cavalry action at High Wood on 14th July 1916, involving the 7th Dragoon Guards and 20th Deccan Horse with machine guns and RHA artillery support, was a tactical success. This action highlights how smaller scale operations using mobile troops with adequate support in firepower would achieve results on the battlefields of 1918.

Historians have for too long dwelt on the horse losses and the perceived poor the showing of the actual cavalry units during 1916 and 1917. In 1917 the Battle of Arras highlighted the charge of the British 6th and 8th Brigades through driving snow at Monchy forcing them to dismount. The planned for breakthrough at Cambrai, 20th November 1917 raised expectations that the massed cavalry would exploit the situation; this failed to happen once again. Many of the failures to achieve objectives can see in poor command and control structures, poor communication and horses unfit to perform tasks required of them.

Commanders apparently gave little thought, when planning offensives, to the fact that if horses were of a poor quality, inadequately fed and not in hard condition, they would not perform as expected. This basic lack of understanding was probably a major cause of the Cavalry's poor showing at times in 1917 and 1918. During the April 1917 offensive, the roads and weather were so bad, that the horses suffered heavily from being in the open. After months of static warfare tasks they were required to perform were unbelievably strenuous. Again, any failure of the cavalry during 1916-1917 should be seen against the often unrealistic expectations and poor planning of the High Command, and horses not in condition for mobile warfare. In March 1918 the Germans produced no cavalry for their great offensive, if they had, the British retreat

8   Crutchley, 1918, p.46.
9   Kenyon, pp.62-69; Crutwell, 1934, p.407.

might have been a rout. During April 1918, the British cavalry were used dismounted and as a reserve to protect the juncture between the two Armies (two divisions had just been dismounted), used as 'putty' to fill cracks, their mobility proving as valuable as at First Ypres in 1914.[10] Badsey wrote, the Battle of Amiens, 8th August 1918, proved that by using the right tactical doctrine and staffwork horsed cavalry could be successfully integrated into the industrialised all-arms battles of the 20th century. Ironically, by the final offensives of 1918 there were too few cavalry available.[11]

Questions continued to be raised around issues of cost and supply to a large cavalry force consuming immense quantities of fodder. Capt. Grimshaw (Indian Cavalry) commented on the absurd irony of the cavalry requiring more motor transport to provide fodder, when the same transport could move the men any distance in one third of the time taken on their horses.[12] In reality cavalry horses consumed only a very small amount of fodder shipped to the theatres of war. It was the everyday work horse of the infantry, ASC and artillery, that kept the war effort moving that consumed the greater quantity. Plans were drawn up for withdrawing, or separating cavalry from their horses along with discussions about breaking up the Cavalry Corps. On 4th March 1916, Lt-Col. Yardley (DADR, GHQ Troops and British Cavalry, March to May, 1916) was notified that for administrative purposes cavalry divisions and Signals would come under the orders of Armies and GHQ to which they were attached. Each of the four Armies was to have a cavalry division, with one at GHQ as a Reserve. At midnight on 5th March 1916, the Cavalry Corps ceased to exist for administrative purposes, until reinstated in September 1916. On the 12th March, cavalry divisions were requested by the Director of Remounts to make arrangements for a provisional system of supplying remounts on their attachment to Armies and GHQ. All remained strongly in favour of the existing system of remount supply.[13]

Shortage of Horses 1916

March appears to have been a difficult month for supplying cavalry remounts. The 4th Cavalry Brigade was informed that no remounts were available to replace any castings and the DADR reported that cavalry divisions had not received any remounts since the previous month, owing to shipments not arriving from England. Divisions were notified not to evacuate any horses that could be used for training personnel. Stock in hand had been used to supply the Canadian Cavalry Brigade (formed as a mounted brigade in the UK in 1915 but sent to France without horses and were remounted in the UK, 1916) and the extra horses required on the formation, in March 1916, of

---

10 Home, 1985, p.268, Feb/March, 12th April 1918; Farndale, 1986, p.164; for cavalry performance being disappointing see Terraine, 1980, p.165; VR 1917, Vol.XXIX, 14th April, p.432.
11 Badsey, 2008, p.297.
12 Grimshaw, 1986, pp.79-80, June and August 1915; Home, 1985, p79, 11th August 1915.
13 WO95/7, Yardley; Home 1985, p.101, 124.

Machine Gun Squadrons (Cavalry) – (MGSC). The Machine Gun Corps was authorised by Army Order 414, December 1915. Prior to this many regular infantry and cavalry divisions had formed ad hoc brigade machine gun companies and squadrons from existing battalion or regiment machine gun sections. For the cavalry this necessitated an extra 71 riding (R1) and 42 pack horses for each brigade, with a surplus of 18 light draught horses, as each MGS(C) consisted of 299 horses. With 15 cavalry squadrons in France in December 1916 this amounted to 4,485 horses. Each cavalry brigade had one MGS(C), with three in a cavalry division. The wartime establishment of a MGS(C) was amended several times during the war; on 22 June 1916 it was a headquarters and six sections of two guns each:

	RH	Draught	Pack horses/mules	Bicycles	Total
HQ	16	6	–	3	22
Attached	–	–	–	3	–
6 sections	168	72	42	6	282
Totals	184	78	42	12	304

HQ personnel included: quartermaster sergeant, farrier sergeant, corporal shoeing-smith, six drivers 1st line transport, a saddler and saddle tree maker both with bicycles. 26 squadrons in 1918, in all theatres, totalled about 7904 animals.[14]

Discussions continued into 1916 about the cost and efficient use of the available, but growing shortage of horses. In May 1916, the Army Council was informed of a War Committee recommendation that an independent investigation be made into the number of horses and mules required for the military forces in France and the UK. The Council pointed out that recent demands had largely been for replacing wastage and not for additional new supply. Few horses had been purchased for some months, but a monthly provision of 10,000 horses was required for the next six months to meet wastage. Certain measures of reorganisation had been carried out and the establishment of horses in the Army had been reduced by 43,450. One measure was to substitute bicycles for horses, for example army chaplains amongst others.[15] Haig was asked to reduce the cavalry and to make further economies on shipping tonnage. As keeping one horse in France cost double keeping one in England, a temporary reduction could make savings. Haig replied that although cavalry could not be used tactically, or strategically, under the existing conditions of trench warfare, it would be a

14 WO95/70, Yardley, 1st March 1916; I am indebted to Robert Alexander of the Machine Gun Corps Association for help on the establishment of the MGC(C).

15 WO163/21, Army Council Minutes, meeting, 22nd May 1916, 'Proposal of the War Committee for Investigation into the Number of Horses and Mules Required for France', (121/France/74); and appendices re Haig CAB22/3, 17-24th May 1916, ref. proposed addition of 60,000 horses and mules for the BEF and problems of shipping.

serious error to conclude that large bodies of mounted troops would not be required during subsequent developments. As cavalry were the only arm that could exploit a successful breakthrough it would be unpardonable to deprive the Army of the only means of achieving this result; a view in which the CIGS concurred.[16]

A further suggestion was that the size of divisional columns should be reduced and baggage sections of divisional trains abolished and substituted by Corps of mechanical baggage columns. The lorries of an ammunition park could normally deliver ammunition directly to brigade ammunition columns, with small horsed divisional ammunition columns being retained for use when this procedure was not practicable. In addition, a pool of officers' chargers in each headquarters unit would be substituted for the existing system of allotting a definite number of riding horses for each mounted officer. Haig replied that the General Staff was working on the reduction of divisional ammunition columns, that the substitution of mechanical baggage columns for the baggage sections of divisional trains was not considered practicable and that the system of pooling officers' chargers had been tried and found unsatisfactory. The number of chargers had been drastically reduced by Field Marshall French when C-in-C of the BEF, and Haig concurred with his decision that the present number allowed was the very minimum. A reorganisation of divisional ammunition columns was completed by 2nd June, with all divisions then in France placed on these new establishments.[17]

The recommendation of the War Committee on the reduction of horses was referred to Haig's attention (semi-officially). He replied to the CIGS that an investigation of the nature proposed was objectionable, as it would impair the confidence and sense of responsibility essential to good and economical administration. Accurate returns were submitted on the actual number of horses with units, in remount depots and hospitals, as was information on the care of horses and administrative arrangements and he and his staff constantly studied every possible economy. Despite very strongly worded correspondence between the Army Council and War Committee of the Cabinet the enquiry into the use of all horses employed in the Army proceeded. In August, Birkbeck produced a statement giving the position of remount supply (see below).[18]

The assets were calculated on a monthly shipping programme from America of 12,000 animals. The normal shipping programme being 8,000 or fewer. The increased need was foreseen in April when the Admiralty was asked to arrange for the monthly shipment of 12,000. However, the War Committee had cut back on the allocation of shipping and the Admiralty had arranged a shipping programme for May of 1,839, for June 7,191, for July, 9,684 and August 4,747. The QMG drew attention to Birkbeck's statement and the serious shortage in establishments at the front, as the demands in

---

16   WO107/16, 24th August 1917; WO163/21 Army Council meetings, 25th January, 22nd May and 2nd August 1916; Singleton, 1993, p.193.
17   WO95/69, 2nd June 1916.
18   WO163/21, Army Council Minutes, 25th May 1916; proposal of War Committee for an investigation into the number of horses and mules required in France (121/France/74).

	Assets	*Liabilities*	
Ready for issue:			
September	10,000	Pressing demands to complete establishment of new units overseas and home formations.	30,000
October	14,000	Further possible demands not hitherto provided for.	40,000
November	16,000		
December	16,000	Normal wastage for 4 months.	28,000
Totals	56,000		98,000

May had not been met due to opposition from the War committee. The Admiralty was asked to provide shipping for 10,000 horses in September and 12,000 per month afterwards. Although the September programme was being met, assurances were required that this would also apply to the planned increased rate and any additional numbers purchased in America, in excess of 12,000 monthly. Allowing for normal wastage and with increased shipments, the urgent demands in the UK for completion of unit and formation establishments, were to be met by the end of December. The Admiralty, after an approach from the Army Council, agreed to provide the necessary shipping for the transport of remounts from America.[19] The Council asked the QMG, Haig and representatives of the Director of Staff-Duties to enquire and report on whether, at least during the winter, reductions could be made in the establishment of horses maintained in France. The question of shipping remounts directly to France was to be reopened.[20] By August 1917 it appears the shortage of riding horses at least, had been relieved, as Maxwell (QMG, BEF) proposed to Cowans that two riding horses be allowed to each corps and division (as provided in wartime establishments) and reissued in exchange for cycles. Each divisional commander should also, if he considered it necessary, be allowed to draw on loan, four additional cobs and sets of saddlery for use of his chaplains.[21]

The Remount Department faced simultaneously coping with a shortage of horses and cutbacks in personnel with the transfer of category 'A' and 'B' men. Correspondence between the WO and BEF provides a glimpse of the frustrations that existed over

---

19   WO163/21 (116/Gen. No/6367), Army Council Minutes, 'The Remount Situation', Précis 835 (5), forming the subject of correspondence with the Admiralty from whom a communication was received while the Council was considering Précis 835, to the effect that the necessary tonnage would be forthcoming.

20   WO163/21, Army Council Minutes, 20th November 1916, 'The Reduction of the Establishment of Horses', (121/France/74). The Under Sec. of State, QMG and Finance Member with the Director Remounts were to consult the Admiralty on the subject.

21   WO107/16, 24th August 1917.

issues of personnel and animals. Cowans wrote to Lt-Gen. Clayton (IGC, BEF) about Birkbeck's idea for cutting the 'remount squadron' from three, to two officers and commenting that 'other similar things might be looked into.'[22] Clayton replied that he did not know why attacks were continually made about the number of people employed on lines of communication. A remount squadron was supposed to look after 500 horses, with one officer continually away from the depot on convoy duty to the front. This left only two officers for 500 horses, and one of these might occasionally be sick, leaving only one for supervision. He considered the results obtained with regard to horses "little short of marvellous". Of the horses admitted to hospitals since the beginning of the campaign about 84% had been returned to the ranks; only 4.5% had died, 7% destroyed and 4.5% cast and sold. These results, when compared with the enormous wastage of horseflesh during the 1899-1902 campaign, would he believed, make people open their eyes. The original number of category 'A' remount personnel to be replaced was 2,892, reduced by medical examination to 2,000. 1,800 veterinary personnel were to be replaced and 378 ASC horse transport drivers. By 12th October, 1916 all category 'A' remount personnel had been replaced by 'B' men from the UK and replacement veterinary and horse transport drivers was completed.[23]

For Lt-Col. Yardley DADR (GHQ Troops and British Cavalry) the daily routine of remount work continued. This included detraining remounts, inspection of horses going to wrong units, managing complaints about the unsuitability of animals or animals not arriving at their destinations, managing transfers and dealing with injuries sustained in transit, checking for castings and routine office work including remount demands and returns.[24] Yardley's area covered about 70 miles of front with many scattered units and over 3,000 horses. It is perhaps ironic that having to cover a vast distance to provide mobility for the Army, DADRs should have faced personal transport difficulties. Garratt wrote to the QMG that it was not possible for DDRs to carry out their duties in an army of any size without a motor car.[25] In the Fourth Army, with some 17 divisions, the DDR only had use of a car every other day as it was shared alternately with the DDAVC. This was insufficient to carry out duties. The QMG would not however, sanction the use of a motor car, when required, by the DDR.

The Somme Offensive (1st July-18th November), 1916

The stationary character of warfare placed a different strain upon the QMG's department. The Somme offensive called for a change in the transportation system. In November a Director General of Transport was appointed, whose brief did not cover

---

22   WO107/15, January 1916, Clayton's reply 7th January 1916.
23   WO107/16, 28th September 1916, from Cowans to Haig; 2nd October 1916, Cowans to Clayton and 12th October; WO95/69, June 1916.
24   WO95/70, Confidential War Diary.
25   WO95/69, 21st and 23rd June 1916.

the Directorate of Horse and Motor Transport.[26] In April, 1916 the daily provision considered necessary for the build up to the Somme offensive was for the railway to provide two trains, moving 720 remounts daily for the Third and Fourth Armies. Fourth Army and the GHQ Reserve for example, had a strength of some 100,000 horses.[27]

Remounts and the AVC had not only to provide for British units, such as the Naval Division, but also for Australian and New Zealand forces arriving in France. Garratt's diary enables one to build up a picture of some of the demands for horsing these units, which were taken from existing units in France and the UK.[28] The 5th Australian Division, due to arrive from Egypt, 1st June, was to bring 450 heavy draught horses with them, and the 4th Australian Division (New Zealand) 449 horses. Horsing the 4th Division began on the 13th June and was completed on the 24th. The concentration of divisions in the Fourth Army area made it necessary to rail horses and mules from Calais and Boulogne to Abbeville, as depots in the southern section were not capable of supplying wastage as well as horsing the divisions arriving from Egypt. A request was made for the loan of horses for training Australian and New Zealand artillery reinforcements at Etaples base camp and for the WO to send light draught animals to Havre as soon as possible, so as not to interfere with sending up the artillery of the 5th Australian and 11th Divisions to concentration areas.[29] Horsing the 11th Division, 328 heavy and 35 light horses, was to be completed as soon as possible and heavy draught animals were to be withdrawn from First Army units if necessary. The horses of the 5th Australian 1st Line Transport were reported to have been an average lot, but the mules were very good. Auxiliary Horse Transport Companies at Rouen requested 457 light draught and 27 heavy draught animals, but this request could not be met owing to a shortage of personnel. Such was the pressure for animals that GHQ ordered the demobilisation of the Lifeguard Reserve Squadron (cavalry) and their horses handed to Remounts at Rouen. (See Map 5 British Remount Depots (BEF), 1918 and Map 6 British Veterinary Establishments (BEF), 1918).

During the July Somme offensive, Remounts continued the routine work of keeping the whole BEF mobile as well as meeting the requirements of units involved in the offensive. The GOC Reserve Army requested a reserve of 3,000 cavalry in case of forward movement and the WO reported that 1,500 R1 and 500 R2 horses could be sent, if ships were available, by the end of the week of 3rd July. Requests were made for the WO to forward 1,000 R1 and 250 R2 horses to Rouen, and then 500 cavalry and 250 R2s in addition to all other demands to Havre. The Indian Lahore divisional artillery (attached to 3rd Cavalry Brigade) demanded over 100 horses to replace those evacuated for mange. On the 16th July Garratt records that mounted cavalry were reported to have been used for the first time since trench warfare began, at High Wood, and 143 horses were required to replace casualties, of which 28 were light draught the rest riding horses, including 54 for the British and 61 for the Indian cavalry. Remounts were sent from Rouen on the 16th.

Owing to a scarcity of heavy draught horses the original establishment of 363 for divisional trains, was amended, Remounts receiving a copy of the amended Establishment on July 9th. The very large remount issues were due to horsing the 5th Australian and 11th Divisions. As the number of available, fit, heavy draught horses was very small, Garratt wrote on 13th July, to the QMG about the necessity of withdrawing them from some units to create a reserve to replace casualties in heavy batteries. Instructions were issued to all Armies to substitute light for heavy draught in certain divisional train vehicles, releasing 35 heavy draught in each train. Casualties amongst horses of French batteries with British divisions were to be replaced by British Remounts and the French Remount Mission was requested to reciprocate. If these demands were not enough, enquiries were made for Remounts to provide sound, workable horses for forest work.[30]

The work of caring for, and replacing the sick animals continued, the number of horses returned to remount depots from hospitals rose to about 500 per week by 6th July. Discussions took place between Garratt and Moore about preventing skin diseases in remount depots after suspicious cases had been received. For example, a case of glanders was reported amongst transport horses for issue to the 4th Australian Division, with about 100 being segregated; cases of mange were reported amongst remounts sent to the front and colic was reported at Boulogne. The DDVS agreed to make a close inspection of all depots and the cleansing and disinfecting of trucks. A circular was sent to all remount depots on the importance of disinfecting equipment. The work of inspecting and improving depots continued, along with attempts to reduce casualties during transportation. Sawdust was required for bedding at Calais; drainage pipes required altering at the Boulogne depot stables to stop flooding; sand and cinders were required for bedding at the stables in Dieppe; bracken was cut for bedding at Sergueux and the standings at Abbeville depot improved by ramming chalk and ashes into the floor (see Map 4). On 30th July a circular was sent to all remount depots stating that owing to the heat, strict attention was to be given to watering animals proceeding by train, and to the ventilation of railway trucks.[31]

The figures opposite, suggest the continued build up of animals through June, heavy casualties in July, lessening in August, with 11,717 remounts received from overseas in July to replace casualties, dropping to 5,124 in August:[32]

---

30   WO95/69, QMG, 17th July and 12th July.

31   *VR*, 1917, 15th December, p.248, ref. AVC personnel on the Somme front setting up the 'Somme Veterinary Medical Association'.

32   WO95/69, June-August 1916.

Remount issues to the front up to 31st May 1916:

Horses	170,144
Mules	24,359
Total	194,503

Remount issues to the front for June, July and August:

June	15,053
July	19,655
August	12,792
Total	47,500

Total issues to Front to 31st August 1916:	242,003

Total received from overseas to end June 1916:	134,536
July	11,717
August	5,124

Total receipts from overseas to 13th August 1916	151,377

Issues to 30th June (difference of 155 to June above)	209,401
Total	229,056

The Somme battlefield was an area thick with animals. A census taken at the cross-roads in Fricourt village (on the little road in from Bray to the south of the village, which became one of the main arteries of the battle) for July 21st-22nd, records the passing, in just less than 24 hours, of 6,162 horse drawn vehicles and 5,404 single horses; 2,746 motor vehicles and 1,043 pedal cycles.[33] One does not know how representative this 24 hours was, but it does give an indication of the number of animals in one sector of the battle area. Casualties were sustained in rear areas from enemy aircraft, Brig-Gen. Home (General Staff Cavalry Corps), for example, records German aircraft over their camp at night with one bomb killing 60 horses. In some cases gun teams were moved too far forward and suffered appalling casualties in horses.[34]

Home wrote that the cavalry saw little mounted action in the Somme offensive. In relation to preparations for Gough's Fifth Army offensive in November, he stated that if a great and unexpected success were not gained the cavalry would be withdrawn to winter areas as the horses had begun to "feel it a good deal" and needed to be looked after if they were to be of use later on. When inspecting the 2nd Cavalry Division on the 4th November, just south of Meaulte, he states, they were in the open and had "a pretty bad time as regards weather and a few good casualties" (presumably from horses

33   Middlebrook, 1991, p.142.
34   Home, 1985, p.122; Farndale, 1986, p.152.

going lame), owing to the mud pulling off shoes. In September, at Morlancourt, horses found themselves bogged in a perpetual sea of ooze and at the height of the battle mud made it necessary to take shells up on mule and horseback, with requests from the front for carriers to hold shells on the animals; for which a scheme was devised of wooden holders connected by chains slung over pack animals backs.[35]

Offensives 1917

The severe winter yet again took its toll on cavalry horses, but more especially on transport animals, the effects of which were to be felt during the spring offensives of 1917. In ASC columns numerous cases of exhaustion were observed in horses. Animals were subjected to a long period, for example six months, of hard work and insufficient food, and especially hard hit were horses which had been in bad condition from the time of requisition, or had fallen away in consequence of gastro-enteric disorder. Most of the animals employed were between 8 to 12 years old, only exceptionally 4 to 8.[36] In December 1916, horses of the 12th Lancers gradually lost condition as the daily ration of oats fell to 7lb, a scale on which they found it hard to endure either long exercise, or extremely cold temperatures. Their horses were well housed in winter quarters, but the circumstances were reminiscent of 1899-1902, with ration scales, enforced by an ignorant High Command. Despite some good horsemastership, troopers were forced to watch the deterioration in circumstances over which they had no control.[37]

An expansion in artillery, for example, put a great strain on horsemastership which began to decline in 1916 and by December had probably reached its lowest ebb. The bad winter caused a deterioration in the condition of their animals raising serious alarm at a higher level as commanders began to realise the importance of horses to their units. This threatened not only infantry transport but also the efficiency of the artillery. Arbuthnot wrote that "screeds on how to look after horses (were) coming from every direction." Generally, animals had a poor time between the summer of 1916 and 1917 and were about as badly treated as they could be, "ending the worst period in the history of our horsemastership". There was a lack of experience, understanding and assistance on the part of higher authorities. Poor horsemanship alone was not the only cause of this suffering. The heavy, continuous work on the Somme during summer/autumn 1916 in horrendous conditions left them run down before the start of winter. The general lack of care and attention, together with poor grooming seriously affected their health and digestion. Overcrowding in the horse lines and a shortage of both officers and men in the artillery batteries skilled in the art of grooming did nothing to aid recovery. Lice and various forms of skin disease, including sarcoptic mange spread rapidly. The King's Troop RHA for example, still cut short the manes of gun horses,

---

35   Home, 1985, p.125, for 31st October; Stewart, 1950, p.280; Marcosson, 1918, p.28.
36   *VR*, 1916, Vol.XXVIII, 3rd June, p.547.
37   Stewart, 1950, p.281.

originally as a prevention against infection from lice. In late winter, AVC opinion prevailed and all horses were 'clipped out', a measure which cost the lives of hundreds of horses and destroyed the condition of the remainder; in hindsight this was viewed as a universal mistake and at the time ignoring years of considered opinion.[38]

The only medicine that could really improve the constitution of horses that outlived the winter was young spring grass, and although the winter regime had failed hopelessly, horsemastership began to re-assert itself and the care of animals improved. The hard winter left transport animals not fully fit for the heavy work of campaigning. Their poor showing is recorded in the movement of guns and supplies into the battle area, forward of the railways, in preparations for the Arras offensive (beginning 9th April). The ditches beside the roads around Arras were full of dead horses and mules, even before the offensive began. The German withdrawal to the Hindenburg Line (25th February – 5th April 1917) brought about unexpected mobile action, placing a greater strain on overworked and underfed draught animals. The cavalry were in operation nearly every day with reconnaissance and other work. For artillery horses hauling the guns at speed on very soft going meant a number died of sheer fatigue. During the Battle of Bullecourt, 11th April (the first Australian attack on the Hindenburg Line, part of the larger British offensive of the Battle of Arras), German heavy artillery began systematically bombarding in depth to destroy the wagons and horses bringing up shells to the front. The strain on animals was terrible and horses moving ammunition were reported "as about done in". [39]

Although the Cavalry Division made no effective contribution to the capture of Vimy Ridge (9th April), they once again suffered heavily, being depleted not only by enemy shelling but also by the weather and inactivity. Several horses of the 12th Lancers, pegged down during a snowy, bitter night, died of exposure; the horses had gone 33 hours without being watered and over 100 were lost, dead and wounded. The week of 12th April saw appalling wet and cold weather conditions in which the poor state of already exhausted horses rapidly deteriorated.[40] Home writes of the 2nd Cavalry Division, 'bitter cold and heavy snow during the night, horses having a bad time owing to the lack of water, with the effect that within three days most of the horses were done in, and in a bad way'.[41] By mid April, the artillery were short of over 3,500 horses. The April offensive marked the end of a unique period of semi-open warfare with field batteries advancing with the infantry, but the price paid by the animals was high and resulted in greatly increased demands for remounts.

38 Arbuthnot, 1919, pp.281, 338-40, 341. My thanks to the King's Troop RHA for information on horsemastership practices.
39 Farndale, 1986, pp.163, 176-7, 167 Bde. RFA War Diary, in action on 2nd April; Mackey, in Purnell, Vol.5, p.2080; Holmes, p.210; Kirk (IWM); VR, 1917, Vol.XXIX, 5th May, p.469.
40 Stewart, 1950, pp.285-7; also Kenyon, pp.90-129.
41 Home, 1985, pp.138-9, 164,; see period 10-13th April 1917, also 29th April, p.140.

There is an interesting letter of complaint to Maxwell from Cowans (10th April), which possibly puts into perspective some of the strain and frustrations in supplying the normal requirements of the BEF and at the same time those of the April offensive. Cowans very strongly attacked, as the 'fault of the WO', the blame for any short-comings, or lack of provision in France. He was not aware, in nearly three years, of any actual deficit in authorised provision; there had not always been 22 days reserves of everything, but that figure was only a figure of speech and the BEF had never been actually short. Supply returns were received daily from Maxwell's Director, and whenever a shortage occurred for example, of oats, of which there had scarcely ever been a satisfactory reserve, it was generally a shipping problem. At that time Maxwell had ten days reserve of oats, and the WO, 40,000 tons in the UK bagged and waiting to be shipped, a situation well known to Maxwell's Supply Directorate. Cowans was constantly being informed that horses were short of rations and doing far more than an ordinary day's work, that they all looked starved and in poor condition. There were 37,000 animals in hospitals every week. Letters were received making the most extravagant statements about the shortage of horses, but when the Director of Remounts and remount officers of Armies were consulted a totally different statement was received. Although Cowans stated he was currently sending Maxwell more horses weekly than he actually received during the Somme fighting period and was, spending most of his day to day work on the wastage of horses in France and meeting Maxwell's demands, yet he then gets a telegram without details, with regard to the shortage of horses in France.[42]

The disasters of 1916 were repeated in the autumn of 1917 at the Third Battle of Ypres, or Passchendale (June – November), when once again extreme strain was placed on supply and artillery animals. There were greater demands for ammunition, more enemy shelling of roads and bombing of wagon lines. The Artillery lost many horses from air attacks when moving positions, thereby reducing their ability to support the infantry advance.[43] Arbuthnot believed that not enough justice was given to the Artillery at Ypres during the autumn of 1917 and the magnificent work of drivers and horses. Their experiences were appalling, as day and night the endless stream of animals went forward to gun positions laden with packs of ammunition, with shelling turning roads into a shambles.[44] Casualties from shelling and bombs during this period were pretty heavy, but the condition of survivors was good largely due to improved horsemastership and the men's experience of working with animals. Home inspected the 4th Cavalry Brigade during October and November, commenting that the horses looked fairly well, but "had not got much to go on and wanted more flesh if they were going to stand exposure and cold".[45] He states that the weather in November

---

42   WO107/16, 10th April 1917.
43   Farndale, 1985, pp.199, 213, 292; Misc. 846 (IWM).
44   Arbuthnot, 1919, p.340.
45   Home, 1985, p159, 19th October 1917 and 21st November, p.156.

was vile, horses were not getting water and so suffered a good deal and orders about clipping, based on inexpert advice, again began to threaten the wagon lines. A question in the House of Commons, 6th August, elicited a response that clipping would be regulated in the coming winter; only 'half-clipping' was eventually ordered.[46]

The figures below show the receipt of horses in France from overseas and issues to the front, from June to December 1917. The Issues were not all newly landed animals, but include those returned from hospitals and remount depots. The figures should be used with caution as the additions for each month do not always agree. For example, July issues, the addition totals 21,825, which is not the total given. The carried forward totals at the end of one month, for receipts and issues, invariably differ, for example, the total receipts for July total 53,447, but the total carried forward into August is 54,577. Over the course of a year these errors are compounded.[47]

		Horses	*Mules*	*Total*
Receipt of Animals into France from Overseas				
To end	May 1917	(187,256)	(45,435)	(232,691)
During	June 1917	10,534	5,102	15,636
	July	8,040	3,387	11,427
	August	3,354	1,043	4,397
	September	3,248	1,206	4,454
	October	4,961	2,224	7,185
	November	8,588	3,031	11,619
	December	9,687	3,833	13,520
Total		48,412	19,826	68,238
Issues to the Front				
To end	May 1917	(321,930)	(65,613)	(387,543)
During	June 1917	18,307	6,309	24,616
	July	17,322	4,503	21,835
	August	10,940	2,461	13,401
	September	11,104	1,939	13,043
	October	13,022	2,954	15,976
	November	14,938	3,493	18,431
	December	12,898	2,805	15,703
Total		98,531	24,464	123,005

46   *VR*, 1917, Vol.XXX, 11th August, p.67, ref. clipping.
47   WO95/70.

The pattern for receipts and issues correspond and show the build up for the Third Ypres offensive and heavy fighting in June. The numbers rise again in October and November to supply the new offensives, and reflect the replacement of heavy casualties, as remounts became available; reducing again in December with the close of the offensive.

The highest total of animals with the BEF reached 460,000, in June 1917, as did the highest losses. The largest shipment of horses in any week was 10,500 in 1917.[48] Dead wastage for the week ending 6th December increased by nearly 1,000 owing to battle casualties; wastage was 4,653, falling to 2,942 the following week (figures include all evacuations as well as dead wastage). Wastage, including evacuations to hospitals, was considerably larger in artillery units, as with every 100 remounts supplied about 70% were for artillery. When fighting was heavy this percentage was of course greater. Changes and reorganisation to establishments continued, with consequent effect on the demand and supply of animals. For example, in December, establishments for the Signal Service were revised with a reduction of 572 horses. The QMG advised that it had practically been agreed to reduce the number of infantry battalions in each brigade by one, calculations being made on a reduction of 140 battalions, including divisional ammunition columns and trains; releasing some 1,540 riding, 5,988 draught, 2,380 heavy draught and 980 pack animals.[49]

With all the pressures to meet requirements for the 1917 offensives in France and Flanders, demands were also made upon the Remount Department at the WO and BEF, to supply our Allies and other theatres of war. It is important to note that in addition to supplying remounts for the British Armies, in all theatres, and the Home Front, the British Remount Department supplied remounts to: Canadian contingents from January 1915, Australian and New Zealand (ANZAC) forces on their arrival in Europe, in 1916, the Belgian army from March 1916, American forces from 1918, the Portuguese and some French Units.

During December 1917, requests were made to supply 600 light draught animals to complete Portuguese divisions. The QMG informed Remounts that the Portuguese were not to receive any future issues until notified by the WO, but if it was necessary to clear the depot some mules might be issued. The Belgium Government requested an increase in their monthly supply of light draught from 300 to 900, but the QMG pointed out this was a very large increase and supply was by no means unlimited. 150 were handed over to the Belgian Remount Commission, but there is no record whether this was in addition to the 300 issued monthly by Remounts. 1,000 horses were withdrawn from the Cavalry Corps for Palestine. The DDR in Italy, was informed that no remounts could be forwarded, though some cavalry horses had gone to Italy from France. Three ships with over 3,000 animals, were notified as likely to sail from Marseilles to Egypt on about the 15th December, but none had gone by the 17th, causing congestion at Havre. On the 21st December, the WO made an urgent

48   Chapman, 1924, p.217.
49   WO95/70.

request for 500 heavy draught for Egypt in place of light draught, to be shipped at the end of the month if possible. On 23rd December, Remounts at Marseilles reported 700 riding horses had embarked for Egypt, the first ship since 1st December, with a further 300 heavy draught requested on the 29th. The figures below show horses supplied from France, to Egypt and Italy, from July 1917:[50]

Issues to Other Theatres from France, 1917

		Horses
To Egypt	July	650
	August	1,405
	September	663
	October	759
	November	1,333
	December	2,456
Total		7,266
To Italy	November	1,000
	December	1,266
Total		2,266

Personnel were also required. The Italian Expeditionary Force (IEF), for example, requested an additional remount squadron and on 14th December the WO informed No.3 Base Remount Depot to hold a squadron in readiness. On 17th December, No.33 Remount Squadron at Dieppe was detailed for Italy. It was suggested that horses going to Italy, should go via Marseilles with the IEF sending conducting parties from Genoa to Marseilles when they required a train load. On 25th December, No.35 Remount Squadron arrived at Havre, from Southampton, to replace No.33 entraining to Italy with 750 animals. Unfit Indian drivers (up to 700) were to be temporarily attached to Remounts at Marseilles for training in riding and stable duties, enabling the depot to handle at least 3,000 animals without an increase in British personnel. There were insufficient farriers for the increased number of animals passing through the depot and an additional 12 were requested.[51]

Horsing the American Expeditionary Force 1918

The major challenge facing Remounts and AVC during 1918 was horsing infantry and artillery divisions of the American Expeditionary Force (AEF). Attempts by

50   Ibid.
51   Ibid., December 1917.

Remounts to meet this new demand provide a detailed analysis of the horse situation and pressures on supply. In 1917 the US veterinary and remount services were no better than those of the British Army in the 1899-1902 War, based on a regimental system with the veterinary service attached to, and under the jurisdiction of, the remount service. An army veterinary corps was only established in 1916 and the Remount Service, as a real service, was formed during the War.[52] When the US declared war, 6th April 1917, no veterinary service existed to compare with the other major powers. When the HQ of Gen. J.J. Pershing's (C-in-C AEF, Europe) sailed for France in May 1917, it did not include any veterinary personnel and no plans existed for any such provision. These were developed independently by the AEF in Europe. In response to questions raised by the US Surgeon General about a lack of veterinary support Pershing replied, 24th September 1917, that he was organising advanced hospitals for 1,000 animals, and base hospitals for 500 animals (which did not appear until 1918). The US Third Cavalry upon arrival would be used exclusively in remount services to which veterinary hospitals would be attached. The British Remount and Veterinary services were to be the model for the AEF. The Americans considered the British AVC to be an efficient service, carefully and thoroughly planned, which had in operations during the war achieved most flattering and successful results.[53]

Initial approaches to Cowans to supply the AEF were not received favourably. He considered that as long as establishments in France remained the same he saw no prospect of giving the Americans any material assistance in horsing their artillery.[54] A forecast of the horse situation on 31st August 1917, in relation to horsing the Americans showed a deficit of demand over supply of 1,900:

Liabilities		Assets	
Deficit UK, 30th June 1918	10,000	Depots UK	28,500
France wastage July and Aug.	18,000	Due from USA to end of Aug.	20,000
Required in Reserve (UK, France, Egypt)	35,000	Purchases, UK	9,000
Egypt (due away now)	3,000	Reduction 60 pounder guns in France (if carried out)	9,000
Wastage UK (July and Aug) on some 60,000 animals	2,400	Balance: Deficit	1,900
	68,400		68,400

52 Armstrong, 1921, p.13.
53 Merillat and Campbell, 1935, pp.101, 103; Ford, 1927, pp.419, 430, 434.
54 WO107/16, 8th July 1917, to Sec. of State from Cowans, 'Horsing USA and British Position of Horses' (Lord Milner spoken to by Cowans re. horses and artillery); the table is attached to this letter.

The UK requirement included, completing the Third Cadre Division, making replacements in units at home that had been drawn upon to complete demands in France, and bringing other units up to establishment which were also affected by heavy demands from France. Egypt had absorbed surplus animals from the transfer of personnel to France and there was a probable deficit of some 12,000 animals at the beginning of December. Cowans considered the only solution was for the Americans to ship their own animals to France, of which they had a considerable number. "You will remember they were willing to sell us 29,000, the figure rose to 60,000, recently reduced to 10,000; this last reduction made it seem likely they actually intended to ship some of these animals".[55] Units in France and the UK had already been stripped to supply 18,000 animals for the Americans.

Lt-Col. V.C. Mather, Chief Remount Officer, First Army, AEF, stated that he was "suddenly made directly responsible by Pershing for our animal supply at the front. Not withstanding, knowing that the British Government was practically at the limit of its resources for artillery horses, it was with no doubt of response that I sounded the 'call of the blood' during these critical days. Cowans, Haig and Travers Clarke (QMG, BEF) all immediately acted and the two English Divisions at home were stripped of their horses for our benefit."[56] In March 1918 Garratt received the requirements for horsing American divisions if supplied by Remounts. A request that 2,000 light draught horses be provided, in addition to those already obtained from the transport of reduced battalions, was considered possible by the QMG, if done gradually. On the 21st March, the QMG ordered that no more horses for American divisions were to be ordered from the UK. They were only to receive surplus regimental transport held in reserve by divisions, or those from the reduction of infantry battalions. The first demand for riding horses was received in April, for the American 77nd Divisional HQ Staff. [57]

A document from the WO to the British Mission, AEF, states that the British front was rather short of artillery. It suggested that the artillery of the five American divisions attached to the British Army, the personnel of which had arrived in France and were thought to be in the French area receiving their equipment and training, should complete their training in the British area as soon as they were fully equipped. Also, the heavy artillery batteries due to receive equipment from the British, should carry out their training and receive equipment in the British area. The advantages of these suggestions were that the five divisions, attached to the British, would be ready to take their place in the line as fighting divisions complete with their artillery at an earlier date. Little was known about their state of training, whether they had received their full complement of guns and howitzers from the French, if all personnel had arrived from America and what the situation was regarding horses, tractors, lorries etc. The

55   WO107/16.
56   Chapman, 1924, p.214.
57   WO95/70, 5th and 7th March 1918.

Americans considered the quickest and most satisfactory procedure was for all artillery to be equipped in their own areas.[58]

Pershing was willing to transfer his artillery if the British could find the horses, in return for which he agreed a lengthy notice period for the withdrawal of complete divisions from the British front. The whole transaction and speedy entry of completed American divisions into the line depended on the supply of artillery horses; each divisional artillery brigade requiring 3,500. The Americans also preferred to equip the heavy artillery in their own areas, carrying out first practices where all facilities existed. Heavy batteries or regiments would be moved up to the British front under orders from the French Gen. Foch if urgently required. It was estimated that horses for the field artillery of two divisions could be available by 1st August with sufficient horses for the other three by mid September, provided the rate of shipment from the UK continued and wastage remained normal. This scheme presumed all divisional 6" howitzer regiments, trench mortar battalions and motor transport ammunition echelons were being equipped with motor transport; none of which could be provided in France. The Americans were being consulted about whether they could provide the motor vehicles.[59]

At the beginning of July a total of 120,000 horses were required for US troops in France, of which, by mid-August 80,000 should have been obtained from the French by requisition. Three divisional artillery brigades were to be horsed by the British, a total of about 11,000 horses, in addition to a supply of mostly mules from Spain. The total requirement for the troops already in France was at that stage unknown, and the large number of troops expected in the future were not provided for. Pershing appealed to Lord Milner (Secretary of State for War from 19th April, 1918), but was informed that no horses could be produced from England. Figures obtained by Wagstaff (Deputy Director Military Operations (DDMO), WO, located with the British Mission at the AEF, GHQ) from the Remount Department showed that very little could be supplied, although possibly by increasing the price, accepting an inferior type of animal, or moving to requisition, some 8,000 to 10,000 horses might be forthcoming in the UK. Wagstaff thought that even 10,000 horses procured immediately would be of great value to the Americans and requested notification from the WO whether this scheme was possible and what the conditions would be, "I write to you as an 'operations' matter and it needs some pushing from the Director

---

58   WO106/518, Secret Operations: From General Wagstaff, HQ, AEF France, to: DMO (WO), 15th July 1918. "I forwarded with my BM306 on 8th June to DSD a statement of American field and horse artillery. Also on 1st July a further statement on artillery was embodied in my monthly report to you. I forwarded a report on HA to DSD on 6th July."; WO106/518, "Consequent on withdrawal of DAN [?] and its artillery from the British zone."

59   WO106/518, Wagstaff, to WO, 15th July, a later document, 26th July, gives 2,805: Secret Operations, from GHQ France, to WO, 18th July 1918, GHQ France to WO, 17th July.

of Military Operations (DMO) to get it through"[60] The scheme was not acceptable as it involved impressment which would probably not have produced very satisfactory results. However, if it were possible to ship 3,000 animals a week to France 1,250 could have been available for American troops, if only 2,500 could be shipped then only 750 would be available. By the end of July, France was thought to have supplied some 6,250 horses, enough for two divisional artilleries; by mid August three were to be completed and five more by the end of September.

The British Mission with the AEF was informed that arrangements were being made to horse the five American divisions in the British sector, forwarding a statement of the horse situation showing a very large deficit of demand over supply, the supply being entirely dependent on continued purchases in America. The WO believed the supply of horses from England was not worth considering as it entailed a very large increase in petrol consumption, which was already causing anxiety, particularly if the foreshadowed expansion of tanks and aeroplanes materialised.[61] On the 3rd July the QMG authorised the issue of riding horses to the Corps HQ American Army, 25 riding horses for the officers of 2nd Corps, AEF, and four horses in addition for the Corps Commander and his personal staff. The anticipated November reduction in the number of British infantry divisions was not expected to make up the deficiency. The overall horse supply position was considered far from satisfactory but it was thought it could possibly be relieved by extending the use of mechanical transport. By 6th July the WO proposed not to take any more American Divisions, but instead to horse the artillery of five American divisions. The new establishment for their divisional transport required an additional 94 animals, creating a very large demand for heavy draught animals for 3 inch' guns for which the QMG suggested light draught of the heavy type would be equally suitable. All five divisions could be horsed in seven weeks using this substitute. The AEF requested a British veterinary and remount officer be attached to their headquarters (Services of Supply) so they could benefit from their experiences. Garratt agreed and Maj. Massey was seconded from Remounts. Cowans noted from a 'Progress Report' and letter from the British Military Attaché in Washington, showing "what Col. Aitken, AVC, had been able to accomplish in organising a veterinary service on modern lines for the US Army and as far as it goes it is most satisfactory".[62]

The AEF demands for horsing their forces by the British continued to change on a regular basis, presenting a confusing picture. The WO considered that after July no more than 2,000 animals weekly from the UK could be provided toward the 3,000 required by the AEF, causing a possible delay in horsing the American artillery by

---

60   WO106/518, Wagstaff to WO, 20th June, Wagstaff to WO, 20th July and (WO, 1332), Minute Sheet, 26th July 1918.
61   Ibid., 3rd August, Secret: WO to Wagstaff.
62   WO95/70, 9th July; Ford, 1927, p.430; WO107/16, letter to Travers Clarke from Cowans, 28th February 1918 re France.

mid September. The QMG inquired into the possibility of using four instead of six horses for American artillery but the weight ratios per horse proved too excessive. By 4th August a decision was reached for one division and a howitzer regiment to transfer complete with horses, leaving only four divisions and howitzer regiments to be horsed. There are interesting WO references as to what and how much the Americans should be charged for maintenance costs in remounts depots in France, for services and branding. Garratt records that depots were full with 19,538 animals, but he was informed that probably only three US divisions would require horsing, meaning 2,887 fewer animals than previously demanded (11,548). The situation changed again, as three of the divisions in the British area moved immediately, leaving only two for horsing, further reducing the outstanding demand by 5,774. Remounts were informed that the remaining two US divisions would probably join their artillery to be horsed in the British sector, requiring 5,774 animals (Riding 1,812; LD 3,122; HD 849). Fox states that the "final triumph of our Army horse administration was in the summer of 1918, when it was able to take up a big part of the burden of horsing the American units arriving in France".[63]

American extravagance in horseflesh staggered the allies. The lack of shipping for remounts to France probably saved the AEF a major catastrophe of 1899-1902 War proportions.[64] Animal management was poor; in remount annexes horses were watered from troughs, the contents of which was at least 5% nasal discharge. Their remount service was the worst offender against the dictates of common sense in animal management, remount depots were of the early 1899-1902 War corral type construction with hospitals in the centre, from which infected animals could not escape spreading disease. In remount stations in France, hundreds of horses stood in mud so deep they could not lie down, remaining there day and night until they died of exhaustion. In August 1918, the Chief Surgeon, AEF, remarked that 70% of their animals were suffering from sickness compared to 7% in the BEF from all causes.[65]

In addition to animals with the AEF in France, at least 350,000 were under training in depots in the US, prior to shipping to France. In November 1918 a report to the QMG gave the number of horses and mules, at remount depots, forts, posts and garrisons in the US, in transit to, or from these places, in France and on board ship in transit to France, to be some 113,725 cavalry and riding horses, 186,348 draught horses, 144,611 draught mules, 17,298 pack and riding mules, and 152,880 unclassified; a total of 477,262 animals on hand.[66] Up to 11th January 1919 the US shipped overseas a total 67,948 animals (5,489 cavalry, 33,396 draught, 28,088 draught mules and 975 pack mules); 600 horses and mules were lost in transit, less than 1% of the

---

63   WO95/70, 13th July; Col. Sanders, ADR (WO), also August 1918; Fox, 1920, p.7.
64   Merillat and Campbell, 1935, p.546.
65   Ford, 1927, p.430, 9 August 1918.
66   Moore, 1934, p.10; Merillat and Campbell, 1935, p.551.

total number shipped. The total number of animals purchased overseas by the US was 152,336:

Purchases of horses in:

France	109,848	
Spain	1,531	
GB	11,898	123,277 horses

Purchases of mules in:

France	9,341	
Spain	12,941	
GB	6,777	29,059 mules

On the 25th December 1918 there was a total 191,631 animals with the AEF in France:

Cavalry	26,023
Draught	109,528
Draught mules	48,614
Pack and Riding mules	7,466

with a total loss overseas of 42,311 animals (36,189 horses, 6,122 mules).

Retreat 1918

In January the Germans adopted a definite policy of searching out and bombing horse lines. As the severity of these air attacks developed, horse lines were concealed, protected by bomb proof earthworks and the animals separated into small groups.[67] The search for improved efficiency continued. Early in 1917 horse advisors were appointed to each Corps to make a distinct improvement in horse management by means of frequent inspections and instructional leaflets. In rapidly raised and trained armies from a largely industrial population, it was difficult to teach efficient and economic horse management during the short period of training possible at home and at bases in France. During March, Moore and the Inspector of QMG Services (Horse Feeding and Economies) suggested that horse advisors might help the DDRs of armies in identifying any animals for casting.[68] During the spring and summer of 1918 horsemastership in the Artillery recovered its position of importance, and cavalry officers were attached as 'horse masters' to brigades and corps.[69] In the autumn of 1918, 'half clipping' was ordered well in advance of winter. Overall, however, horse-

67 Fox, 1920, p.9; White, 1921, p.560 (DSO Dorsetshire Regiment).
68 RCT Archives, B10754, p.90; WO95/70, 9th March 1918.
69 Arbuthnot, 1919, pp.340-1.

mastership remained indifferent during 1918-19 owing to such issues as the shortage of hay, demobilisation of personnel, scattered country billets, foul stuffy stables and absence of grooming.

In March 1918 reductions were made in the number of cavalry units, some were to be dismounted: Bedfordshire, Essex, Leicester and N. Somerset Yeomanry, Household Cavalry and Yorkshire Dragoons, were to be replaced by the Canadian Cavalry Brigade fully horsed by 11th April. These arrangements were to be carried out when the tactical situation allowed. Home states two divisions had been disbanded by April. [70] All horses of dismounted units which could not be absorbed were to be used to fill vacancies bringing the Cavalry Corps up to war establishments, or sent to remount depots. All Yeomanry horses were to be taken into remount depots to be mallein tested before entraining. The Deputy Director Remounts, (DDR) Cavalry Corps was instructed to select any black horses from the 1st Life Guards and Blues suitable for repatriation and any officers who had brought out chargers, formerly their private property (20 in number), were to be allowed to send them home provided they purchased them back. The QMG countermanded this. Two trains of horses from the Household Cavalry Brigade were sent to Dieppe and one train, chiefly of Bedfordshire Yeomanry horses to Marseilles.[71] These arrangements had the effect of reducing demand for riding horses which were in short supply. Garratt was requested to provide the QMG with options for marching remounts up to the front if circumstances made it necessary. As remounts were already being marched from Calais, Boulogne and Abbeville, it was proposed that Dieppe could be added, although it was necessary to rail horses from Rouen and Havre. On 18th March, Garratt visited Fifth Army HQs to discuss the supply of remounts in the event of a German offensive and selection of sites for advanced remount depots.

The German spring (Ludendorff) offensive launched on 21st March (concluding in July) threw the Fifth and Third Armies into retreat, creating another brief period of fluid warfare, which for the Remount and Veterinary services was similar to that of 1914. They had to move and re-establish their bases, stores and equipment and at the same time be sufficiently organised to receive remounts, continue supplying units and receive casualties, when communication was extremely difficult, if not, at times, chaotic. Field remount sections of both armies were ordered back to Abbeville, remounts due to be trained or walked up to the front were cancelled. It was not possible to entrain remounts to the Third Army. Owing to the difficulty in obtaining trucks and moving remounts by train, a staging camp was re-opened at Eu, halfway between Dieppe and Abbeville. The Remount Department could not obtain an account of losses or the probable number of animals required by Fifth Army. If it became necessary to evacuate Dieppe, remounts were to be sent by road, via St Valery, to Etaples

70   Home, 1985, p.162.
71   WO95/70, 13th March 1918.

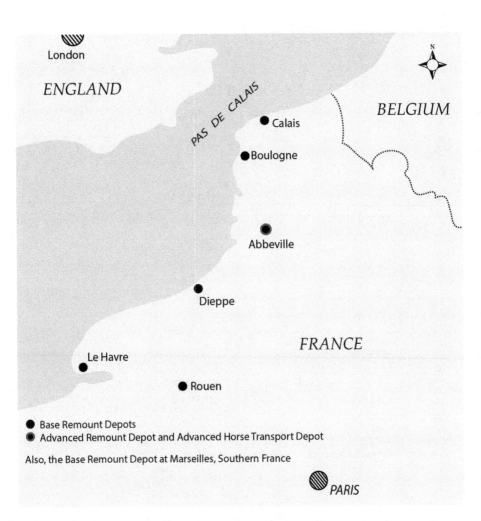

Map 5: British Remount Depots (BEF), 1918

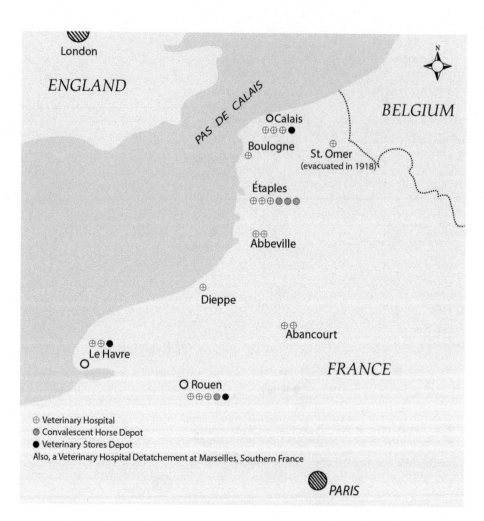

Map 6: British Veterinary Establishments (BEF), 1918

(see Maps 4, 5 and 6), where there was only room for a staging camp for 500 animals.[72] All fit horses were to go north and hospitals south. In addition to dealing with the crisis of the retreat, Garratt had to discuss with the QMG reinstating the much needed supply of horse ships from America, which had been stopped.[73]

The DDR, Cavalry Corps, reported that no horses were required owing to the loss of men, however the QMG requested that 1,000 riding horses were always to be held in reserve depots (exclusive of those at Marseilles). Remounts were instructed to mount two Yeomanry regiments (Essex and North Somerset that had just been dismounted) at Abbeville. The horses and about 1,000 saddles were to be supplied from Rouen and Dieppe. Arrangements were made with HQ, Line of Communications to send 15 lorries to bring in men to draw the horses. Maj-Gen. May, DQMG, asked for an extra 500 riding horses to be ordered from home as one cavalry division was to be used mounted immediately.[74] In addition, 140 machine gun packs were urgently requested for the Household Cavalry Brigade. On the 5th April, the DDR Cavalry Corps required remounts, to be drawn by the 12th April, for the:

1st Cavalry Division	455	
2nd Cavalry Division	350	
Canadian Cavalry Brigade	209	
Total	1,014	(959 riding)

A further 200 remounts were requested and on the 21st, 200 cavalry reinforcements were to be horsed at Abbeville. The Cavalry Corps kept about 1,000 reinforcements at Abbeville for use in conducting horses to their divisions and the Reserve Army.

In the event of Abbeville, Gournay, Serqueux and Dieppe remount depots being evacuated the decision was made to gradually clear all depots in the danger area, leaving Abbeville to last.[75] Abbeville became the railhead for remounts from Havre, Rouen and Dieppe (see Maps 4, 5 and 6). Remounts at Abbeville were located in hospital horse tents and veterinary stabling made vacant with the moving of all unfit horses south; the remount depot trebled in size with up to 2,000 animals being accommodated. Remounts from Abbeville for Fifth Army went to Picquingny, NW. of Amiens. Remounts for the Fourth Army were to be trained, with staging posts, owing to a shortage of trucks, from Boulogne, Havre and Rouen, detraining at Abbeville and sent by road to Picquingny where the Army would take over. During April, the

72   WO95/70, Col. Yardley, 27th March (DDR Fifth Army) and 1st April.
73   WO95/70, 29th March 1918; Conference, HQ Line of Communications, 30th March, and GHQ. QMG conference 31st March, ref. final instructions for evacuation of bases if necessary, and 31st March.
74   Ibid., 31st March; Blaxland, 1968, p.42, ref. 5th Cavalry Brigade and the long separation from their horses as they plugged the line, dismounted.
75   Ibid., 2nd April, Conference, HQ Lines of Communication and 23rd April, ref. plans for evacuation of Abbeville.

Fourth Army made heavy demands for artillery horses, for example, requesting 1,000 horses on 7th April, with plans made for the provision of remounts if Fourth Army had to fall back on the GHQ Line. The 52nd Division, due at Marseille, was to be horsed at Abbeville, requiring some 4,000 horses by 27th April, to move on the 28th. During April the demand for remounts, particularly riding horses was at crisis point and all methods were adopted to meet demand. On hearing the question of remounts was acute, Home wrote that there were lots of horses in England, but the authorities had starved them during the winter and so they were not fit to be shipped to France for work. He considered this all hinged on the decision that cavalry were no longer worth keeping; he also refers to delays in shoeing 2nd Cavalry Division horses.[76]

Daily replacements for divisions in each Army amounted to about 200 horses. During the week ending 13th April, 5,568 animals were issued to field remount sections of the four Armies at the front, mostly by conducting parties of remount personnel. Garratt and the QMG decided that 4,000 animals were required weekly for two weeks by when, it was hoped to reduce to the normal level of 3,000. All shipments to Egypt were halted with fit animals held at Marseilles and Havre, in 'the pool' for Egypt and Italy, to be used to meet the crisis in France if necessary. Surplus riding horses, withdrawn from the reduction in the transport of infantry battalions, were to be taken into remount depots. To maximise effective use of all available riding horses, a list of all those on temporary loan was sent to the QMG; this revealed the only large numbers were riding horses with chaplains (240) and mounted police. A reduction of those on the wartime establishment of veterinary hospitals was proposed, with a request to the Director of Transport to reduce the number in auxiliary horse transport companies on lines of communication. The Small Arms Ammunition (SAA) sections of five divisions (14th, 16th, 30th 39th and 66th) were to be broken up and the horses utilised in making up deficiencies in authorised establishments, or withdrawn to remount depots. Even with all these measures, on 30th April, the largest outstanding deficit was some 1,700 animals, for each of the Third and Fourth armies. On the same date the number of animals in remount depots had decreased from 17,000 to 12,000. No.5 Remount Squadron was to hand over St Germer to the French Army who were to take over all the country between Beauvais and Gournay, including 200 acres of grass taken near Aumale. On 19th April, the QMG sanctioned Dieppe remount depot being returned to a strength of 3,000 animals, having been reduced to 600, provided they could be evacuated by road if need arose. Stables lent by the AVC at Havre to the Remount Department were handed back, owing to great congestion in veterinary hospitals which meant relinquishing about 300 stables with mules being put in kraals.[77]

The QMG reported that although it was difficult to give an accurate forecast of requirements, it was not possible to function on the resources then in France, "the

---

76   Home, 1985, p.168, 16th April.
77   WO95/70, 30th April.

bosche has seriously inconvenienced us in this respect".[78] The remount situation showed liabilities totalling 13,879 animals including the provision of some 4,000 horses for the 52nd and 450 for the 74th Divisions, with 1,200 horses for nine Yeomanry regiments, all of which were to arrive in France from Egypt:

	Riding	Light	Heavy	Pack	Mules	Total
Demands received from fighting units	1,043	2,934	737	27	1,268	6,009
For 52nd Division from Egypt	871	1,585	472	109	1,000	4,037
For 74th Division from Egypt		472				472
For nine Yeomanry Regiments from Egypt forming:						
Army Machine Gun battalions	175	915	85			1,175
For 77th American Division	690	1,038	362	96		2,186
Totals	2,779	6,472	2,128	232	2,268	13,879

To meet this liability there were roughly 6,000 fit and 900 unfit animals in remount depots with 4,350 due to sail that week. The actual wastage, for the week ending 4th April, was 5,486 animals, about 1.4% weekly of the fighting strength of animals in the country. The average weekly receipts from hospitals was expected to be about 2,500. As fighting was expected to continue, it was crucial that the 52nd and 74th Divisions were equipped at the earliest possible opportunity. Demands were calculated at a weekly rate of 4,000 animals for the following fortnight at least, although after that, a reduction to the normal weekly figure of 3,000 was considered possible. It was, however, impossible to forecast accurately as so much depended on battle casualties. Certain complete first line transport units had been set aside for issue to the Americans, but the transport of depleted divisions could not be totally withdrawn owing to deployment on new defensive lines, and their ultimate disposal was dependent on the utilisation of American personnel.

The completion of reductions in army units and their horse establishments of, for example, the 4th and 5th Cavalry Divisions, three Corps Cavalry regiments, four Yeomanry regiments, three Household Cavalry regiments, Reserve Parks, and infantry units, released 29,000 animals, of which 8,850 had gone to Egypt with the 5th Cavalry Division. Against this, Pioneer and Machine Gun battalions had absorbed 1,850 horses, with approximately 8,800 animals, saved from the reduction

---

78   WO107/16, 15th April, Travers Clarke to GHQ (BEF); WO107/16, 15th April, Remount Statement.

in number of infantry battalions, made available for the Americans.[79] In total about 9,500 horses (net), had been released. However, it was not possible whilst operations continued to implement proposals to convert into motor transport, horse drawn 6" howitzer batteries, first line wagon and ammunition columns of 60 pounder gun batteries, which would have released 8,700 heavy draught horses. Other reductions relating to ammunition echelons of field artillery were also under consideration but held in abeyance, giving an eventual saving of 7,600 animals.

In July the war establishment of machine gun battalions was increased, each requiring five riding, four light and two heavy draught horses, a total increase for 50 divisions and eight army machine gun battalions of 638. Further demands included completely re-horsing the SAA of the 25th Division Ammunition Column which had lost all vehicles, harness and horses in recent fighting. Although battalions arriving from Salonika brought some animals with them issues were still required, for example, small draught mules were withdrawn to be utilised as pack mules, and replaced with light draught mules. British divisions in the French area, east of Paris, on the 27th July, were supplied with remounts by rail from the Havre depot. Such demands were not helped by a serious outbreak of influenza in the Directorate HQ with some 5% of animals being hospitalised; Boulogne was also badly affected. Temporary assistance was provided by keeping artillery drivers, sent down with horses on the reduction of field artillery, and not sending them back immediately to their reinforcement base. On the 5th July, congestion in remount depots caused the cancellation, for example, of 1,100 light draught animals due at Havre by 13th July. Such was the pressure to meet demands and the potential difficulty of getting a sufficient supply of horses in the future, that the QMG considered lowering the standard and using every available horse.[80] Reductions of over 100 horses in the Cavalry Corps was considered, by reducing the number of chargers of divisional and brigade commanders and staff; the 1/1 Northumberland Fusiliers (originally a Corps Cyclist Regiment), with one squadron mounted in March, was still awaiting the issue of riding horses to be fully horsed; on 16th July the QMG issued instructions to complete. Whilst Remounts was keeping the BEF horsed, others matters of a less immediately crucial nature were being addressed, for example, possible reductions in the personnel of remount depots if, it was decided at a later date, to reduce the armies in the field. The proposal meant reductions initially of 30,000 then 20,000 men with a possible reduction in the Remount Establishment by four squadrons (about 788 men), if both were implemented.[81]

By the summer of 1918 animal wastage had been cut to the lowest percentage in the campaign, with battle losses compensated for by a very low sickness rate, achieved to some extent by skilful care and improved horsemastership. Although Home states

79   WO107/16, 15th April, Remount Statement.
80   WO95/70, 1st July 1918 and Director of Remounts with QMG, 9th July.
81   WO95/70, 25th July.

that there were many very bad horsemen (at the base cavalry depot), who required a good deal of training before they were fit to be called cavalrymen; no doubt owing to the necessity of having to rapidly expand the cavalry after some units were dismounted and had lost trained men.[82] In May 1918 the sickness rate was 8.73% (12.05% in May 1917), in June, 7.7%, lower than at any period since August 1914; falling to 7.5% in July, 1918. Losses in battle showed a marked reduction, as did losses from enemy bombing. The sickness rate was only 9% on the 11th November 1918. Shortage in the supply of animals, compared with demand, was principally due to the needs of the American units, with nearly 25,000 animals being made available by reductions, for example, in the horse strength of artillery units. Providing mechanical transport for 6 inch howitzer and some 60 pounder gun batteries saved a further 14,000 animals. Savings were also made by initiating a Category 'B' animal, those not quite fit for arduous work with a fighting unit, where withdrawn to less demanding units.[83]

In early 1918 it was proposed to reduce the number of horses in France. Cowans wrote of "having a rather hectic time at the WO" getting rid of horses and reducing hay and oats, which made the feed situation almost desperate.[84] To help the situation Cowans passed suggestions to Travers Clarke (QMG, BEF) such as: obtaining returns from divisions or armies showing their weekly strength in horses, giving the average strength in exercising order, and the number of horses out of work every week, or pooling artillery and even infantry brigade horses. Cowans had no doubt Clarke had thought of these ideas, but added he was even having to give up horse ships so the Army could get rice from Burma for human consumption.

During the latter stages of the war military authorities were hard pressed to keep up the supply of fodder and for animals to be properly fed. With the effect of German submarine activity, and bad harvests at home and around the world, such as in the US and Italy, the supply of forage became acute and rations were cut to a bare minimum. The fodder crisis probably had a greater impact on the Central Powers, but with a possible slight easing of supply for the Germans from captured British stores in their March 1918 offensive. With hugely over stretched transport resources, road, rail and shipping, animal fodder was not seen as a priority, yet without the 'work horse' the war effort would have ground to a halt.

The WO resorted to requisitioning at home when necessary, for example in 1914, 1915 and 1916, chiefly from farms near military centres. An advert in the West Somerset Freepress, April 1915, requested tenders for daily supplies of hay to the twelve Somerset Mule Depots and two convalescent depots, for up to three and six tons daily. Also for daily grain supplies of crushed oats and bran, with very specific regulations for the quality of all feedstuffs.[85] The Army had assumed that the ordinary

82   Fox, 1920, p.7; Home, 1985, p.174, 5th and 13th June.
83   Fox, 1920, p.9.
84   WO107/16, Cowans to Lt-Gen. Travers Clarke, GHQ France, 18th February 1918.
85   *West Somerset Freepress*, 3rd April 1915. My thanks to Maggie Robertson.

commercial trade of the country would always provide whatever fodder was required, no thought was given to the increased quantities required when initially an additional half million mouths were imported by the Army for heavy war work. Crisis in the supply of hay came with the failure of the 1918 harvest and introduction of rationing for horses, though army and agricultural horses were exempted.[86] On active service, officers chargers and other light horses would get a daily ration of about 12lbs each of oats and hay. The standard daily ration for heavy draught horses on active service was 17lbs of oats and 15lbs of hay; for mules of 15 hands upwards on heavy draught work and lighter horses it was 12lb of oats and hay. Rations were frequently cut to 10 lbs and even as low as 7lbs which was far too small a ration to sustain heavy war work. [87]

The general situation in 1918 called for drastic action and in May an Inspector of Horse Feeding and Economics (IMQG – Horse feeding) was appointed, to advise on all matters connected with the feeding of animals in Army and Lines of Communication areas. He was to satisfy himself that the condition of animals was maintained at a high standard; reporting monthly to the QMG on methods for improving economy, in feeding and use of animals. An organisation developed for growing fodder in Army and Line of Communication areas. Remount and Veterinary Service statistics for 1918 show marked economies and improved animal condition, but as with other statistics they should be treated with care. A QMG's Report gives the highest monthly consumption of forage during 1914 as 590 lbs, rising in 1918 to 132,250,000 lbs (about 60,000 tons). The Prime Minister, in March 1916 stated 1,000 tons of hay was shipped daily to France (possibly 31,000 tons for the month).[88]

The French issued a smaller ration to their horses and repeatedly made efforts to persuade the British to reduce to the same level. Travers Clarke informed Cowans that the Inter Allied Command of Supply was departing from what he understood to be their charter, by dealing with a standard ration for horses.[89] In July the War Cabinet yielded to strong representations that the British Army wasted resources and transport in its feeding of animals and ordered a significant reduction in horse rations. The British Command in the field continued to argue against such cuts, pointing out the vast amount of extra work being thrown upon animals, for example with the reduction of field artillery ammunition teams from six horses to four; but the French persisted, even persuading the Americans to agree to reduced ration levels, a decision they later reversed. Reduced rations increased the sickness rate and affected the ability and performance of horses in the advances between August and November 1918. Taking an average of 25,000 light and heavy horses the weight of the daily rations issued at the time of the fodder controversy was:

86   Horn, pp.91-2; Thompson, 1983(b), pp.53, 72.
87   Hobday, 1918, p.45; Marcosson, 1918, p.54.
88   RCT Archive, File No1, B1 0754, p.10; Horn, 1984, p.91.
89   WO107/16, from QMG France to QMG WO, 13th August 1918.

lbs.
American   23.6
British   22.2
French   16.1

A daily average of 22lbs of fodder was not excessive for a horse doing hard work, but after the heavy horses had received their higher ration, the light horse got less. Maj-Gen.Vaughan, IQMG (Horse feeding) viewing chargers at the Rouen remount depot sent out from England, thought they were too big and leggy and the reduced ration would be insufficient for them.[90]

Offensives 1918

On the 8th August the Allies launched the offensive (The Hundred Days) that culminated in the November Armistice. Yet on 1st August, the Director of Remounts was involved in discussions about probable future reductions of the BEF, for example, a proposal to abolish the Cavalry Corps and keep one division mounted.[91] The Cavalry were heavily involved in the August offensive, putting great strain on Remounts to provide large numbers of riding horses. Home noted 18 miles of cavalry moving through part of Amiens (the first battle of the offensive) between 10 p.m. and 6 a.m. and on the 9th August, he also noted the perpetual difficulty of getting water for horses.[92] Garratt records visiting all the squadron stables of No.1 Base Remount Depot, inspecting riding horses for immediate issue to the Cavalry Corps, as he understood they might be required immediately to replace casualties. He found 500 horses fit for issue and 60 or 70 for the RHA. This urgency for riding horses was not helped by the accidental poisoning of about 100 horses at No.2 Base Remount Depot, Havre, 8th August; in one squadron they appeared to have been poisoned by castor oil being mixed with linseed cake from Spain (by accident in the mills). Only one died. The DDR Cavalry Corps reported about 1,500 casualties with the 3rd Division suffering most heavily with about 700. Of some 2,000 riding horses in remount depots suitable for cavalry only about 700 were fit for issue. The Canadian Cavalry Corps suffered most heavily in the early days of the offensive and two trainloads, about 700 remounts, were immediately supplied. Heavy casualties were also sustained among artillery horses. The Fourth Army units lost many horses from bomb attacks. The Remount Department (WO) was informed of casualties and probable requirements.

Supply and demand was continually changing, with demand constantly outstripping supply. The DDR Cavalry Corps estimated 2,000 riding horses were required, of which the WO reported that over the following five weeks they could only supply

90   Fox, 1920, pp.8-9; WO95/70.
91   Home, 1985, p.178, ref 3rd August.
92   Ibid., p.179, 8th August.

a weekly maximum of 100. By 20th August he was still requesting replacements for battle casualties, as well as for a large number of veterinary evacuations; about 800 riding horses were required to complete, of which Remounts could supply about 500 by the end of that week. The 1st Cavalry Corps sustained about 400 battle casualties on the 21st August, with a further 200 or 600 expected. Large casualties were also expected from the two cavalry divisions to be used in the advance on Bapaume.[93] To meet such demands the decision was made to reduce the standard of remounts, in quality, but not condition, which was considered important, for example, remount depots at Boulogne and Calais were to select R2 army horses suitable for cavalry. A list of all HQ staff riding horses was drawn up, totalling 3,990, of which 25% were to be withdrawn if the situation required; reductions in riding horses in Cavalry Corps units were also approved by the WO. Home wrote that the Army was not "too pleasant to work with" as they considered horses to be machines, for example, batteries of the 2nd Cavalry Division (with Third Army) had to march 40 miles, he thought unnecessarily, and the Third Army "was not good and wasteful of horses". During March and April, casualties were in excess of 2,800, of which 1,700 had been replaced. Home did not expect to receive the 1,000 shortfall; "horses were not considered in the slightest". He wrote that the Chief (Haig) was preparing a scheme for the cavalry (to take place about the 14th), and could only hope he would not gallop the legs of the horses, as they required a bit of nursing if they were to do any fast work in the future. In late October, he states that the Cavalry was sitting doing nothing as the German rear guard defence was in very great depth. In November a new danger appeared for cavalry as there were many accidents with horses striking unexploded shells.[94]

Again, during these crises other routine work continued. The QMG authorised the issue of 50 horses, to be used for harvesting in the recently captured countryside; a further 150 were required, 29th August, from Abbeville, equipped with harness, from the advanced horse transport depot. The WO requested 500 heavy draught horses be supplied to Canadian forestry companies, arriving from England for aerodrome work, at least 300 were to be found from workable sound horses from hospitals, 30% of which could be blind. Blind and partially blinded animals were normally issued to transport units on lines of communication, forestry and agricultural units, but the numbers were rapidly increasing and the question of their disposal became a problem. Moore estimated that roughly 2,000 were in hospitals and convalescent horse depots. Steps were taken to ascertain which units at the front could take a proportion of these animals and after close investigation it was proposed to summon a conference of DDRs to decide the best way to issue them.[95]

The pressure to meet demands for animals was still evident in October 1918, with a very limited reserve in England. The WO was forwarding 1,500 horses via France,

---

93   WO95/70, 23rd August; GOC Cavalry Corps to Director of Remounts.
94   Home, 1985, p.182, 7th September, p.186 and p.189 for 1st November.
95   WO95/70, 10th August, ref. DVS.

spread over two weeks, for Gen. Allenby (commanding the Egyptian Expeditionary Force in Palestine from 1917). It was noted they could be stopped at Marseilles for use in France, if necessary, as it was thought Allenby would not be needing many more, as he was also getting 1,500 from India. In addition, if agreement was reached to temporarily put aside Home Defence, some 5 to 6,000 animals could be obtained from divisions in England; 100 fit horses weekly were already being taken from these divisions. The WO could never ship more than about 5,000 animals weekly from England, but they could be transported to France quickly enough if the cavalry had to make a move. Cowans believed the reserve was as easily looked after by the divisions in England as they would be in remount depots in France, which had some 4,500 waiting to go forward to the front. Cowans assured Garratt that "if you have any push I think you may comfort the Chief that he won't be let down". In October, the deficiency in France, was he believed under 3,000, which if spread over the 350,000 in the country was not very much. The UK remount situation, available for France was:[96]

	Riding	LD	HD	Total
Numbers Promised	400	1,600	500	2,500
Hope to send	800	2,000	200	3,000*
Despatch night of IV (?)	488	743	284	1,520

* really 3,150, awaiting shipment, 11th October

The figures below give total receipts of horses from overseas into France and issues to the front for March to December 1918 (the same caution applies to using these figures as for 1917).[97]

Receipts of Animals into France from Overseas

	Horses	Mules	Total
To the end of February	(248,775)	(71,571)	(320,346)
During March	3,180	2,292	5,472
April	7,425	2,475	9,900
May and June	12,563	5,822	18,385
July	6,408	2,280	8,688
August	7,848	1,729	9,577

96   WO107/16, 'Horse Situation', 8th October 1918, letter from Cowans to Travers Clarke, 11th October Cowans to Travers Clarke, 8th October 1918, Remount Situation.
97   WO95/70.

	Horses	Mules	Total
September	6,594	1,518	8,112
October	9,553	2,543	12,096
November	8,953	2,260	11,213
December	651	651	
Total	63,175	20,919	84,094
	(311,950)	(92,490)	(404,440)

Issues to the Front

	Horses	Mules	Total
To the end of February	(440,839)	(94,367)	(535,206)
During March	11,153	2,301	13,454
April	17,700	5,501	23,201
May and June	26,326	8,719	35,045
July	9,854	2,051	11,905
August	12,464	3,706	16,170
September	15,597	5,486	21,083
October	19,177	5,351	24,528
November	13,125	3,328	16,453
December	3,500	721	4,231
Total	128,896	37,174	166,070
	(569,735)	(131,541)	(701,276)

Receipts for the months following the British retreat in March show the replacement of heavy wastage and supply of new units; those for August and October, the replacement of wastage from the offensive. The Issues follow a similar pattern, high in April to replace losses and again in the months of July to October, during the offensives, lowering in November, to virtually nothing in December after the Armistice:

Issues to Other Theatres from France

	Horses	Mules	Total
EGYPT:			
July 1917 to end of July 1918	11,603	3,564	15,167
During August (includes 87 donkeys)	412	175	587
Total	12,015	3,739	15,754
ITALY:			
November 1917 to end of March 1918	2,970	2,734	5,704
April, 1918	288	288	576
May to July	85	304	389
August, September	8		8
October	48		48
Total	3,399	3,326	6,725
SALONIKA:			
January 1918	543		543
October	493	315	808
Total	1,036	315	1,351
INDIA:			
June, 1918 (includes 39 donkeys)	40		40

The horse services played a crucial role in the British Army's success of 1918. The extent of their achievement has been acknowledged in the claim that the ultimate defeat of the Central Powers was due to an inability to obtain horses for remounting their armies. The British Commander in Chief, Douglas Haig, stated that "if in March 1918 the equine force of Germany had been on the same scale and as efficient as the British equine force, the Germans would unquestionably have succeeded in breaking through between the French and British armies, and inflicted a defeat so great that recovery might not have been possible".[98] In March 1918 the Germans produced no cavalry for their great offensive, if they had done, the allied retreat might have been a rout.[99]

98   *Veterinary Medicine*, 1919, 14th February, p.561, in Merillat and Campbell, 1935, p.561.
99   Farndale, 1986, p.164.

10

Supplying the Demand

What most people don't realise is that, in the First World War, everything that moved had a horse attached. There were a few staff cars, but for the most part the war was conducted on the backs of horses[1]

With the expansion of the BEF, the raising of the Kitchener New Armies and the opening of new theatres purchasing arrangements had to be extended. The insatiable demand for animals was met from a number of sources: domestic and foreign markets, the efficiency of the Remount Department and AVC, and increased mechanisation. The Mobilisation Scheme allowed for horses and mules to be obtained from abroad, including the immediate despatch of a remount commission to North America, with the first batch of 10,000 horses from North America arriving in England in October 1914.

Foreign Markets

Purchasing Commissions were sent to the US, Canada, Australasia, Portugal, Spain and South America. Some 627,303 animals were landed in England for re-distribution, giving some indication of the supply from foreign markets. In addition, remount commissions shipped substantial numbers direct to the various theatres of war. In total, approximately 780,000 horses and mules were purchased abroad, for all theatres of war.

Camels, oxen and donkeys were purchased for use in those theatres to which they were particularly suited. Animals from Australasia (Australia and New Zealand) were used in Egypt, India and Mesopotamia. South Africa supplied thousands of horses, mules, donkeys and oxen to East Africa. The supply of horses and mules for India and Mesopotamia was arranged by the Indian Government, as far as possible by purchase

---

1   Swarbrick, in Arthur, 2006, pp.231-2. As a naval man he did not see the vast numbers of motor vehicles employed on the Western Front.

in India, Australia Argentine and China. The number of mules obtainable in China and India was limited, supply was therefore supplemented from South America. All arrangements for the purchase of mules from various countries and for their shipment to India was made by the WO, directly with the Ministry of Shipping. As the great majority of the animals came from the southern hemisphere, they required a considerable time for acclimatisation in India; with shipment impossible during the summer months India had to estimate requirements nearly two years in advance.[2]

Remounts to the Desert Mounted Column in Palestine, were nearly all from Australia and Canada (British units took their horses with them), Australian Walers (saddle horses) forming the majority of horses in the Desert Corps. The Remount Branch of the Australian Military Forces was formed in 1911-12 and purchased in Australia 42,926 horses for their own troops, until January 1917, at a lower price than those purchased in North America. The Branch assisted Imperial Remount Commission officers operating in Australia when buying horses for service in Europe and India; a further 93,000 were exported by the end of 1917.[3] Depots in Egypt and Salonika were initially supplied with horses mainly direct from Australasia and with mules from North America. Probably the largest ever remount depot, 640 acres, was at El Kantara, Egypt, on the eastern side of the Suez Canal, accommodating some 8,000 animals. Owing to difficulties of transportation, shipments from Australia to Egypt were stopped, the last horses shipped arrived May/June, 1917; 8,000 remounts that had been purchased in Australia, were never shipped owing to the shortage of shipping. Later, all direct shipments of animals from America to the Mediterranean were also stopped. The supply to Egypt and Salonika was then provided through the UK and France, necessitating an increase in depot accommodation in France.[4] Some 28,000 horses were shipped by remount commissions, from Australia and New Zealand to France and Egypt; about 5,000 Walers in total were landed in France.[5]

British authorities strongly advocated that the Remount Commissions to North America should have their HQs on British soil, even though the bulk of their purchases would be in the US. On 4th August, the Secretary of State for the Colonies informed Canadian ministers that Maj-Gen Sir F.W. Benson, head of the British Remount Commission, was proceeding to Canada to make arrangements, if events proved necessary, for the purchase of horses for H.M's Army. He arrived on 17th August to be joined, initially, by a staff of eight officers. Benson died (after an illness) on 20th August 1916, and was replaced by Maj. Sir C. Gunning, who was already with the Commission.

2   Galtrey, 1918, pp.14, 16-17; *Statistics*, p.861.
3   Kent, 1982, pp.9-10.
4   Kantara (El Quantara el Sharqiyya, N.E. Egypt); Preston, 1921, p.317; *Statistics*, p.862.
5   WO163/20, (34/2487), Army Council Minutes, 'Report by the Inspector General of the Overseas Forces', Ian Hamilton, 1914; Inspection of Australia and (34/2577) Report of New Zealand. The latter gives details of mechanical transport as well as horse supply, and demands of the New Zealand forces on mobilisation.

When the Commission was formed, it was uncertain whether or not the US would sanction, or even tolerate the presence of its purchasers, and it was only on sufferance that an officer started purchasing in Kansas City in September 1914. He was the first of what was to become a much larger purchasing staff, whose purchases reached figures of then unimaginable magnitude. Support was given to Benson, including veterinary assistance and provision of stockyards established at St John, Halifax, Montreal and Toronto, under armed militia guard; the Commission's HQ was in Toronto. The Commission Report states there was little doubt that when constituted the magnitude of its subsequent operations was never contemplated, otherwise a very much larger staff would have been employed. The Commission engaged thirteen transport ships for three voyages, each to carry 10,000 horses monthly to England. In October 1914, 9,801 remounts were shipped for the British Army.[6]

The Commission was increased, by the addition of a Commission to South America, mainly in Argentine and Uruguay. The Uruguay Remount Commission arrived in Montevideo on 12th December 1914 with three veterinary and five other officers. Their work was delayed for some weeks whilst ascertaining the stamp and extent of horse resources; purchasing was then done through local contractors. The Commission's headquarters was established at Fray Bentos, from where, all horses had an 18 to 24 hour rail journey to Montevideo, the port of embarkation. Horses were examined at Fray Bentos and again before embarkation. A large percentage of the horses presented for purchase were rejected. No more than 35% passed all requirements of height, age, stamp and soundness, the main reasons for rejection being lack of height, for veterinary reasons and cataracts. Many of the horses in Uruguay had been imported from neighbouring districts in the Argentine. Considerable difficulty was found in obtaining a heavy type of horse for artillery. The country was exceptionally free of infectious and contagious diseases and as the risk of glanders seemed remote, mallein testing was not carried out before shipment. A total of 2,232 horses were shipped to England, in six vessels fitted and chartered for the task.

Responsibility for all arrangements for boats, fittings and placing vessels at the disposal of the North American Commission rested with the Admiralty, however, it was unable to carry out this programme which was passed to the WO, or the Commission. In most cases animals were transported on the upper decks, open to the weather, to reduce difficulties in ventilation, even though improvements were made to the ventilation of the horse decks by increasing the use of electric fans and a new type of wind sail. The *S.S. Hesperides*, for example, is recorded as having to fit windsails to the lower deck where horses were stalled. *Hesperides* was sunk in April 1917 on a voyage from Buenos Aires to Liverpool with a general cargo, by the German submarine U-69. Embarkation duties rested entirely with the senior veterinary officer

6   *Report of the Purchasing Commission to Canada and America (RPCCA)*, August 1914-Februaury 1919, p.5, AMSM, Box 22; Official History of Canadian Forces, Appendix 257, pp.187-8 (Canadian War Museum).

at Montevideo. Attendants to accompany shipments were difficult to obtain and largely composed of Russian and Italian men wishing to return to Europe, but with no knowledge of horses. They worked under a foreman who had previous experience in the shipping of horses. The required number of attendants for each boat was probably only achieved due to reservists travelling home to rejoin their units. Arrangements for shipping, although the best under the circumstances, was far from satisfactory. It was not possible for example for a veterinary surgeon to accompany every shipment and it was recognised that limiting losses at sea would depend on a quiet passage and absence of any form of contagious disease.[7]

The general system of fitment left much to be desired. No exercise was possible, nor could the feet of animals be reached, and it was only with difficulty, and the carpenter's assistance, that animals could be removed from their stalls if the need arose. The practice of shipping animals in specially fitted pens, rather than in single stalls, was gradually introduced after trials on the *S. S. Devonian* during November 1915, and by the end of the war this arrangement became an Admiralty regulation for all remount ships. It was also less expensive to fit ships with pens. Records state that animals in pens fared better in heavy weather and landed in better condition than those carried in stalls. 5% of single stalls were retained for the accommodation of vicious animals.[8]

The most important foreign market was North America, from which, by the end of December 1918, a total of some 703,705 animals (428,608 horses, 275,097 mules) were shipped from the Atlantic seaboard to UK ports for re-distribution, or, direct to other theatres of war. Nearly 72,000, for example, were shipped directly to France and the Mediterranean, although most were employed in England and France. To avoid a rise in prices when Canada entered the war, the Commission suspended purchases in Canada.[9] Birkbeck gives a total of 688,619 shipped from North America by 10th December 1918:[10]

	Horses	*Mules*	*Horses and Mules*
To the UK	411,473	205,231	616,704
To France and the Mediterranean direct	7,691	64,224	71,915
Total	419,164	269,455	688,619

The Commission was not the only foreign purchaser. Daniels, an American horse dealer, writes of purchasing for the Italians, English, Belgians and French, shipping "thousands of horses, thousands of them". In April 1917, Daniels became a Horse

---

7   Blenkinsop and Rainey, 1938, pp.504-7, 644.
8   Ibid., p.645; *RPCCA*, p.11.
9   *Statistics*, p.396, dated 11th November 1918, however, on p.861 a total of 617,935 (411, 206 horses and 206,729 mules) is given, but no date for the figures.
10   In Jessel, 1920, p.110, '*The Remount Service*,' 10th December 1918.

Merchant Navy – horses and mules crossing the Atlantic to La Pallice, the port of La Rochelle, France. Taken by Captain Joseph Clarke (1870-1941). The animals are accommodated in a specially constructed open shelter on the side of the after deck, or weather deck, the unprotected deck behind the bridge of a ship towards the stern. Ironically, in 1941, La Pallice was home to a massive German U-boat base. (Dr W.M. Goodchild, 1997)

Inspector in the US Army at Camp Dodge near Des Moines, 40 miles from his farm.
[11] The French had agreed not to purchase in Canada, but the export of army horses consigned from the US through Canada to France, in bond, was authorised. In August 1915, when prices had settled, French purchasers, with agreement from the Army Council, were allowed to purchase in the Canadian horse markets. A French officer at St Louis spent 12 million dollars on cavalry horses and mules. The Commission noted that in May 1917 the French, Belgium and Italian Governments had increased their purchases, but this was felt to be a help to the Commission as it allowed dealers to dispose of rejected animals.[12]

In November 1914 Birkbeck wrote that the future of the American horse supply was problematical.[13] There had been political difficulties with supply during the 1899-1902 War, and in 1914 the British Government was unsure of the American Government's view on military purchases in the US. The estimated horse population

11   Daniels, 1989, pp.92, 100.
12   *Official History of the Canadian Forces*, 1938, Vol.1, p.188; Order in Council, 3rd October 1914; *VR*, 1914, Vol.XXVII, 28th November, p.306; *RPCCA*, p.9.
13   WO107/17, 26th November 1914.

was over 30 million, of which eight million were said to be broken horses and barring political complications there appeared to be an inexhaustible source of supply. France, Italy and Belgium purchased approximately 600,000 and the US on entering the War about 500,000. Canada only produced about 31,402 for the British Remount Commission and about 10,000 for the French, as its supply was limited. Benson decided to establish a separate Mule Commission from the Horse Commission in respect of finance, headed by Col. C.H. Bridge, who had joined the Commission in October, with a staff of five buyers. Specifications and prices ($175, for mules) were agreed and the Commission proceeded to the US establishing its headquarters at Kansas City, moving in 1916 to Montreal. In April 1916 prices were agreed with dealers in the US for the purchase of heavy artillery horses at $220, field artillery $200 and cavalry horses $185; in Montreal, $225 for heavy, $210 for field and $185 for cavalry horses. In December 1916, a deterioration was noticed in the size and quality of 'gunner' mules (used by the British for pack, mountain, or ammunition columns, not for pulling gun teams), coinciding with an unprecedented increase in the price of cotton, that inflated the mule market out of all recognition. Supply of mules was limited and of poorer quality making them virtually unobtainable to army purchasers, especially with the French and US also purchasing large numbers. At this time the French Remount Commission protested that the British were spoiling the market by purchasing animals at a higher price and at no better quality than those purchased by themselves. Late in 1917 new areas were opened up for the purchase of mules in Atlanta (Georgia) and Nashville (Tennessee).[14]

The decade preceding the outbreak of war was one of change in the US as automobiles had driven light horses from city streets. By 1916 half the draying was done by motor trucks, which also served as a means of transportation for the family; this had confined horses to the farms where motor power had probably supplanted only a few horses. The saddle horse had therefore declined as a commercial factor in the North American horse market. Considerable numbers of animals were purchased in the US during the 1899-1902 War, mainly riding and the light draught horses, the type most required by British and Allied forces for field artillery and light transport. The heavy artillery horse was difficult to obtain in any numbers. The light draught type were of good quality and formed the country's commercial stock. Mules were purchased in the mid-western states of Missouri and Kansas, and the southern states of Tennessee, Texas, Alabama and Georgia (see Map 7).[15] Purchasing operations were extended

---

14   Lyddon, 1938, p.206; *RPCCA*, pp.5-6, 19. "Cotton mules" were originally used in the U.S. to carry big cotton sacks as they walked down furrows while slaves picked the cotton. Plantation owners bred the Cotton mule to stand low to the ground as a time-saving device, so the slaves didn't have to stand to put the cotton into the sacks. Mules were also used in the ploughing/planting and haulage of cotton.

15   Merillat and Campbell, 1935, p.503, 551; Bate, in Galtrey, 1918, pp.30-2; VR, 1915, Vol. XXVIII, 25th December, p.291. In the late 19th century there were about 2.2 million mules in the US, worth about $103 million. With the cotton boom numbers rose to about

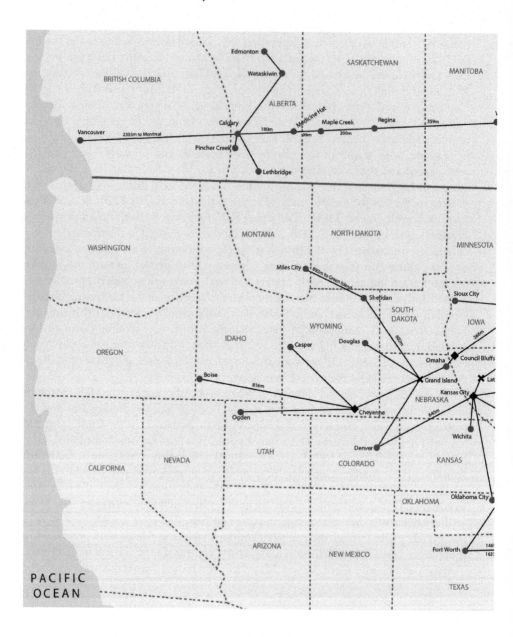

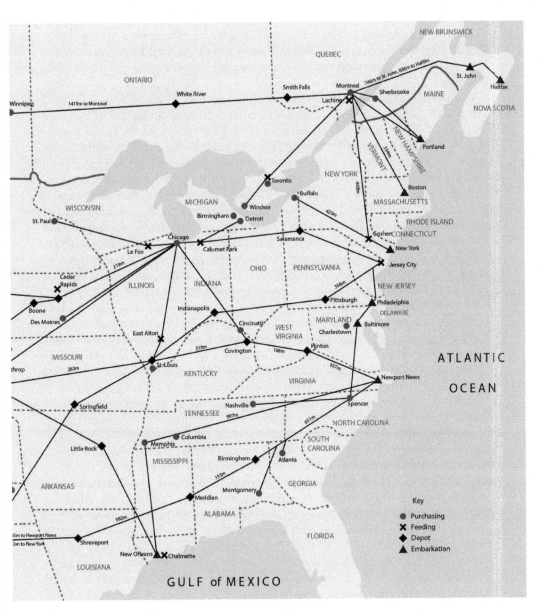

Map 7 – Remount Procurement in Canada and the United States

to other centres and by 1st November 1914, purchasing officers were also located in Kansas City, Denver, St Louis, Chicago, Fort Worth (Texas) and Toronto, purchasing from six major civilian dealers. The Commission HQs was moved to Montreal in November.

Animals embarked from the Atlantic seaboard ports of St John (New Brunswick) and Halifax (Nova Scotia), but these ports proved difficult during the winter, with the port of Montreal frozen up between November and April. With the closure of St John and Halifax in January 1915 arrangements were made for embarkation depots at Newport News (Virginia), Portland and Boston. From December 1916, with increased demands for both horses and mules, grain ships were employed to take a small number of animals on their top decks. As these mainly took their cargoes in New York, Philadelphia, Baltimore, Boston and Portland, a special horse depot was established in the Jersey City stockyards. During the course of the war some of the depots and ports were opened, closed and re-opened as demand and availability changed, and with different areas of North America producing a certain class or stamp of animal. The numbers of Commission staff would also increase and decrease subject to purchasing, administrative, veterinary and WO demands.[16]

In the early stages of their activities, the Commission covered practically the whole continent in search of suitable animals. On 1st April, 1915 purchasing officers were located at points in Chicago (Illinois), Cincinnati (Ohio), two centres in St Louis (Illinois), St Paul (Minnesota), Lathrop (Missouri), Denver (Colorado), Miles City (Montana), Grand Island (Nebraska), Cheyenne (Wyoming) and Montreal. They purchased from thirteen dealers in the latter locations plus Kansas City (Missouri), Oklahoma City, Sheridan (Wyoming), Windsor (Ontario) and Toronto. Experience proved it was more profitable to concentrate all activities in the draught horse producing areas of the mid-western states. The main purchasing centres then used by the Commission were Chicago, St Paul, Sioux City (Iowa) and Des Moines (Iowa), St Louis, Kansas City, Toronto and Montreal in Canada. The majority of purchases were made from a small number of large, reliable horse dealers who had their show-yards in the large towns. Animals were collected and moved by rail, with offloading and feeding stations en route to depots and embarkation ports. Some depots were in existing stockyards, especially at ports of embarkation, others were specially built, or expanded such as Lathrop, Chalmette (New Orleans), Lachine (Montreal), Columbia (Tennessee), East Alton (Illinois) and Calumet Park (Indiana). With an increase in shipping from New York, in July 1917 the Commission took over an Italian Remount Commission depot at Goshen about 60 miles from the port. With a reduction in demand from the WO and a reasonable reserve in hand, the Commission ceased

---

4.1 million, worth about $120 each in a normal market. Possibly a quarter of all the mules were in Texas, with the stockyards at Fort Worth a major centre for buying and selling.

16   Lyddon, 1938, p.206; *VR*, 1917, p.516, Vol.XXIX, 9th June; *RPCCA*, pp.6-7, 15, 17.

purchasing on 15th November 1915, until 17th March 1916, when nearly all depots had been emptied.[17]

To assist in the classification of animals on arrival at depots, purchasers were instructed to brand heavy artillery horses with an H on their near cheek and cavalry with a C. The manes of cobs were hogged (cut short), leaving only a tuft of mane; cavalry manes were left intact, but heavy and field artillery horses were also hogged. This practice is still used by The King's Troop RHA on their gun team horses, although not for the officers' chargers which are left uncut.[18]

The area of operation was divided into two zones, purchase and embarkation. A system of remount depots was situated in each of these zones, where possible in places with suitable railway facilities. With the huge increase in the number of animals dealt with, arrangements at the detraining points were inadequate and so facilities had to be constructed by the Commission.[19] An enormous expanse of country was covered from the mid-west purchasing areas to the embarkation points on the Atlantic seaboard. These long distances, covered by rail, on average 1,200 miles, were thought to be responsible for the virulence of 'shipping fever', a type of influenza resulting in pneumonia and similar pulmonary diseases, with over 70% of horses moved by rail contracting the fever. As the main sources of infection was the dealers' yards, stockyards and railway cars, animals were moved through these points as quickly as possible. The period from purchase, to date of embarkation, was a minimum of seven weeks.[20] The law in Canada and America, under normal conditions, did not allow for any animal to be aboard a train for more than 28 hours without being off-loaded to feed, water and rest; this was extended to 36 hours under war conditions. In winter, journeys could be in temperatures of 25 degrees below zero and 110 in the shade in summer. Both the American and British Remount Commissions suffered from considerable numbers of animals dying on trains shortly after arriving at their destination. Subsidiary remount depots were formed at suitable points, on selected railways, to be used as off-loading and feeding stations. In theory, every horse was examined at each stage of the journey so that only fit horses arrived at embarkation depots, where they received a final rest of several weeks before embarkation. Only fit animals were meant to be embarked by the embarkation officer and remount official.[21]

In consequence of the heavy mortality rates at sea, and on arrival in England, amongst remounts from Canada during the winter of 1914-15, a Deputy Director AVS (DDAVS) was sent out to inspect and report upon the veterinary services with the Commission. One of his findings was an absence of veterinary staff at the Commission's headquarters in Montreal. Capt. A.F. Deacon, AVC, with remount

17   Bate, in Galtrey, 1918, p.27; Lyddon, 1938, p.206; Barratt (IWM), diary of shipments 1915-16; *RPCCA*, pp.1, 15, 19.
18   I am grateful to The King's Troop RHA, Woolwich, for this information.
19   Lyddon, 1938, p.207; Blenkinsop and Rainey, 1925, pp.30-2.
20   Blenkinsop and Rainey, pp.468-9.
21   Bate in Galtrey, 1918, pp.30-2.

experience, was appointed PVO and sailed for Canada in April 1915, to organise the veterinary services and advise the GOC on technical matters. The mortality rate among animals arriving in the UK was considerably reduced during the summer of 1915, although a major outbreak of gangrenous dermatitis in a number of depots seriously interfered with shipments.

The status of the PVO and of the whole veterinary service with the Remount Commission was reminiscent of the 1899-1902 War and complicated by mixed lines of accountability. Veterinary officers employed in command of remount depots and on embarkation duties were considered to be serving under the GOC and not under the PVO, who was in full possession of information relating to veterinary matters. The results of this lack of status and the inability to ensure expert recommendations were carried out, was demonstrated in the excessive losses at Lathrop during the winter of 1916-17 and at Calumet the following winter. In May 1918 necessary improvements, advocated from July 1917, were adopted with obvious benefits to health. In the meantime, the mortality among animals in the Commission's hospitals remained abnormally high, increasing during the latter half of 1916 from 6% admissions in June, to 23% in November, when the decision was made to replace the PVO by a senior AVC officer with extensive service with the BEF. Col. A. Olver, DDVS, was appointed to the Commission. Arriving Montreal in June 1917 he set about visiting depots in the neighbourhood.[22] At Lachine, one of the largest shipping depots, he found, for example, that the practice of holding large numbers of animals together, in more or less open paddocks and corrals, a practice that had generally been abandoned elsewhere, caused the paddocks to become extremely muddy and insanitary during wet weather, or a thaw. He recommended covered accommodation with hard standings for all remounts as soon as possible. He also found the hospital accommodation to be insanitary. Financial considerations ruled out many of the necessary improvements; many animals therefore spent the winter in the open, on muddy ground, causing large numbers of cases of gangrenous dermatitis, for example at Lachine and Newport News during late 1917, with even more serious losses from pneumonia. In September 1917, with veterinary evidence that the Commission's depots were grossly infected and insanitary, sanction was given to improve the organisation of depot hospitals. This included a definite establishment of subordinate civilian personnel for the veterinary care of animals, and improved sanitation at all depots, with the responsibilities of the Commission for sick animals and depots clearly defined.[23] These changes brought about a significant improvement in the condition of the hospitals and sanitation in general. However, in February 1918 the DGAVS (WO) reported that heavy mortality and sickness still existed among animals arriving in the UK, again highlighting the need for more satisfactory accommodation.

22   Blenkinsop and Rainey, 1925, pp.450-2.
23   Report of the Surgeon General of the US Army, 1918 (Department of Army, Washington), p.423; Blenkinsop and Rainey, pp.454-5.

During August 1917 attention was drawn to fact that the reserve of horses had fallen so low that animals not fully recovered from illness were being shipped from the US to fill the vessels. It was generally considered necessary to have accommodation available for a reserve of two months purchases; this was gradually built up during the last months of 1917. This resulted in a consequential increased pressure on accommodation that eased in November when a new depot was opened at La Fox, near Chicago, for 1,800 animals under cover.

The entry of America into the war on 6th April, 1917, meant the Commission had to relate to the British Embassy in Washington. The American Government entered the horse market as a purchaser with a consequent rise in prices. It took immediate steps to control purchases by forming an advisory Committee, with the British Remount Commission represented by Maj. Gunning and Col. Bate, RFA. Additional domestic demands were placed on the US national herd already facing a boom in the cotton industry and increased demands for animals for agriculture. By the end of 1917 there was a great shortfall in the US hay crop, causing a considerable rise in prices and forage charges.

Relationships with the US military establishment and the purchase of remounts by the Commission was something of a roller coaster ride. With the US Remount Department purchasing heavily, they indicated that British purchasing seriously interfered with their own activities and demanded a period of restriction, or a total cessation of British purchasing. An agreement was eventually reached, with the proviso that British prices were regulated to conform with the wishes of the US, that no new dealers were employed without US sanction and all purchases and movements were reported to them weekly. The price of cavalry horses was reduced from $175 to $165. US purchasing did not materially affect the number of heavy or artillery horses collected for inspections, as US specifications for such animals was different, requiring a much lighter horse they purchased fewer heavy types.

The state of the mule market was much more serious as US specifications for the three classes of mule clashed with the British:

Type of mule	Pounds weight	Height in hands	Cost in dollars
Wheel Mules	1,250	15.75 to 16.5	$230
Lead Mules	1,000	15.00 to 15.75	$190
Pack mules	950 to 1,150	14.50 to 15.5	$175

The 'gun mule' required by the Commission, for which the US fixed the price at $190, weighed 1,100 lbs, height 15.1 hands, clashing in category with the US wheel and lead mules.

At the end of November 1917, the US Remount Department requested an officer from the Commission, Col. Bate, be attached to them for assistance in the coordination of purchasing. In February 1918 the US 'requested' that all, or any, British remount ships be handed over, or transferred to them for the transportation of animals to France; the WO refused this request. During August several conferences were held with the US Department to discuss future purchasing, the main item being the very large reserve of animals held by the US Department for which they lacked ships. The attitude adopted was to refuse the Commission permission to continue purchasing unless they agreed to a transfer of shipping. After considerable discussion "harmony was maintained" and a "general feeling of reciprocity was finally established", when the Commission agreed to support the US application to transfer ships. However, in September the US realised the impossibility of such a transfer and gave approval for the resumption of purchasing. [24]

1918 opened with the most severe weather conditions in living memory, the *Montreal Star* reported on the phenomenal heavy snowfall. Movements of animals were greatly disrupted, and for a time impossible. Some depots were entirely cut off by deep snow, with resulting overcrowding. Animals suffered considerably when trains already en route for the ports were delayed for several days, and a lack of coal supplies to ships in New York caused delays, with as many as ten horse ships unable to leave harbour. The hay crop had also failed and the cost of feeding consequently increased. The WO ordered the Commission to close down purchasing operations and arrange for 12,000 animals to be available in depots, involving expenditure to improve accommodation for holding this number of horses during the spring thaw. From mid February to mid May 1918, no purchasing took place and mortality, mainly pneumonia cases, remained high. Instructions were received early in May to resume purchasing in nego-tiation with the American Government.[25] Improvements continued to be made in both accommodation and organisation during 1918, with consequent reductions in mortality. In August, at Lachine, a large number of animals were however destroyed during a serious outbreak of glanders. Daniels wrote of this outbreak, "I'll never forget glanders. Destroyed some 1,700 horses; when all done and buried had to disinfect all pens in the whole of Camp Dodge".[26]

On the 11th November, 1918, the Commission held 10,855 horses (7,093 in Canadian depots) and 15,977 mules (493 in Canadian depots). Following the November Armistice the Commission was ordered to dispose of its animals, close down and return to the UK. The Canadian Government did not wish to purchase any of the surplus stock and would not allow their sale in the country, except for cast animals and those that could not travel. The US also did not wish to purchase animals but allowed the Commission to sell on the open market. Remounts in Canada were moved into the US for sale. Sales were held at Chicago, St. Louis, Fort Worth (Texas), Atlanta (Georgia), Birmingham (Michigan), Newport News, Boston (Massachusetts), Buffalo (New York) and Jersey City (New Jersey). Prices were low as

24   Lyddon, 1938, p.209; *RPCCA*, pp.21-22, 24.
25   Lyddon, p.210; Blenkinsop and Rainey, p.459; *Montreal Star* in *RPCCA*, p.17.
26   Daniels, 1989, pp.103-4.

the sales took place in mid-winter. Sales continued into January 1919 but with competition from the US Government releasing 45,000 surplus animals onto the market. The final sale was in Montreal on 4th February and by the end of the month the Commission had returned to England, having spent about £36.5 million during the war, which included the purchase of horses and mule, railway fares, feeding, buildings and labour.[27]

Relationships with the Canadian Government appear to have been generally good. During the first three months of the Commission gifts of 1,321 horses were received from individuals, a township and the Saskatchewan Government (1,280). During December 1914, when the Canadian Government was purchasing for their own forces, the Commission was requested to give them "a fair field for about eight weeks or more". During this period all purchasers were moved to the US. In March 1915, the Government again gave permission to purchase in Canada, however in the April, the Commission was again requested to either cease buying, or place all orders in the hands of Canadian Authorities, as it was felt buying interfered and competed with Canadian purchasers. The decision was taken to cease buying in Canada; the official reason given was better arrangements for financing in the US. However, the Canadian Government then ceased purchasing military horses for overseas in the summer of 1915 and in the August, arrangements were made for the Commission to purchase all animals for British and Canadian forces overseas. Canadian farmers and dealers expressed their dissatisfaction when purchasing was reduced or stopped, causing considerable discussion between the Canadian Government and the Commission, with questions being raised on several occasions in the House of Commons, Ottawa. In April 1916 the Mule Commission HQ, now under Gen. Benson, moved to Montreal, although purchases were in the US. For financial reasons the WO reduced expenditure in Canada and then ceased purchasing on 15th August 1917.[28]

The Maritime Contribution and Submarine Menace

The magnitude of the maritime contribution to the shipping of military horses is too often overlooked. Continuing the supply of remounts to all theatres of war meant maintaining a supply of transport in the face of new methods of warfare, for example the submarine, and growing demands from other military services for the same transport. E. G. Barrett, kept a diary written between October 1915 and September 1916, whilst he was stationed at various French ports, Brest, Bordeaux, La Pallice (La Rochelle) and St. Nazaire, receiving and checking deliveries of horses shipped from New York, to France; it provides an example of the numbers of horses shipped, deaths, and the ports of arrival.[29]

27   *RPCCA*, pp.28-29.
28   *RPCCA*, pp.7, 8-9,12-13, 17,
29   IWM (74/991), Barratt, E.G.

- The total number shipped was   29,498 with a total loss of 2,196
- The smallest number shipped was   266 with a total loss of   11
- The largest shipment was   1,364 with a total loss of   101
- The greatest single loss per shipment out of 1,084 was   125

Also recorded is a bonus paid in New York, for example to captains and first officers; horse attendants received $5 per man if deaths on voyage did not exceed 30, and $2.50 if not exceeding 40.

Nicholas Swarbrick, radio operator in the Merchant Navy, served on the *Westfalia*, crossing the Atlantic from the Canadian ports of Halifax and later from Montreal, with his main cargo of horses. He refers to the u-boat menace, "I am not quite sure how many torpedoes missed us but ships were being sunk all around me." During October 1916 German submarine activity off Newport News was the cause of considerable anxiety with several ships being delayed, and again in December, 1916 when the *S.S. Georgic* was sunk carrying horses, wheat and oil. Throughout January and February there were large shipments with 73 ships despatched from various ports, but despite submarine activity only two ships were lost, the *St. Ursula*, which had unloaded her cargo of horses before being hit, and *Japanese Prince*, which lost all 310 horses. Between January and 30th April 128 ships (175 by end of June) carried 71,787 animals with the loss of five ships and 2,033 horses and mules. In August 1917 the *Argalia* and *Athenia* were sunk on their return journeys with a loss of 899 horses; the *Devonian* was also sunk.[30]

Some ships had near misses, such as HM Horse Transport the *S.S. Anglo California*, captained by Lt. Frederick Parslow. The vessel, on charter to the Admiralty had been converted for use as horse transporter with stalls, fodder stores and the required veterinary officer. On 4th July 1917 Parslow was taking a cargo of 927 horses from Montreal to Avonmouth when attacked by the submarine *U-96*, possibly also the *U-20*, near Fastnet, about ninety miles SW of Queenstown. Parslow attempted to flee the U-boat, which eventually opened fire damaging the vessel. Despite the option to surrender, Parlow, knowing help was on the way from Royal Navy destroyers, continued to outmanoeuvre the U-boat whilst still taking direct hits from shell and small arms fire. After three hours under action the vessel was saved by the arrival of the destroyers, the U-boat escaping. Possibly 30 animals were killed. At some point in the engagement Parlow had been killed. In 1919 he was awarded a posthumous Victoria Cross for his bravery, when the rules were changed to allow such awards to the Merchant Navy. The *Anglo-California* does not appear to have been a lucky horse ship as on 24th August 1915, when about to leave port with 916 horses, a fire broke out in No.1 hold where some of the forage was stored; 12 horses were suffocated the remainder were unharmed.[31] The *Anglo-California*, was sold in 1916 to the Cunard

30   *RPCCA*, pp.15, 17-18,20; Swarbrick, in Arthur, 2006, p.230.
31   Bourke, EJ, *The First World War at sea off West Cork*, National Maritime Museum of Ireland;

Line and renamed the *Vandalia*, was torpedoed and sunk by *U-96* on 9th June 1918, in St George's Channel between England and Wales.

The cargo liner *S.S. Armenian* had been fitted out to transport horses and was used in the 1899-1902 War. In October, 1914, she was deployed taking the Grenadier Guards to Belgium, and then as a horse transport. On 28th June 1915 whilst crossing the Atlantic from Newport News to Avonmouth, with a consignment of 1,400 mules, she was engaged and sunk by the *U-24*, off the Cornish coast, heading into the Bristol Channel. Warning shots were fired, but the *Armenian* refused to stop whereupon the *U-24* opened fire; after numerous hits the *Armenian* was abandoned and then sunk by one or two torpedoes. 29 crew, mostly American muleteers, and all the mules were lost.

Baron Von Spiegel, captain of *U-202* writes of an attack in April 1916 on an unnamed cargo vessel; an account which is difficult to verify. "The steamer appeared to be close to us – I saw with amazement – a shiver went through me – a long line of compartments of wood spread over the entire deck, out of which were sticking black and brown horse heads and necks. Oh, great Scott! Horses! What a pity! Splendid animals! What has that to do with it? I continually thought. War is war. And every horse less on the Western Front is to lessen England's defence. I have to admit, however, that the thought which had to come was disgusting, and I wish to make the story about it short. The vessel was hit abaft the second funnel ... All her decks were visible to me ... a storming, despairing mass of men were fighting their way on deck ... jostling one another on the sloping deck. All amongst them, rearing, slipping horses are wedged ... then a second explosion, followed by the escape of white hissing steam from all hatchways and scuttles. The white steam drove the horses mad. I saw a beautiful long-tailed dapple-grey horse take a mighty leap over the berthing rails and land into a fully laden boat. At that point I could not bear the sight any longer, and I lowered the periscope and dived deep."[32]

Another notable encounter, 19th August 1916, off the Scilly islands involved the steamer *Nicosian*, carrying a cargo of munitions and 250 mules and fodder from New Orleans. Stopped by the *U-27* she was about to be sunk when saved by the British decoy, or 'Q-ship', *HMS Baralong* under Lt. Herbert RN. At a War Cabinet meeting on 11th January 1917, the First Sea Lord stated that the Admiralty desired to increase the number of coastal steamers from two to ten, fitted out as decoy vessels (Q-ships) to engage enemy submarines. He found the employment of such vessels was, on the whole, a most effective method of dealing with U-boats. The Shipping Controller stated that he fully realised the importance of this work, having already released two

www.searlecanada.org, Sunderland Site, page 079, shipbuilders, p.69; Wikipedia, SM.U-38, Frederick Daniel Parslow, SS Anglo-Californian; *RPCCA*, p.10.

32   Spiegel, 1917, pp.53-59; Wikipedia, SS Armenian; *U-boat Attack, 1916*, www.eyewitnesstohistory.com (1997); History Channel – Deep Wreck Mysteries – *Search for the Bone Wreck*.

SS Armenian – *constructed as the* Indian *by Harland and Wolff,* Belfast *for the Leyland Line in 1895, changed to the* Armenian *on delivery as a cattle and cargo carrier between Liverpool and Boston. Returned to commercial service in 1902 after the 1899-1902 War and transferred to the White Star Line, until 1910, as a cargo vessel between Liverpool and New York. Laid up March 1914 before doing war service from August 1914. Sunk June 1915. (Author's collection)*

A remount at Ormskirk Depot 20th May 1915. Reputedly a survivor of the sinking of SS Hortilius, *8th May 1915. I have not been able to locate any other reference to this vessel or its sinking. (Army Medical Services Museum)*

ships to the Admiralty, but felt that the responsibility for the release of further vessels from the carrying trade should rest with the War Cabinet, in view of the great pressure being exerted by the French and Italian Governments to obtain tonnage, particularly for the conveyance of coal. The War Cabinet decided that six further coasting vessels, making eight in total, should be released by the Shipping Controller to become decoy ships.[33]

With the entry of the US into the war and the introduction of the Convoy System in April, 1917, losses amongst merchant shipping and of horse-ships on the homeward journey was reduced, notably with the aid of US naval vessels providing escorts. Losses fell instantly to 0.24%, or 120 times less than before the introduction of the system.[34] Of the 703,705 animals shipped from Atlantic seaboard ports, 13,724 were lost at sea, of these, some 6,667 were lost through enemy action. Ten horse ships were sunk crossing the Atlantic. The first losses were in 1915 when 2,233 horses and mules were sunk and 49 killed by enemy shellfire. Only 300 horses were lost in 1916; the worst losses were in 1917 with 2,932 sunk and 14 mules killed by shellfire. Losses during 1918 were 1,139.

Despite all the setbacks, between October 1914 and December 1918 an average of over two ships, every three days was dispatched by The North American Remount Commission to Europe, mostly carrying from 500 to 1,000 animals per ship. There are records of 196 ships being used for transporting remounts during 1918. For 191 of these ships that carried animals from Canada and America during 1918, 76 completed the voyage without losing a single animal Excluding losses from the ten ships sunk by enemy action, the average loss in horses and mules on voyage was under 1%; in comparison, at depots, on rail etc, prior to shipment it was approximately 5%.

Domestic Market

Following mobilisation, impressment virtually ceased and all purchases were obtained on the open market. By 31st March 1920 some 468,323 horses had been purchased in the UK.[35] The fugues below, to 31st December 1918, include the purchase of some 174,665 riding horses:[36]

---

33 Hoehling, 1965, pp.103-4; Hough, 1983, Q Ships pp.303-4; CAB/23/1, War Cabinet, 32, 11th January 1917, P.M10, p., also WC.63/64, P.M.3, 1/132 February, re submarine losses, p.2.

34 Corbett & Newbolt, 1931, Vol.V; Hough, p.308; Blenkinsop and Rainey, p.646.

35 *Statistics*, p396, this source also gives a total of 467,973 but without a date; Birkbeck, in Jessel, 10th December 1918, gives 468,088. Moore, 1934, pp.9-10, between August 1914 and mid 1918 about 450,000, see Appendix giving the Return of Horses purchased in the UK from 1st August 1914 to 31st March 1915; MAF52/3/TL3770 for 19th November 1919 gives about 450,000.

36 *Statistics*, p.397.

1st, mobilisation period (5th to 16th August 1914, inclusive)	49,131
2nd, Completion of mobilisation period to 31st March 1915	57,271
3rd, 1st April 1915 to 31st March 1916	21,337
4th, 1st April 1916 to 31st March 1917	20,583
5th, 1st April 1917 to 31st March 1918	10,646
6th, 1st April 1918 to 31st December 1918	15,697
Total:	174,665

The Report on the Census of Horses, carried out in the UK during April and May 1917, gives the number of horses purchased from the beginning of the War as approximately 400,000.[37] Birkbeck estimated that 17% of the working horse population of Great Britain was mobilised for the war effort and that the WO was prepared to put that same number back into the economy if required.[38]

It was not only the loss of horses from civilian life and for breeding that caused concern and made the continued supply of horses difficult to maintain. The Board of Agriculture and Fisheries (BAF), for example, issued a statement to clarify the misconception about the number of heavy draught horses actually required by the military. *The Veterinary Record* states that farmers considered veterinary surgeons going to war left them in the lurch, "a rather dirty trick".[39] The cost of fodder also increased. Members of horse societies and the horse world generally were involved in war duties including some on remount duties. Stallion leaders and other skilled manual workers and tradesmen were lost to the war effort, farmers faced a shortage of farm workers, and a depletion of civilian blacksmiths, wheelwrights, harness makers and other ancillary tradesmen. The very fabric of the nation's horse world had been disrupted; the Army was forced reluctantly to temporarily release some skilled workers in 1916 and 1917, to assist the industry.

Representative horse shows were cancelled or reduced, racing was stopped except at Newmarket and in Ireland policies were adopted that affected horse breeding and hunting.[40] The *West Somerset Freepress* records that on the 15th August 1914, the Devon and Somersetshire Staghounds were discontinuing hunting and putting down fourteen couples of surplus hounds to help reduce expenses. A Mr Amory from the Tiverton Foxhounds was sending eight of his hunters to the WO and other members of the hunt were also offering horses. On the 10th October on article headed the '*Supply of Horses*', noted that "a few days after the outbreak of war every Hunt was called upon

---

37   WO107/27, p.5; Hume, 1980, p.42 states almost 600,000 animals were purchased as remounts in UK, based on different dates, and as many again imported into England from overseas.

38   Birkbeck, in Jessel, 1920, p.113.

39   *VR*, 1914, Vol.XXVII, 29th August, p.149, also 20th February, p.444.

40   Hansard (C), 1915, Vol.LXIX, 18th February, (c)1305; *VR*, 1915, Vol.XXVII, 19th June, p.643; MAF52/3/TL21438, 19th July 1915; *The Field*, 21st August 1915, 'Horses For the Army'; Chivers, 1976, pp.300-1.

to supply a number of horses for Army purposes. In some cases only half of the Hunt horses were requisitioned at the first call, but in many other instances nearly all the mounts were taken out of the stables," and that "many of the smaller hunts would not be hunting during the winter of 1914-15 as they had lost their masters, huntsmen and whippers-in to military service."[41]

The speed of mobilisation and scale of requisitioning took many agriculturists by surprise as Army personnel impressed, or purchased on the open market, vast numbers of horses. This included men and horses taken for short periods to work on military projects such as camp building. Mobilisation took place at harvest time when the demand for draught horses was at its peak, a situation that led to angry questions in the House of Commons. In September the point was being made defensively that the Army had only taken about 9,000 heavy horses from farms, a little over 1% of the number recorded in June 1914, as being used on the land.[42] There were of course regional variations, for example, in areas where there was little arable land. The process did not stop. By 16th November the total number requisitioned had risen to 2% of the June total and by June 1915 about 8%. On the 14th June, the estimated number of horses used for agriculture, including mares kept for breeding, but excluding saddle horses, carriages or trap horses and 'vanners' was 793,436, so with only about 9,000, or 1% taken for the war effort, the Army was not interfering seriously with the cultivation of the land.[43]

The drop in the number of saddle horses on farms to 25%, had been drastic. After the first months of war, efforts were made to secure the bulk of army horses from overseas and British stock gradually recovered. The first two years of the war undoubtedly affected the number of good horses available, and although numbers recovered by 1916, they were still below the 1914 level.[44] In 1917, the Remount Department was purchasing about 3,000 horses monthly, mostly from industry and urban transport locations, which were replenishing their supplies by purchasing farm horses. The *Sale of Horses Order* was introduced in June 1917 to stop this trade, and the sale of farm horses was forbidden without a license from the County Agricultural Executive Committee, and only granted if the animals were surplus to farm requirements and being sold to another farmer, or authorised person.[45]

It would be wrong to see the purchase of agricultural horses by the Army as the major concern of agriculturists during the war years and the only catalyst for the use of tractors. Very clearly the shortage of labour was equally important, if not more so. Mont Abbott, an Oxfordshire farm labourer, saw the shortage of men as being central to farmers turning to the tractor and steam plough. The tractor was in its infancy in

41   I am grateful to Maggie Robertson for this information.
42   Horn, 1984, pp.88-9; for example Hansard (C), 1915, Vol.LXV.
43   *VR*, 1914, Vol.XXVII 29th August, p.149.
44   Horn, 1984, pp.90-91.
45   Dewey, 1989, pp.61, 192-3.

1914, home production was slow, around 1,500 in 1917; the importation of tractors from America helped.[46] Collins commented, that tractors tended to be adopted when the supply of horses became inelastic, as in 1917-18, when arable cultivation expanded and 10,000 tractors were imported.[47]

The Army also assisted the economy by returning animals no longer suited for military work, set aside for casting and from hospitals, to the UK for civilian work. Board of Agriculture officials made regular visits to remount depots in France to view possible horses for return to the UK. When the Food Production Department of the Board of Agriculture was established (1st January 1917, which on 19th February was constituted as a separate department), the Remount Department purchased 6,792 horses for the Department and transferred 3,200 army horses no longer suitable for military purposes. Arrangements were made for the Food Production Department to loan their draught horses, to farmers, after being conditioned at POW ploughing camps, such as Dulverton, Somerset. Once fit the animals were returned to Remount Depots and replaced by others. The QMG also sanctioned thirteen draught horses for work under the Assistant Director of Roads Seine Imperieure, Rouen, to be found from horses returned from the Agricultural Directorate. [48]

The Somerset War Agricultural Committee between September 1917 and March 1918 purchased 403 horses and were loaned 50 WO remounts; 40 horses had died or were sold off. Many of the horses are referred to by their army number. Horses and equipment were loaned out at a set fee by the Committee and Remount Depots. In October, 28 teams comprising 57 horses had been loaned with requests from farmers for many more. The Committee's records suggest a quite involved organisation, establishing their own horse depots and isolation units for sick animals, a ploughing school or instruction centre for motor ploughing and a tractor training school, all of which were linked closely to the personnel, equipment and facilities of local Remount Depots. Reference is also made to training and employing women farriers and the employing a horse breaker. Some of those purchased had been repatriated from the Western Front. There are references to unbroken Argentinean and US horses, loaned by the Remount Depots soon after landing, for example, "50 American horses fresh from the boat and not equal to long hours of work". Prices were laid down for the hire of horses for harrowing, rolling, cultivating and drilling; in December, the minimum prices for ploughing were:

Light land ...	2 horses ...	20/- ... per acre
Medium	2	22/6
Heavy	3	25/-
Heavy	4	27/6

46   Stewart, 1988, pp.37, 45, 73, 83-4; Dewey, 1989, pp.60-61.
47   Collins, 1983, pp.73, 92; also Horn, 1984, p.91.
48   WO95/70, 20th April.

The *Ormskirk Advertiser* notes for 5th April 1917, that no fewer than 43 complete horse teams and soldier ploughmen, from the Ormskirk Remount Depot, were on loan to local farmers with another 50 on agricultural leave, two being employed as stallion men. A man and pair of horses were charged out at 12/- for eight hours work.[49]

The outbreak of war did not halt the debate in the UK on horse breeding for military purposes. Cubitt (Secretary to Army Council) wrote that the experience of mobilisation clearly demonstrated the Army Council's well founded anxiety as to the quality of the national horse supply, as the number of unsound and utterly worthless animals, which ought never to have been bred was deplorably large.[50] Birkbeck states the Army secured sufficient horses on mobilisation, but the quality of many of them was unsuitable for military service, particularly in the Territorial Army, which received very many bad horses.[51] He considered they had not realised just how many very bad horses there were in the country, which had been drained of good horses.

Fears for future supply were raised when the Development Commission reduced the Light Horse Breeding (LHB) Grant for 1915-16 by £5,000 (to £26,500) and informed the Board of Agriculture that the whole grant could be withdrawn for 1916-1917.[52] Later, in 1915, the Commission was so dissatisfied with the results from the use of the grant they announced their intention to cut it by £25,000 immediately.[53] The Board was, however, satisfied that owing to the depletion of the country's horse stock as a result of the war, it was even more necessary for the industry to receive substantial government support. At a county meeting at Dorchester in December 1916, there was a very strong and unanimous feeling that unless the Government prohibited the export of horses to foreign countries, for say three to five years, the future of light horse breeding would be seriously imperilled, matters required urgent attention in view of the demands that would arise from the effects of the war.[54] Birkbeck informed Cowans of the Commission's decision and requested the Secretary of State record with the Cabinet, that for national defence it was absolutely essential the LHB Scheme be continued and developed, with a sufficient annual grant from the Treasury.[55] Thoroughbred sires of sufficient quality and numbers were required to

49   *Statistics*, p.862; *VR*, 1914, Vol.XXVII, 19th December, pp.337-8; Chivers, 1976, p.302; Tylden, 1965, p.39; Horn, 1984, p.91; *VR*, 1915, Vol.XXVIII, 18th December, p.275; *Somerset War Agricultural Committee Minutes* with thanks to Maggie Robertson; Nigel Neil, *Horses in War*, 2012, p.45.

50   Army Council, WO, to Sec. of Treasury, 16th December 1919, ref. letter No.L19342, 19th November 1919, from Sec. of BAF, in MAF52/3/TL3770.

51   MAF52/2/A43091/1915, 6th August 1915, Evidence to the Selborne Committee on the 'Supply of Horses for Military Purposes'.

52   D1/1, 25 November 1914; D2/15, 28th November 1914.

53   MAF52/3/TL21438, 19th July 1915; WO163/29, p.134

54   D2/15, 3rd December 1914, BAF to Treasury; *VR*, 1914, Vol.XXVII, 19th December, p.338, also 1916, Vol.XXVIII, 4th March, p.403.

55   Birkbeck to Cowans, WO32/9128, 2nd December 1914.

attract high-class mares, with a major proportion of the annual grant being spent on subsidising privately owned stallions.

Birkbeck considered a unique opportunity existed for the purchase of good sires at the Newmarket sales, as there was no foreign competition and the owners of good class racehorses were willing and anxious to sell for prices that would not have been considered the previous year. He was keen for Lord Kitchener to be stirred into immediate action, enter the market and purchase at extraordinary prices, thus solving the sire question forever and with it the question of suitable remounts for the Army for years to come. With the enormous wastage early in the war, the WO saw the situation as infinitely more serious, if heavy expenditure was to be avoided in establishing large military stud farms, the supply in civilian life had to be maintained. Although the number of motor vehicles was increasing this did not materially reduce the number of horses required in wartime; motor vehicles were subject to very definite limitations and the type of horse they replaced was the heavy draught, of which at that time, there was an ample supply in the country. No form of motor vehicle existed which could take the place of the artillery horse; the greatest shortage was of riding horses.[56]

In June 1915, Lord Selborne, President of BAF, took up the matter, requiring a very definite written statement from Lord Kitchener on the WO views about encouraging light horse breeding and their requirements, also stating what costs they might be prepared to share financially.[57] The Army Council expressed its willingness to cooperate with the Board, to the extent of even being prepared to consider purchasing remounts directly from breeders at three years of age, and a larger proportion annually from Great Britain. Kitchener did not hesitate in stating that expenditure on the Scheme was of paramount military importance, as proved by experiences in the war, and could not be delayed.[58] In August 1915, Selborne appointed a Committee, to consider and advise the Board on the steps to be taken in securing the production and maintenance, in England and Wales, of a supply of horses, suitable and sufficient for military purposes, especially on mobilisation.[59] In December the Army Council concurred generally with recommendations in the Committee's Report to put the light horse breeding industry on a proper footing.[60] In particular the WO was to purchase a much larger number of horses in England and Wales, increase the number

56 Correspondence between WO and BAF, 1st August 1914, 13th December 1914; MAF52/2/A43091/15 and WO32/9128, Gen.No116/5719

57 MAF/52/2/A43091/1915, 5th June 1915; Financial Sec. WO and Parliamentary Sec. of BAF.

58 MAF52/2/A43091/1915, 9th July 1915, Cubitt, WO to Sec. BAF; WO107/27, 116 Gen.No/6178, 12th July, notes on Lord Selborne's memorandum; WO107/27, 20th July, Kitchener to Selborne.

59 3rd August 1915, chairmanship of Lord Middleton: WO107/27, Selborne Commission on 'The Supply of Horses for Military Purposes'.

60 Summarised in para.80, sections 1 to 9, pp.14-15; VR, 1915, Vol.XXVIII, 11th December, p.266 and 18th December.

of horses on peacetime establishments, purchase more horses directly from breeders, purchase remounts when rising four and purchase specially selected fillies to be left with breeders until they produced foals.

In October 1915, Col. Hall Walker (later Lord Wavertree) offered his stud farms and stock at Russley Park (Wiltshire) and Tully (County Kildare, Ireland) valued at £150,000, to the Government for £75,000 (or less).[61] Cowans was of the opinion that it was initially an option for the Board to take up, not the Army, which had never been involved in the horse breeding business. Only if the Board turned it down would he consider the option, although the WO finance section was against it. At one stage, Cowans became so frustrated with the Board's attitude that he produced notes on a scheme to be run by the WO, proposing the Army take over the whole of the LHB Scheme and the Hall Walker stud. Selborne was prepared to take on the stud during the war period, but considered that military horse breeding should then become the responsibility of the Army Council and charges transferred to the WO Vote. On 1st January 1916, the Hall Walker Stud (later to become the Irish National Stud) was purchased by the Government, with the Board administering horse-breeding for military considerations. The training establishment at Russley Park, Wiltshire, was intended to become a government stallion depot when its use as a wartime remount depot ceased.

At the close of 1915 the horse-breeding situation had been clarified. The Report of Lord Middleton's Committee indicated the steps necessary to put light horse breeding on a proper footing. The Board had purchased the Hall-Walker establishment and was therefore in possession of a foundation stud of thoroughbreds and a stallion depot for the accommodation of sires that might be purchased, in addition to, or as substitute for, those subsidised under their Premium Scheme.[62]

A joint Committee of the Board and Army Council was established in April 1917, under the chairmanship of Sir G. Greenall, and reported in the October in favour of a scheme for 'boarding out' surplus horses, to be called up for Territorial training, and a scheme for the distribution of surplus mares to approved breeders. These schemes, with modifications and with support from the WO, were approved by the Treasury subject to reconsideration within a year. Some 15,000 horses had been 'boarded out' by December 1919.[63] The Hunter Improvement Society and National Light Horse Breeding Society made strong representations to the WO and the Board about the future of light horse breeding.[64] At a deputation received by Lord Lee, President of the Board, Lee, accompanied by Lord Peel, Under Secretary of State for War, indicated

61   WO107/27, correspondence relating to the purchase; *VR*, 1915, Vol.XXVIII, 18th
       December, pp.275-6 and 1916, 11th March, p.411.
62   MAF52/3/TL3770, letter from WO dated 16th December 1918.
63   WO107/27, WO letter 9th November 1918; Treasury approval given 7th December 1917;
       MAF52/3/TL3770, letter to WO 16th December 1918.
64   WO107/27; MAF52/3/TL3770; Macgregor-Morris, 1986, pp.115-18.

his intention to apply for funds to enlarge the scope of breeding operations and put the light horse breeding industry on a satisfactory basis. [65]

The Army Council restated the need to preserve the national supply of horses required by the Army on mobilisation, recognising that mobilisation on a large scale was considered improbable within ten years, as horse breeding made slow progress and the effect of any action by the Board would hardly be felt before 1930. It recognised that the first demand on mobilisation was for riding horses for mounted troops, though probably less in number than in 1914, but even that reduced demand would be very difficult to meet in 1919. Years of careful work was required to restore the supply to an adequate level. There was an awareness of the increasing difficulty, as mechanical vehicles improved and became cheaper, of obtaining light draught horses, as numbers in use would decrease. The Council did not believe that horses could be replaced by motor vehicles to the same extent with armies in the field, where the importance of movement across country was essential. The Army Council acknowledged, subject to provision in Army Estimates, that the Middleton Committee's recommendations should be implemented when the purchasing of remounts resumed in 1921 and that purchasing should not be confined to the cheapest market in Ireland, but undertaken with a view to assisting the Board's policy; also breeders should be relieved of their riding horses at 3.5 years old.

The WO acknowledged the valuable work carried out by the horse societies in taking over several hundreds of four-year-old cavalry remounts, keeping them free of cost for a year or more, returning them broken and in condition, many to be issued as officers chargers. The English Hunts placed their horses at WO disposal, for example, with the formation of the Third Cavalry Division, at Windmill Hill, on Salisbury Plain at the end of September 1914. Similar provision was made for many of the horses for the 7th Brigade, composed of the Household Cavalry, with Lord Derby assisting with a number of horses from his own stables. Many private owners refused to take any payment for their animals. A WO letter sent to the Masters of Foxhounds noted the importance of maintaining the Hunts, noting that the Director of Remounts had urged on the Director General of Recruiting this necessity, as the preservation of hunting was important in the continued breeding and raising of light horses for cavalry purposes. Lord Derby supported this claim but hoped the Hunts would employ men ineligible for military service. [66]

A useful, but very small source of supply was the confiscation of several horses owned by the German Government. A Mr Dawson informed the authorities of some valuable horses at Newmarket belonging to the German and Austrian Governments and intended for export as stallions. The horses were named as Andular, Aides and Boland, belonging to the Austrian Government, leased or lent to Baron Springer,

65   MAF52/3/TL3770, 16th December 1918; *VR*, 1917, Vol.XXIX, 14th April, p.431.
66   *VR*, 1915, Vol.XXVII, 1st May, p.569; Chapman, 1924, p.91; WO letter in *Upton News*, 20th March 1915, I am grateful to Brian Hill for this information.

trained by Butlers at Newmarket. A horse, Cyklon, belonged to the German Government and ran in Count Lehrdorff's colours, trained by R. Day at Newmarket. There were other foreign owned horses at Newmarket, but as far as was known these were the only ones owned by foreign governments. Birkbeck informed Dawson that the stallions were of no use to the Army, but the Board might like them, depending on the legal situation. In September the horses were found to be enemy public property and could be confiscated by HM Government. The Board received notification from Weatherby and Sons, London (founded 1770, bloodstock agents), listing horses that were entered in the name of Baron Springer (Andular, Aides, Apart, Boland, all leased from the Austrian Government, and Invention, Claserie, Flightiness) and for Count Lehrdorff (Cyklon, Longobarde, Grillpazer).

The Board was authorised to seize on behalf of HM Government, as enemy public property, the stallions Adulator, Aides, and Boland in the custody of Mr Butlers of Newmarket. A Report on the horses at Newmarket showed that in May 1913, Apart had broken a leg and had been shot. Aides and Boland were sold at Newmarket for £630; Cyklon and Longobarde, property of the German Government, sold for £600 in October 1914. Adular was to be kept for light horse breeding at Compton Stud, for the Board's LHBS at Gillingham, Dorset. Mr Weatherby confirmed that Mentor, Closerie and Flightiness, purchased in England 1913, by Baron Springer were his own property. Grillpazer was believed to be the property of the German Government and possibly sent back to Germany sometime ago.

The *West Somerset Freepress* records that a sale of three horses, by the Army Purchasing officer, belonging to Count Hochberg of Croydon Hall, was stopped as they were the private property of the Count, who had left the Hall the previous week. Presumably for Germany.[67]

Efficiency of the Remount Department and AVC

The 1899-1902 War clearly highlighted that to keep a force supplied and mobile it was not simply the supply of large numbers of animals that was important, but crucially, their level of acclimatisation, condition, the standard of horsemastership and veterinary care. In addition, the level of co-operation and understanding between the Remount and Veterinary Services, and the Higher Command, was vital, in knowing what animals could achieve and at what cost, both financially and in terms of their health.

The Remount Service made strenuous efforts to provide efficient remount depots supplied with covered shelters, stabling, hard standings, adequate supplies of water

67   MAF52/2/TL/22037, File II.TL22038 and File III TL22039; Letter from N. Dawson at the Household Brigade Boat Club, Maidenhead, dated 23rd August 1914, to Harry; Birkbeck, 29th August 1914, (A41759); *West Somerset Freepress*, 8th August 1914, my thanks to Maggie Robertson.

and forage, adequate and effective exercise, trained personnel and good transport facilities. In general, remounts were conditioned, acclimatised and hardened before issue. Depots and units were inspected regularly, but the Service did not escape criticism. Very early in the war Home wrote, "Remounts are again in trouble. This department seems to collect fat headed idiots (General Allenby's expression); too much department with a big 'D' and too little war with a small 'w'." Col. Hall Walker commented adversely following an inspection of Reserve Parks in France, September, 1915, recording a waste of 7,000 horses absorbed by 21 Reserve Parks, including for example, a lack of exercising.[68] Administration was well planned with returns made to the QMG's Department and to the WO, with the Director of Remounts (BEF) providing daily 'State of the Day, Reports,' showing demands and what was in stock, 'Weekly Requisitions' for horses and 'Monthly State of All Animals', by classes, divisions and units.[69]

The huge expansion in remount purchases created increased demands for accommodation, personnel to handle the animals, fodder, supply of harness and saddlery, and specialist veterinary equipment and medicines. With the release from remount depots and hospitals in the UK of men fit for the 'firing line', routine work had still to be carried out, in spite of the difficulties presented in the handling of horses by men of inferior physique and often lacking previous experience.

The Veterinary service made similar efforts in relation to their hospitals, convalescent depots and rest farms. Liaison between both services was generally good. The number of already trained and experienced animals taken into care by the AVC and then returned to active service clearly indicates their success. The increase in personnel and units from 1914 was huge, however, for the majority of the war the AVC was working on an establishment of officers 30% below that conceived in pre-war establishments. Many retired officers offered their services for example, Maj-Gen. Sir Frederick Smith, who took charge of veterinary services in Southern Command, where the majority of remounts in the UK were located. Civilian surgeons were employed, but their numbers were small compared to the demand. Early in 1918 the distribution of officers was carefully reviewed, with changes made to economise on personnel and increase professional efficiency. The ensuing redistribution made it possible to considerably increase the number of officers in India, Mesopotamia and the Sudan, without adding to the existing cadre of the Corps. At the same time, the number of civilian veterinary practitioners employed in the UK and Ireland was greatly reduced. The supply of young graduates from British schools was practically exhausted by July 1918 and a Veterinary Tribunal, formed in September, to place these practitioners with the RAVC, came too late to be of real value.[70]

---

68   Home, 1985, p.25, for 25th September 1914; WO107/15, Col. Hall Walker, France, 14th September 1915. For more positive view see *VR*, 1915, Vol.XXVIII, 3rd July, p.7
69   WO107/15.
70   Chapman, 1924, pp.96-98; F. Smith Archive, RCVS, Cabinet 39.

The AVC was responsible for training and keeping the Army supplied with farriers and shoeing-smiths, a vital trade when one considers the QMG's Department provided over 60 million shoes for horses and mules.[71] The increased demand could not be met from the civilian trade, so a School of Farriery was established at Romsey in 1915, two more were added and one in France, with 1,317 pupils passing through them. A history of the Northumberland Hussars Yeomanry references in June 1915 a remount depot, established at Newton Hall, Stocksfield, for which the regiment was responsible. 1,800 horses were conditioned and distributed to the various cavalry, yeomanry and artillery units in the Northern command and a school of farriery and cold shoeing was established there by the GOC Northern command, to meet the shortage of personnel in this special branch of the service. It continued in use until the regiment's departure for York (April 1916) by which time hundreds of NCOs and men from Yeomanry, RFA, RASC, and infantry units had attended courses. Gradually the insufficiently trained 'cold shoers' were replaced by competent shoeing-smiths as by August 1918, some 2,534 were qualified (2,353 British and 181 Indian).

AVC personnel undertaking the care of animals also became casualities. Although their numbers are rarely mentioned they were not inconsiderable: [72]

Other ranks and NCOs

	UK	ANZAC	Canada	India	South Africa
AVC	497	18	24	–	–
RAVC (1918+)	205	–	–	–	–
Shoeing Smiths	619	31	13	30	6
Farriers	29	14	9	23	2
Vet. Assistants	–	–	–	8	-
Vet. Officers*	56	4	2	3	2
Mule Corps Muleteers/drivers	}	3,325 total			
Zion Mule Corps	}	13 total			
Macedonian Mule Corps	}	48 total			

• 9 Killed in action, 24 Died of wounds, 34 Died of disease.

Generally, there was no breakdown in the supply of veterinary equipment and medicines to meet all requirements of war. Considerable progress was made in the

71   RCT. Archive. File No1, B1 0754, p.45; Chapman, p.98; *Statistics*, pp.187, 864.
72   Pease, 1924, p.259. I am grateful to Brian Hill for this information; Commonwealth War Graves Commission and Royal College of Veterinary Surgeons, I am grateful to Andy Chelmsford for this information.

Farriers at work, Rouen, France. (Army Medical Services Museum)

Discarded horseshoes … a small part of the 60 million. (Royal Logistic Corps Museum)

treatment and prevention of animal diseases; equipment was modified and improvements in medical and surgical science was, as far as possible, introduced. The application of modern scientific methods, in the control and treatment of diseases, and the surgical treatment of wounds, gave results undreamed of in the early days of the war.[73] The technical equipment of the AVC was in considerable demand by the French, American and Portuguese Expeditionary Forces, which were supplied, on repayment of stores, to the value of nearly £6,000.[74]

When large numbers of animals are collected together in depots and camps, moved by rail and sea, and generally exposed to bad weather, respiratory sickness, infectious diseases and injury naturally occur. In the UK and France during the winter of 1914-15, before the adequate provision of stabling and hospital accommodation could be made, respiratory sickness and mortality amongst the heavy draught horses was very high.[75] One of the most difficult tasks performed by the AVC, but by far the most important, was the control of contagious disease, necessitating, frequent, and careful repeated inspection of all animals. Shortage of personnel did not assist the Corps in this crucial task.

The highly infectious disease of glanders (affecting bronchial tubes, lungs, glands and skin) and the parasitic skin disease of mange, the principal scourges of animals in former campaigns, were kept under control. There was negligible loss due to glanders. Mallein testing was applied to all 300,000 animals of the BEF in the autumn of 1915 without any interruption to army work. Mange first appeared in France, late November 1914, with mules suffering far less than horses. The maximum incidence of mange and allied skin diseases, in France, was reached in March 1917, when 3.8% of the total number of animals on strength were affected. In October and November, this was reduced to 1%. On the cessation of hostilities only 0.4% of animals were unemployable due to skin disease. Infectious respiratory diseases, such as strangles and catarrhal fever, were the most serious causes of sickness in the early part of war, with influenza and pneumonia prevailing heavily in remounts from overseas.

During 1916 Australian remounts in Egypt developed influenza. Of 3,900 horses and mules, 3,221 (86%) contracted the disease, of which 561 (14%) had severe catarrhal or pneumonic complications. The mildest cases took six weeks before being fit for re-issue. In North America, 1918, there was a severe outbreak amongst remounts sent from collecting centres in the West to the Eastern depots for shipment. In India, April 1915, a shortage of veterinary officers meant a lack of effective control and the disease appeared in Calcutta amongst Australian remounts, but not before animals in the infectious stage had been re-drafted to other depots and units. By September, 16,921 cases had been reported:[76]

73   *Statistics*, p.187; Misc. 846 (IWM), gives a comprehensive nomenclature of diseases under 13 classes.
74   RCT. Archive. File No, B1 0754, p.46.
75   Moore, 1934, p.11.
76   *VR*, 1939, No8, Vol.51, 25th February, p.253.

	No of cases	Mortality	% of admissions
Horses	16,045	886	5.5
Mules	804	5	0.6
Donkeys	72	2	2.8

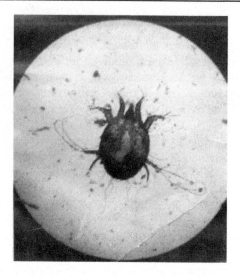

Sarcoptic mange mite.
(Army Medical Services Museum)

Horses, though not many mules, suffered badly from specific, or periodic ophthalmia, with hundreds going blind. This eye disease was very serious in France, appearing early in March 1917, caused by a germ in the mud of Flanders (see Marlborough's Despatches of 1708-9). By the end of the war, casualties of this disease numbered thousands, including some of the best draught horses.[77] Fit, but blind horses were used for work on lines of communication, or returned to the UK.

The worst period in France for the poor condition of horses was early 1917, when the monthly wastage rose to 7%. Cowans was so concerned that he visited France to enquire into the cause, finding that artillery horses suffered most, owing partly to overwork but chiefly from clipping and lack of adequate shelter in the bitter winter of 1916-17. Fearing a serious outbreak of mange, veterinary surgeons insisted that all horses were clipped for disinfection purposes; subsequently horses were only clipped trace high (the line where, for example, the straps or chains which take the pull from the breast collar harness rest on the horse), or not at all. The most serious losses occurred on the Somme, 1916 where shelter was not available, whereas in the Ypres salient matters were never quite so bad. Horse wastage never rose to be as high again and Cowans later provided specific funds and materials for horse shelters. By the middle of 1918, the decrease in contagious

77   Chapman, 1924, p.100; Moore, 1934, p.16.

disease was marked and continued to drop. The percentage of animals affected, or isolated, under suspicion of glanders or mange in France and the UK declined from about 3% in March 1918, to under 1% in March 1919.[78] Disease was kept under control by prompt action in isolating affected animals by the various diseases, disinfection of water troughs and other vehicles of contagion.[79] The main causes of wastage were battle casualties, debility, exhaustion, mange and allied skin diseases such as ophthalmia. Losses from gas (385) were small compared to high explosives and gunshot. In France, nails picked up from littered campaign areas and storage depots, amounted to about 400 cases weekly from the winter of 1915-16 onwards.[80]

Experience gained from the 1899-1902 War, showed that the policy of retaining ineffective animals with fighting formations was unsound. The problem of evacuating sick and wounded animals to base hospitals was largely overcome by the creation of small Mobile Veterinary Sections (see Sketch, Veterinary Origination in the Field, 1918, Chapter 7, Moblisation) that kept in close touch with fighting formations, relieving them of ineffective animals and conveying them to base hospitals on lines of communication. These Sections, used the first time in August 1914 as line of communication units, had an establishment of one officer and 13 other ranks, and were included in the war establishments of the BEF on the basis of one per cavalry brigade and infantry division. Owing to the mobile nature of warfare during the early phases of the campaign, and difficulty of intercommunication, it was not possible to adequately control the movements of these units. As a result they were often completely cut off from any administrative officer who could give them instructions. Despite these difficulties, they gave immediate evidence of their value in the chain of veterinary organisation, by collecting and evacuating large numbers of animals that would otherwise have been lost.[81]

With the growth of the Army in France and divisions organised into Corps, it became necessary to form an additional link in the chain of evacuation, so that mobile veterinary sections were not absent from their formations. Veterinary Evacuating Stations were formed to solve this problem on the understanding that the personnel were found from existing establishments. In May 1918, eighteen stations were placed in the field, designated Army Troops and allotted to Corps as the military situation required, with an establishment of one officer and 38 other ranks, each provided with a motor horse ambulance capable of accommodating two patients, a gift from the RSPCA. The normal allocation was one per corps in France and also later Italy. Hostilities ceased only six months after their formation, but the stations and veterinary sections proved absolutely essential for the efficient clearance of ineffective animals. From August 1914 to January 1919 over 500,000 sick and injured animals were collected and moved by Mobile Veterinary Sections and Evacuating Stations to hospitals.

78   Chapman, pp.100-1; *Statistics*, p.865.
79   RCT. Archive. File No, B1 0754, p.43.
80   Moore, 1934, p.14.
81   RCT Archive. File No1, B1.0754, p.43.

Wounded horses being loaded onto horse drawn ambulance carts; a hospital in France, possibly Rouen. (Army Medical Services Museum)

A summary of the work done by hospitals and convalescent horse depots of the BEF up to the armistice shows:[82]

Admitted	725,216	Cured	529,064
		Died	18,975
		Destroyed (including animals destroyed and sold for food)	127,741
		Sold to agriculturists	29,524
		Remaining under treatment	19,912
		Total:	725,216

---

82   Ibid., pp.43-44; Forgrave, 1987, pp.10-11; Chapman, pp.99-101; Blenkinsop and Rainey, pp.90-91.

Other notable developments included, the adoption of motor horse ambulances to Corps headquarters in the field; establishing the Central Veterinary Research Laboratory at Aldershot and the formation of field laboratories with each expeditionary force; the installation in UK hospitals of electrically driven machinery for clipping and grooming purposes; the application of mechanical methods for the preparation of animal food in veterinary institutions and the setting up of an extensive organisation for the economic disposal of animal carcasses.[83]

More than 70 veterinary hospitals with accommodation for over 100,000 animals were established during the war. 551,960 horses and mules were admitted to hospitals and convalescent horse depots in France, between August 1914 and mid-February 1918, of which 394,768, or 71.5% passed out as cured.[84] Moore gives figures for the period 18th August 1914 to 22 January 1919, of 725,216 animals, which covers the severe fighting of 1918.[85] The numbers successfully treated, up to the second year of the war was 84%, down to 82%, 80% and 78% and gradually lower, as weakened resistance and the recuperative powers of individual animals from the strain of active service became more evident. These figures do not include minor ailments dealt with at the front, usually 2% of strength. A weekly average of 3,500 animals were evacuated to hospitals in France, each eventually capable of dealing with 2,000 patients, with a staff of seven officers and 631 other ranks.

A hospital had eight sub-divisions, each as self-contained as possible, capable of dealing with 250 animals, with each sub-division normally dealing with conditions of a similar nature, for example, respiratory, debility, mange and cases of lameness. From August 1914 to 31st March 1919, the total number of admissions and re-admissions to hospitals and convalescent depots of the Home Commands, BEF, Egypt, Salonika and Mesopotamia amounted to 2,526,549 (admissions, not individual animals), of which 78%, or approximately 2 million, were cured and returned to service. The maximum number of animals under treatment at any one time in hospitals and convalescent depots, at home and overseas, reached 90,000, falling considerably before hostilities ceased on 11th November 1918, to under 60,000, including about 3,000 camels. On 15th March 1919 approximately 22,500 animals remained under treatment.[86]

The annual mortality, from disease and injury, of all animals with British forces at home and with expeditionary forces, was less than 14% for the whole period of the War, despite 89.5% deaths for 1916 in East Africa. The average mortality from all causes in horse and mule freight shipped and transports conveying animals on ocean routes was under 10%.[87]

83   *Statistics*, pp.187, 864; *VR*, 1915, Vol.XXVII, 19th June, p.643.
84   *Statistics*; *VR*, 1914, Vol.XXVII, 19th December, p.338; Blenkinsop and Rainey, pp.561-2.
85   Moore, 1934, p.16.
86   Forgrave, 1987, pp.10-11; Moore, 1934, p.11; *Statistics*, p.863.
87   Chapman, 1924, pp.99-101.

Canadian Veterinary Corps Hospital, Shorncliffe, England.
(Department of National Defence Library and Archives, Canada)

Type of horse shelter, No.5 Veterinary Hospital, Rouen, France. (Army Medical Services Museum)

Reference must be made to the work of voluntary agencies such as the Blue Cross Society, and in particular the RSPCA. The RSPCA offered their services in August 1914 but were turned down, as the WO did not deem it necessary for charitable societies to augment the veterinary work already arranged by army services. In November 1914, the Army Council reconsidered and accepted the Society's offer which was designated by the WO as the Voluntary Aid Society to veterinary services in the field. The WO and IGC in France agreed to accept the Society's offer of ten motor lorries, ten motor ambulances, nine corn and chaff cutters, 2,000 shelters (stabling accommodation), 5,000 horse rugs, 5,000 headstalls, 5,000 halters and 5,000 sets of bandages. A Society representative in France personally superintended, for example, the erection of No.8 Veterinary Hospital at Forges-les-Eaux and stabling for 500 animals at Gournay. The RSPCA provided their own trained veterinary staff, helped recruit new staff and set up an official fund *For sick and Wounded Animals*, raising over £1/4 million.[88]

By the end of the war some 13 hospitals (for 13,500 horses) were equipped, each with an operating theatre, forage barns and dressing sheds; a complete convalescent depot was funded and tented hospitals to accommodate a further 6,800 horses; 180 horse and 26 motor ambulances plus a great variety of equipment.[89] A reference in the *Veterinary Record* mentions the work of Lady French and Mrs Adelaide M. Moore (wife of Maj. Gen Moore DGAVC, BEF) in raising money for the RSPCA. Mrs Moore established a fund, for such things as money and clothes for AVC personnel.

Mechanisation

The importance of mechanical vehicles during the war deserves greater acknowledgment. Singleton, in an article on the military use of horses, wrote that the internal combustion engine had a poor record of reliability, and in 1914 the British army could muster a mere 507 assorted vehicles.[90] Nothing could be further from the truth. The Army had reorganised its transport and supply arrangements prior to 1914, with motor transport columns rapidly replacing ASC horse transport columns.[91] The conservative British Army did not take such a monumental step based upon unreliability and the availability of only 507 vehicles. The arrangements for the provision of motor vehicles on mobilisation was on exactly the same basis as the horse.

A WO document records that, for the first time in modern warfare mechanical transport had been used extensively for the carriage of supplies and ammunition for

88   *VR*, 1914, Vol.XXVIII, 29th August, p.139, 1915, Vol.XXVI, 13th March, p.485.
89   Moore, 1930, p.119; Cooper, 1983, pp.40-42; *Statistics*, p.864; RCT. Archive. File No1, B1 0754, p.46; Moss, 1961, pp.122-3; Blenkinsop and Rainey, pp.56-8; *VR*, 1914, Vol.XXVII, 28th November, p.305, 1915, Vol.XXVIII, 3rd July, p.9.
90   Singleton, 1993, p194, from WO161/18, 'History of the Department of the Senior Inspector of Mechanical Transport, 1918'.
91   WO107/63, 'Report of the Motor Transport Committee', Annual Report, 1911-12.

Operating theatre, No.5 Veterinary Hospital, Rouen, France. (Army Medical Services Museum)

the army in the field, and with the extreme mobility and other advantages gained from motor transport its use was extended far more than anticipated. The principal vehicle was the 3 to 4-ton lorry on solid rubber tyres, encouraged under the pre-war Subsidy Scheme. It was a relatively economical and reliable performer when road conditions were good. However, mainly on account of its great axle-weight and low torque-weight ratio, it was very poor for negotiating rough and soft ground, making the ability to move off the road negligible. Where conditions of war necessitated some degree of cross country ability, vehicles of lighter axle weight, higher torque-weight ratio, shod with pneumatic tyres, such as the light Fiat lorry and the Ford car, were used relatively successfully.[92] Galtrey wrote, "you may ask if it is not a fact that motor haulage has largely displaced horses. Obviously from the figures it has not done so. To a limited extent it has done so or there would be no reason for the existence of the bewildering growth of the ASC motor transport companies and the immense 'parks' of motor lorries in France and other countries, and again the tractors which are now part of all heavy siege artillery units".[93]

The outstanding feature of mechanical transport was its phenomenal growth from 842 vehicles on peacetime establishments to 121,702 of all types, in all theatres on

92   WO107/19.
93   Galtrey, 1918, p.14.

11th November 1918. Yet, at no time during the war did supply meet demand.[94] Of the 842 motor vehicles on the 1914 peacetime establishment, the War Department owned only 80; 727 being subsidised. On mobilisation, all subsidised vehicles were immediately called in and the balance, traceable by the Subsidy Scheme register, were impressed. Despite the impressive quantity of mechanical vehicles on 4th August 1914, the BEF's road transport needs in France were still met largely by animal transport. Only in operations in Mesopotamia, Egypt and Palestine was the mobility offered by mechanical vehicles significantly achieved.

On leaving England, the BEF was fully equipped with mechanical transport according to the authorised establishments. To 10th September 1914, this included:[95]

Motor lorries	1,468
Motor cycles	326
Motor ambulances	58
Total	1,852

The maximum number of mechanical vehicles, 125,149 was reached on the 1st March 1919, including:

Motor lorries	53,107
Pneu-tyred vehicles and ambulances	31,098
Motor cycles	36,953
Total	121,158

In addition, there was the massive increase in drivers, mechanics, depot staff, new depots, workshops and training:

BEF	4,229
UK	11,797
Indian and Colonies	798
Total	16,824

As the BEF grew in size and requirements, additional motor transport was sanctioned for a range of new purposes. Problems arose with the increase in divisions and therefore the number of vehicles on the roads. In September 1914, when the BEF was on the Aisne, the army of six divisions with a front of 20 miles had about 1,200 lorries, equating to 200 lorries per division and 60 lorries per mile of front. In September 1916, the Fourth Army with a front of 15 miles had 4,691 lorries, 235 lorries per

94   *Statistics*, p.852
95   WO107/19, 13th September 1914.

division and over 300 per mile of front, in addition to over 1,000 motor cars and nearly 2,000 motor cycles.[96]

Marcosson wrote that when the real story of the 'Great War' was written technical experts would probably call it an 'artillery war', but it would always be known as the 'war of mechanical transport'.[97] An interesting contrast is to be found in correspondence from Cowans to Maxwell where he notes that in relation to financial cutbacks, the Prime Minister stressed the urgency for a reduction of expenditure, suggesting that horses in reserve parks might replace a good deal of the mechanical transport at the front, thus saving wear and tear on motor lorries and expenditure on petrol. Reserve parks were viewed as some sort of rest park where horses not being used and, or, in good condition were eating forage.[98]

During the summer of 1916, demand for motor transport from overseas increased. In addition to the output of British manufacturers contracts were placed in America for large numbers of vehicles, but for financial reasons these contracts were cancelled; they were re-opened later in the year for about 70 lorries per week. It was impossible, for example, to cancel the American contracts for Holt Caterpillar tractors and four-wheeled drive vehicles (which pulled the big guns) as they were not a type produced in the UK. The outstanding success for the use of motor vehicles was in the Eastern Theatres under conditions thought impossible in pre-war days. They were put to the hardest test in the Palestine campaign during the advance over some of the most difficult country a lorry could encounter. In the advance from Jerusalem 75% of vehicles were out of action, a position Allenby considered so serious that he decided on a retirement unless the transport could be got moving again. In 1917, when chairman of the Motor Transport Board, Cowans wrote that the tendency to substitute motor, for horses transport, was more and more marked. Experiments in for example the transportation of field guns and machine gun battalions by motor vehicles was a change that was about to take place just prior to the Armistice, but it was ultimately decided not to proceed further with this alteration. The question of providing a large number of cross-country tractors for use in special operations in the spring of 1919 was also under consideration.[99]

At Passchendaele in November 1917, the system of light railways sustained accurate and heavy concentrated enemy artillery fire. Practically immobilised, they were unable to cope, with for example, the immense volume of ammunition, engineering stores, and supplies required to be moved in forward areas. The bulk of maintenance work fell to mechanical and animal transport. In his despatch of 15th December 1917, Haig paid great tribute to the work of the motor transport service.

96   Henniker, 1937, pp.147-8.
97   Marcosson, 1918, p.78.
98   WO107/15, 28th November 1915.
99   Chapman, 1924, pp.124-5, 128-34.

A complete reorganisation of motor transport was carried out by the QMG in 1917 and successfully tested during the German offensive of 1918, when the main railways were shelled, became disorganised and the great lateral supply line St Just – Amien and St Pol – Hazebrouck was abandoned, leaving only one lateral route open, Eu – Abbeville – Etaples. Again, the maintenance of the armies in the field relied upon motor and animal transport. As the railheads were far back, long-distance haulage was carried out by motor transport, which was crucial from the time the Amiens-Arras railway line was rendered useless until it was reinstated in July 1918. With the advance to victory, reconditioning of the railways was a slow process and the advance of railheads could not keep pace with that of the armies, so once again troops were supplied over long distances by motor transport.[100] The area covered by the 1918 offensive contained many narrow roads and one way paved tracks in bad repair that had been systematically broken up. Dense traffic, constant congestion around rail heads and lorry routes, and the irregular arrival of trains at railheads, made working conditions for the vastly increased number of motor transport columns more difficult than in 1914. In the Fourth Army area, the repair of mine-craters in the roads could not keep pace with the advance, with the range of the columns limited by the extent to which roads had been made passable. Ironically, shortly before the Armistice, horse transport from ammunition columns was being used to carry loads forward.[101]

The increased use and efficiency of motor transport was essential in keeping British armies mobile and supplied, its use should be seen as complimentary to that of animals, as without either, the allied military efforts would have been brought to a standstill.[102]

---

100 RCT Archive, File No1, B1 0754; Chapman, p.230.
101 Henniker, 1937, p.461.
102 RCT Archive, C6/2531, Capt.C.H. Kuhne, RASC, London, 1927, p.1; the MT Inspection Branch formed, 1915, the Census Branch July 1915, Motor Transport Experimental Section, early 1916 the Motor Drivers Section of Women's Legion founded, Corps of Women Drivers, ASC; WO163/21, Army Council, Minutes of 24th August 1916, Agenda (4), 'Transfer of Responsibility for the Supply of Mechanical Transport from the WO to the Ministry of Munitions', (Précis No.834); RCT. Archive. B1.0754, 'Report of QMG's Staff', document DT-12521/7/6, 'Organisation and Development of QMG's Services During the War', HQ of Transport Directorate; *RASCQ*, 1924, Vol.12, July, p.327, letter to Editor from Lt-Col. A Berger, RASC; *VR* 1915, Vol.XXVII, 19th June, p.643; WO95/4202, ref. value of horse transport compared with MT in Italy on River Piave.

11

Supply to Other Theatres

"We cannot do without horses in army work despite the advance of mechanised operations."[1]

The largest demand for animals came from the Western Front, but it is important to note that in addition to supplying remounts for the British Armies, in all theatres, the Remount Department supplied to other allied forces: Australian and New Zealand, Canadian, Belgian, American, Portuguese and some French units.[2]

Canada

In Canada, for example, an element of competition in purchasing was introduced when the Canadians entered the war and had to complete establishments for their own forces (2nd Division and mounted rifles regiments), and provide 1,500 remounts monthly for the Canadian Expeditionary Force (CEF); though these went into a general pool in England. In August 1915, it was agreed that the British Remount Commission would be responsible for all purchases in Canada and supplying CEF requirements overseas from the WO pool; Canadian purchases were then limited to such horses as were needed in Canada for training purposes. Purchases fluctuated, and eventually practically ceased on transfer of operations to the U.S. Throughout the war the Commission purchased only about 31,402 horses in Canada, with the Canadian authorities purchasing 24,672 horses between 4th August 1914 and the end of November 1915.[3]

---

1   *VR*, 1940, Vol.52, 7th February, p.131. Lecture given by Maj- Gen. Sir J. Moore, 'The Horse as an Economic Factor', to the Newcastle Congress, 1928, of the Central Veterinary Society.
2   WO107/17; *Statistics*, p.862; Chapman, 1924, p.91; Blenkinsop and Rainey, 1925 is the major source for the text in this chapter.
3   *Official History of the Canadian Forces*, 1938, p.188.

Gallipoli, or Dardanelles Campaign: 25th April 1915 – 9th January 1916[4]

The first landings by a joint force of French, with British and Anzac units from the Mediterranean Expeditionary Force (MEF), took place at Cape Helles and Sari Bair (ANZAC Cove), on 25th April 1915; a second major British landing took place at Suvla Bay on 6th August. The MEF HQ was at Alexandria, 650 miles from the Gallipoli Campaign HQ on the island of Mudros, which was about 60 miles from Helles. The campaign was difficult for the horse services especially for the AVC with very extended lines of communication causing great difficulties in administration.

The landing force departed from the island of Lemnos. Animals were transferred from horse transports to lighters of various sizes, capable of carrying 24 to 76 horses. Disembarkation and landing took place with comparatively few casualties, but during the first week on shore there were many casualties from rifle, machine gun and shell-fire, as ten days after landing the enemy began regularly shelling the beaches. In one incident 80 hopelessly wounded animals had to be shot. The selection of sites for horse lines was limited since all were in range of enemy fire. On 10th May, the DVS and AQMG (MEF) selected fresh sites for the horse lines of all mounted units, after which, casualties were appreciably reduced; similar action was taken with lines dug under the edge of cliffs at Anzac and Suvla. The horse numbers allowed on the Peninsula were restricted, due to a water problem and limited space, for example, Artillery were only allowed to land one team per battery. Most 42nd Division animals were disembarked and returned to Alexandria, with some units leaving large detachments of men in Alexandria to look after their animals. A lack of roads and the light sandy soil soon churned up the ground making the draught work for horses and mules very heavy especially during and shortly after the landings. Work eased at the end of April with the arrival of the Indian and Zion Mule Corps (a Jewish unit, raised March 1915).[5] The wounded animals in the Indian Transport Corps at Cape Helles, between 25th April 1915 and 29th January 1916, were numbered about 500 (25%) and at Anzac, from 25th April to 15th August:

	Horses	Mules	Total	%
Killed	2	259	261	16
Wounded	4	599	603	31
Total	6	858	864	

The 7th Indian Mountain Artillery brigade, with only 56 mules from each battery, landed on the 25th April at Anzac Cove and were immediately sent into action,

4   Blenkinsop and Rainey, 1925, Chapter X, pp.106-127.
5   Half of the Zion Mule Corps, commanded by Col. Paterson, landed at Cape Helles 26th April, the remainder went to ANZAC Cove probably on 27th. My thanks to Brian Hill.

however most of their mules were subsequently sent back to Mudros for lack of water. Watering was a serious problem at Cape Helles due to a lack of pumps, troughs and with watering parades attracting enemy fire. Only the excellent condition of the animals when landed enabled them to survive the deprivation without any appreciable effects. In addition to the 950 mules already at Anzac, eventually 3,700 mules and 1,750 water carts were provided for Anzac and Suvla; 100 local small donkeys were also purchased. Horses suffered from the extreme of temperatures, from summer heat to the extremes of autumn cold; a lack of rugs and shelter from the wind and cold resulted in a considerable loss of condition. Forage supply was of a good quality, consisting of oats, crushed barley and maize, compressed forage and hay. There were difficulties with its landing and distribution, especially in rough weather, resulting in animals occasionally being on half rations; leading to the ingestion of sand and an increase in cases of sand colic (accumulation of sand in the large colon – see Glossary). Despite repeated requests for reinforcements, there remained a shortage of personnel in the horse lines, with some work, such as shoeing, neglected.[6] There were problems with the weight of shoes; the DVS ordered the type used in India and South Africa but only a small number arrived before evacuation.

Animals maintained their condition and health extremely well considering the conditions of the campaign. Not until September and October was there any appreciable loss of condition, in some cases through work, others from an unavoidable shortage of personnel in horse lines, and exposure. Very few cases of debility were evacuated to base hospitals until November and December. Sanitation was affected by the limited space available, as it was almost impossible to change the ground, or location, on which the animals were kept. Horse manure was burnt in incinerators, dumped as far from the lines as possible, or thrown over the cliffs. Disposal of carcasses was even more difficult and cremation was impracticable, eventually, when personnel and equipment was available, the Navy towed carcasses two miles out to sea on barges or rafts, cut them open, weighted them down with stones and threw them overboard. Due to enemy submarine activity horse transports were unable to get alongside the Peninsula, or any of the islands, or anchor near the coast. Every animal evacuated had to be slung on board and for those placed on small ferry steamers this was repeated for re-loading onto lighters; the operation was then repeated when transferring to transports at Mudros Bay. This difficulty had to be taken into consideration when selecting sick animals for evacuation; those too ill, or seriously injured for slinging, were destroyed.

Restrictions on the number of animals used on the Peninsula, compared with the number originally intended for use, in conjunction with the constant shifting of animals to and from base detail camps, at Alexandria, Port Said, Mudros and Imbros, made it impossible to ascertain the exact number of animals landed, killed,

6   Kingston (IWM reference 88/27/1) a farrier, NCO; Stuttard, 18th Mobile Section, RAVC (IWM reference 90/7/1).

died and wounded during operations. The completion of returns, collated from many widely distributed camps and the loss of correspondence en route, involved delays and frequent discrepancies. In August, there were some 8,863 animals and 19 veterinary officers allotted to the Corps on the Peninsula, in addition to about 5,000 animals at Alexandria, 3,080 in Mudros and nearly 20,000 in other parts of Egypt belonging to formations involved in the Gallipoli operations. There was little alteration in this strength until the evacuation of the Peninsula.[7] Approximately 50% of admissions to hospitals for treatment were from injuries, including wounds from shell and rifle fire, with 25% due to digestive trouble and 10% to debility.[8] The number of inefficient animals in hospitals and convalescent horse depots reached its maximum in December 1915 and in view of the conditions, the numbers were not excessive. Sand Colic was very prevalent in base camps at Alexandria throughout the summer of 1915 and was indirectly responsible for the number of debility cases, although indifferent horsemastership was more often the cause. The bulk of contagious diseases were attributed to influenza in animals from horses transports, but this was probably "shipping fever", a type of pneumonia, not influenza.

Embarkation for the evacuation of Suvla and Anzac began on 11th December 1915, taking place at night. Animals were taken off in small steamers and lighters and landed at Kephalos, Mudros and Tenedos, or transferred directly to larger horse transports for despatch to Eygpt and Salonika, most having at least two transfers of ships. A veterinary officer was stationed at each point of embarkation, with one left till last on Gallipoli to superintend the humane destruction of animals left behind. In the confusion of evacuation and for some time after, the submission of accurate returns was impossible. On 4th December the strength of animals at Suvla was 2,525 and Anzac 2,020 (total 4,545), with all surviving animals at Suvla being evacuated, but not all from Anzac. About 56 Indian Mule Cart Corps animals and some donkeys were not evacuated. James lists 3,684 horses and mules evacuated and 508 animals slaughtered and left behind. The Evacuation of Helles, animal strength 4,296, began on 29th December and was completed by the early morning of 9th January 1916; 907 were destroyed, missing or abandoned. In No.16 veterinary hospital, with capacity for 250 animals, sick animals were destroyed and buried.[9]

Salonika, or Macedonian Front: 21st October 1915- 30th September 1918[10]

The British Army was one of six nationalities (Greece, Serbia, Russia, France, Italy) involved in this campaign; initially consisting of two divisions of the Salonika Force

---

7   Taken from tables in Blenkinsop and Rainey, pp.116-7, complied soon after the Suvla landings, 6th August 1915.
8   Tables in Blenkinsop and Rainey, pp.124-7, weekly statistical returns.
9   James, 1965, p.347.
10   The main source for this section is WO95/4202, War Diary of the DDR and ADR, Italy; also Blenkinsop and Rainey, pp.359-384, especially pp.277-88.

(MEF), landing in November 1915 and increasing by the autumn of 1916, to six divisions and two mounted brigades. The lack of railways and roads in the British sector led to an increase in animal transports to the extent that by 1916, instead of 6,000 animals per division there were 10,000. The roads were poor and had to be metalled and constantly repaired by the horse transport companies. Most of the gun positions were on the hilltops, or forward slopes and only accessible to pack transport; in the river valley, the deep sand often made the passage of wheeled transport difficult. There was a remarkable variety in climate, severe cold winters, snow, rain, winds and heat, and mud in winter on un-metalled roads was possibly worse than on the Western Front.

With long road communications horse transport companies were overworked and being widely scattered, general supervision and management was difficult. Once artillery batteries were in position, using every available man, the gun horses were mostly idle and horse management became a problem. In the early period of the campaign, wastage at the front and on the road lines of communication was very heavy. Demands were placed on the reserve of animals at the base, many of which were unfit. The standard of horse management and fitness of reserve animals was greatly improved with regular and regulated exercise, along with the paving of horse lines and erection of wind breaks; although the problems of horse management on lines of communication always remained below that at the front.

The supply of forage for such a large force, and so far overseas, especially with the constant sinking of supply ships, caused problems, for example, one effect of the shortage of hay was a widespread epidemic of sand colic. During 1918, when shipping losses reached a climax, the Salonika Force cultivated forage on a large scale, hospitals contributed by ploughing and sowing 1,500 acres, from which they reaped about 600 tons for themselves.

In a force composed of different nationalities there were many opportunities for the spread of infection with the exchanging of positions and use of the same roads. Outbreaks of mange were practically confined to the first eighteen months, and from 1917 to the close of hostilities, only 32 cases occurred. Other diseases caused few problems, for example, ulcerative lymphangitis and specific ophthalmia; pneumonia was unknown as animals always lived in the open. There were no intermediate convalescent depots and hospitals were based close to the town of Salonika. Five remount centres were erected, with the usual problems created by a shortage of remount and veterinary personnel.

The supply of remounts began arriving during the middle of winter, then arrived rapidly and almost without interruption until the following autumn; only small numbers of horses were then received and no mules. The supply of remounts was calculated on an anticipated monthly wastage of 15% of horses, and 5% of mules, the loss of remounts through sickness on transport ships was negligible, and they were virtually free from mange. More than 50,000 remounts arrived in less than a year creating a difficult situation for accommodation and management, for example in water supply. The remount situation was partly relieved with the transfer of 12,000 surplus reserve animals to Egypt. For nearly two years remounts contributed over a third of the sick in hospitals, which were returning 86.6% of their patients to the field; a weekly average of 200 so that remount squadrons had a good supply. With the submarine threat and shortage of horse transports, the transfer of debility cases to Egypt was impracticable. Sickness reached 12% of strength, suddenly rising to 17% when two divisions and almost two mounted brigades were transferred to Egypt, along with a large number of remounts. In the bad year of 1916, net wastage, including remounts, was 24%, of which casualties in remount depots accounted for at least one third. In 1917, the net wastage, including remounts, fell to 12% and in 1918, the numbers returned from hospitals outnumbered the total wastage at the front and in remount depots by 3,909. This was partly due to the reduction in the Salonika Force, showing that wastage at the front itself was extremely low. Total wastage in veterinary hospitals for 1916-18 was only 11.3% of admissions.[11]

Italian Front: 23rd May 1915 – 6th November 1918[12]

Austro-Hungarian and German forces heavily defeated the Italian army with enormous loss at the Battle of Caporetto, October-November 1917. The Italians were then reinforced by French and British forces from France. Concentration of the British Italian Expeditionary Force (IEF) was completed between 16th November and early December 1917, mainly of formations and units from the XIVth Army Corps (animal strength of 17,960) and XIth Army Corps (animal strength of 7,949, less 5th Division which arrived later); Army Headquarters, Army Troops and Lines of Communication units (animal strength of 2,685).

During the period of concentration, 436 cases (3.76% of strength) required treatment, of which 140 (0.8% of strength) were cured and 61 (0.38%) died. Animals were railed from France between October and December; journeys that were poorly organised with some cases of mange and 76 cases of pneumonia, of which 39 were fatal. During the road march, after the long train journey, laminitis inevitably occurred (a painful inflammatory condition of the foot tissues), following a period of forced-inertia and unsuitable diet, when horses were put to work before the circulatory system of the feet had been restored. There were also 37 cases of digestive problems, 19 fatal. During December the number of remount squadrons increased from two to three (No's 10, 19 and 33), providing a reserve of 1,500 animals. Due to the volume of veterinary evacuations and remount squadron personnel having to provide conducting parties to forward areas and Marseilles, in January 1918, the DDR (Col.H. Palmer) requested, unsuccessfully, a fourth squadron, which would have increased the reserve of animals and men. There were initial problems and some confusion over good sites for the location of remount camps, which in some cases had to be moved between

---

11 Blenkinsop and Rainey, pp.277-88.
12 Ibid., Chapter XV, pp.359-384; WO95/ 4202, War Diary DDR Italy.

winter and summer sites. Water supplies were monitored and all use of village troughs prohibited, for protection against local infection, and there was never sufficient cover, or hard standings.

During the first phase of operations, 5th December 1917 to 30th March 1918, there were a number of problems, for example, with the Italian authorities not recognising the need to evacuate sick animals by rail. Also owing to a shortage of coal, cold shoeing was the only option, with unsatisfactory results. Hard standings were required as the soil in the River Po valley was mostly clay and unsuitable for horses. In March, Palmer records borrowing two lorries over two weeks for transporting sand and stones from a river bed to make hard standings. Horsemasters, or Corps Horse Advisors, appointed in France, accompanied some units to Italy and provided courses of instruction in shoeing, horsemastership, sanitation and disinfection, fitting of saddlery and harness, veterinary first aid, march discipline and equitation. In January, Palmer requested the exchange of light draught horses for heavy draught, required for heavy artillery batteries, and in February some 1,400 pack mules to replace draught horses and GS wagons for mountain warfare. Early in March, the IGC requested a reduction in the Remount Establishment but Palmer considered it advisable to keep all three squadrons. He further requested that no more 'B' class Rough Riders (breaking and schooling horses) be re-classified as 'A' men and sent to fighting units, as there were only 13 in the country to re-train awkward and vicious animals and if more were taken the re-training of animals, young mules especially, would present difficulties.

A remount train of mules from France was cancelled due to the German March offensive and early in April hay trains were cancelled, with forage rations reduced as a temporary measure. Blenkinsop and Rainey state that owing to enemy submarine activity forage rations were reduced by 2lb oats and the DDR records for 3rd April, that owing to the non-arrival of hay trains from France, the forage ration was reduced, as a temporary measure; heavy draught to 12lbs, other animals over 15 hands to 9lbs and animals under 15 hands to 8lbs, a level of forage that was particularly hard on light draught mules doing pack work. The normal full ration was restored after a short time, supplemented by straw, lucerne or Alfalfa (perennial flowering plant in the pea family cultivated as an important forage crop) and green fodder. There was no shortage of water in the plains and only in certain sectors of the mountainous plateau.[13]

During this phase of operations, 4,976 animals were received from France and 897 returned from hospitals; wastage amounted to 26 killed and 45 wounded. Mange was prevalent during December 1917 and January 1918 mainly among animals that had not been clipped before leaving France. The casting and selling of animals, other than for veterinary reasons, was to be on the same basis as in France; some old and worn out horses were cast and sold for meat and one for work on the land.

With the Austrian defeat at the Battle of Piave in June 1918, the second phase of operations, 31st March to 15th October 1918, saw the British line move north,

---

13   Blenkinsop and Rainey, p.369; WO95-4202, 3rd April 1918.

taking over a mountain sector, with an increased demand for pack animals and requirements for a new pattern shoe suitable for this terrain, with all the additional work entailed in such a change. Heavy draught horses were used in the plain region to take supplies from railhead to divisional refilling points; some 1,400 pack mules were supplied to replace draught horses and GS wagons for mountain warfare. Col. Swabery, Director of Transport, converted an auxiliary horse transport company into one of pack mules by exchanging the heavy draught horses for the mules of the divisional ammunition column. All pack work was done my mules, with an increase of 40% per battalion. It was necessary to train animals to a high degree of physical fitness before they could endure the strenuous uphill work, in altitude and temperatures to which they were unaccustomed. Supplies had to be hauled from the plain to the plateau, a height difference of some 3,000 feet, on a general slope of 1 in 10 with many zig-zag and hairpin bends. Units made permanent standings for animals and in the summer erected temporary shelters as protection from the sun; the area provided good summer grazing. The AVC structure consisted of an evacuation station clearing sick animals to veterinary aid posts and mobile veterinary sections to hospitals, with a central dressing station established for animals of infantry brigades in the line. There was good co-operation between allied formations irrespective of the nationality of the casualty; 84 animals of the French, 929 of the Italians and 4,443 British received treatment; the veterinary evacuating station conducted 1,078 animals to the base, a weekly average of 60.

During March-April 1918, the IEF was reduced to three divisions and Palmer was again questioned about reducing the Remount Establishment by one squadron which he advised against, as owing to the situation in France it might not be possible to despatch any more remounts to Italy. There were 16,600 animals with units in the forward area and on lines of communication. Keeping the IEF horsed to establishment, required a monthly average of 700 remounts (4%). There were few battle casualties and little disease at that time, but if the situation changed, Palmer considered the wastage rate could exceed 7%, requiring about 1,100 animals monthly, with a reserve of 1,200 animals from the three remount squadrons. The IEF was able to be independent of France for about three months, provided 800 animals monthly were returned from hospitals. In June, the average wastage was recorded as 1,232 animals, 7.7%. Palmer had requested notice of the future situation for the supply of remounts from France and in June was notified that no difficulty was anticipated in supply to Italy, providing the BEF received shipments from the UK

The C-in-C (Italy), decided to reduce remount personnel, No.33 squadron, by 42 other ranks; Nos. 10 and 19 were maintained at war establishment. In August Palmer agreed to release No.33 squadron to France, less their horses, one officer and 33 other ranks for the Field Remount Section and closure of a remount depot, but only if no American troops were sent to Italy. However, in the November, the DDR received instructions to have ready for issue 174 animals for horsing the regimental transport of one American infantry headquarters and four infantry regiments. October was a bad month for horses and remount personnel due to heavy rains with consequent deep mud in depots and an outbreak of influenza amongst the men. With 150 men in hospital and two deaths, rising to 164 and seven deaths, Palmer requested the temporary transfer of 100 dismounted yeomanry to assist at depots. He records that the majority of remount personnel were old and unsound and he did not think they would stand the winter living in wooden huts, but by late October he notes animals were looking well and the men's health was improving.

During this phase, 965 animals were received from France and 4,658 from hospitals. 62 animals were killed by shellfire and 99 wounded (35 seriously), the majority occurred amongst animals working between the wagon lines and units, others were killed in the wagon lines. 8.53% of horses and 7.53% of mules in the forward area were evacuated to hospitals for debility. In April, nine animals were sold for work on the land and two blind animals for meat; France took 50 blind horses and eleven were swopped for heavy draught at the base transport depot. In June, France reported only heavy draught blind animals were wanted. In July animals were selected for the butcher, the balance were all blind heavy horses, many of excellent type, however, it was decided not to sell blind animals. Palmer requested that the Director of Transport sanction sending them to divisional transport, auxiliary horse transport companies in exchange for sound animals. The Italian authorities were informed that no blind horses were to be sold except to horse butchers, as instructed by the WO. In September the WO sanctioned the sale of animals no longer fit for service to farmers for agricultural purposes, with guarantees of subsequent good treatment; it is also noted that 38 animals were sold for extraordinary high prices.

Palmer's diary contains some interesting references to the disposal of animals no longer fit for military service and plans for demobilisation. There was clearly a high demand through the Italian authorities for working animals. In July the Agricultural Society at Cremona (base remount depot and hospital) guaranteed that animals sold by the Army were to be available for veterinary inspection, and that they would not change hands without sanction from the Society. There were discussions in June with Italian authorities in Rome and with the ADR Italian Army, about disposal of IEF animals on demobilization; the outcome being that the Italian Government could purchase them at a flat rate and sell them alongside those of the Italian Army on the open market, probably through two main horse dealers in Rome and Milan. Palmer submitted a scheme for the demobilization and disposal of animals based on that of the BEF in France.

In the final phase of operations, 16th October to 4th November 1918, owing to the complete rout of the enemy at the Battle of Piave, there were few animal casualties and the mobile veterinary sections of the divisions were able to deal with their sick. The Battle of Vittorio Veneto, 24th October and 3rd November 1918, saw the final Austrian defeat and surrender. On 11th November Palmer requested that remounts due from France be held there owing to the number of captured enemy horses. On the 14th November, the Remount establishment consisted of one depot at Cremona with No.10 and 19 Remount squadrons, a headquarters, and a Field Remount Section from No.33 squadron (one officer and 30 other ranks). There were two base veterinary hospitals, No.1 and 22, which from 1st January to 14th November 1918, admitted 9,270 animals, of which 70.47% were discharged to remounts; 1.13% died, or were destroyed in hospital, 12.60% were cast and sold for destruction.

For the period 24th October to 4th November, 1918, 117 animals were killed and 223 wounded. Between 16th and 31st October, aid posts dealt with 408 cases (91 Italian and 8 French), however this increased during the period 1st June to 7th November, with 929 casualties from the Italian army and 84 from the French being dressed and cleared, in addition to 4,443 British; totalling 5,456.

No.1 and 2 Animal Collecting Camps were established for demobilisation, the former at the Cremona Remount Depot for animals on lines of communication, and the latter, with personnel from yeomanry squadrons, for animals with GHQ, Corps HQ and Corps troops. Each division was to form two collecting camps, each for 2,000 animals. To estimate damage to the ground, trees and buildings on the site used by No.19 squadron, Palmer with an officer from the Hirings and Requisition Branch, visited the Marchese Cornaggia, landlord of the Bidella remount depot. After examining the ground and he was told to submit his claim for compensation. The casting and selling of animals continued, but on 14th December Palmer cancelled a sale that was poorly attended on finding the Italian Government was selling 600 horses at very low prices in Milan. Sales to farmers had not been a successful as they would not bid against each other and few were sold, so the GOC (Italy) sanctioned the sale of animals to people other than farmers. Horses sold to City Companies and Municipalities with public money were thought to be better treated, with lighter work and shorter hours than those sold to farmers. During December, 861 animals were cast or sold. The British Remount Department in Egypt requested permission to transfer a large number of surplus draught horses to sell in eastern Italy, but this was refused on cost grounds. At the end of February 1919, 2,765 animals were in hospitals and 6,273 had been sold for £477,516 averaging £76 each. In March, orders were published for the repatriation of about 30 officers' chargers at a price agreed by a remount officer, and details for about 1,600 animals to be kept in Italy for the Army of Occupation, with a small reserve. At the end of March the total number of animals sold was 12,903.

During the whole campaign veterinary hospitals dealt with 14,358 animals, excluding 4,785 admitted from the forward area to be treated with mallein before transferring to depots for sale. The output from hospitals, on percentage of field strength, rose over 1% in April 1918, the highest being 1.61% for the week ending 20th June 1918. The average weekly number of horses sick in hospitals was 11.64% of the total horse establishment, and 6.6% for mules. The annual rate of wastage amongst horses was 13.52% of which 5.2% died, or were destroyed, with 8.32% cast and sold; for mules the corresponding figures are, 6.76%, 4.16% and 2.6% respectively.

Persian Campaign (South Persia), December 1914 – 30 October 1918[14]

British dominance over the Persian Gulf was crucial to the security of trade routes to India. The Anglo-Russian Treaty of 1907 divided Persia into northern and southern spheres of interest. In 1914 Persia declared for neutrality, but this was not respected by Turkey, or Germany, who moved into the central and southern regions. The series of engagements in this Campaign were essentially part of the ongoing struggles between the British, Russian and Ottoman Empires, with Germany acting as agent provocateur hoping to free Persia from British and Russian influence, divide Britain and Russia, ultimately leading to an invasion of India.[15]

An ADVS taken from an already greatly depleted veterinary staff in India was sent to South Persia, arriving April 1917, and included in the Establishment of the South Persia Rifles, a locally recruited militia in 1916, commanded by British officers. The ADVS arrived to find one Indian veterinary assistant and no hospital except a small and very dirty dark stable in the infantry barracks. The main work for the ADVS was the number of cases of foot lameness in transport mules, extensive galls from the pack saddlery and "palans" (twin side mounted stretchers or panniers) in the mules and camels.[16] The mules were very small, undersized, of poor physique and not shod, so during long and arduous marches, over hard stony ground they suffered from bruised feet and laminitis; mule equipment was far too big and caused excessive pressure on the ribs and withers. A hospital was eventually located in the former stables of a prince and governor, with accommodation for 69 animals including sixteen loose boxes, two colic boxes and a forge There was further outside accommodation for 62 animals and an adjoining isolation stable; all areas had a good supply of water. As the veterinary services developed, two further hospitals were established with a veterinary officer and field veterinary section at each. Poor horsemastership among the personnel was the cause of problems, poor grooming and bedding materials, and a lack of drainage with consequent cracked heels. Shoeing arrangements were not always satisfactory, with no good British farriers. Contagious diseases included glanders, sarcoptic mange and fever. Sanitation was unknown so little was done in the country to suppress outbreaks of known diseases as animals were only killed for food.

---

14   Blenkinsop and Rainey, Chapter XVIII, pp.428-438.
15   Overview of Persian Campaign see Purnell, 1966, volumes 1 and 3.
16   My thanks to Andy Chelmsford for information on pack saddlery.

North Russian Expeditionary Force and British Mission to South Russia, 1918-1920[17]

The October Bolshevik Revolution of 1917 and the civil war that followed brought Allied intervention in support of the White Russian faction fighting against the Bolshevik Red Army, from the final months of the War in 1918 through to 1920. For British forces, involvement in North and South Russia was not as significant in comparison with other theatres of war, although Britain played a leading role in foreign intervention and in supplying military equipment and training. It is interesting that none of the lists of units, or Orders of Battle for the Russian campaigns give any RAVC or Remount units.

The North Russian Expeditionary Force (NREF), formed two training missions, the Syren Force (at Murmansk) June 1918-October 1919 and the Elope Force (at Archangel) May 1918- August 1919. Until evacuation in October, 1919 the NREF employed 50 cobs and 711 mules imported from England; 1,363 Russian ponies belonging to British troops and 90 imported French mules and 1,502 Russian ponies belonging to the Russians. The English cobs were only suitable as officers' chargers and the imported mules were unsatisfactory especially as pack animals. The local Russian pony proved to be the best animals for use on this campaign. The condition of the animals was generally satisfactory; forage and feeding was on the whole good, except for the local ponies which suffered in condition when oat rations failed to reach the front. Shoeing of animals with the British force was done with difficulty owing to a lack of staff, tools and materials.

The whole of the veterinary staff for North Russia was supplied by the British with the exception of a few Russian veterinary officers. The veterinary staff of the Elope Force included an ADVS (who was appointed to the allied forces: British, French and American, and acted as technical advisor to the GOC), eight veterinary officers and 27 staff-sergeants. A veterinary school and hospital was established, which was also used for the treatment of British and allied animals and for training Russian personnel to be veterinary assistants, sergeants, shoeing-smiths and in stable management. A Russian mobile veterinary section was also trained for duties at the front. All animals with the force were malleined with only one reaction to the test. The French mules suffered a bad outbreak of sarcoptic mange. A number of animals suffered from a strange disease known as Hvorst poisoning supposedly from eating "mares tail" grass, this was never proven, but could have been related to a dietary-deficiency disease.[18]

---

17   Blenkinsop and Rainey, Chapter XIX, pp.439-444, Chapter XX, pp.445-449.
18   Writing in 1954 (p.308), Forsyth states that Equisitales (or Equisetum – Horsetails) was widely distributed in Britain, especially on damp land and was a frequent cause of poisoning in horses, usually through hay containing the dried plants. I am grateful to Vic Simpson for this source.

Climatic variations were significant in North Russia, with ice, thaw and tropical conditions, especially affecting communications and transport.

With the evacuation from North Russia in October 1919, all cobs and majority of mules were shipped back to England, without casualties. During the campaign casualties from death, destruction and sickness were infinitesimal.

Early in 1919, a British Military Mission arrived in South Russia, with the purpose of providing war materials, including veterinary equipment and stores, to the South Russian forces and technical advice on use of equipment and materials. The veterinary branch of the Mission included an ADVS and a Base Depot of stores, with a captain and quartermaster; this establishment was increased in September 1919 with another officer, quartermaster and six other ranks. When the Mission left for the Crimea in March 1920, numbers were reduced to the original number of officers and three sergeants. The Russian forces already had two general hospitals for 500 animals each, in addition to some infantry and cavalry divisional hospitals, each capable of dealing with 150-250 animals. The total strength of animals was said to be about 200,000 animals, but with no mobile veterinary sections in the Russian force mange, glanders and rinderpest were prevalent. The ADVS inspected the existing methods of management and treatment of sick animals in the base area, reporting on the almost hopeless state of veterinary conditions. Horse-shoes were scarce and none had been issued by Russian authorities. He noted that 'in the Don Army veterinary organization was quite good on paper, but in practice it could scarcely said to exist at all'. On evacuation to Sevastopol in the Crimea, all stores at the base veterinary depot were given to the completely disorganised veterinary services of the South Russian army. The ADVS found veterinary conditions with forces in the Crimea at their lowest ebb.

In July 1920 veterinary work in South Russia ceased when the Mission embarked for Constantinople. Blenkinsop and Rainey stated that "Military veterinary history hardly contains an instance of a more hopeless task than that which the ADVS of the British Mission was required to undertake, " and that "the animal strength of an army in the field, under conditions of modern warfare, could only be maintained when a well organised veterinary corps acts independently, liberally supplied with personnel and material".

South Africa and German South West Africa: September 1914 – July 1915[19]

The South African Afrikaner-led government of Louis Botha entered the War in 1914 with Britain. However, some Boer and Africaan elements opposed this move, including some in the South African army, the Union Defence Force of South Africa, who refused to fight against the Germans. These supporters of the recreation of a Boer South African Republic rose in revolt, thereby renewing resistance against the British. Hostilities began in September 1914 with a Boer rebellion, the

---

19   Blenkinsop and Rainey, Chapter XVI, pp.385-406.

Maritz Rebellion, led by Gen. Maritz, head of a commando of Union forces on the border of German South West Africa, who had allied himself with the Germans. He was defeated on 24th October and took refuge with the Germans. The Union forces continued their operations in German South West Africa until July 1915.

German South West Africa (Namibia), sharing a common border with South Africa, was a German colony from 1884 until their defeat in 1915, when it was taken over by the Union of South Africa, as part of the British Empire and administered as South West Africa. German forces, or Protection Forces, were the African colonial armed forces of Imperial Germany, with one command in each of the three German colonial regions, East, West, and Southwest Africa. The Protection Forces in German Southwest Africa were structured into twelve companies of mounted infantry totalling 1,500 men, primarily Germans, with a Company, stationed in the northern desert area of the colony, mounted on imported camels. The structure of this Command included two Horse Depots, a camel stud farm and nine veterinarians. The last German commander surrendered on 9th July 1915.[20]

In July 1914 the British Remount Service had one depot in South Africa, at Robert's Heights, Pretoria, with a DADR and Superintendant, Maj. H. Findlay, with an attached veterinary officer Capt. J.J. Aitken, AVC, an NCO and storeman.[21] On mobilization there was a total of 8,000 horses and mules on establishment, with the veterinary service expanded by the addition of seven civilian practioners engaged for military service, and a base veterinary depot. Remounts were purchased throughout the country and placed in new remount depots, for example, Kimberley, Maitland and Standerton. Veterinary Regulations (War) were only finalised and issued on 8th October 1914, when the DVS was instructed to form and organize a veterinary service. The organisation of the South African Veterinary Corps (SAVC) was quickly formed from nothing as an emergency organization. All officers and subordinate personnel of the SAVC consisted of volunteers, with the establishment increasing to 47 officers, 450 NCOs and men, and 650 black South Africans.

With the outbreak of the Maritz Rebellion and expansion of mounted units there was an increased demand for remounts and veterinary services. Eight base hospitals, fifteen mobile veterinary sections and details for all mounted units, remount and

20   For an overview on German South East Africa and German East Africa Campaigns see Purnell, 1966, volumes 1, pp.354-360; 4, pp.1370-76; 6, pp 2318-2323; 8, pp.333-36.

21   Nothing is recorded for South Africa in *WO Monthly Listings* after October 1914. Harold Findlay, Bt., served as a Lt. in the relief of Kimberley during the 1899-1902 War. A Capt., Brevet Major with 2nd Battalion, East Kent Regt., 1899-1902 and special service officer for mounted infantry; mentioned in Despatches 1901 and 1902. Staff Officer for remounts on South African staff from 3/3/11. Promoted Temp.Maj. 5th August 1914 to 5th Nov 1914 whilst DADR with BEF. Brevet Lt- Col. February 1917; Nov. 1916, Remount Section, DDR, Maj, Temp. Lt-Col. as AQMG to Sept. 1918. Mentioned in Despatches 1915. *WO Monthly Lists*; *London Gazettte Supplement*, 18.12.1919 pp.15734-5, 1.2.17, p.1114 and 3.12.01, 29.7.02, 22.6.15, p.5977; *Medal Index Cards*. My thanks to Brian Hill.

transport depots, shipping details and purchasing boards were quickly trained and equipped. The number of animals increased to some 160,000. The SAVC between August 1914 and 31 January 1916 dealt with 75,159 horses, mules and donkeys; 60,977 were discharged, 6,100 died (8.12% over the 17 months). A further 15,862 died other than in hospitals from, for example, starvation, exhaustion, horse-sickness and anthrax (transport oxen), bringing the total deaths and destructions to 21,962 (13.72% over the 17 months).

The Union Army was divided into four forces, Eastern, Central, Southern and Northern, each area with differing climatic conditions and terrain. The Eastern force with its base at Kimberley crossed 400 miles of desert to the border with German territory and became part of Southern Force; rest camps and hospitals on grazing farms were established. The Central force marched through 60 miles of desert to be faced by entrenched German positions; hospitals were posted along the lines of communication. Water supply was a serious problem with animals restricted to watering only once daily; supply consisted of condensed sea water and water carried from Capetown by transport ships. Glanders soon appeared but was quickly suppressed, mallein testing being rigidly enforced, with only 44 animals destroyed. When this Force merged with the Southern Force for the general advance, its ADVS assumed duties for the whole combined force.

The Southern Force mobilized under Lt-Col. Maritz, who rebelled with part of this force during October. The campaign was hard on the animals with a shortage of rations and with the strain of hard work their condition deteriorated. In January 1915 rebel forces were repulsed and a separate German force beaten, with the rebels surrendering in February after which full rations were again issued. Glanders appeared in March 1915 but was quickly dealt with; further cases appeared in May 1915 on demobilisation of the Force. There was an outbreak at Maitland Transport and Remount Depot containing some 9,000 animals, all were mallein tested and branded, then moved to clean ground at Vredehoek; the depot was disinfected and cleaned so that glanders did not reappear. Mange appeared in June 1915, but was contained by dipping, a total of 1,648 cases were treated. A range of other diseases were encountered, in relatively small numbers and successfully treated, for example, anthrax in oxen, strangles, horse-sickness and sand colic. The number of cases of saddle injuries was excessive, reflecting badly on horsemastership in the Southern Force, probably due to badly fitting saddles.

The first section of the Northern Force sailed from Capetown in December 1914, to Walvis Bay, South East Africa, with about 2,000 animals of which six died in transport. After landing the animals rapidly lost condition mainly due to a lack of water. In total 43,000 were landed at the Bay with generally good horsemastership on board ships but with frequent cases of for example, a lack of watering in the lower decks. Prior to the general advance in March 1915 animals were well cared for and in excellent condition. The advance went through desert without food and water. Large numbers of animals were left behind as the mounted troops outpaced the transports; animals became emaciated and useless for further service. A second advance began in May leaving about 10,000 debilitated animals behind. The advance was rapid in some cases covering 40 miles per day, again with transports loaded with forage being left behind. When the German forces surrendered, horse and transport animals were exhausted, with hundreds left on the roadside to be collected by mobile veterinary sections. Worse was to come when troops were ordered to return to railway lines, often a journey of about 250 miles, departing for the Union and demobilization, leaving their animals behind. Left anywhere on the veldt, mobile veterinary sections took between 7-10 days to arrive due to jams on the rail line; leaving many worn out animals to die.

There were probably some 60,000 animals, many of them debilitated, left behind for the remount depots and veterinary service to deal with during July to October, with several thousand dying of starvation. Attempts to trek debilitated animals back to the Union beacuse of a lack of rail and ship transports, left many dead along the route. The Remount Department attempted to distribute animals to farms but many were too weak to travel; on some farms grazing was poor and water some miles away, and yet ironically there were huge quantities of forage at rail centres, including some 15,000 tons at the supply depot, unable to move because of broken down engines. Another attempt at trekking animals to supplies of fodder at the coast ended in many deaths; about 946 cases of clinical glanders were destroyed, many of which were German horses. In total some 17,571 animals were lost from the original 60,000. Inspections were made by Remount and Veterinary officers of hospitals, depots and remount farms, during August and began closing them down as part of the demobilisation process. In January 1916 all remount depots in occupied territories were closed down, with veterinary, remount and transport establishments handed over to civilian authorities. Total losses during the rebellion and in German South West Africa campaign amounted to 21,962, an annual death rate of 9.09%.

East African Campaign: 3rd August 1914 – November 1918[22]

The German East Africa colony came into existence during the 1880s and ended with Germany's defeat in 1918. The colony included what are now Burundi, Rwanda and Tanganyika (the mainland part of present Tanzania). The Campaign was a series of battles and guerrilla actions that began in German East Africa and ultimately affected portions of Mozambique, Northern Rhodesia, British East Africa, Uganda and the Belgian Congo. Conflict effectively ended in November 1917, but the Germans entered Portuguese East Africa and continued the campaign living off Portuguese supplies. An Indian Expeditionary Force arrived in October 1914 with the general officer assuming supreme command in East Africa. [23]

---

22   Blenkinsop and Rainey, Chapter XVII, pp.407-427.
23   For an overview on East African and German East Africa Campaigns, see Purnell, 1966, volumes 1, pp.354-360, pp.354-360; 4, pp.1370-76; 6, pp 2318-2323; 8, pp.333-36.

Many of these areas were unknown to British veterinary services and therefore the Campaign added hugely to scientific veterinary knowledge, notably in relation to the enormous tsetse-fly infested belts stretching inland from the coast. The soil of East Africa was heavily infected with a large variety of pathogenic organisms that quickly infected wounds; poisonous plants were also a problem. Horse-sickness was common in wet seasons and near water and swamps in dry weather; rinderpest and East Coast fever attacked cattle and transport oxen. In addition there were the usual diseases, often imported by military forces, of glanders, strangles, epizootic lymphangitis and a catarrhal pneumonia among asses. The greatest mortality rate was caused by animal African trypartosomiasis, a parasitic disease spread by the tsetse -fly, followed by horse-sickness.

Disease was, however, only one cause of loss, heavy rains, starvation and poor management were also contributors. There were adequate supplies of good quality forage at bases and on lines of communication, until early in 1917. The problem was the provision of rail and road transport to move supplies to animals in the forward areas. Even in South Africa and East Africa motor vehicles had already replaced some animals for a proportion of transport work. Horsemanship and horsemaster-ship amongst mounted regiments from South Africa was poor, technical personnel such as shoeing-smiths and saddlers were considered to be useless encumbrances. During October 1916 when regimental personnel took 1,720 animals from remount depots and moved them about 200 miles, 155 were lost; however, during the same period remount personnel moved forward 2,528 horses and mules over the same route, without loss.

Wastage varied over the four years of the campaign. During the period August 1914 to March 1916 the campaign was waged in tsetse-fly free areas, when wastage was the lowest and not abnormal for an African campaign; but during the period March 1916 to January 1917 the wastage was horrendous as units moved into the fly infested regions. From the period January 1917 to the end of the campaign the incidence of disease did not differ. Limiting the use of animals in the tsetse-fly free areas was the only possible advice that could be given by the veterinary services, if mounted troops were to be used. This advice was adopted until early 1916, so that of some 20,000 animals with military forces, there was only a very small death rate, probably less than 10% monthly. After March 1917, the average quarterly wastage was:

Horses	Mules	Donkeys
38.7%	32.23%	36.8%

The veterinary services had informed the Director of Remounts that an estimated wastage of 30% per month could be expected with an ultimate dead wastage of 100%. From March 1916 to January 1917, when animals were not limited to tsetse-fly free areas, the result was a dead wastage of nearly 100% per month, in the field, with the exception of 444 horses, 80 mules and 329 donkeys sold and cast during the campaign.[24] There is no parallel for such a colossal wastage of animals in any campaign, much of which could have been prevented. Out of a total of approximately:

Horses	Mules	Donkeys	Total
31,000	33,000	34,000	98,000

At the end of the campaign there remained only:

827	897	1,402	3,216

At the outset of war there was no military veterinary organisation in the East African Protectorate. This was created from the civil veterinary department (fourteen colonial service officers) becoming the East African Veterinary Corps and commanded by the chief veterinary officer, with the title of Director of Veterinary Services and Remounts. His first task was the purchase of large numbers of horses, mules, donkeys, transport oxen, slaughter cattle, sheep and goats. He also arranged for the construction of depots at the two main remount purchasing centres. During 1914-15 the Director was involved in the planning of the campaign's line of advance as the unsuitability of certain areas for animals was appreciated. The situation altered early in 1916 when an ADR was sent out by the WO to take charge of the Remount Service. The veterinary and remount services were separated until re-united later in the campaign; the Deputy Director of Supplies and Transport took over live-stock. The veterinary services included the EAVC (1914), the AVC (1915), SAVC (1915) and ANVC (1917). Veterinary organisation in South African units was based on a regimental system.

Mesopotamian Campaign: 6th November 1914 – 14th November 1918 [25]

The entry of the Ottoman Empire into the War in October 1914, strategically threatened the production and supply of oil. Control of the oil fields by the British was a crucial objective. The Anglo-Persian Oil Company had exclusive rights for most of the Persian deposits (largely present day Iraq), with a contract to supply the navy with oil. Allied forces were mostly drawn from India and Australia, those of the enemy mainly Turks from the Ottoman Empire. Indian Army forces, already in Bahrain protecting oil refineries, advanced into Mesopotamia and captured Basra; they advanced again during 1915 but were besieged in the town of Kut and surrendered in April 1916. In December the British renewed their advance taking Baghdad in March 1917, continuing to the Caspian Sea and taking the oilfields of Mosul in November 1918. The

---

24   Trench, 1988, p.68; Blenkinsop and Rainey, p.417.
25   Blenkinsop and Rainey, Chapter XIII, pp.289-348.

Ottoman forces were finally defeated at the Battle of Sharquat, 23rd October – 30th November.[26]

No remount personnel were with the Force. Veterinary staff undertook Remount functions until December 1915, when they were taken over by remount officers from India. Before 1916 the number of veterinary officers, trained personnel, equipment and transport was inadequate. This was the cause of considerable loss, presumably from military activity, as although no veterinary statistics exist for this period the sickness rate is stated as low. The situation improved with a period of stability and the arrival of two Indian divisions from France in January 1916, complete with veterinary resources. Blenkinsop and Rainey state that the organisation of the AVC in India at the outbreak of the War was much inferior to AVC in the U.K. As the two Corps operated different systems a period of time was required for adjustment and integration.[27] During the second phase of operations, autumn 1916 to the Armistice, there were exceptionally long, fast, hard marches with vast distances covered without water and shortages of forage, yet exhaustion was not a major cause of wastage, suggesting animals were in good, hard condition at the beginning of the campaign. There was good co-operation with veterinary units, regular inspections, speedy evacuation of animals and good horsemastership. The highest incidence of disease was Equine Piroplasmosis, a blood-borne disease caused by two parasitic organisms and primarily transmitted to horses by ticks; only 20 cases of glanders occurred and were eradicated and several cases of anthrax, but generally diseases were controlled, or stamped out.

During 1916 the situation regarding the shortage of veterinary personnel was serious and the formation of mobile veterinary sections was delayed owing to this shortage. In 1917 there was a serious shortage of veterinary officers although in April 1917 drafts of trained syces (horse-keepers) from India assisted greatly. The shortage remained in 1918 but conditions improved. The scale of forage altered according to supply and although the full ration scale was good, often it was not available owing to transport difficulties. There was the usual shortage of trained shoeing-smiths and as India could not supply sufficient numbers, courses were provided for training British and Indian personnel in cold shoeing.

Sinai and Palestine Campaigns: 28th January 1915 – 30th October 1918[28]

On the outbreak of war the existing British garrison in Egypt was, with most its animals, recalled to England to join the BEF. An infantry division and brigade of yeomanry were sent to Egypt in September 1914, to be followed by other units, forming the Suez Canal Defence Force, with about 6,500 animals, including camels.

---

26   For details of this campaign, see Pirie Gordon, 1919, pp.95-107; Preston, 1921; Bullock, 1988, p.24; Blenkinsop and Rainey, pp.128-279.
27   Blenkinsop and Rainey, p.298.
28   Ibid., Chapter XI, pp.128-276.

Between February and April 1915 fresh mounted units arrived, so that by early 1915 there were about 20,000 horses and mules and 3,000 camels, but with the inevitable shortage of veterinary facilities and personnel to cope with the rapid expansion.

The Egyptian Expeditionary Force (EEF) was formed in March 1916 from the Mediterranean Expeditionary Force (MEF) and the Egyptian Force, with the purpose of guarding the Suez Canal and Egypt.[29] The Force consisted of units from the British Empire, except Canada, and was opposed by German, Turkish and Austro-Hungarian forces. The Force was to see action in the Sinai, Palestine and Senussi Campaigns. The Campaign began in January 1915, when a German led Ottoman force invaded the Sinai Peninsula attacking the Suez Canal. The Peninsula was retaken in 1916 by the Anzac Mounted Division and a British infantry division. The advance continued successfully so that during January 1917, with the newly formed Desert Column, victory was complete. The Desert Column had been formed in December 1916, under of Lt-Gen. Chetwode, as part of Eastern Force, until mid 1917 when Gen. Allenby took command of the EEF, and in August the Desert Column was reformed and renamed the Desert Mounted Column, commanded by Lt-Gen. Chauval. This mounted corps contained Australian light horse, British yeomanry, French chasseur, Indian lancers and New Zealand mounted rifle units; formed into three mounted divisions, Anzac, Australian and Yeomanry. Victory was followed by defeats at the First and Second battles for Gaza, but victory in October at the Third Battle of Gaza led to the capture of Jerusalem in December, 1917. With the German spring offensive on the Western Front in March 1918, reinforcements were sent from the region halting any further advance of the EEF until September. When the EEF advance resumed they destroyed three Ottoman Armies and by 30th October 1918 the Ottoman Empire agreed to an Armistice, having lost the Sinai Peninsula, Palestine, Syria and Lebanon.[30]

Between 30th January 1915 and 28th February 1916, 7,440 casualties were sustained, 5,178 of which were successfully treated. The Western Frontier Force, along the Italian-Egyptian border, under the command of the EEF, in operation from November 1915 to March 1916, was formed in response to the German and Ottoman inspired Bedouin and Senussi uprisings. Animal casualties amounted to 1,471, of which 1,154 were successfully treated. The majority of these were injuries (863), with digestive complaints forming the largest incidence of sickness (272). Animals suffered

---

29   By 1915, there were problems in maintaining control of the various administrative services in the Near East from London; involving a complicated system with the MEF (which included Australian and New Zealand forces, the forces in Egypt and Salonika, the latter administered by the MEF), organised with a staff known as the 'Levant Base', responsible for the administration of all forces operating in Egypt and the Levant. By March 1916 this was replaced by absorbing three forces into one command, the Egyptian Expeditionary Force.

30   For an overview of Desert Mounted Corps/Column and Sinai and Palestine Campaigns, see Purnell, 1966, volumes. 4, 5, 6, 7.

from the effects of severe work, wet weather and swampy condition of the ground, scarcity of water and poor handling by inexperienced troops. At one point the Cavalry were too exhausted for the pursuit.

With the evacuation of Gallipoli, December 1915 and January 1916, animals arrived in Egypt for treatment, convalescence and training. Remount depots had to supply units with serviceable animals as replacements for those hospitalised; additional work that had to be absorbed by already overworked services. In September 1915, permission was given for the creation of an Australian Remount Unit, which was sent to Egypt, arriving in December 1915, to take charge of Australian horses. The evacuation of Gallipoli and the return of the dismounted mounted troops made Australian Remount units somewhat redundant and were incorporated into the British Remount Service under Brig-Gen. Bates, Director of Remounts, Egypt, but operated separately and dealt chiefly with the provision of horses and mules for Australian and New Zealand Forces.[31] By December 1915 there were over 44,000 horses and mules in Egypt, of these 4,800, or 11%, were sick. With insufficient accommodation only 3,450 could be hospitalised or put in convalescent horse depots; 1,350 were left with units. The WO ordered all hospitals in Egypt to take 1,250 cases each. There was a serious shortage of qualified European veterinary surgeons and staff, with Egyptian personnel forming 75% of hospital establishments, requiring training and supervision in horse management.

The veterinary personnel under the DVS of the EEF, Maj-Gen. Butler, were a mixture from different forces, differing considerably in their organisations. The AVC (Regulars, Special Reserve and Territorials), Australian, New Zealand and South African Corps, Indian Subordinate Veterinary Corps, and Egyptians. Butler undertook a complete reorganisation that by February 1916 provided a unified, coherent and co-ordinated organisation, this was especially important with the movement of personnel and units between different theatres of war. For under strength services, sickness among personnel was always a serious problem, especially when demands increased, and ongoing training needs such as the constant shortage of shoeing-smiths.

During 1916, the total wastage of horses and mules, from all causes, was 12,770, or 12.15% of the average total strength of 105,121. The veterinary service treated 125,676 cases with 50,872 hospitalised, 91.66% returned to duty, with 81% of those in hospitals successfully treated.

About 170,000 Egyptian camel drivers and 72,500 predominantly pack camels were employed in The Camel Transport Corps (CTC) from December, 1915 to demobilization in 1919. The Imperial Camel Corps (ICC), was formed in December 1916 and disbanded May 1919, with some 4,800 camels. These units necessitated the creation of a special organisation for camel remount depots and veterinary services. Camels were prone to suffering from sarcoptic mange and sore backs and were placed for treatment either in the Camel Transport Corps Depot, or the Camel Veterinary Hospital. The

31   Kent, 1982, pp.10-11.

formation of the CTC and ICC placed serious strains on the AVC, which had to provide personnel for training and purchasing duties. Camel remount depots were formed in November 1915 and struggled to find either the quality or quality of equipment required; some 10,000 poorly made and often badly fitting saddles were hastily purchased from camel owners. By the end of 1916 two camel remount depots and three camel veterinary hospitals had been established with a fourth formed in 1917. By the 8th March, 1916, 600, or 2.5% of the then camel strength were sold, or destroyed.

With the huge increase in animals the disposal of manure and carcasses became a major problem, which if not controlled properly, was a serious potential health hazard to both men and animals. Initially, carcasses were buried away from camps, or dumped to disintegrate naturally. Others were disembowelled and left to dry in the sun, filled with straw then burnt. Manure was placed in large dumps away from camps, but later it was dried on platforms and burnt in square type incinerators. The manure from 100 horses, with bedding straw in it, when spread out in a suitable thickness to allow turning to dry, covered an area 72' x 27' feet (22 metres x 8 metres). Animals dying or destroyed in Cairo and Alexandria were sold to the Cairo Manure Company and municipal authorities of Alexandria.[32]

The plentiful supply of good quality water was a major factor in the Palestinian campaigns and formed an important element in strategic and tactical planning. Forage was often of good quality but in short supply, animals had to perform very heavy and severe work on rations reduced in nutritive value, and in quantity, far less than allowed in peacetime. From September 1918 the quality improved, supplemented when available, with good grazing.[33]

By the end of 1916 there were three remount squadrons in Egypt. The last horses shipped to Egypt arrived in May or June 1917, most of which were issued before the October Beersheba-Gaza operations began. From that date until the end of war no more horses arrived in the country. A shortage of shipping meant that shipments from Australia were ended in January 1917; 8,000 horses ordered by the British in response to Australian pressure, were never shipped to Egypt. This was treated with dismay by the Australian and New Zealand troops and was all the harder to comprehend during the slow build up to the second and third battles of Gaza.[34] At the opening of the final Palestine offensive in September 1918, remount depots were emptied and scarcely a single fit horse was left behind; when remount stocks in Palestine were exhausted, casualties were replaced by horses that had already seen service, with the sick or wounded transferred to remount depots for reissue when fit.[35]

The percentage of animals returned from hospitals to Remounts as fit for re-issue was 80% of horses and 70% of camels. There can be no doubt that the tremendous

32   Kent, p.14; Blenkinsop and Rainey, pp.171-5.
33   Preston, 1921, pp.313-4.
34   Kent, p.13.
35   Preston, p.317; Kent, p.13.

accomplishments of the EEF were in no small part due to the Remount and Veterinary services and the willingness of army staff to understand the importance of keeping animals in good condition. Animals not fit for general duty were formed into a 'B' class and used on lines of communication; draught horses in moderate condition were used by veterinary units for transport work until fit for issue to Remounts. Animals over 15 years of age in hospitals were inspected and those not likely to be fit for duty destroyed.

The average strength of the EEF during January to June 1917, which included the first Palestine offensive between March and April, was 59,357 horses and mules, and 44,077 camels. The wastage from all causes was 2,799 horses and mules, or 4.71%, and 5,580 camels, or 12.66%. The total receiving treatment was 110,759 (38,368 horses and mules; 72,391 camels).

The second Palestine offensive, Beersheba-Gaza-Jerusalem, beginning in October 1917, was extremely strenuous for all animals. Weather conditions varied from intense heat to frost, and from drought to severe exposure from torrential rain and wet conditions. During periods of heat many horses went without water for 48 hours, while military requirements combined with floods and mud prevented the regular supply of rations. Casualties were naturally heavy and only the constant attention by troops and all those involved prevented greater loss. During this period, the mobile veterinary sections and field veterinary detachments were especially effective in saving many animals that otherwise would have been lost, thereby allowing Remounts to keep field units up to strength. Exhaustion, short rations, and lack of water on more than one occasion slowed the advance and stopped the cavalry from following up the retreating enemy. In December 1917, the Desert Mounted Corps rested in the Gaza area, their horses in poor condition; remount depots were empty except for a few animals returned from hospitals and with no prospect of fresh remounts arriving into the country. All horses of the Corps had to be nursed back into condition before the Cavalry could take part in any further serious work.[36] The average strength from July to December 1917 was 82,515 horses, mules and donkeys, and 48,191 camels. The wastage from all causes was 6,597 horses, mules and donkeys, or 7.99% of average strength, and 6,173 camels, or 5.6%. The total number of reported cases received for treatment was 139,780 (66,620 horses, mules and donkeys, and 73,160 camels).

During February and May 1918 operations were taking place in the Jordan Valley when demands came in during the March-April from the BEF for men and guns. 'A' class men were taken for combat duties and 'B' class men trained to replace them and between January and June, 3,959 horses and mules were embarked for other theatres. The average strength between January and June was 156,728 (59,625 horses, 43,375 mules, 10,487 donkeys and 42,881 camels). Wastage from all causes was 7,049 horses, mules and donkeys, or 6.19% of average strength, and 8,474 camels, or 19.76%.

36   Preston, 1921, p.123.

157,801 cases were reported treated (82,977 horses, mules and donkeys, and 74,824 camels).

On 9th September the approximate ration strength of the force was 74,800 horses, 39,100 mules, 35,000, camels, 11,000 donkeys. Prior to the final advance, all animals in poor condition, or unlikely to withstand the strain of operations were evacuated to hospitals, unfortunately the number of remounts for replacement was limited. The continuous work demanded during the final offensive, in Palestine and pursuit through Syria, September to 31st October 1918, kept hospitals full. Though considerable casualties were sustained during the advance the general health of the animals remained good. For July to December 1918 the average strength was 58,871 horses, 44,501 mules, 11,562 donkeys and 34,154 camels. Wastage from all causes, for horses, mules and donkeys was 12,289,(10.69%), and 4,493 camels,(13.15%). The main increase in loss was in horses, 9,816, (16.17%), of which 3,579, (3.25%) were with cavalry units in the field.

During these advances, the problem for transport and artillery animals was keeping pace with the faster moving cavalry; transport horses were generally too heavy for this work. Mules were used for transport work, but following the experiences of 1917, for work that required keeping up with cavalry, they were replaced by horses. The same was true for field artillery horses that carried and pulled greater loads than cavalry horses, but were required to support the cavalry in action; probably 90% of artillery and transport draught horses had strained hearts during the severe work in the desert sands. [37] Animals were affected by a number of contagious diseases, such as glanders, anthrax, mange, piroplasmosis (tick fever); epizootic lymphangitis that affected horses and mules, whilst trypanosomiasis (parasitic disease transmitted by tsetse fly) and mange were more frequent among camels. An effective system of mallein testing throughout the Army prevented the spread of glanders; every animal was tested, and retested on entry to hospital or remount depot, although isolated cases were found the disease was kept under control. Horses generally remained remarkably free from disease.

When the campaign changed from one of entrenched positions to extreme mobility, the wastage became proportionately higher. Up to the end of 1918, the veterinary services admitted and treated for sickness and injuries 447,757 horses, mules and donkeys, and 266,070 camels. Of these totals 144,864 equines (32%), and 61,232 camels (23%), were serious and moved to hospital requiring longer treatment. The total loss of animals from all causes was 46,615 horses, mules and donkeys, and 31,969 camels. Of the 144,864 equines sent to hospital 118,553, (12.80%) were cured and sent to remount depots; 18,553, (12.80%) died or were destroyed, and 7,987, (5.51%) remained under treatment. Of the 61,232 camels, 38,333 (62.6%) were cured and 20,070, (32.78%) died, were destroyed, or cast and sold. On 31st December, 2,827, (4.6%) were still in hospital. The total annual losses during the entire campaign,

37   Ibid., pp.312, 324-6.

calculated on average strength with the Army did not exceed 16% of horses, mules and donkeys, and 30% of camels.

Transport and mounted troops are only as effective as the ability of their animals to perform their required tasks; the campaigns in this theatre of war depended upon the constant availability of fit, trained animals to replace those killed, wounded or exhausted by work. From the beginning of 1916, to the Armistice, there were never less than 100,000 horses and mules serving in Egypt and Palestine as riding, draught and pack animals. Wastage was always an important consideration, as without sufficient replacements, the mounted arm was paralysed. During 1918, it was almost impossible to keep up with remount demands and many were issued before they were ready. Allenby severely over stretched resources during his dash to Damascus, and if the Turks had not sought an armistice it is probable he would have been forced to halt his advance anyway, as he had exhausted his supply of horses and men.[38] Without a reliable supply of replacements the long-range mobility that the mounted arm provided would have been lost and it was a measure of the Remount and Veterinary Service's success, that strategic and tactical considerations were never compromised by a shortage of horses and mules.[39]

Mechanical transport played a vital role and was of great value in the advances from October 1917. Initially used for localised station transport, then with light ambulances and light patrol cars, then used in the Western Desert and in the advance across the Sinai. Heavy transport was used in the Palestine campaign. The number of vehicles used in the campaigns grew from a few hundred to nearly 6,000, with all the necessary organisation and personnel. Mechanised transport became a mainstay for supplying the Army to the extent that Field Marshall Wavell declared it to be a triumph and a vindication of that arm in modern warfare.[40] He anticipated that in the future highly mobile, lightly armoured, mechanised tanks would replace the cavalry, but was aware that in 1918 the limiting factor on mechanised forces was supply and repair.

38   Allenby replaced Gen. Sir A. Murray as C-in-C, from June 1917.
39   Kent, 1982, pp.9, 13, 15; Kingston (IWM reference 88/27/1).
40   Wavell, 1928, pp.234-40, in the conclusion to his account of the Palestine campaign; Kent, 1982, p.15.

Demobilisation and Conclusion

I have often heard the remark: "But surely horses have ceased to be in modern warfare. One never, or very rarely hears of cavalry. And isn't all the rest done by motors?" This belief is typical of the folk left behind.[1]

Perhaps few people have an adequate conception of the enormous number of animals which took part in the late war, and of the great service rendered by them, they should be counted as elements in victory.[2]

Demobilisation

The subject of demobilisation at the close of the War arouses controversy, but it must be understood within the correct context; with sentiment not sentimentality. The British Armies alone employed some 896,000 animals in all theatres on 11th November 1918, the majority of which were surplus to military requirements at the end of hostilities. In addition, there were those of the Allied and Central Powers.

What was to be done with so many surplus animals scattered around the world? They were owned by the military authorities, or governments that had purchased them, not necessarily their country of origin, for which many, when purchased, where surplus to social or economic requirements. It was the responsibility of the military authorities to dispose of their horses as quickly and humanely as possible. This was not a simple task and they faced many problems. For example, the availability of transport to move so many animals in a relatively short period; the continued cost of maintaining animals, even for a short period; cost of transportation; the fear that imported animals would spread disease into national herds; not flooding home markets with surplus animals and protecting the horse breeding industry of a country; keeping a balance of supply and price in the market place. For example, owing to their large horse population, the US Government was content to leave their animals in Europe at the end of war. [3]

Hume wrote that the demobilisation of army animals at the end of the war was not an event in which Great Britain can take a pride. There is some truth in this statement

---

1   Galtry, 1918, p.1.
2   Moore, 1934, p.8.
3   Merillot and Campbell, 1935, pp.551-2 (Statistical Section of Remount Division).

but it needs to be seen within the context of 1918-1919. In all countries and communities there are those who value animals other than as beasts of burden and those who do not, irrespective of their level of wealth or poverty. The destiny of animals sold by the British authorities into civilian working life was mixed. Once sold, pledges of humane treatment could not be guaranteed by military authorities. The question arises as to whether those authorising sales understood the appalling servile conditions to which some animals would be subjected, or had other realistic options for their disposal in such large numbers.

During the War, the AVC was responsible for the disposal of military animals no longer fit for service.[4] The Disposal of Animals Branch of the AVC was formed in August 1918, and quickly became an important economic contributor to the Corps work, making it probably one of the few services that helped to pay for itself, for example:[5]

- From its inception to 11th November 1918, the Branch dealt with 64,334 animals, realising approximately £858,377.
- Between 11th November 1918 and 15th March 1919, 35,000 animals were disposed of for human food purposes, either by sale or issue to POWs, with a financial return of about £780,000, an average of about £22 per animal.
- By-products from animals raised over £35,000.
- Between 11th November 1918 and 31st March 1920, 49,751 animals were disposed of for human food consumption, realising £1,009,243, an average of £20 5s 9d per carcass sold, in addition by-products from animal carcasses realised £33,573 12s 6d.
- Horses sold as fit for work by various AVC units realised £6,064,329 9s 3d, an average price of £36 4s 0d per animal.

A daily manure output of 32lbs (14.5 kg) created a disposal problem for large hospitals and remount depots. In some locations, convenient chalk or clay pits were used as dumps, and where the offal of dead animals was buried with manure, methane gas was generated. A number of hospitals collected gas generated by the decay of flesh and manure and used it for heating purposes. In France, seven horse carcass economisers (slaughterhouses) were installed near groups of hospitals to make use of the by-products.[6]

The sale of cast horses was the subject of an Army Council meeting in November 1916, the précis of which provides an interesting insight into various viewpoints on the subject. During the summer of 1915, public feeling was aroused by letters in the press

---

4   RCT Archive. B1 0754, p.45; WO107/16, 13th December 1918, letter from Cowans to Ian Malcolm Esq., London, ref. complaints about the destruction of animals in France. Cowans sets out the humane measures in practice by the AVC; *Statistics*, p.188.
5   RCT Archive. File No1, B1 0754, p.45; Moore, 1934, pp.26-28; *Statistics*, p.866.
6   RCT Archive. B1 0754, p.45; Moore, 1934, pp.23, 27.

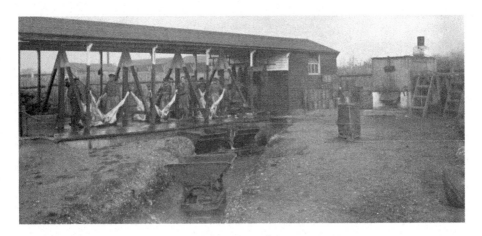

Rouen, France. Carcasses of horses unfit for service after being wounded being butchered to be used as rations for German POWs. (Army Medical Services Museum)

describing the fate of worn-out army horses sold in foreign countries. Questions were asked in the House of Commons and some Members called for the destruction of all cast horses serving abroad. Their arguments, the précis states, were purely sentimental, as once a cast horse was sold its ultimate fate was beyond control. The Secretary of State promised to further consider the question of sales in France and prohibit sales in the Eastern theatres of war, for example Egypt. In October, 1916 the RSPCA passed a resolution stating they would give no further help, or countenance the continued use of the Society's *Sick and Wounded Horse Fund* to assist the Army veterinary service, "until the WO discontinued the sale of cast horses abroad." The Secretary of State informed the House of Lords that orders had been issued stopping unfit horses and mules being sold in the Eastern theatres; pointing out that £40,000 had been raised from previous sales and that as a private individual he would not be sorry if the State were prepared to sacrifice the sum in order to prevent any possible cruelty to animals.

The Under Secretary of State and Finance Member decided all cast horses and mules in the Eastern theatres of Egypt, Salonika and Mesopotamia were to be destroyed. The same policy was to be adopted in France (and where possible carcasses sold for food), subject to consideration of a proposal to sell suitable breeding mares under adequate guarantees. The GOC-in-Chief pointed out this decision would amount to an estimated loss of £1,000 per week, create ill-feeling in France as farmers would be hampered in cultivating their land and the output of foodstuffs diminished. He suggested all horses fit for work be returned to England. [7]

7   WO163/21Army Council Minutes, Precis 845,29.11.16, House of Commons 12th October ref. Col. Lockwood and Sir George Greenwood and 25th October, 18th October House of Lords.

In November 1916 the Army Council reversed its previous decision and decided that discretionary powers for the sale, or destruction, of cast horses in France should be left to the GOC-in-Chief. Suitable horses could be sold for employment in agricultural work if the French Government gave guarantees that proper care would be taken of them.[8] In December 1918 the Army Council submitted a revised procedure to the War Cabinet, stating that animals no longer required by Armies in the Eastern Theatre were to be disposed of to the best advantage by sale or otherwise. At the same time GOCs were instructed to exercise a very literal discretion in destroying horses, instead of selling, especially those of British origin that were impossible to repatriate, or were not worth the freight costs and for which good homes could not be found on the spot.[9] In January 1919, the Council decided that horses and their equipment should be maintained for 67 divisions and 10 cavalry divisions until peace was signed. About 25,000 of the best horses were retained for the post-war Army and Army of the Rhine. On 31st March 1920 there were 3,976 horses (including 975 mules) with the Army of the Rhine, 1,719 (including 918 mules) with the Army in France and Flanders, 27,806 in Egypt (including 1,983 camels and 82 donkeys), and 5,801 with the Army of the Black Sea (including 3,294 mules). Surplus horses in the UK were sold as they became available, as were those in France and on the Rhine.[10] In Egypt, horses were disposed of, if the GOC considered they could be spared.

On demobilisation, the disposal of surplus animals was organised so that all horses and mules were classified into four groups, with units retained in Armies of Occupation and in the UK having the first choice horses from Groups A and B:

- A   Practically sound 5 to 8 years
- B   Practically sound 9 to 12 years
- C   Unsound, but fit for work, or over 12 years
- D   Unfit for work, to be destroyed

The WO had approached the Board of Agriculture and Fisheries (BAF) in April 1915 with a plan that at the end of hostilities 25,000 animals would be set aside for the whole of the UK. The remainder would be sold off of at the rate of 250 per week in each of ten big yards (2,500), 100 in each of 50 big markets (5,000) and 50 in 50 small markets (2,500). In Great Britain ex-army heavy draught horses were in greatest demand. Chivers gives figures for just one weeks sales: Tuesday 25th March, 1919, 120 "superior heavy and light draught horses" offered at Tomkin's Repository, Reading; at Ormskirk Remount Depot "100 staunch heavy draught horses, 200 light 'vanners'

---

8   Ibid., 29th November 1915, agenda: 'Sale of Cast Horses'; *VR*, 1915, Vol.XXVII, 29th May, p.615, 1916, XXVIII, 21st October, p.174 and November, p.189.
9   WO163/23, Army Council Minutes, 2nd December 1918, Agenda, 'Disposal of Horses in the East'.
10   Ibid., 1st January 1919, Agenda, 'Sale of Horses'; *Statistics*, p.404; Moore, 1934, pp.26-27.

and 50 riding and driving animals, smart cobs and carriage horses"; Wednesday at Holywell Stables, Oxford, " 50 very active heavy and light draught horses": Thursday Old Brewery Yard, Banbury, "50 upstanding draught horses"; Friday at Tomkin's again, "120 very powerful draught horses": Saturday, at Leicester Repository, "125 high class specially selected draught horses" and Raven's Repository, Shrewsbury, "150 grand army horses".[11]

At the end of October 1918, the Railway Executive Committee informed the WO that it intended to bring 125,000 army horses from France for sale in England; 1,200 per week for ten weeks. Repatriation of horses and mules from France began on 9th January 1919 and during the following two months, 35,000 were sent to Southampton, Tilbury and Hull, or by train and ferry to Richborough. Elaborate plans were made for the return of horses at 400 per day. As the Ministry of Shipping could not meet requirements, horses were not landed at stipulated ports, but had to travel by train ferry from Calais to Richborough. Repatriated animals were quarantined for two weeks, before moving to sale yards, with the result that not a single case of contagious disease was introduced into the UK. Before the Armistice, some 26,835 horses no longer fit for military service but sufficiently "reconditioned" to work on farms had been sold into civilian work in Great Britain. The sale of remaining surplus animals began soon after the Armistice, starting with the destruction of those over twelve years of age. [12]

By mid March 1919, over 60,000 horses and 1,500 mules were sold in the UK and thousands in France and Belgium. They fell under three headings; by auction to farmers and breeders, or for food, or dealt with in horse carcase economisers for by-products. In France and Belgium the sale of horses raised just over £2 million, fetching an average price of £40, and the sale of mules £25,000 with an average price of £44. The average price for horse sales in the UK was lower, about £33 and £17 for mules.[13] By 15th March 1919, 225,812 had been disposed off across all theatres, raising a total of £7,639,560.[14]

The Board of Agriculture was strongly opposed to the repatriation of animals from any theatre of war except France, for fear of introducing disease and the cost of transport. Animals in Egypt, Mesopotamia, Italy, Black Sea and East Africa were therefore disposed of locally.[15] The Commander-in-Chief in India arranged for the demobilisation of troops in Mesopotamia by withdrawing certain units to India completely horsed. He then disposed of animals surplus to the requirements of the Army of Occupation, at the same time meeting the needs of local inhabitants for working animals.

11 MAF 52/2/A4 3091/1915, 27.4.1915; Chivers, 1976, p.307.
12 Pratt, E., 1921, Vol.1, pp.190-9; Chivers, 1976, p.755. For the use of horses returned to England during the War for work on farms see the *Somerset War Agricultural Committee Minutes* (CSH/WA/1B-2).
13 Chapman, 1924, pp.264-5; Moore, 1934, p.25.
14 *Statistics*, p.862.
15 Ibid.

It is perhaps the plight of the animals in Egypt that has been brought to public attention due to the work of Mrs Dorothy Brooke and her *Old Warhorse Memorial Hospital* in Cairo. She had been actively interested in animal welfare, when in 1930 she moved to Cairo with her husband Geoffrey Brooke, posted as a Brigadier commanding the Cavalry Brigade in Egypt. She witnessed the conditions in which the old War Horses (identified by their distinctive British Army branding) had to work and live, in indescribable conditions, a far cry from, for example, the rolling hills of England. She was moved so much she began a search to rescue what remained of the 1914-18 army horses which 16 years previously had been sold into "bondage" in Egypt. She was advised that if any survived, as rumour suggested, they would be over 22 years of age. Under normal conditions a horse can live to the age of 25-30. There was no law in eastern countries compelling the destruction of sick and worn out animals, they were not sold or retired, when they were of no further use to their owners they were often left to starve to death. In the East, the principal issue was that if a beast of burden fails to do its work, the owner with often a large extended family, starved. The half-starved animal represented his only bit of capital, the only means of obtaining the barest living; if an animal did not work there was no income, and the normal charges for treatment and board at, for example, the Cairo S.P.C.A. Hospital were beyond the means of the average owner.

On being shown her first old War Horse, which she named "Old Bill", she wrote that "he was without exception the most dreadful looking horse I had ever seen in my life … I shall never forget the shock he gave me." She paid £9 to purchase the horse, being told that although the owner was a very poor man, "the horse would go on for a long time yet as he was comparatively strong, but half-starved as the peasants could not afford food for the large old army horses". While she arranged to buy Old Bill, he was given everything she could think of to afford him some luxury but life held little pleasure for him, so she took the decision to let him rest.

Requiring funding to purchase the surviving horses, of which the initial estimate was about 200, at £20 each, Dorothy Brooke wrote to the *Morning Post* (absorbed into the *Daily Telegraph*). Her letter was published and over £600 was immediately forthcoming in public donations, which led to the creation of the "*Old War Horse Fund*," that would receive the equivalent to £20,000 in today's money. Donations were also received from Australia, New Zealand and Canada; all spent on the purchase or expenses attached to the horses and creation of the original *War Horse Memorial Hospital* in 1934. The purchasing of the horses took place with Dorothy and her buying committee, every Thursday for nine months, for four years. The locals came to know her, and her quest, for which they called her the "Mad English lady". The going was hard, harrowing, at times unsafe, fighting apathy, bureaucracy and constant appeals for funding. Some 5,000 old warhorses and mules were eventually purchased. Only five were capable of the journey to England. At the 1934 International Horse Show, Olympia, at a parade for old war horses, one had been was sent by Dorothy, paid for by the Leamington and Warwickshire branch of the RSPCA, for which she wrote, " I am sending him as a representative of all his poor companions who have suffered

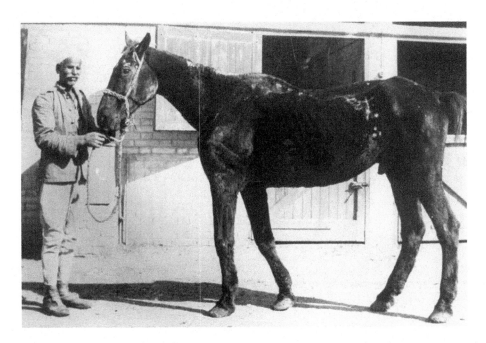

"Old Bill", Dorothy Brooke's first war horse, that "would go on for a long time yet as he was comparatively strong". This picture accompanied the appeal Dorothy sent out to The Morning Post in April 1931. (Brooke Hospital for Animals)

in this country – as a sort of "Unknown Warrior" – to the people who have helped to save the thousands of horse and mules we have purchased." The hospital in Cairo still operates as *The Brooke Hospital for Animals*, in its original location, known locally as "The Street of the English Lady", with the UK based Brooke Hospital for Animals operating in eleven countries in Latin America, Asia, the Middle East, and Africa, dedicated to improving the lives of working horses, donkeys and mules in the world's poorest communities.[16]

Col. Palmer, the Director of Remounts in Italy continually attempted to safeguard army horses that were sold off. In February 1919, he asked the Italian Mission whether he could devise any plan whereby animals sold could be regularly inspected by the Italian authorities and their treatment monitored. He pointed out this precaution in no way implied that the British Government thought the Italians ill-treated their animals, "but in all countries some individuals do". The Mission agreed they would do their best through their Society for the Prevention of Cruelty to Animals. Palmer also

---

16 This section is taken from Spooner, *For the Love of Horses, Diaries of Mrs. Geoffrey Brooke*. I am indebted to Lally Baker of the UK Brooke Hospital for Animals for all her enthusiasm and material supplied.

Dorothy Brooke in the yard of the Society for the Prevention of Cruelty to Animals in Cairo with some of the old war horses she rescued in the 1930s. (Brooke Hospital for Animals)

Army mule, blind in both eyes and broken hind leg. (Brooke Hospital for Animals)

wrote that animals were sold at a low price to the Italian Government to help poor farmers in devastated districts and that it would be "interesting to see how long these poor farmers keep these animals, if they ever received them, and I much doubt if they ever will ... many animals sold to farmers at a moderate price to help agriculture had been at once re-sold by farmers presumably at profit."[17]

Remount Departments and the AVC were heavily worked during demobilisation. Sales of animals in army areas in France were carried out through veterinary evacuating stations and mobile sections.[18] The disposal of carcasses, together with the movement of vast numbers of animals to the UK, required careful veterinary inspection, quarantine and testing for disease; work that was carried out with little check on the rapid demobilisation of remount and veterinary personnel required for this work. However, there were problems with personnel, for example, with reference to strikes, largely over delays in demobilisation, Cowans wrote in January 1919, "as you have seen we have had a good deal of unrest here, particularly in the RASC, and I am afraid we shall have to recall some regular officers to take charge of the various depots around London until they are reduced in size, and to keep the men in hand," and in Kettering, Northamptonshire, there was a short lived strike of the ASC at the local remount depot.[19]

Conclusion

The performance of the Remount and Veterinary Services during the War more than compensated for the shortcomings of the 1899-1902 South African War. The British Army, in every theatre, had the best veterinary service of any nation.[20] Fox wrote that no two officials at GHQ or with the BEF, had more right to be proud of their Departments than Maj-General Moore, DGAVC (BEF) and Brigadier-General Garratt, Director Remounts (BEF), "it is admitted all over Europe that horsemastery in the 'improvised' British Army reached the highest standard of the campaign".[21] Such praise should also be extended to Gen. Cowans, QMG (WO) and Maj-Gen. Birkbeck, Director of Remounts (WO).

The success of staff work in 1914 exceeded anything previously accomplished, including the speed with which well-organised and staffed remount camps and veterinary hospitals were established all over the country. To provide wartime establishments, reserves and wastage for the BEF and TF, from very low to non-existent peacetime establishments, was a triumph, when the only source for the equine demands of mobilisation was the horse stock of the UK national herd. The Remount

---

17   WO95/4202, 22nd and 28th February 1919.
18   Chapman, 1924, pp.264-5.
19   *Statistics*, p.188; WO107/16, 9th January 1919, Travers Clarke from Cowans (confidential), ref: Strikes; Rothstein, 1980, p59, re Kettering, 16th January 1919.
20   Caldwell, 1929, p.397.
21   Fox, 1920, p.6.

Department provided the Army in France and Flanders with more than 570,00 horses and 131,00 mules, and it's work also enabled the Americans to be supplied with horses at a critical juncture of the War. Close partnerships with the AVC and other departments meant sufficient remounts were procured and wastage in the field kept to a minimum.[22]

However, there were problems, for example, as demands increased, there were delays in supply due to a lack, or shortage of transport and provision of the right stamp and class of animals. The achievement of the horse services is evident in figures giving the numbers supplied and returned from hospitals to active service, the number and geographic spread of theatres of war, problems of submarine warfare and dwindling world horse markets with both the allied and Central Powers purchasing. As Maj-Gen. Sir John Moore wrote, "they should be counted as elements in victory".[23]

The annual totals, in all theatres, for the number of horses and mules in military service include:[24]

	Aug.1914	Aug.1915	Aug.1916	Aug.1917	Aug.1918
United Kingdom	25,000	234,161	146,752	137,595	91,289
France	232,635	409,730	449,880	391,458	
Egypt	68,155	53,233	71,788	106,316	
Salonika		58,988	81,200	41,618	
Mesopotamia		64,657	80,947		
East Africa	1,076	4,681	23,731	4,244	1,766
Italy			19,310		
Total	26,076	539,632	692,434	809,364	732,704

It is, perhaps, in the Palestinian campaign of 1917-18 that the success of the Remount Department and AVC is highlighted. Preston wrote that, "the (remount) depots were admirably managed, the whole remount service was a model of effectiveness".[25] During the advance of some 20,000 mounted troops in Chauvel's Desert Mounted Column, when stocks of remounts were exhausted, casualties were taken from veterinary centres and reissued by the Remount Department. There was no constant influx of fresh animals (an interesting contrast with the 1899-1902 War), animals worked under severe conditions and privations, and by force of circumstances the horses of some units went without water for as long as 84 hours, others between 77

---

22   Chapman, 1924, p.6, 331; RCT Archive, B1 0754, p.10.
23   Moore, 1934, p.8.
24   Birkbeck, in Jessel, 1920, p.110.
25   Preston, 1921, p.317.

and 60 hours. Considerable exhaustion and wastage was experienced and the margin of success was very close.[26]

The health of animals at home and in all theatres was maintained at a higher standard than in any former war. This standard showed a steady improvement in the later stages of the war, with the result that following demobilisation, there was no check on account of disease in the disposal of surplus animals. Wastage was naturally high, 529,564 horses and mules in all theatres were cast, sold, died, destroyed and missing:

- The average annual mortality among horses and mules in the various theatres of war and the UK, fluctuated between 9% and 17%; the average being less than 14%.[27]
- The highest annual wastage in the UK was 12%, which compared extremely well with a total of 14.8% annual wastage in peacetime prior to the war, made up of 8.23% for sick, dead and casting for disease, and 6.57% from other causes. [28]
- Total losses in France-Flanders and the UK, were 256,204.[29]
- The highest percentage loss of horses and mules in all theatres, 28.5%, was on the Western Front during 1917, except for the exceptional losses in the East African Campaign in 1916, mainly due to tsetse fly.

In Eastern theatres, losses were far less, owing in part to less fierce and only intermittent fighting and differences in climate, for example:

Italy	less than 1% per month
Salonika	8% to 10% per annum
Egypt	10% to 14% per annum
Mesopotamia	8% to 10% (from when the WO took over administration from the Indian Government)

It is interesting to compare the number of horses used by the major protagonists in the war and losses they incurred:

France	put	1,800,000	horses into the field and lost	758,507
Germany		2,500,000		900,000
Austria		2,005,837		1,500,000

The greater part of these losses, at least 80%, were from preventable causes.

---

26 Moore, 1934, p.17; Tylden, 1965, p.41.
27 *Statistics*, pp.188, 861, 865.
28 Birkbeck, in Jessel, 1920, p.112.
29 Tylden, p.39.

Figures available to compare British and French losses, but only up to 1st October, 1917 show:[30]

	Dead or Missing	Cast	Total Loss
British Army in France and GB	225,856	30,348	256,204
French Army in France	376,201	165,513	541,714

The ratio of castings to deaths, to the same date was 1: 7.4 in British Army and 1:2.3 in the French.

Of 688,619 horses and mules shipped from North America to the UK, France and the Mediterranean, Birkbeck gives losses of 13,629, or nearly 2% of the total; the average loss in transit for the whole war was less than 1%:[31]

			Percentage Lost	
	Horses	Mules	Horses	Mules
To United Kingdom:				
Lost at sea owing to: sickness	4,866	1,841	1.18	0.89
: enemy action	4,773	1,894	1.11	0.92
To France and Mediterranean:				
Lost at sea owing to: sickness	45	210	0.58	0.32
: enemy action	Nil	Nil	Nil	Nil
Totals	9,684	3,945		

The higher mortality figures for the British Remount Commission in Canada and America, during the earlier stages of its operations, showed a marked improvement during 1918-19, as the result of a thorough reorganisation, more effective control of veterinary arrangements and the adoption of more scientific methods.[32]

Poverty, debility and exhaustion through hard work, lack of water and short rations, were the most frequent and serious form of inefficiency in the field. On the Somme in 1916, 16,074 cases of debility were recorded. During operations in front of Arras in 1917, the strain of service on the 195,000 animals was severe; appalling weather conditions, exhaustion and debility meant admissions to convalescent horse depots rose to an unprecedented 20,319. Owing to the static nature of the warfare, wastage from battle casualties on the Western Front during 1914-15 was extraordinarily low.

30   Chivers, 1976, 754.
31   Birkbeck, in Jessel, pp.110-11; Galtrey, 1918, p.104.
32   Statistics, p.865.

However, casualties and losses correspondingly increased with the advent of offensive operations in the summer of 1916, the enormous increase in artillery and the development of bombs and gas. During the period 1st July to 31st December 1916, losses from gunfire and gas were:

	Killed or destroyed	Wounded	Total
Gunshot	3,941	6,063	10,004
Gas	33	352	385
Totals	3,974	6,415	10,389

The first three months of 1917 were not marked by severe fighting and battle casualties only totalled 1,977 (717 killed and 1,260 wounded); however, the Arras operations in April 1917 cost 4,625 animals (2,070 were killed and 2,555 wounded). From 1st May 1917 to 11th November 1918, covering the battles of the Somme and Ancre, there were 2,046 casualties from gunshot wounds and from 1st July 1916 to 11th November 1918 total casualties of 137,931:

Gas	211	killed	2,220 incapacitated.
Gunshot and bombs	58,090	killed	77,410 wounded

In August and September 1917, bomb casualties amounted to about 400 per week. Heavy casualties were sustained in the rear areas during May 1918, as the German's pursued their policy of shelling and bombing horse lines and transport areas. These casualties began to decline and in October 1918 only amounted to about 16 per week. Maj. White (Dorsetshire Regiment) refers to German long range shelling and bombing in 1917-1918 and the enormous and ongoing work to erect satisfactory splinter proof banks around horse lines. Mortality amongst horses affected by gas was high and even in mild cases, recovery was slow. Stabled horses were most severely affected and movement after an attack was found to aggravate the condition. Gas masks were used with limited success against some gases and although several methods were recommended for skin protection against the irritant action of mustard gas none proved entirely satisfactory. In the Australian army the majority of losses from gas were due to mustard gas, dichloroethylsulphide.[33]

An adequate supply of water was one of the biggest problems experienced in most theatres. It is difficult to comprehend why this vital issue, so well understood from experiences in the 1899-1902 War, did not receive sufficient consideration in pre-war planning. It would appear that units and formations were not provided with water

---

33 RCT Archive, File No.1 B1.0754, p.44; Moore, 1934, p.16; White, 1921, *RASCQ*, October, p.560; *VR*, 1936, Vol.48, 31st October, p 1311, 'Gas Warfare as Affecting Horse and Mules', M. Henry, 1935, *Australian Veterinary Journal*, 11th April, p.143.

troughs or force pumps and no steps were taken to arrange for water to be carried on transport vehicles. Often all that was available was a canvas water bucket, too small for heavy draught horses to drink from. The Royal Engineers built watering places, but these were seldom sufficient for the large number of animals in an area and often located at considerable distances from camps. Officers commanding horse transport units in France found that when moving large columns, the head of the column would halt near water, unhook the horses then take them to drink. Other units in the same column halted but were unable to water or feed, as the whole road would be blocked for hours. Leading units would then move on, splitting up the column resulting in much more than its normal road space being utilised. Eventually horse transport trains improvised means of carrying water on their wagons.[34]

With the vast wartime expansion in horses and untrained personnel in horse transport and artillery units the standard of horsemastership, such as grooming, suffered. This was clearly evident from 1916 onwards and some responsibility must lie with the High Command. Lessons were learnt and moves made to improve the situation, but as with the massive expansion of the 1899-1902 War, there was a shortage of skilled trained personnel such as veterinary staff and farriers. Drafts of new drivers were taught the elements of driving but little of practical use about horse and stable-management. In general, stable routines of watering, feeding and exercise went well and valuable lessons were learnt in the economy of rations. However, horsemastership is not just the process of following a prescribed routine, it is also includes the quality of the work such as grooming and understanding the individual likes and dislikes of a horse. The serious decline in the art of grooming caused problems as did the controversial question of clipping animals. Lt-Col. Arbuthnot RFA, stated that "our system proved the best in the world, it evoked the admiration of the Frenchman, the American and the Italian, but we had our bad times, we were too dependent on the one man expert who becomes rare in wartime, we need to have a greater interest and more widespread horse-knowledge among both officers and men."[35]

Tylden wrote that "the RAVC and Remount Department could hardly have done better work and came out of the war with vastly increased prestige … the mistakes of the 1899-1902 War in South Africa had been amply vindicated." However, an article in the *Veterinary Record*, 'An Undetected War Scandal' about the loss of animals other than by enemy action, provides a completely contrary view, suggesting the AVC failed in its task of animal welfare.[36]

The wartime services of the AVC and ASC were recognised with the status of 'Royal' Corps in November 1918.[37] There was no such recognition for the Remount Department. A Committee on 'Remount Duties', looked at the future organisation

34   'Watering', *RASCQ*, 1924, April, pp.199-200.
35   Arbuthnot, 1919, pp.341-3, reference Artillery; Hobday, 1918, p.41.
36   Tylden, 1965, p.44; *VR*, 1917, Vol.XXX, 11th August, p.6.
37   RAVC and RASC created by Army Order 363, 27th November 1918.

No. 6 Veterinary Hospital, Rouen. This photograph shows only a small section of motor and horsed vehicles making ready to collect stores, but note the number of animals and range of wagons, carts and a motor vehicle about to enter the road supply system. (Army Medical Services Museum)

and staffing of the Remount Department and possible amalgamation into the RAVC; reporting on 31st December 1936 its findings were not implemented. However in 1941 the RAVC and Remount Department were amalgamated to form a Veterinary and Remount Directorate, the "duties and functions of the existing Remount Service ... will be performed in future by the personnel of the RAVC".[38]

Military finance was based on the 'Ten Year Rule' adopted in August 1919, stating armed forces were to draft their estimates for expenditure on the assumption that the British Empire would not engage in any large scale war within the next ten years; thereby restricting the Army to policing the Empire. The 'Rule' was abandoned in March, 1932.[39] Demobilisation, post-war financial stringency and the process of mechanisation (which was limited by the 'Ten Year Rule'), meant a continual decline in the number of personnel required by the horse services. Military personnel were rapidly substituted by civilians, a process Beadon refers to as the "fashionable pursuit of demilitarisation." The exception to this were the overseas remount depots and until 1920 Woolwich, which retained about 80 military personnel to mitigate against the risk of strikes. Gen. Birch, replacing Birkbeck as Director of Remounts in 1919, advocated replacing all military personnel, hence the change at Woolwich in 1920.[40]

38   Special Army Order 8th January 1941; *VR*, 1941, 8th March, Vol.53, p.145.
39   For example Larson, 1984, p.26.
40   Beadon, 1931, Vol.II, pp.12-14.

The continued requirement for horse services was recognised by the Prince of Wales in 1923, "so long as we have a standing army we shall always want remounts".[41] However, only two remount depots survived into the post-war period, Melton Mowbray and Arborfield; Woolwich closed in 1921 and Dublin 1922. In November 1919, the WO transferred to BAF the Hall Walker stud at Russley Park, which had been on loan to them as a remount depot and managed by Lady Birkbeck. When originally taken from Hall-Walker in 1916, the depot was to have been a stallion depot for light horse breeding. BAF decided it could not be used for that purpose and until its future was decided, Birkbeck was acting as 'caretaker' in a private capacity.[42]

Cumberlegge wrote in 1911 that it was "the introduction of motor transport on a large scale that is bringing home to the modern soldier how quickly and extensively machinery is replacing manual and animal labour in every detail of military life. The importance of the change is as yet scarcely recognised, except by individuals. Yet it is certain that motor transport will, in the near future, assume a higher degree of mobility to modern armies than has never before been dreamed of, and its effect on the strategy and tactics of the next years will as certainly be remarkable".[43] During the War there were 405 Horse Transport Companies (HTC), equipped with the GS wagon, reduced to 31 with the RASC in 1921.The last Regular Army Company, No.4 HTC, was replaced in 1929; the horsed transport of the Territorial Force and other units had largely been replaced by 1939. A RASC training company for pack transport was retained.[44] However, animals did not disappear completely, some transport and pack animals were retained and the heated debate over mechanisation of the Cavalry continued throughout the inter-war years.

The 1914-1918 War had shown the importance of producing good quality, active horses of strong constitution. The WO continued its representations to the Board of Agriculture and Fisheries (BAF) on the necessity for maintaining an adequate supply of horses suitable for military purposes on mobilisation. Field Marshall Haig's letter to the President of BAF, December 1918, (see Appendix VI) on the future of the horse for military purposes is illuminating and should not be taken out of context as proof of a blinkered cavalryman with an infatuation for the horse on the battlefield. Haig was writing for a specific audience to safeguard the supply of horses and was fully aware of the value and progress of mechanisation. The Army had proved by 1914 and during the War that it was not backward in adopting new technology. In 1919, the Army would have been irresponsible not to seek a continuing supply of horses and as Badsey wrote, "to predict in 1918 that cavalry had a future was to be accurate." Haig was not isolated in his opinion, Moore commented in 1936 on the American

---

41   HRH Prince of Wales, President of HIS, AGM, 1923, in Macgregor-Morris, 1986, p.130.
42   MAF52/3/TL3770, 16th March 1920, extract from minutes ref. light horse breeding.
43   Cumberlegge, 1911(b), 'Looking Ahead', p.566.
44   Sutton and Walker, 1990, p.127; Stokes, 1920, pp.174-8; 'Sparking Plug' 1920, pp.116-8; Editorial, *RASCQ*, 1925, p.342; White, 1921, pp.553-4.

veterinary view of mechanisation in their own forces, under the heading, "Can the Army Be Mechanised Too Much?" "In this we yield no ground ... horses and mules in a field army will be used in the next great war ... perhaps in greater numbers than ever before; no other conclusion is tenable in the light of our studies and experiences ... it is hoped our country (US) will not be swayed beyond the horizon of commonsense in this significant factor of national defence."[45]

With the continued advance of mechanisation and decline in the UK national herd, from about 2 million in 1920 to just over 1 million in 1924, the stamp and types of horses required for military purposes were becoming ever scarcer. In 1942, of an estimated US equine population of about 14million (compared to Birkbeck's estimation of over 30 million in 1914), only 400,000 were in non-agricultural use, of some six million farms only 1.5% had tractors, nearly five million still depended on horses.[46]

With the close of hostilities, the Allied armies abruptly ceased to purchase horses, returning many for civilian use in Europe or the UK where, with sensible planning, it would have been recognised the majority were not required. From 1915 onwards heavy horses, such as the Shire, were bred to meet wartime demands for agriculture and the Army. The first wartime foals reached age five and were therefore ready for work on the land in 1921, by which date, some 141,000 army horses, fit for work, yet some of poor quality, had been sold on the open market in Great Britain.

The War did not deal kindly with the horse breeding industry. The financial position of light horse breeding had been unsound before the War and was now viewed as in grave danger of collapse.[47] The high-class market disappeared leaving the Army with a virtual monopoly. Breeders had been told for years that light horse breeding must be kept alive in case of national necessity and when this arose patriotic breeders were ill rewarded. Nothing caused greater discontent than the WO commandeering horses, despite many protests, and exploiting breeders by purchasing horses at 30% below their cost of production. Impressment was carried out somewhat ruthlessly at times; there was no impressment in Ireland. Hundreds of former breeders were driven out of the industry and their confidence shaken. If the country's horse production was to be stimulated the WO would have to change completely its policy of only buying in the cheapest markets.[48] From the WO point of view, they considered their attitude was reasonable and financially their method of purchasing was the most economic; but it did not encourage breeders.

45 MAF52/3/L19000/1919, 1st December 1918, letter from Field Marshall Haig, GHQ France, to the Rt.Hon. R.E. Protheroe, President of BAF 1916-1919; Badsey, 2008, p.242; Moore in *VR*, 1936, 8th February, Vol.XVI, p.165.
46 Chivers, 1976, a drop of 9.09% in horses of all kinds in GB, from Board of Trade 3rd Census, 1920 and 4th census, June 1924; *VR*, 1938, p.535, the horse population of the U.K. and Ireland fell from approximately 2 million in 1914 to just over 1 million by 1938.
47 MAF52/3/TL3770, H.I.S. to Winston Churchill, 11th July 1919.
48 Ibid., and MAF52/3/TL3770-L18519/1919, to WO from BAF, 9th July 1919.

In July 1919, breeders requested the WO update and re-issue the publication '*Types of Horses Suitable for Army Remounts*' (re-issued 1920), which provided information about government requirements for the future in respect of riding and artillery horses, the age on purchase and price to be given, also an estimate of what number of each type would be purchased in England and Wales. The Army was requested to purchase at prices that allowed a reasonable profit on cost of production and a reasonable number of horses at rising four years old.[49] The WO forwarded reports to BAF on the suitability for war purposes of the various types of horses used by the Army, both were in agreement that the well-bred hunter on short legs and of moderate height was the ideal riding horse. The classes to be considered were:[50]

Officers' chargers:	hunters below 16 hands at maturity
Officers' cobs:	riding cobs and ponies from 14.2 to 15.1 hands
Cavalry troopers:	misfit hunters about 15.2 hands
Field Artillery:	light draught, old omnibus type, between 15.2 and 15.3 hands

Annual requirements for the peacetime regular army were estimated at 1,500 riding and 1,500 artillery horses, about 3,000 animals, similar to pre-war requirements. In addition 2,000 light draught horses were to be purchased for the 'Boarding Out' Scheme. The Director of Remounts, Gen. Sir Noel Birch, RA, was considerably anxious about the supply of horses for the Territorial Force as the pre-war method of provision, through contractors, did not appear feasible and the 'Boarding Out' Scheme had not proved the success Birkbeck had anticipated. Only 15,000 horses have been put out and many of the horses and allottees were unsuitable, though Birch considered the Scheme should provide for 50,000.[51] In December 1919 the WO agreed, on the basis of the Middleton Commission recommendations (1915), that when purchasing resumed in 1921 they would buy a limited number of horses direct from breeders in Great Britain at 3.5 years old and at a fixed price agreed with BAF.[52] However, some BAF officials regretted the narrow view taken by the WO, in expressly rejecting the idea of basing their prices on cost of production, declaring an intention to continue buying at market rates. BAF questioned whether it would continue in light horse

---

49 MAF52/3/TL3770--L17623/1919, BAF memo 12th May 1919; MAF52/3/ TL3770-L18519/1919, BAF to WO, 9th July 1919.
50 Macgregor-Morris, 1986, p.122, from BAF Journal, 1919; MAF52/3/TL3770 (WO116/ GN/6723(QMG4), 11th July 1919.
51 MAF52/3/TL3770 (WO.116/GN/6723(QMG4), August 1919; MAF52/3/TL3770, draft letter 15th April 1920.
52 Ibid., letter from Winston Churchill to Lord Ernle, 22nd July 1919; 5th December 1919, letter from Gilbey to Lord Lee. Lord Middleton chaired the Committee appointed by Lord Selborne, August 1915, Report, MAF52/3TL21438.

breeding, as it was uneconomic and of little concern to agriculture, except for the National interest.[53]

In 1921 the Treasury raised with BAF the issue of continuing the Light Horse Breeding Scheme (LHBS), which BAF did not consider was essential from a purely agricultural viewpoint. In consequence, the Treasury decided they could only agree to a continuation of the Scheme for purely military requirements if all expenditure was met from approved Army Estimates. Abolishing the Scheme meant the practical cessation of light horse breeding which the Army had always maintained was of vital importance. As a result of their representations to the Treasury the WO (QMG4) had no option but to continue the Scheme from 1 April 1923, as a charge on Army Votes (budgets).[54]

A Committee was established, in October 1922, under the chairmanship of the Director of Remounts, Col. C.E.G. Norton, to review the existing administration, cost and practical working of the LHBS and to report in what direction, if any, it should be amended, or extended, to serve more directly the country's military require-ments. The Committee reported on 5th March 1923 and amongst its recommen-dations was support for the Scheme's administration transferring to the WO. The Scheme was to be extended into Scotland where BAF did not have control of horse breeding, but where the powers of the WO did extend. Provision was made in the 1923 Army Estimates of £35,500 for the Scheme. The existing Remount Department provided the framework on which the Scheme was to develop, with officers combining their existing duties with those of the Schemes administration.[55] The policy adopted was to find the most practical and economic methods for 'grading up' the quality of the country's horses, ensuring that the right stamp and types were available for the Army on any future mobilisation.[56]

Following the 1914-18 War, remount purchases were small and the peace-time requirement was not going to materially affect the horse breeding industry. Commercially, the Army would remain a very small and declining customer, as mech-anisation continued to replace horses for military purposes. However, for the breeder and dealer, the WO was regular in the annual number of remounts required and paid cash. The Army establishment in 1914 was about 28,742 horses, in October 1934 it had fallen to 12,605 and in 1938 to 5,205, down to 4,455 in 1939 when there were still 16 cavalry regiments.[57]

53   Ibid., BAF note, 2nd September 1919, and document, 'Horsebreeding', 8th September 1919, 5th November 1919, 16th March 1920.
54   WO163/29, Army Council 1923, Précis No.1145, 'The Future of the LHBS', pp.134, 141.
55   MAF spent £37,703 in 1922-33; WO163/29, Army Council Records, 1923, Précis No.1145, p.136.
56   WO163/29, Report of the Norton Committee, 1923, pp.145-6.
57   Ibid., p.148; *VR*, 1938, 15th October, p.1415, 1939, 11th March, p.333, 2nd December, p.48.

War is not glamorous, nor is the suffering of animals who participate without choice, but they were an integral part of the military system and their work and those of the 'horses services', that supported them deserve greater and wider acknowledgment.

The light and heavy draught horses of the ASC, Artillery, specialist and infantry units were the cornerstone of military success in 1918. There are very few memorials to the service of horses and mules from either the 1899-1902 or 1914-18 wars. For 1889-1902, in England, there are four specifically horse trough memorials: at Burtsow and Morden in Surrey; Jewry Street, Winchester; Martock, Somerset and at Barnard's Green, Malvern to a single horse killed in the War. In South Africa the magnificent Port Elizabeth horse memorial is a fitting tribute to those animals that served in the War, with a small memorial plaque at Fort Nonquai, Eshowe. For 1914-18, in England there about four: a horse trough at Wall on the Isle of Wight, a plaque in St Jude's on the Hill Church, Hampstead, London, the base of Newton Village war memorial Cambridgeshire, and the National Animal war memorial in London. The magnificent 58th London Division memorial at Chipilly, Northern France is not a horse memorial but is one of the finest memorials to portray an army draught work horse, the Artillery horse.

There is one grave stone memorial in England, to a donkey, "Our Jimmy," in Central Park Peterborough, of which there are conflicting stories. He was said to have been born on the Somme in June 1916 where his mother was killed and he became a German pack donkey. When German positions were taken by the 1st Scottish Rifles (old 26th Cameronians) they found Jimmy, weaned him and adopted him as their mascot, which suggests he was too young to be a pack animal. He was wounded on several occasions and wore a brow-band with four wound stripes and chevrons denoting length of foreign service. He was either demobilised from Swaythling remount depot, in 1919, to a dealer and then purchased through public subscription by the Peterborough Branch of the RSPCA, or sold to the RSPCA by the Cameronians after their post-war stay in the town. His final years were spent peacefully grazing and on flag days would pull a little cart giving rides for children to raise money for the RSPCA, he died in 1943. Jimmy was not to become the star of a Spielburg epic war film, but he did have his story recorded as a strip cartoon in the "Warlord" comic "Mascots at War" series.[58]

---

58   For South Africa and other 1899-1902 memorials I am grateful to Margaret Harradine, for St. Jude's on the Hill, Raymond Lowe; for material on "Jimmy", Rory Duncan of DC Thomson & Co, and Caroline Devine and her campaign to preserve his memorial.

Page one of the strip cartoon featuring 'Our Jimmy' in the Warlord comic, No.15, 1975. (© D.C. Thomson & Co. Ltd. 2013)

Recent media and literary attention has focused too heavily on the emotional aspect of the horse in war and therefore failed to understand, or acknowledge, their strategic and tactical role. The horse, mule, donkey, camel, bullock, dog and reindeer were the principal forms of military motive power and mobility. Within this context, most histories still fail to view the role of animals in war as an integral part of a wider transport system including, water, rail and motor transport, or to acknowledge the role of the domestic and business world in the supply of animals for military purposes. Such oversights I hope this study has begun to address.

> *And some there be, which have no memorial:*
> *Who are perished as though they had not been*
>   (Eccleiasticus 44.9)

> *Our Servant the Horse ... Lest We Forget*
> (1934, Maj-Gen. Sir John Moore, DVS., BEF)

Appendix I

Biographies

Biddulph, R. Gen. Sir (1835-1918)

Commissioned into Royal Artillery 1853, served in the Crimean War and Indian Mutiny. 1893 briefly Quartermaster-General to the Forces. His final appointment, 1904, was Army Purchase Commissioner when he abolished the purchasing of commissions.

Birkbeck, Maj-Gen. Sir William Henry (1863-1929)

Commissioned into the 1st King's Dragoon Guards 1883. As a major in 1898 he graduated from the Staff College with Maj. Allenby and Capt. Haig. Served with the 1888 Hazara and 1889-90 Chin-Lushai Expeditions. Promoted captain 1890, major 1897 and lieutenant colonel 1900. Served as Staff Officer (major) Remounts, Cape Town then from February 1900 Assistant Inspector of Remounts in South Africa 1899-1902. In 1905-6 attached to the Japanese 3rd Army in Manchuria. Commandant of the Cavalry School at Netheravon 1906-11. January 1911 placed on half pay; in the September he was informed by the WO that in the event of mobilisation he would be appointed Director of Remounts with the Field Force. September 1912 appointed Director of Remounts at the WO until 1920. Retired 1920 and killed in a walking accident at St, Briac near Dinard, 1929.

Blenkinsop, L. Maj-Gen. Sir (1862-1942)

Entered the AVD 1883. Advising Veterinary Surgeon to Punjab Government and Professor Lahore Veterinary College, 1891-93. SVO for British troops 1898 Nile Expedition. SVO in Egypt 1896-99. Major in 1900, colonel 1908. 1899-1902 South Africa; SVO to the Cavalry Division under Lt-Gen. Sir J. French until September 1901, when appointed SVO Remounts to December 1902. PVO 3rd Army Corps Irish Command 1904-6. South Africa 1906-9. Northern Command 1910, Southern Command 1910-12 and Aldershot Command 1913. Director of Veterinary Service in India 1916-17. DGAVS (WO) 1917-21. Retired pay 1921. Col-Commandant RAVC 1921-32.

Bridge, C.H. Brig-Gen Sir (1852-1926)

Served in West Indies, Woolwich and Dublin; Commissariat and Transport Staff Egyptian Campaign 1882; Adjutant Aldershot 1885; DAQMG Army Headquarters 1886-88; assisted in formation of the ASC; Lt-Col ASC 1889; commanded ASC Aldershot 1891-96; served in South Africa; Matabeleland Campaign 1896; Brevet Col. 1898; Director of Transport, South African Field Force 1899-1901; AAG Aldershot 1901-2; Director of Transport 1902; retired 1903; re-employed AIR; organized Remount Depot Arborfield Cross; Inspector Remount Depots from 1906; Brig-Gen 1914; head of Mule Purchasing Commission America 1914-16; retired 1916.

Brodrick, W. St John Fremantle, 1st Earl of Midleton (1856-1942)

Entered Parliament as Conservative member for West Surrey in 1880. From 1886 to 1892 Financial Secretary to the War Office; Under-Secretary of State for War, 1895-1898; Parliamentary Under-Secretary of State for Foreign Affairs, 1898-1900; Secretary of State for War, 1900-1903; and Secretary of State for India, 1903-1905.

Cowans, Gen. Sir John Steven (1862-1921)

Graduated Sandhurst 1881 and commissioned into the Rifle Brigade in India; served as aide-de-camp to Sir John Ross and commanded the Poona Division of the Bombay Army. 1891 passed Staff College with distinction. Held several staff appointments (Staff Captain, Army HQs 1893-4) becoming Deputy Assistant Quartermaster General (WO) 1898-1903. Promoted major 1898, lieutenant colonel 1900 and colonel 1903. Brigade Major, Aldershot 1894-7; AQMG 2nd Division, Aldershot 1903-6. Director General Military Education Indian Army 1906, Director of Staff Duties and Training Army HQ India 1907-8; commanded Bengal Presidency Brigade, Calcutta 1908-10. Brigadier General 1908 and Director General of Territorial Force 1910-12; QMG of Forces WO 1912-19. Promoted general and retired 1919. Managing Director of a company formed to develop Mesopotamian oil fields in 1920. Died April 1921.

Duck, F. Veterinary-Col., Sir (1845-1934)

Gazetted Royal Artillery, 1867. Involved with transport duties for the Abyssinian campaign 1867-8. In India 1868-74. In the Cape from 1878 to 1885. In 1880 veterinary surgeon attached to the Frontier Light Horse with charge of all mounted corps. Reported for gallantry and recommended for the VC. Saw service in the Gaika and Galika Wars, first Secocooni War, Zulu War, Boer War and Bechuanaland Expedition. In June 1890 promoted to Investigating Veterinary Surgeon. In 1894 to India as PVS. Director General of AVD in India. 1898 appointed Director General of AVD in UK. Retired in 1902.

Eassie, F, Brig-Gen. (1864-1943)
Entered the army 1889. Served Chin Hills, Burma 1890; Manipur Expedition, Chin Hills 1890-94; Chitral 1895, South Africa 1899-1902 with the Remount Department. Promoted from major to Lt-Col in October 1913. Director of Veterinary Services Salonika 1915-18. Deputy Director of Veterinary Services. Retired 1921.

Brett, R.B., 2nd Viscount Esher (1852-1930)
Held a militia commission after studying at Trinity College Cambridge. Parliamentary Private Secretary to Lord Harrington, Secretary of State for War 1882-5. Member of Lord Elgin's Commission inquiring into the failings of the Army in South Africa and influenced many post Anglo-Boer War military reforms; chaired the War Office *Reconstitution Committee* and member of the Committee of Imperial Defence from 1905.

Fitz-Wygram, F.J. Lt-Gen., Sir (1823-1904)
Cornet 6th (Inniskilling) Dragoons July 1843, served with the regiment in the Crimean War; Lt-Col. 15th Hussars 1860 and Colonel 1891. Lt-Gen. Commanded Cavalry Brigade Aldershot 1883 and placed on retired list 1889. Inspector General of Cavalry 1879-1884. Obtained a diploma from the Royal College Veterinary Surgeons and became its President 1875-1877; aided the establishment of the Veterinary School, Aldershot. A leading exponent, practitioner and author on the study and system of horsemastership. Member Parliament 1884-1900.

Fleming, G. Dr. (1833-1901)
Entered the army 1855 and proceeded to the Crimea, serving with the Land Transport Corps. 1857 served with the Military Train in China, present at Taku Forts and capture of Peking. Left China 1862 and joined 3rd Hussars in 1864; transferred to RE. In Syria for a short time purchasing animals for the Abyssinian War. 1877 appointed to the 2nd Life Guards. 1879 promoted Inspecting Veterinary Surgeon. Appointed PVS, head of the AVD in 1883 (at the age of 50). Retired 1890. Died in 1901. Smith, 1927, p.177, states "he suffered under the disadvantage of not having served in India".

Garratt, F.S. Hon. Brig-Gen., Sir
Served in the Afghan War 1879-80. South Africa 1899-1902; commanded the 6th Dragoon Guards, in command of a column June 1901 to 31st May 1902, then groups of columns. Director of Remounts, BEF 1914-19. The Army Lists for January 1914 show him on the Reserve Officers List under Colonels (substantive), late Staff, Hon. Brig-Gen. On 5th August 1914 he is listed under Temporary Appointments as Director of Remounts, graded as Brig- Gen. Still shown on the active list in March 1919, but in April was listed under Non-effective Officers, retired pay, late staff, although in May 1919 he is still listed as Director of Remounts. In the June 1919 listings he does not appear under Remounts and in July appears under Non-effective Officers.

Haldane, R.B. 1st Viscount Haldane (1856-1928)
Secretary of State for War, 1905-1912. His first army estimates significantly reduced the manpower and expenditure of the Army, but he implemented a wide-ranging set of reforms in preparation for a European war in support of the French against the Germans. The main element of this planning was establishing a BEF of six infantry divisions and one cavalry division. He established the Imperial General Staff replacing the Defence Committee of the Cabinet, which only met in emergencies, and the Colonial Defence Committee; created the Territorial Force of 14 divisions and 14 mounted Yeomanry brigades at home, the Officer Training Corps and Special Reserve. Haldane worked closely at the War Office with Maj-Gen. Haig. He was also instrumental in the creation the Advisory Committee for Aeronautics, 1909.

Head, Alfred. S., Lt. AVC (1874 -1952)
Aged 18, spent a couple years in America and Canada. Qualified Royal Veterinary College, London in 1897 and 1898 an assistant to Hoadley veterinary practice in Helston, Cornwall. Joined the Regular Army, AVD, posted to 6th (Inniskilling) Dragoons in 1899 and left for South Africa, arriving Cape Town in November. In 1903 he was seconded to the Egyptian army and attached to the Camel Corps, Sudan, as a veterinary officer. Returned to England in 1906 and retired from the Army in 1909, joining his now father-in-laws practice of Hoadley in Helston. Qualified as a Fellow RCVS in 1908. The Army Lists for June 1914 shows him as a Maj. on the AVC Reserve of Officers (from 29th November 1903). On 7th November 1914 he is listed as Assistant Director Veterinary, Staff officer and in December as temporary Lt-Col. (TF). Served two years in France, including the action at Mons and mentioned in despatches by Sir John French. 1916 recalled to the UK and appointed CO to Pitt Corner Veterinary Hospital, Winchester, until 1919 when he retired as Lt. Col. November 1918 on the Reserve of Officers AVC (Hon. Lt-Col. retd TF) and January 1919 under Non-effective Officers, retired pay, late AVC. Returned to practice in Helston. During the 1939-45 War he was active in forming a local Home Guard battalion, commanding it until 1943.

MacMunn, G.F. Lt-Gen., Sir (1869-1952)
Joined the Royal Artillery 1888. Served in Upper Burma and Irrawaddy Column 1892; Sima Column 1893; Kohat Field Force 1897; North West Frontier 1897-8, including the Tirak Expedition in command of the Imperial Service mountain battery. In South Africa with the Artillery and on the Staff 1899-1902. GSO2 India 1910-12. Deputy Assistant Director of Remounts (WO) March 1912 to June 1914; Assistant Director of Remounts (WO) June 1914 to July 1915. 1915-19 served in Dardanelles and Mesopotamia. AQMG, MEF 1915, DA and QMG, MEF 1915-1916. Inspector-General of Commands, IEF, "D" and Mesopotamian EF. Promoted Major-General 1917. C-in-C Mesopotamia April 1919 to January 1920. QMG India 1920-24. Retired pay 1925. Col-Commandant R.A. 1927-39.

Methuen, P.S., Field Marshal, 3rd Baron Methuen (1845-1932)

Royal Wiltshire Yeomanry. Scots Guards as an ensign in 1864, Captain 1867, adjutant 1st battalion 1868. Ashanti campaign of 1873-1874 on the staff of Sir Garnet Wolseley. Lt-Col. 1876, Regimental Major 1882. Brigade Major, Home District from 1871, Assistant Military Secretary in Ireland from 1877, Military Attaché Berlin from 1878 and assistant adjutant and QMG, Home District from 1881. Commandant of headquarters in Egypt 1882, at Battle of Tel el-Kebir. Expedition of Sir Charles Warren to Bechuanaland, 1884-1885 commanding Methuen's Horse. Deputy Adjutant-General, South Africa from 1888. Maj-Gen 1888 and GOC Home District 1892-1897. 1897 press censor at headquarters on the Tirah expedition, promoted Lt-Gen 1898. Command of the 1st Division on outbreak of war, 1899. Experienced both defeats and successes; greatest defeat was the Battle of Magersfontein. The only British general to be captured by the Boers during the War, March 1902; released due to the severity of his injuries. Appointed Col. Scots Guards 1904, then general, and in June given the command of the IV Army Corps, reconstituted as Eastern Command in 1905. 1908 General Officer C-in-C South Africa. Appointed governor and C-in-C of Natal, 1910 and Field Marshal 1911.Appointed governor and C-in-C Malta 1915. Retired 1919.

Moore, J. Maj-Gen., Sir (1864-1940)

Commissioned into the army as Veterinary Surgeon 1889. Promoted surgeon 1st Class 1899, Major 1900. Lt-Gen. 1906, Colonel 1913, Brig-Gen 1914 and Maj-Gen 1918. India 1890, including four years on horse remount purchasing duty at Calcutta. Served with the Indian contingent in Sudan 1896. Attached to 3rd Dragoon Guards as Veterinary Officer, Woolwich 1896 and York 1897-8. Employed with the Remount Purchasing Commission in the Argentine,1898 and had charge of a shipment of horses to South Africa. Rejoined his regiment in Ireland. Saw service in Rhodesia and Transvaal July 1899. Relief of Mafeking 1900. Returned to England October 1900 and proceeded with a Remount Purchasing Commission to the USA, Commandant Lathrop Remount Depot, until close of the War. June 1902 returned to England and attached to Remount Department (WO) for the Registration of Horses, Army Reserve. 1904 proceeded to Canada and the USA to prepare a scheme for horse purchase in the event of war. Visited Mexico to report on Remount possibilities there. 1905-1910 India. 1906 appointed Inspecting Veterinary Officer, Eastern Command, India and in 1907 Deputy Principal Veterinary Officer at HQs Simla. Assistant Director Veterinary Services, Northern Command, York, transferring to the Irish Command. December 1913 posted to the Aldershot Command as DDAVS. August 1914 DVS (BEF). 1919-21 DAVS India. Retired 1921. Col-Commandant RAVC 1932-34.

Pringle, R., Maj-Gen., Sir (1855-1926)
Joined as Veterinary Surgeon AVD 1878. Promoted 1st Class 1888, Major 1898 and Veterinary Lt-Col. 1901. Served in the Afghan War 1879-80, Wuzeree Expedition 1881, Zhob Valley Exhibition 1884 and South Africa 1900-1901. December 1900, commanded Elandsfontein, the largest remount depot in South Africa. PVO to 3rd Army Corps 1902, Inspecting Veterinary Officer India 1903-7 and PVO Aldershot Command 1908-10. Appointed Director-General Army Veterinary Service, October 1910, at the age of 55. His period of office expired in 1915, but was extended owing to the War. Retired on health grounds in October 1917. See Smith, 1927, pp.233, 236-7, for the controversy over his appointment and extension.

Rainey, J.W., Lt-Col. (1881-1967)
Royal Veterinary College Edinburgh. Served (corporal) 74th Irish Yeomanry, South Africa 1901-2. Entered AVD 1905. Captain AVC 1910. Served in 1914-19 War, promoted Brevet Major. Assistant Director General AVS 1917-19. Government Veterinary Officer Fiji Islands 1920-21.

Rasch, F.C., Sir (1847-1914)
6th Dragoon Guards. 1867 Major 4th Essex Regiment. MP for S.E. Essex 1886-1900.

Ravenhill, F.G., Col. (1833?-1895)
Gentleman Cadet 1847, promoted Captain 1867, Major 1872, Lt-Col. 1877 and Maj-Gen. 1893. 1881 shown in the Distribution Lists with C Brigade R.H.A. From 1 April, although still with that brigade, he was "Inspector and Purchaser of Horses". April 1882 retired temporarily on half pay. On the Quarterly Distribution List in October 1888, still on the half pay listed as "Inspector and Purchaser of Horses, Woolwich". Still on the Half Pay List, he moved to the Remount Establishment in January 1891 and remained there until his retirement in April 1894. October 1887, Inspector General of Army Remounts (WO) with temporary rank of Maj-Gen. Ravenhill was the architect of the Horse Registration Scheme and Remount Department.

Seely, J.E.B., Maj-Gen. (1868-1947)
Colonel in Hampshire Yeomanry. Commanded 41st Company Imperial Yeomanry in South Africa 1900-1901. Under Secretary of State for War 1911-12. Secretary of State for War June 1912 to March 1914 when he resigned. On special service with BEF in 1914. Brigadier commanding Canadian Cavalry Brigade 1915-18. Major General 1918.

Smith, F., Maj-Gen. Sir (1857-1929)

Entered the AVS in 1876, gazetted to the R.A. 1877. 1877-86 in India. 1880 Vet-Capt. with 12th Royal Lancers. 1886 Professor of the Army Veterinary School Aldershot. Established the Army Vaccine Institute, Aldershot 1888. Promoted Major 1896, Veterinary Lt-Col 1899, Colonel 1905 and Maj-Gen. 1907. Served in Sudan 1898; South Africa 1899-1902, SVO Orange Free State, PVO 1902-1904, returning to England as PVO Eastern Command. As DGAVS 1907-10 he fought to remove the subordination of the AVS from the Remount Department and place it directly under the QMG. 1914-18, DDAVS Southern Command then ADGVS. Died July 1929.

Stanley, E., 17th Earl of Derby, (1865-1948)

Joined the Grenadier Guards as a lieutenant serving between 1885 and 1895. Aide-de-Camp to the Gov-General of Canada 1888 and 1891. Fought in the 1899-1900 War. Private secretary to the Commander-in-Chief of the British forces in South Africa 1900.

Stevenson, R., Col.

Joined 18th Hussars, then 3rd Dragoon Guards, 5th Dragoon Guards. Promoted to 13th Hussars, then to Carabiniers. Assistant Inspector Remounts, WO, January 1899; responsible for the inspection of Registered Horses. July 1899 South Africa as Senior Remount Officer. Left for England 20 November 1899.

Truman, W.R., Maj-Gen. (1841-1905)

Enlisted in the Army 1862 as Cornet in 7th Dragoon Guards. Captain 13th Hussars in 1873; 1874 to 5th Dragoon Guards; 1883 Lt-Col; 1887 Col. 7th Dragoon Guards. 1878-1883 adjutant to Warwickshire Yeomanry. 1891 to 1893 Officer Commanding No.14 (York) Regimental District, in addition to becoming Assistant Inspector Remounts, 1891. January 1899 succeeded Maj- Gen. Ravenhill as Inspector General of Remounts. Died 1905.

Annesley, A., 11th Viscount Valentia (1843-1927)

Educated Royal Military Academy, Woolwich; joined 10th Hussars in 1864 and promoted to Lieutenant 1868. Served with the Yeomanry Cavalry, Acting Adjutant General in South Africa; mentioned in dispatches. Retired from the Army in 1872. 1895 elected MP for Oxford until 1917.

Welby, G.E., 5th Baronet (1865-1938)

Private secretary to Edward Stanhope, Secretary of State for War 1887-1892, and to Lord Lansdowne, Secretary of State for War, 1895-1899/1900. Assistant Under-Secretary of State for War from 1900 to 1902.

Appendix II

Points of the horse

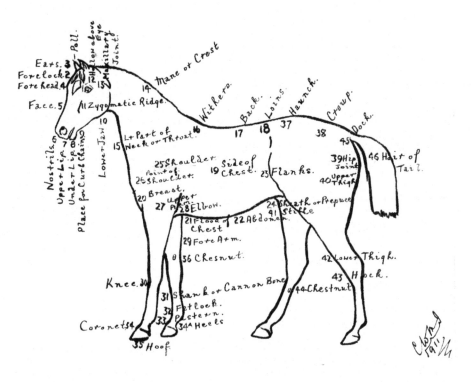

Points of the horse. Taken from the training notes of Private Cyril Jackson, "A.Co." Transport Section, 7th (Robin Hood) Bn., Sherwood Foresters, Notts and Derby Regiment (TF), 1911. (Author's collection)

Appendix III

Remount Service – Southern Home Command October 1919

DISTRICT REMOUNT OFFICERS

No.1 Circle
No.1 (Berkshire) District
Badcock, Bt. Lt-Col., G.H, OBE (temp. Lt-Col.) retired Indian Army
No.2 (Buckinghamshire) District
(July 1914) Maj. P.W.North., 3rd Bn. R.Berkshire Regt., Capt. retired pay (Reserve of Officers)
(Oct 1919) Seymour, Temporary Lt Col.
No.3 (Hampshire) District

No.2 Circle
No.4   (S. Gloucestershire) District
No.5   (N. Gloucestershire) District
No.6   (W. Somersetshire) District
No.7   (E. Somersetshire) District
No.8   (Wiltshire) District

No.3 Circle
No.9   (S. Oxfordshire) District
No.10   (N. Oxfordshire) District
No.11   (S. Warwickshire) District
No.12   (N. Warwickshire) District
Paul, G.D. (Temp. Capt), Lt. Staffordshire Yeomanry (TF)
No.13   (Central Warwickshire) District
No.14   (N. Worcestershire) District
No.15   (S. Worcestershire) District

No.4 Circle

No.16	(E. Cornwall) District
No.17	(W. Cornwall) District
No.18	(W. Devonshire) District
No.19	(E. Devonshire) District
No.20	(Dorsetshire) District

Appendix IV

Remount Directorate, BEF, 1918

ORGANISATION OF THE REMOUNT SERVICE, BRITISH ARMIES IN FRANCE, NOVEMBER, 1918.

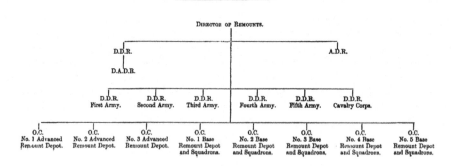

(Taken from Report upon the Work of the Quartermaster General's Branch, *HMSO, 1919.*
Copy held in RLC Museum, ref RCT. B10754)

Appendix V

Directorate Veterinary Services, BEF, 1918

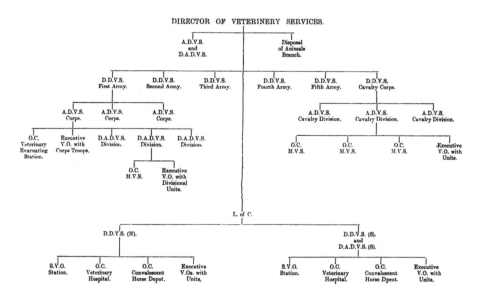

(Taken from Report upon the Work of the Quartermaster General's Branch, *HMSO, 1919.*
Copy held in RLC Museum, ref RCT. B10754)

Appendix VI

Supply of Horses for Military Purposes

NA. KEW: MAF52/3/L19000/1919.
Letter from: Field Marshall Sir Douglas Haig (GHQs France)
To: The Rt. Hon. Rowland Edmund Protheroe (President of the Board of Agriculture 1916 to 1919).
Dated: 1 December 1918

1   I desire to bring to your notice the urgent necessity for considering without delay what steps are essential to secure the supply of horses for war purposes in the future. The subject is in my opinion, of such vital importance that I make no excuses for addressing you personally and at some length on the subject.

    I realise that there is a considerable body of public opinion which holds the view that the recent developments in the means of transportation both by land and air have rendered the maintenance of the horse breeding industry of less importance than was formerly the case, and it is for this reason that, before considering the types of animals which in my opinion it is necessary to keep up, I desire to put before you briefly certain conclusions at which I have arrived.

2a   Cavalry has been, is, and will continue to be indispensable in modern warfare. That this opinion is held by the Commanders of Formations in the Field is illustrated clearly by the fact that I have been unable from the resources at my disposal to meet the demands of Corps and Divisional Commanders for mounted troops, both in offensive and defensive operations.

    In an advance, mounted troops are essential. However great may be the development of the Air Force in the future, it cannot eliminate the necessity for cavalry. This has been proved on many occasions during the recent British advance which commenced on August 8th this year, and it is my considered opinion that had I had at my disposal a much larger force of cavalry the fruits of victory would have been more rapidly gathered.

In rearguard actions, when fighting becomes loose and units scattered, the value of cavalry has been constantly proved both in the retreat from Mons and during the retirement of the Fifth Army in the spring of the present year.

Again, mounted troops will often be able to move quickly and independently of roads or railways to threatened localities, and the value of a mobile reserve of this nature is apparent.

In open country, such as the theatre of war in which General Allenby's forces were operating, cavalry may well still exercise a decisive influence.

In all cases traffic control, which is all important in the rear of the battle zone, cannot be satisfactorily carried out in the absence of mounted men.

2b   Horse and Field Artillery and the echelons of transport which accompany the fighting troops must be horse drawn. These details have constantly to move across country and round craters in roads, and to pass over bridges, which in many cases have been hastily constructed and are insufficient for the passage of heavy vehicles.

The supply of light natures of ammunition, both rifle and gun, is impossible in the absence of horse drawn transport, and the use of pack transport for carriage and ammunition and food has proved the only sure method of supply on many occasions during the present campaign.

While the heavier types of guns can, generally speaking, be drawn by mechanical transport in the shape of tractors, either ordinary or of the caterpillar type, it is essential that the light and medium natures up to and including 60pdrs and possibly an equal number of 6" Howitzers should be horse drawn and able to move across country in immediate support of an advance.

2c   For short haulage i.e. that requiring continual starting and stopping, the use of horses transport is more economical than any other.

Horses can live on the country in the harvest season – this fact was recognised by the Germans in the date chosen for the commencement of the present campaign.

2d   The limiting factors of the aeroplane are weather considerations, petrol capacity, and suitable landing grounds. Those of mechanical transport, roads, petrol capacity and an adequate supply of spare parts. Given sufficient food and reasonable shelter, the horse has proved to be the most reliable means of all transport for an Army in the Field under all conditions of weather and terrain.

3   In view of these considerations, it remains to consider what types of horse are required to meet the demands of a modern army in the Field. From the above remarks it is clear that two are essential, viz.: the rider and the light draught horse and the kind of animal that will best suit army needs as follows:-

(a) The Hunter for the Cavalry and for riding purposes generally, of the same type but with shorter legs than was generally the fashion in the English hunting field before the war.
(b) The light draught, well ribbed-up strong constitutioned horses for Field Artillery and general transport work, and which framers will normally use for agricultural purposes.

The maintenance of an adequate supply of horses of the above two types is, in my opinion, essential if we are to look forward with any confidence to meeting our obligations as a military power in years to come, and the demobilisation of the present armies in the field will afford an opportunity which may never occur again for laying a sure foundation of our military horse supply.

4   There are at present in the British Army in France a very large number of horses of the types I have mentioned, and, as I think you know, steps have already been taken on this side to brand mares of the types required with a view to their being retained by the British Government at the conclusion of hostilities.

The importance of this matter was not lost sight of by the Germans who, since 1870, by means of State Stud Farms and laws which provided that only state certified stallions could cover privately owned mares, built up their remount depots and introduced throughout Germany a breed of horse suitable for military purposes. This was a further development of a horse breeding scheme commenced nearly a century before.

The German machinery was, however, not devised to meet the strain of a long war, with the result that at the conclusion of hostilities much of his transport was rendered immobile owing to lack of remounts. If his horse situation had been satisfactory we could not have brought his offensive last April to an end so speedily. He had not the mounted troops nor a sufficiency of Artillery horses to exploit his original success.

In our case the command of the seas has enabled us to meet the needs of our Armies by the collection of horses from all parts of the world, but, in spite of this, our horse situation before the armistice was far from satisfactory, while the expense involved both in cost and freight has been enormous. It is, moreover, an unsound policy to depend wholly on supply from America or our own colonies while the riding horse bred in the UK is far the best of its kind.

I would, therefore, urge that the Government take steps at once, not only to provide for the disposal of branded mares to qualified owners in the UK, but, also, by the provision of State Stud Farms and State Certified Stallions. to ensure that the breeding of horses for military purposes is a matter not only of patriotism but of profit amongst the farmers in the UK, and the Board of Agriculture affords to my mind the best medium for directing and controlling the breed of horses.

If action on these lines is not taken and every provision is not made by the Sate to undertake, assist, and encourage the breeding of the stamp of horse which we require, and which is essential for the welfare of the Nation in war, I fear it is probable that the extension of the use of mechanical transport for commercial purposes will have disastrous effects on the horse breeding industry.

While I admit that the mechanical transport had many uses and advantages with an army in the field it can yet never take the place of the horse in war, and I am of opinion that immediate action on the part of the Government in this matter is of vital importance for the future welfare of the British Empire.

D. Haig, 1/12/18.

Bibliography

This bibliography is organised as follows:

1. Archival Sources: National Depositories

1.1 National Archive, Kew
1.2 Imperial War Museum (London)
1.3 Ministry of Defence (Whitehall)
1.4 National Army Museum (Chelsea)
1.5 Royal Artillery Institution (Woolwich)
1.6 Australian War Memorial (Canberra)
1.7 Canadian War Museum (Ottawa)
1.8 Department of the Army, Centre of Military History (Washington DC)
1.9 The Williams Research Centre, Historic New Orleans Collection
1.10 South African National Museum of Military History (Johannesburg)
1.11 African Library, Port Elizabeth, South Africa
1.12 Zululand Historical Museum, Eshowe, South Africa

2. Archival Sources: Local Depositories

2.1 Bishop Stortford Local History Society: Gilbey Rooms
2.2 Cambridge University Library
2.3 Cambridge University Library of the School of Clinical Veterinary Medicine
2.4 Hampshire County Record Office (Winchester)
2.5 Hereford and Worcester County Record Office
2.6 Huntingdon Research Centre (Veterinary)
2.7 Royal College of Veterinary Surgeons Library
2.8 Somerset Heritage Centre (Taunton)
2.9 Warwick University Library
2.10 Winchester Public Library
2.11 Shakespeare Birthplace Trust Record Office (Stratford on Avon)
2.12 Royal Logistic Corps Museum (Royal Corps of Transport Archive)
2.13 Army Medical Services Museum (Aldershot)

3. Printed Works

3.1 Official Publications
3.2 Private Papers
3.3 Contemporary Journals
3.4 Contemporary Printed Books and Articles (works up to and including 1930)
3.5 Later Books and Articles
3.6 Later Journals
3.7 Unpublished Theses
3.8 Miscellaneous Works of Reference

Please Note: articles from the following journals quoted directly in the main text are to found under Printed Works by author and date, not under their repository.

- *Army Service Corps Journal*
- *Army Service Corps Quarterly*
- *Royal Army Service Corps Quarterly*
- *The Waggoner* (Journal of the Royal Army Service Corps)

1. ARCHIVAL SOURCES: NATIONAL DEPOSITORIES.

1.1 National Archive, Kew

1.1.1 War Office Papers

War Office Administrative Directories: 1913, 1914, 1917, 1918, 1919.

WO24

/899 1913-14	WE 1913-14; 1914 Expeditionary Forces, Remounts.
/900	Line of Communication Units (under orders of IGC).
/911/351/78	Machine Gun (Cavalry) Squadron, 1916

WO32

/5073 1912	Précis for the Army Council No.557, Report of Mr Acland's Committee on the 'Horsing of the Cavalry Division,' 1911.

WO32 (code 22A)

/7272 1902	Report of Ebrington Committee on 'Provision of Horses for the Imperial Yeomanry' (see also WO33/246).
/8755 1887/91	Scheme for purchasing and forming a reserve of horses for the Army. Formation of Remount and Registration Establishment.
/8756 1901/2	Report of the Committee on the 'Supply of Remounts,' (Stanley Committee).

/8757	1902	Report of the Committee on 'Horse Purchase in Austro-Hungary.'
/8758	1902	Report of the 'Court of Enquiry into Administration of the Remount Department.'
/8759	1902	Report of Remount Commission in USA and Canada.
/8760	1902	'Court of Enquiry Remounts,' proceedings for Parliament. Presentation of Report to Parliament.
/8761	1903	Report on 'Remount Operations during Boer War 1899-1902' (Birkbeck).
	1902	'Conditioning and Training Animals and Notes,' Circular No.63, 6 April, Bowkers Park, South Africa.
/8762	1903/4	Provision of horses for officers of mounted infantry or alternative pay arrangements.
/8763	1904	Proposed increase of pay when supplied with a Government Horse.
/8764	1904	Rate of pay for mounted infantry officers when supplied with horses at public expense.
/8766	1905	Officers of mounted infantry, mounted at public expense and its effect on pay arrangements.
/8767	1912	Report of Commission on the 'Scheme for Registration of Horses related to Mobilisation of RH and FA,' (Birkbeck).
/8768	1901/4	Formation of a Reserve for the Remount Department, Amendment to Reserve Forces Act.
/8769	1903	Duties of Assistant Inspectors of Remounts. Memo for future organisation of Remount Department, 1902.
/9127	1912	Horse Impressment Scheme: Rules for Purchasers.
	1912	*Instructions for purchasing officers employed on mobilisation.* London: HMSO.
/9128	1913/14	Reduction of grant for Light Horse Breeding. Minutes of evidence taken before the Development Commission.
	1913	Gilbey, W., *Horses Taken for the Army.* London: Vinton and Co.
/9129	1911/12	Proposed New Scheme for Classification and Supply of Horses on Mobilisation.
/9130	1911/12	Proposed Scheme for Classification and Supply of Horses on Mobilisation (Conference at WO).
/9131	1911/12	Reports from Commands on the proposed scheme for classification and supply of horses on mobilisation.
	1912	'Types of Horses for the Army.' BAF pamphlet.
/9132	1912/13	Purchasing and collection, re proposed new scheme for horses classification and impressment.
/9133	1913	Revised railway arrangements for transport of horses to Aldershot on mobilisation.

/9134 1911/14   Horse Registration Scheme; classification and supply on mobilisation. First case of horse owner refusing permission to inspect his premises.

WO33

/42	1884	Sir Fitz-Wygrams Committee Report on 'Supply of Horses.'
/190	1901-2	Report of the Commission of WO Establishments, 1901-2.
/194	1901	Report of the Remount Commission.
/196		Minutes of proceedings of the Committee on Drafts etc. 1899-1901.
/224	1901	Report on the 'Supply of Remounts for the Army.'
/242	1901	Reports on English and foreign horses and cobs in South Africa.
/246	1902	Report of the Commission on the 'Provision of Horses for the Imperial Yeomanry.'
/271	1899/1902	Report on the 'Work of the Army Remount Department (Truman, 1901).
/463	1908	Reports on 'Experiments with Various Bullets Against Animals.'
/600	1912/13	Detailed statement and instruction for remounts required by the Army on mobilisation.
/608	1912	Mobilisation tables: Eastern Command
/611	1914	Mobilisation appointment: Part 1, Expeditionary Force.
/612	1912	Report of Commission. on 'War Establishments at Home,' (Pres: Col. W Adye).
/618	1912	Report of Foreign Manoeuvres.
/621	1913	Interim report of the sub-committee of the War Establishments Commission, on the 'Present Military Organisation in the UK,' and recommended adjustments.
/628	1913/14	Remount Statement.
/664	1914	Amendments re General Mobilisation.
/669	1914/15	Amended edition of the Remount Statement, 1914-15.
/673	1914	Second report of the Commission on War Establishments.
/743	1916	Index to War Establishments, 16 February.

WO95

/27	War Diary QMG/GHQ France.
/65	Director of Veterinary Services Aug. to Dec. 1914.
/66	Jan. to Dec. 1915.
/67	Jan. to Dec. 1916.
/68	Jan. 1917 to Nov. 1920.
	ADVS Dec. 1918 to Mar. 1919.
	DADVS June to Aug. 1919.
/69	Director of Remounts, GHQ (France and Belgium), Aug. 1914 to Dec. 1916.
/70	Director of Remounts, Jan. 1917 to Dec. 1919.

/70		Deputy Ass. Director of Remounts, Lt. Col. Yardley, DADR. GHQ Troops and British Cavalry, March to May 1916.
/71		Director of Transport, Sept. 1914 to Sept. 1919.
/72		ADT Aug. to Sept. 1914.
		DADT Aug. 1914 to June 1919.
		ADT of T (Indian Section) Jan. to Feb. 1915.
/201		DDR (First Army), Feb. to Dec. 1918.
		DDVS (First Army), Nov. 1915 to Mar. 1919
/289		DDR (Second Army), Feb. 1915 to Dec. 1918.
		DDVS, (Second Army), Feb. 1915 to Mar. 1919.
/383		DDR (Third Army), Aug. 1915 to Dec. 1918.
		DDVS (Third Army), Nov. 1915 to Sept. 1919.
/453		DDR (Fourth Army), Feb. 1916 to Dec. 1919.
		DDVS (Fourth Army), Feb. 1916 to Oct. 1919.
/536		DDR (Fifth Army), June 1916 to Feb. 1919.
		DDVS (Fifth Army), July 1916 to Aug. 1919.
/581		DADR (Cavalry Corps), Feb. 1915 to Feb. 1916 and Sept. 1916 to Mar. 1919.
/581		DDVS (Cavalry Corps), Aug. 1914 to Feb. 1916 and Sept. 1916 to Mar. 1919.
/586		ADVS (Indian Cavalry), Sept. 1914 to Nov. 1915.
/4202		GHQ, DDR (Italy), Assistant Director of Remounts.
/5466		Romsey Remount Depot
		Shirehampton Remount Depot
		Home Mechanical Transport Depot ASC.

WO105

/40	Roberts Papers.

WO106

/518	Horsing American Artillery Divisions with British and Provision of Horses, 1918.

WO107

/13	Sept. to Dec. 1914	Inspector Stores and Equipment. General Correspondence.
/14	Jan. to June 1915	Stores and Equipment.
/15	July 1915 to June 1916	General Correspondence.
/16	July 1916 to March 1919	General Correspondence.
/17	1914	New Armies; horses, statements and returns.
/18	1914/15	New Armies; mechanical transport, statements and returns.
/19	1914/15	Mobilisation: reports to Secretary of State, WO.
/21	Aug 1914 to Nov. 1915	Directors Meetings; stores and equipment.

/22	June 1915 to Feb. 1916	Director of Supply and Transport; general correspondence
	June 1916	MEF: Egypt and Salonika.
/23	6 March to 28 Sept. 1915	New formations; weekly returns.
/26	1915	Committee meetings on Light Horse Breeding. Remount depots and Commands.
/27	1915	Breeding of light horses; correspondence.
	1915	Report of Committee on 'The Supply of Horses for Military Purposes.' (chairman: Lord Middleton).
	1917	Reports of the 'Census of Horses in GB and Ireland.'
/63	1911/1912	Report of Mechanical Transport Committee.

WO108 (Boer War Papers)

/75	Col. Birkbeck's report, July, 1900 (also in PP. Cd 963, 1902).
/79	Proceedings of Army Board.
/233	Telegrams, ref. USA and Boers.

WO161

| /7 | 1914 | History of military and mechanical transport dating from 1914. |
| /18 | 1918 | History of the Department of the Senior Inspector of Motor Transport, 1918. |

WO163 (Army Council Records)

/19	Index: decisions and précis prepared for Army Council, 1914-20.
/20	Army Council Records, 1914.
	34/2204, Report of the Inspector General of Home Forces, 1912-13, (Gen. C. W. Douglas).
	Précis 820, 34/2228, Annual Report of the Inspector General of Home Forces, Oct. 1913.
	34/2497, Report of the Inspector General of Overseas Forces, Inspection of Australia (I. Hamilton), 1914.
	34/2577, Report of the Inspector General of Overseas Forces, Inspection of New Zealand (I. Hamilton), 1914.
	Précis No.782, 1914, p.73, 'Forage allowance for officers chargers taken away from their Stations during leave.'
	(also Précis No.409, 1909.
	Précis No.789, 1914, p.154, 'Impressment of Horses etc on Mobilisation,'
	(continuation of Précis No. 681, 1913, pp. 9, 221).
/21	Army Council Records, 1915-16.
	Précis 834, p.50, 'Transfer of responsibility for the supply of motor transport from the WO to the Ministry of Munitions.'
	Précis 835, p.50, 'The Remount Situation,' 1916.
	Précis 845, p.68, 'Sale of cast horses.'

/22	Army Council Records 1917.
/23	1918.
/24	1919
/25	1920
/26	1921

Précis 1072, p.105, 'Use of Government Horses for Polo.'
Précis 1073, 'Army Expenditure 1921-22.'

/27   (Index, 1922-34)
/28   Army Council Records 1922

Précis 1086, p.35, 'Provision of horses for Territorial drills and
Précis 1091, p.73, 'Reduction of Cavalry.'
Précis 1094, p.78, 'Reduction of Cavalry.'
Précis 1110, p.149, 'Reorganisation of Cavalry.'

/29   Army Council Records 1923

Précis 1145, pp.133-58, 'The Future of Light Horse Breeding,
Report of the Norton Committee.'

/30   Army Council Records 1924
/37   1931

Précis 1357, 'Reduction in Army Expenditure; saving on LHB
subsidy.'

1.1.2 Ministry of Agriculture and Fisheries Papers (BAF)

MAF 52/2/TL22037	Confiscation of Horses Owned by Enemy Governments, 1914-23.
	File II, TL22038; File III, TL22039.
52/2/A43091/1915	Army Horse Supply Committee: minutes and reports.
52/3TL21438	Supply of Horses for Military Purposes: Selborne Committee Report (Chairman: Middleton)
52/3/L19000/19	Supply of Horses for War Purposes, 1918.
52/2/TL3770	Light Horse Breeding, Increase in Premiums, 1916-20. (includes reports on types of horses used in the war).
MAF 60/564	5th Report of the Central Council, Forage Department; Civil Supplies to Forage Committee, 4 September, 1918.
MAF 60/60	Feeding of oats to horses engaged in winter racing, Dec. 1917.
MAF 60/140	Control of Hay, memo, June 1919.

1.1.3 Development Commission Papers (D)

D1	/1	Minutes of Meetings 1912-14.
	/2	1915-18.
	/3	1919-29.

D2	/11-23	Reports to the Treasury by the Development Commission for Advances from the Development Fund, 1914-18.
	/15	Minutes of evidence taken before the Development Commission, July 1914.
D3	/1-9	Annual Reports of Development Commission, 1911-1919
	/2	2nd Report of the Development Commission to 31 March 1912
	/4	4th Report to 31 March 1914
	/10	(includes a review of 20 years), 1920
	/11-12	Annual Reports, 1921-1922
D4		Development Commission correspondence and papers, 1910-70
	/100	Papers for: 1910-11
		Colonel E.J. Granet's evidence to the Development Commission, 21 September 1910, pp.14-16, Q1024-1106.

1.1.4 Cabinet Papers (CAB)

CAB 22		Papers of the Committee of Imperial Defence, War Council.
	22/3	Meetings 17 May, 18 May, 24 May 1916.

1.1.5 Foreign Office Papers (FO)

FO371   General Correspondence, after 1906 (card index,1906-20)

1.1.6 Treasury Papers (T)

T1	Treasury Board Papers, 1557-1920
T2	Treasury Registers of Papers, 1777-1920
T24	Treasury, outletters, War Department, 1855-1920.
T102	National Wartime Committee, 1917-18.

1.2 Imperial War Museum (London)

Army Form series G 1098-77, Sept., 1918, *Establishment of the Remount Service Headquarters and squadrons.*

Barratt, E.G. Ms diary containing details of horse shipments from New York to France 1915-18. Ref: 74/991

Fyrth, Captain W. Reference 97/4/1. Ms diary of service in the AVC attached to 8th Brigade RFA (5th Division), August-November 1914.

Holden, J.A., Ref: 97/37/1A Remount depot El Kantara.

Kingston, A.J. Reference 88/27/1. Service as a farrier NCO 1914-19 with 53rd Division. Includes Gallipoli, Salonika and Egypt.

Kirk, Major, H. Account of his service with RAVC through to the Army of the Rhine.

O'Rorke, Lieutenant Colonel F.C. Reference PP/MCR/54. Diary of an AVC officer 1914-18.

Stuttard, Private C.E., AVC. Ms diary January-November 1915 with 18th Mobile Section RAVC (29 Division). In Gallipoli from May 1915.
Todhunter, Lieutenant Colonel B.E. Reference 87/53/1. Purchasing Officer for the Essex Yeomanry August 1914 to July 1915.
Reference Misc.521. Pocket diary for 1916-19 of service of unknown AVC officer on the Western Front.
Reference Misc.846. Field message book 1917 from B and C Batteries, 256th Brigade to the veterinary officer commanding 51st Mobile Veterinary Section, 256th Brigade.

1.3 Ministry of Defence (Whitehall Library)

War Office, 1936, *Report of the Committee on Remount Duties*, 31 December. (Chairman: V.A.G.A. Warrender).
R:AO11, *Abstract of the Recommendations of Commissions Committees and Conferences relating to Army Affairs 1900-1920*.
R:AO11, *Abstract of the Recommendations of the Principal Commissions and Committees which have reported on Army Matters 1806-1900*; London, HMSO, 1901.

1.4 National Army Museum (Chelsea)

Acc.No. 8407-20 (Remounts 1913-18).
Documents relating to the service of Lt.Col. A.W.C McFall OBE., 1881-1920.
Acc.No. 8401-30-1, (Remounts 1927), *Types of Horses Suitable for Army Remounts*, WO, 1927.

1.5 The Royal Artillery Institution (Woolwich)

Ref.G26, Monograph works on horse management and veterinary science
Fox, F., ("GSO"), 1920, 'Army Animals in France,' *The Gunner*, Vol.II, pp.6-9.

1.6 Australian War Memorial (Canberra)

Index of records relating to horses services, transport and Light Horse.

1.7 Canadian WAr Museum (Ottawa)

Official History of the Canadian Forces in the Great War, 1938, Vol.1, Appendix 257.
Report of the Ministry: Overseas Military Forces of Canada 1918. London: Ministry of Military Forces of Canada.

1.8 Department of the Army, Centre of Military History (Washington, DC)

HRC 461, Bibliography of material on the US Remount Service.

Order of Battle of the United States Land Forces in the World War, American Expeditionary Forces (General Headquarters, Armies, Army Corps, Services of Supply and Separate Forces). (Washington: Government Printing Office, 1937).

Report of the Surgeon General, US Army (Annual Reports, War Department, Fiscal Year Ended 30 June 1918). Washington: Government Printing Office, 1918.

1.9 Williams Research Centre, Historic New Orleans Collection

The *Times Picayune* newspaper, New Orleans, 1901.

1.10 South African National Museum of Military History

Material on Port Elizabeth and 1899-1902 War.

1.11 African Library, Port Elizabeth, South Africa

Material on the Port Elizabeth Horse Memorial and Remount Depots 1899-1902 War.

1.12 Zuluand Historical Museum, Eshowe, South Africa

Material on the Eshowe horse memorial, and 1899-1902 War.

2 ARCHIVAL SOURCES: LOCAL DEPOSITORIES

2.1 Bishop Stortford Local History Society: Gilbey Rooms

Extract from *Sports and Sportsman* of the obituary to Sir Walter Gilbey. Pamphlet, 1873, in 'Gilbey Scrapbook,' by Thacker, W., *The Troop Horse*.

2.2 Cambridge University Library

2.2.1 Official Publications (OP)

OP3100.2.01	'Types of Horses Suitable for Army Purposes, 1920', London, HMSO
OP.3100.8.100:	'Organisation of the Remount Service and its Duties in Peace and War.' (lecture 1925 on Remounts).
OP.3100.8.0273	Army Lists (monthly), 1880-1913.
OP.4100.8.073	'Veterinary Manual (War),' 1915.
OP.4100.8.139	'Notes on Feeding, Management and Issue of Army Horses,' 1916.
Op.4100.8.255	'Farriery,' 1884.
OP.4100.8.0124	'AVS,' 1894.
OP.4100.8.0134:	'Remount Manual (War),' 1913, (WO).

OP.4100.8.0135   'Remount Regulations,' 1913, (WO).
OP.5100.8.25:   'Remount Manual,' 1906, (WO).
2.2.2 *Veterinary Record [VR]* (ref. L442.b.8): *v*olumes 26 to 28, 1913 to 1920.

2.3 Cambridge University, Library of the School of Clinical Veterinary Medicine

Veterinary Journal [VJ]: *v*olumes 1887-1888.
Veterinary Record [VR]: *v*olumes 1 to 11 (1888 to 1899); volumes 12 to 18 (1899 to 1906).

2.4 Hampshire County Record Office (Winchester)

Romsey Remount Depot (plans and photographs).

2.5 Hereford and Worcester County Record Office

HWRO705: 445 BA 5247/19 (6944); Elgar Letter to Schuster.

2.6 Huntingdon Research Centre (Veterinary)

Veterinary Record: *v*olumes 45 to 54, 1933 to 1942.

2.7 Royal College of Veterinary Surgeons Library

Fredrick Smith Archive
Types of Horses Suitable for Army Remounts, 1909, Board of Agriculture and Fisheries, London, HMSO

2.8 Somerset Heritage Services: Archives

DD\CPHS/36: Correspondence with E.A Mattock
CSH/WA/1B.2: Somerset War Agricultural Committee meetings, 1917-1919

2.9 Warwick University

D521/E2. Economic and Social History of the World War, British Series. Dictionary of Official Wartime Organisations, Dearle, Carnegie Endowment for International Peace, Oxford University Press, 1928.

2.10 Winchester Public Library

SH35.5. Jessel, H.M., *The Story of the Romsey Remount Department*. London: Abbey Press, 1920.

2.11 Shakespeare Birthplace Trust (Stratford upon Avon)

BRR 60/9   Stratford Corporation Horse Book; Impressment Order to the Corporation.

DR 227/48   Flowers Brewery, Stratford upon Avon; Horse Stock Book.

2.12 Royal Logistics Corps Museum (Royal Corps of Transport) Archive

A1/0752-4   'Mobilisation of Motor Transport; French Organisation of Services 1914.'

A6/0718   Wyatt, H., 'Motor Transport in War.'

A6/1387   Nugent and Bagnall-Wild, 'Notes on the Design of Traction Engines.' HMSO: 1905

A6/1396   Extract from MTC annual report 1910-11, 'Motor Cycles.'

A6/1911   Kidner, R.W., 'The First Hundred Road Motors.' Oakwood Press, 1950.

A6/3521   'Caterpillar Traction,' *The Waggoner*, 1965, pp.242-3.

                'Steam Sappers: The Earliest Mechanical Transport,' *The Waggoner*, 1973, March, (see letter to Editor of *Royal Engineers Journal*, August 1877).

                'Tracks versus Wheels,' *The Waggoner*, 1958, May, p.136.

A6/8919   Motor Transport Corps, 1905; work performed.

A6/8920   Motor Transport Corps reports 1908-9.

A6/8921-24   Motor Transport Corps reports, 1909-13.

A18/3376   Mechanical Transport. (File B1/ Great War General)

B1/0754   'Report upon the Work of the Quarter Master General's Branch of the Staff (file No.1) and Directorates Controller. British Armies in France and Flanders, 1914-18.' HMSO, 1919.

B1/0754   Plans of base remount depot and veterinary hospitals (types of buildings).

(file No.2)   Veterinary hospitals and remount depots (constructional details). Horse carcass economiser, accessory buildings (10 and 30 horses).

                Details of stocks for shoeing restive horses.

                No.4 FSD Bethune, sketch of chaff cutting installation.

B1/1339   Allotment of ASC units; amendments to 1 Oct., 1915, WO.

B1/1340   Ibid., to 1 Aug. 1918 (Horse Transport, MT and Support).

B1/1394   Historical Record of Advanced MT Depot, No.1 54 Company and No.2 365 Company, ASC.

B1/1444   Provisional War Establishments: Corps troops and 3 divisions (HQ ASC (MT); Supply Column; Ammunition Column.

B1/6091   Army Horse Show, 25 June 1917

B1/7928   Instructions Officers Commanding Horse Transport Formations, Second Army.

B1/7951	Statistics of Military Effort of the RASC, 1914-19.
B1/8190	'Companies Proceeding Overseas and Allotment, at Outbreak of War; Horse Transport Companies and MT Companies.'
B1/8198	Report from the 'Directeur Des Services Automobiles' about the use of motor cars during the operations round Verdun in Feb-March 1916.
B1/8203	Organisation of the French Automobile Service.
B1/8210	Allotment of ASC units; with amendments to 25 Nov. 1916.
B1/8392	Fletcher, D., 1987, *War Cars (British Armoured Cars of the First World War)*. London: HMSO.
File B2/	Mobilisation 1914-15 and Great War
B2/1310	Records of a supply officer, 5th Cavalry Brigade, to 6 March 1915.
B2/1461	Orders to impressing officers on day 1 of mobilisation.
B2/1550	'Yorkshire Waggoners with the ASC,' *Journal Royal Army Service Corps*, 1935, November, pp.496-507. 'The Yorkshire Waggoners,' *The Waggoner*, 1957, July, p.324.
Box 1, 3970	Letter Sykes, July, 1974
B2/1638	Record of N0.2 Reserve Horse Transport Depot, Blackheath, opened 24 Feb.1915.
B2/3965	*The Times History and Encyclopaedia of the War*. Part 125, Vol.10, January 1917, 'Mechanical Transport.'
B2/7290	Motor Transport bases in England.
B2/7705	*From Mons to Loos: The Diary of a Supply Officer.* London: W. Blackwood and Sons, 1917.
B2/8204	Requisition form re Army Act.
B2/8205	Ref. mobilisation of motor cars and lorries, WO.
B4/4600	Badcock, G.E., 1925, *History of the Transport Services of the Egyptian Expeditionary Force 1916-18*. London: Hugh Rees.
B6/2451	'History of MT of the Desert Mounted Corps during operations in Palestine and Syria, 1918.'
B11/3858	RCT Training Centre, file on the 'Disbandment of H Squadron: the Last HT unit of the Corps in the UK, 1971.'
B11/8541	Standing Orders: Army Remount Service, Romsey remount depot, 1916.
C1/1467	ASC Training Establishment, School of Instruction.
C3/1396	Extract from Motor Transport Commission, Annual Report, 1910-11. 'Motor Cycles.'
C3/0713	Scholfield, G.P. (Major), RE, *Report on Steam Road Transport in South Africa*. London: HMSO, 1903.
C3/1643	Hobbs, P.E.F., 'The New System of Transport as Carried Out By the Blue Force During Army Manoeuvres, 1912.' *Army Review*, 1913, Vol.IV, No.2, April, pp.413-430.

C4/1034	'Mechanical Transport: RASC.'
	'The History and Development of Mechanical Transport RASC,' Outline Scheme of Compilation 1914-19. Part.III: 'Other Theatres.' Sect.II: Mesopotamia and Persia.
C6/2531	Kuhne, C.H., 1927, (Transport 1913-39). 'The Institution of Automobile Engineers.' Lecture given in London.

2.13 Army Medical Services Museum (Aldershot)

| Box 22 | *Report of the Purchases of Horses and Mules by the British Remount Commission to Canada and USA*, Aug.1914-Feb.1919; 1919, Canada (RPCCA), Gunning, C. |
| Box 6 | Eassie Sytem plus various photographs |

3 PRINTED WORKS

3.1 Official Publications

3.1.1 Public General Acts

1881	Army (Annual) Act
1888	National Defence Act
1907	Territorial and Reserve Forces Act.
1911	Army (Annual) Act.
1912	Army (Annual) Act.

3.1.2 Parliamentary Papers Command Papers (PP. Cd.)

Cd.466	1901, Committee on the Organisation, Arms and Equipment of the Yeomanry Force.
Cd.468	1901, Yeomanry Cavalry Training Return 1900 (WO, February 1901, E. Wood, Adjutant General, 'State of Corps of Yeomanry Cavalry in Great Brtitain, Annual Inspection, 1900).
Cd.580	1901, Report of the Committee Appointed to Enquire into War Office Reorganisation
Cd.581	Minutes of Evidence, Appendices, Digest and Index.
Cd.803	1901, Imperial Yeomanry; First Report, 15 May.
	1903, Imperial Yeomanry, Second Report, 1 January.
Cd.882	1902, Report of the Committee on Horse Purchase in Austro-Hungary. (President: Welby).
Cd.884	1902, Return of Numbers of Troops and Horses that have Embarked for South Africa from 1 January 1900 to 31 December 1902.
Cd.892	1902, Army Returns of Mounted Forces in South Africa, 1899-1902. (Continuation of Cd.579, 1901)

Cd.963	1902, Army (Remounts) Reports, Statistical Tables and Telegrams Received from South Africa, June 1899 to 22 January 1902. (Birkbeck)
Cd.990	1902, Return of Military Forces in South Africa, 1899-1902, (continuation of Cd.892).
Cd.991	1902, Report on Trials of Self Propelled Lorries for Military Purposes at Aldershot, from 4 to 19 December 1901.
Cd.993	1902, Report of a Court of Enquiry on the Administration of the Army Remount Department, since January, 1899. (President: General Sir R. Biddulph).
Cd.994;	Evidence with Appendices.
Cd.995	1902, Report by Officers Appointed by the Commander in Chief to Inquire into the Working of the Remount Department Abroad.
Cd.1413	1903, Return Showing State of the Six Army Corps.
Cd.1496	1903, General Annual Report on the British Army for 1902
Cd.1497	1903, Return Showing Peace Establishment for Effective Strength of Troops Belonging to the First, Second, Third and Fourth Army Corps.
Cd.1789	1903, Report of His Majesty's Commission Appointed to Inquire into the Military Preparations and Other Matters Connected With the War in South Africa. (President: Lord Elgin)
Cd.1790-91	Evidence Vols.1 and II.
Cd.1792	Appendices, IV
Cd.1932	1904, Report of the War Office (Reconstitution) Committee, Pt.1, 11 January.
Cd.1968	1904, ibid., Part II, 26 February.
Cd.1968-1	1904, ibid., Map accompanying Part II.
Cd.2002	1904, ibid., Part III, 9 March. (Chairman Lord Esher)
Cd. 2993	1906, Memorandum by the Secretary of State on Army Re-organisation 30 July 1900.
Cd.5419	1888, Royal Comission on Horse Breeding, 1st Report, Vol.XLVIII.
Cd.5425	1910, Statistical and General Report of the AVS for 1909.
Cd.5595	1888, Royal Commission on Horse Breeding, 2nd Report, Vol.XLVIII
Cd.8134	1914-16, Report of the Committee Appointed to Consider and Advise What Steps Should be Taken in England and Wales to Secure an Adequate Supply of Horses for Military Purposes, Vol.XXXIX.
Cd.8916	1917, Horse Breeding Commission.

3.1.3 British Parliamentary Papers

1873, Vol. XIV.1, Select Commitee of the House of Lords to enquire into the 'Condition of the Country with Regard to Horses, and its Capabilities on Supplying any Present or Future Demand on them.'(Chairman: Lord Rosebery).
Army Appropriation Accounts:
For years   1913-14   Ref. 1914-16, Vol. xxxix.

1914-15	Ref. 1916, Vol xvii.
1915-16	Ref. 1917-18, Vol xix.
1916-17	Ref. 1918, Vol xv.
1917-18	Ref. 1919, Vol xxxii.

Hansard (C)   **(Column (c)**

1875	Vol.CCXXIII	27 April	1694	Development and Road Improvement Act.
1887	Vol.CCCXVIII	19 July	1343	Purchase of horses in Canada.
		29 July	494	Cavalry remounts.
1895	Vol.XXXVI	26 August	798-9	Army horses.
1897	Vol.XLVI	4 March	1597	Horse purchases.
1898	Vol.LIV		601	Horses on the Cavalry Estbl.
1898	Vol.LV		100	Cavalry Horses
1898	Vol.LVII		174-5	Officers Chargers
1898	Vol.LXI		1212	Retaining Fee for Horses for Military Purposes.
			1200	Purchase of Horses for Army Purposes.
			1365-6	Horses for Military Manoeuvres.
1902	Vol.CII	3 February	240-43	Yeomanry Scandal
	Vol.CV	17 March	287	ref. Tomkinson and Truman.
1906	Vol.CLIII	8 March	634	Haldane and mobilisation.
1914	Vol.LXV	5 August	1965	Agric. horses impressed for war purposes.
		6 August	2064-5	Requisition of horses (merchants and farmers).
			2121-3	Commandeering of private horses.
		8 August	2203-4	Agricultural horses and food distribution.
		10 August	2262-3	Horses, Agricultural Districts and Impressment.
			2302-3	Impressment of carthorses.
			2312-3	Impressement of carthorses
			2322	Requisition of pit horses.
1915	Vol.LXIX	8 February	242	Shelter for Army horses at home and mortality due to exposure.
		15 February	902	Purchase of horses by WO in Ireland.
		17 February	1135	Death by exposure at home camps

		18 February	1305	Remount Department employing unskilled men of military age.
1915	Vol.LXXV	9 November		Sir F. Crawley and Col. H.W. Walker
1917	Vol.XCVII	6 August	21-23	BEF (horses), ref.clipping.

Hansard (L)

1887	Vol.CCCXVIII	8 September	1623-27	ref. registration scheme.
1902	Vol. CIV	13 March	1236-38	Lord Ribblesdale and Devonshire's reply.

3.2 Private Papers

Diary of Capt. A.E. Deprez RA (in possession of Anne Daniels)

Nuneaton RE Company (in possession of Beryl Kerby)

Papers of Maj-Gen. W.H. Birkbeck (in possession W. Birkbeck)

Letters of Capt. W.M. Mitchell, AVC (in possession of Helen Gibson)

Papers of Joseph Clark, Merchant Navy (in possession of Dr W.M. Goodchild)

Papers of Cyril Jackson, A.Co., Transport Section 7th Notts. and Derby Regiment, 1911 (in author's possession).

Photograph of horse taken on mobilisation and returned as too old (in possession of Anthea Cox)

Roy Baker, RAVC, 1939, papers and photographs (in his possession, Kineton, Warwickshire)

Papers of Lt. Head (in possession of John Head)

Correspondence Col. Hume, 1989

Correspondence Brian Bird, 2012 (photographs E.J.Bird/Walter Bird in family possession)

Travis Hampton, *A Medical Officer's diary and narrative of the First World War* (in possession of Simon Butler)

3.3 Contemporary Journals

3.3.1 *Army Service Corps Journal* (held in Royal Logistics Corps Museum)

(Articles quoted directly in the text will be found in 'Printed Sources: Contemporary Books and Articles)

1902	March	pp.252-3, 'Blue Paper Remounts.'
	June	pp.132-33, Review of: Hayes, H., *Horses on Board Ship: A Guide to their Management*. London: Hurst and Blackett.
	December	p.128, ref. mules and remount depots in South African War.
1903	October	pp.21-31, 'The 1903 Manoeuvres from Supply and Transport Point of View'

1904	January	pp.165-171 'Notes on Some Transport Difficulties'
	April	p.21 *Le Mesurier, F.A.*, 'Army Transport as Connected with Home Defence.' p.23 ref. Esher Commission, Third Report, Section II: The QMG.
	May	pp.58-71, *Mc.Nalty, C.E.I.*, 'Mechanically Propelled Vehicles for Military Purposes.' Summary of lecture given February.
	November	pp.412-6, 'The 1904 Manoeuvres from a Supply and Transport Point of View.'
1905	January	pp.23-33, *Denny, W.A.C.*, 'The Component Part of an Army in the Field.' Paper at the Canadian Military Institute.
	May	pp.230-45, *Rawnsley, C.*, 'The Organisation of Lines of Communication, with Special Reference to the South African War.' Lecture, Cairo, 9 Jan. 1905.

3.3.2 *Army Service Corps Quarterly* (held in Royal Logistics Corps Museum)

(Articles quoted directly in the text will be found in 'Printed Sources: Contemporary Books and Articles)

Volume 1:

Courtney, E.A.W. July, 1906, 'Embarking and Disembarking Transport at Portsmouth.' Editor 'The Automobile in War,' pp.421-31.

Hayter, H.R. January, 1907, 'Mechanical Transport from a Company Officers Point of View,' pp.652-665.

Volume 2:

Richards, H.A.D. April, 'The Necessity For, and Practice of Requisitioning as the Means for Supplying an Independent Cavalry Division and a Brigade of RHA in The Field,' pp.61-62.

Edye, M.W.J.,January, 1908, 'Instructions for Slinging Horses.'

Cumberlege, H.C.F. July, 'The Past and Present Vehicles of the ASC, Part.1 (part II, October 1908; part III, January 1909: Volume III; part IV, April, 1909.)

   October   'Military Motors in Many Lands,' pp.701-5.

Hutchinson, T.M. 'The Hornsby Chain Tractor,' pp.768-78.

Volume 3:

(no author given) January, 1909, 'Further Development of the Hornsby Chain Truck Type of Vehicle.'

Blunt, G.C.G. July, 'Notes on the Movement by Rail and Embarkation of Heavy Traction Engines,' pp.246-55.

Hazelton, P.O. January, 1910, 'Mechanical Transport in the Colonies,' pp.481-7

Reid, H.G. 'The Australian ASC,' pp.453-58.

(no author given),'Census of Horses and Vehicles, 1909,' p.515, in the *Times*.
Scott, M. de B April, 'The Work of the Transport Service in the Field With German Army Corps,' pp.568-76.
Scott, M. de B 'The Evolution of Organised Military Transport,' pp.591-98.

Volume 4

(no author given) October, 'A New Horse Ambulance.'
(no author given) 'Experiments in Systems of Supply and Transport on the French Manoeuvres, 1909.'
Aylmer, G. January, 1911, 'Mechanical Transport in India,' pp.197-203
'WED,' July, 'Testing of War Department Motors at Brooklands,' pp.502-12.

Volume 5:

Williamson, W.A.F. 'Oats: Our Sources of Supply.'
(no author given) 'Strength and Organisation of the Armies of France, Germany, Austria, Russia, Italy, Mexico and Japan.'
'Graphite' 'Refilling Points.'

Volume 6:

Cumberlegge, H.C.F. January, 1913, 'The ASC in European Warfare.'
Bennett-Stanford, J.M. 'The Transport of the Yeomanry Brigade on the 1912 Manoeuvres and a Few of its Difficulties.'
White, W.N. 'The Supply of a Territorial Division during Annual Training.'
Hazelton, P.O. 'General Conditions to be fulfilled by Industrial Vehicles Put Forward by Manufacturers in 1913 With A View to Qualification for Receipt of Premium.'
Hogg, I.G. April, 'The Cavalry Division Training, 1912.'
Young, J.M. July, 'Outline of a Supply System and Methods of Accounting During Army Exercises, 1913.'
Lawson, H.S. 'Furze as Horse Food.'
Fuller, J.F.C. 'Mobilisation of a Territorial Infantry Battalion,' pp.386-7.
Stringer, F.W. 'Some Facts About Our Supplies of Food Supply.'
Wyatt, H. October, 'On the Means of Rendering Adequate MT Available for Military Purposes Throughout the Empire,' pp.360-64.

Volume 7:

Atkinson, J. January, 1914, 'The Mobilisation of a Mounted Brigade or Brigade Company ASC (TF).'
Ridler, J. 'Some Changes in Service Harness and Saddlery During Recent Years: Their Effect on Horse Transport.'
'Hydrocarbon' 'Mechanical Transport for India,' pp.84-92.
Marsh, J.T. 'The New Transport System (Australia),' pp.84-92.

Young, J.M. 'The Work of the Main Supply Depot During Army Exercises, 1913,' pp.1-15.

Carter, E.E. April, Lecture on: 'The System of Supply for Home Defence,' pp.184-5.

Carter, E.E. July, 'The Services of Maintenance in the Field: Some object lessons from the Army Exercises, 1913.'

Editorial, ref. War Establishment changes and abolition of mounted infantry, pp.95-108.

Leland, F.W.G. July, 'A Mechanical Transport Supply Column From a Mechanical Transport Officers Point of View,' pp.223-46.

Carter, E.E. 'The Services of Maintenance in the Field: Some Object Lessons from the Army Exercise, 1913,' pp.204-7.

3.3.3 *Royal Army Service Corps Quarterly* (Royal Logistics' Corps Museum)

(Articles quoted directly in the text will be found in 'Printed Sources: Contemporary Books and Articles)

Volume 8:

Hazelton, P.O. January, 1920 'Supplies and Transport in E. Africa.'

McGwire, J.E.M. 'Some Notes on the Antecedents and Origin of the RASC.'

Roberts, A.H. 'Supply Systems in the Alps.'

Beadon, R.H. 'Some Transport Considerations in the Modern Battle.'

Baring-Gould, E.S. April, 'History of MT of the Desert Mounted Corps.'

Reid, F.J. 'The Investigation Dept., Supply Directorate, France. Its Inception and Development.'

Wakelin, A.B. 'A MT Vehicle Reception Park.'

Whittaker, F.A.E. 'Transport Work in N. Russia.'

'MT' 'Some Transport Considerations in the Modern Battle: An Argument.'

Blunt, G.C.G. 'History of the Organisation and Development of the No.2 Base MT Depot, on the Northern Lines of Communication.'

Elliott, W.E. July, 'A Divisional Train of the Future: Two Replies.'

White, W.N. 'The Last Phase in France and Flanders.'

Davies, G.F. 'Lecture on Supplies and Transport: Egyptian Expeditionary Force.'

Hazelton, P.O. October, 'Organisation and Administration of Supply and Transport the East African Campaign.'

Beadon, R.H. 'The Allied Supreme Command and its Extension into the Administrative Sphere.'

Wakelin, A.B. 'A Divisional Train of the Future,' pp.272-74.

Wlin, A.B. 'A Divisional Train of the Future.' 'Camel Transport Corps, EEF, 1915-19,' (Compiled in the Supply and Transport Directorate, EEF)

Volume 9:

Hedges, K.M.F. January, 1921, 'The Future Design of Motor Vehicles.'
Giblett, R.H. 'Should The Army Tell,' pp.373-76.
Swabey, W.S. April 'RASC Work in Italy.'
Parker, W.M. 'Supply Services in Mesopotamia.'
Cooper, H.I. 'Mechanical Transport and the Maintenance of the Frontiers of the Empire.'
Boyd, C.T. 'From Vimy Ridge to Asiage with the 48th Divisional Supply Column.'
Hubbard, R.K. 'Ways and Means: on the future design of the Military Motor Vehicles.'
Swabey, W.S. July 'Working of MT in Italy,-Section 'A.'
Montagu of Beaulieu 'The Future of Road Transport.'
Verney, R.H 'War Experience and Motor Vehicle Design.'
Giblett, R.H. October, 'The Military Importance of the Motor Coach.'
White, O.W. 'The Abolitions of Horse Transport in the Administrative Services.' pp.553-582

Volume 10:

White, W.N. January, 1922, 'The Organisation and Maintenance of a Base,' pp.49-69.
Clayton, F.T. April, 'The History of the RASC.'
Christmas, D.H. 'Mechanical Transport in India.'
Kuhne, C.H. 'First Line or Heavy Artillery Mechanical Transport.'
Wakelin, A.B. 'Mechanically Mad,' pp.125-6
Anderson, N.G. July, 'Ammunition Supply in the Field.'
Dobbs, C.E.S. 'The Supply of Corps Troops in the Field.'
Mills, M.N. 'Maintaining the Motor Transport of a Field Army.'
Beadon, R.H. 'The Future of the RASC.'
(No author given) 'Notes from the General Report on the Transport Services With the British Forces in Italy, November 1917 to November 1918.' Compiled by the Supply and Transport Directorate, IEF.

Volume 11:

Wilmet, January, 1923, '1914-18: L'Effort Automobile Interallie.' (Inspector General du Materiel Automobile).
Reckitt, J.T. 'The Training of MT Drivers During the Great War.'
Jackson, R.R.B. April, 'Supply Service (Intendance) in the Field.' (Translated, French Staff College,1920-1)
Jackson, R.R.B. 'With the 5th Cavalry Division in France.'
Evan Gibb 'The Organisation of Labour in the Great War.'
G. Le Q.Martel 'Cross Country Tractors.'
Dempsey, H.H. 'The Transport of a Division,' pp.226-43.

Volume 12:

Striedinger, O. January, 1924, 'Cape Helles: A Retrospect.'
Blunt, G.C.G. 'The Commercial Development of Cross Country Vehicles for Military Service.'
Kuhne, C.H.April, 'MT and its Future Development in the Army.'
Dobbs, C.E.S. July, 'The Territorial Divisional Train.'
'Pera' 'Motor Cars in War.'
Doran, J.C.M. 'Petrol Supply in the Field.'
Berger, A. Letter to Editor re transport and MT, EF, 1917.
Kuhne, C.H.   October, 'The Movement of Troops by MT.'
Berridge, H.H. 'Petrol Supply for an Infantry Division in the Field.'

Volume 13:

(no author given) January, 1925, 'MT at the Aldershot Command Exercises,' pp.54-69.
Cooper, H.J. 'Some Further Thoughts for the Future,' pp.97-113.
Elliott, W. 'Maintaining Allenby's Armies.'
(no author given) Extract from 'Parliamentary Notes on Motor Vehicles 1918 and 1924,' p.167.
(no author given) Extract from review of a book in *JRE*, ref. 'French Mechanisation of Cavalry,' p.176.
'RHB,' April, 'Sir John Cowans: The Greatest Quartermaster General.'
Stokes, H.W.P. July, 'Notes on the Stable Management of the Transport Horse,' pp.428-38.
'PEFH' and 'HAS,' October, 'Lt.Gen. SirF Clayton,' pp.486-9.
Rowcroft, E.B. 'Ammunition Supply,' pp.490-507.
(no author given) December, 1924, 'Lt. General Sir R. Maxwell (QMG, BEF, France, Jan. 1915 to Dec., 1917), pp.536-42.

Volume 14:

Watson, H.N.G. April, 1926, 'North Russia (1918-19).'
Tapp, H.A. 'Feeding of Corps Troops.'
Flood, A.W. 'The Supply Reserve Depot.'

Volume 15:

White, W.N. April, 1927, 'Administration of MT as represented by the Load Carrying Vehicle.'
Kuhne, C.H. 'The Development of Motor Vehicles for General Load Carrying Duty in the Army.'
'Chough,' July, 'Mechanisation.'

3.3.4 *Motor Traction*, 1909 (held in Cambridge University Library, reference L225:8.b.4)

20 February	Vol.VIII	pp.169-70	'The WO Tractor Trials.'
27 February		p.184	'The WO Tractor Trials.'
6 March		pp.208-11	'The WO Tractor Trials of 1901.'
13 March		pp.228-31	'The WO Tractor Trials.'
20 March		pp.258-9	'The WO Military Trials at Aldershot.'
		pp.260-2	'The WO Tractor Trials.'
3 April		pp.296-7	'Motor Traction for Military Purposes.'
24 April		pp.233-6	'Motors in Warfare.'
1 May		pp.386-7	'The Motor Mobilisation Trial in Yorkshire.'
29 May		pp.475-7	'Motors in Warfare.'
21 August	Vol.IX	pp.152-3	'Motor Transport at Salisbury Plain.'
28 August		p.170	'Motor Transport at Salisbury Plain.'
16 October		p304	'Warfare in the Future.'

3.3.5 *Veterinary Journal*

1887	Vol.V	p.426	Summary of veterinary statistical report, first one on horses of the British Army.
	Vol.xxiv		Duck, F., 'Working of the AVD in the Field.'
1888	Vol.xxix	p.42	Fleming, G., 'Physical Condition of Horses for Military Purposes.'

3.3.6 *Veterinary Record [VR]*

Volume 1:

1888	11 Aug.	p.55-6	'Registration of Army Horses.'
		p.57	'Export and Import of Horses.'
1889	12 January	p.324	'Cavalry Without Horses.'
	16 February	p.393-4	Fleming, G., 'Army Horse Supply.'
	9 March	p.241	ref. Aldershot Vaccine Station, also p.431.
	16 March	p.442-3	Fleming, G., 'Reports on African Horse Sickness.'
	16 February	pp.393-4	Fleming, G., 'Army Horse Supply.'

Volume 2:

1890	22 February	p.440	Agricultural Returns; import and export of horses.
	21 June	p.687	'AVD- A New Warrant.'

Volume 3:

1890	5 July	p.11	'The French Army Remounts.'
	9 August	p.74-5	'Annual Report, AVD.'
	16 August	p.91	'Army Remounts.'
	13 September	p.137	ref., Smith, F., and Army Vaccine Institution.
	27 September	pp.162-3	'French Army Veterinary Service.'
	18 October	pp.198-9	'Sore Backs in Army Horses – Treatment.'
	13 December	p.300	Board of Trade returns ref. exports and imports.

Volume 4:

1891	9 May	p.572	'Tramway Horses.'
	23 May	pp.593-5	'On Horse Breeding.'
	25 July	p.52	'Army Veterinary Department.'
	26 September	p.174	AVD, 'Registered Army Horses.'
	14 November	pp.269-70	'Annual report AVD.'

Volume 5:

1892	6 February	pp.418-9	'Cold Shoeing in the Army.'
	16 July		ref. AVD and mobilisation.
	3 September	p.129	'The Army Veterinary Report.'
	29 October	pp.242-3	'Horse Supply in India.'

Volume 6:

1893	21 January	pp.409-10	'Army Farriers and Farriery.'
	23 September	p.181	Smith, F., 'The Loss of Horses in War.'
		p.180-1	'Annual Report of AVD,' ref. horse strength.
	18 November	p.280	Ref. export of horses.
	30 December	p.363-4	'AVD, 'Origin and Development.'
		p.364	'Remount Establishment.'

Volume 7:

1894	12 January	p.390	ref. purchase of remounts in Syria.
	1 September	p.144	'Stable Management.'
	15 September	p.171	ref. Army Veterinary School.
1895	26 January	p.411	'Australian Horses.'
	11 May	p.619	ref. AVD and Chitral Expedition.
	7 September	p.127	AVD, 'Purchase of Army Horses in the Country.'

Volume 8:

1895	19 October	p.199	'Military Registration of Horses,' and 'Art of Army Shoeing.'
	14 December	p.304	AVD, 'Our Military Horses.'
1896	7 March	p.460	'Horses for Cavalry Service.'

Volume 9:

1896	15 August	p.84	'The Loss of Horses in War.'
	31 October	p.221	'Horse Breeding in Ireland.'
	7 November	p.235	'The Army Veterinary Report.'
1897	3 April	p.571	'Army Horses- A New Regulation.'
	8 May	p.639	AVD 'Remounts from the Argentine.'

Volume 10:

1897	3 July	pp.7-8	'Horse breeding in Ireland: The Supply of Army Remounts.'
	17 July	p.43	'How the Army Veterinary Department Might Be Further Utilised.'
	13 November	pp.261-2	'Army Veterinary Report.'
	4 December	p.323	'Army Veterinary Department.'
1898	26 March	p.571	Ref. officers using troop horses.
	16 April	p.616	ref. purchase of remounts in Syria.
	18 June	p.739	'Army Veterinary Department.'

Volume 11:

1898	16 April	p.616	Purchase of remounts in Syria.
	28 May	p.699	ref. Kitchener's despatches.
	16 July	p.43	'Horse Mortality in Natal.'
	30 July	p.68	'Horses Registered for Military Purposes.'
	19 November	p.297	'Horses and Motor Cars.'
	3 December	p.334	'The Export of Horses.'
	31 December	p.395	'The Annual report, AVD.'

Volume 13:

1900	3 November	pp.234-5	'Army Remounts.'.
	15 December	p.326	'Commandeering 'Bus Horses.'

Volume 26:

1913	12 July	p.36	Change in length of service of DGAVC.
	26 July	p.67	'Stampede of Army Horses at Aldershot.'

	23 August	p.136	ref. Greek army purchases from Ireland.
	30 August	p.150	'Price of Army Horses.'
	6 September	p.154	ref. German purchases.
	13 September	p.179	'Boarding Out of Horses.'
	11 October	p.36	ref. Maj. Eassie to Lt.Col. Regular Forces, AVC.
	22 November	pp.338-9	'The Treatment of Army Horses in Recent Army Manoeuvres.'
	13 December	pp.375-7	O'Rorke, F.C., 'Notes on the Treatment of Remounts.'
1914	7 February	p.523	'Purchase of Army Horses.'
	28 March		ref. photograph of army horse sickness.
		p.634	'The Horse Owner and the Motor (effects on trade and horse supply).
	18 April	p.687	ref. Light Horse Breeding
	4 April	p.652	'Prohibition of Export of Russian Horses.'
	2 May	p.712	'Cavalry Remounts- Canadian Horse breeding Scheme,' and 'The Mule in USA.'
	29 August	p.139	'Horses in Warfare.'
		p.149	'Horses for the Army.'
	19 September	p.186	'Remounts.'

Volume 27:

1914	24 October	p.243	'Need for Veterinary Surgeons in the Regular Army' Army.'
		pp.244-5	ref. work of AVC, Fund for AVC with EF.
		p.245	'The RSPCA Unit.'
		p.245-6	'Alleged Fraud in Requisitioning Horses (discharged).'
	31 October	pp.255-6	'Two Claims Against the Army Council.'
	28 November	p.306	'The Army Mule.'
		p.305	ref. Fund for AVC with EF.
	12 December	pp.326-8	'East Kent Farmer Sues Army Council.'
	19 December	pp.337-8	'The Horse Supply.'
		p.338	'The AVC at Work.'
	24 December	p.243	'The Need of Veterinary Surgeons in the Regular Army with Suggestions as to How to Remedy It.'
1915	9 January	p.369	'Germans Still Buying Thoroughbreds.'
	23 January	p.397	ref. auction of army horses for breeding.
	20 February	p.443	'Veterinary Work of the EF.'
		p.444	ref. 'Farmers and the AVS.'
	27 February	p.452	ref. 1/1 North Midland Division, MVS.
	13 March	p.485	'Comforts for Troop Horses.'

Volume 28:

1 April	p.452	'The Army Horse Ration.'
3 June	p.547	'Exhaustion of Horses in War.'
30 September	p.140	'A Veterinary Hospital.'
21 October	p.174	'Sale of Army Horses.'
4 November		'Casting Army Horses.'

Volume 29:

1917	14 April	p.431	'The Future of Army Horse Supply.' 'The Army Veterinary Service.'
		p.432	'The Use of Cavalry,' 'The Shortage in the AVC.'
	5 May	pp.469-70	'More about the Horse in War.'
		p.470	'Army Veterinary Servcie.'
	9 June	pp.516-7	'Remount Work in USA.'

Volume 30:

	14 April	p.432	'The Use of Cavalry.' (HG Wells)
	11 August	p.67	Parliamentary 'Clipping of Army Horses.'
		p.69	'An Undetected War Scandal.'
	15 September	pp.114-5	'Mr. H.G. Wells on the Horse.'
	10 November	pp.192-3	'A Visit to an English Veterinary Hospital.'
	15 December	p.248	'The Somme' Veterinary Medical Association.
1918	9 February	p.331	Wilson, A.L., 'Evacuated to Hospital.' (poem)

3.4 Contemporary Printed Books and Articles

(Up to and including 1930)

Abbott-Brown, C., 1916, *How To Do It: the ASC Subalterns and NCOs Vade Mecum*. London: Forster Groom.

Alderson, E.A.H., 1900, *Pink and Scarlet*. London: Heinemann.

Amery, L.S., 1903, *The Problem of the Army*. London: Edward Arnold

Amery, L.S., 1909, *Times History of the War in South Africa 1899-1902*. Vols. III and V1. London: Sampson Low.

Ansell, G.K., 1907, 'A Suggestion on the Question of Veterinary Hospitals etc.' *Cavalry Journal*, Vol.II, pp.245-6.

Arbutnot, A.G., 1919   'Horsemanship During The War.' *Journal of the Royal Artillery*, Vol.46, November, pp.337-43.

Archdale, A.Q., 1912, 'The Scarcity of Horses in the British Empire.' *Journal of the Royal Artillery Institution*, No. 5, Vol.XXXVIII, pp.231-239

Armstrong, F.S., 1921, 'The Remount Service,' in *Quartermaster Review*, Vol.1, No.1, July-August, pp.13-18. Washington: Quartermaster Association.

Armstrong, W.H.M., 1908, 'The Age of Mechanical Appliances.' *Army Service Corps Quarterly*, Vol.2, April, pp.495-512.

Aspinall-Oglander, C.F., 1929, 1932, *Military Operations in Gallipoli (British Official History)*. 2 Volumes. London: Heinemann.

Baden-Powell, (ed.), 1908, *Army Annual Year Book*, 1908. London: Wm. Clowes and Son.

Baden-Powell, (ed.), 1909, *Army Annual Year Book*, 1909. London: Wm. Clowes and Son.

Bagnall-Wild, R.K., 1910, 'Mechanical Transport for Military Purposes.' *Journal of the Royal Engineers*, December.

Balfour, C.D., 1909, 'From Southampton to South Africa with Horses' *Journal Royal Artillery Institution*, Vol.XXXV, pp.45-48

Bannatine-Allason R.,   1924, 'Reminiscences of 40 Years of Peace and War.' *Journal of the Royal Artillery*, Vol.L, No.12, pp.466-77.

Barbor, R.D., 1913, 'Army Administration in the Crimea.' *Journal of the Royal United Services Institute*, Vol.LVII, No425, July, pp.865-894.

'A Battery Commander' 1912, 'Morals and maxims for Stable Management and Horse Mastership.' *Journal Royal Artillery Institution*, Vol.XXXVIII, pp.35-50

Battine, C.W., 1908, 'The Use of the Horse Soldier in the Twentieth Century.' *Cavalry Journal*, Vol.III, January, pp.82-86.

Bedford-Pim, E.H., 1910, 'Horsing of a Territorial Battery.' *Journal Royal Artillery Institution*, Vol.XXXVI, pp.204-208

Bernhardi, Von F., 1906, *Cavalry in Future Wars*. London: John Murray.

Bernhardi, Von F., 1910, *Cavalry in War*. London: The Pall Mall Military Series.

Bethune, E.C., 1906, 'The uses of Cavalry and Mounted Infantry in Modern Warfare.' *Journal Royal United Services Institute*, Vol.1 Pt.1, February, pp.619-36.

Biddulph, R., 1904, *Lord Cardwell at the War Office*. London: Murray.

Birkbeck, R., 1900, *The Birkbecks of Westmoreland and Their Descendants*. Mitchell and Hughes, privately published.

Birkbeck, W.H., 1907, 'Notes on the French Remount System.' *Cavalry Journal*, Vol. II, January, pp.327-342.

Birkbeck, W.H.,1908, 'The Provision of Horses for the Army in War.' *Cavalry Journal*, Vol.III, July, pp.327-342.

Birkbeck, W.H., 1909, 'The Cavalry Division in the Egyptian Campaign of 1882.' *Cavalry Journal*, Vol.IV, pp.403-22.

Birkbeck, W.H., 1909, 'The Prussian System of Horse Breeding and Remounts.' *Cavalry Journal*, Vol.IV, pp.161-70.

Birkbeck, W.H., 1909, 'Russo-Japanese War.' *Cavalry Journal*, Vol.III, Pt.1, pp.501-17, Pt.II, pp.32-46, Pt.III, 186-94, Pt.IV, pp.298-307.

Birkbeck, W.H., 1914, 'The French Horse Breeding and Remount Organisation.' *Cavalry Journal*, Vol.9, Part 1, pp.341-46.

Birkbeck, W.H., 1920, 'The French Horse Breeding and Remount Organisation.' *Cavalry Journal*, Vol.10, Part II, pp.82-96.

Blenkinsop, L.J. and Rainey, J.W., 1925, *Official History of the Great War: Veterinary Services*. London: HMSO.

Board of Agriculture and Fisheries, 1912, *Types of Horses Suitable for Army Remounts*. London: HMSO (1912, revised edition).

Bridge, C.H., 1909, 'The Breeding and Supply of Horses.' *United Services Magazine*, Vol.XXXIX, June, pp.282-301

Bridge, C., 1909, 'What the French are doing to Encourage the Breed of Saddle Horse.' *Cavalry Journal*, Vol.IV, pp.335-46.

Bridges, G.T.M., 1908, 'The French Cavalry School.' *Cavalry Journal*, Vol.III, July, pp.300-11.

British Dominions General Insurance, 1914, *War Facts and Figures*. London: British Dominions General Insurance Ltd.

Brownlow, A.L, 1918, *The Breaking of the Storm*. London: Methuen.

Brunker, H.M.E. and Baden-Powell (eds), 1910, *Army Annual Year Book*, 1910. London: Wm. Clowes and Son.

Brunker, H.M.E.(ed), 1911, *Army Annual Year Book*, 1911. London: Wm. Clowes and Son.

Brunker, H.M.E.(ed), 1912, *Army Annual Year Book*, 1912. London: Wm.Clowes and Son.

Brunker, H.M.E.(ed), 1913, *Army Annual Year Book*, 1913. London: Wm.Clowes and Son.

Budworth, C.E.D., 1901, 'Harness and Blankets.' *Proceedings Royal Artillery Institution*, Vol.XXVII, pp.625-627.

Burnett-Stuart, J., 1928, 'The Progress of Mechanisation.' *Army Quarterly*, Vol.XV1, April, pp.30-51

Caldwell, G.L., 1929, 'History of Cavalry Horses.' *Cavalry Journal*, July, pp.385-403.

Carey, W.L.J., 1906, 'Some Notes on Motor Cars for Military Purposes.' *Journal of the Royal Artillery*, Vol.XXXIII, Oct, pp.213-221.

Carter, E.E., 1912, 'The New Transport System: Its Principles and Their Applications.' *Journal of the Royal United Services Institute*, Vol.LV1, Pt.1, May, pp.671-703.

Chapman-Huston, D. and Rutter, O., 1924, *General Sir John Cowans*. London: Hutchinson. Vol.I, II.

Charteris, J., 1929, *Field Marshal Earl Haig*. London: Cassell.

Childers, R.E., 1910, 'War and the Arme Blanche: The General Staff Views on Mr.Childers Book.' *Journal of the Royal United Services Institute*.

Childers, R.E., 1911, *War and the Arme Blanche*. London: Arnold.

Childers, R.E., 1911, *German Influence on British Cavalry*. London: Arnold

Clarkson, T., 1910, 'The Use of Motors For the Transport of Troops.' *Journal of the Royal United Services Institute*, Vol.L1V, Pt.1, April, pp.450-64.

Cochrane, R.C., 1902, 'Glanders in South Africa.' *Journal of Comparative Pathology and Therapeutics*, Vol.XV.

Cochrane, R.C., 1913, 'Veterinary Hospitals During the War.' *United Services Magazine*, Vol.XLVIII, November, pp.162-70.

Coleman, F., 1916, *With Cavalry in 1915*. London: Sampson Low, Marston Co.

Compton, T.E., 1920, 'The Campaign of 1918 in France.' *Journal of the Royal United Services Institute*, Vol.LXV, February, pp.164-184.

Conan Doyle, A., 1900, *The Great Boer War*. London: Smith, Elder and Co.

Cooper, H., 1922, 'An Outline of The French System of Mechanical Transport.' *Royal Army Service Corps Quarterly*, Vol.10, January, pp.16-30.

Corbin, H.C., 1903, 'Horse Management in South Africa' *Proceedings Royal Artillery Institution*, Vol.XXIX, pp.17-23

Courtney, E.A.W., 1914, 'The Divisional Train.' *Army Service Corps Quarterly*, Vol.7, April, pp.152-55.

Crawshay, M., 1913, 'A Government Stud Farm in Hungary.' *Cavalry Journal*, Vol.8, pp.281-7.

Cree, G., 1914, 'A Single Divisional Field Ambulance.' *Army Service Corps Quarterly*, Vol.7, July, pp.252-73.

Crutchley, C.E., 1918, *Machine Gunner 1914-18*. Bailey Bros. and Swinfen.

Cumberlege, H.C.F., 1910, 'Large or Small Engines for Mechanical Transport Equipment,' *Army Service Corps Quarterly*, Vol.4, July, pp.28-28.

Cumberlege, H.C.F. 1911(a), 'Notes on the Employment of Mechanical Transport as Supply Columns at the Irish Command Manoeuvres, 1910.'*Army Service Corps Quarterly*, Vol.4, January, pp.232-45.

Cumberlege, H.C.F. 1911(b), 'Looking Ahead.' *Army Service Corps Quarterly*, Vol.4, October, pp.565-71.

Cumberlege, H.C.F. 1912, 'Transport Tactics.' *Army Service Corps Quarterly*, Vol.5, April.

Davidson, A.E., 1913, 'The Provision Of Motor Vehicles Required On Mobilisation By The Chief Military Nations Of The World.' *Army Service Corps Quarterly*, Vol.6, October, pp.352-60.

Davies, F.G.H., 1909, 'Training Remounts in the Indian Cavalry.' *Cavalry Journal*, Vol.IV, pp.505-8.

Day, H.C., 1922, *Cavalry Chaplain*. London: Heath Cranton.

Deane, C.B., 1906, 'Thoroughbred Horses.' *Cavalry Journal*, Vol.1, pp.204-11.

Dewar, G.A.B., 1922, *Sir Douglas Haig's Command, Dec 1915- Nov 1918*. London: Constable.

Dickinson, W., 1863, 'On the Breeding of Horses.' *Journal of the Royal Agricultural Society England*, 1st Series, Vol.XXIV, pp.267-8

Editorial, 1908, Notes: 'The National Horse Supply.' *Cavalry Journal*, Vol.III, April, pp.246-8

Editorial, 1925, Ref. 'Horse Transport.' *Army Service Corps Quarterly*, Vol.13, July, p.342.

Edmonds, J.E., 1922, 1925, *Military Operations, France and Belgium 1914* (*British Official History*). 2 volumes. London: Macmillan.

Edmonds, J.E. and Wynne, G.C., 1927, 1928, *Ibid.*, *1915*. Vol.1 Edmonds; vol.2 Wynne.

Edye, M.W.J., 1911, 'Notes on the Irish Manoeuvres, 1910.' *Army Service Corps Quarterly*, Vol.4, April, pp.384-6.

Evans, R., 1926, *A Brief Outline of the Campaign in Mesopotamia 1914-18*. London: Sifton Praed and Co.

Falls, C., 1930, *Military Operations Egypt and Palestine (British Official History)*, 3 vols. London: HMSO.

Fitz-Wygram, F., 1881, *Horses and Stables*. London: Longmans and Green.

Forbes, A., 1929, *A History of the Army Ordnance Services*, Vol.I London: Medici Society.

Ford. J.H., 1927, *The Medical Department of the United States Army in the World War. Vol.II, Administration American Expeditionary Forces*. Washington: Government Printing Office.

Fox, F., 1920, *GHQ (Montreuil Sur Mer)*. London: P.Allan.

Fox, F., 1920, *"The Gunner"*, Army Animals in France, Vol.II

Fulton, J.D.B, 1906, 'Draught -horses and the Army.' *Proceedings Royal Artillery Institution*, Vol. XXXII, pp.542-544.

Furse, G.A., 1882, *Military Transport*. London: HMSO.

Furse, G.A., 1883, *Mobilisation and Embarkation of an Army Corps*. London: William Clowes and Sons.

Furse, G.A., 1899, *Provisioning Armies in the Field*. London: William Clowes and Sons

Galtrey, S., 1918, *The Horse and the War*. London: "Country Life".

Galvayne, R., 1902, *War Horses Present and Future, or Remount Life in South Africa*. London: R.A. Everett and Co.

Gartside-Spaight, C.W. 1906(a), 'Military Resources in Ireland.' *Army Service Corps Quarterly*, Vol.1, January, pp.156-83.

Gartside-Spaight, C.W. 1906(b), 'Irish Remounts.' *Army Service Corps Quarterly*, Vol.1, April, pp311-40.

Gibb, H., 1925, *Record of the 4th Irish Dragoon Guards in the Great war*, Canterbury.

Gilbey, W., 1900, *Small Horses in Warfare*. London: Vinton and Co.

Gilbey, W., 1901, *Horse Breeding in England and India and Army Horse Abroad*. London: Vinton and Co.

Gilbey, W., 1913, *Horses for the Army*, (revised from 1902 edit.) London: Vinton and Co.

Gillson, G, 1906, 'My First Experience in Search of Remounts.' *Cavalry Journal*, Vol.1, pp.327-32.

Godley, A.J., 1906, 'The Development of Mounted Infantry Training at Home.' *Cavalry Journal*, Vol.1, pp.52-55.

Goldman, C.S., 1902, *With General French and the Cavalry in South Africa*. London: Macmillan.

Gordon, W.J., 1893, *The Horse World of London*. London: J.A. Allen.

Green, A.F.U., 1905, 'Some Speculations With Regard to Possible Developments of Mechanical Appliances in Warfare.' *United Services Magazine*, Vol.XXX1, September, pp.599-613.

Haig, D., 1901, *Cavalry Studies*. London: Hugh Rees.

Haldane, R.B., 1920, *Before the War*, London.

Haldane, R.B., 1929, *Richard Burton Haldane: an autobiography*. London: Hodder and Stoughton (3rd Edit.)

Hambro, P., 1913, 'Remount Training.' *Cavalry Journal*, Vol.8, pp.43-50.

Hardy, S.J., 1912, 'The Training of a Remount.' *Cavalry Journal*, Vol.7, pp.1-18.

Harris, Lord, 1908, 'The Yeomanry.' *Cavalry Journal*, Vol.III, July, pp.393-401.

Hayes, M.H., 1902, *Horses on Board Ship*, London: Hurst and Blackett

Hayter, H.R., 1910, 'The Employment of Mechanical Transport for Military Purposes.' *Journal of the Royal United Services Institute*, Vol.LIV, June, pp.720-36.

Hazelton, P.O., 1911, 'Mechanical Transport and The Expeditionary Force.' *Army Service Corps Quarterly*, Vol.4, July, pp.482-92.

Head, A.S., 1903, 'The Wear and Tear of Horses During the South African War.' *Journal of Comparative Pathology and Therapeutics*, Vol.XV1, No4, 31 December, pp.299-311.

Head, A.S., 1904, 'Tsetse-Fly Disease Among Mules in the Sudan.' *Journal of Comparative Pathology and Therapeutics*, Vol.XVII, No.3, September, pp.206-208.

Head, A.S., 1906, 'Cattle Plague in the Anglo-Egyptian Sudan.' *Journal of Comparative Pathology and Therapeutics*, Vol.XIV, No.1, March, pp.12-18

Head, A.S., 1908, 'Rinderpest.' Unpublished, RCVS Fellowship Thesis, 1st Series

Henderson, H.D., 1914, 'The Territorial ASC and Its Training For Work.' *Army Service Corps Quarterly*, Vol.7, April, pp.184-87.

Hibbard, B.H., 1919, *Effects of the Great War upon Agriculture in the United States and Britain*. New York.

Hobbs, P.E.F., 1913, 'The New System of Transport as Carried Out By the Blue Force During Army Manoeuvres 1912.' *Army Review*, Vol.1V, April, No.2, pp.412-30, and *RCT Archive C3/1643*.

Hobday, E.A.P., 1918, 'Horse Management In The Field.' *Journal of the Royal Artillery*, Vol.XLV, No.2, May, pp.41-59. (lecture at Royal Artillery Institute, 14 March, 1918)

Holden, H.C.L., 1913, 'The Standardisation Of Mechanically Propelled Commercial Vehicles for Military Purposes In Time Of War.'*Army Service Corps Quarterly*, Vol.6, October, pp.345-52.

Hotham, J, 1903, 'Hints to Officers Proceeding to Purchase Remounts in a Foreign Country.' *Proceedings Royal Artillery Institution*, Vol.XXIX, pp.450-454.

Hotham, J., 1905, 'South Africa as a Breeding Ground for Remounts' *Proceedings Royal Artillery Institution*, Vol.XXXI, pp.4953

Hotham, J., 1906, 'National Horse Supply' *Proceedings Royal Artillery Institution*, Vol. XXXII, pp.189-192

'HT,' 1924,, 'Watering.' *Royal Army Service Corps Quarterly*, Vol.12, April, pp.199-200.

Hunt, F.D., 1913, 'The Ahmednagar Stallion Breeding Stud (India).' *Cavalry Journal*, Vol.8, pp.169-73.

Jessel, H.M., 1920, *The Story of the Romsey Remount*. London: Abbey Press.

Johnson, R.F., 1901, 'Engine Traction for Artillery.' *Proceedings Royal Artillery Institution*, Vol.XXVII, pp.589-594.

Kavanagh, McM, C.T. 1913, 'Horse Breeding in India: Mona Depot.' *Cavalry Journal*, Vol.8, pp.76-78.

Kenyon, R., 1901, 'The Boer War 1899-1900, Conveyance of Horses' *Proceedings Royal Artillery Institution*, Vol.XXVII, pp.89-96

Knox, W.G., 1909, 'The Farmer and the Horse Question.' *The National Review*, Vol.53, June, pp.675-80.

Lane, A.H., 1912(a), 'Horses for War Purposes. *United Services Magazine*, Vol.XLV, April, pp.38-47.

Lane, A.H., 1912(b), 'Some Notes on Horse Management on Active Service.' *United Services Magazine*, Vol.XLV, April, pp.201-4.

Leland, F.W., 1920, *With the Motor Transport in Mesopotamia*. London: Groom and Co.

Levita, C.B., 1906, 'Horse-Shoes for Military Purposes.' *Cavalry Journal*, Vol.1, pp.346-55.

Ludendorff, E. 1919, *My War Memories*. 2 Vols. London: Hutchinson.

Lyon, C.S. and Unwin, W., 1908, 'Mechanical Transport Its Future Administrative Development.' *Army Service Corps Quarterly*, Vol.2, January, pp.411-31.

Mackenzie.C.G., 1899, 'Our Working Horses.' *Proceedings Royal Artillery Institution*, Vol. XXVI, pp.121-126

Mackenzie.C.G., 1899, 'Horse Buying and Breeding in South Africa' *Proceedings Royal Artillery Institution*, Vol. XXVI, pp.547-559

MacMunn, G.F., 1914, 'The Horse Mobilisation of the Army.' *Journal of the Royal Artillery*, Vol.XL, No10, June, pp.433-450. (lecture given at the RA Institute, Woolwich, 23 October 1913).

MacMunn, G.F., 1930, *Behind the Scenes in Many Wars: Military Reminiscences of MacMunn*. London: J. Murray.

Mann, M., 1924, *Regimental History of the 1st The Queen's Royal Dragoon Guards*. Norwich: Michael Russell (for) 1st The Queen's Royal Dragoon Guards, 1993.

Marcosson, I.F., 1918, *The Business of War*. London: John Lane. The Bodley Head.

Maude, F.N., 1903, *Cavalry: Its Past and Future*. London: John Lane The Bodley Head.

Maurice, F., 1906-8, *History of the War in South Africa*. Vol.1 1906; Vol.II 1907; Vol. III 1908; Vol.IV 1910 (Grant, M.H.)

Maydon, J.G., 1901, *French's Cavalry Campaign*. London: C. Arthur Paterson.

Mayhew and Skeffington Smyth, 1909, 'Motor Cars With the Cavalry Division.' *Cavalry Journal*, Vol.IV, pp.438-42.

Moore, J, 1934, 'In the Beginning', *Journal of the Royal Army Veterinary Corps*, Parts I & II

McNalty, C.E.I., 1904, 'Motor Transport.' *Army Service Corps Journal*, May, pp.58-71; part II continued June, pp.109-119. (lecture at Aldershot, 22-23 February, 1904).

McNalty, C.E.I., 1905, 'The Supercession of Steam as a Source of Power for Military Self Propelled Vehicles.' *Army Service Corps Quarterly*, Vol.1, October, pp.73-78

Moberly, F.J., 1923, 1927, *The Campaign in Mesopotamia (British Official History)* 4 volumes. London: HMSO.

Molyneux, E.M.J., 1904, 'The British Cavalry: Some Suggestions.' *Journal of the Royal United Services Institute*, Vol.XLVIII, Pt.2, pp.1164-1171.

Moore, J.,1930, 'In the Beginning.' *Journal of the Royal Army Veterinary Corps*, Vol.1, Part 1, pp.10-27, and Part II, pp.110-123.

Morrison, E.W.B., 1901, *With the Guns in South Africa*. Spectator Printing Co.

Mossley, H.S., 1920, 'Care of Animals in a Mountain Region in Italy.' *Cavalry Journal*, Vol.10, pp.542-552.

Nolan, L.E., 1853, *Cavalry: its history and tactics*. London: Thomas Bosworth.

Nolan, L.E., 1861, *The Training of Cavalry Remounts*. London: John W. Parker.

Parker St.John, W.T. 1911, 'Some Views on the Possibilities of Mechanical Transport.' *Army Service Corps Quarterly*, Vol.4, April, pp.365-75.

Paterson, J., 1927, *The History and Development of Road Transport*. London: Sir Isaac Pitman and Sons.

Paul, G.R.C., 1911, 'Notes on Recent Developments In Road Transport.' *Army Service Corps Quarterly*, Vol.4, October, pp.535-51.

Pirie Gordon, H. (ed.) 1919, *The Advance of the Egyptian Expeditionary Force, July 1917 to October 1918*. London: HMSO (2nd Edition).

Pollok, A.B., 1913, 'Breeding Horses.' *Cavalry Journal*, Vol.8, pp.156-168.

Pratt, A.S., 1918, 'Horse Management.' *Journal of Royal Artillery*, No.10, Vol. XLIV (44), pp.329-341

Pratt, E.A., 1921, *British Railways and the Great War*. Vol.1. London: Selwyn and Blount.

Prease, A., 1915, Horse Breeding in Relation to National Requirements. *Journal of the Farmers Club*, February, pp.21-50.

Preston, R.M.P., 1921, *The Desert Mounted Corps*. London: Constable and Co.

Reckitt, J.T., 1925, 'The Light Lorry Subsidy.' *Journal of the Royal Army Service Corps*, Vol.X111, October, pp.544-50.

Ribblesdale, Lord, 1890, 'Report of the Royal Commission on Light Horse Breeding.' *Journal Royal Agricultural Society England*, 3rd Series, 1, pp.289-305.

Richardson, 1903, *With the Guns in South Africa*. London: Richardson and Co.

Ricketts, P.E., 1914, 'An Indian Cavalry Stud Farm.' *Cavalry Journal*, Vol.9, pp.59-65.

Rimington, M.F., 1912, *Our Cavalry*. London: Macmillan.

Ryan, J.A., 1905, 'Observations on Military Service in Europe.' *Journal of the Military Services Institute of the USA*. Vol.XXXVII, September – October, NoCXXXVII, pp.205-33.

Sandys, E.S., 1908, 'Some Notes on Field Troops, Royal Engineers, and Their Use.' *Cavalry Journal*, Vol.III, July, pp.365-9.

Scolfield, G.P., 1903, *Report on Steam Road Transport In South Africa*. London: HMSO. (in *RCT. Archive*. C3/0713).

Scott, F.J., 1923, *Records of the 7th Dragoon Guards*. Sherborne: F. Bennett.

Seely, J.E.B., and Sessions, H., 1903, *Adventure*. London: William Hienemann. *Two Years with Remount Commissions*. London: Chapman and Hall.

Sessions, H., 1909, 'Mule Breeding.' *Cavalry Journal*, Vol.IV, pp.427-34.

Shelton, A.C., 1916, *On the Road from Mons with an Army Service Corps Train*. London: Hurst and Blackett.

Smith, F., 1894, 'The Loss of Horses in War.' *Journal of the Royal United Services Institute*, Vol.XXVIII, pp.267-312.

Smith, F., 1894, The Effect of the Lee Metford Bullet on the Horse. *Journal of the Royal United Services Institute*, Vol.XXXVIII, pp.41-50.

Smith, F., 1919, *Veterinary History of the War in South Africa*. London: H. and W. Brown.

Smith, F., 1927, *History of the RAVC, 1797-1919*. London: Bailliere, Tindall, Cox.

'Sparking Plug,' 1920, 'A Divisional Train of the Future.' *Royal Army Service Corps Quarterly*, Vol.8., April, pp.116-8.

Spiegl, Baron, Von, E, 1917, *The Adventures of the U-202* New York: Century Co; EBook #32216, 2010

Spiers, E.L., 1930, *Liaison 1914*. London: Heinemann.

Statistics, 1922, *Statistics of the Military Effort of the British Empire, 1914 to 1920*. London: HMSO.

Stirling, C., 1902, 'The Mobility of Artillery' *Proceedings Royal Artillery Institution*, Vol.XXVIII, pp.15-16

Stokes, H.W.P., 1920, 'Our Transport Horse of the Future.' *Royal Army Service Corps Quarterly*, Vol.8, July, pp.174-8.

Thacker, W, 1903, 'The Troop Horse.' *Proceedings Royal Artillery Institution*, Vol. XXIX, pp.220-226

Vaughan, J., 1920, 'Horse Management.' *Cavalry Journal*, Vol.10, pp.7-14.

Verney, RH., 1912, 'The Motor Omnibus in War.' *Army Service Corps Quarterly*, Vol.5, January, pp.1-7.

Verney, R.H., 1913, 'Territorials as Reservists for Manoeuvres.' *Army Service Corps Quarterly*, Vol.6, July, pp.237-42.

Vincent, B., 1901, 'Experiences with a Horse Transport from India to China.' *Proceedings Royal Artillery Institution*, Vol.XXVII, pp.553-558.

Vincent, B, 1904, 'Artillery remounts from an Australian Point of View.' *Proceedings Royal Artillery Institution*, Vol.XXX, pp.274-277.

Waldron, F., 1901, 'Horses for Embarkation to South from England' *Proceedings Royal Artillery Institution*, Vol.XXVII, pp.103-105

Walker, R., 1909, 'Some Possibilities of Modern Forms of Transport.' *Journal of the Royal Engineers*, Vol.9, April, pp.269-80.

Wallace, E., 1915, *In The King's Army: From Citizen to Soldier*. London: George Newnes

Wavell, A.P., 1928, *The Palestine Campaign*. London: Constable.

Weber, W.H.F., 1919, 'The Development of Mobile Artillery, 1914-18.' *Journal of the Royal United Services Institute*, Vol.64, February, pp.49-58.

Welby, J.E., 1897, 'Notes on LHB.' *Journal Royal Agricultural Society England*, 3rd Series, Vol.VIII, pp.313-18.

Welby, J.E., 1913, 'The Government Scheme for the Improvement of Livestock.' *Journal of the Royal Agricultural Society England*, Vol.LXXIV p.31.

White, O.W., 1921, 'The Abolition of Horse Transport in the Administrative Services.' *Royal Army Service Corps Quarterly*, Vol.9, 21 October, pp.553-82.

Williams, V.A.S., 1909, 'Canada as a Country for Breeding Remounts.' *Cavalry Journal*, Vol.IV, pp.290-2.

Wilson, F.M., 1914, 'The Present System Of Cavalry Supply Column Applied To Two Days on the 1913 Manoeuvres.' *Army Service Corps Quarterly*, Vol.7, July, pp.247-51.

Wood, E., 1906, 'British Cavalry 1853-1903.'*Cavalry Journal*, Vol.I, pp.146-54.

Wyndham, G.P., 1909, 'Horse Supply of Russia.' *Cavalry Journal*, Vol.IV, pp.977-89.

Yardley, Watkins, J, 1904, *With The Inniskilling Dragoons: The Record of a Cavalry Regiment During the Boer War, 1899-1902*, London: Longmans, Green & Co.

3.5 Later Books and Articles

Allen, T *Animals at War 1914-1918*, York, 1999

Anglesey, Marquis of *A History of the British Cavalry* 1816 to 1919.

 1973, Vol.1, *1816 to 1850*

 1975, Vol.2, *1851 to 1871*

 1982, Vol.3, *1872 to 1898*

 1986, Vol.4, *1899 to 1913*

 1994, Vol.5, *1914 to 1919, Egypt, Palestine and Syria*

 1995, Vol.6, *1914 to 1918, Mesopotamia*

 1996, Vol.7, *The Curragh Incident and Western Front 1914* London: Leo Cooper

Arthur, M., 2003, *orgotten Voices Of The Great War*, London: Ebury Press

Arthur, M., 2006, *Last Post*, London: Phoenix

Ascoli, D., 1983, *A Companion to the British Army*. London: Harrap.

Ashby, M.K., 1961, *Joseph Ashby of Tysoe 1859-1919*. Cambridge: Merlin Press

Badsey, S.D., 1996, *Cavalry and the Development of Breakthrough Doctrine* Chapter 7, pp.138-174, in Griffith, P., 1996.

Badsey, S.D., 2008, *Doctrine and Reform in the British Cavalry 1880-1918*. Basingstoke: Ashgate Publishing

Baker, P.S., 1933, *Animal War Heroes*. London.

Barker, T.C., 1982, *The Spread of Motor Vehicles Before 1914*, in Kindleberger and Tella, *Economics in the Long View*, Essays in Honour of W.W. Rostow, Vol.II, London.

Barker, T.C., 1983, *The Delayed Decline of the Horse in the 20thC*, in Thompson, F.M.L. (ed.), 1983, Chapter 6, pp.101-112.

Barker, T.C., 1985, 'The International History of Motor Transport.' *Journal of Contemporary History*, Vol.20, pp.3-19.

Barker, T.C. and Robbins, M., 1974, *A History of London Transport*, Vol.II. London: Allen and Unwin

Barnett, C., 1970, *Britain and Her Army 1509-1970*. London: Allen Lane.

Barthrop, M., 1991, *The Anglo-Boer Wars*. London: Blandford.

Bartlett, Moyse, H., 1971, *Nolan of Balaclava (Louis Edward Nolan and His Influence on the British Cavalry)*. London: Leo Cooper.

Beadon, R.H., 1931, *A History of Transport and Supply in the British Army*, Vol.II. Cambridge: Cambridge University Press.

Beeston, A & Neil, N., 2012, *Horses For The War*. Lathom Park Trust

Blake, R., 1952, *The Private Papers of Douglas Haig 1914-1919*.London: Eyre and Spottiswoode.

Blaxland, G., 1968, *Amiens 1918*. London: Frederick Muller.

Boddy, C. and Wilson, R., 1988, *A History of the Wolds Wagonners Special Reserve*. Beverley: Museum of Army Transport.

Bond, B.J., 1965, *Doctrine and Training in the British Cavalry 1870-1914*, in Howard, M. (ed), *The Theory and Practice of War*. London: Cassell, pp.118-19.

Bond, B.J., 1980, *British Military Policy Between the Two World Wars*. Oxford: Clarendon Press.

Boraston, J.H., 1979, *Sir Douglas Haig's Despatches*. London: Dent.

Bostock, H.P., *The Great Ride; Personal Account of the Palestine and Sinai Campaigns*. Canberra.

Bourke, EJ, *The First World War at sea off West Cork*, National Maritime Museum of Ireland.

Bourne, J.M., 1989, *Britain and the Great War*. London: Edward Arnold.

Brereton, J.M., 1976, *The Horse in War*. London: David and Charles.

Brereton, J.M., 1983, *A History of the 4/7th Royal Dragoon Guards and Their Predecessors 1685-1980*. Catterick: The Regiment.

Brock, M and E., 1982, *H.H. Asquith: Letters to Venetia Stanley*. Oxford

Bucholz, A., 1991, *Moltke, Schlieffen and Prussian War Planning*.New York: Berg.

Bullock, D.C., 1988, *Allenby's War (The Palestine-Arabian Campaign, 1916-18)*. London: Blandford Press.

Butler, S., 2011, *The War Horses*, Somerset: Halsgrove

Caidin, M.and Barbree, J, 1974, *Bicycles in War*. New York: Hawthorn Books.

Chadwick, G.A., 1992, *The Anglo-Boer War: Remount Depots in Natal*. South Africa: Booklet given by Col. Young, RCT.

Chappell, 1983, *British Cavalry Equipment 1800-1941*. London: Osprey.

Charlton, P., 1986, *Pozieres 1916*. London: Leo Cooper/Secker Warburg.

Chivers, K., 1976, *The Shire Horse*. London: J. Allen.

Chivers, K., 1983, *The Supply of Horses in Great Britain in the 19thC*, in Thompson, F.M.L. (ed), 1983 (b), Chapter 3, pp.31-49.

Clabby, J., 1963, *History of the RAVC, 1919-1961*. London: J.A. Allen.

Collins, E.J.T., 1983, *The Farm Horse Economy of England and Wales in the Early Tractor Age, 1900-40.* in Thompson, F.M.L (ed) 1983, Chapter 5, pp.73-97.

Condell, D and Liddiard, J., 1987, *Working for Victory? Images of Women in the First World War.* London: Routledge and Keegan Paul.

Cooper Duff, A., 1935, *Haig.* London: Faber and Faber.

Cooper, L., 1965, *British Regular Cavalry 1644-1914.* London: Chapman and Hall.

Cooper, J., 1983, *Animals in War.* London: Heinemann.

Corbett, J & Newbolt, H., 1931, *Naval Operations*, Vol.V. London: Longmans, Green

Crouch, J.D., 1984, 'The Use of Motor Transport in the Boer War.' *Soldiers of the Queen,* Journal of the Victorian Military History Society, March, pp.3-6.

Crutchley, C.E., 1973, *Machine Gunner 1914-18.* Bailey Bros. and Swinfen.

Crutwell, C.R.M.F., 1934, *A History of the Great War.* Oxford: Clarendon Press.

Dakers, C., 1987, *The Countryside at War 1914-18.* London: Constable.

Daniels, L.J., 1989, *Tales of an Old Horse Trader.* Manchester: Carcanet.

Dewey, P.E., 1989, *British Agriculture in the First World War.* London: Routledge.

DiNardo, R.L. and Bay, A., 1988, 'Horse Drawn Transport in the German Army.' *Journal of Contemporary History*, Vol.23, No.2, January, pp.129-142.

Smith-Dorrien, H., 1925, *Memories of Forty-Eight Years Service.* London: J. Murray.

Dunlop, J.K., 1938, *The Development of the British Army, 1899-1914.* London: Methuen.

Edmonds, J.E. and Miles, W., 1932, 1938, *Military Operations, France and Belgium 1916 (British Official History).* Vol.1 Edmonds; vol.2 Miles. London: Macmillan.

Edmonds, J.E., Falls, C., and Miles, W., 1932, 1948, Ibid., *1917.* Vol.1, 1932, Falls. London: Macmillan; vol.2, 1948, Edmonds. London: HMSO; vol.3, 1948, Miles. London: MSO.

Edmonds, J.E., Maxwell-Hyslop, R., 1935, 1939, 1947, Ibid., *1918.* Vol.1-3, 1935-39, Edmonds. London: Macmillan; vol.4, 1947, Maxwell-Hyslop. London: HMSO.

Edmonds, J.E., and Davies, G.R., 1949, *Military Operations in Italy 1915-19 (British Official History)* London: HMSO.

Falls, C., 1934, 1935, *Military Operations in Macedonia (British Official History).* 2 volumes. London: HMSO.

Farndale, M., 1986, *History of the Royal Regiment of Artillery: Western Front 1914-18.* Woolwich: Royal Artillery Institution.

Farrar Hockley, A.H., 1964, *The Somme.* London: Pan.

Forgrave, B.T.G., 1987, *A History of the Royal Army Veterinary Corps.* Melton Mowbray: RAVC.

Forsyth, A.A., 1954, *British Poisonous Plants.* London: HMSO

French, G., 1931, *The Life of Field Marshal Sir John French, First Earl of Ypres.* London: Cassell.

French, G., 1937, *Some War Diaries: Addresses and Correspondence of Field Marshal the Earl of Ypres.* London: Herbert Jenkins.

French, E.G., 1951, *Goodbye to Boot and Saddle.* London: Hutchinson.

Glover, M., 1980, *Warfare from Waterloo to Mons.* London: Guild Publishing.

Gray, E.A., 1985, *The Trumpet of Glory*, London: Robert Hale

Griffith, P (ed.) 1994, *Battle Tactics of the Western Front: The British Army's Art of Attack 1916-18*. New Haven: Yale University Press.

Griffith, P., 1996, *British Fighting Methods in the Great War.* London: Frank Cass

Grimshaw, R., 1986, *Indian Cavalry Officer, 1914-15*. Kent: Costello.

Gullett, H.S., *Official History of World War One: The AIF in Sinai and Palestine.* Canberra

Hamilton, J.A.B., 1967, *British Railways in World War One*. London: Allen and Unwin.

Harrison, B., 1982, *Peaceable Kingdom: Stability and Change in Modern Britain.* Oxford: Clarendon Press.

Henniker, A.M., 1937, *Transportation on the Western Front 1914-18*. London: HMSO.

Hibbs, J., 1968, *The History of the British Bus Service*. Newton Abbot: David and Charles.

Hibbs, J. (ed), 1971, *The Omnibus.* (Readings in the History of Road Passenger Transport). Newton Abbot: David and Charles.

Higham, R., 1966, *The Military Intellectuals in Britain, 1918-39*. Rutgers University Press.

Hills, R.J.T., 1972, *The Royal Dragoons*. London: Leo Cooper.

Hoehling, A.A., 1965, *The Great War at Sea*. London, Corgi

Holland, C., 2012, *Local Aspects of the Great War: Coventry and Warwickshire.* Warwickshire Great War Publications.

Holmes, R., 'Canadian Onslaught at Vimy.' *Purnell's History of the First World War*, Vol.5, Issue 10, pp.2096-2103.

Holmes, R., 1981, *The Little Field-Marshal, Sir John French*. London: J. Cape.

Holmes, R., 1995, *Riding the Retreat: Mons to Marne 1914*. London: J. Cape.

Home, A., 1985, *The Diary of a World War 1 Cavalry Officer*. Kent: Costello.

Hordern, C., 1941, *Military Operations in East Africa, Aug 1914-Sept 1916 (British Official History)*. London: HMSO.

Horn, P., 1984, *Rural Life in England in the First World War*. Dublin: Gill and Macmillan.

Hough, R., 1983, *The Great war at Sea 1914-1918*. Oxford University Press.

Hume, R., 1980, 'Arborfield and the Army Remount Service, 1904-18.' *Journal of the Royal Electrical and Mechanical Engineers*, No30, April, pp.35-43, Pt.1. (Part II in 1981, April, No31, pp.14-18).

Hume, R, 2010, *The Story of the Army Remount Department*, Army Medical Services Museum

Idriess, I.L., *The Desert Column: Personal Account of the Palestine and Sinai Campaigns.* Canberra.

James-Rhodes, R., 1984, *Gallipoli*. London: Pan.

Jones, I., 1983, 'Beersheba Light Horse Charge.' *Journal Australian War Memorial*, No.3, October.

Jordon, M., 1994, *The Story of Compton Bishop and Cross*

Kent, D.A., 1982, 'Australian Remount Unit in Egypt 1915-19.' *Journal of the Australian War Memorial*, No1, October.

Kenyon, D., 2011, *Horsemen In No Man's Land: British Cavalry & Trench Warfare 1914-1918*, Pen and Sword Military

Larson, R.H., 1984, *The British Army and the Theory of Armoured Warfare, 1918-40*. Newark: University of Delaware Press.

Laux, J.M., 1985, 'Trucks for the West During the First World War.' *Journal of Transport History*, Vol.6, No.2, September, pp.64-70.

Lawford, J. (ed), 1976, *The Cavalry*. Maidenhead.

Lee, E., 1985, *To the Bitter End*. London: Viking.

Liddle, P., 1976, *Men of Gallipoli*. London: Allen Lane.

Lyddon, W.G., 1938, *British War Missions to the US, 1914-18*. London: Oxford University Press.

Lucy, J.F., 1938, *There's A Devil In The Drum*. London: Faber and Faber.

MacGregor-Morris, P., *The History of the Hunters Improvement Society 1885-1985*, 1986. Cornwall: Trematon Press.

Mallinson, A., 1992, 'Charging Ahead.' *History Today*, Vol.42, January, pp.29-36.

Marse, C.H., 1948, *The Predecessors of the Royal Army Service Corps, 1757-1888*. Aldershot: Gale and Polden.

McKay, J.P., 1976, *Tramways and Trolleys: Rise of Urban Mass Transport in Europe*. New Jersey: Princetown University Press.

Macksey, K. 'Breakthrough at Arras.' *Purnell's History of the First World War*, Vol.5, Issue 10, pp.2077-95.

Mason, I.L., and Maule, J.P., 1960, *The Indigenous Livestock of East and South Africa*. Commonwealth Agricultural Bureaux: Technical Commission No.14.

Merillat, L.A., and Campbell, D.M., 1935, *Veterinary Military History of the United States*, Vol.1 Veterinary Magazine Corps, Chicago.

Middlebrook, M., 1991, *The Somme Battlefields*. London: Viking.

Mileham, P.J.R., 1983, *The Yeomanry*. Yeomanry Association.

Mitchell, E., *The Story of Australia's Mounted Troops*. Canberra.

Money-Barnes, R., 1968, *The British Army of 1914*. London: Seeley.

Moore, J., 1934, *Our Servant the Horse: An appreciation of the part played by animals during the war, 1914-18*. London: H. and W. Brown.

Moore-Colyer, 1992, 'Horse Supply and the British Cavalry: A Review, 1066-1900.' *Journal Army Historical Review*, LXX (284), Winter, pp.245-60.

Morpurgo, M. 2007, *WarHorse*, London: Egmont.

Moss, A.W., 1961, *Valiant Crusade, History of the RSPCA*. London: Cassell

Nicholls, B., Malins, P. and Macfetridge, C., 2006, *The Military Mule in the British Army and Indian Army*. Doncaster:British Mule Society

Nicholson, M., 1995, *What did you do in the War Mummy?* London: Chatto and Windus.

Norman, T., 1984, *The Hell They Called High Wood*. London: W. Kimber.

Nutt, T.P., 1989, *When Boongate Was Bungate*. Peterborough: Westcombe Industries.

Orchard, V., 1953, *Tattershall's*. London: Hutchinson

Packer, C., 1964, *Return to Salonika*. London: Cassell.

Pakenham, T., 1979, *The Boer War*. London: Weidenfeld and Nicolson.

Parkinson, R., 1977, *Encyclopaedia of Modern War*. London: Routledge and Keegan Paul.

Pease, H (ed)., 1924, *The History of the Northumberland (Hussars) Yeomanry*. London: Constable

Pitt, B., 1984, *1918 The Last Act*. Macmillan.

Plowden, W., 1971, *The Motor Car and Politics 1896-1970*. London: Bodley Head.

(Purnell), *History of the First World War*. Vols.1-8. London: Purnell.

Reith, J., 1966, *Wearing Spurs*. London: Hutchinson.

Robson, H.B., 1959, 'Horses in War: A reappraisal of the cavalry 1914-18.' *Army Quarterly*, Vol.LXXV111, No.2., pp.232-7.

Rothstein, A., 1980, *The Soldiers Strikes of 1919*. London: Journeyman.

Royal Corps of Transport, 1981, *A Short History Of The Royal Corps Transport and its Predecessors, 1794-1981*. Aldershot: RCT Regimental Museum.

Rogers, H.C.B., 1959, *Mounted Troops Of The British Army, 1066-1945*. London.

Seeley, J., 2011, *Warrior: The Amazing Story Of A Real War Horse*, Berkshire: Racing Post Books (reprint from the original, *My Horse Warrior*, 1934)

'Schweizer Kavallerie,' 1931, 'Statistics of Horses Used in the War.' *Cavalry Journal*, Vol.XXI, (Taken from, *'Schweizer Kavallerie'*), p.486.

Singleton, J., 1993, 'Britain's Military Use of Horses 1914-18.' *Past and Present*, No.139, May, pp.178-203.

Smith, D.J., 1977, *Horse Drawn Transport of the British Army*. Bucks: Shire Publications.

Smith, D.J.M., 1980, 'Foden Steamers.' *Transport History*, Vol.II, No.2, Autumn, pp.169-75.

Smithers, A.J., 1970, *The Man Who Disobeyed: Sir Horace Smith-Dorrien and His Enemies*. London: Leo Cooper.

Smithers, A.J., 1978, *Toby*. London: Gordon and Cremonesi.

Spiers, E.M., 1979, 'The British Cavalry, 1902-14.' *Journal of the Army Historical Review*, Vol.LV11, pp.71-79.

Spiers, E.M., 1985, 'Review of Work on the British Army 1856-1914.' *Journal of the Army Historical Review*, Vol.LXIII, pp.194-207.

Spooner, G. *For Love of Horses: Diaries of Mrs Geoffrey Brooke*, London: The Brooke Charity

Stewart, P.F., 1950, *History of the X11th Royal Lancers*. Oxford University Press.

Stewart, S., 1988, *Lifting the Latch*. Oxford: Oxford University Press.

Summerhays, R.S., 1973, *Horses and Ponies*. London: Frederick Warne.

Sutton, J and Walker, J., 1990, *From Horse To Helicopter*. London: Leo Cooper.

Sutton, J., 1998, *Wait for the Waggon*. Leo Cooper.

Symons, J., 1963, *Buller's Campaign*. London: Cressett Press.

Taylor, W.L., 1965, 'The Debate over Changing Cavalry Tactics and Weapons.' *Military Affairs* (Journal American Military Institute), Winter.

Tennant, E., *The Royal Deccan Horse in the Great War*. Aldershot.

Terraine, J., 1963, *Douglas Haig: The Educated Soldier*. London: Hutchinson.

Terraine, J., 1978, *To Win A War: 1918, The Year of Victory*. London: Sidgwick and Jackson.

Terraine, J., 1980, *Smoke and the Fire*. London: Sidgwick and Jackson.

Thomas, K., 1983, *Man and the Natural World*. London: Allen Lane.

Thompson, F.M.L., 1976, '19thC Horse Sense.' *Economic History Review*, 2nd series, XXIX, February, pp.60-79.

Thompson, F.M.L., (ed.) 1983(a), *Horses in European Economic History*. Reading: British Agricultural Society.

Thompson, F.M.L., 1983(b), *Horses and Hay in Britain, 1830-1918*, in Thompson, F.M.L. (ed), 1983, Chapter 4, pp.50-72.

Thompson, F.M.L., 1968, *Victorian England: the horse drawn society*. Bedford College, University of London.

Trench-Chenevix, C., 1970, *A History of Horsemanship*. London: Longman.

Trench-Chenevix, C., 1988, *The Indian Army and the King's Enemies, 1900-47*. London: Thames and Hudson.

Trew, C.G., 1939, *From Dawn to Eclipse*. London: Methuen.

Turner, E.S., 1980, *Dear Old Blighty*. London: Michael Joseph.

Tylden, G., 1965, *Horses and Saddlery*. London: J.A. Allen.

Van Emden, R., 2011, *Tommy's Ark*, London: Bloomsbury

Ventham, P. and Fletcher, D., 1990, *Moving The Guns: The Mechanisation of the Royal Artillery, 1854-1939*. London: HMSO.

Warner, P., 1984, *The British Cavalry*. London: J.M.Dent.

Warren, F. (ed.A.Bird) 1990, *Honour Satisfied (War Diary of 2nd Lt. F. Warren)*. Swindon: Crowood Press.

Watteville de.H., 1954, *The British Soldier*. London: Dent.

Wavell, A.P., 1940, *Allenby: A Study in Greatness*. London: Harrap.

Wavell, A.P., 1943, *Allenby in Egypt*. London: Harrap.

Whetham, E.H., 1978, *The Agrarian History of England and Wales*, Vol.V111. Cambridge: Cambridge University Press.

Whetham, E.H., 1970, 'The Mechanisation of British Agriculture, 1910-45'. *Journal of Proceedings of the Agricultural Economics Society*, Vol.XXI, No.3, pp.317-31.

Williams, M., 1985, *Ford and Fordson Tractors*. Dorset: Blandford Press.

Winter, J.M., 1975, *War and Economic Development*. Cambridge: Cambridge University Press.

Winton, G., 2000(a), 'The Supply and Transport of Horses for Military Purposes, from the American Continents, 1914-1918', Paper given to The *World Maritime Millennial Conference*, Massachusetts, USA

Winton, G., 2000(b), 'The British Army, Mechanisation And a New Transport System, 1900-14', *Journal of the Society for Army Historical Research*, Vol.78, No.315

Winton, G., 2007, 'The 1914-1918 War: A Horse War?', *Western Front Association*, London, Firestep, Vol.8, No.1

Winton, G, 2012, 'The 1914-1918 War: A Horse War?', revised and reprinted in *Emma Gee*, Journal of The Machine Gun Corps, Summer

Winton, M.V., 1980, *Saskatchewan's Prairie Soldiers 1885-1980*. Canada.

Wortley, L., 1996, *Lucy Kemp Walsh 1869-1958*. Suffolk

Wrangel, A., 1982, *The End of Chivalry. (The Last Great Cavalry Battles 1914-18)*. Leo Cooper, Secker Warburg.

Young, M., 1996, *London Omnibuses at War*. (unpublished, private copy given by Lt. Col. M Young, RASC)

3.6 Later Journals

3.6.1 *Veterinary Record*

Volume 34:

1933	22 April	p.371, Ref. London van horses.
	22 July	p.707, Ref. LHB and the WO.
	26 August	pp.829-41, Curson, H.H., 'The Volunteer Veterinary Services of the Empire and the Second Anglo-Boer War (1899-1902).' Canada; Australia; New Zealand; South Africa; Appendices.

Volume 35:

1934	13 January	pp.51-2, Moore, J., 'Haig Memorial (equine statue).'
	24 February	p.227, Tipper, L.C., 'The Case for the Retention of the Horse on the Streets.'
	3 March	p.251, Ref. WO grant to LHB.
	12 May	pp.525-6, Ref. Statistics if animal and AVS strength.
	28 July	p.852, Chivers, J.S., 'The Breeding and Use of Percheron Horses.'

Volume 47:

1935	5 January	pp.4-14, Curson, H.H., 'The Veterinary Profession in South Africa.' (Veterinary account of the Zulu War 1879).
	27 April	p.512, 'Census of Horses,' 5th census made by the Army.
	4 May	pp.521-22 ,'The Veterinary Profession in the Great War.' p.532, 'The Cost of Feeding Army Horses.' (Moore, J.)
	3 August	pp.895-6, 'The Future of the Horse.'

Vol. XVI: (?)

1936	22 February	pp.221-229, (I) 'Veterinary Military History of the United States.'
	29 February	pp.245-254, (II)
	7 March	pp.288-294, (III)

Volume 48:

1936 8 February   p.165, 'Can the Army be Mechanised too Much?' (Moore, J.)
      31 October   p.1311, 'Gas Warfare as affecting Horses and Mules.'

Volume 49:

1937 1 May   p.567, 'Return of the Horse to Favour in the German Army.'
      29 May   p.686, 'WO Horse Purchases.'
      28 August   p.1126, 'The Future of Horse Breeding.'
      23 October   p.1368, Ref. change in rank of DGAVS.

Volume 50:

1938 2 July   pp.805-16, 'Animals in Chemical Warfare.'
      15 October   p.1415, 'Dangers of Horse Population Reduction.'
      20 August   p.1083, 'A German View of Cavalry.'

Volume 51:

1939 18 February p.225, 'Draught Horses in Peace and War.'
      25 February p.253, Todd, A.G., and Soutar, J.J.M., 'Influenza: Prevention of
                   Animal Diseases under War-time Conditions.'
      11 March   p.333, 'Army Establishment of Horses.'
      30 September p.1204, 'Return of the Horse.'
      28 October   p.1285, 'The Present Prospects of the Commercial Horse.'
                   pp.1301-2, Parliament: 'Requisitioning of Horses.'
      2 December   p.1420, 'Survival of Cavalry.'

Volume 52:

1940 10 February p.118, 'Protective Plates for Horses in War.'
      17 February pp.130-32, 'Maj. Gen. Sir John Moore.' (Obituary)
                   pp.119-120, 'The Horse in War-Time, (1) The Economics of
                   Horse Maintenance.'
      9 March   pp.175-6, 'The Horse in War-Time, (II) The Farmers' Friend
                   Indeed.'
      9 March   pp.176-179, (III) 'Remounts: Purchasing Duty and Examination
                   for Soundness and Serviceability.'
      24 August   p.607, 'Horsed Units In The Army.'

Volume 53:

1941 8 March   p.145, 'A Happy Extension Of RAVC Activities.' (amalgama-
                   tion ARD/RAVC)

Volume 54:

1942   9 December   p.535, 'Equine Population of the USA.'

Volume 128:

1991   18 May   pp.470-474, 'Two Hundred British Veterinary Years.' (Pattison, I.)

3.6.2 *The Waggoner*

(Journal of the Royal Army Service Corps, held in the Royal Corps of Transport Archive). (Articles quoted directly in the text will be found in 'Printed Sources: Later Books and Articles).

Guthkelch, C.N. March, 1981   The Motor Volunteer Corps: A Corps of Gentlemen Motorists, pp.23-4.

3.7 Unpublished Theses

Badsey, S.D., 1982 'Fire and Sword: the British Army and the Arme Blanche Controversy, 1871-1921'. Cambridge: Cambridge University (PhD thesis).

Groot de, G.J., 1984 'The Pre-war Life and Military Career of Douglas Haig, 1861-1914.' Edinburgh: Edinburgh University (PhD thesis).

Page, A.H., 1976 'The Supply Services of the British Army during the South African War.' Oxford University (PhD thesis): Bodleian Library, 11690, C2300 (reference 0236 71/81)

Winton, G., 1997 'Horsing the British Army 1878-1923. Birmingham University (Ph.D thesis)

3.8 Miscellaneous Works of Reference

Dictionary of National Biography

Gradation List of Officers of the British Army

Who Was Who

Who Was Who British MPs

This England, 1983, Winter, 'The London Bus Horse.'

Cavalry Journal, 1908, April, pp.246-8. Notes: 'The National Horse Supply', and 'Shire Horses'.

Ibid., Recent Publications, p.241, *Journal of the US Cavalry Association*, reference the British Remount System.

WWW.searlecanada.org, Sunderland Site, page 079, shipbuilders, p.69

Wikipedia, SM.U-38, Frederick Daniel Parslow, SS Anglo-Californian

Wikipedia, SS Armenian; *U-boat Attack, 1916*

History Channel – Deep Wreck Mysteries – *Search for the Bone Wreck*

Index

People

Places

England

Other Theatres of War

EAST AFRICAN CAMPAIGN

GALLIPOLI, OR DARDANELLES CAMPAIGN

INDIA

ITALIAN FRONT

MACEDONIA, 381, 397

MESOPOTAMIAN CAMPAIGN

NORTH RUSSIAN EXPEDITIONARY FORCE AND BRITISH MISSION TO SOUTH RUSSIA EXPEDITIONARY

PERSIAN CAMPAIGN (SOUTH PERSIA)

9 781909 384484